MACMILLAN/McGRAW-HILL

MATHEMATICS IN ACTION

Alan R. Hoffer   Steven J. Leinwand   Gary L. Musser

Martin L. Johnson   Richard D. Lodholz   Tina Thoburn

MACMILLAN/McGRAW-HILL SCHOOL PUBLISHING COMPANY

New York / Chicago / Columbus

CONSULTANTS

Zelda Gold, Mathematics Advisor, Los Angeles Unified School District, Panorama City, California • Audrey Friar Jackson, Math Specialist K-6, Parkway School District, Chesterfield, Missouri • Susan Lair, Department Chairperson, Wedgwood Middle School, Fort Worth Independent School District, Texas • Gail Lowe, Principal, Conejo Valley United School District, Thousand Oaks, California

ACKNOWLEDGMENTS

The publisher gratefully acknowledges permission to reprint the following copyrighted material:

"And the Walls Came Tumblin' Down," from MUSIC AND YOU, Gr. 7, B. Staton, M. Staton, M. Jothen, and V. Lawrence, Authors. Copyright © 1988 Macmillan Publishing Company.

Chart of "Ten Major Box Office Failures" from ANATOMY OF THE MOVIES by David Pirie. Copyright © 1984 by Shuckburgh Reynolds, Ltd. Reprinted with permission of Macmillan Publishing Company.

Excerpt from Washington, D.C. Metro Subway Map. Used by the kind permission of the Washington Metropolitan Area Transit Authority.

"Floor Areas of Famous Buildings," adapted from COMPARISONS, The Diagram Group. Copyright © 1980. Published by St. Martin's Press and used with their permission.

"Mass of the Planets," from THE WORLD ALMANAC, 1989. Copyright © Newspaper Enterprise Association. New York, N.Y. 10166. Used by permission.

COVER DESIGN B B & K Design Inc.   **COVER PHOTOGRAPHY** Scott Morgan

ILLUSTRATION Len Antinori; 398 • George Baquero; 138, 139, 140, 141 • Blaise Zito Assoc.; 130 • Alex Bloch; 382, 383 • Dan Bridy; 331, 344, 502, 515, 560 • Robert Burger; 174, 175, 214, 215 • Rick Buterbaugh; 248, 518 • Circa 86, Inc.; 74, 323 • Mona Conner; 252, 253 • Margaret Cusack; 342, 343 • Everett Davidson; 144, 184, 206 • Daniel Del Valle; 382, 383 • Bob Deschamps; 386, 387 • Eldon Doty; 43, 279, 417, 535 • Mary Young Duarte; 156 • Jeff Faria; 60 • David FeBland; 172, 173 • Anne Feiza; 203, 453, 491 • Gregg Fitzhugh; 82, 308, 309 • Robert Frank; 374, 375 • Barbara Friedman; 24, 208 • Simon Galkin; 64, 65, 68, 104, 105, 136, 142, 143, 181 • Chris Gall; 254, 255, 286, 554 • Donald Gambino; 481 • John Paul Genzo; 282 • Patrick Gnan; 423, 473 • John Gurney; 152, 153, 304 • Abe Gurvin; 312, 524 • Gary Hallgren; 8, 9 • Bryan Hendrix; 132, 133 • Mark Herman; 18, 19, 222, 480 • Erasmo Hernandez; 289, 438 • Christopher Hill; 356, 357 • Neal Hughes; 96 • Diane Jaquith; 56, 57 • Dave Joly; 86, 92, 93, 188, 189, 247 • Terry Kovalcik; 52, 296, 512, 513 • Mike Kowalski; 212, 335, 354, 470 • Lingta Kung; 150, 396, 397 • MKR Design; Handmade props • Jeff Nishinaka; 1 • Donna J. Pallotta; 360, 428, 429 • Hima Pamoedjo; 147, 224, 258, 344, 478 • Wayne Parmenter; 462 • Bob Pasternak; 6, 7 • Steve Petruccio; 466 • Al Pisano; 218, 219 • Scott Pollack; 384, 385 • William Reiser; 48 • S. D. Schindler; 167 • Marsha Serafin; 268 • Bob Shein; 84, 85 • Aki Shirakawa; 338, 495 • Terry Sirrell; 2, 3 • Steve Smallwood; 498 • Bruce VanPatter; 178, 179 • Anna Walker; 10 • Kay Wanous; 336 • Cameron Wasson; 260, 376, 520, 521 • Fred Winkowski; 306, 307 • Mark Yankus; 552, 553 • Rusty Zabransky; 10, 22, 24, 26, 30, 66, 106, 190, 224, 225, 266, 310, 404, 440, 478, 566 • Ron Zalme; 20, 21, 294, 295, 468, 469 • Maggie Zander; 361, 568 • Jerry Zimmerman; 124, 125 • Robert Zimmerman; 506, 507

PHOTOGRAPHY After Image, Inc. / David Lissy, 55 • Clara Aich, 4, 5 • Allsport USA, 126 • Peter Arnold / Hanson Carroll, 170; NASA, 241 • The Bettmann Archive, 130B • Lee Bolton Picture Library, 32L • Ken Cavanagh for Macmillan / McGraw-Hill School Division, 33, 69T&B, 157, 193, 227, 269T&B, 407, 443L, 525 • Bruce Coleman Inc. / Jen & Des Bartlett, 558M; Jeff Foott, 362M; Joe McDonald, 107T; David Overcash, 177; Robert D., 361; John Shaw, 360; Waina Cheng Ward, 547 • Comstock, 181, 210; Henry George, 131 • Courtesy of Chrysler, 508M, B • Folio / James A. Cook, 326L; Cameron Davidson, 236R • Four By Five, 473 • FPG International / Richard Laird, 226 • F-Stop Pictures / Don & Pat Valenti, 558TM • The Granger Collection, 442T • Richard Haynes, Jr. , 26 • Grant Heilman Photography / Runk / Schoenberger, 94B, 558MB; Barry L. Runk, 94T, M • The Image Bank / Ira Block, 542; Kay Chernush, 476; Gary Faber, 390; G.V. Faint, 220M; D. Hiser, 402; Don Klumpp, 244, 434; Barry Rokeach, 435; Pamela J. Zilly, 107B • Index Stock International / John D. Luke, 108B • NASA, 12, 225 • Ron Kimball, 508T • Bill Kontzias, 109 • Odyssey / Robert Frerck, 480 • Stephen Ogilvy, 46, 47, 59, 256, 359, 394, 395, 400, 401, 424, 474, 541, 545, 567 • Omni-Photo Communications, Inc. / Ken Karp, 14, 27, 31, 32, 50, 62, 388, 406, 425, 460, 479, 481, 488, 496, 510, 514, 515, 540, 566, 567 • John Lei, 30, 186, 191, 293, 441, 443R • Photo Researchers / Gregory G. Dimijian, M.D., 558B; George Holton, 176, 192B, 442; Stephen J. Kraseman, 402; Peter Miller, 262; Hank Morgan, 122; N. Smythe / National Audubon Society, 558T; Stan Wayman, 565 • Research Plus, 298; Kurt Anderson, 239, 267; Gene Anthony, 284; Franklin Avery, 81, 107, 205, 225, 325, 359; Laurence Bartone, 11, 31, 45, 67, 121, 155, 169, 191, 281, 311, 373, 405, 493, 523, 537, 567; Karen Rantzman, 419, 441, 445, 479 • John Running, 108T • Joseph Sachs, 67, 106, 107, 155, 225, 242, 243, 267, 290, 302, 310-311, 313, 358, 405, 430, 522, 523 • J. Gerald Smith Photography, 17, 18, 28, 29, 54, 55, 90, 91, 148, 149, 250, 251, 264, 265, 288, 302, 427, 504, 505, 516, 517, 550, 551, 564 • Tom Stack & Associates / Ed Robinson, 556; John Shaw, 327 • The Stock Market / Tom Bean, 192T; Berenholtz, 182; Randy Duchaine, 442B; Steve Elmore, 128; Charles Krebs, 406; NASA, 240; Stan Osolinski, 88; William Roy, 220B; Marmel Studio, 220T • Viesti Associates / J.J. Barrelle, 336MR; Joe Gillespie, 336L; Joe Viesti, 336ML • Kay Wanous, 336R • Woodfin Camp & Associates / Craig Aurness, 548; John Blaustein, 134

Macmillan/McGraw-Hill School Division
866 Third Avenue
New York, New York 10022

Printed in the United States of America
ISBN 0-02-108495-5
9 8 7 6 5 4

CONTENTS

THINKING MATHEMATICALLY

LETTER TO STUDENTS 1
APPLYING MATHEMATICS 2
USING NUMBER CONCEPTS 4
COLLECTING AND INTERPRETING DATA 5
VISUAL REASONING 6
ESTIMATING 8
LOGICAL REASONING 10

CHAPTER 1

Understanding Numbers and Interpreting Data 11
MATH CONNECTIONS STATISTICS / PROBLEM SOLVING

Decimal Place Value 12
Making Frequency Tables 14
PROBLEM SOLVING USING THE FIVE-STEP PROCESS 16
Making Line Plots 18
THINKING MATHEMATICALLY USING NUMBER CONCEPTS 20
Interpreting Bar and Line Graphs 22
Making Bar Graphs 24
Making Line Graphs 26
PROBLEM SOLVING STRATEGY: CONDUCTING AN EXPERIMENT 28
DECISION MAKING CHOOSING A DISC JOCKEY 30
CURRICULUM CONNECTION SOCIAL STUDIES 32
TECHNOLOGY COMPUTER GRAPHING: TRIPLE-LINE GRAPH 33
EXTRA PRACTICE 34
PRACTICE PLUS 38
Chapter Review 40
Chapter Test 42
ENRICHMENT FOR ALL OCTAL NUMBERS 43
Cumulative Review 44

CHAPTER 2

Applying Addition, Subtraction: Whole Numbers, Decimals 45
MATH CONNECTIONS PERIMETER / ALGEBRA / PROBLEM SOLVING

Mental Math: Adding and Subtracting 46
Estimating Sums, Differences by Rounding 48
Front-End Estimation: Sums and Differences 50
Adding and Subtracting Whole Numbers and Decimals 52
PROBLEM SOLVING STRATEGY: USING ESTIMATION 54
THINKING MATHEMATICALLY INVESTIGATING PATTERNS 56

★★★★★ *TAAS REVIEW Booklet*
for Chapter 1
pp. 2, 22-23, 44-45

DECISION MAKING
Choosing a Disc Jockey,
pages 11 and 30

★★★★★ *TAAS REVIEW Booklet*
for Chapter 2
pp. 2, 6, 8, 16, 18, 26, 28, 34, 42-43, 46

Metric Units of Length: Perimeter	58
Using Addition and Subtraction with Equations	60
Using Addition and Subtraction with Inequalities	62
PROBLEM SOLVING STRATEGY: GUESS, TEST, AND REVISE	64
DECISION MAKING CHOOSING WHAT TO DO FOR LUNCH	66
CURRICULUM CONNECTION LITERATURE	68
TECHNOLOGY COMPUTER SPREADSHEET: NUTRITION ANALYSIS	69
***EXTRA* PRACTICE**	**70**
PRACTICE *PLUS*	**74**
Chapter Review	76
Chapter Test	78
ENRICHMENT FOR ALL GENERATE MAGIC SQUARES	**79**
Cumulative Review	80

DECISION MAKING
Choosing What to Do
for Lunch,
pages 45 and 66

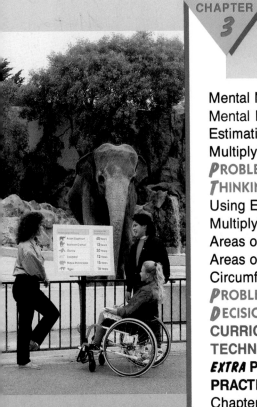

DECISION MAKING
Choosing a Save-an-
Animal Project,
pages 81 and 106

TAAS *R*EVIEW Booklet
for Chapter 3
pp. 2, 4, 7, 18-19, 30,
34, 46

TAAS *R*EVIEW Booklet
for Chapter 4
pp. 2, 4, 6, 8, 16, 22-23,
31, 34-36, 42-43, 46

iv

CHAPTER

3 / **Applying Multiplication: Whole Numbers, Decimals** **81**

MATH CONNECTIONS AREA / CIRCUMFERENCE / PROBLEM SOLVING

Mental Math: Multiplying by Powers of 10	82
Mental Math: Decimals and Powers of 10	84
Estimating Products: Whole Numbers and Decimals	86
Multiplying Whole Numbers and Decimals	88
PROBLEM SOLVING STRATEGY: SOLVING A MULTISTEP PROBLEM	90
THINKING MATHEMATICALLY INVESTIGATING PATTERNS	92
Using Exponents	94
Multiplying Greater Numbers: Scientific Notation	96
Areas of Rectangles	98
Areas of Parallelograms, Triangles, and Trapezoids	100
Circumferences and Areas of Circles	102
PROBLEM SOLVING STRATEGY: DRAWING A DIAGRAM	104
DECISION MAKING CHOOSING A SAVE-AN-ANIMAL PROJECT	106
CURRICULUM CONNECTION ART	108
TECHNOLOGY CALCULATOR: CARPET SALE	109
***EXTRA* PRACTICE**	**110**
PRACTICE *PLUS*	**114**
Chapter Review	116
Chapter Test	118
ENRICHMENT FOR ALL ESTIMATING AREAS	**119**
Cumulative Review	120

CHAPTER

4 / **Applying Division: Whole Numbers, Decimals** **121**

MATH CONNECTIONS ALGEBRA / METRIC MEASUREMENT / STATISTICS / PROBLEM SOLVING

Mental Math: Dividing by Powers of 10	122
Mental Math: Decimals and Powers of 10	124

Estimating Quotients 126
Dividing Decimals by Whole Numbers 128
PROBLEM SOLVING FINDING NEEDED INFORMATION 130
THINKING MATHEMATICALLY MEASURING 132
Dividing Decimals by Decimals 134
Rounding Decimal Quotients 136
Dividing Greater Numbers: Scientific Notation 138
Using Multiplication and Division with Equations 140
Using Multiplication and Division with Inequalities 142
Metric Units of Capacity and Mass 144
Converting Metric Measures 146
PROBLEM SOLVING STRATEGY: USING ESTIMATION 148
Mean, Median, Mode, and Range 150
Effects of Change on Data 152
DECISION MAKING CHOOSING A VACATION 154
CURRICULUM CONNECTION SOCIAL STUDIES 156
TECHNOLOGY COMPUTER SPREADSHEET: STATISTICS 157
***EXTRA* PRACTICE** **158**
PRACTICE *PLUS* **162**
Chapter Review 164
Chapter Test 166
ENRICHMENT FOR ALL PERPETUAL CALENDAR **167**
Cumulative Review 168

DECISION MAKING
Choosing a Vacation,
pages 121 and 154

CHAPTER
5 **Algebra: Equations and Formulas 169**
MATH CONNECTIONS VOLUME / PROBLEM SOLVING

Order of Operations 170
Variables and Formulas 172
Writing Algebraic Expressions 174
Writing Algebraic Sentences 176
THINKING MATHEMATICALLY LOGICAL REASONING 178
PROBLEM SOLVING STRATEGY: USING NUMBER SENSE 180
Solving Equations: Adding and Subtracting 182
Solving Equations: Multiplying and Dividing 184
Applying Equations: Volumes of Prisms 186
PROBLEM SOLVING STRATEGY: USING A FORMULA 188
DECISION MAKING WHERE TO HOLD THE END-OF-YEAR PARTY 190
CURRICULUM CONNECTION SCIENCE 192
TECHNOLOGY COMPUTER SPREADSHEET: FUNCTIONS 193
***EXTRA* PRACTICE** **194**
PRACTICE *PLUS* **198**
Chapter Review 200
Chapter Test 202
ENRICHMENT FOR ALL PERFECT, DEFICIENT, AND ABUNDANT NUMBERS **203**
Cumulative Review 204

*****★★★★★** **T**AAS **R**EVIEW Booklet
for Chapter 5
pp. 6, 8, 19, 42-43

DECISION MAKING
Where to Hold the End-of-
Year Party,
pages 169 and 190

v

TAAS REVIEW Booklet
for Chapter 6
pp. 4-5, 7

DECISION MAKING
Choosing a Science Project
to Demonstrate,
pages 205 and 224

TAAS REVIEW Booklet
for Chapter 7
pp. 2-3, 8, 10, 27, 29,
42-43, 46

DECISION MAKING
Planning a Cable TV Show,
pages 239 and 266

CHAPTER 6
Patterns and Number Theory 205
MATH CONNECTION PROBLEM SOLVING

Sequences 206
Sums of Sequences 208
PROBLEM SOLVING STRATEGY: FINDING A PATTERN 210
Mental Math: Divisibility 212
Primes and Prime Factorization 214
PROBLEM SOLVING STRATEGY: MAKING AN ORGANIZED LIST 216
THINKING MATHEMATICALLY LOGICAL REASONING 218
Greatest Common Factor 220
Least Common Multiple 222
DECISION MAKING CHOOSING A SCIENCE PROJECT TO DEMONSTRATE . . . 224
CURRICULUM CONNECTION MUSIC 226
TECHNOLOGY COMPUTER EXPLORATION: STAR POLYGONS 227
***EXTRA* PRACTICE** **228**
PRACTICE *PLUS* **232**
Chapter Review 234
Chapter Test 236
ENRICHMENT FOR ALL PASCAL'S TRIANGLE **237**
Cumulative Review 238

CHAPTER 7
Fractions: Addition and Subtraction   239
MATH CONNECTIONS ALGEBRA /
PROBLEM SOLVING

Equivalent Fractions 240
Mixed Numbers and Improper Fractions 242
Fractions, Mixed Numbers, and Decimals 244
Terminating and Repeating Decimals 246
Ordering Mixed Numbers and Decimals 248
PROBLEM SOLVING STRATEGY: SOLVING A SIMPLER PROBLEM . . . 250
THINKING MATHEMATICALLY ESTIMATING 252
Estimating Sums and Differences 254
Adding and Subtracting Fractions 256
Adding and Subtracting Mixed Numbers 258
Renaming Before Subtracting 260
Solving Equations: Adding and Subtracting Fractions 262
PROBLEM SOLVING STRATEGY: USING DIFFERENT STRATEGIES **264**
DECISION MAKING PLANNING A CABLE TV SHOW **266**
CURRICULUM CONNECTION MUSIC **268**
TECHNOLOGY COMPUTER EXPLORATION: FRACTIONS AND DECIMALS **269**
***EXTRA* PRACTICE** **270**
PRACTICE *PLUS* **274**
Chapter Review 276
Chapter Test 278
ENRICHMENT FOR ALL PARADOXES **279**
Cumulative Review 280

CHAPTER 8

Fractions: Multiplication and Division 281

MATH CONNECTIONS ALGEBRA / CUSTOMARY MEASUREMENT / PROBLEM SOLVING

Multiplying Fractions 282
Multiplying Fractions by Mixed Numbers 284
Multiplying Mixed Numbers 286
PROBLEM SOLVING STRATEGY: SOLVING A SIMPLER PROBLEM 288
Dividing Fractions: Using Common Denominators 290
Dividing Fractions: Using Reciprocals 292
THINKING MATHEMATICALLY USING NUMBER CONCEPTS 294
Dividing Mixed Numbers 296
Mixed Number Divisors 298
Solving Equations: Multiplying and Dividing Fractions 300
Customary Units of Measure 302
Converting Customary Units 304
PROBLEM SOLVING STRATEGY: WORKING BACKWARD 306
Mental Math: Scaling Up and Down 308
DECISION MAKING CHOOSING AND BUYING CARPETING 310
CURRICULUM CONNECTION SCIENCE 312
TECHNOLOGY CALCULATOR: SCHOOL RECORDS 313
EXTRA PRACTICE 314
PRACTICE PLUS 318
Chapter Review 320
Chapter Test 322
ENRICHMENT FOR ALL RENAMING REPEATING DECIMALS AS FRACTIONS 323
Cumulative Review 324

CHAPTER 9

Geometry 325

MATH CONNECTION PROBLEM SOLVING

Lines and Angles 326
Measuring Angles 328
Construct Congruent Segments and Angles 330
Lines: Intersecting, Perpendicular, Parallel 332
Construct Perpendicular and Parallel Lines 334
PROBLEM SOLVING STRATEGIES REVIEW 336
Construct Segment and Angle Bisectors 338
Triangles 340
THINKING MATHEMATICALLY VISUAL REASONING 342
Polygons 344
Congruence and Similarity 346
Symmetry and Reflections 348
Translations and Rotations 350
PROBLEM SOLVING STRATEGY: USING SPATIAL THINKING 352
Pythagorean Theorem 354
Square Roots 356
DECISION MAKING PLANNING A WALL MURAL 358

TAAS REVIEW Booklet
for Chapter 8
pp. 7-8, 17, 42-43, 46

DECISION MAKING
Choosing and Buying
Carpeting,
pages 281 and 310

TAAS REVIEW Booklet
for Chapter 9
pp. 11-15, 37-38, 39-40

DECISION MAKING
Planning a Wall Mural,
pages 325 and 358

CURRICULUM CONNECTION SCIENCE 360
TECHNOLOGY COMPUTER EXPLORATION: SYMMETRY 361
EXTRA PRACTICE 362
PRACTICE *PLUS* 366
Chapter Review 368
Chapter Test 370
ENRICHMENT FOR ALL CONSTRUCTING TRIANGLES 371
Cumulative Review 372

IAAS REVIEW Booklet
for Chapter 10
pp. 3, 7, 42-43

CHAPTER
10 / **Ratio, Proportion, and Percent** **373**
MATH CONNECTIONS ALGEBRA / GEOMETRY / PROBLEM SOLVING

Ratios and Equal Ratios 374
Using Rates: Mental Math 376
Solving Proportions 378
Scale Drawings and Similar Figures 380
PROBLEM SOLVING STRATEGY: USING PROPORTIONS 382
THINKING MATHEMATICALLY INVESTIGATING PATTERNS 384
Percent 386
Decimals and Percents 388
Fractions and Percents 390
Percents Greater Than 100 and Less Than 1 392
Percent of a Number 394
Percent of a Number: Mental Math and Estimation 396
Percent of a Number: Using Equations and Proportions 398
Exploring Proportions and Percents 400
PROBLEM SOLVING CHECKING FOR A REASONABLE ANSWER 402
DECISION MAKING CHOOSING A VCR 404
CURRICULUM CONNECTION ART 406
TECHNOLOGY COMPUTER SPREADSHEET: COMPOUND INTEREST 407
EXTRA PRACTICE 408
PRACTICE *PLUS* 412
Chapter Review 414
Chapter Test 416
ENRICHMENT FOR ALL GOLDEN RATIO 417
Cumulative Review 418

DECISION MAKING
Choosing a VCR,
pages 373 and 404

IAAS REVIEW Booklet
for Chapter 11
pp. 20, 22-23, 44-45

CHAPTER
11 / **Statistics** **419**
MATH CONNECTION PROBLEM SOLVING

Reading and Interpreting Histograms 420
Reading and Interpreting Circle Graphs 422
Making Circle Graphs 424
PROBLEM SOLVING STRATEGY: MAKING A GRAPH 426
THINKING MATHEMATICALLY LOGICAL REASONING 428
Representing Data 430
Misleading Statistics 432

Making Stem-and-Leaf Plots 434
Making Box-and-Whisker Plots 436
PROBLEM SOLVING STRATEGY: DRAWING A VENN DIAGRAM 438
DECISION MAKING CHOOSING A BUDGET 440
CURRICULUM CONNECTION SOCIAL STUDIES 442
TECHNOLOGY COMPUTER GRAPHING: CIRCLE GRAPHS 443
***EXTRA* PRACTICE** **444**
PRACTICE *PLUS* **448**
Chapter Review 450
Chapter Test 452
ENRICHMENT FOR ALL ESTIMATING WILDLIFE POPULATIONS **453**
Cumulative Review 454

CHAPTER
12

Measurement: Surface Area and Volume **455**

MATH CONNECTIONS ALGEBRA / PROBLEM SOLVING

Spatial Visualization 456
Surface Area: Prisms 460
Surface Area: Pyramids 462
Surface Area: Cylinders 464
PROBLEM SOLVING STRATEGY: MAKING A TABLE 466
THINKING MATHEMATICALLY VISUAL REASONING 468
Volume: Cylinders 470
Volume: Pyramids 472
Volume: Cones 474
PROBLEM SOLVING STRATEGY: MAKING A PHYSICAL MODEL 476
DECISION MAKING CHOOSING A DRAMA CLUB OUTING 478
CURRICULUM CONNECTION SOCIAL STUDIES 480
TECHNOLOGY CALCULATOR: VOLUME OF A CONE 481
***EXTRA* PRACTICE** **482**
PRACTICE *PLUS* **486**
Chapter Review 488
Chapter Test 490
ENRICHMENT FOR ALL EXPLORING THE LATERAL AREA OF A CONE **491**
Cumulative Review 492

CHAPTER
13

Probability **493**

MATH CONNECTION PROBLEM SOLVING

Modeling an Experiment 494
Probability of Simple Events 496
Probability of Mutually Exclusive Events 498
Experimental Probability: Using Random Digits 500
Statistics and Probability: Making Predictions 502
PROBLEM SOLVING STRATEGY: CONDUCTING A SIMULATION 504
THINKING MATHEMATICALLY EXPERIMENTING AND PREDICTING 506

DECISION MAKING
Choosing a Budget,
pages 419 and 440

TAAS R*EVIEW* Booklet
for Chapter 12
pp. 11, 19, 37-38

DECISION MAKING
Choosing a Drama Club
Outing,
pages 455 and 478

TAAS R*EVIEW* Booklet
for Chapter 13
pp. 21, 41

Representing Outcomes. 508
Probability of Independent Events. .510
Dependent Events 512
Probability of Dependent Events 514
PROBLEM SOLVING STRATEGY: USING MORE THAN ONE STRATEGY 516
Counting Outcomes: Permutations .518
Counting Outcomes: Combinations .520
DECISION MAKING CHOOSING A CANDIDATE 522
CURRICULUM CONNECTION SOCIAL STUDIES 524
TECHNOLOGY COMPUTER SIMULATION: DEPENDENT PROBABILITY 525
EXTRA PRACTICE 526
PRACTICE PLUS 530
Chapter Review 532
Chapter Test 534
ENRICHMENT FOR ALL BUFFON'S NEEDLE PROBLEM 535
Cumulative Review 536

DECISION MAKING
Choosing a Candidate,
pages 493 and 522

TAAS REVIEW Booklet
for Chapter 14
pp. 9, 10

DECISION MAKING
Choosing a Bicycle Route,
pages 537 and 566

CHAPTER

14 / Algebra: Integers and Coordinate Graphing. 537

MATH CONNECTIONS GEOMETRY / PROBLEM SOLVING

Comparing and Ordering Integers 538
Adding Integers with Counters 540
Adding Integers 542
Subtracting Integers with Counters .544
Subtracting Integers 546
Adding and Subtracting Integers 548
PROBLEM SOLVING STRATEGY: WRITING AND SOLVING AN EQUATION 550
THINKING MATHEMATICALLY USING NUMBER CONCEPTS 552
Multiplying Integers 554
Dividing Integers. 556
Scientific Notation. 558
Graphing Sentences. 560
Graphing Ordered Pairs 562
PROBLEM SOLVING STRATEGIES REVIEW 564
DECISION MAKING CHOOSING A BICYCLE ROUTE 566
CURRICULUM CONNECTION SCIENCE 568
TECHNOLOGY CALCULATOR: ORDER OF OPERATIONS 569
EXTRA PRACTICE 570
PRACTICE PLUS 574
Chapter Review 576
Chapter Test 578
ENRICHMENT FOR ALL GRAPHING TRANSLATIONS AND REFLECTIONS 579
Cumulative Review 580

Databank 581   Table of Measure 592
Glossary 587   Index 593

Thinking
MATHEMATICALLY

What will the twenty-first century be like? Are you ready for the changes to come? Mathematics can help you prepare for your future. For example, you will live in a world where calculators and computers are commonplace. Does that mean that you do not need to learn math? Actually, it means just the opposite! You need to learn when and how to use technology. You need to understand what it does. In short, you need to think mathematically.

What does it mean to think mathematically? It means knowing how to add, subtract, multiply, and divide—but it is much more than that. It includes comparing, estimating, organizing, reasoning, and many other skills you will use to solve problems. And *that is* what thinking mathematically is really about: facing tough problems and finding real solutions.

The lessons in this first chapter introduce you to many aspects of thinking mathematically. Do not worry if you cannot find all the answers—you are learning more than a few facts. You are learning a whole new way of thinking.

Alan Hoffer

Martin Johnson

Steve Leinwand

Richard Lodholz

Gary L Musser

Tina Thoburn

Applying Mathematics

Suppose you are hungry. What would you choose from this menu? Decide on a reasonable order.

1. How much will your order cost?

2. How much change will you get from $20?

Suppose that you and your family go to the Munchie Barn for dinner.

3. About how much money should you bring? How did you find your answer?

4. What is a reasonable order for your entire family?

5. What is the average cost per person for dinner? How did you find your answer?

6. Suppose that you earn $4.25 per hour. About how much time do you have to work to pay for your family's meal?

Three of your friends placed orders at Munchie Barn:

7. Which friend(s) spent the most? the least?

8. How much would it cost to treat all three of your friends to lunch?

Suppose you have $20.

9. Could you buy a regular burger for everyone in your class? How much change would you get, or how much more money would you need?

10. Could you buy a small salad for everyone in your class?

11. How can you spend as close to $5 as possible? What if you buy more than one of an item?

12. Every May the Munchie Barn has an Eat-a-Thon. All prices are reduced by 25 cents. How much would you save on your original meal? Which items are the biggest bargains during the May sale? Explain.

Write some problems of your own based on this menu. Ask others to solve your problems. Check their answers.

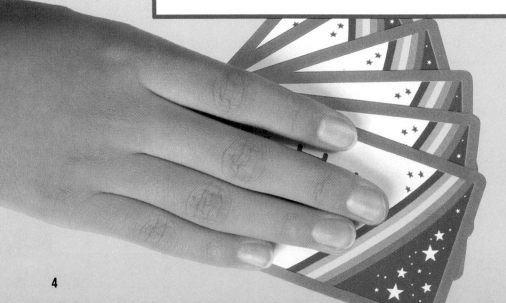

Using Number Concepts

You can use your understanding of decimals to solve some puzzles.

A. Make a card for each of the digits 0 to 9. Draw an addition board like the one at the right where your cards can fill the spaces.

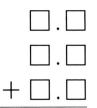

1. Pick any six cards to make a sum of exactly 6.5. Which cards did you pick? What numbers did you make?

2. Use the *same* six cards. Make three different numbers with a sum of 6.5. What did you change?

3. Leave the cards you used for the whole number (ones) part in their spaces. Find three different digits to use for the decimal part (tenths). Which digits did you use? Is there another set of possible digits for the tenths?

4. What other set of digits can you use for the whole numbers? What are all the possible sets of digits that can be used for the tenths with these whole numbers?

B. Use the same cards and the same addition board.

5. Pick six cards to make a sum of 8.5. Which cards did you pick?

6. Try to analyze this puzzle as was done in Part A. What are all the possible sets of digits that can be used for the whole numbers? For each set of whole number digits, what are the possible sets of digits for the tenths?

7. Summarize your results in a list or table.

Educated Guessing

Collecting and Interpreting Data

Think about each statement and guess whether it is probably true or false.

a. At least two people in my class have the same birthday.

b. At least two people in my class were born on the same day of the month, regardless of which month, for example, May 12 and July 12.

c. At least two people in my class were born in the same month.

d. At least four people in my class were born in the same month.

e. At least six people in my class were born in the same month.

f. More people in my class were born before June 1st than after June 1st.

Now take a poll of your class to find out the facts about other students' birth dates. Record your information. You may wish to use a calendar.

1. Which of the statements are true? Which are false?

2. How do the facts compare with your original guesses?

3. Suppose you were going to conduct the same survey in another class. Would you make the same guesses before polling? Why or why not?

4. Suppose you were going to conduct the same survey of your entire school. What do you think the results would be now? Why?

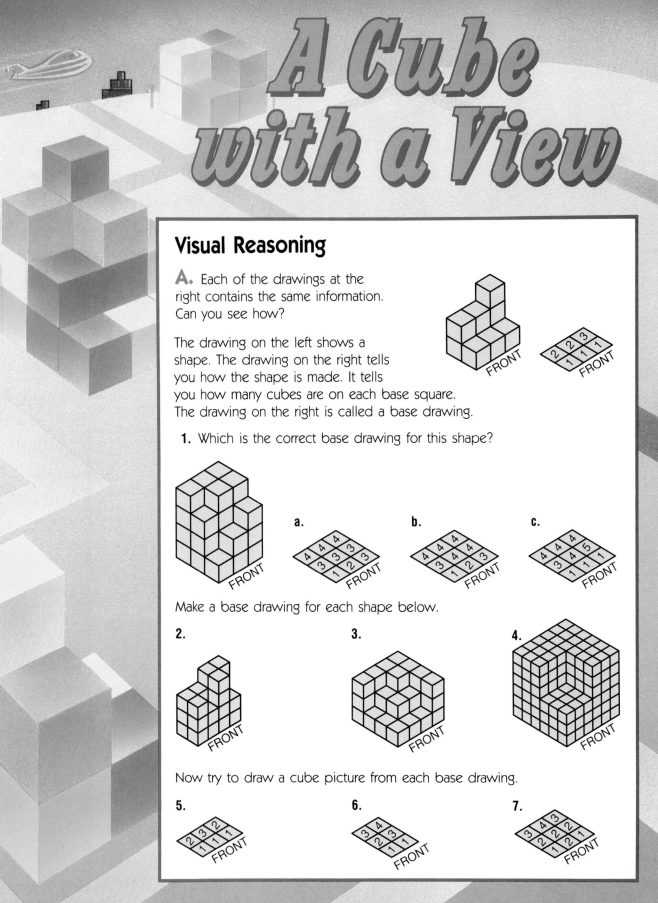

A Cube with a View

Visual Reasoning

A. Each of the drawings at the right contains the same information. Can you see how?

The drawing on the left shows a shape. The drawing on the right tells you how the shape is made. It tells you how many cubes are on each base square. The drawing on the right is called a base drawing.

1. Which is the correct base drawing for this shape?

a.

b.

c.

Make a base drawing for each shape below.

2.

3.

4.

Now try to draw a cube picture from each base drawing.

5.

6.

7.

B. You have probably solved puzzles where you count squares or triangles. Now try counting cubes.

Suppose you want to find the total number of cubes (all sizes) in a $3 \times 3 \times 3$ cube. You could work as follows:

How many $1 \times 1 \times 1$ cubes? There are 27. Why?

How many $2 \times 2 \times 2$ cubes?

There is 1 shown. There are 8 in all. Be sure you can find them.

How many $3 \times 3 \times 3$ cubes?

There is only 1.

So $27 + 8 + 1 = 36$ cubes in all.

8. How many cubes (all sizes) in a $4 \times 4 \times 4$ cube? Find how many of each size, then find the sum.
    ___ $1 \times 1 \times 1$ cubes
    ___ $2 \times 2 \times 2$ cubes
    ___ $3 \times 3 \times 3$ cubes
    ___ $4 \times 4 \times 4$ cubes
    ___ cubes in all

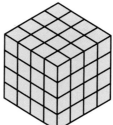

9. Look at how many cubes of each size there were in the problems above. What pattern do you see?

10. What size cubes will you count for a $5 \times 5 \times 5$ cube? Use the pattern to predict how many of each size and how many in all. Draw pictures to convince yourself your answers are correct.

11. Use a calculator to help you. What is the total number of cubes (all sizes) in a $10 \times 10 \times 10$ cube?

YOUR LIFE IN MATHEMATICS

Estimating

A. Sometimes math can help you view your life in a different way. These pages will help you look at the "big picture" of your life. You will estimate and then use a calculator to find statistics that pertain to you. So find out more about *your* life in mathematics.

1. How old are you?

You probably gave your age in years, but how old are you in each of the following units of time?

      months   weeks   days   hours   minutes   seconds

2. How many times does your heart beat in a minute? How many times does it beat in a day? About how many times has your heart beaten in your life?

3. Estimate how much time you spend doing these activities each day.
- going to and from school
- attending school
- exercising/playing sports
- sleeping
- eating
- watching television
- reading
- brushing your teeth

How much time do you spend on each activity in a week? in a year? Make a graph showing your results for a year. What type of graph will you use?

4. Find out how far you can count in 30 seconds. How long would it take you to count to 100,000? How long would it take you to count to 1,000,000?

5. About how far can you walk in 10 seconds? Experiment to find out. Then figure out how long it would take you to walk a mile.

About how long would it take you to walk across the United States (about 3,000 miles) if you didn't stop? What if you walked for only 8 hours a day?

B. Here are some other aspects of your life to explore.

6. Consider the five foods you eat the most. Do you drink more water or soda? Do you eat more bread or cheese?

Make a list of the five foods or drinks that you consume the most of in a week. Then estimate how much of each food you consume during that time.

Next, use a calculator to help you estimate how much of each food you eat in a year. Do your answers surprise you?

7. How long does it take you to sign your name? sign one hundred autographs? one thousand? ten thousand?

8. Estimate how many hours you spend each week in a car or bus. Then find about how long you spend riding over the course of a year. Could you take a bus from Seattle to Miami in that amount of time? What information do you need to find out?

9. About how long would it take you to read an entire encyclopedia? How will you find a reasonable estimate?

10. How many pages of paper do you use in a week? month? year?

HOOK, LINE & SINKER

Logical Reasoning

To solve these problems, you need to find a secret 3-digit number with no repeated digits. You find the number by looking at the scores for several guesses.

The scores:

    hook: One digit is correct and in the correct position.

    line: One digit is correct, but it is in the wrong position.

    sinker: No digits are correct.

For example, a score of "hook, line" means that two digits are correct, but only one is in the correct position. A score of "two hooks" means that two digits are correct *and* in the correct position.

Use the reasoning given to complete the first problem. Then solve the other problems.

Guess	Score	Reasoning
071	hook, line	(Two digits are correct; one digit is in correct position.)
072	hook	(One of the digits is 1; eliminate 2.)
042	hook	(Eliminate 7 and 4; 0 is another digit and it is in the correct position.)
689	sinker	(Eliminate 6, 8, 9.)
685	sinker	(Eliminate 5.)

1. What is the remaining digit? What is the secret number?

2.

864	line
146	sinker
357	two lines
175	line
385	three lines

3.

689	line
869	hook
839	hook
247	line
379	hook
571	hook

4.

123	sinker
456	line
623	line
789	two lines
937	hook
738	two lines

CHAPTER 1

Understanding Numbers and Interpreting Data

MATH CONNECTIONS: STATISTICS • PROBLEM SOLVING

CODES	CASSETTES	CD'S
A	$4.98	$ 8.95
B	$5.98	$11.50
C	$6.75	$13.75
D	$7.98	$14.90
	$8.85	$16.00

1. What information do you see in the picture?
2. How can you use this information?
3. Can you buy both a code C cassette and a code C CD for $20?
4. Write a problem using this information.

UNDERSTANDING A CONCEPT

Decimal Place Value

A. Pluto is the planet farthest from the Sun. Its maximum distance from the Sun is 4,587,000,000 mi. Traveling this distance at a mile a second would take you about 146 years!

You can use this **place-value chart** to help you read and write numbers. It shows the names of the **periods,** or groups of three digits.

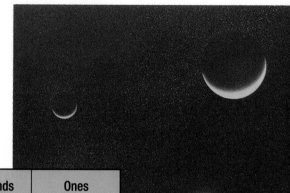

Trillions			Billions			Millions			Thousands			Ones		
H	T	O	H	T	O	H	T	O	H	T	O	H	T	O
					4	5	8	7	0	0	0	0	0	0

Standard form: 4,587,000,000

Short word name: 4 billion, 587 million

Read: four billion, five hundred eighty-seven million

1. What is the value of the digit 5 in this number?

B. You also can use a place-value chart to help you read decimals. The Moon revolves around the Earth once every 27.321661 days.

Standard form: 27.321661

Short word name: 27 and 321 thousand, 661 millionths

Read; twenty-seven and three hundred twenty-one thousand, six hundred sixty-one millionths

hundreds	tens	ones		tenths	hundredths	thousandths	ten-thousandths	hundred-thousandths	millionths
	2	7	.	3	2	1	6	6	1

2. How do you read the decimal part of the number?

You can write a number in **expanded form** to show the place values of the digits. Write 27.321661 in expanded form.

$$(2 \times 10) + (7 \times 1) + (3 \times 0.1) + (2 \times 0.01) + (1 \times 0.001) + (6 \times 0.0001) + (6 \times 0.00001) + (1 \times 0.000001)$$

3. Is 27.32166100 **equivalent** to 27.321661? Why or why not?

4. The distance from the Sun to Pluto is about 4.6 billion mi. Use this notation to record a distance of 7,500,000,000 mi.

T RY OUT Write the value of the digit 9 in the number.

5. 29,841.03   **6.** 38.023974   **7.** 34.682159   **8.** 149.265

P RACTICE

Write the short word name for the number.

9. 46,867   **10.** 9.000017   **11.** 735,054   **12.** 0.3652

13. 209.00294   **14.** 68,253.457   **15.** 3,097,023.036541

Write in standard form.

16. 45 billion, 87 million, 33

17. Seven hundred six thousand

18. 3 thousand, 3 and 13 thousandths

19. Twenty-seven and five tenths

20. Seven and nine hundred five thousandths

21. Six thousand, four hundred twenty-two millionths

22. $(5 \times 10) + (3 \times 1) + (0 \times 0.1) + (7 \times 0.01) + (0 \times 0.001) + (2 \times 0.0001)$

Write the number in expanded form. Then find the value of the underlined digit.

23. 9̲5,987,076,000   **24.** 487,045.6779̲4̲4

Write the letters of the equivalent decimals.

25. 0.3   **a.** 0.30   **b.** 3.0   **c.** 0.03   **d.** 0.3000

26. 0.45   **a.** 0.4500   **b.** 0.045   **c.** 4.50   **d.** 0.450

27. 0.036   **a.** 0.0036   **b.** 0.03600   **c.** 0.36000   **d.** 0.0360

28. 34.32   **a.** 34.32000   **b.** 340.320   **c.** 034.320   **d.** 34.0032

Solve.

29. The planet Neptune is about 2,795,460,000 mi from the Sun. Write the short word name for this number.

30. The diameter of the Sun is about 1.4 million mi. What is this in standard form? Write 2,800,000,000 mi in decimal form.

Critical Thinking

31. There are two 8s in 483.00284. Do they have the same value? Explain.

32. A calculator displayed the numbers | *0.4898* |, | *0.9975* |, and | *0.2689* |. Which fractions or whole numbers are good approximations of these displays?

DEVELOPING A CONCEPT

Making Frequency Tables

It is often helpful to group data into **intervals.** The **width** or size of all the intervals must be the same. These are the batting averages of the Homer High baseball players Coach Sluggs has listed for today's game:

.310, .240, .370, .310, .220, .288, .355, .235, .340, .337, .273, .410, .252, .392, .266.

The coach wants to have more than half the players batting .300 or higher. How can he organize the data into a table to check on the progress of his players?

WORKING TOGETHER

1. What intervals could you use to group the data?

2. What is the lowest average? the highest average?

3. What is the second highest average?

4. Is an average of .310 less than, equal to, or greater than an average of .300? How do you know?

5. What title will you give your table?

6. Did Coach Sluggs achieve his goal?

Coach Sluggs organized the data into a **grouped-frequency table** like this one.

SHARING IDEAS

7. How does your table of batting averages compare with the coach's table?

8. How do the intervals you used compare with the intervals the coach used?

9. How many averages were at least .300?

Which data source is better for answering the following questions, **a.** the list of data or **b.** the table?

10. How many averages were between .300 and .349?

11. How many averages were between .225 and .325?

12. Was any average greater than .420?

13. Did any player have an average greater than .450?

BATTING AVERAGES		
Interval	Tally	Frequency
.200–.249	///	3
.250–.299	////	4
.300–.349	////	4
.350–.399	///	3
.400–.449	/	1

PRACTICE

14. Copy and complete the frequency table on the right. The won/lost averages for all the teams in the league are:

.500, .569, .362, .506, .462,
.400, .377, .269, .500, .673.

LEAGUE RECORD		
Won/Lost Average	Tally	Frequency
.250–.399		
.400–.549		
.550–.699		

15. The list below shows the number of shots the Homer High basketball team took in each game. Make a grouped-frequency table to display this data.

58, 49, 62, 59, 47, 60, 50, 58, 45, 61,
50, 52, 47, 68, 65, 49, 48, 53, 46, 55

Solve Problems 16–18 by either referring to the list or frequency table from Problem 15. Tell which source of data you used.

16. How many times did the team take 50 shots or more?

17. What was the greatest number of shots the team took? the least number?

18. Did the team ever take more than 68 shots?

Make a grouped-frequency table for Problems 19 and 20.

19. Use the Olympics sports information found on page 581 of the Databank to make a grouped-frequency table.

20. *Write a problem* based on your favorite sport. Gather numerical data into a table that compares players. Have other students solve the problem.

LOGICAL REASONING

1. How many 4-digit numbers can be made using the cards below?

2. How many whole numbers between 1 and 400 have 8 as the sum of their digits?

3. How many whole numbers between 1 and 400 have 9 as the sum of their digits?

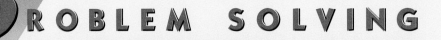

PROBLEM SOLVING

Using the Five-Step Process

A traveling circus with 1,525 seats stops in a town for one show. The circus gives each spectator a paper hat with the town's name on it. Hats come in boxes of 100 and can be bought only in full boxes. How many boxes of hats does the circus need?

Study how a five-step process can be used to solve this problem.

UNDERSTAND

What do I know?

I know that there are 1,525 seats. Each person gets one hat. Hats come in boxes of 100.

What do I need to find?

I need to find the number of boxes needed.

PLAN

What can I do?

I can round the number of seats up to the next greater hundred. The number of hundreds is the number of boxes of hats needed.

TRY

Let me try my plan.

1,526 rounds up to 1,600.
Think: There are 16 hundreds in 1,600. So the circus needs 16 boxes of hats.

CHECK

Have I answered the question?

Yes, I have answered the question.

Does the answer make sense?

My answer makes sense since 15 boxes (1,500 hats) or less would not guarantee enough hats if all seats are filled.

EXTEND

What have I learned?

I have learned that overestimating ensures that the minimum amount needed is reached.

How can I apply what I have learned?

I can apply what I have learned to a similar problem. For example, if the greatest total attendance at another town is 1,789, the circus would need to order 18 boxes of hats.

PRACTICE

Answer questions a through h to solve Problem 1.

The Barnum School held a circus show for charity in a local stadium. For every $10 the school earned, the stadium owners contributed $1. The school earned $484. How much did the stadium owners contribute?

a. What do I know?
b. What do I need to find?
c. What can I do?
d. Let me try my plan.
e. Have I answered the question?
f. Does the answer make sense?
g. What have I learned?
h. How can I apply what I have learned?

Use the five-step process to solve the problem.

2. There are 264 walkers from Lincoln School in the Charity Walkathon. Each walker gets a T-shirt. If the shirts come in full boxes of 10, how many boxes of T-shirts does the charity need?

3. In the afternoon 241 parents will attend the school play. In the evening 391 will attend. Each parent will get a pin. If pins come in boxes of 100, how many boxes of pins will the play committee need?

4. There are 12,312 people coming to a game at the stadium on Friday. Each person will get a souvenir hat. If the hats come in full boxes of 1,000, how many boxes of hats will the stadium need?

5. The fifth grade is planning a weekend trip with Busy Travel Agency. A total of 158 students plan to go. For every 10 students, one chaperone can go for free. How many chaperones can go for free?

DEVELOPING A CONCEPT

Making Line Plots

This table lists the total number of medals won by each of the competing countries in a recent Winter Olympics.

How well did the United States do when compared to the other countries?

You can make a **line plot** to visualize the data in order to make comparisons more easily.

TOTAL NUMBER OF OLYMPIC MEDALS

Country	Medals	Country	Medals
Austria	10	Japan	1
Canada	5	Liechtenstein	1
Czechoslovakia	3	Norway	5
Finland	7	Sweden	6
France	2	Switzerland	15
East Germany	25	Soviet Union	29
West Germany	8	United States	6
Italy	5	Yugoslavia	3

TOTAL NUMBER OF OLYMPIC MEDALS

Step 1 Draw a horizontal line.

Step 2 Draw a scale of numbers on the line using a ruler. Choose a scale that includes the whole range of data values. Most frequently, multiples of 1, 2, 5, or 10 are used.

Step 3 For each entry in the table, place an X above the line at the corresponding number.

Step 4 Write a title above the graph.

SHARING IDEAS

1. Describe the scale used.

2. What was the least number of medals won by any country? the greatest number of medals won by any country?

3. How many countries won fewer than 10 medals? 10 or more medals?

4. Ralph said the data clustered between 1 and 10. What did he mean?

5. Joan said that the United States was in the top half of the medal winners. Was she correct? Explain.

6. What type of data can be easily organized by using a line plot?

7. What suggestions would you give to help someone make a line plot?

PRACTICE

Choose one of the two following exercises. Collect the data for the survey. Make a line plot.

Before you collect the data, predict the answers to these questions.
a. What do you think will be the least number?
b. What do you think will be the greatest number?
c. Do you think the data will be clustered? If so, where?

8. Find the number of hours that 15 students learned about current events last week from television, newspapers, and other sources.

9. Use a television guide for Monday to find the total number of hours given to news, sporting events, general information, movies, comedies, dramas, and children's programming.

10. Write two statements to summarize the survey results. Did you get the results you expected? Explain.

11. Use the Olympics information found on page 581 of the Databank. Round each distance to the nearest foot. Then make two line plots.

Mixed Review

Write the value of the digit 6 in the number.

12. 239,164.75   **13.** 82.0563   **14.** 4.315769   **15.** 8.40692

Write in standard form.

16. 36 million, 3 thousand, 57   **17.** Seven hundred fifty-six millionths

TARGET

Using Number Concepts

A. Suppose you throw darts at Target A. All your darts hit. Your score is the sum of the numbers in the circles you hit.

1. What is the highest score you can get with 5 darts? 6 darts?

How can you get each of the following totals using the fewest darts? (You can hit a circle more than once.)

2. 19   **3.** 20   **4.** 21

5. 30   **6.** 25   **7.** 40

8. Are there any scores between 10 and 50 that you cannot get? How do you know?

9. You throw 3 darts that hit Target A. What scores are possible? (*Hint:* Make a list.)

B. Now you're ready for some harder targets. Suppose you throw darts at Target B.

10. Can you score exactly 100? How many darts will you need?

11. You can use any number of darts. What scores are possible from 1 to 100?

12. Make up some questions of your own to ask about Target B. Try them out on a friend.

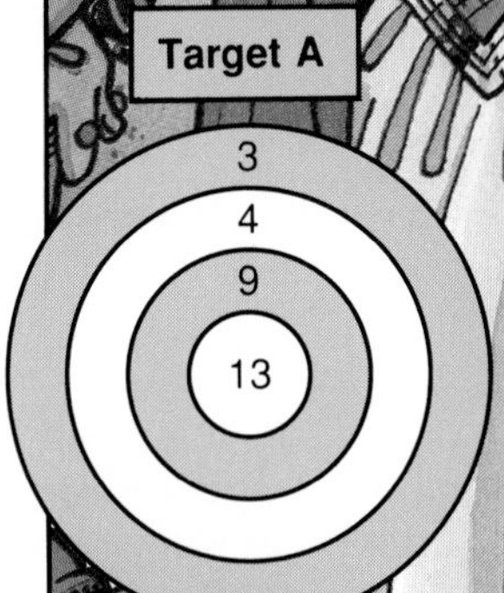

Target A

3
4
9
13

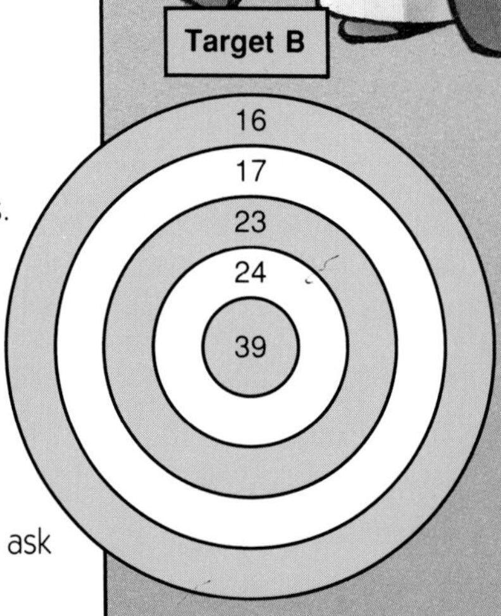

Target B

16
17
23
24
39

PRACTICE

Target C

| 1 |
| 2 |
| 3 |
| 5 |
| 10 |
| 20 |
| 25 |
| 50 |

C. Look at Target C.

- Bill, Jill, and Phil each threw 6 darts and scored with each throw.

- Each player scored 71 points.

- Bill had more than 20 points after his first two throws.

- Phil got only 3 points with his first throw.

- Jill never scored less than 5 points on a throw.

13. Which player hit a bull's-eye?

21

UNDERSTANDING A CONCEPT

Interpreting Bar and Line Graphs

A. Milt's mother said that he spent more time watching sports on TV than doing his homework. To prove that this was not the case, Milt made a **double-bar graph.** You can use a double-bar graph to compare data.

1. Why do you think Milt made a double-bar graph instead of two single-bar graphs?

2. On which day did he spend more time watching sports than doing homework?

3. Did Milt prove his case? Why or why not?

4. **What if** the teachers at Milt's school decide to give weekly tests on Fridays? How could Milt's Thursday activities justify his mother's complaint?

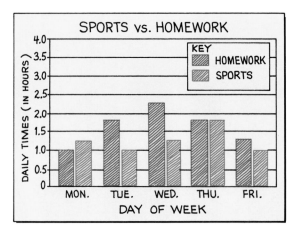

B. You can use a **line graph** to show changes or trends over periods of time. This **double-line graph** shows changes in running distances for two members of a track team.

5. What information is given on the vertical axis? on the horizontal axis?

6. On which days was the difference in their distances the least? What was the difference?

7. Which runner ran the most consistent distances for the week?

8. **What if** the trend continues from Friday to Saturday? Would you expect Samantha and Annie each to run at least 5.5 km on Sunday? Explain.

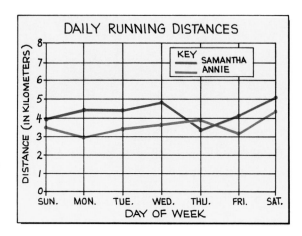

TRY OUT   Refer to the graphs above to answer the question.

9. How much time did Milt spend on homework on Monday?

10. How much time did Milt spend watching sports on Wednesday?

11. Which runner ran about 4 km on Friday?

12. On which days were the distances less than 1 km apart?

PRACTICE

Use the information in the graph to answer the question.

A **calorie** is a measure of energy. The graph shows how many calories men and women of average weight use while performing certain activities.

13. What information is given on the two axes?

14. How many calories do women use when walking for an hour? when sitting for an hour?

15. What conclusion can you reach about the number of calories used by men and by women when doing these five tasks?

16. What is the relationship between the activity performed and the number of calories needed?

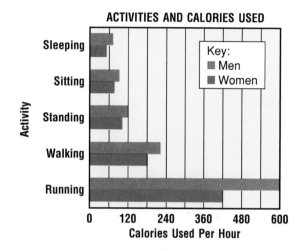

Mickey Mantle and Willie Mays were great baseball players. The graph compares their batting averages over an 11-year period.

17. What information is given on the two axes?

18. Which line shows Mays's average?

19. In which year did the two have the same average?

20. Daria looked at the graph and said, "Mantle had greater peaks and valleys, but Mays was steadier." Do you agree or disagree? Why?

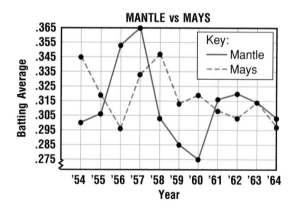

Critical Thinking

Depending on the relationship you want to show among data, either a bar graph or a line graph may be useful. Decide which kind of graph will be better for each situation. Explain your decision.

21. comparing trends for high and low temperatures for two cities over the same time period

22. comparing sales of ten different car models

23. comparing the sales of one car model over seven years

24. comparing the sizes of cassette collections of other students

Making Bar Graphs

Two new television shows, *On the Phone* and *As the Wheels Spin,* are designed for a teenage audience. This table shows the number of teenagers in four cities who watched the programs on the day they were first shown.

NUMBERS OF TEENAGE VIEWERS

City	On the Phone	As the Wheels Spin
Cleveland	20,298	25,492
San Diego	24,693	29,909
Miami	20,148	30,367
El Paso	14,983	19,702

As producer of *On the Phone,* you want to display the results of the comparison between the viewing audiences for the two shows in a bar graph. How should you do it?

WORKING TOGETHER

Before you draw the graph, you must make a few decisions.

1. Why would you make a double-bar graph to display this data?

2. How will you label each axis?

3. Will you round the numbers? If so, to what place?

4. What scale will you use?

5. What title will you use for the graph?

Donald made this double bar graph to display the data.

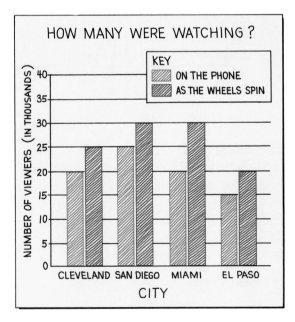

6. Compare Donald's graph with your graph. How are they the same? How are they different?

7. Why do you think Donald chose the scale he did? Was it a better choice than your scale? Why?

8. How could you change Donald's graph to make the bars run horizontally?

9. Using Donald's graph, what predictions can you make about the success of the two television shows?

PRACTICE

Use the data to make a single- or double-bar graph.

10.

TEENAGE TELEVISION
VIEWING TIME (in hours)

Time Period	Male	Female
Daytime: Mon.–Fri.	2.1	2.5
Evening: Mon.–Fri.	4.3	3.8
Daytime: Sat.–Sun.	7.0	7.4
Evening: Sat.–Sun.	1.5	1.2

11.

1950 POPULATION OF
SURVEYED CITIES

City	Population
Dayton, OH	178,920
Yonkers, NY	186,080
Anchorage, AK	235,000
Amarillo, TX	165,850
Oakland, CA	356,960
Tampa, FL	277,580

Solve.

12. How do you think teenagers' and adults' favorite television programs will compare? Take a survey to find what teenagers say are their favorite television programs and what adults say are theirs. Record your results in a table like the one in Exercise 10. Make a double-bar graph to compare the results of your survey. Describe your results.

13. What changes would you predict in the population of the cities from the 1950 census to the present? Find the present populations of the cities listed in Exercise 11. Use an almanac or another reference source. Make a double-bar graph to compare the population in 1950 to the present population for the cities. Describe your results. How did your prediction compare with the actual numbers?

Critical Thinking

14. How do changes in the way data are rounded affect the appearance of a graph?

DEVELOPING A CONCEPT

Making Line Graphs

Jeanna is researching the tuition costs at various local colleges. This table shows the tuition and fees for East Coast College and Northern College over a five-year period.

You want to display the results of this comparison in a line graph. How should you do it?

TUITION AND FEES

Year	East Coast College	Northern College
1	$6,950	$5,100
2	$7,900	$5,502
3	$8,525	$5,980
4	$9,175	$6,175
5	$9,495	$6,490

WORKING TOGETHER

Before you draw your graph, you must make a few decisions.

1. Why would you make a double-line graph to display this data?

2. How would you label each axis?

3. Would you round the numbers? If so, to what place?

4. What scale would you use?

5. What title would you use for the graph?

Jeanna made this double-line graph to display the data.

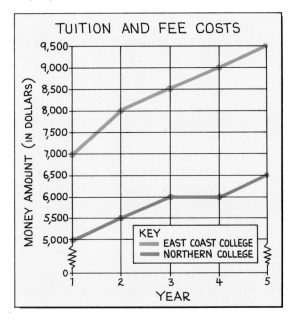

SHARING IDEAS

6. Compare your graph with Jeanna's graph. How are they the same? How are they different?

7. Is it easier to use Jeanna's scale or your scale on the vertical axis? Why?

8. Why is there a break in the vertical axis on Jeanna's graph?

9. To which places did Jeanna and you round the data? Is one way better than the other?

10. Using Jeanna's graph, what predictions can you make about the differences in tuition and fees for the two colleges next year? in five years?

PRACTICE

Use the data to make a single or a double-line graph.

11. BOARDING COSTS: SOUTHERN COLLEGE

Year	Cost
1965	$500
1970	$700
1975	$1,000
1980	$1,500
1985	$2,200
1990	$3,500

12. PERCENT OF HIGH SCHOOL GRADUATES GOING TO COLLEGE

Year	North High	South High
1965	45	30
1970	50	45
1975	68	62
1980	73	69
1985	75	72
1990	80	75

Critical Thinking

For Problems 13 and 14, use the graphs you made in Exercises 11 and 12 to answer the questions.

13. Name some of the facts that may have caused college boarding costs to more than double from 1980 through 1990.

14. Predict what percent of North High graduates will go to college in the year 2010. Why can't the percent of North High graduates going to college continue to climb 5% each five years?

15. Contact a local college. Find out the costs for tuition compared to room and board for the past five years. Make a double-line graph. Write three conclusions that you can draw from your graph.

PROBLEM SOLVING

Strategy: Conducting an Experiment

To solve a problem you may need to conduct an experiment.

Suppose that you have two number cubes. The faces on each cube are numbered 1 through 6. If you roll the cubes several times, which sum of the numbers on a roll will occur most frequently?

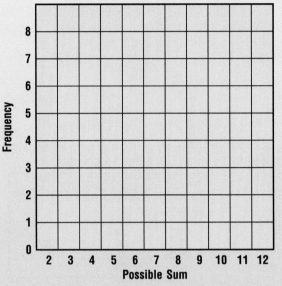

EXPERIMENT: NUMBER CUBE SUMS

Plan your strategy.

You can guess, but conducting an experiment will help you solve the problem in a more informed way. You also need to plan how to record the results of your experiment.

Try your plan.

Get two number cubes and roll them 20 times. Write the sum of each set of numbers rolled. Copy the graph and record the results of your experiment. Draw a bar above each sum to show how many times it occurred.

1. Which sum did you guess would occur most often?

2. Which sum occurred most often in your experiment?

3. Compare your results with others in your class. Are they similar?

4. How does using a bar graph help you?

5. If you rolled the cubes 50 more times, how would your results change?

PRACTICE

Conduct an experiment to solve.

6. Do people naturally prefer rounded objects or squared objects? Try the following experiment. In a bag place one hand-size ball and one similar-size box. Ask 20 people to pull one item from the bag. Record and interpret your results using a frequency table.

7. How do most students in your school travel to school? Survey 20 students about how they travel to school. Record and interpret your results on a bar graph.

8. Which color do most students prefer? Try the following experiment. Color six circles each a different color: red, orange, yellow, green, blue, and purple. Ask 20 students to pick their favorite color. Use a bar graph to record and interpret your results.

9. Draw a circle the size of a quarter. Drop a penny 20 times from 1 ft above the circle. How many times do you think the penny will land inside the circle, outside the circle, or on the circle? Use a bar graph to record and interpret your results.

10. What is the number of letters that occurs most often in last names of people in your neighborhood? Try this experiment. Using a local phone book, count the number of letters in the last name of the first person on every tenth page. Use a bar graph to record and interpret your results.

11. How high can you lift your leg in front of you during the course of three minutes? Have a friend check the height of your foot every 15 seconds. Use a line graph to record and interpret your results.

12. Were most of the students in your class born in the city in which your school is located? How about their parents? Survey 20 of the students about what city they and their parents were born in. Use a bar graph to record your results.

13. ***Write a problem*** that can be solved by conducting an experiment and interpreting the results on a graph. Ask others to solve it.

DECISION MAKING

Problem Solving: Choosing a Disc Jockey

SITUATION

The seventh grade is planning a class party. The students want to hire a disc jockey. They found the names of three DJs from three different sources and the recommendation of friends.

PROBLEM

Which DJ should they hire?

DATA

	Twins DJ	Rockin' Robin DJ	Sound City DJ
Basic Cost	$22.00 per hour 3 hours minimum	$80.00 for first 3 hours $10.00 each additional hour	$30.00 per hour 2 hours minimum
Extra Charges	$10.00 for weekends *	$15.00 for weekends *	$15.00 for Friday $20.00 for Saturday
Services	Has all top-40 hits for the past 5 years.	Includes hits from the '50s and '60s.	Plays "guess the song" and gives out prizes.
Added Attraction	Sings a song with students and teachers' names. ($15.00)	Plays part of a song to "remind" students of each 7th grade teacher. ($20.00)	Has a light show that lights up the entire gym. ($40.00)
Other Information	Has not been seen by anyone in the class. Nonrefundable deposit of $20.00.	Rated "fair" by students, "good" by parents. Nonrefundable deposit of $25.00.	Rated "really good" by students. All deposits are refundable.

Weekend is from Friday night to Sunday night.

USING THE DATA

What is the basic cost to hire the DJ for 2 hours on a Friday night?

1. Twins DJ   **2.** Rockin' Robin DJ   **3.** Sound City DJ

What is the basic cost to hire the DJ for 3 hours on a Friday night?

4. Twins DJ   **5.** Rockin' Robin DJ   **6.** Sound City DJ

What is the total cost to hire the DJ for 4 hours on a Friday night, including the added attraction?

7. Twins DJ   **8.** Rockin' Robin DJ   **9.** Sound City DJ

MAKING THE DECISIONS

Complete the table.

Which DJ should the class choose to get the lowest cost basic service?

	3 hours	4 hours	5 hours
Friday	**10.**	**11.**	**12.**
Saturday	**13.**	**14.**	**15.**

16. The class has not seen Twins DJ. Why might they choose Twins DJ over Rockin' Robin or Sound City?

17. *What if* the majority of students prefer disco music? Which DJ would they be more likely to choose? Why?

18. *What if* the students have a budget of $100 and definitely want to have a light show? How can they do it?

19. Which DJ would parents most likely prefer? Why?

20. *What if* the students want to book the first DJ who is available weeks in advance? Which DJ would they feel more comfortable booking? Why?

21. *Write a list* of the other factors the class should consider when deciding which DJ to hire.

22. Which DJ would you choose? Why?

Math and Social Studies

One of the most complex calendar systems was that of the Mayans, who lived in the Yucatan area of Central America. The Mayan calendar was later adopted by the Aztecs.

The Mayans used three simultaneous systems for counting days. One system was the 365-day period. Since no leap years were used, the calendar slipped backward every century by about 24 days in relation to the sun. This 365-day cycle had 18 months of 20 days each. The extra 5 days at the end of the year did not belong to any month.

Each day of the 20-day cycle was given a name. Then the cycle of 20 names started over. The Aztecs also gave their days numbers, but these only went from 1 to 13 before starting over. You can see that the names and numbers were out of phase with each other most of the time.

What if you start the 20-name cycle and the 13-day cycle on the same day? How many days will it be before the two cycles start again on the same day?

Think: name days × numbered days

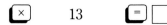

20 ⊠ 13 ▣ ⟨ 260. ⟩

The cycles will start together after 260 days.

ACTIVITIES

1. The Mayans also used what is called the "long count." Write a report on its meaning and purpose.

2. For an oral report, find out about the Julian calendar. Compare it with either the Mayan calendar or a present-day calendar.

Computer Graphing: Triple-Line Graph

The tables below show the average monthly temperatures, in degrees Fahrenheit, for three cities. The data has been divided into two parts: winter months and summer months.

AVERAGE WINTER TEMPERATURES (in °F)

Month	Dallas	Eureka	Tampa
October	68	54	74
November	56	51	67
December	48	48	61
January	44	47	60
February	49	49	61
March	56	48	66

AVERAGE SUMMER TEMPERATURES (in °F)

Month	Dallas	Eureka	Tampa
April	66	49	72
May	74	52	77
June	82	55	81
July	86	56	82
August	86	57	82
September	79	57	81

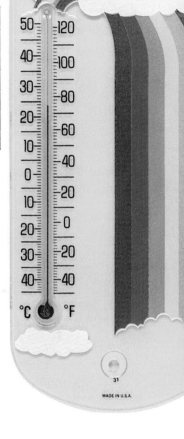

For this activity you will use the computer program TEMPERATURE GRAPH to draw a triple-line graph displaying the data in each table.

AT THE COMPUTER

1. In the first column on the computer screen, enter the names of the winter months in order from October to March. Enter the average monthly winter temperatures for each city in the correct places on the screen, and have the program draw the triple-line graph. Which two cities does the graph show to have comparable temperatures for the winter months?

2. Which city shows the greatest variation in temperature? Which shows the least variation? How does the shape of a line graph display small variations and large variations?

3. You can alter the graph to make the variations in temperature more obvious. Since no temperature is below 40°, you can use 40 as the starting point on the vertical axis. Choose a new interval so that the variation is as pronounced as possible. What interval did you choose? How did the changes make the temperature trend easier to see?

4. Now return to the opening screen and clear the data. Enter the data for the summer months, and have the program draw the graph. How does the summer graph differ from the winter graph? How is it similar? In what part of California would you expect Eureka to be?

5. Alter the graph as you did in Problem 3 for the winter months. What number did you use as your starting point? Why? What size interval did you use? Why?

EXTRA PRACTICE

Decimal Place Value, page 13

Write the short word name for the number.

1. 259,617   **2.** 175,089   **3.** 2,350,706   **4.** 56,007   **5.** 302,008

6. 8.00015   **7.** 0.004126   **8.** 109.0028   **9.** 4,516.007   **10.** 345.05078

11. 45.3409   **12.** 4,123,056.056   **13.** 200.008   **14.** 67,708.1532   **15.** 456,789.081

Write in standard form.

16. 5 billion, 8 million, 25

17. 2 hundred 4 and 32 thousandths

18. two hundred three million

19. sixty-two and three tenths

20. $(8 \times 100{,}000) + (7 \times 10{,}000) + (6 \times 1{,}000) + (3 \times 100) + (0 \times 10) + (5 \times 1)$

21. $(3 \times 1) + (5 \times 0.1) + (6 \times 0.01) + (7 \times 0.001) + (0 \times 0.0001) + (9 \times 0.00001)$

Write the number in expanded form. Then find the value of the underlined digit.

22. <u>8</u>7,205,017,000   **23.** <u>9</u>,017,362,048   **24.** 380,<u>9</u>01,007

25. 287,156.390<u>1</u>87   **26.** 78,417.5<u>4</u>017   **27.** 9,340.7802<u>4</u>

Making Frequency Tables, page 15

1. Make a grouped-frequency table for the field goals made by the players.

2. Make a grouped-frequency table for the field goals attempted by the players.

3. Make a grouped-frequency table for the field goal averages of the players.

4. How many players made this number of field goals?
   a. less than 126   **b.** at least 126

5. How many players attempted this number of field goals?
   a. 168   **b.** more than 168

6. How many players had a field-goal average of:
   a. less than 0.518?
   b. more than 0.518?

Player	Field Goals Made	Field Goals Attempted	Average
A	225	376	0.598
B	75	153	0.490
C	186	373	0.499
D	42	86	0.488
E	251	418	0.601
F	126	305	0.413
G	134	304	0.441
H	141	308	0.458
I	71	124	0.573
J	68	148	0.459
K	52	94	0.553
L	87	168	0.518

EXTRA PRACTICE

Problem Solving: Using the Five-Step Process, page 17

Use the five-step process to solve the problem.

1. There are 16,412 runners scheduled to run in a marathon. Each runner gets a tee shirt, which come in full boxes of 100. How many boxes of tee shirts are needed?

2. The Metro Glass Company agreed to contribute $.50 for every dollar donated to the children's fund. The fund received $1,341 in donations. How much did Metro Glass Company contribute?

3. A bakery sells muffins 6 to a box. Nora needs 80 muffins for an office meeting. How many boxes does she need to buy?

4. For the tennis tournament, the High Hill Racquet Club needs to buy 50 tennis balls. The tennis balls come in boxes of 3. How many boxes do they need to buy?

Making Line Plots, page 19

Use the data at the right to answer Questions 1–5.

1. Make a line plot for the data.

2. What is the least number of people in each family?

3. What is the greatest number of people in each family?

4. Is the data clustered? If so, where?

5. Write a statement to summarize the results.

Number of People in Families of 30 Students

4	3	9	3	3	7	4	4
4	5	3	6	5	5	3	4
3	5	5	5	4	6	4	3
3	4	6	4	7	8		

Use the data at the right to answer Questions 6–10.

6. Make a line plot for the data.

7. What is the longest period on the plot?

8. How many years are represented by no more than one student?

9. What is the most frequent term of residence shown?

10. Write a statement to summarize the results.

Number of Years 24 Students Have Lived at Present Address

0	3	6	2	4	3	2	7
1	4	12	4	10	0	5	1
2	1	4	3	8	4	9	6

EXTRA PRACTICE

Interpreting Bar and Line Graphs, page 23

1. What information is given on the vertical axis? the horizontal axis?

2. Why is a double-bar graph better than a double-line graph for this data?

3. In what age groups are there more females than males? more males than females?

4. In what age group is the difference in the number of males and females the greatest? the least?

5. In what age group is there the most amount of people? the least?

6. In 20 years, when the 25–44 age group reaches age 45–64, will the number of males and females still be about the same? Why?

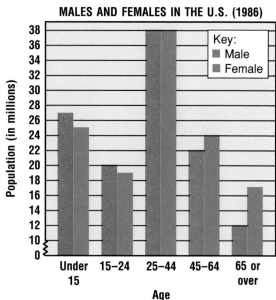

Making Bar Graphs, page 25

Use the data to make a single- or double-bar graph.

1.

PARTICIPATION IN AFTER-SCHOOL ACTIVITIES

	Athletics	Music, Art, Drama	Writing	Other	None
Students	52	34	22	46	15

2.

SWIMSUIT SALES

	April	May	June	July	August	September
Tank	$3,200	$4,600	$5,600	$6,100	$4,800	$2,400
Two-piece	$2,600	$3,200	$5,800	$5,900	$5,100	$2,100

3.

VACATION—HOTEL REGISTRATIONS (IN 1,000S)

	Jan.	Feb.	Mar.	Apr.	May	June	July	Aug.	Sept.	Oct.	Nov.	Dec.
Mountains	180.7	192.3	171.9	150.0	158.0	168.8	174.2	179.4	147.5	151.6	155.4	161.8
Seashore	111.9	114.5	98.2	93.5	102.1	198.7	209.5	218.3	189.6	103.7	84.6	92.9

Making Line Graphs, page 27

Use the data to make a single- or double-line graph.

1. STUDENT COUNCIL SHIRT SALES

Month	Sales
Sept.	$654
Oct.	$835
Nov.	$1,038
Dec.	$1,258
Jan.	$1,450
Feb.	$1,150
Mar.	$1,000
Apr.	$615
May	$438

2. BOB'S TEST SCORES VS. CLASS AVERAGE

Test Number	Bob's Score	Class Average
1	88	90
2	90	85
3	95	90
4	76	85
5	85	80
6	90	85
7	90	85
8	95	90
9	85	85

Problem–Solving Strategy: Conducting an Experiment, page 29

Choose one of the following Questions.

1. What letter appears most often in written material? Take a 20-line sample from a newspaper, magazine, or book. Record your results in a frequency table.

2. Which television show do most of the students in your class prefer? Make a list of five popular shows. Survey 20 of the students. Make a bar graph to show your results.

3. How well can the students in your class estimate the length of a piece of string? Cut a string less than 30 in. long. Ask students to take a quick look and estimate its length. Use a bar graph to show your results.

4. Which sport do most of the students in your class prefer? Survey 20 of the students. Make a bar graph to show your results.

5. Ask students to name their five favorite entertainers. Make a bar graph showing the top half of the list. Make additional bar graphs of this data by gender of entertainer and by gender of voters.

Practice PLUS

KEY SKILL: Making Frequency Tables (Use after page 15.)

Level A

1. These are the field-goal averages of players on a basketball team:

   0.589, 0.527, 0.456, 0.342, 0.675, 0.545, 0.576, 0.424, 0.589, 0.356, 0.478, 0.512, 0.457, 0.379, 0.617, 0.685, 0.495, 0.225.

   Make a grouped-frequency table to organize the data.

2. How many players had a field-goal average of
   a. less than 0.500?   **b.** greater than 0.600?   **c.** 0.478?

3. Did you use your data list or grouped-frequency table to answer questions 2a, 2b, and 2c?

Level B

4. Make a grouped-frequency table for free throws made by the players.

5. Make a grouped-frequency table for the free-throw averages of the players.

6. How many made a number of free throws of
   a. less than 100?   **b.** at least 100?

7. How many players had a free-throw average of
   a. less than 0.700?   **b.** between 0.600 and 0.799?

BASKETBALL STATISTICS

Player	Free Throws Made	Average
A	98	0.715
B	121	0.864
C	215	0.907
D	66	0.516
F	186	0.899
H	155	0.816
I	105	0.614
J	139	0.755

Level C

BASKETBALL STATISTICS

Player	A	B	C	D	E	F	G	H	I	J
Rebounds	502	366	547	170	504	703	536	628	240	1,066
Field-Goal Average	0.464	0.453	0.518	0.478	0.557	0.527	0.604	0.589	0.438	0.483
Free-Throw Average	0.826	0.758	0.649	0.798	0.772	0.912	0.797	0.734	0.856	0.727

8. Make a grouped-frequency table for:
   a. rebounds made.   **b.** field-goal averages.   **c.** free-throw averages.

9. Write questions based on the information in your grouped-frequency tables.

KEY SKILL: Interpreting Bar and Line Graphs (Use after page 23.)

Level A

1. How many cocker spaniels were registered in 1987?

2. How many poodles were registered in 1982?

3. Of which breed of dog were less than 30,000 registered in 1987?

4. Which breed of dog had the least change in number of registrations from 1982 to 1987?

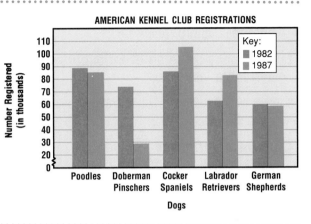

Level B

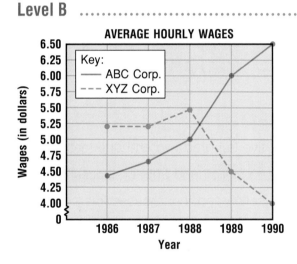

5. Which company had an hourly wage of $5.00 in 1988?

6. Which company shows a consistent increase in the average hourly wage?

7. During which year was the difference in the hourly wage the least? the greatest?

8. During which years was the difference in the hourly wage less than $1?

9. What would you expect the hourly wage for ABC Corp. to be in 1991?

Level C

10. During which month was the difference in the amount of precipitation the greatest? the least?

11. During which months is the difference in precipitation less than 0.5 in.?

12. If you were planning a trip to Phoenix and Honolulu, during which months might you plan to go? Why?

13. What is the relationship between the amount of precipitation and the season?

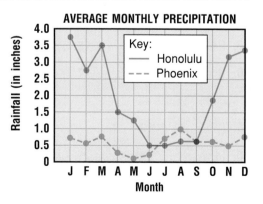

CHAPTER REVIEW

LANGUAGE AND MATHEMATICS

Complete the sentence. Use the words in the chart on the right.

1. A ▦ shows the names of the periods in our number system. *(page 12)*

2. How many times an event occurred is shown by a ▦ table. *(page 14)*

3. Trends of two sets of numbers over time are shown by a ▦. *(page 22)*

4. ***Write a definition*** or give an example of the words you did not use from the chart.

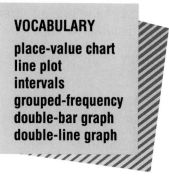

VOCABULARY
place-value chart
line plot
intervals
grouped-frequency
double-bar graph
double-line graph

CONCEPTS AND SKILLS

Write the short word name. *(page 12)*

5. 0.2654   **6.** 0.603   **7.** 504.68   **8.** 403,002

9. 30.145   **10.** 6.2067   **11.** 64,307.1   **12.** 0.00045

Write in standard form and in expanded form. *(page 12)*

13. fourteen hundredths   **14.** five hundred two and one tenth

15. twelve hundred   **16.** 45 million and 205 ten-thousandths

17. three thousand and five hundredths   **18.** seven and four thousandths

What is the value of the underlined digit? *(page 12)*

19. 3,5̲06,222.4   **20.** 2,3̲04.467   **21.** 0.003̲41

Round to the nearest hundred. *(pages 24–27)*

22. 249   **23.** 2,361   **24.** $624.52   **25.** $52,087

26. 963   **27.** 108   **28.** $75   **29.** $42

CRITICAL THINKING

30. How many times greater is 6 million than 6 millionths? *(page 12)*

31. Which is the larger number: 550 ten-thousands or five and one-half million? *(page 12)*

MIXED APPLICATIONS

A science class made a grouped frequency table to show the mass of 10 rocks. The masses were 2.3, 4.1, 0.2, 0.75, 3.8, 0.5, 1.0, 5.2, 0.9, and 12.3 g. *(page 14)*

32. How many rocks would be in the 0–2 g interval?

33. How many rocks were more than 4 g?

34. Which rock had the greatest mass?

This line plot shows the number of assignments the students in Ms. Burke's class turned in last week. *(page 18)*

35. How many students did not turn in any assignments?

36. How many students turned in three assignments?

37. How many students are in her class?

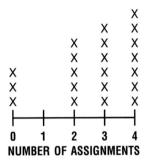

This bar graph shows the costs of two different brands of radios at three stores. *(pages 22–25)*

38. What information is shown on the horizontal axis?

39. At which store does brand A cost the least? the most?

40. At which store can you buy a radio for the least cost?

41. At which store is the difference between the costs the least?

Jake made this graph to determine if there was a pattern between the number of video games he played and the number he won. *(pages 22, 26)*

42. What information is given on the vertical axis?

43. About how many games did he win in February?

44. During which month(s) did he play more than 20 games?

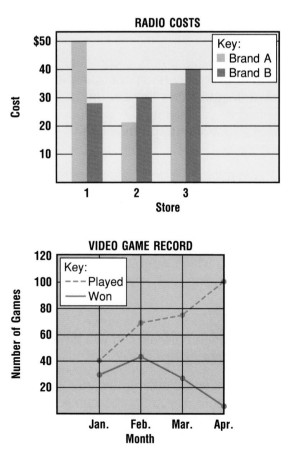

CHAPTER TEST

Write the short word name.

1. 0.402　　　　　**2.** 5.037　　　　　**3.** 5,678.02　　　　　**4.** 230,004.9

Round to the nearest hundred.

5. 648　　　　　**6.** 72　　　　　**7.** 960　　　　　**8.** 42.73

Round to the nearest ten dollars.

9. $512.34　　　　　**10.** $1,007.80　　　　　**11.** $13.62　　　　　**12.** $4.48

A gym class made a grouped-frequency table to show the weights of running shoes. The weights were 12.5, 14.6, 11.7, 10.9, 13.9, 15.6, 17.1, 10.8, 13.8, 14.0, 18.6, and 10.9 oz.

13. How many shoes would be in the 10–11 oz interval?

14. How many weigh between 13 and 15 oz?

15. How many weigh more than 13 oz?

16. How many weigh less than 14 oz?

17. What is the weight of the lightest shoe?

18. What is the weight of the heaviest shoe?

Todd made this graph to compare the amount of money he spent going to movie theaters and the amount he spent renting movies during the last four weeks. Use the graph to answer questions 19–24.

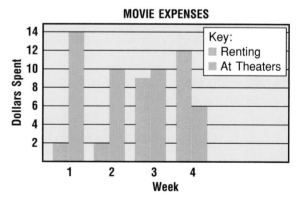

19. What information is given on the vertical axis?

20. How much did he spend at theaters during week 1?

21. During which week did he spend the most going to theaters?

22. During which week was the difference between the two amounts he spent the least?

23. During which week was the difference between the two amounts he spent the greatest?

24. As the amount he spent renting movies increased, how did the amount he spent at theaters change?

25. The faces on each of two number cubes are numbered 1 through 6. If you roll the cubes several times, which product of the numbers on a roll will occur most often? Use a frequency table to record and interpret your results.

OCTAL NUMBERS

The decimal number system uses the base 10. Computers often use **octal numbers,** which use groups of 8 instead of 10.

Octal numbers use only the digits 0, 1, 2, 3, 4, 5, 6, and 7. Look at the following dot arrangements to see how base 10 and base 8 numbers compare.

Group by 10	Group by 8

Think: 2 groups of 10 with 7 left over
Write: 27_{10}

Think: 3 groups of 8 with 3 left over.
Write: 33_8

Octal numbers have their own place values based on groups of 8.

13067_8 means:

Place value	4,096	512	64	8	1
Octal number	1	3	0	6	7

Use your calculator to multiply each digit by its place value to find the base 10 value of this octal number.

Add the products.

$$
\begin{array}{rcl}
1 \times 4{,}096 &=& 4{,}096 \\
3 \times 512 &=& 1{,}536 \\
0 \times 64 &=& 0 \\
6 \times 8 &=& 48 \\
7 \times 1 &=& \underline{7} \\
&& 5{,}687
\end{array}
$$

$13067_8 = 5{,}687_{10}$

Use the grouping by 8 to write an octal number.

1.

2.

Write as a base-10 number. Use your calculator.

3. 20_8 **4.** 32_8 **5.** 402_8 **6.** 345_8 **7.** 627_8

8. 2504_8 **9.** 1723_8 **10.** 30521_8 **11.** 45672_8 **12.** 72346_8

Write the letter of the correct answer.

1. What is the short word name for 0.06?
   a. 6 tenths
   c. 60 tenths
   b. 6 hundredths
   d. not given

2. What is the standard form for three hundred two and twelve thousandths?
   a. 302.012
   c. 300.2012
   b. 302.12
   d. not given

3. What is the standard form for $(7 \times 10) + (3 \times 1) + (4 \times 0.1)$?
   a. 730.4
   c. 73.4
   b. 73.04
   d. not given

This frequency table shows the number of films seen by the drama club members in March.

FILMS SEEN

Number of Films	Members
0	8
1	3
2	4
3	0
4	6

4. How many members saw four films?
   a. 2
   c. 6
   b. 4
   d. not given

5. How many members did not see any films?
   a. 0
   c. 6
   b. 3
   d. not given

6. How many members are in the club?
   a. 6
   c. 21
   b. 10
   d. not given

7. How many members saw more than one film?
   a. 7
   c. 21
   b. 8
   d. not given

This graph shows the percent of boys and girls in the gym classes who wear certain colors of tennis shoes.

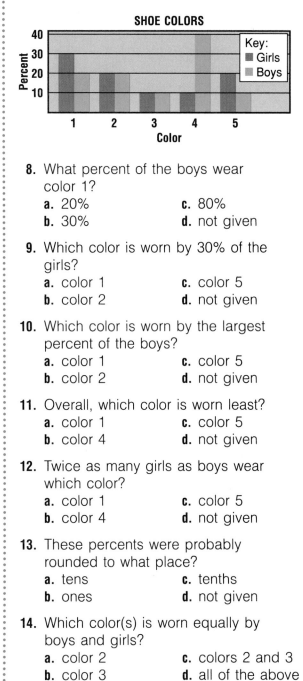

SHOE COLORS

Key:
■ Girls
□ Boys

8. What percent of the boys wear color 1?
   a. 20%
   c. 80%
   b. 30%
   d. not given

9. Which color is worn by 30% of the girls?
   a. color 1
   c. color 5
   b. color 2
   d. not given

10. Which color is worn by the largest percent of the boys?
    a. color 1
    c. color 5
    b. color 2
    d. not given

11. Overall, which color is worn least?
    a. color 1
    c. color 5
    b. color 4
    d. not given

12. Twice as many girls as boys wear which color?
    a. color 1
    c. color 5
    b. color 4
    d. not given

13. These percents were probably rounded to what place?
    a. tens
    c. tenths
    b. ones
    d. not given

14. Which color(s) is worn equally by boys and girls?
    a. color 2
    c. colors 2 and 3
    b. color 3
    d. all of the above

Applying Addition, Subtraction: Whole Numbers, Decimals

MATH CONNECTIONS: PERIMETER • ALGEBRA • PROBLEM SOLVING

Pizza	Hamburger
Salad	Salad
Fruit	Fruit
Juice	Milk
$3.05	**$2.95**

1. What information do you see in this picture?

2. How can you use this information?

3. If pizza costs $.95, salad costs $.85, and fruit costs $.65, how much would you expect juice to cost?

4. Write a problem using this information.

UNDERSTANDING A CONCEPT

Mental Math: Adding and Subtracting

A. Eleanor and Shelley collect coins. They have 78 coins from Canada, 49 from Mexico, and 22 from the United States. How many coins do they have in all?

Add: 78 + 49 + 22

You can use **addition properties** to help you add mentally. Group for 10s and 100s.

Property	Example
Commutative	31 + 28 = 28 + 31
Associative	(11 + 42) + 6 = 11 + (42 + 6)

$$(78 + 49) + 22 = (49 + 78) + 22 \leftarrow \text{Commutative Property}$$
$$= 49 + (78 + 22) \leftarrow \text{Associative Property}$$
$$= 49 + 100$$
$$= 149$$

Eleanor and Shelley have 149 coins in all.

1. How can you use the addition properties to add 6.4 + 1.3 + 2.6 + 3.7 mentally?

B. You can also use **compensation** to add mentally.

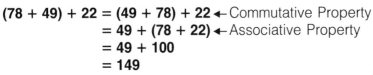

Add: 597 + 346 *Think:*   597 + 346

$$\begin{array}{cc} +3\downarrow & \downarrow-3 \\ 600 + 343 & = 943 \end{array}$$

So 597 + 346 = 943.

2. How can you use compensation to add 762 + 48?

C. You can use **equal additions** to subtract mentally.

Subtract: 7.8 − 4.9 *Think:*   7.8 − 4.9

$$\begin{array}{cc} +0.1\downarrow & \downarrow+0.1 \\ 7.9 - 5.0 & = 2.9 \end{array}$$

So 7.8 − 4.9 = 2.9.

3. How would you use equal additions to subtract 683 − 97 mentally?

4. 62 + (12 + 38)   **a.** 112   **b.** 102   **c.** 108   **d.** 12

5. 50.7 + 24.3   **a.** 74   **b.** 750   **c.** 75   **d.** 85

6. $134 − $47   **a.** $84   **b.** $87   **c.** $93   **d.** $94

7. 58.4 − 19.6   **a.** 38.4   **b.** 39   **c.** 38   **d.** 38.8

PRACTICE

Add or subtract mentally.

8.
```
  63
  37
+ 54
```

9.
```
  4.8
  2.6
+ 7.2
```

10.
```
 $144
   56
+ 237
```

11.
```
  36.1
  12.2
+  7.9
```

12.
```
  427
  645
+ 573
```

13.
```
  396
+ 258
```

14.
```
  237
+  83
```

15.
```
  3.9
+ 6.5
```

16.
```
 $4.63
+  3.48
```

17.
```
  29.8
+  8.6
```

18.
```
 $5.74
−   .96
```

19.
```
  8.3
− 2.4
```

20.
```
  482
− 395
```

21.
```
 $6.59
−  2.93
```

22.
```
  78.4
−  7.8
```

23.
```
  4,673
− 1,598
```

24.
```
 $8.32
−  4.98
```

25.
```
  6,541
−   799
```

26.
```
  0.83
− 0.48
```

27.
```
  67.5
−  9.7
```

28. $43 + $25 + $37

29. 7.6 − 2.4

30. 27.3 + 19.7

31. 352 + 48

32. 393 − 154

33. $5.61 − $4.70

34. 3 + 4 + 7 + 6 + 8

35. 14 + 16 + 21 + 9

36. 3.4 + 2.6 + 5.0

Critical Thinking

37. Give an example to illustrate that subtraction is not commutative.

38. Give an example to illustrate that subtraction is not associative.

Mixed Applications

39. Eleanor spent $4.50 for an 1888 silver dollar and Shelley spent $2.99 for a Canadian coin. How much more did Eleanor spend?

40. Make a bar graph to show how many coins from each country the girls had in their collection.

41. Eleanor read that collectors hold about 45.5 million coins. Write the number in standard form.

42. *Write a problem* that could be solved using mental math. Ask others to solve your problem.

UNDERSTANDING A CONCEPT

Estimating Sums, Differences by Rounding

A. Bruce and Sun Li were interested in finding out how many people went to the movies in their town in one week. They collected attendance figures from the four theaters. About how many people went to the movies during the week in their town?

THEATER ATTENDANCE	
Starlight	6,105
Mart	988
City Center	475
Palace	9,769

Estimate: 6,105 + 988 + 475 + 9,769

Here are the ways Bruce and Sun Li estimated the sum by rounding.

Bruce's estimate	Sun Li's estimate
Round to the greatest place of the greatest number.	Round to the greatest place of the least number.

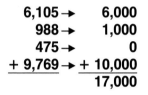

6,105 →	6,000	6,105 →	6,100
988 →	1,000	988 →	1,000
475 →	0	475 →	500
+ 9,769 →	+ 10,000	+ 9,769 →	+ 9,800
	17,000		**17,400**

Bruce estimated that about 17,000 people went to the movies, while Sun Li estimated that about 17,400 people went to the movies.

1. Use Bruce's way to estimate: 7.934 + 0.61 + 2.136. Then estimate using Sun Li's method. Which estimate is closer to the exact answer? Why?

B. You can also estimate differences by rounding.

Estimate: 7.63 − 0.425

Method 1	Method 2
Round to the greatest place of the greater number.	Round to the greatest place of the lesser number.

7.63 →	8	7.63 →	7.6
− 0.425 →	− 0	− 0.425 →	− 0.4
	8		**7.2**

2. What is the advantage of rounding to the nearest whole number? the nearest tenth?

3. Estimate: 1.321 − 0.846. Use both methods. Which method results in the more useful estimate? Why?

Write the letter of the correct answer. Estimate by rounding.

4. 2,105 + 398 + 929 + 4,751   **a.** 6,000   **b.** 8,000   **c.** 10,000   **d.** 18,000

5. 5.82 − 1.317   **a.** 3   **b.** 7   **c.** 3.5   **d.** 5

6. 6.527 + 0.57 + 3.495   **a.** 10.6   **b.** 15   **c.** 9   **d.** 15.7

7. 4,729 − 2,951   **a.** 1,000   **b.** 2,000   **c.** 200   **d.** 3,000

PRACTICE

Estimate by rounding.

8.
```
  5,386
    259
+ 2,707
```

9.
```
    914
  7,652
+ 1,093
```

10.
```
$129.25
 301.50
 686.99
+  59.49
```

11.
```
  1,004
  5,768
  2,909
+ 8,333
```

12.
```
  17.95
  22.86
  39.03
+ 11.19
```

13.
```
  7.32
+ 6.554
```

14.
```
  1.809
+ 0.682
```

15.
```
  4.5
  3.279
+ 1.08
```

16.
```
  1.732
  0.414
+ 2.64
```

17.
```
$2.59
 3.15
+ 2.70
```

18.
```
$1.49
− 0.86
```

19.
```
  4.9
− 1.843
```

20.
```
  3.268
− 0.24
```

21.
```
  0.415
− 0.287
```

22.
```
  0.317
− 0.067
```

23.
```
  3.17
− 1.954
```

24.
```
  45.9
− 18.43
```

25.
```
  32.685
− 24.2
```

26.
```
  1.05
− 0.51
```

27.
```
  6.4
− 0.117
```

28. 6.93 + 5.864   **29.** 5.62 − 1.729   **30.** $63.58 + $7.95 + $19.29

31. 2.912 − 1.124   **32.** 1.233 + 3.59 + 0.486   **33.** $7.25 − $0.89

Critical Thinking

34. ***What if*** you estimated the sum 46,930 + 45 + 239 by thinking 50,000 + 50 + 200? Is this a useful estimate? Why or why not?

Mixed Applications

Solve. You may need to use the Databank on page 581.

35. Two stars of a recent movie each received $3,550,000 to make the movie. About how much was their total cost to the producers?

36. About how much was the total cost of making the ten biggest box office flops?

UNDERSTANDING A CONCEPT

Front-End Estimation: Sums and Differences

A. Marla plans to work in her neighborhood theater group to put on a play. The group's budget is $3,500. Can it afford to purchase materials for scenery at $1,760, tools at $445, costumes at $287, and props at $539?

You can use **front-end estimation** to find the answer.

One Column with Adjustment		Two Column
Add the front digits.	Then adjust the estimate.	Add the two front digits.

One Column with Adjustment — Add the front digits:
$1,760
287
445
+ 539
$1,000

Then adjust the estimate:
$1,760 ⎫ about 1,000
287 ⎭
445 ⎫ about 1,000
+ 539 ⎭
$3,000

Two Column — Add the two front digits:
$1,760
287
445
+ 539
$2,800

Both estimates are less than $3,500. The group can afford the purchases.

1. Which method of front-end estimation would you use to estimate 5,673 + 428 + 13,630 + 2,471 + 7,590? Why?

B. You can also use front-end estimation to estimate differences.

Estimate: 5.604 − 0.937

One Column with Adjustment		Two Column
Subtract the front digits.	Then adjust the estimate.	Subtract the two front digits.

5.604
− 0.937
5

5.604
− 0.937
< 5   *Think:* 6 < 9 The exact answer is less than 5.

5.604
− 0.937
4.7

2. Is the exact answer greater than or less than 4.7? Why?

3. Estimate: 96,487 − 93,513. Which method results in a more useful estimate? Why?

TRY OUT Estimate.

Use the front digits and adjust.

4. $2,379 + $764 + $281 + $1,888   5. 7.874 − 0.946

Use the two front digits.

6. 35.68 + 29.042 + 7.197 + 17.76   7. $3,645 − $1,999

PRACTICE

Estimate. Use the front digits and adjust.

8. 379
   621
 + 410

9. $1.75
   .82
 + 3.96

10. 44,417
   26,709
 + 9,681

11. 684
   259
   511
 + 1,803

12. 2.168
   3.945
   0.897
 + 1.308

13. 8.735
 − 0.952

14. 4.862
 − 1.67

15. $29.45
 − 6.30

16. 35,283
 − 22,768

17. 0.755
 − 0.68

Estimate. Use the front two digits.

18. $2,176
   345
 +   862

19. 3.762
   2.5954
 + 0.945

20. 7.689
   0.125
   1.409
 + 0.813

21. 1,845
   3,086
   2,424
 + 1,297

22. 3.599
   0.68
   0.915
 + 2.849

23. 5.619
 − 0.832

24. 9.56
 − 3.14

25. $72.65
 − 9.25

26. 48,659
 − 21,953

27. 0.629
 − 0.51

Estimate the sum or difference. Choose the letter of the best estimate.

28. $348 + $529 + $641   **a.** < $1,000   **b.** < $1,500   **c.** > $1,500   **d.** > $2,000

29. 8.34 − 5.16   **a.** < 2.0   **b.** < 3.2   **c.** > 3.2   **d.** > 5.0

30. 3.345 + 0.75 + 1.082   **a.** < 4   **b.** < 5   **c.** > 5   **d.** > 6

31. 6,708 − 889   **a.** < 5,000   **b.** < 5,900   **c.** > 5,900   **d.** > 6,000

Critical Thinking

Which front-end estimation method would you use in each case? Why?

32. Kevin ran 7.6 miles on Monday and 7.35 miles on Tuesday. About how many more miles did he run on Monday?

33. Charlene ran a mile in 8.6 minutes 3 months ago. Her goal has been to shorten her time by 2 minutes. This week she ran a mile in 6.75 minutes. Did she meet her goal?

Mixed Applications

34. Make a line graph to show the profits the play group made on its plays: Play 1, $224.50; 2, $510; 3, $1,088.75; 4, $1,694.30.

35. The budget for a major play is $8,200,000. Write the short word name for this number using decimal notation.

Adding and Subtracting Whole Numbers and Decimals

A. Students collected newspapers for three months to raise money to buy computers. The first month they collected 7,923 lb; the second month, 3,284 lb; and the third month, 4,659 lb. How many pounds of paper did they collect in all?

Tanya used a calculator, and Sean used paper and pencil.

Tanya	Sean
7,923 [+] 3,284 [+] 4,659 [=]	15866.

Sean
```
  1  1 1
  7,9 2 3
  3,2 8 4
+ 4,6 5 9
 15,8 6 6
```

Tanya and Sean both found the answer to be 15,866 lb.

1. **What if** Tanya had pressed 723 [+] 3,284 [+] 4,659 [=] on her calculator? What would be her display? How would an estimate help her see that she entered a number incorrectly?

2. **What if** the numbers of pounds were 7,900; 3,000; and 4,600? How could you have done the problem mentally?

B. Tanya used a calculator and Sean used paper and pencil to find this difference: $3,875 − $985.29.

Tanya	Sean
3,875 [−] 985.29 [=]	2889.71

Sean
```
        171614  9
      2  7 6 4  1010
   $3,8 7 5.0 0
   −    9 8 5.2 9
   $2,8 8 9.7 1
```

Both Tanya and Sean found the answer to be $2,889.71.

3. What is your estimate? How does it compare with the exact answer? What can you conclude?

4. Does using a calculator ensure a correct answer? Why or why not?

TRY OUT Find the answer.

5. 1.36 + 45.2 + 3.002

6. 19.2 − 4.9823

7. 4,578 + 6,035 + 5,711

8. 8,792 − 641.25

PRACTICE

Add. Use mental math, calculator, or paper and pencil.

9. 3,400
  + 2,600

10. $287.35
  + 176.93

11. 187,452
  + 35,810

12. 146
  83
  +   7

13. 7.258
  4.782
  + 5.267

Subtract. Use mental math, calculator, or paper and pencil.

14. 98,000
  − 42,000

15. $854
  − 26.20

16. 73,596
  − 42,967

17. 11.4
  − 5.7

18. $176
  − 32.96

Add or subtract. Which method did you use?

19. $900.89 − $450.59

20. 3,628 + 2,719 + 1,307

21. 5,683 − 2,174

22. 46,000 + 188,000 + 3,000

23. 2,908,867 − 366,532

24. $187,452 + $35,810

25. 4.9 + 98.56 + 302.631 + 3.756 + 2.8 + 143

26. $19,000,891 + $31,980,000 + $26,980,875

27. 54 thousand
  + 36 thousand

28. 12.8 million
  − 7.9 million

29. $6.49 billion
  + 3.35 billion

Mixed Applications Solve. Which method did you use?

30. The regular price of a computer was $4,278. The school got it for $3,875. How much of a discount did the school get?

31. Students at Brook School raised $1,213.55; $623.56; and $800. Did they raise enough to purchase a computer for $2,700?

32. For one project, Chris brought in 33.4 lb of aluminum; Sandy, 89.3 lb; and Shari, 66.6 lb. How many pounds of aluminum did the students collect?

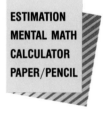

ESTIMATION
MENTAL MATH
CALCULATOR
PAPER/PENCIL

MENTAL MATH

One way to add mentally is to use a zigzag method.

—4-5—
—2-3—
+ —5-6—

Think: 45 + 20 = 65
65 + 3 = 68
68 + 50 = 118
118 + 6 = 124

Add mentally.

1. 34 + 26 + 62

2. 23 + 18 + 21 + 43

3. 125 + 251 + 347

4. 143 + 27 + 173

PROBLEM SOLVING

Strategy: Using Estimation

A. Merriweather Town runs a refreshment stand within its sports facilities. Last year the stand sold 851 hot dogs in March, 1,176 in April, and 1,330 in May. John, the manager, must order hot dogs for the same months this year. How many hot dogs should he order?

John plans to use estimation to help him solve the problem. To make sure that he has enough hot dogs for all the fans, he decides to *overestimate*.

John tries his plan. He overestimates by rounding up the numbers of hot dogs sold and then adds to get the total.

$$851 \longrightarrow 900 \qquad\qquad 900$$
$$1,176 \longrightarrow 1,200 \qquad\quad 1,200$$
$$1,330 \longrightarrow 1,400 \qquad +1,400$$
$$\overline{3,500}$$

John estimates the total number of hot dogs he should buy for March, April, and May of this year is 3,500.

1. What might happen if John underestimates the number of hot dogs?

2. **What if** the weather last year had been bad? How might that have affected John's estimate?

B. Each year the concession stands give to the athletic clubs money left over after expenses. Last year the refreshment stand gave $275, the program stand gave $125, and the T-shirt stand gave $560. Donna, the concession director, wants to donate *at least* $700 this year. How can she be sure that she has enough money left over to meet her goal?

Donna plans to use estimation to help her solve the problem. She decides to *underestimate* last year's donations.

$$\$275 \longrightarrow \$200 \qquad\qquad \$200$$
$$\$125 \longrightarrow \$100 \qquad\qquad 100$$
$$\$560 \longrightarrow \$500 \qquad\quad +500$$
$$\overline{\$800}$$

Donna estimates that the concessions should be able to donate *at least* $700 this year.

3. What might happen if Donna overestimates last year's donations?

PRACTICE

Use estimation to solve. Did you overestimate or underestimate? Why?

4. Rae is going to the store to buy 3 packages of hot-dog buns. Last week the buns cost $.89. Estimate how much money Rae should take to the store.

5. At last year's concert in the big field, attendance included 743 adults, 1,235 teenagers, and 690 children. How many people should the groundskeepers expect this year?

6. Last year the booster club sold programs and made a profit of $336 at football games, $264 at baseball games, and $416 at track and field events. How should the club estimate its profit for this year?

7. Last year a concession stand took in $3,250 in sales and had $1,720 worth of expenses. How should its director estimate the profit for this upcoming year?

Strategies and Skills Review

Solve. Use mental math, estimation, a calculator, or paper and pencil.

8. In last year's triathlon the winner scored 8.6, 7.8, and 9.2 in the three events. What total score should Marisol aim for if she hopes to win next year's triathlon?

9. How many hot dogs does a sports fan eat at a game? Try this experiment. Survey 20 people about the number of hot dogs they ordered at the last game they attended. Use a bar graph to record and interpret your results.

10. Lisa can run a mile twice as fast as Jim. If it takes her 5 minutes to run a mile, what is the combined time it would take for each to run a mile?

11. **_Write a problem_** in which the solution requires an overestimate or an underestimate. Ask others to solve it.

Investigating Patterns

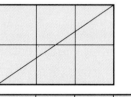

A. If you have a 2 × 3 rectangle and you draw a diagonal (a line from one corner to the opposite corner), then the diagonal goes through 4 squares.

The diagonal also goes through 4 squares in a 2 × 4 rectangle.

1. Work with a partner. Use graph paper and a straightedge. Investigate this diagonal pattern for other rectangles. Keep the width the same: 2 units. Vary the length from 1 to 12 units: 2 × 1, 2 × 2, 2 × 3, . . ., 2 × 12.

2. Organize your results in a table like this.

3. What is the sequence of numbers in the second column? How would you describe this sequence?

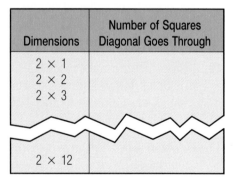

Dimensions	Number of Squares Diagonal Goes Through
2 × 1	
2 × 2	
2 × 3	
2 × 12	

4. What do you think the next four numbers are? Draw pictures to check your guess.

5. Suppose the diagonal of a 2 × n rectangle goes through 32 squares. What values are possible for n?

B. Try another experiment with your partner.

6. Investigate the diagonal pattern for rectangles of width equal to 3 units. Vary the length from 1 to 12 units: 3×1, 3×2, 3×3, ..., 3×12.

7. Organize your results in a table like the one you used before.

8. What is the sequence of numbers in the second column this time? Describe this sequence.

9. What do you think the next three numbers are? Draw pictures to check your guess.

10. Suppose the diagonals of three rectangles go through 24, 23, and 24 squares, respectively. If the rectangles are each 3 units wide, what are their lengths?

11. Pick another group of rectangles to investigate. (Rectangles of width 4 are interesting.) See what patterns you find and what predictions you can make.

Metric Units of Length: Perimeter

A. The **meter (m)** is the basic unit of length in the metric system. Basketball player Michael Jordan is about 2 m tall. During warm-ups, a player jogged the 86 m distance around the basketball court in about half a minute.

The **decimeter (dm), centimeter (cm),** and **millimeter (mm)** are used to measure shorter distances. The **kilometer (km)** is used to measure longer distances.

1 m = 10 dm
1 m = 100 cm
1 m = 1,000 mm
1 km = 1,000 m

A spoke in a bicycle wheel is about 3 dm long.
A basketball hoop is about 46 cm across.
The distance from New York to Phoenix is about 3,931 km.

1. Which unit would you use to measure the length of a pencil?

B. To find the **perimeter** or distance around a figure, you can use a metric ruler.

2. What is the length to the nearest centimeter of each side of the figure on the right?

3. What is the approximate perimeter?

4. ***What if*** you had to find the perimeter of a rectangle? Would you need to measure all four sides? Why or why not?

5. How could you find the perimeter of a square? of a regular octagon?

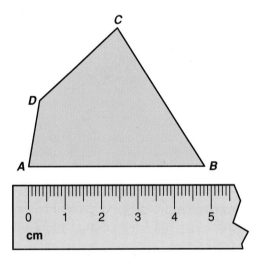

TRY OUT
Which of the units, mm, cm, dm, m, or km, would you use to measure each?

6. The distance you can walk in 20 minutes.

7. The width of a standard doorway.

8. The size of a television screen.

Use the figure on the right for Problems 9–10.

9. Estimate and then measure the length of each side of the figure to the nearest centimeter.

10. Find the perimeter in centimeters.

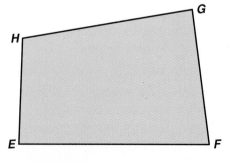

PRACTICE

Which of the units, mm, cm, dm, m, or km, would you use to measure each?

11. the width of a book

12. the length of a football field

13. the thickness of a dime

14. the perimeter of a tennis court

15. the distance between Washington, D.C. and San Francisco, California

Estimate each length. Then measure to the nearest centimeter and to the nearest millimeter.

16. 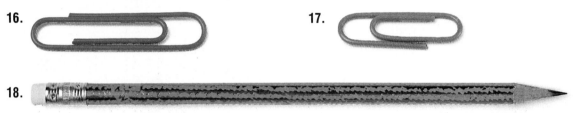 **17.**

18.

Measure the length of each side of the figure to the nearest centimeter. Then find the perimeter.

19.  **20.** **21.**

Mixed Applications

22. Estimate the perimeter of a field with sides of 1.7 km, 2.6 km, 1.8 km and 2.1 km.

23. The sides of a triangular island are 9.7 km, 4.8 km, and 10.3 km. Find the perimeter.

24. A basketball hoop is 3.048 m high. A player with extended arms is 1.92 m high. How far does she have to jump to reach the hoop?

25. *Write a problem* involving perimeter. Solve your problem. Ask others to solve it.

Mixed Review

Find the answer. Which method did you use?

26. 46 + 38 + 54

27. 39.883 + 35.9 + 148.26

28. 157 − 39

29. 37,088 + 183,701

30. 58.98 + 199.24 + 32.86

31. 12.6 − 4.8

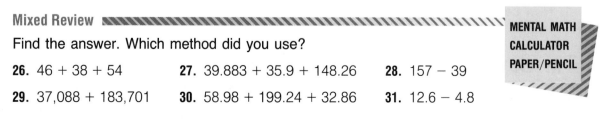

MENTAL MATH
CALCULATOR
PAPER/PENCIL

UNDERSTANDING A CONCEPT

Using Addition and Subtraction with Equations

A. Hanna's Computer Company hired 54 new employees on April 12. Now there are 162 workers with the company. How many people worked for the company before April 12?

You can find the number of workers before April 12 by writing and **solving** an equation.

Let n = the number of workers before April 12.
$n + 54$ = the total number of workers

Write the equation. $n + 54 = 162$

To find the **solution** to the equation you need to find the value of the variable that makes the equation true.

To do this, **isolate the variable** using a **related sentence.**

Solve.	$n + 54 = 162$
Think: Use a related sentence.	$162 - 54 = n$
Simplify.	$108 = n$

Check your answer by substituting 108 in the original equation.

$$n + 54 = 162$$
$$108 + 54 \overset{?}{=} 162$$
$$162 = 162 \quad \text{It checks.}$$

There were 108 workers before April 12.

B. You can use a related sentence to solve a subtraction equation.

Solve.	$n - 36 = 89$
Think: Use a related sentence.	$89 + 36 = n$
Simplify.	$125 = n$

1. How can you check that your solution to the equation is correct?

TRY OUT Solve the equation. Check the answer.

2. $n + 28 = 76$　　**3.** $n - 31 = 78$　　**4.** $n + 4.9 = 8.2$　　**5.** $n - 31.6 = 83.7$

PRACTICE

Solve the equation. Check the answer.

6. $n + 37 = 71$

7. $n + 292 = 403$

8. $n + 23.6 = 82.4$

9. $n - 42 = 83$

10. $n - 167 = 48$

11. $n - 4.5 = 17$

12. $n + 9.8 = 17.6$

13. $n + 215 = 349$

14. $n - 82 = 112$

15. $n + 214 = 386$

16. $n - 53.45 = 82.14$

17. $n - 69.2 = 56.8$

18. $n - 167 = 312$

19. $n + 63 = 78$

20. $n + 16.37 = 54.96$

21. $n + 54.9 = 93.7$

22. $n - 123 = 198$

23. $n - 57 = 23$

Write an equation for the problem. Solve the equation.

24. What number plus 9 is equal to 26?

25. What number minus 16 is equal to 59?

26. What number minus 16 is equal to 14.4?

27. What number plus 72 is equal to 143.1?

28. What number minus 23.7 is equal to 34.78?

29. What number plus 0.06 is equal to 4.02?

30. A number plus 5.9 is equal to 11. What is the number?

31. A number minus 14 is equal to 26. What is the number?

Critical Thinking

32. Suppose that $a + b = c$. What happens to c if a increases and b remains the same?

33. Suppose that $a - b = c$. What happens to c if a increases and b remains the same?

Mixed Applications

Solve. Which method did you use?

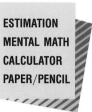

ESTIMATION
MENTAL MATH
CALCULATOR
PAPER/PENCIL

34. On a four-day walkathon to promote computer use in schools, Kim, from Hanna's Computer Company, hiked 14.8 km, 18.5 km, 21.2 km, and 22.5 km. How far did he hike?

35. The value of stock in Disks-Are-Us dropped 17.7 points from the previous day to 97.2. What was the previous day's value?

36. A gift for a retiring employee is going to cost $315. So far, fellow workers have raised $85.45, $77.75, and $98.90. Have they raised enough money for the gift?

37. Helen's total sales for a four-day saleathon were $4,040.75. After three days Janet's total sales were $3,385.55. How much must Janet sell on the fourth day of the saleathon to tie Helen?

Using Addition and Subtraction with Inequalities

A. The world record for balancing on one foot is 34 hours. Duane is determined to break the record. The last time his mother checked, Duane had been balancing for 21 hours.

WORKING TOGETHER

1. What are the three possible outcomes of Duane's efforts?

Look at the following number sentences.

$$n + 21 < 34 \qquad n + 21 = 34 \qquad n + 21 > 34$$

2. What does n represent in each sentence?

3. The symbols $>$ and $<$ are **inequality symbols.** Which of the three number sentences are **inequalities?**

4. Which number sentence shows that Duane tied the record?

5. Which number sentence shows that he fell short of the record?

6. Which number sentence shows that he broke the record?

B. You can use a related equation to solve an inequality.

Solve.	$n + 21 > 34$
Think: Use a related equation.	$n + 21 = 34$
Solve the equation.	$34 - 21 = n$
	$13 = n$
Write the solution to the inequality.	$n > 13$

Check your answer by substituting any number greater than 13 in the original inequality.

$$n + 21 > 34$$
$$17 + 21 \overset{?}{>} 34$$
$$38 > 34 \quad \text{It checks.}$$

7. How much longer must Duane balance to break the record?

8. ***What if*** Duane had failed to tie or break the record? Write an inequality to show the number of additional hours he would have balanced on one foot.

9. Which of these values for n would satisfy the conditions in Problem 8: 11, 13, or 15? Why?

10. How would you use the method in B to solve $n + 34 > 76$?

11. What related equation did you write?

12. Was this the same equation your classmates wrote?

13. What was your answer?

PRACTICE

Solve the inequality. Check the answer.

14. $n + 8 > 14$

15. $n + 103 > 150$

16. $n - 9.6 > 2.1$

17. $n - 9 < 21$

18. $n - 213 < 116$

19. $n + 2.6 < 7.8$

20. $n - 36 < 49$

21. $n + 4.7 > 10.2$

22. $n - 189 < 267$

23. $n - 18.1 > 25.6$

24. $n + 206 > 411$

25. $n - 2 > 8.41$

Write an inequality for the problem. Solve the inequality.

26. What number plus 4 is greater than 7?

27. What number minus 16 is less than 31?

28. What number minus 3.2 is greater than 4.9?

29. What number minus 46 is greater than 99?

30. What number plus 2.5 is less than 9.2?

31. What number plus 15 is less than 22?

Critical Thinking

32. Must the answer to an inequality be a whole number? Why?

Mixed Applications

33. Tom Luxton played the accordion for 84 hours. Norma has played nonstop for 39 hours. How much longer must she play to tie the record?

34. The record for baton twirling is 122.5 hours. Karl has been twirling for 30 hours nonstop. How much longer must he twirl to break the record?

35. Sarah went to the music store. She spent $172.99, $49.75, and $16.95. How much did she spend in all?

36. *Write a problem* that can be solved by using the inequality $n + 22 < 47$. Solve your problem. Ask others to solve it.

Mixed Review

Find the answer. Which method did you use?

MENTAL MATH
CALCULATOR
PAPER/PENCIL

37. $68 - 42$

38. $87.043 - 9.999$

39. $165 - 55

40. $96.5 - 8.3207$

41. $4,812 - 800.85

42. $20 - 6.735$

UNDERSTAND
✓PLAN
✓TRY
CHECK
✓EXTEND

PROBLEM SOLVING

Strategy: Guess, Test, and Revise

According to Gwynne's history book, the three kingdoms of Saul, David, and Solomon lasted a total of 100 years. David's kingdom outlasted Saul's by 18 years, and Solomon's lasted 4 years longer than David's. How long did each kingdom last?

Plan a strategy.

To solve the problem Gwynne plans to use the guess, test, and revise strategy.

Try the plan.

Gwynne tries her plan. First she guesses that Saul's kingdom lasted 40 years. If her guess is right, then:

David's kingdom lasted 58 years. $40 + 18 = 58$
Solomon's kingdom lasted 62 years. $58 + 4 = 62$
Next she tests her guess. $40 + 58 + 62 = 160$

Since all three kingdoms lasted a total of 100 years, Gwynne knows that her guess is too high. She must revise her guess and try again.

Suppose Gwynne guesses that Saul's kingdom lasted 10 years.

1. How long would each of the other two kingdoms have lasted?

2. How long would the three kingdoms have lasted?

3. Was Gwynne's second guess just right, too high, or too low?

4. Why should Gwynne now pick a number between 10 and 40?

Try a guess of 20. If Saul's kingdom lasted 20 years, then David's lasted 38 years and Solomon's lasted 42 years.

Test the guess. $20 + 38 + 42 = 100$

So 20 is correct.

5. **What if** there had been four kingdoms that lasted a total of 74 years? If each kingdom lasted 3 more years than the previous one, how long did each kingdom last? Use the guess, test, and revise strategy to find the answer.

PRACTICE

Solve.

6. Gilgud rode her horse a total of 36 mi in 4 days in a mountainous kingdom. Each day she rode 2 mi farther than the previous day. How far did she ride each day?

7. A wall around part of a kingdom was 96 ft long. It was built in three sections. The second was 6 ft longer than the first, and the third was 9 ft longer than the second. How long was each section?

8. Within the Roman Empire three aqueducts had a total length of 545 ft. If two were the same length and one was 20 ft longer, how long was each aqueduct?

9. In ancient Greece two city-states had 27 temples. One had 5 more temples than the other. How many temples did each city-state have?

Strategies and Skills Review

Solve. Use mental math, estimation, a calculator, or paper and pencil.

10. To dress three members of the royal family, the tailor needed 21 yd^2 of cloth. If the second and third persons required 2 more square yards than the next younger person, how much cloth did the tailor use for each?

11. The junior high class is planning an "Ancient Kingdom Festival." The class plans to serve a sweet cake to each person attending. If the class expects to have at least 67 adults and 158 students, how many sweet cakes will be needed?

12. Did your ancestors come from another land? What about the ancestors of your friends? Survey 20 friends to find out where their ancestors came from. Display your results in a bar graph.

13. *Write a problem* that uses the guess, test, and revise strategy to find a solution. Ask others to solve the problem.

COOPERATIVE LEARNING

DECISION MAKING

Problem Solving: Choosing What to Do for Lunch

SITUATION

Three friends who are going on a class trip must decide what to do about lunch. They can bring lunch from home, buy food from a truck stand, or eat in the cafeteria on location. A friend who had already been on the trip gave them the notes below.

PROBLEM

What should they do for lunch?

DATA

	LUNCH FROM HOME	TRUCK STAND	CAFETERIA
Menu	sandwich fruit fruit drink	tacos burritos juice	turkey grilled cheese salad milk
Cost of Meal	$1.70-$1.95	$2.80-$3.50	$3.40-$5.00
Cost of Drink	$.45	$1.00	$.75
Dessert	You can buy dessert at the truck stand or at the cafeteria.	fruit salad $.85	frozen yogurt $.75
Other Factors	You will have to carry lunch with you all morning. The food may be warm.	You will not have to carry food. Food will be served hot. The nutritional value of the food is questionable.	You will not have to carry food with you all morning. The cafeteria offers a wider choice of foods. There may be a long wait at lunch hour.

USING THE DATA

What is the total cost of the least expensive lunch and drink without dessert?

1. home   **2.** truck stand   **3.** cafeteria

What is the total cost of the least expensive lunch and drink with dessert?

4. home   **5.** truck stand   **6.** cafeteria

What is the total cost of the most expensive lunch and drink with dessert?

7. home   **8.** truck stand   **9.** cafeteria

MAKING DECISIONS

10. When would a lunch from home save one of the friends about $3 over the cost of a cafeteria lunch?

11. *What if* the friends did not want to bring drinks with their home lunches? What would be the least expensive cost if each friend bought a drink and a dessert at the truck stand? at the cafeteria?

12. *What if* each friend had $8.00 to spend on a cafeteria lunch and on souvenirs? Each needed exactly $2.25 for souvenirs. What could each have eaten for lunch?

13. *Write a list* of other factors the friends should consider when deciding how to have lunch.

14. *What if* the cafeteria offered a discount to groups? Would that affect your choice? Why or why not?

15. Which lunch would you choose? Tell why.

Math and Literature

An author who plans to write a biography must do a great deal of research. The biographer might use an encyclopedia to start but will need to consult other sources as well. The biographer, for example, may interview people who knew the subject and may study the correspondence of the individual. Biographers also like to note events in the world at different periods in the person's life. These details of history and of the person's life help make the subject alive for the reader. A *time line* is one way to organize such data.

Madeleine L'Engle, born November 29, 1918, has been writing books for young people and adults for many years. Her first book, *The Small Rain,* was published in 1945, four years after graduating from Smith College. The Newbery Medal winner *A Wrinkle in Time* was published in 1962. It was the first of a trilogy of science-fiction books about the same characters. These three books are now published together as *The Time Trilogy.* L'Engle published another book, *Two-Part Invention,* in 1988.

What if you wanted to examine the time span between L'Engle's first book and her award-winning book? How many years had elapsed?

Think: How many years are there between 1945 and 1962?

Subtract: 1962 − 1945 = 17

Seventeen years had elapsed.

ACTIVITIES

1. Copy the time line of L'Engle's life. Fill in other dates including the publication dates of her other books and the dates of major world events.

2. Make a time line of your own life. Include important dates in your life and important historical events.

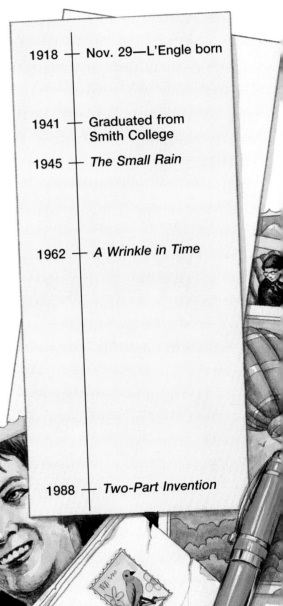

1918	Nov. 29—L'Engle born
1941	Graduated from Smith College
1945	*The Small Rain*
1962	*A Wrinkle in Time*
1988	*Two-Part Invention*

Computer Spreadsheet: Nutrition Analysis

The Food and Nutrition Board of the National Academy of Sciences has determined that children between the ages of 11 and 14 require a minimum of about 45 grams of protein per day. The chart below shows various foods and their protein content for given portions of the food. Each food has been numbered so that you will be able to identify it when you use the computer spreadsheet MENU PLAN.

A *spreadsheet* performs various calculations on data.

FOOD	PORTION	PROTEIN
Dairy products		
1 Cheddar cheese	1 oz	7 g
2 Cottage cheese	1 cup	26 g
3 Butter	1 tbs	0
4 Milk	1 cup	8 g
Grains		
5 Corn muffin	1	3 g
6 Whole wheat bread	1 slice	3 g
7 Roll	1	3 g
8 Pizza	1 slice	6 g
9 Noodles	1 cup	7 g
10 White rice	1 cup	4 g
Meat, poultry, fish		
11 Tuna fish	3 oz	24 g
12 Lamb chop	3 oz	18 g
13 Liver	3 oz	22 g
14 Frankfurter	1	7 g
15 Hamburger	3 oz	23 g
16 Chicken drumstick	1	12 g
17 Chicken soup	1 cup	7 g
18 Beef/vegetable stew	1 cup	16 g

FOOD	PORTION	PROTEIN
Vegetables		
19 Broccoli	1 stalk	6 g
20 Carrot	1	1 g
21 Spinach	1 cup	6 g
22 Lima beans	1 cup	10 g
23 Peas	1 cup	8 g
24 Baked potato	1	4 g
25 Potato salad	1 cup	7 g
26 Tomato	1	1 g
27 Tomato juice	1 cup	2 g
Fruit		
28 Orange	1	1 g
29 Apple	1	0
30 Banana	1	1 g
31 Cantaloupe	$\frac{1}{2}$	2 g
32 Orange juice	1 cup	2 g
33 Lemonade	1 cup	0
Other		
34 Mayonnaise	1 tbs	0
35 Peanut butter	1 tbs	4 g
36 Egg	1	6 g

AT THE COMPUTER

Plan breakfast, lunch, and dinner for a day, using foods from the chart. In column A enter the identifying number for the food you choose. In column C enter the number of portions. For example, if you would like the portion given in the chart, enter the number 1; if you would like three times as large a portion, enter 3; if you would like half as large a portion, enter 0.5. Keep your menu balanced. The program will display the total grams of protein in column D. If the grand total is less than 45 grams, substitute items until it is 45 grams or more.

EXTRA PRACTICE

Mental Math: Adding and Subtracting, page 47

Add or subtract mentally.

1. 77
        25
     + 23

2. 2.8
        6.4
     + 1.2

3. $134
         27
      + 266

4. 2.69
        1.28
     + 0.31

5. 435
        716
     + 284

6. $996
      + 458

7. 547
      + 94

8. 2.9
      + 9.6

9. $7.73
      + 5.49

10. 89.8
       + 7.8

11. $8.64
       − .98

12. 27.3
       − 6.7

13. 551
       − 495

14. $2,614
       − 1,398

15. 7,255
       − 899

16. $46 + $35 + $14 + $25

17. $7.42 − $3.99

18. 34.2 + 12.3 + 65.8

Estimating Sums, Differences by Rounding, page 49

Estimate by rounding.

1. 3,825
         614
     + 5,071

2. $229.35
         213.60
      + 49.89

3. 68,017
        23,385
     + 14,842

4. 7.6
        2.416
     + 3.02

5. 3.814
        0.218
     + 4.74

6. 0.624
      − 0.089

7. 35.8
      − 17.33

8. 39.802
      − 28.1

9. $2.07
       − .78

10. 5.3
       − 0.227

11. 8.52 − 2.869

12. $53.78 + $8.95 + $29.39

13. 2.311 + 6.59 + 0.387

Front-End Estimation: Sums and Differences, page 51

1. $ 33,307
         365,699
      +   8,579

2. 3.279
        4.086
     + 0.9897

3. 5.173
      − 2.89

4. 45,172
      − 32,098

5. 0.866
      − 0.57

Estimate. Use the front two digits.

6. 4,841
         249
     +   752

7. 5.271
        0.78
     + 3.756

8. 6.817
      − 0.028

9. $62.15
       − 8.45

10. 78,954
       − 34,865

EXTRA PRACTICE

Adding and Subtracting Whole Numbers and Decimals, page 53 ....

Add or subtract.

1. 7,300 + 2,700   **2.** 178,325 + 56,920   **3.** 245 + 345   **4.** 8.6 + 5.6

5. 88,000 − 34,000   **6.** 39.24 + 56.32   **7.** 56,498 − 29,897   **8.** 764 − 36.2

9. 286 − 42.8761   **10.** 826,000 − 56,999   **11.** 13.6 − 4.8   **12.** $800.79 − $350.29

13. 36,789 − 5,999   **14.** 25.6 − 7.9   **15.** 789 − 23.8976   **16.** $7,003 − $5,678

17. 4,390 + 72,856 + 298,452 + 992   **18.** 76,000 + 288,000 + 4,000

19. $3,809,678 − $466,532   **20.** 587,552 + 45,920

21. 5.9 + 89.65 + 502.731 + 2.576 + 253   **22.** $18,000,992 + $46,890,000

23. 4.6 + 3.7 + 2.2 + 6.8 + 5.3 + 2.4   **24.** 34.56023 + 45.8976 + 59.07865

25. 10.73 + 411.3 + 8.22 + 7   **26.** 473.225 − 304.82

27. $43.02 + $112.17 + $4,281.25   **28.** $119 − $48.39

Problem−Solving Strategy: Using Estimation, page 55 ....

Use estimation to solve Questions 1−6. Did you overestimate or underestimate?

1. Beth is going to stay at a cabin in the mountains for 3 nights. It costs $79 per night. Estimate how much she should take to pay for the cabin.

2. Last season at a campground there were 243 adults, 562 teenagers, and 186 children. How many people should the director expect this year?

3. Last year the campground took in $5,880 and had expenses of $1,420. How should the director estimate the profit for this year?

4. Last year the refreshment stand made a profit of $3,256. The gift shop made a profit of $4,876. How should the manager estimate the profit for this year?

5. Batteries cost $.96. Susan needs 3 for her flashlight. Estimate how much money she should take to the store?

6. Last year the Smiths spent $345 on lodging and $285 on food during a ski trip. How much should they budget for this year?

EXTRA PRACTICE

Metric Units of Length: Perimeter, page 59 ···

Which of the units, mm, cm, dm, m, or km would you use to measure each?

1. the width of a penny

2. the length of the Golden Gate Bridge

3. the distance from Atlanta to Houston

4. a 12-year-old student's height

5. the width of a student's desk

6. the thickness of a dime

Estimate each length. Then measure to the nearest centimeter or millimeter.

7. _____

8. _____

Measure the length of each side of the figure to the nearest centimeter. Then find the perimeter.

9.   **10.**   **11.**

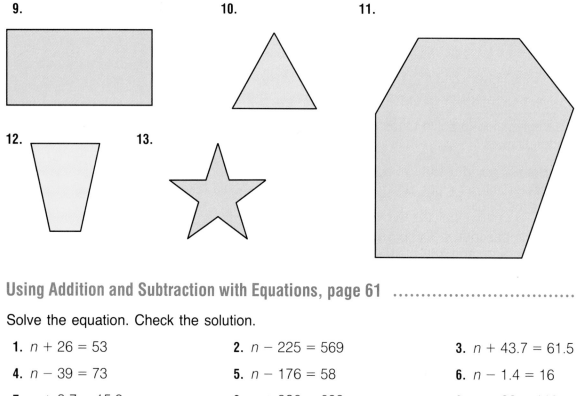

12.   **13.**

Using Addition and Subtraction with Equations, page 61 ·······························

Solve the equation. Check the solution.

1. $n + 26 = 53$

2. $n - 225 = 569$

3. $n + 43.7 = 61.5$

4. $n - 39 = 73$

5. $n - 176 = 58$

6. $n - 1.4 = 16$

7. $n + 8.7 = 15.9$

8. $n + 326 = 688$

9. $n - 66 = 119$

10. $n + 215 = 590$

11. $n - 29.85 = 62.13$

12. $n + 3.8 = 7.2$

13. $n + 36.8 = 84.6$

14. $n + 57 = 108$

15. $n - 67 = 11$

16. $n - 88.34 = 57.28$

17. $n + 78.45 = 96.7$

18. $n - 87 = 43$

Using Addition and Subtraction with Inequalities, page 63 ·····························

Solve the inequality. Check the solution.

1. $n + 9 > 15$

2. $n - 8.7 > 3.1$

3. $n + 203 > 260$

4. $n - 8 < 23$

5. $n - 316 < 158$

6. $n + 24 < 46$

7. $n + 2.7 < 5.9$

8. $n + 326 > 688$

9. $n - 186 < 269$

10. $n + 215 < 322$

11. $n - 27.1 > 32.7$

12. $n + 13.8 > 17.2$

Write an inequality for the problem. Solve the inequality.

13. What number plus 3 is greater than 7?

14. What number minus 18 is less than 41?

15. What number minus 4.6 is greater than 6.9?

16. What number plus 3.5 is less than 8.4?

17. What number minus 57 is greater than 88?

18. What number plus 17 is less than 44?

19. What number plus 7.6 is greater than 12.8?

20. What number minus 848.27 is less than 1,042?

Problem–Solving Strategy: Guess, Test, and Revise, page 65 ·······················

Solve.

1. An automobile manufacturer makes three models of vans: the Oryx, the Kudu, and the Gnu. The three models have a total length of 36 ft. The Oryx is 4 ft shorter than the Gnu, and the Kudu is 2 ft longer than the Oryx. How long is each van model?

2. To increase sales last month the manufacturer offered a rebate of $500 for each model sold. The rebates for the month totaled $150,000. The rebates for the Oryx were twice as much as for the Kudu and the Gnu. How much was rebated for each model?

3. Last year a total of 3,000 vans were sold. The Oryx sold 500 more than the Kudu, and the Gnu sold 1,000 less than the Oryx. How many of each model were sold?

4. The two best salespeople sold a total of 32 vans last month. One salesperson sold 8 more vans than the other. How many vans did each salesperson sell?

Practice PLUS

KEY SKILL: Adding and Subtracting Whole Numbers and Decimals (Use after page 53.)

Level A

Add or subtract.

1. 8,725
    + 1,894

2. 45,327
    − 9,439

3. 8.26
    − 0.79

4. 22.57
    + 7.4

5. 1,300 + 2,700   6. 8,000 − 5,999   7. 146 + 254   8. 7,013 − 6,297

9. 1.5 + 3.5   10. 3,584 + 8,258   11. 704,341 − 59,487   12. 84 − 35.8

13. 12.4 − 5.8   14. 818,000 − 57,896   15. $76 + $25 + $24

16. Students at South Jr. High want to raise $3,000 for computer software. So far they have raised $1,689. How much more do they need?

Level B

Add or subtract.

17. 72,934
    + 12,908

18. 145,764
    − 5,835

19. 4,845.6
    − 69.831

20. 0.941
    + 16,975.004

21. 4,200 + 3,800   22. 17,000 − 4,999   23. 825 + 575 + 450   24. 14,542 − 9,875

25. 1.4 + 2.5 + 3.6   26. 23,584 + 8,347   27. 172 − 45.1457   28. 941 − 25.2

29. $102,764 − $53,875   30. 25,001 − 4,126   31. 277,000 − 41,799

32. Students collected soup labels to buy gym equipment. The first month they collected 8,268 labels; the second month, 5,765, and the third, 3,000. How many did they collect in all?

Level C

Add or subtract.

33. 76,935
    − 12,642

34. 38,499
    + 192,582

35. 52,456.483
    + 16,984.27

36. 453,890.12
    − 96,767.834

37. 56,000 + 44,000   38. 88,000 − 7,999   39. 1,300 + 2,500   40. 14,542 − 9,875

41. 5.2 + 6.7 + 8.8   42. $800.79 − $350.79   43. $3,807,549 − $968   44. 32,031 − 28,747

45. 286 − 52.6714   46. 5.4 + 98.26 + 524.387   47. 25,000 + 185,000 + 7,000

48. The Newspaper Club needs $13,000 to buy a desk-top publishing system. So far they have raised $8,872.85. How much more do they need?

PRACTICE PLUS

KEY SKILL: Metric Units of Length: Perimeter (Use after page 59.)

Level A

Which is the best unit, mm, cm, dm, m, or km, to measure:

1. the width of your bedroom?

2. the length of a pencil?

Measure the length to the nearest centimeter and to the nearest millimeter.

3. _____

4. _____

Level B

Which of the units, mm, cm, dm, m, or km, would you use to measure:

5. the length of a car?

6. the distance between NY and TX?

Measure the length of each side of the figure to the nearest centimeter. Then find the perimeter.

7.

8.

9.

10. The sides of a garden are 5.8 m, 4.3 m, 3.9 m, and 5.5 m. What is the perimeter in meters?

Level C

Which of the units, mm, cm, dm, m, or km, would you use to measure:

11. the thickness of a quarter?

12. the length of this page?

Measure the length of each side of the figure to the nearest centimeter. Then find the perimeter.

13.

14.

15.

16. A rectangular corral is 27.8 m by 34.2 m. What is its perimeter?

CHAPTER REVIEW

LANGUAGE AND MATHEMATICS

Complete the sentence. Use the words in the chart on the right.

1. The distance around a figure is its ■.
   (page 58)

2. The symbols > and < are called ■
   symbols. *(page 62)*

3. The basic unit of length in the metric
   system is the ■. *(page 58)*

4. The equation 5 + 0.3 = 0.3 + 5
   illustrates the ■. *(page 46)*

5. ***Write a definition*** or give an example
   of the words you did not use from
   the chart.

> **VOCABULARY**
>
> **commutative property**
> **associative property**
> **meter**
> **perimeter**
> **equation**
> **inequality**

CONCEPTS AND SKILLS

Estimate by rounding. *(page 48)*

6. 2,347 + 6,782 + 413

7. 46.8 − 32.97

8. $563.48 + $4.72 + $327

9. 43.07 − 3.912

Estimate using front-end estimation. *(page 50)*

10.	**11.**	**12.**	**13.**	**14.**
282	67.8	$3.75	8.65	6.195
27	− 24.99	.89	− 4.18	− 0.382
+ 302		+ 1.94		

15. 8 + 0.7 + 2.32 + 1.09

16. 10 − 0.99

17. 745 + 308 + 237

18. 4.862 − 1.67

19. 25 − 13.42

20. 3.43 + 0.57 + 8.01

Add or subtract. *(page 52)*

21.	**22.**	**23.**	**24.**	**25.**
34,567	56.7	8,063	500	72.86
78,081	6.51	− 267	− .86	8.47
+ 3,402	+ 2			+ 26.54

26. $.25 + $3

27. 3 − 0.5

28. $203 − $.48

29. 10 − 3.2

30. 9.01 − 2.004

31. 176 − 97

32. 11 − 5.73

33. $115 + $1.56

34. 8.3 − 4.596

35. 6 − 2.09

Measure to the nearest centimeter and then to the nearest milimeter. *(page 58)*

36. ——

37. ——————————————

38. ——————

Use *mm, cm, m,* or *km* to complete the sentence. *(page 58)*

39. The length of a new pencil is about 200 ▪.

40. The length of a staple is about 12 ▪.

Solve. *(pages 60–63)*

41. $n + 8 = 302$

42. $n - 145 > 26$

43. $n + 3.6 < 47$

44. $n - 5 = 1.2$

45. $n + 0.56 > 1$

46. $n - 32 < 8.3$

47. What number plus 5 is equal to 7.3?

48. What number plus 0.7 is equal to 1?

Critical Thinking

49. *What if* $n + x = 5$? If n increases, will x increase or decrease? *(page 60)*

50. *What if* $n - 0.5 < 0.2$? Can n be a whole number? *(page 62)*

51. What would be the best value to use in the "equal addition" method to subtract 99.8 from 142.3 mentally? *(page 46)*

52. Which front-end estimation method would be best to use when adding 3.43, 567, and 10.8? *(page 50)*

Mixed Applications

53. The drama club was selling tickets for a play. One day it had sales of $15.75, $23, $6.75, $8, $18, $3.25, and $10.25. Estimate the total sales for that day by rounding to the greatest place of the greatest number. *(page 48)*

54. The computer club wants to buy a computer that costs $1,899.99, a printer that costs $785, a dust cover that costs $9.60, and software that costs $190. How much money does it need to buy all of that equipment? *(page 52)*

55. A trailer can hold 8.5 T. There is already 2 T of grain on the trailer. Write and solve an equation to show how many more tons of grain can be put on the trailer. *(page 60)*

56. Jan put ribbon around the perimeter of rectangular paperweights. Each paperweight was 45 mm long and 30 mm wide. How many millimeters long was each piece of ribbon? *(page 58)*

57. A German castle has 2 walls that are a total of 12 ft thick. One is twice as thick as the other. How thick is each wall? *(page 64)*

Chapter Test

1. Estimate by rounding to the greatest place of the greatest number.
   9,781 − 6,307

2. Estimate by rounding to the greatest place of the least number.
   $6.82 + $.36 + $2.24

3. Estimate using front-end estimation.
   Method: One-column with adjustment.
   7.68 + 0.9 + 2.46

4. Estimate using front-end estimation.
   Method: Two-column.
   78,487 − 6,751

Add or subtract.

5. $\begin{array}{r} 4{,}362 \\ 828 \\ +\ 246 \\ \hline \end{array}$

6. $\begin{array}{r} 80.2 \\ -\ \ .64 \\ \hline \end{array}$

7. $407.52 + $63 + $8.48

8. 315 − 0.72

Measure the segment to the nearest millimeter.

9.

10.

Use *mm, cm, m,* or *km* to complete the sentence.

11. The length of a spoon is about 150 ■.

12. The length of your little toe is about 30 ■.

Solve.

13. $n - 53 = 187$

14. $n + 1.86 < 12$

15. $n - 7 > 8.3$

16. Jack made four measurements. They were 6.96 m, 1.24 m, 0.81 m, and 7.3 m. Estimate the total of the measurements by rounding to the greatest place of the least number.

17. Tisha's record for running is 4.5 km. Tad has already run 2 km. Write an inequality to show how much farther he must run to beat Tisha's record.

18. Computer X costs $1,809.99, and Computer Y costs $2,199.98. How much more does Computer Y cost?

19. The sides of a triangle measure 5 cm, 8.75 cm, and 10.4 cm. What is the perimeter of the triangle?

20. A 40-ft tower was made from three sections. Two sections were the same height and one was 5 ft shorter. How long was each section?

GENERATE MAGIC SQUARES

In a **magic square** the sum of the numbers in each row, column, and diagonal are the same. You can make your own 3-by-3 magic square by following these steps.

Choose a sequence of 9 numbers that differ by the same number.

Example: 1, 3, 5, 7, 9, 11, 13, 15, 17

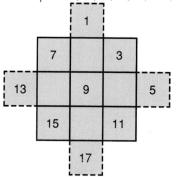

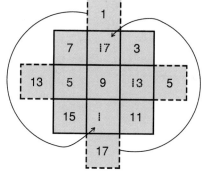

7	17	3
5	9	13
15	1	11

Draw a 3-by-3 square. Add the extra boxes. Begin with the top box. Write the numbers diagonally from upper left to lower right.

Flip each outside number to the opposite inside box. See what happens for 1 and 17 in the diagram.

Remove the outside boxes to see the magic square.

1. What is the magic sum for this square?

2. Multiply each entry in the square by 2. Is the new square a magic square?

3. *What if* you multiplied each entry by 30? Is that square a magic square?

Make a magic 3-by-3 square with these numbers.
What is the magic sum for each square?

4. 3, 6, 9, 12, 15, 18, 21, 24, 27   **5.** 1.5, 3.5, 5.5, 7.5, 9.5, 11.5, 13.5, 15.5, 17.5

6. Choose nine numbers to make your own magic square.

7. *What if* you add the corresponding entries of two magic squares? Do you get another magic square?

8. Can you see any relationship between the middle number of a magic square and the magic sum?

9. Use a different sequence of numbers to create a magic square with a magic sum of 39.

Choose the letter of the correct answer.

1. What is the standard form for twenty thousand, one hundred and two hundredths?
   a. 20,100.002
   b. 20,100.02
   c. 20,000.102
   d. not given

This frequency chart shows the number of colleges to which the members of the honor society wrote for information.

COLLEGE

Number of Colleges	Members
1	4
2	6
3	2
4	11

2. How many members wrote to four colleges?
   a. 1
   b. 4
   c. 11
   d. not given

3. How many members wrote to more than one college?
   a. 4
   b. 8
   c. 11
   d. not given

4. How many members are in the club?
   a. 11
   b. 23
   c. 33
   d. not given

5. Estimate by rounding to the greatest place of the least number.
   $8.03 + $.47 + $7 + $3.96
   a. $19.00
   b. $19.50
   c. $24.00
   d. not given

6. Estimate by using the front digits and adjusting.
   3.681 + 9.54 + 0.87
   a. 12
   b. 16
   c. 14
   d. not given

Add or subtract.

7. $501 + 6.2 + 8$
   a. 5.61
   b. 5.71
   c. 515.2
   d. not given

8. $2.01 + 6$
   a. 2.07
   b. 2.61
   c. 8.01
   d. not given

9. $230 - 8.62$
   a. 221.38
   b. 222.48
   c. 632
   d. not given

Solve for n.

10. $n - 65 = 100$
    a. 165
    b. 45
    c. 35
    d. not given

11. $n + 4.6 < 5$
    a. $n < 4.1$
    b. $n < 5.1$
    c. $n < 9.6$
    d. not given

12. $n + 6.8 = 10$
    a. 16.8
    b. 5.8
    c. 3.2
    d. not given

Solve.

13. Three speech club members wrote 726, 302, and 389 words for a 5,000-word speech contest. Round each amount to the nearest hundred and find about how many more words they need to write.
    a. 3,600
    b. 3,500
    c. 1,400
    d. not given

14. Three of the speech club members are timing their speeches. The first speech is 3.45 minutes, the second speech is 4.5 minutes, and the third speech is 2.6 minutes. What is the total time for the three speeches?
    a. 11 minutes
    b. 10.55 minutes
    c. 12.06 minutes
    d. not given

CHAPTER 3

Applying Multiplication: Whole Numbers, Decimals

MATH CONNECTIONS: AREA • CIRCUMFERENCE • PROBLEM SOLVING

Endangered Animals		Average Life Expectancy
	Asian Elephant	40 Years
	Bactrian Camel	12 Years
	Gorilla	20 Years
	Leopard	12 Years
	Black Rhinoceros	15 Years
	Tiger	16 Years

1. What information do you see in this picture?
2. How can you use this information?
3. Compare the life expectancies of the Asian elephant and the leopard in two ways.
4. Write a problem using this information.

UNDERSTANDING A CONCEPT

Mental Math: Multiplying by Powers of 10

A. Patterns can help you to find some products mentally.
Tom used a calculator to find the products.

17 [×] 10 $\boxed{170.}$ 17 [×] 100 $\boxed{1700.}$ 17 [×] 1000 $\boxed{17000.}$

Susan used a calculator to find these products.

3.76 [×] 10 $\boxed{37.6}$ 3.76 [×] 100 $\boxed{376.}$ 3.76 [×] 1000 $\boxed{3760.}$

1. What pattern could Tom have used to find his products mentally?

2. What pattern could Susan have used?

3. Use these patterns to find the product mentally.
   a. 31×100 **b.** 51.723×10 **c.** $7.6 \times 10,000$

B. Sometimes the multiplication properties can
be used to multiply mentally.

Property	Example
Commutative	$3 \times 7 = 7 \times 3$
Associative	$(3 \times 4) \times 5 = 3 \times (4 \times 5)$
Distributive	$5 \times (50 + 6) = (5 \times 50) + (5 \times 6)$

Tom and Susan multiplied $4 \times 8 \times 25$
to find the volume of a box.

Tom started to multiply mentally. $\underline{4 \times 8} \times 25$

Then he used his calculator. 32 [×] 25 [=] $\boxed{800}$

Susan used the multiplication $4 \times 8 \times 25$
properties to rearrange the factors. $\underline{4 \times 25} \times 8$

Then she multiplied mentally. $100 \times 8 = 800$

4. Which properties did Susan use?

TRY OUT   Write the letter of the correct answer. Multiply mentally.

5. $750 \times 1,000$ **a.** 750   **b.** 7,500   **c.** 75,000   **d.** 750,000

6. 0.005×10 **a.** 0.005   **b.** 0.05   **c.** 0.5   **d.** 5

7. $20 \times 0.09 \times 5$ **a.** 0.09   **b.** 0.9   **c.** 9   **d.** 90

8. $2.5 \times 7.5 \times 4$ **a.** 0.75   **b.** 7.5   **c.** 75   **d.** 750

PRACTICE

Find the product mentally.

9. 10 × 28

10. 100 × 4.5

11. 1,000 × 39

12. 1,000 × 807

13. 100 × 4.2

14. 10 × 0.006

15. 1,000 × 0.0085

16. 0.207 × 100

17. 50 × 9.44 × 2

18. 5 × 98 × 200

19. 4 × 6 × 25

20. 2.5 × 30 × 4

21. 10 × 0.003

22. 2 × 4.3 × 5

23. 8 × 75 × 125

24. 5 × 8 × 0.2

25. 10 × 59.23

26. 0.2403 × 1,000

27. 25 × 365 × 4

28. 5 × 48 × 2

29. 500,000 × 100

30. 5 × 180.9 × 20

31. 250 × 3.5 × 4

32. 1,000 × 0.0086

33. 24.96 × 10,000

34. 0.042 × 100,000

35. 0.25 × 5 × 0.4

36. 0.125 × 4 × 16

37. 4.8 × 2.5 × 4

38. 1.25 × 273 × 8

39. 0.025 × 8 × 12

40. 0.17 × 0.2 × 0.5

41. Use the distributive property to multiply: 8 × 6.5; and 12 × 4.5.

Mixed Applications

Solve. Which method did you use?

> **MENTAL MATH**
> **CALCULATOR**
> **PAPER/PENCIL**

42. In November, the school bookstore had sales of $3,902.54 and expenses of $2,888.92. How much money did the bookstore make after expenses?

43. Tom and Jo bought 400 pens at a cost of $60 and sold each pen for $.25. How much money did they make on the sale of the pens?

44. The bookstore sold 100 copies of a book called *Fantastic Facts and Figures*. The book sold for $8.97. What were the total sales?

45. During one four-month period, sales at the bookstore were $3,902.54; $2,834.33; $933.93; and $1,390.75. Find the total sales for the period.

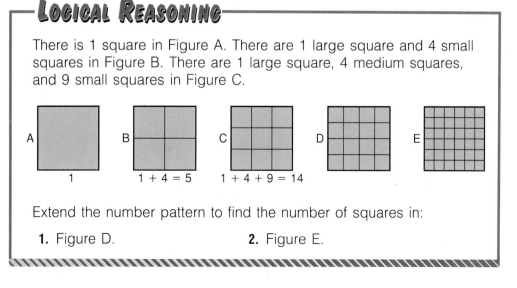

LOGICAL REASONING

There is 1 square in Figure A. There are 1 large square and 4 small squares in Figure B. There are 1 large square, 4 medium squares, and 9 small squares in Figure C.

A   1
B   1 + 4 = 5
C   1 + 4 + 9 = 14
D
E

Extend the number pattern to find the number of squares in:

1. Figure D.

2. Figure E.

Mental Math: Decimal Powers of 10

A. Mark and Elisa wanted to multiply 2,500 by 0.1, 0.01, and 0.001.

Elisa used fractions.

$$0.1 \times 2{,}500 = \frac{1}{10} \times 2{,}500 = \frac{2{,}500}{10} = 250$$

$$0.01 \times 2{,}500 = \frac{1}{100} \times 2{,}500 = \frac{2{,}500}{100} = 25$$

$$0.001 \times 2{,}500 = \frac{1}{1{,}000} \times 2{,}500 = \frac{2{,}500}{1{,}000} = 2.5$$

 Mark used his calculator.

0.1 ⊠ **2,500** ⊟ $\boxed{250.}$

0.01 ⊠ **2,500** ⊟ $\boxed{25.}$

0.001 ⊠ **2,500** ⊟ $\boxed{2.5}$

1. What pattern do you see in Mark's and Elisa's answers?

2. How would you use this pattern to find 0.3 × 0.01 mentally? What is the product?

B. You can use the same pattern to multiply by multiples of decimal powers of 10.

Multiply: 0.04 × 500

$$\begin{aligned}
0.04 \times 500 &= (4 \times 0.01) \times 500 \\
&= (4 \times 500) \times 0.01 \\
&= 2{,}000 \times 0.01 \\
&= 20
\end{aligned}$$

3. How would you find 30 × 0.8 mentally? What is the product?

TRY OUT Choose the letter of the correct answer.

Multiply mentally.

4. 0.01 × 8.56   **a.** 85.6   **b.** 8.56   **c.** 0.856   **d.** 0.0856

5. 0.001 × 0.49   **a.** 4.9   **b.** 0.49   **c.** 0.049   **d.** 0.00049

6. 0.07 × 400   **a.** 2,800   **b.** 280   **c.** 28   **d.** 2.8

7. 0.003 × 4.2   **a.** 0.0126   **b.** 126   **c.** 0.126   **d.** 12.6

PRACTICE

Multiply mentally.

8. 0.1 × 795   **9.** 0.001 × 6,409   **10.** 0.01 × 3.8   **11.** 0.001 × 45,267

12. 0.01 × 0.9   **13.** 0.1 × 0.05   **14.** 0.001 × 968   **15.** 0.01 × 4.01

16. 0.9 × 70   **17.** 0.02 × 14   **18.** 0.005 × 6,000   **19.** 0.04 × 25

20. 0.008 × 6   **21.** 0.7 × 0.05   **22.** 0.006 × 700   **23.** 0.03 × 0.6

24. 0.001 × 5.8   **25.** 0.04 × 1.2   **26.** 0.8 × 500   **27.** 0.01 × 0.217

28. 0.007 × 0.6   **29.** 0.001 × 84   **30.** 0.06 × 40   **31.** 0.1 × 0.0011

Mixed Applications

32. The pet store where Aaron works did $835,000 in business last year. This year, the store plans to do $940,000 in business. How much more money will the pet shop take in this year?

33. The pet shop has 180 neon fish, 225 guppies, 58 angel fish, 163 yellowtails, and 175 goldfish. Make a bar graph to show this data.

34. Last year, the price of a huskie was $455.70. This year the price is $500. By how much has the price increased?

35. Sandra bought dog food for $22.99, a collar for $3.99, a bowl for $6.40, and a leash for $6.88. About how much did Sandra spend?

Mixed Review

Use the graph at the right to answer the following questions.

The graph shows the first-month sales in New York City and Los Angeles of the Tidal Waves' latest cassette tape.

36. Were more tapes sold in New York City or in Los Angeles during the first week?

37. How many tapes were sold in New York City during the third week?

38. How many more tapes were sold in New York City than in Los Angeles during the second week?

39. What is the total number of tapes sold in both cities during the first month?

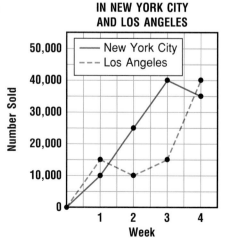

FIRST-MONTH SALES IN NEW YORK CITY AND LOS ANGELES

— New York City
‑ ‑ ‑ Los Angeles

Estimating Products: Whole Numbers and Decimals

A. Ace Rent-A-Car is replacing 48 of the oldest cars in its fleet with the latest models. The owner sells each old car for about $8,750. If he sells 48 cars, about how much money will he earn?

Estimate: 48 × $8,750.

Here are two ways to estimate the product:

Front-End Estimation	**Rounding**
Use the front digits.	Round to the greatest place of each factor.
48 × $8,750	48 × $8,750
Think: 40 × $8,000 = $320,000	*Think:* 50 × $9,000 = $450,000

1. Is the exact answer greater or less than the front-end estimate? the estimate by rounding? Why?

B. You can use the same method to estimate decimal products.

Estimate: 0.152 × 1,597

Front-End Estimation	**Rounding**
Use the front digits.	Round to the greatest place of each factor.
0.152 × 1,597	0.152 × 1,597
Think: 0.1 × 1,000 = 100	*Think:* 0.2 × 2,000 = 400

2. Between which two numbers does the exact answer fall? Why?

TRY OUT   Write the letter of the correct answer.

Estimate by using the front digits.

3. 0.7 × 56   **a.** 30   **b.** 35   **c.** 42   **d.** 45

4. 63 × $32,972   **a.** $1,000,000   **b.** $1,500,000   **c.** $1,800,000   **d.** $2,000,000

Estimate by rounding.

5. 0.882 × 4,326   **a.** 4,600   **b.** 3,600   **c.** 3,000   **d.** 2,600

6. 51 × 619   **a.** 30,000   **b.** 3,000   **c.** 300   **d.** 300,000

PRACTICE

Estimate by using the front digits.

7. 413
     × 9

8. 2,506
     × 3

9. 94
     × 33

10. 118
      × 83

11. 832
      × 402

12. 0.362
      × 8.3

13. 24.90
      × 3.42

14. 845
      × 21.8

15. 924.25
      × 43.8

16. 513.4128
      ×   6.29

Estimate by rounding.

17. 592
      × 8

18. 8,402
      × 5

19. 49
      × 23

20. 183
      × 55

21. 242
      × 361

22. 0.152
      × 3.9

23. 262.5
      × 4.3

24. 1.2982
      × 0.304

25. 18.5
      × 12.6

26. 0.224
      × 3.1

Estimate.

27. 9 × 546

28. 18 × 249

29. 22 × 4,550

30. 36 × 94

31. 0.512 × 6.3

32. 945 × 8.56

33. 421.62 × 19.5

34. 86.212 × 32.9

Write the letter of the best estimate.

35. 2.867 × 5,019   **a.** < 10,000   **b.** > 10,000   **c.** > 15,000   **d.** > 20,000

36. 401 × 832   **a.** < 300,000   **b.** < 320,000   **c.** > 320,000   **d.** > 350,000

37. 0.86 × 7.35   **a.** < 1   **b.** < 7   **c.** > 7   **d.** > 10

38. 0.324 × 57   **a.** < 5   **b.** < 10   **c.** > 15   **d.** > 50

Critical Thinking

39. Is 52 × 762 greater than or less than 35,000? Is it greater than or less than 48,000? Why?

Mixed Applications

Solve. Which method did you use?
You may need to use the Databank on page 583.

40. When renting a car in Spain, Ramona bought 22.5 gal of gas. About how much did she spend?

41. A car rents for $14 a day plus $.15 per mi after the first 100 miles. If you rent a car for 5 days and drive 300 miles, will you spend more than $90? Why or why not?

ESTIMATION
MENTAL MATH
CALCULATOR
PAPER/PENCIL

UNDERSTANDING A CONCEPT

Multiplying Whole Numbers and Decimals

A. Monica and Eleanor are planning a 14-day trip to Yellowstone National Park. They plan to allow $125 per day for lodging, meals, and other expenses. How much are they allowing for the trip?

Eleanor used her calculator to find the amount, and Monica used paper and pencil.

Eleanor	Monica
14 ⊠ 125 ⊟ │ 1750. │	$\begin{array}{r} 1\,2\,5 \\ \times\ \ \ 1\,4 \\ \hline 5\,0\,0 \\ 1\,2\,5\ \ \\ \hline 1{,}7\,5\,0 \end{array}$

They are allowing $1,750 for the trip.

1. Is $1,750 a reasonable answer? Why or why not?

2. **What if** Monica and Eleanor had planned a 20-day trip? How could you find the product mentally?

B. Recall that you multiply decimals the same way you multiply whole numbers.

Multiply: 15.7 × 1.15

Estimate

10 × 1 = 10

◄——15.7 × 1.15

20 × 1 = 20

Exact answer

$$\begin{array}{r} 1.1\,5 \\ \times\ \ 1\,5.7 \\ \hline 8\,0\,5 \\ 5\,7\,5\ \ \\ 1\,1\,5\ \ \ \\ \hline 1\,8.0\,5\,5 \end{array}$$

3. How can you use the estimate to place the decimal point?

4. Compare the total number of decimal places in the factors with the number of decimal places in the product. What is a rule for finding the number of decimal places in the product?

5. How many decimal places would be in the product 0.03 × 1.5? What is the product?

TRY OUT Find the product.

6. 17 × 168

7. 241 × 359

8. 2.4 × 0.0415

9. 18.98 × 178.2

PRACTICE

Place the decimal point in the answer.

10. $4.23 \times 12.9 = 54567$　　**11.** $18.4 \times 21.66 = 398544$　　**12.** $4.7 \times 0.016 = 752$

Find the product. Use mental math, a calculator, or paper and pencil.

13. 19×187　　　　**14.** 46×318　　　　**15.** 449×208　　　**16.** $\$57.88 \times 45$

17. $35 \times 2{,}500$　　　**18.** $\$300 \times 32$　　　**19.** $88 \times 24{,}101$　　**20.** $987 \times 7{,}890$

21. 8×7.5　　　　　**22.** 12×3.4　　　　**23.** 7×5.3　　　　**24.** 5×6.9

25. 2.5×0.4　　　　**26.** 12.5×0.08　　　**27.** 0.48×0.06　　**28.** 3.33×0.6

29. 0.38×0.025　　　**30.** 709×341　　　**31.** $\$520 \times 16$　　　**32.** 0.014×0.0682

Find the product. Do only those that have a product between 100 and 1,000.

33. 2.8×48.75　　　　　**34.** 10.44×8.3　　　　　**35.** 39×53

36. $2{,}328.5 \times 0.33$　　　　**37.** 463×1.845　　　　　**38.** 2.341×503.99

Critical Thinking

Tell if the statement is true or false. Give examples to support your answer.

39. When you multiply a whole number by a decimal less than 1, the answer always is less than the whole number.

40. When you multiply a whole number by a decimal greater than 1, the answer always is greater than the whole number.

Mixed Applications

41. Al has $\$1{,}000$ in travelers' checks. His hotel room at Yellowstone costs $\$89.75$ per night. How much does Al have left after paying for 8 nights?

42. *Write a problem* using the numbers 26.5 and 3.8. Solve your problem. Ask others to solve it.

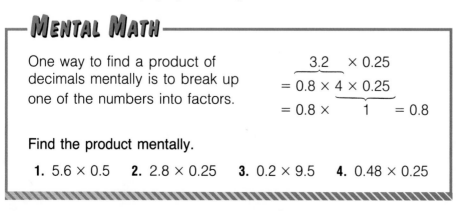

MENTAL MATH

One way to find a product of decimals mentally is to break up one of the numbers into factors.

$$3.2 \times 0.25$$
$$= 0.8 \times 4 \times 0.25$$
$$= 0.8 \times 1 = 0.8$$

Find the product mentally.

1. 5.6×0.5　　**2.** 2.8×0.25　　**3.** 0.2×9.5　　**4.** 0.48×0.25

PROBLEM SOLVING

Strategy: Solving a Multistep Problem

Two seventh-grade classes are raising money for charity. Class 7-1 has 20 students. Each student collected an average of $12.50. Class 7-2 collected $187.34. The money raised by the two classes is to be divided evenly between two charities. How much will each charity receive?

Plan your strategy.

You can write subproblems to help you solve the problem.

Try your plan.

Subproblem 1: What was the total amount collected by Class 7-1?

Think:

The number of students in Class 7-1	$\times$	Average per student		
20	$\times$	$12.50	=	$250.00

Subproblem 2: What was the total amount raised by both classes?

Think: The total amount is the sum of the amounts raised by each class.

$$\$250.00 + \$187.34 = \$437.34$$

Subproblem 3: How much should each charity receive?

Think: Each should receive half of the total amount.

$$0.5 \times \$437.34 = \$218.67$$

Each charity should receive $218.67.

1. ***What if*** there were three charities instead of two to share equally the money raised? What would each charity receive?

2. ***What if*** Class 7-2 did not hand in $187.35, but instead handed in two envelopes, one containing $53.65 and the other containing $144.85? How would your plan change? How much would each of three charities receive?

PRACTICE

Use subproblems to solve.

3. A charity group went on a camping trip. The campers hiked 8 mi the first day and 7 mi the second day. On the third day they hiked 2 mi an hour for 6 hours. How many miles did they hike in the three days?

4. Some friends did odd jobs to earn money for charity. They divided their earnings evenly between two charities. One week they mowed 7 lawns at $6 per lawn and raked 5 lawns at $3.50 per lawn. They earned another $4.50 for weeding a large lawn. How much did they give each charity?

5. The Charity Singers visited a house every 20 minutes in a 5-hour period. They received about $3.75 from each house. How much did they raise in all?

6. A school charity group gave $25 to each of three charities. The group also gave a total of $85 to some other charities. How much did the group donate in all?

Strategies and Skills Review

Solve. Use mental math, estimation, a calculator, or paper and pencil.

7. To raise money for a "Clean Up Our Parks" program, students bought cookies at $1.59 a box and sold them at $2.59 a box. They sold 1 box at each of 250 homes and 100 boxes at the school office. How much money did the students raise?

8. A television station planned to donate 327 minutes of time for the governor to talk about keeping the streets free from drugs. If 80 minutes of time were planned for each of three weeks, how much time would be left?

9. The hospital volunteers are sponsoring a bikeathon. Jill bikes 27 mi in 3 hours. Each hour she travels 4 mi less than the hour before. How many miles does she travel each hour?

10. If you toss a paper cup 20 times in the air, how will the cup fall most frequently: on its side? on its bottom? on its top? Try this experiment and show your results in a frequency table.

11. This year a charity is sponsoring a square dance. The charity has already sold 75 adult tickets at $7.50 each. The charity hopes to raise $1,000. How would you estimate to find how many more tickets the charity needs to sell?

12. **Write a problem** that contains several subproblems and uses a plan to find the solution. Ask others to solve the problem.

Investigating Patterns

A. Suppose you arrange 6 red checkers in a row. Then you can put a border of black checkers around the red row so it looks like this:

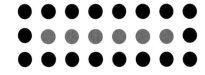

Count. You need 18 black checkers to make the border.

1. What if you put the 6 red checkers in 2 rows with 3 in each row (a 2 × 3 arrangement)? How many black checkers do you need for the border now?

Explore what happens when you use 8 red checkers.

2. How many black checkers do you need to make a border for each arrangement? Draw pictures.

Red	Black
1 × 8	
2 × 4	

3. Try arrangements of 12 red checkers. Keep drawing pictures to help you.

Red	Black
1 × 12	
2 × 6	
3 × 4	

B. Look at your tables and the pictures you drew. Can you find some patterns in the arrangements?

4. When you arrange the red checkers in a single row, how is the number of black border checkers related to the number of red checkers?

5. Can you predict how many black border checkers you would need for a single row of 25 reds? Draw a picture to see if you are correct.

6. When there are two rows of red checkers, how many black checkers are always used to make the "sides"? Now compare the number of black checkers you need to complete the border with the number of red checkers in each row.

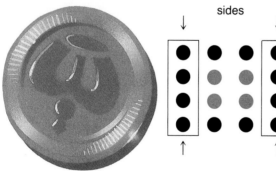

sides

7. Predict how many black checkers you would need to border a 2 × 17 arrangement of red checkers.

8. What relationships can you find when there are 3 rows of red checkers? *N* rows of red checkers?

9. How many black checkers would you need to border a 3 × 10 arrangement of red checkers? How does the total number of red checkers compare with the total number of black checkers?

10. Work with a partner to solve this problem. There is one other arrangement in which the number of red checkers is equal to the number of black border checkers. Can you find it?

UNDERSTANDING A CONCEPT

Using Exponents

A. Jeff did a study about rabbits for a science project. He found that a colony of rabbits doubled in number every month. If there were 2 rabbits at the beginning of the first month, how many were there at the beginning of the 5th month?

Beginning of 1st Month	Beginning of 2nd Month	Beginning of 3rd Month	Beginning of 4th Month	Beginning of 5th Month
2	2×2 $= 4$	$2 \times 2 \times 2$ $= 8$	$2 \times 2 \times 2 \times 2$ $= 16$	$2 \times 2 \times 2 \times 2 \times 2$ $= 32$

There were 32 rabbits at the beginning of the 5th month.

A short way of writing $2 \times 2 \times 2 \times 2 \times 2$, or expressing 2 as a factor 5 times, is to use **exponential form.**

$$2 \times 2 \times 2 \times 2 \times 2 = 2^5 \leftarrow \textbf{exponent}$$
$$\uparrow\underline{\qquad}\textbf{base}$$

2^5 is read "two to the fifth power."

Some numbers in exponential form can be read in special ways.

For example, 2^2 is read as "2 squared" or "2 to the 2nd power." 2^3 is read as "2 cubed" or "2 to the 3rd power."

1. How would you find the value of 7^4?

2. Express the rabbit population at the beginning of the 12th month in exponential form and in standard form.

3. During which month would the population exceed 50,000?

B. You can use patterns to find the value of any nonzero number to the zero power.

$2^5 = 32$	$2^4 = 32 \div 2 = 16$
$2^4 = 16$	$2^3 = 16 \div 2 = 8$
$2^3 = 8$	$2^2 = 8 \div 2 = 4$
$2^2 = 4$	$2^1 = 4 \div 2 = 2$
$2^1 = 2$	$2^0 = 2 \div 2 = 1$

4. What is 6^0? 12^0? any number greater than zero to the zero power?

TRY OUT   Find the value.

5. 4^3

6. 10^0

7. 5^4

8. 10^7

9. 11^2

PRACTICE

Write the number in exponential form.

10. $2 \times 2 \times 2 \times 2 \times 2 \times 2 \times 2 \times 2$ **11.** $10 \times 10 \times 10 \times 10$

12. $45 \times 45 \times 45 \times 45 \times 45$ **13.** $3{,}098 \times 3{,}098 \times 3{,}098$

Find the value.

14. 7^3 **15.** 10^3 **16.** $2{,}078^1$ **17.** 4^0 **18.** 10^5 **19.** 3^4

20. 2^9 **21.** 6^4 **22.** 19^2 **23.** 1^{25} **24.** 9^0 **25.** 8^3

Which is greater?

26. $(0.2)^5$ or $(0.3)^5$ **27.** $(0.2)^4$ or $(0.4)^2$ **28.** $(0.5)^3$ or $(0.3)^5$

Critical Thinking

29. Why is 2^8 the same as 16^2? To what power would you raise 4 to get the same number?

Mixed Applications

30. A project involved one branch of a tree that added 5 new branches on each branch each year. Express in exponential form the number of branches that grew on the original branch after 10 years.

31. The number of students from each of the four junior highs in Jeff's city at the science fair were 1,089, 782, 1,287, and 99. How many were there in all?

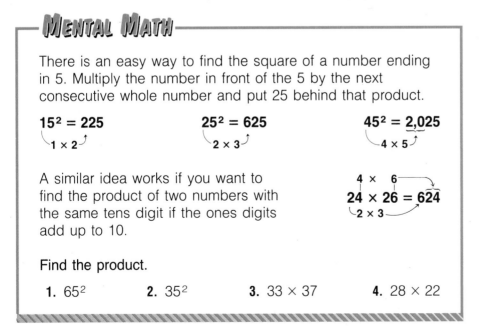

MENTAL MATH

There is an easy way to find the square of a number ending in 5. Multiply the number in front of the 5 by the next consecutive whole number and put 25 behind that product.

$15^2 = 225$ **$25^2 = 625$**   **$45^2 = 2{,}025$**
   1 × 2   2 × 3   4 × 5

A similar idea works if you want to find the product of two numbers with the same tens digit if the ones digits add up to 10.

         4 ×   6
$24 \times 26 = 624$
       2 × 3

Find the product.

  1. 65^2 **2.** 35^2 **3.** 33×37 **4.** 28×22

Multiplying Greater Numbers: Scientific Notation

A. Here are some astronomical numbers.

Our galaxy, the Milky Way, contains at least 100,000,000 stars.	Astronomers believe that the galaxies were formed about 14,000,000,000 years ago.	The diameter of one of the largest stars, Betelgeuse, is about 621,000,000 mi.

You can write these numbers in a more compact form called **scientific notation.**

A number written in scientific notation is expressed as a product of two factors. The first factor is equal to or greater than 1 but less than 10. The second factor is a power of 10.

Standard Form	Scientific Notation
100,000,000	1.0×10^8
14,000,000,000	1.4×10^{10}
621,000,000	6.21×10^8

Alex has a quick way of changing numbers between standard form and scientific notation.

700,000 = 7 0 0 , 0 0 0 . = 7.0 × 10^5

6.2 × 10^6 = 6 . 2 0 0 0 0 0 = 6,200,000

1. Write a rule for changing a number from standard form to scientific notation.

2. Write a rule for changing a number from scientific notation to standard form.

B. The diameter of our Moon is 2.0×10^3 mi. The diameter of our Sun is about 4.0×10^2 times as great. Find the diameter of our Sun.

Lucille and Scott used two different methods.

Lucille	Scott
$2.0 \times 10^3 = 2,000$	$(2.0 \times 10^3) \times (4.0 \times 10^2)$
$4.0 \times 10^2 = 400$	$(2.0 \times 4.0) \times (10^3 \times 10^2)$
$2,000 \times 400 = 800,000$, or 8.0×10^5	$8.0 \times 10^{3+2} = 8.0 \times 10^5$

SHARING IDEAS

3. Is Lucille's or Scott's method easier? Why?

4. How did Scott multiply $10^3 \times 10^2$? How does the answer relate to the number of zeros in 800,000?

5. Find $(9.5 \times 10^4) \times (4.0 \times 10^2)$. Are there 6 zeros in the product? Why or why not?

PRACTICE

Write in scientific notation.

6. 528,000 **7.** 18,000,000 **8.** 637,000,000 **9.** 213,000,000,000

Write in standard form.

10. 6.0×10^4 **11.** 3.2×10^6 **12.** 8.1×10^8 **13.** 5.37×10^7

Find the product in scientific notation.

14. $(2.0 \times 10^3) \times (3.0 \times 10^6)$ **15.** $(1.5 \times 10^5) \times (8.0 \times 10^2)$

16. $(1.2 \times 10^3) \times (3.5 \times 10^4)$ **17.** $(4.7 \times 10^5) \times (8.2 \times 10^7)$

18. $(6.5 \times 10^0) \times (7.9 \times 10^{10})$ **19.** $(8.1 \times 10^9) \times (9.3 \times 10^5)$

20. $(6.4 \times 10^6) \times (3.85 \times 10^7)$ **21.** $(5.4 \times 10^5) \times (1.23 \times 10^6)$

Multiply using a calculator. Write the product in scientific notation.

22. $400 \times 95,000$ **23.** $3,500 \times 29,000$ **24.** $5,123 \times 76,000$

Mixed Applications

25. Pluto has a diameter of about 1.5×10^3 mi. The United States is about 3,000 mi across. Which is the greater distance? About how many times as great?

26. The Sun is about 93 million mi away from Earth. If Curtis could drive his car there at a rate of 60 mi per hour, about how long would the trip take?

27. Voyager 1 traveled by Saturn at a speed of about 43,000 mi per hour. At that rate how far could it travel in 365 days?

28. *Write a problem* that involves using a calculator to multiply very large numbers. Solve your problem. Ask others to solve it.

Mixed Review

Find the answer. Which method did you use?

MENTAL MATH
CALCULATOR
PAPER/PENCIL

29. $432,400 + 6,897$ **30.** $560,000 - 40,000$ **31.** $898 - 402$

32. $45 + 62 + 15 + 68$ **33.** $870 + 210 + 190 + 30$ **34.** $1,782 - 539$

Areas of Rectangles

Kitty's Chicken Farm had 32 ft of fencing to make a rectangular pen. The builder of the fences drew some pens. Which pen has the greatest area?

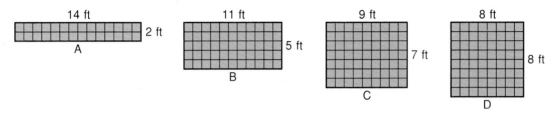

Recall that the **area of a plane figure** is the measure of the surface enclosed by the figure. Area is measured in square units such as square feet and square centimeters.

To find the **area of a rectangle,** you can use the formula $A = \ell \times w$, where ℓ is the length and w is the width.

To find the **area of a square,** you can use the formula, $A = s^2$, where s is the length of a side.

Find the area of each pen.

A	B	C	D
$A = \ell \times w$	$A = \ell \times w$	$A = \ell \times w$	$A = s^2$
$= 14 \times 2$	$= 11 \times 5$	$= 9 \times 7$	$= 8^2$
$= 28 \text{ ft}^2$	$= 55 \text{ ft}^2$	$= 63 \text{ ft}^2$	$= 64 \text{ ft}^2$

The builder decided to construct a square pen with 8-foot sides.

1. Are there other pens that the builder could draw? What are their areas? Which pen gives the greatest area?

2. What if there had been 48 ft of fencing? What shape pen would give the greatest area? What is the greatest area?

3. If you are given a perimeter, will a square or a rectangle give you the greatest area?

TRY OUT   Find the area.

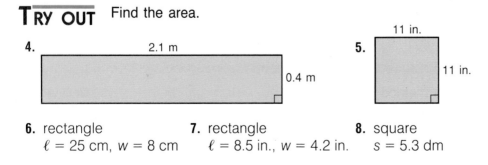

4.   2.1 m   0.4 m

5.   11 in.   11 in.

6. rectangle
   $\ell = 25$ cm, $w = 8$ cm

7. rectangle
   $\ell = 8.5$ in., $w = 4.2$ in.

8. square
   $s = 5.3$ dm

PRACTICE

Find the area.

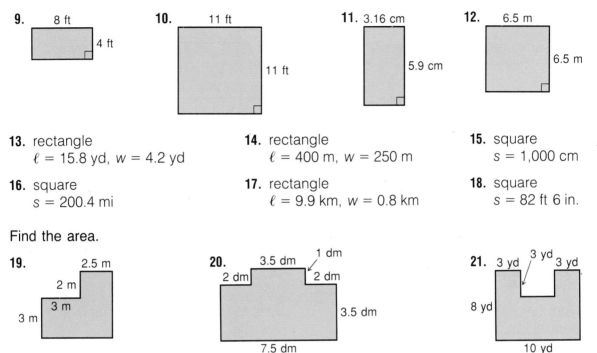

9. 8 ft / 4 ft

10. 11 ft / 11 ft

11. 3.16 cm / 5.9 cm

12. 6.5 m / 6.5 m

13. rectangle
$\ell = 15.8$ yd, $w = 4.2$ yd

14. rectangle
$\ell = 400$ m, $w = 250$ m

15. square
$s = 1,000$ cm

16. square
$s = 200.4$ mi

17. rectangle
$\ell = 9.9$ km, $w = 0.8$ km

18. square
$s = 82$ ft 6 in.

Find the area.

19. 2.5 m / 2 m / 3 m / 3 m

20. 3.5 dm / 1 dm / 2 dm / 2 dm / 3.5 dm / 7.5 dm

21. 3 yd / 3 yd / 3 yd / 8 yd / 10 yd

Solve.

22. If the area of a rectangle is 36 ft² and the length is 9 ft, what is the width?

23. If the area of a square is 225 m², what is the length of one side?

Critical Thinking

24. How does the area of a square change if the length of a side is tripled? if it is multiplied by 4? Write a general rule.

25. How does the area of a rectangle change if both the length and the width are cut in half?

Mixed Applications

Solve. Which method did you use? You may need to use the Databank on page 582.

26. The swimming pool in Michelle's yard is 30 ft by 15 ft. How many square feet of plastic are needed for a solar cover?

27. Michelle spent $1.55 each for 20 chickens and $15.29 each for 3 ducks. About how much did she spend in all?

28. Michelle bought 25 yd of fencing at $4.88 per yd. How much did she pay?

29. What is the area of a basketball court in Michelle's school?

ESTIMATION
MENTAL MATH
CALCULATOR
PAPER/PENCIL

Areas of Parallelograms, Triangles, and Trapezoids

A. Carole and Steven make wooden signs. They make signs of different shapes. In order to determine how much varnish to buy, they need to find the area of these two signs.

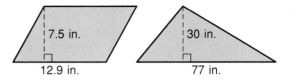

Recall that:

the **area of a parallelogram** is equal to the area of a rectangle that has the same base (*b*) and height (*h*).

the **area of a triangle** is $\frac{1}{2}$ the area of a parallelogram that has the same base (*b*) and height (*h*).

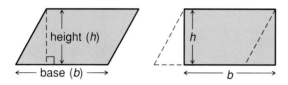

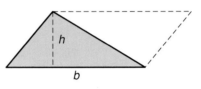

Find the area of the sign that is a parallelogram.

$A = b \times h$
$\quad = 12.9 \times 7.5$
$\quad = 96.75 \text{ in.}^2$

Find the area of the sign that is a triangle.

$A = \frac{1}{2} \times b \times h$
$\quad = \frac{1}{2} \times 77 \times 30$
$\quad = 1,155 \text{ in.}^2$

1. What is the total area of the two signs for which Carol and Steven need to buy varnish?

B. You can develop the formula for finding the area of a trapezoid from the formula for finding the area of a parallelogram.

The **area of a trapezoid** is $\frac{1}{2}$ the area of a parallelogram that has the same height and a base equal to the sum of the two bases of the trapezoid.

$b = b_1 + b_2$

Find the area of the trapezoid.

$A = \frac{1}{2}(b_1 + b_2) \times h$
$\quad = \frac{1}{2}(26 + 62) \times 19$
$\quad = \frac{1}{2}(88) \times 19$
$\quad = 836 \text{ in.}^2$

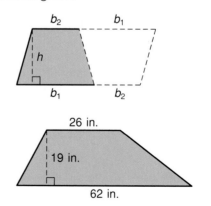

T̲RY OUT Find the area.

2.

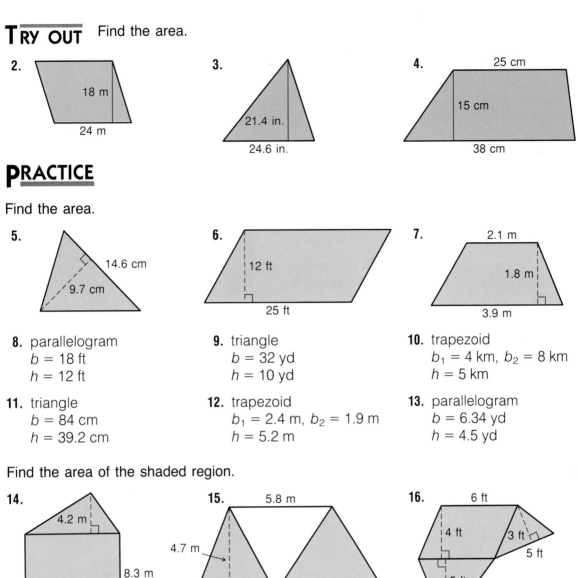

18 m
24 m

3.

21.4 in.
24.6 in.

4.

25 cm
15 cm
38 cm

P̲RACTICE

Find the area.

5.

14.6 cm
9.7 cm

6.

12 ft
25 ft

7.

2.1 m
1.8 m
3.9 m

8. parallelogram
$b = 18$ ft
$h = 12$ ft

9. triangle
$b = 32$ yd
$h = 10$ yd

10. trapezoid
$b_1 = 4$ km, $b_2 = 8$ km
$h = 5$ km

11. triangle
$b = 84$ cm
$h = 39.2$ cm

12. trapezoid
$b_1 = 2.4$ m, $b_2 = 1.9$ m
$h = 5.2$ m

13. parallelogram
$b = 6.34$ yd
$h = 4.5$ yd

Find the area of the shaded region.

14.

4.2 m
8.3 m
10.1 m

15.

5.8 m
4.7 m
10.7 m

16.

6 ft
4 ft
3 ft
5 ft
5 ft

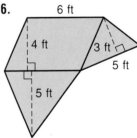

Critical Thinking

17. How does doubling the base of a triangle affect its area?
Suppose both the base and the height are doubled. How does
the area change?

18. Give two ways to quadruple the area of a parallelogram.

Mixed Applications

19. If the area of a parallelogram is
400 m² and its height is 25 m, what is
its base?

20. If the area of a triangle is 9.92 dm²
and its base is 6.4 dm, what is its
height?

UNDERSTANDING A CONCEPT

Circumferences and Areas of Circles

A. How does the distance around a circle (**circumference**) compare with the circle's diameter?

Tony measured the circumferences and diameters of several different size cans. He made this table to show his findings.

Can	C	d	$\frac{C}{d}$
Bean can	23.5 cm	7.6 cm	3.09
Soda can	18.7 cm	6.0 cm	3.12
Tuna can	26.5 cm	8.5 cm	3.12
Coffee can	49.2 cm	15.6 cm	3.15

The value of C divided by d is called pi (π). π is approximately equal to ($\approx$) 3.14.

Since $\frac{C}{d} = \pi$, you can find the circumference of a circle by rewriting the formula as **$C = \pi d$.**

Find the circumference of a circular fish pond that has a diameter of 8.2 ft. Use the formula $C = \pi d$.

$C \approx 3.14 \times 8.2$
≈ 25.748

The circumference of the pond is approximately 26 ft.

B. You can find the area of a circle by cutting it into sections and rearranging them. The sections of the circle below have been rearranged into a figure that approximates the shape of a parallelogram.

$$A = b \times h$$
$$= \tfrac{1}{2}C \times r$$
$$= \tfrac{1}{2}(2\pi r) \times r \quad \boxed{C = 2\pi r}$$
$$= \pi r^2$$

Find the area of the fish pond. The diameter is 8.2 ft.

First find the radius. Then use the formula $A = \pi r^2$.

$r = \frac{d}{2} = \frac{8.2}{2} = 4.1$ $A \approx 3.14 \times (4.1)^2 = 3.14 \times 16.81$
≈ 52.7834

The area of the pond is approximately 53 ft².

TRY OUT Find the circumference and the area of the circle.

1. 18 m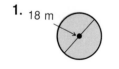

2. 3.6 yd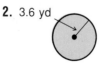

3. $d = 27$ in.

4. $r = 2.3$ km

PRACTICE

Find the circumference and the area of the circle.

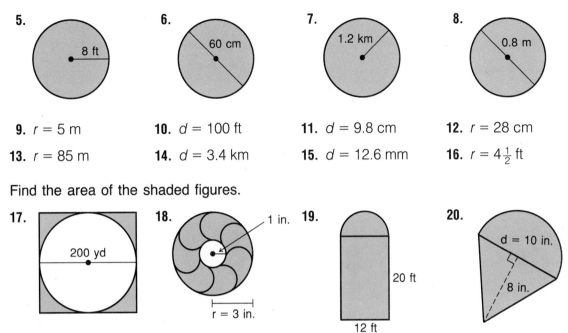

5. 8 ft

6. 60 cm

7. 1.2 km

8. 0.8 m

9. $r = 5$ m

10. $d = 100$ ft

11. $d = 9.8$ cm

12. $r = 28$ cm

13. $r = 85$ m

14. $d = 3.4$ km

15. $d = 12.6$ mm

16. $r = 4\frac{1}{2}$ ft

Find the area of the shaded figures.

17. 200 yd

18. 1 in. $r = 3$ in.

19. 20 ft   12 ft

20. $d = 10$ in.   8 in.

Critical Thinking

21. If you double the length of the radius of a circle, how does the circumference of the circle change? How does the area of the circle change?

Mixed Applications

Solve. You may need to use the Databank on page 582.

22. Tony is a loyal fan of the Houston Astros. He wants to find the floor area of the Astrodome. What is the area?

23. Tony spent $3.49, $5.29, and $15.85 on food and drinks at different games at the stadium. How much did he spend in all?

24. The diameter of a large pizza at the stadium is twice that of a small pizza. If the small pizza costs $6, how much should the large one cost?

25. The stadium nets about $35,000 each game. If there are 86 games in a year, about how much is the total net?

Mixed Review

Find the answer. Which method did you use?

MENTAL MATH
CALCULATOR
PAPER/PENCIL

26. $8,000 \times 45,000$

27. $39,804.09 + 386.92$

28. $369 + 231 + 87$

29. $34.0987 - 0.86$

30. $5,000 - 365.96

31. $143.25 - 39.75

PROBLEM SOLVING

Strategy: Drawing a Diagram

A train line connects six cities. Two train tracks connect Carson City. One goes to New City, and one goes to Old City. One track goes from New City to Rapid City. Train tracks connect Old City to Rapid City, New City, Ringwood, and Ferndale. In how many ways could you travel from Carson City to Rapid City?

Plan your strategy.

One way to solve the problem is to make a diagram and then trace the routes.

Try your plan.

Here is one possible route from Carson City to Rapid City:
Carson City → New City → Old City → Rapid City.

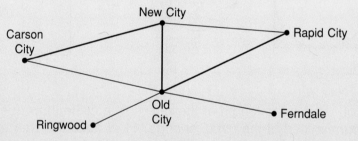

1. Copy the diagram and trace the routes from Carson City to Rapid City.

2. List each route.

3. In how many ways could you travel from Carson City to Rapid City?

4. ***Write a problem*** that could be solved with this diagram. Ask others to solve it.

5. ***What if*** all tracks to and from New City were closed and a track from Ferndale to Rapid City were opened? In how many ways could you now travel from Old City to Rapid City?

PRACTICE

Draw a diagram to solve.

Bus routes connect these cities: Arlington and Demarest, Demarest and Benton, Eaton and Coatsville, Benton and Coatsville, and Demarest and Eaton.

6. In how many ways could you travel from Eaton to Benton? What are they?

7. Another route is started from Demarest to Arlington to Coatsville. In how many ways could you travel from Eaton to Benton? What are they?

In the Old West, telegraph lines connected these towns: Sandstone with Mesa, Butte, and Medicine Wells; Butte with Platte and Soda Wash; and Soda Wash with Medicine Wells and Platte.

8. In how many ways could messages have been sent from Mesa to Platte? What are they?

9. **What if** the wires between Butte and Platte had been down? In how many ways could messages have been sent from Mesa to Platte? What are they?

Strategies and Skills Review

Solve. Use mental math, estimation, a calculator, or paper and pencil. You may need to use the Databank on page 582.

10. Use a map of the streets in Washington, D.C., to find six possible named-street routes to travel from the corner of New York Av. and Massachusetts Av. to the corner of Florida Av. and Maryland Av.

11. Lia hiked for 3 days and traveled 29 mi. She hiked 5 fewer mi on the second day than the first day. She hiked 3 more mi on the third day than on the second day. How many mi did she hike each day?

12. Chad has two jobs. He works 9 hours a week for a bus company at $4.15 per hour. He also works 7 hours a week for a taxi company at $3.95 per hour. How much does he earn each week?

13. **Write a problem** that requires the use of a diagram to find the solution. Ask others to solve the problem.

DECISION MAKING

Problem Solving: Choosing a Save-an-Animal Project

SITUATION

The Service Club is planning a Save-an-Animal Project. The 15 members of the club are considering three possible projects.

PROBLEM

Which project should they choose?

DATA

Project 1: Raising Money

- Club members will raise money and donate it to an organization to save animals. The goal is to raise $400.00
- Each club member will spend 20 hours on fund raising.
- Each club member will donate $7.50 in initial fund-raising expenses.
- Each member will be reimbursed with money raised.

Project 2: Donating Time

- Each club member will donate time to help with mailings, general office work, and other odd jobs at a local animal shelter.
- Each club member will work at the shelter for 2 hours a week for a 6-week period.
- Each club member will spend about $3.00 a week for transportation.

Project 3: Writing Letters

- Each club member will write to 10 members of Congress about saving endangered animals.
- Each club member will spend about 8 hours writing letters.
- Each club member will spend about $2.50 for stamps.

USING THE DATA

How many hours would each member devote to the project?

1. raising money   **2.** donating time   **3.** letter writing

How many total hours would the club devote to the project?

4. raising money   **5.** donating time   **6.** letter writing

How much money would each member spend on the project?

7. raising money   **8.** donating time   **9.** letter writing

MAKING DECISIONS

Which project should they choose to:

10. help experienced people save endangered animals?

11. donate money to a worthy cause?

12. put pressure on others to save endangered animals?

13. get friends involved in saving animals?

14. learn firsthand about saving animals?

Use the data to answer the questions.

15. *What if* club members can't afford to spend money? Which project should they choose?

16. *What if* club members don't have much free time? Which project should they choose?

17. *Write a list* of other factors the club members should consider in choosing a project.

18. Which project would you choose? Why?

Math and Art

Weaving a beautiful fabric is an art that must begin with much preparation and planning. A *loom* is used for weaving. The term used for the fabric is *web*. The web is created by interlacing, or weaving, the lengthwise *warp* yarns and the crosswise *weft* yarns. An essential part of preparation for weaving is deciding how much yarn is needed to produce a web of the desired size.

As the weft yarn is passed over and under each warp yarn, it pushes the yarns up and down a little bit. This is called "warp takeup." When warp length is figured, an extra one-tenth of the desired length must be added for warp takeup. When the tension of the loom is released and the piece is finished by steaming or washing, most yarns shrink and so another one-tenth of the length is added. Additional length of each warp yarn is needed to attach the yarn to the loom at each end. This is called "loom waste." Usually 0.75 yd (27 in., 70 cm) is allowed for loom waste for each length.

If the weaver plans to hem the piece at each end, the depth of each hem must also be added.

What if you wanted a finished piece of fabric 10 yd long? What length would each warp yarn be if the fabric is not hemmed?

Think: 10

$$
\begin{array}{r}
10 \\
1 \quad \longleftarrow \ (0.1 \times 10) \\
1 \quad \longleftarrow \ (0.1 \times 10) \\
+ \ \underline{0.75} \\
12.75
\end{array}
$$

Each warp yarn would be 12.75 yd long.

ACTIVITIES

1. Find the total length of warp yarn you need to make a web that is 10 yd long and has 430 warp yarns.

2. Write a brief report on one of these topics:
   a. Tapestry masterpieces
   b. Backstrap or other looms

Calculator: Carpet Sale

The Wilsons want to carpet a room that measures 3.7 yards by 5 yards. The following Carpetland Annual Sale ad appeared in today's newspaper.

ONE DAY ONLY!

GET YOUR STAIN-RESISTANT
WORRY-FREE CARPETS NOW!
AN IRRESISTIBLE LINEUP
AT THE LOWEST PRICES!

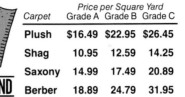

CARPETLAND

Carpet	Price per Square Yard Grade A	Grade B	Grade C
Plush	$16.49	$22.95	$26.45
Shag	10.95	12.59	14.25
Saxony	14.99	17.49	20.89
Berber	18.89	24.79	31.95

What will it cost the Wilsons to cover the floor with the least expensive saxony carpet if they have to pay 0.06 of the cost in sales tax?

Use a calculator.   3.7 $\boxed{\times}$ 5 $\boxed{\times}$ 14.99 $\boxed{\text{M+}}$ $\boxed{\times}$ 0.06 $\boxed{\text{M+}}$ $\boxed{\text{MRC}}$ $\boxed{293.9539}$

It will cost $293.95 to cover the floor.

USING THE CALCULATOR

Use your calculator to solve the problem. Estimate first.

1. The Cohens' den measures 12 feet by 15 feet. What will it cost to cover it with the most expensive plush carpeting if they pay 0.06 of the cost in sales tax? [*Hint:* 9 square feet = 1 square yard]

2. The Toons are choosing between the $17.59 saxony and the $18.89 berber carpeting for their living room that measures 30.6 square yards. How much will they save by buying the saxony?

3. The Clancys are choosing between the least expensive berber and the most expensive shag for their two bedrooms. One bedroom measures 18 feet by 12 feet, and the other is 9 feet by 15 feet. How much less will it cost them to carpet both rooms with shag carpeting?

4. The Lewis family bought 135.5 square yards of carpeting at a cost of $2,526.45, which included $143 sales tax. Which irresistible saxony carpet did they choose?

5. The dimensions of the living room at the Gonzales home are shown at the right. What will it cost to carpet it with wall-to-wall $22.95 plush?

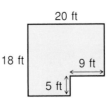
20 ft
18 ft
9 ft
5 ft

EXTRA PRACTICE

Mental Math: Multiplying by Powers of 10, page 83 ....

Find the product mentally.

1. 10×17 **2.** 100×14.57 **3.** $1{,}000 \times 25.04$ **4.** 100×7.8

5. $1{,}000 \times 349{,}542$ **6.** 10×0.07 **7.** $53{,}000 \times 100$ **8.** $1{,}000 \times 0.065$

9. $20 \times 44 \times 5$ **10.** $50 \times 8.33 \times 2$ **11.** $5 \times 78 \times 200$ **12.** $2 \times 5.4 \times 5$

13. $8 \times 95 \times 125$ **14.** $0.25 \times 6 \times 0.4$ **15.** $250 \times 6.5 \times 4$ **16.** $1.25 \times 373 \times 8$

17. $2.5 \times 4 \times 0.3$ **18.** $4 \times 58 \times 0.25$ **19.** $5 \times 8 \times 0.2$

20. $54.98 \times 10{,}000$ **21.** $0.0052 \times 100{,}000$ **22.** $0.0019 \times 0.2 \times 0.5$

Mental Math: Decimals and Powers of 10, page 85 ....

Find the product mentally.

1. 100×3.4 **2.** 0.405×100 **3.** $1{,}000 \times 606$ **4.** $1{,}000 \times 0.0073$

5. $7 \times 40 \times 115$ **6.** $9 \times 6 \times 0.3$ **7.** $5 \times 2.6 \times 2$ **8.** $30 \times 8.33 \times 3$

9. $6 \times 150.8 \times 30$ **10.** $0.16 \times 3.7 \times 5$ **11.** $0.0021 \times 0.6 \times 0.5$

12. Use the distributive property to multiply 7×8.4 and 14×6.5.

Estimating Products: Whole Numbers and Decimals, page 87 ....

Estimate by using the front digits.

1.	**2.**	**3.**	**4.**	**5.**
459	671	534	0.7236	3.098
$\times \quad 3$	$\times \quad 61$	$\times 487$	$\times \quad 9.6$	$\times \quad 526$

Estimate by rounding.

6.	**7.**	**8.**	**9.**	**10.**
856	734	8.907	0.548	92.34
$\times \quad 3$	$\times \quad 26$	$\times \quad 7.7$	$\times \quad 431$	$\times \quad 29.7$

Estimate.

11. 8×868 **12.** 73×428 **13.** $66 \times 5{,}216$ **14.** 48×79

15. 0.907×6.7 **16.** 745×51.4 **17.** 217.83×18.4 **18.** 32.756×28.3

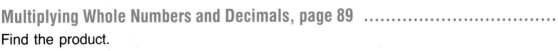

Multiplying Whole Numbers and Decimals, page 89 ....

Find the product.

1. 49 × 63

2. 73 × 489

3. 205 × 371

4. $400 × 42

5. $400 × 52

6. 77 × 43,101

7. 35 × $67.99

8. 55 × 35,000

9. 927 × 7,240

10. 805 × 407

11. 24 × 3,027

12. 499 × 21

13. 9 × 5.3

14. 8 × 3.5

15. 7 × 10.8

16. 5 × 201.9

17. 6.6 × 0.25

18. 1.08 × 9.2

19. 3 × 411.2

20. 4.6 × 58.95

21. 3.25 × 14.8

22. $4,500 × 1.66

23. 9.2 × 31.7

24. 2.05 × 87.7

25. 6.7 × 29.04

26. 10.88 × 9.2

27. 549 × 19.8

28. $2.88 × 1,200

29. 2.4 × 3,012

30. $500 × 8.24

31. 6 × 7.4

32. 1.23 × 5.99

33. 62.7 × 4.35

34. 0.17 × 840.23

35. 99 × 4.31

36. 4.71 × 8.24

Problem–Solving Strategy: Solving a Multistep Problem, page 91 ....

Use subproblems to solve.

1. Sarah earned $28.20 on Monday. On Wednesday she worked 6 hours and Friday she worked 8 hours. She earns $4.30 per hour. How much did she earn in the three days?

2. John had a chicken sandwich for $2.09. John's friend had a tuna sandwich for $1.85. They each had a glass of milk at $.90 each. The tax and tip was $1.50. If John paid with a $10 bill, how much change did he receive?

3. Meg bought roses for $12.98 and 6 packages of tulips at $2.49 a package. How much did she spend in all?

4. Advance tickets for a concert cost $4. At the door they cost $5. $12,000 worth of tickets were sold. In all, 100 tickets were sold at the door. How many advance tickets were sold?

5. Sailboat rental is $24 a day. Christine rented a sailboat for half price for 3 days. The next 2 days she rented the sailboat at full price. What was the cost of renting the sailboat for the 5 days?

6. Jay drove 225 mi on Monday and 355 mi on Tuesday. On Wednesday he averaged 50 mi per hour for 5 hours. How many miles did he drive in the three days?

EXTRA PRACTICE

Using Exponents, page 95

Write the number in exponential form.

1. $2 \times 2 \times 2 \times 2 \times 2 \times 2 \times 2$

2. $10 \times 10 \times 10 \times 10 \times 10 \times 10$

3. $2{,}125 \times 2{,}125 \times 2{,}125 \times 2{,}125$

4. $415 \times 415 \times 415$

Find the value.

5. 2^7 **6.** 25^1 **7.** 7^0 **8.** 9^2 **9.** 8^3 **10.** 10^7

11. 6^3 **12.** 1^{28} **13.** 10^9 **14.** 15^2 **15.** 4^5 **16.** 3^4

Multiplying Greater Numbers: Scientific Notation, page 97

Write in standard form.

1. 2.1×10^5 **2.** 4.0×10^9 **3.** 5.2×10^3 **4.** 5.87×10^6

Write in scientific notation.

5. 7,290,000 **6.** 29,000 **7.** 425,000,000 **8.** 35,000,000,000

Find the product and write in scientific notation.

9. $(3.8 \times 10^2) \times (2.2 \times 10^4)$

10. $(2.2 \times 10^0) \times (1.5 \times 10^9)$

11. $(5.3 \times 10^3) \times (7.2 \times 10^6)$

12. $(1.2 \times 10^8) \times (15.3 \times 10^7)$

13. $(7.14 \times 10^5) \times (4.5 \times 10^8)$

14. $(2.3 \times 10^4) \times (1.04 \times 10^7)$

15. $(3.5 \times 10^3) \times (2.2 \times 10^4)$

16. $(8.2 \times 10^3) \times (5.4 \times 10^6)$

Areas of Rectangles, page 99

Find the area.

1.

12 m
14 m

2.

1.5 cm
1.5 cm

3.

13 ft
13 ft
2 ft
5 ft 5 ft

4.

7 m
3 m
5 m
4 m

Find the area of the following rectangles.

5. $\ell = 3.75$ m
$w = 4.2$ m

6. square
$s = 12$ ft

7. square
$s = 8.7$ cm

8. $\ell = 9.2$ km
$w = 5.6$ km

Areas of Parallelograms, Triangles, and Trapezoids, page 101 ·························

Find the area.

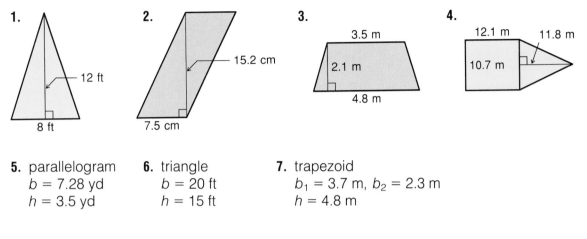

1. 12 ft   8 ft

2. 15.2 cm   7.5 cm

3. 3.5 m   2.1 m   4.8 m

4. 12.1 m   11.8 m   10.7 m

5. parallelogram
$b = 7.28$ yd
$h = 3.5$ yd

6. triangle
$b = 20$ ft
$h = 15$ ft

7. trapezoid
$b_1 = 3.7$ m, $b_2 = 2.3$ m
$h = 4.8$ m

Circumferences and Areas of Circles, page 103 ·································

Find the circumference and
the area of the circle.

Find the area of the shaded region.

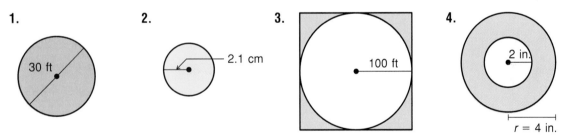

1. 30 ft

2. 2.1 cm

3. 100 ft

4. 2 in. $r = 4$ in.

Problem–Solving Strategy: Drawing a Diagram, page 105 ·····························

Draw a diagram to solve.

Train routes connect these stations: Grand Junction and Lemoine,
Lemoine and Vernon, Hudson and Grantville, Vernon and Grantville,
and Lemoine and Hudson.

1. In how many ways could you travel
from Grand Junction to Hudson?

2. List each route from Grand Junction
to Hudson.

3. Another set of tracks is opened from
Lemoine to Grantville. In how many
ways could you travel from Grand
Junction to Hudson? What are they?

Practice PLUS

KEY SKILL: Multiplying Whole Numbers and Decimals (Use after page 89.)

Level A

Place the decimal point in the answer.

1. $5.9 \times 3.84 = 2\,2\,6\,5\,6$ **2.** $8.1 \times 1.6 = 1\,2\,9\,6$ **3.** $4.23 \times 1.04 = 4\,3\,9\,9\,2$

Find the product.

4.   18
   $\times\ 5$

5.   12
   $\times\ 0.3$

6.   1.4
   $\times\ 8$

7.   29.1
   $\times\ 0.34$

8.   725
   $\times\ 5.3$

9. 7×6.2 **10.** 6.2×20 **11.** 134×223 **12.** 13.8×7

13. $42 \times \$200$ **14.** 9×5.8 **15.** 4.7×19.02 **16.** $77 \times 28{,}203$

17. Ben bought 8 pens at $1.20 each. What was the total cost of the pens?

Level B

Find the product.

18.   40
   $\times\ 0.9$

19.   85.1
   $\times\ 6.1$

20.   38
   $\times\ 2.09$

21.   7.6
   $\times\ 8$

22. 7×6.3 **23.** 15×7.2 **24.** 6×202.3 **25.** 667×309

26. $44 \times 2{,}000$ **27.** 6.8×13.7 **28.** $88 \times 5{,}682$ **29.** 8×12.5

30. $35 \times \$27.44$ **31.** 38.134×52 **32.** $35 \times 3{,}000$ **33.** $58 \times 3{,}287$

34. 16×506 **35.** 233×25.6 **36.** 109.4×35 **37.** 6.3×7.084

38. Kim bought 2.5 pounds of beef. It cost $3.58 per pound. What was the total cost of the beef?

Level C

Find the product.

39.   3.7
   $\times\ .009$

40.   63
   $\times\ .6$

41.   28
   $\times\ 38$

42.   726
   $\times\ 10.4$

43. 12×5.6 **44.** 7×6.8 **45.** $5{,}000 \times 74.8$ **46.** 887×465

47. $65 \times 2{,}000$ **48.** 503×8.9 **49.** 23.7×5.6 **50.** $7{,}000 \times 64.85$

51. $\$87.66 \times 35$ **52.** 29.034×7.6 **53.** $64{,}302 \times 55$ **54.** $4.55 \times 2{,}500$

55. Tracy put 18.5 gal of gas in her car. It cost $1.24 per gal. What was the cost of the gas?

KEY SKILL: Areas of Parallelograms, Triangles, and Trapezoids (Use after page 101.)

Level A

Find the area.

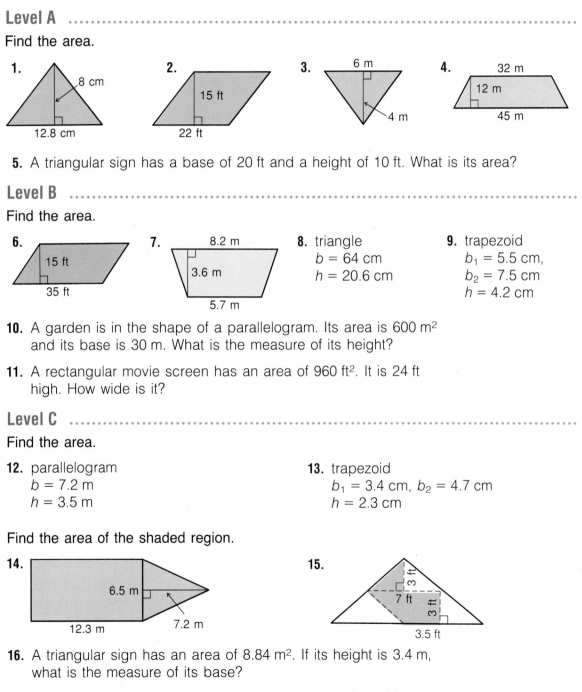

1. 8 cm / 12.8 cm

2. 15 ft / 22 ft

3. 6 m / 4 m

4. 32 m / 12 m / 45 m

5. A triangular sign has a base of 20 ft and a height of 10 ft. What is its area?

Level B

Find the area.

6. 15 ft / 35 ft

7. 8.2 m / 3.6 m / 5.7 m

8. triangle
$b = 64$ cm
$h = 20.6$ cm

9. trapezoid
$b_1 = 5.5$ cm,
$b_2 = 7.5$ cm
$h = 4.2$ cm

10. A garden is in the shape of a parallelogram. Its area is 600 m² and its base is 30 m. What is the measure of its height?

11. A rectangular movie screen has an area of 960 ft². It is 24 ft high. How wide is it?

Level C

Find the area.

12. parallelogram
$b = 7.2$ m
$h = 3.5$ m

13. trapezoid
$b_1 = 3.4$ cm, $b_2 = 4.7$ cm
$h = 2.3$ cm

Find the area of the shaded region.

14. 6.5 m / 12.3 m / 7.2 m

15. 3 ft / 7 ft / 3 ft / 3.5 ft

16. A triangular sign has an area of 8.84 m². If its height is 3.4 m, what is the measure of its base?

17. A town is building a trapezoidal swimming pool. One side is 50 m long and the other is 40 m long. The area is 1,350 m². How wide is the pool?

CHAPTER REVIEW

LANGUAGE AND MATHEMATICS

Complete the sentences. Use the words in the chart on the right.

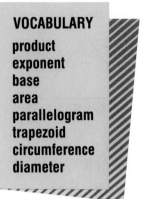

VOCABULARY

product
exponent
base
area
parallelogram
trapezoid
circumference
diameter

1. A ■ has exactly one pair of parallel sides. *(page 100)*

2. In a number that is in exponential form, the ■ tells the number of times that the ■ is used as a factor. *(page 94)*

3. The ■ of a plane figure is a measure of its surface. *(page 98)*

4. The distance around a circle is called its ■. *(page 102)*

5. *Write a definition* or give an example of the words you did not use from the chart.

CONCEPTS AND SKILLS

Choose the letter of the best estimate of the product. *(page 86)*

6. 324×1.2 **a.** 32.4 **b.** 64.8 **c.** 324 **d.** 648

7. 4.9×7.09 **a.** 35 **b.** 28 **c.** 3.5 **d.** 2.8

8. $0.5 \times .496$ **a.** 250 **b.** 25 **c.** 0.25 **d.** 0.0025

9. 803×0.75 **a.** 6,000 **b.** 600 **c.** 6.0 **d.** 0.06

Find the product. *(page 88)*

10. 23×117

11. 52×406

12. $99 \times \$31,042$

13. $\$30.46 \times 12$

14. 7×8.4

15. 4.5×3.8

16. 4.8×0.25

17. 0.2×0.3

18. $867 \times 8,207$

19. 10.1×56.78

20. $1.0 \times 9,876.54$

21. 2.5×604

Write in scientific notation. *(page 96)*

22. 48

23. 45,000

24. 2,400,000

Find the product in scientific notation. *(page 96)*

25. $3.267 \times 1,000$

26. $0.456 \times 10,300$

27. $(1.01 \times 10^3) \times (4.5 \times 10^3)$

28. $(5.6 \times 10^0) \times (9.9 \times 10^1)$

29. $(23 \times 10^2) \times (4.2 \times 10^4)$

30. $(2.0 \times 10^1) \times (16.3 \times 10^2)$

31. $(2.5 \times 10^4) \times (2.5 \times 10^4)$

32. $(8.1 \times 10^4) \times (2.06 \times 10^5)$

Find the circumference of the circle. Use $\pi = 3.14$. *(page 102)*

33.
4 km

34.
12 cm

35. $d = 0.5$ m

36. $r = 2\frac{1}{2}$ ft

Find the area. *(pages 98, 100, 102)*

37. square
$s = 3$ ft

38. rectangle
$l = 4.5$ m
$w = 3.9$ m

39. triangle
$b = 3$ feet
$h = 1$ ft 6 in.

40. circle
$r = 8$ cm

41. trapezoid
$b_1 = 8$ in. $b_2 = 7$ in.
$h = 2$ in.

42. parallelogram
$b = 10$ km
$h = 35$ km

Find the area of the shaded figure using $\pi = 3.14$. *(pages 98, 100, 102)*

43.
5 cm
12 cm

44.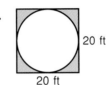
20 ft
20 ft

Critical Thinking

45. If a number greater than one is multiplied by a number greater than one, is the product always greater than one? *(page 88)*

46. If a number that is greater than zero and less than one is multiplied by itself, can the product be greater than one? *(page 88)*

47. One wheel has a radius twice as long as another. How much farther does a point on the rim of the larger wheel move in one revolution compared to a point on the rim of the smaller wheel? *(page 102)*

48. What is the value of $(10^3 \times 10^2)^2$? *(page 96)*

Mixed Applications

49. The circumference of a wheel is 10π cm. What is the radius? *(page 102)*

50. What is the length of a room that has a width of 5 m and an area of 35 square meters? *(page 98)*

51. A city bus has 42 stops on its route. If it makes 8 routes in one day, how many stops does it make? *(page 104)*

52. Light bulbs sell for $2.25 for a pack of 2 bulbs. If each pack costs the store $1.75, how much does the store make on each bulb? *(page 90)*

CHAPTER TEST

Choose the letter of the best estimate of the product.

1. 6.981×10.2
    a. 0.7   **b.** 7   **c.** 70   **d.** 700

2. 0.992×0.511
    a. 0.05   **b.** 0.5   **c.** 5   **d.** 50

Find the product.

3. 41×203 **4.** $68 \times \$20,500$ **5.** $550 \times 4,201$ **6.** $\$21.50 \times 100$

7. 608×0.37 **8.** 0.9×0.1 **9.** 3.25×0.4 **10.** 0.75×0.40

Write in scientific notation.

11. 68,000   **12.** 4,500,000

Find the product in scientific notation.

13. $(8.9 \times 10^2) \times (1.0 \times 10^6)$ **14.** $(2.7 \times 10^5) \times (3.1 \times 10^5)$

15. $(1.57 \times 10^4) \times (3.0 \times 10^7)$ **16.** $(2.02 \times 10^1) \times (3.3 \times 10^2)$

Find the area.

17.

$2\frac{1}{2}$ in.

3 in.

18.

7 m

6 m

8.2 m

19.

4 m

7.5 m

20.

25.1 m

25.1 m

21. What is the circumference of a circle with $d = 7$ ft?

22. What is the area of a circle with $r = 2$ ft 6 in.?

Solve.

23. The home economics class sells lunches to elderly people for $1. Since each lunch costs \$2.50 to make, they lose money on each lunch. How much do they lose if they make and sell 5 lunches?

24. A school was having a walkathon for charity. For each mile walked, a student earned \$.75. Chris and Terri walked 4 miles each. How much did they earn for the charity?

25. Five islands are connected by five bicycle bridges: Little Shrimp and Big Clam, Rocky Oyster and Big Clam, Great Mussel and Red Lobster, Rocky Oyster and Red Lobster, Great Mussel and Big Clam. Draw a diagram and describe all the bike routes from Great Mussel to Rocky Oyster.

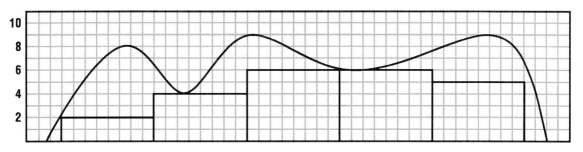

ENRICHMENT FOR ALL

ESTIMATING AREAS

You can use rectangles to estimate the area under a curve. In the drawing below, 1 square equals $\frac{1}{64}$ in.^{2}. The area is estimated using 5 rectangles each with a width of 8 squares. The area under the rectangles is:

$(2 \times 8) + (4 \times 8) + (6 \times 8) + (6 \times 8) + (5 \times 8) =$
$16 + 32 + 48 + 48 + 40 = 184$ squares $= \frac{184}{64}$ or $2\frac{56}{64}$ in.^{2}

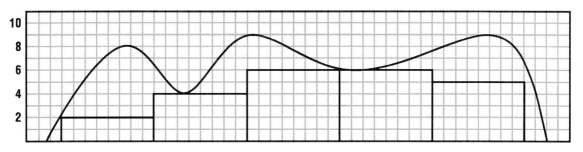

1. Below, the area under the curve is estimated using 10 rectangles each with a width of 4 squares. What is the total area of these rectangles?

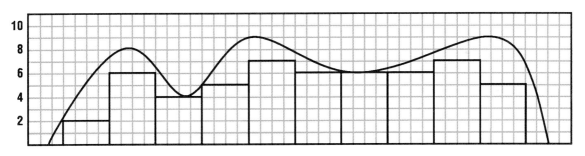

2. Below, the area under the curve is estimated using 20 rectangles each with a width of 2 squares. What is the total area of these rectangles?

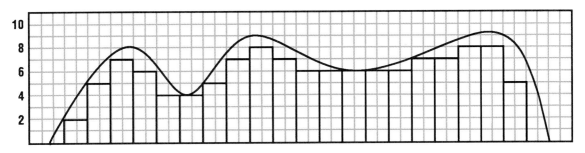

3. What happens to the estimated areas as the number of rectangles increases?

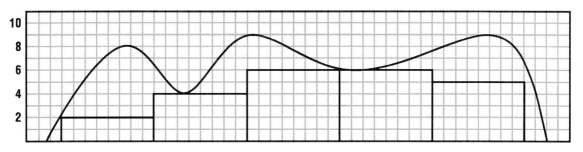

Applying Multiplication: Whole Numbers, Decimals   **119**

CUMULATIVE REVIEW

Choose the letter of the correct answer.

Chris measured the amount a baby bird was fed. In the first 5 feedings the bird drank 0.95, 1.4, 2.9, 3.8, and 3 mL.

1. What was the most the bird drank in one feeding?

   a. 0.95 mL   **c.** 3.8 mL
   b. 2.9 mL   **d.** not given

2. How many times did the bird drink between 1 and 2 mL?

   a. 1   **c.** 3
   b. 2   **d.** not given

3. What was the total amount the bird drank?

   a. 9.35 mL   **c.** 17.9 mL
   b. 12.05 mL   **d.** not given

4. Round each value to the nearest whole milliliter and find the total amount it drank.

   a. 10 mL   **c.** 13 mL
   b. 11 mL   **d.** not given

5. $70 - 0.85$

   a. 0.15   **c.** 70.85
   b. 69.25   **d.** not given

6. Solve: $n + 2.8 < 15$

   a. $n < 12.2$ **c.** $n < 13.8$
   b. $n < 13$ **d.** not given

7. Which is the best estimate of 0.9×43.7?

   a. 0.4   **c.** 40
   b. 4   **d.** not given

8. 0.3×0.2

   a. 0.06
   b. 0.5
   c. 0.6
   d. not given

9. $\$2.70 \times 0.5$

   a. $1.05
   b. $1.35
   c. $13.50
   d. not given

10. $(1.2 \times 10^3) \times (3.0 \times 10^6)$

   a. 3.6×10^7
   b. 3.6×10^8
   c. 3.6×10^9
   d. not given

11. $(2.0 \times 10^2) \times (9.5 \times 10^0)$

   a. 1.9×10^2
   b. 1.9×10^3
   c. 1.9×10^4
   d. not given

12. What is the circumference of a circle with $r = 1.5$ cm?

   a. 7.07 cm   **c.** 94.2 cm
   b. 18.8 cm   **d.** not given

13. What is the area of a triangle with $b = 5$ m and $h = 3$ m?

   a. 7.5 m²   **c.** 15 m²
   b. 8 m²   **d.** not given

14. What is the area of a trapezoid with $b_1 = 2$ ft 6 in., $b_2 = 3$ ft, and $h = 4$ ft?

   a. 5.5 ft²   **c.** 22 ft²
   b. 11 ft²   **d.** not given

Applying Division: Whole Numbers, Decimals

MATH CONNECTIONS: ALGEBRA • METRIC
MEASUREMENT • STATISTICS • PROBLEM SOLVING

1. What information do you see in this picture?
2. How can you use this information?
3. How much more is it for a family of 4 to go to the beach than to the Everglades, not including car rental?
4. Write a problem using this information.

Mental Math: Dividing by Powers of 10

A. The Space Shuttle can carry 29,500 kg of cargo. Companies interested in space research divide this amount of cargo among them. How much cargo weight would each company be assigned if there were 10 companies? 100 companies? 1,000 companies?

You can use patterns to help you find quotients mentally.

29,500. ÷   1 = 29,500
29,500. ÷   10 = 2,950
29,500. ÷   100 = 295
29,500. ÷ 1,000 = 29.5

If 10 companies share the cargo space, each would be assigned 2,950 kg of mass. Each of 100 companies would be assigned 295 kg, and each of 1,000 companies would be assigned 29.5 kg.

1. Compare the position of the decimal point in the dividend to the position of the decimal point in the quotient. What happens when you divide by 10? by 100? by 1,000?

2. How could you use the pattern to find 29,500 ÷ 10,000? What is the quotient?

B. You also can use patterns to help you divide decimals by powers of 10.

36.8 ÷   1 = 36.8
36.8 ÷   10 = 3.68
036.8 ÷   100 = 0.368
0036.8 ÷ 1,000 = 0.0368

3. What happens when there are not enough places to move the decimal point as far to the left as needed?

4. What would be the next number sentence in the pattern?

TRY OUT   Write the letter of the correct answer.
Find the quotient mentally.

5. 7,950 ÷ 100   **a.** 795   **b.** 79.5   **c.** 7.95   **d.** 0.795

6. 550,000 ÷ 100   **a.** 55   **b.** 55,000   **c.** 550   **d.** 5,500

7. 28.3 ÷ 1,000   **a.** 2.83   **b.** 0.283   **c.** 0.0283   **d.** 0.00283

8. 0.49 ÷ 100   **a.** 0.049   **b.** 4.9   **c.** 49   **d.** 0.0049

PRACTICE

Find the quotient mentally.

9. 4,800 ÷ 100   **10.** 5,000 ÷ 1,000   **11.** 58 ÷ 10   **12.** 300 ÷ 1,000

13. 8,300 ÷ 100   **14.** 45,000 ÷ 10   **15.** 6 ÷ 10   **16.** 75 ÷ 10,000

17. 588 ÷ 100   **18.** 870 ÷ 100,000   **19.** 49 ÷ 1,000   **20.** 500 ÷ 100,000

21. 3.6 ÷ 10   **22.** 30.87 ÷ 100   **23.** 0.8 ÷ 100   **24.** 23.9 ÷ 10

25. 5.5 ÷ 1,000   **26.** 460.33 ÷ 1,000   **27.** 0.09 ÷ 10   **28.** 0.0062 ÷ 1,000

29. 76 ÷ 10,000   **30.** 500.3 ÷ 10,000   **31.** 0.04 ÷ 100   **32.** 45.05 ÷ 100,000

33. 4,500 ÷ 100   **34.** 5.4 ÷ 1,000   **35.** 187 ÷ 10   **36.** 8.42 ÷ 1,000

37. 0.764 ÷ 100   **38.** 66,000 ÷ 1,000   **39.** 4,150 ÷ 100   **40.** 6.903 ÷ 10

41. 0.32 ÷ 1,000   **42.** 75,000 ÷ 10,000   **43.** 0.048 ÷ 10   **44.** 1.64 ÷ 1,000

Mixed Applications

Solve. Which method did you use?

45. The Space Shuttle weighs 4.5×10^6 lb. How much would a fleet of 10 shuttles weigh?

46. The Saturn V rocket is 110.6 m long, and the Jupiter C rocket is 20.8 m long. How much longer than the Jupiter C is the Saturn V?

47. Each of two solid rocket boosters has a mass of 589,670 kg. About how much is the total mass of the two boosters?

48. One year the Shuttle Supply Store did $3,985,299 in business. The next year its business increased by $532,182. What were the store's earnings for the second year?

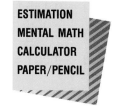

ESTIMATION
MENTAL MATH
CALCULATOR
PAPER/PENCIL

MENTAL MATH

You can use mental math to multiply by multiples of 5. The number 5 can be thought of as 10 ÷ 2.

Multiply: 36 × 5   **Think:** 36 × 10 ÷ 2 = 360 ÷ 2 = 180

You can use this idea to multiply by 25 mentally.

Multiply: 36 × 25   **Think:** 36 × 100 ÷ 4 = 3,600 ÷ 4 = 900

Multiply mentally.

1. 28 × 25   **2.** 46 × 50   **3.** 44 × 250   **4.** 680 × 250

Mental Math: Decimals and Powers of 10

A. How can you find the following quotients:
$1 \div 0.1$, $1 \div 0.01$, and $1 \div 0.001$?

Here is one way:

$1 \div 0.1$ ***Think:*** 1 has how many tenths? 10.
So $1 \div 0.1 = 10$.

$1 \div 0.01$ ***Think:*** 1 has how many hundredths? 100.
So $1 \div 0.01 = 100$.

$1 \div 0.001$ ***Think:*** 1 has how many thousandths? 1,000.
So $1 \div 0.001 = 1,000$.

Here is another way:

Think of multiplying mentally.

$$1 \div 0.1 = 1 \div \frac{1}{10} = 1 \times \frac{10}{1} = \frac{10}{1} = 10$$

$$1 \div 0.01 = 1 \div \frac{1}{100} = 1 \times \frac{100}{1} = \frac{100}{1} = 100$$

$$1 \div 0.001 = 1 \div \frac{1}{1,000} = 1 \times \frac{1,000}{1} = \frac{1,000}{1} = 1,000$$

1. Tell how multiplication can help you divide mentally by 0.1, 0.01, and 0.001.

2. Use the multiplication method to help you find the following quotients mentally: $48 \div 0.01$ $7.9 \div 0.001$

B. You can also use the multiplication method when the divisor is a multiple of 0.1, 0.01, or 0.001.

Divide: $0.36 \div 0.004$

$$0.36 \div 0.004 = 0.36 \div \frac{4}{1,000} = 0.36 \times \frac{1,000}{4} = \frac{360}{4} = 90$$

3. How would you use this method to divide $3.2 \div 0.08$ mentally? What is your answer?

T_RY OUT   Write the letter of the correct answer. Divide mentally.

4. $490 \div 0.01$ **a.** 49   **b.** 4.9   **c.** 49,000   **d.** 4,900

5. $2.3 \div 0.001$ **a.** 0.23   **b.** 2,300   **c.** 0.0023   **d.** 0.023

6. $720 \div 0.008$ **a.** 90,000   **b.** 9,000   **c.** 900   **d.** 0.0009

7. $6.3 \div 0.9$ **a.** 700   **b.** 70   **c.** 0.7   **d.** 7

PRACTICE

Divide mentally.

8. 490 ÷ 0.1   **9.** 0.23 ÷ 0.1   **10.** 1.8 ÷ 0.1   **11.** 0.012 ÷ 0.1

12. 0.16 ÷ 0.01   **13.** 0.0003 ÷ 0.01   **14.** 50 ÷ 0.01   **15.** 2.5 ÷ 0.01

16. 180 ÷ 0.001   **17.** 35,000 ÷ 0.001   **18.** 6 ÷ 0.001   **19.** 0.09 ÷ 0.001

20. 2.8 ÷ 0.07   **21.** 45 ÷ 0.5   **22.** 490 ÷ 0.007   **23.** 2,700 ÷ 0.9

24. 10 ÷ 0.005   **25.** 48 ÷ 0.06   **26.** 800 ÷ 0.04   **27.** 4.2 ÷ 0.007

28. 963 ÷ 0.01   **29.** 6.4 ÷ 0.8   **30.** 32 ÷ 0.04   **31.** 720 ÷ 0.08

32. 0.66 ÷ 0.001   **33.** 8.1 ÷ 0.9   **34.** 0.88 ÷ 0.01   **35.** 44 ÷ 0.001

36. 1.2 ÷ 0.02   **37.** 6.83 ÷ 0.01   **38.** 0.35 ÷ 0.007   **39.** 800 ÷ 0.02

40. 0.18 ÷ 0.3   **41.** 5.4 ÷ 0.06   **42.** 180 ÷ 0.003   **43.** 2.8 ÷ 0.004

Critical Thinking

If a is a whole number, will b be greater than or less than a? Why?

44. $a \div 0.4 = b$

45. $a \times 0.01 = b$

Mixed Applications

46. John's mice eat 0.83 oz of food each day. How much food do they eat in a week?

47. Candy spends $20.45 on an aquarium, $4.88 on a cover, and $3.99 for each of two gerbils she needs for a science experiment about mazes. How much does she spend in all?

48. In order to do an experiment on levers, Curt plans to divide 12 lb of sand into 0.5-lb packages. How many packages will he need to hold the sand?

49. For another science project Yolanda records the weight of her rabbit for several weeks: 2.1 lb, 2.4 lb, 2.9 lb, 3.1 lb, 3.7 lb, 4.2 lb. Make a line graph to show how the rabbit's weight changed.

UNDERSTANDING A CONCEPT

Estimating Quotients

A. The table below shows the total number of games played and the total number of points scored by the four leading scorers in professional basketball in a recent year. About how many points did Michael Jordan score per game?

Player	Games	Points
Michael Jordan	82	3,041
Alex English	82	2,345
Dom Wilkins	79	2,292
Larry Bird	74	2,076

You can estimate the quotient by using compatible numbers. **Compatible numbers** are numbers that give the remainder 0 when you divide.

Estimate: 3,041 ÷ 82

Round the divisor to the nearest ten, then use compatible numbers.

$$3,041 \div 82$$

Think: 3,200 ÷ 80 = 40

Michael Jordan scored about 40 points per game.

1. Estimate 37,712 ÷ 48. Which compatible numbers did you use? Is there more than one possible estimate? Why?

B. You can use compatible numbers to estimate decimal quotients.

Estimate: 5.28 ÷ 0.58

Round the divisor to its greatest place. Then use compatible numbers.

$$5.28 \div 0.58$$

Think: 5.4 ÷ 0.6 = 9

2. Estimate 52.32 ÷ 7.6. Is there more than one possible estimate? Why?

TRY OUT

Write the letter of the best estimate. Estimate the quotient.

3. 2,678 ÷ 28   **a.** 9,000   **b.** 900   **c.** 90   **d.** 9

4. 0.8634 ÷ 3.9   **a.** 0.02   **b.** 0.2   **c.** 2   **d.** 20

5. 0.38 ÷ 4   **a.** 9   **b.** 0.9   **c.** 0.09   **d.** 0.009

6. 7.54 ÷ 0.92   **a.** 8   **b.** 0.8   **c.** 0.08   **d.** 80

PRACTICE

Estimate the quotient.

7. 6,724 ÷ 83   **8.** 356 ÷ 59   **9.** 5,349 ÷ 87   **10.** 13,864 ÷ 23

11. 820 ÷ 31   **12.** 5,840 ÷ 94   **13.** 783 ÷ 87   **14.** 300,482 ÷ 66

15. 385 ÷ 9.5   **16.** 1,957 ÷ 6.2   **17.** 162 ÷ 5.3   **18.** 29.3 ÷ 3.8

19. 68 ÷ 0.9   **20.** 14.68 ÷ 0.46   **21.** 49.2 ÷ 5.8   **22.** 8.75 ÷ 0.039

23. 4,682 ÷ 63   **24.** 81,530 ÷ 37   **25.** 479 ÷ 8.3   **26.** 37.26 ÷ 7.1

27. 4,344 ÷ 12   **28.** 75,640 ÷ 85   **29.** 67.64 ÷ 19   **30.** 440 ÷ 7.7

31. 736 ÷ 4.2   **32.** 1,760 ÷ 34   **33.** 3.52 ÷ 1.78   **34.** 2.56 ÷ 0.44

35. 2,242 ÷ 58   **36.** 13.32 ÷ 0.37   **37.** 38 ÷ 0.57   **38.** 4.3 ÷ 0.92

39. 418 ÷ 51   **40.** 12,357 ÷ 29   **41.** 3.57 ÷ 0.58   **42.** 26 ÷ 0.49

43. 3.645 ÷ 0.28   **44.** 6.49 ÷ 0.58   **45.** 17,613 ÷ 4.26   **46.** 2.086 ÷ 1.7

Use estimation to write the following quotients in order from least to greatest.

47. 2.76 ÷ 2.8, 0.246 ÷ 3.9, 0.831 ÷ 2.73   **48.** 37 ÷ 4.8, 7.23 ÷ 8.7, 0.683 ÷ 0.04

Mixed Applications

Solve. Which method did you use?

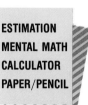

ESTIMATION
MENTAL MATH
CALCULATOR
PAPER/PENCIL

49. One month the basketball coach spent $46.50, $81.25, and $97.63 on equipment for the team. How much did the coach spend in all?

50. Mary saves $137 each month toward the purchase of sports equipment. About how much will she save in a year?

51. A one-month cleaning bill for a basketball team's uniforms was $89.56. The next month it was $106.42. Find the amount of the increase.

52. A basketball team makes insurance payments of $705 twice a year. About how much does the insurance cost per month?

UNDERSTANDING A CONCEPT

Dividing Decimals by Whole Numbers

Rory and Gil are studying architecture. For one project they are working on, they need to know the height of a story of the Chrysler Building in New York City.

Rory telephoned the maintenance manager at the Chrysler Building and was told that the building is 75 stories high. From an encyclopedia, Gil found that it is 315.51 m high. What is the height of a story?

You can divide to find the height of a story.

Divide as you would divide whole numbers. Place the decimal point in the quotient directly above the decimal point in the dividend.

```
        4.2 0 6 8
75)3 1 5.5 1 0 0
   3 0 0
   1 5 5
   1 5 0
       5 1 0
       4 5 0
           6 0 0
           6 0 0
               0
```

The height of a story is about 4.2068 m.

1. Is the answer reasonable? Why?

2. What needed to be placed in the quotient in the hundredths place? Why?

3. What needed to be done to the dividend in order to complete the division?

4. How would you find the quotient using a calculator?

5. Show how you would find 1.6 ÷ 400 using paper and pencil.

TRY OUT Write the letter of the correct answer.

6. 16)163.2
   a. 12.00   **b.** 102.00   **c.** 10.20   **d.** 10.02

7. 30)92.55
   a. 30.85   **b.** 3.085   **c.** 0.3085   **d.** 3.85

8. 4.3 ÷ 200
   a. 0.0215   **b.** 0.215   **c.** 2.15   **d.** 21.5

9. 5.5 ÷ 550
   a. 0.001   **b.** 0.01   **c.** 0.1   **d.** 1.0

PRACTICE Divide. Use a calculator or paper and pencil.

10. $8\overline{)18.16}$

11. $9\overline{)39.24}$

12. $3\overline{)3.009}$

13. $66\overline{)16.5}$

14. $12\overline{)1,027.68}$

15. $14\overline{)529.2}$

16. $90\overline{)21.24}$

17. $23\overline{)4.715}$

18. $25\overline{)426.5}$

19. $28\overline{)15.12}$

20. $32\overline{)98.8}$

21. $40\overline{)4.26}$

22. 1,352.182 ÷ 26

23. 451.22 ÷ 56

24. 4.536 ÷ 72

25. 0.018 ÷ 45

26. 1.8 ÷ 100

27. 6.2 ÷ 400

28. 12.7 ÷ 250

29. 0.45 ÷ 150

Find the answer.

30. What is the quotient of 17.682 divided by 14?

31. If the divisor is 15 and the quotient is 21.05, what is the dividend?

Find the missing number.

32. ■ ÷ 45 = 8.05

33. 249.6 ÷ ■ = 64

34. 106.5 ÷ ■ = 213

Complete. Write >, <, or =.

35. 2.675 ÷ 5 ● 2.675 + 0.5

36. 33.6 ÷ 12 ● 25.2 ÷ 9

37. 2.4 ÷ 200 ● 0.24 ÷ 200

Mixed Applications

Solve. You may need to use the Databank on page 583.

38. The height of a raised ranch house is 18 ft. About how many ranch houses high is the Empire State Building?

39. The largest multistoried garage is 4 stories high with 2.9 acres per floor. Find the total area it occupies.

40. There are plans to construct a building in Chicago 741 ft higher than the World Trade Center. How high will the building be if it is constructed?

41. *Write a problem* based on the fact that the total floor area of the Sears Tower is 4.4 million ft^2. Ask others to solve it.

MENTAL MATH

You can use your knowledge of factors of numbers to multiply mentally by certain decimals.

Since 4 × 0.25 = 1, you can use this fact to find 3.2 × 0.25.

Think: 3.2 × 0.25 = (0.8 × 4) × 0.25 = 0.8 × (4 × 0.25) = 0.8 × 1 = 0.8

Think of factors to find the product mentally.

1. 5.2 × 0.25

2. 1.6 × 0.25

3. 0.55 × 0.2

4. 0.45 × 0.2

PROBLEM SOLVING

Finding Needed Information

A. On May 20–21, 1927, Lindbergh crossed the Atlantic in a 3,610-mi flight from New York to Paris in $33\frac{1}{2}$ hours. Eight years earlier Alcock and Brown made the first transatlantic flight of 1,960 mi.

How many miles longer was Lindbergh's flight?

- **Do you understand the question?**

Yes, I need to find the difference in their distances.

- **List the given information. Cross out the information that you do not need.**

Lindbergh's flight was 3,610 mi.
Lindbergh's flight lasted 33 hours 30 minutes.
Alcock and Brown flew 8 years before Lindbergh.
Alcock and Brown's flight was 1,960 mi.

- **Is there enough information to answer the question?**

Yes, this problem also contains extra information.

- **Solve the problem.**

$3,610 - 1,960 = 1,650$
Lindbergh's flight was 1,650 mi longer.

B. How much longer did Lindbergh's flight last than Alcock and Brown's flight?

- **Do you understand the question?**

Yes, I need to find the difference in their times.

- **Use the list of given information above.**

- **Is there enough information to answer this question?**

- **If not, list the missing information.**

I do not know Alcock and Brown's time.

- **If you can find this information, solve the problem.**

In an encyclopedia you may find that Alcock and Brown's time was 16 hours 12 minutes.

33 hours 30 minutes − 16 hours 12 minutes = 17 hours 18 minutes

Lindbergh's flight lasted 17 hours 18 minutes longer than Alcock and Brown's flight.

PRACTICE

Solve. If there is not enough information to solve, list the missing information.

1. Lynne and her father went to a balloon race. Each balloon traveled about 8 mi in an hour. Lynne's father followed one balloon by car. How many miles did he drive?

2. There were 9 players on the Air Force baseball team. Each played 4 games, with 7 innings per game. Del got 2 hits in each game. How many hits did Del get in all?

3. Elsa went on a bike trip. She traveled 3 days. The first 2 days she traveled 18 mi. On the third day she traveled 14 mi. Four other people went with her. How many people went on the trip?

4. One summer Rick took several trips with a total mileage of 418. He took 2 more trips and traveled 78 more miles than Joe. What was Rick's average mileage for each trip?

Strategies and Skills Review

Solve. You may need to use the Databank on page 583. Use mental math, estimation, a calculator, or paper and pencil.

5. Manuel jogged at an 8-minute-mile pace for 15 minutes and at an 11-minute-mile pace for 12 minutes. He weighs 120 lb. How many calories did he burn?

6. The ship *Queen Elizabeth 2* is 963 ft long. This is 72 ft less than the ship *Norway*. The *QE 2* is also 2,063 T less than the *Norway*. How long is the *Norway?*

7. Betsy was planning a bike trip of 240 mi. On her last bike trip, she traveled 24 mi a day. Should Betsy overestimate or underestimate the number of days her trip will take? About how many days will the trip take?

8. Carl played three space travel games for a total of 420 points. Each score was twice the previous score. What was each score?

9. In 1929 from July 31 to September 4, the *Graf Zeppelin* make the first round-the-world flight by a lighter-than-air craft. About how many days did the flight last?

10. **_Write a problem_** that does not contain enough information. Have other students identify the missing information.

Applying Division: Whole Numbers, Decimals   **131**

How Does It

Measuring

A. Suppose that you have a very, very large sheet of paper. If you cut the sheet in half and stack the pieces, you obviously have a stack of 2 pieces. If you cut this new stack in half and place one stack on top of the other, you now have a stack of 4 sheets.

1. If you repeat the process, how many sheets will there be in the next stack?

2. Suppose you keep cutting and stacking. Copy and complete the table at the right for 1 to 20 cuts. Use a calculator to help you.

3. Look at your completed table. What happens to the number of sheets in the stack each time another cut is made?

4. Exponents are another way of representing the number of sheets in the stack after each cut. For example:

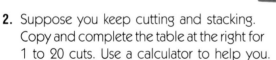

$4 = 2 \times 2 = 2^2$ $8 = 2 \times 2 \times 2 = 2 \times 2^2 = 2^3$

Rewrite the rest of the numbers in the second column of the table using exponents.

5. For each row of the table, compare the exponent with the number of cuts. What relationship do you find?

6. How many sheets would be in the stack after 35 cuts? Write your answer using an exponent.

Number of Cuts	Number of Sheets in the Stack
0	1
1	2
2	4
3	
4	
5	
6	
7	
8	
9	
10	
20	

Stack Up?

B. If you really were cutting and stacking the sheets of paper, your stack would be getting rather tall.

Suppose a 500-sheet package of paper is 2 inches high. Use a calculator to help you with the problems below.

7. How thick is a single sheet of paper? How do you know?

8. If you start cutting one sheet, how high is the stack after 10 cuts?

   How high is it after 20 cuts?
   About how many feet is that?

9. How many cuts could you make before the stack would be taller than you are? taller than your classroom?

10. How high can you count in one minute? Time yourself and find out.

11. Suppose you started counting the sheets in the stack at the rate you just found. About how many minutes would it take you to count the sheets in the stack after 12 cuts?

12. About how many hours would it take you to count the sheets in the stack after 20 cuts?

13. Make up some questions of your own about the stack. Ask a student to solve them.

133

UNDERSTANDING A CONCEPT

Dividing Decimals by Decimals

Lava Falls on the Colorado River are the fastest rapids that have ever been navigated. To find the speed of the rapids, a log was dropped into the water and then retrieved 7.625 mi and 0.25 hour later.

What was the speed of the rapids?

Divide: 7.625 ÷ 0.25

To divide by a decimal, multiply both the divisor and the dividend by the same power of 10.

Step 1	Step 2	Step 3
Multiply the divisor by a power of 10 to make it a whole number.	Multiply the dividend by the same power of 10. Write the decimal point of the quotient.	Divide. Write zeros in the dividend if necessary.

Step 1: $0.25\overline{)7.625}$

Think: $0.25 \times 100 = 25$

Step 2: $0.25\overline{)7.625}$

Think: $7.625 \times 100 = 762.5$

Step 3:
```
        3 0.5
0.25 )7.6 2.5
       7 5
       1 2 5
       1 2 5
           0
```

The speed of the rapids was 30.5 mi per hour.

1. Is the answer 30.5 reasonable? Why?

2. Show how you would find 45.849 ÷ 0.87.

3. Show how you would find 75 ÷ 0.125.

4. How would you find the quotient in Problem 3, using a calculator?

TRY OUT   Write the letter of the correct answer.

5. 2,621.452 ÷ 8.6   **a.** 34.82   **b.** 30.482   **c.** 304.82   **d.** 3,048.2

6. $4.8\overline{)1.2}$ **a.** 25   **b.** 0.25   **c.** 2.5   **d.** 0.025

7. 27.945 ÷ 1.35   **a.** 20.7   **b.** 207   **c.** 2.07   **d.** 27

8. $1.85\overline{)37}$ **a.** 200   **b.** 20   **c.** 2   **d.** 0.2

PRACTICE

Divide. Copy and place the decimal point in the quotient.

9. $0.3\overline{)0.54}$ quotient: 18

10. $0.7\overline{)2.94}$ quotient: 42

11. $2.4\overline{)76.8}$ quotient: 32

12. $1.3\overline{)0.351}$ quotient: 27

13. $0.08\overline{)1.28}$ quotient: 16

14. $0.05\overline{)0.0545}$ quotient: 109

15. $0.042\overline{)0.9156}$ quotient: 218

16. $0.016\overline{)0.0004}$ quotient: 0025

Divide. Use a calculator or paper and pencil.

17. $0.6\overline{)4.5}$

18. $2.4\overline{)\$7.32}$

19. $0.03\overline{)1.08}$

20. $0.05\overline{)\$3.55}$

21. $0.08\overline{)0.002}$

22. $0.28\overline{)\$12.60}$

23. $0.006\overline{)0.543}$

24. $0.004\overline{)2.24}$

25. $40.6 \div 0.7$

26. $0.801 \div 0.9$

27. $4.8896 \div 1.6$

28. $0.442 \div 0.13$

29. $0.0576 \div 0.12$

30. $\$21.50 \div 0.08$

31. $0.749 \div 0.35$

32. $40.365 \div 0.345$

33. $76 \div 0.125$

34. $0.37575 \div 0.045$

35. $1.6872 \div 0.111$

36. $10.4364 \div 2.007$

37. $5.55 \div 1.5$

38. $16.254 \div 8.4$

39. $0.0016 \div 0.04$

40. $6.3 \div 87.5$

41. $45.08 \div 9.8$

42. $0.0027 \div 0.45$

43. $0.051 \div 0.68$

44. $0.1521 \div 0.013$

Find the missing number. Use a calculator or paper and pencil.

45. $7.32 \div \blacksquare = 2.4$
46. $\blacksquare \div 3.7 = 2.5$
47. $21 \div \blacksquare = 0.06$
48. $\blacksquare \div 2.5 = 0.01$

49. $0.352 \div 1.1 = \blacksquare$
50. $1.3 \div \blacksquare = 0.026$
51. $\blacksquare \div 0.008 = 74.1$
52. $0.018 \div 1.2 = \blacksquare$

Mixed Applications

53. The Mississippi River flows at a rate of 2 mi per hour. How many ft per hour is that if there are 5,280 ft in 1 mi?

54. The fastest swim around Manhattan was 28.5 mi in 6.2 hours, and it was made by Shelley Taylor. Estimate her average speed.

55. The land-speed record in 1898 was 39.24 mi per hour. The most recent official record is 622.29 mi per hour. How much faster is the current record than that of 1898?

56. *Write a problem* that involves finding an average rate of speed. Solve your problem. Ask others to solve it.

Mixed Review

**MENTAL MATH
CALCULATOR
PAPER/PENCIL**

Find the answer. Which method did you use?

57. $4,800 \div 0.24$

58. 75.25×3.8

59. $\$9,875.23 - \$986.19$

60. 864×0.25

61. $87 \div 75$

62. $8,460,000 + 640,000$

UNDERSTANDING A CONCEPT

Rounding Decimal Quotients

Victoria and Marie want to find which tulip bulbs are the better buy. One way to find the better buy is to find the cost per bulb to the nearest cent in each ad and then to compare. To do this, divide the total cost by the number of bulbs.

36 bulbs for $6.79

24 bulbs for $4.79

Victoria uses a calculator, and Marie uses paper and pencil.

Victoria	Marie

Victoria:

6.79 ÷ 36 = 0.1886111

4.79 ÷ 24 = 0.1995833

$$\begin{array}{r} \$\ .1\,8\,8 \\ 3\,6)\overline{\$\,6.7\,9\,0} \\ 3\,6 \\ \hline 3\,1\,9 \\ 2\,8\,8 \\ \hline 3\,1\,0 \\ 2\,8\,8 \\ \hline 2\,2 \end{array}$$

$$\begin{array}{r} \$\ .1\,9\,9 \\ 2\,4)\overline{\$\,4.7\,9\,0} \\ 2\,4 \\ \hline 2\,3\,9 \\ 2\,1\,6 \\ \hline 2\,3\,0 \\ 2\,1\,6 \\ \hline 1\,4 \end{array}$$

0.1886111 ⟶ $.19

0.1995833 ⟶ $.20

$.188 ⟶ $.19 $.199 ⟶ $.20

The 36 bulbs for $6.79 is the better buy since $.19 < $.20.

1. How are the quotients found by Victoria and Marie similar? How are they different?

2. Why did Marie divide to only three decimal places?

3. **What if** you need to find a quotient to the nearest thousandth? To how many places do you need to divide?

4. **What if** the price of the 24 bulbs for $4.79 were changed to $4.80? How could you find the cost per bulb mentally?

TRY OUT   Write the letter of the correct answer. Use a calculator or paper and pencil.

5. 1.86 ÷ 0.8 to the nearest hundredth
   a. 23.25   b. 2.32   c. 2.33   d. 0.23

6. 9.542 ÷ 0.16 to the nearest thousandth
   a. 59.638   b. 5.963   c. 5.964   d. 0.596

7. $7.85 ÷ 32 to the nearest cent
   a. $.24   b. $.25   c. $2.45   d. $2.46

8. $25.60 ÷ 1.5 to the nearest cent
   a. $1.70   b. $1.71   c. $17.06   d. $17.07

PRACTICE

Divide. Use a calculator or paper and pencil. Round the quotient to the nearest hundredth or cent.

9. $6.97 \div 8$ **10.** $13 \div 7$ **11.** $\$45.99 \div 8$ **12.** $\$11.98 \div 4$

13. $0.08 \div 12$ **14.** $85.72 \div 27$ **15.** $\$25.65 \div 13$ **16.** $\$9.25 \div 47$

17. $19.22 \div 3.2$ **18.** $11.63 \div 0.07$ **19.** $0.09 \div 0.53$ **20.** $\$92.17 \div 4.6$

21. $4.59 \div 11.2$ **22.** $102.55 \div 0.06$ **23.** $30.09 \div 0.08$ **24.** $\$863.50 \div 4.9$

25. $0.08 \div 0.3$ **26.** $0.07 \div 1.8$ **27.** $0.009 \div 0.04$ **28.** $0.063 \div 0.12$

Round the quotient to the nearest tenth.

29. What is the quotient of 5.062 divided by 7.3?

30. What is the quotient of 96.43 divided by 0.82?

Divide. Do only those problems with a quotient less than 10. Round the quotient to the nearest thousandth.

31. $5.27 \div 23$ **32.** $16.4 \div 1.3$ **33.** $8.81 \div 1.2$ **34.** $48 \div 49$

35. $0.078 \div 0.16$ **36.** $5.997 \div 6$ **37.** $95.90 \div 0.63$ **38.** $7.2 \div 0.7$

Complete. Write $>$, $<$, or $=$.

39. $0.79 \div 0.03 \bullet 0.79 \div 0.3$

40. $0.893 \div 0.63 \bullet 1.786 \div 1.26$

41. $0.06 \div 0.13 \bullet 0.13 \div 0.06$

42. $1.337 \div 0.5 \bullet 0.786 \div 0.23$

Mixed Applications

Solve. You may need to use the Databank on page 583.

43. Alana had 10 acres of property in Idaho. She needs 5 gal of gas to fill the tank of her mower. How much will she pay?

44. Rolfe took his mower in for service. His bill shows $35.80 for parts and 2 hours of labor at $35 per hour. What is his total bill?

45. Red's Nursery sold 458 trees in its first week of business. About how many trees were sold each day?

46. *Write a problem* involving the cost per pound of grass seed at a local store. Have a classmate solve the problem.

Mixed Review

Find the answer. Which method did you use?

MENTAL MATH
CALCULATOR
PAPER/PENCIL

47. $873 + 498$ **48.** $995 - 285$ **49.** 94×186 **50.** $864 \div 90$

51. $37.5 + 2.06$ **52.** $37.5 - 2.06$ **53.** 37.5×2.06 **54.** $37.08 \div 2.06$

UNDERSTANDING A CONCEPT

Dividing Greater Numbers: Scientific Notation

A. The chart shows the volumes of various objects in space. Malcolm wants to find out how much larger the Earth and the Sun are than the Moon.

To find the answer, Malcolm divides. First he writes each number in standard form. Then he divides the whole numbers.

VOLUMES OF OBJECTS IN SPACE	
Moon	2.0×10^{10} km^3
Earth	9.0×10^{12} km^3
Sun	9.8×10^{17} km^3

Earth and Moon

$\dfrac{9.0 \times 10^{12}}{2.0 \times 10^{10}}$ $\dfrac{9,000,000,000,000}{20,000,000,000} = 450$ or 4.5×10^2

Sun and Moon

$\dfrac{9.8 \times 10^{17}}{2.0 \times 10^{10}}$ $\dfrac{980,000,000,000,000,000}{20,000,000,000} = 49,000,000$ or 4.9×10^7

As Malcolm condenses the work for a poster, he realizes there is a shorter method.

$\dfrac{9.0 \times 10^{12}}{2.0 \times 10^{10}} = 4.5 \times 10^{12-10}$ $\dfrac{9.8 \times 10^{17}}{2.0 \times 10^{10}} = 4.9 \times 10^{17-10}$

$= 4.5 \times 10^2$ $= 4.9 \times 10^7$

1. What are some advantages of dividing numbers using scientific notation?

2. Write a rule for dividing numbers in scientific notation.

B. Sometimes you may have to adjust the numbers in scientific notation before you divide.

$\dfrac{4.0 \times 10^{12}}{5.0 \times 10^3}$ **Think:** $4.0 \times 10^{12} = 40.0 \times 10^{11}$ $\dfrac{40.0 \times 10^{11}}{5.0 \times 10^3} = 8.0 \times 10^{11-3}$

$= 8.0 \times 10^8$

3. Why has 4.0×10^{12} changed to 40.0×10^{11}?

TRY OUT   Write the letter of the correct answer.

4. $\dfrac{5.0 \times 10^8}{5.0 \times 10^4}$ **a.** 5.0×10^4 **b.** 1.0×10^{12} **c.** 1.0×10^4 **d.** 10.0×10^4

5. $\dfrac{9.0 \times 10^{16}}{3.0 \times 10^8}$ **a.** 3.0×10^2 **b.** 3.0×10^4 **c.** 3.0×10^8 **d.** 3.0×10^{24}

6. $\dfrac{3.0 \times 10^{10}}{5.0 \times 10^3}$ **a.** 0.6×10^7 **b.** 0.6×10^6 **c.** 6.0×10^7 **d.** 6.0×10^6

7. $\dfrac{1.0 \times 10^{11}}{2.0 \times 10^5}$ **a.** 5.0×10^5 **b.** 0.5×10^6 **c.** 2.1×10^6 **d.** 5.0×10^{15}

PRACTICE

Divide. Write the answer in scientific notation.

8. $\dfrac{8.0 \times 10^{24}}{2.0 \times 10^{11}}$

9. $\dfrac{4.0 \times 10^{16}}{2.0 \times 10^{11}}$

10. $\dfrac{9.0 \times 10^{16}}{3.0 \times 10^{2}}$

11. $\dfrac{3.0 \times 10^{30}}{2.0 \times 10^{23}}$

12. $\dfrac{9.0 \times 10^{18}}{4.0 \times 10^{9}}$

13. $\dfrac{5.0 \times 10^{9}}{4.0 \times 10^{3}}$

14. $\dfrac{3.0 \times 10^{50}}{6.0 \times 10^{25}}$

15. $\dfrac{7.2 \times 10^{47}}{8.0 \times 10^{46}}$

16. $\dfrac{6.4 \times 10^{6}}{8.0 \times 10^{3}}$

17. $\dfrac{5.4 \times 10^{11}}{9.0 \times 10^{9}}$

18. $\dfrac{9.0 \times 10^{15}}{3.0 \times 10^{5}}$

19. $\dfrac{8.0 \times 10^{21}}{4.0 \times 10^{15}}$

20. $\dfrac{9.0 \times 10^{51}}{2.0 \times 10^{25}}$

21. $\dfrac{1.5 \times 10^{9}}{5.0 \times 10^{8}}$

22. $\dfrac{1.6 \times 10^{10}}{2.0 \times 10^{7}}$

Critical Thinking

23. Without dividing, is the quotient $\dfrac{2.7 \times 10^8}{9.0 \times 10^7}$ greater than or less than 1? Why?

Mixed Applications

24. The volume of Earth is about 1.08×10^{27} sugar lumps. Write the number in standard form.

25. The volume of the Milky Way galaxy is 3.0×10^{52} km³. How many times as great as the Sun is it?

CALCULATOR

Some calculators have an [EE] button. You can use this button to work with numbers in scientific notation.

To show 9.0×10^{52}, enter **9** [EE] **52.**

The calculator displays | *9.   52.* |

You can use this to divide numbers in scientific notation.

Divide: $\dfrac{9.0 \times 10^{52}}{3.0 \times 10^{2}}$

Enter 9 [EE] **52** [÷] **3** [EE] **2.**

The calculator displays | *3.   50.* |

So $\dfrac{9.0 \times 10^{52}}{3.0 \times 10^{2}} = 3.0 \times 10^{50}$.

Rework Exercises 8–22 using a calculator. Did you get the same answers?

UNDERSTANDING A CONCEPT

Using Multiplication and Division with Equations

A. Ralph is very excited! He has just placed 147 dominoes one on top of the other. This is three times as many dominoes as he has ever stacked. What was Ralph's previous record?

You can use a number sentence, or an equation, to solve this problem. Recall that multiplication and division are inverse operations.

Let n = Ralph's previous record
   $3n$ = 3 times his previous record

> Write $3n$
> to show $3 \times n$.

Solve. $3n = 147$

Think: Use a related sentence. $147 \div 3 = n$

Simplify. $49 = n$

Ralph's previous record for stacking dominoes was 49.

1. How would you check that your solution is correct?

B. Joan is a domino toppler. She said, "I will not tell you how many dominoes I have toppled, but when you divide the number by 22.5, you get 34." How many has Joan toppled?

2. Write an equation for the problem.

3. Solve the equation using a related sentence.

4. Verify that your answer is correct by substituting it in the original equation.

5. How is solving multiplication and division equations similar to solving addition and subtraction equations?

TRY **OUT**   Solve the equation. Check the solution.

6. $5n = 105$ **7.** $2.2n = 24.2$ **8.** $\frac{n}{3} = 17$ **9.** $\frac{n}{10} = 15.6$

140   Lesson 4–10

PRACTICE

Solve the equation. Check the solution.

10. $4n = 76$

11. $19n = 418$

12. $3.5n = 21$

13. $8.6n = 120.4$

14. $14n = 126$

15. $20n = 270$

16. $9.5n = 209$

17. $3.8n = 26.22$

18. $25n = 40$

19. $9.2n = 115$

20. $16.5n = 188.1$

21. $28n = 420$

22. $\frac{n}{12} = 17$

23. $\frac{n}{18} = 37$

24. $\frac{n}{24} = 18.75$

25. $\frac{n}{12} = 18.75$

26. $\frac{n}{0.8} = 21$

27. $\frac{n}{21} = 17$

28. $\frac{n}{32} = 11.25$

29. $\frac{n}{35} = 21$

30. $\frac{n}{10.5} = 31.2$

31. $\frac{n}{18} = 32$

32. $\frac{n}{11.2} = 31$

33. $\frac{n}{9} = 16$

Write an equation for the problem. Solve the equation.

34. What number multiplied by 6 is equal to 96?

35. What number divided by 6 is equal to 96?

36. What number multiplied by 0.5 is equal to 48?

37. What number divided by 25.5 is equal to 16.8?

38. Multiplying 8.5 by what number is equal to 46.75?

39. What number divided by 14 is equal to 9?

Critical Thinking

40. *What if* $ab = c$? What happens to c if a increases and b remains the same?

41. *What if* $\frac{a}{b} = c$? What happens to c if a increases and b remains the same?

Mixed Applications

Solve. Which method did you use?

ESTIMATION
MENTAL MATH
CALCULATOR
PAPER/PENCIL

42. For her train sets Sonia is saving for a new locomotive that costs $495. She can save $11 each week. Will she have enough saved in a year?

43. Sam wants to earn money to buy a new tent. He earned $42 for 5 hours of work. How much did he earn per hour?

44. Alan spends 6.5 hours each week building model cars. How many hours does he do this in 0.5 year?

45. The city budgeted $85,600 for 21 dirt-bike trails. About how much money was budgeted for each?

Using Multiplication and Division with Inequalities

A. Carla is eating servings of pasta before the big race. She wants to keep her calorie intake under 1,000. One serving of pasta has 200 calories.

1. What are three possible outcomes of Carla's efforts?

Look at the following number sentences.

$200n < 1,000$ $200n = 1,000$ $200n > 1,000$

2. What does n represent in each number sentence?

3. Recall that the symbols $<$ and $>$ are **inequality symbols.** Which of the number sentences are inequalities?

4. Which number sentence shows that Carla went over the limit? reached the limit? stayed below the limit?

B. You can use a related equation to solve an inequality.

How many servings can Carla have and still stay below the limit?

Solve.	$200n < 1,000$
Think: Use a related equation.	$200n = 1,000$
Solve the equation.	$n = 1,000 \div 200$
	$n = 5$
Write the solution to the inequality.	$n < 5$

Check your answer by substituting a number less than 5.

$$200n < 1,000$$
$$200 \times 3 \overset{?}{<} 1,000$$
$$600 < 1,000 \quad \text{It checks.}$$

Therefore, to stay below the limit, Carla must eat less than 5 servings.

5. Which of these values would make Carla go over the limit of 1,000 calories: 1, 5, or 7? Why?

SHARING IDEAS

6. How would you solve the inequality $\frac{n}{2} > 36$?

7. What values did you substitute for n to check the solution?

8. Did all of the values you substituted check out? Why?

PRACTICE

Solve the inequality. Check the solution.

9. $6n > 42$

10. $15n > 4.5$

11. $17n < 323$

12. $9n < 288.9$

13. $13n > 169$

14. $9n > 319.5$

15. $1.8n > 34.74$

16. $14n < 294$

17. $\frac{n}{12} > 67$

18. $\frac{n}{8} > 3.5$

19. $\frac{n}{9} < 41$

20. $\frac{n}{7} < 114.8$

21. $\frac{n}{14} < 21$

22. $\frac{n}{4.9} > 16$

23. $\frac{n}{16.3} < 11.2$

24. $\frac{n}{17.9} > 25.2$

Write an inequality for the problem. Solve the inequality.

25. What number multiplied by 6 is greater than 54?

26. What number divided by 6 is less than 54?

27. What number divided by 2.5 is greater than 22?

28. What number multiplied by 5 is greater than 101?

29. The quotient of a number divided by 4 is less than 37.6. What number satisfies this condition?

30. The product of a number and 0.7 is less than 11.9. What number satisfies this condition?

Critical Thinking   Write *always true, sometimes true,* or *never true.*

Suppose a, b, and c are any numbers greater than 0. Give examples to support your answer.

31. If $a > b$, than $ac > bc$.

32. If $a < b$, then $a \div c < b \div c$.

Mixed Applications

Solve. You may need to use the Databank on page 583.

33. Claudia weighs 100 lb. During which activity will she burn twice as many calories per minute as she would playing table tennis?

34. Write an inequality to show how many minutes of 10 mi-per-hour cycling a 120-lb person must do in order to burn more than 500 calories.

35. Jeffrey weighs 100 lb. During which activities will he burn at least twice as many calories per minute as he would playing table tennis?

36. Make a double-bar graph to compare calories burned per minute during different physical activities. Include in the graph the data for a 100-lb person and a 120-lb person.

UNDERSTANDING A CONCEPT

Metric Units of Capacity and Mass

A. **Capacity** is a measure of how much a container holds. In the metric system capacity can be measured in **liters (L), milliliters (mL),** and **kiloliters (kL).** A teaspoon holds about 5 mL of liquid, a small sink holds about 7.6 L, and a pond holds about 500 kL.

milliliter	liter	kiloliter
0.001 L	L	1,000 L

Lara wants to describe the capacity of each of the following objects. Which unit should she use for each?

milliliter

milliliter

kiloliter

liter

1. Why would you use kiloliters instead of liters to measure the capacity of the pool?

2. Why does it make more sense to measure the capacity of the cup in milliliters rather than in liters?

B. **Mass** is the amount of matter contained in an object. It can be measured in **grams (g), milligrams (mg), kilograms (kg),** or **metric tons** or **tonnes (t).** A penny has a mass of about 3 g, a chicken has a mass of about 3 kg, and a small car has a mass of about 1 t.

milligrams	kilogram	metric ton
0.001 g	1,000 g	1,000 kg

Helmut wants to describe the mass of each of these objects. Which unit should he use for each?

metric ton   kilogram   milligram   gram

3. If Helmut wants to measure the mass of a bag of apples, which unit would be most appropriate to use? Why?

TRY OUT   Write the letter of the most appropriate unit of measure.

4. To measure the capacity of a thimble, use:
   a. kiloliters.   **b.** milliliters.   **c.** milligrams.   **d.** millimeters.

5. To measure the mass of a horse, use:
   a. kilograms.   **b.** kiloliters.   **c.** kilometers.   **d.** grams.

PRACTICE

Write the letter of the best estimate.

6. When baking a cake the baker uses ▦ of butter.
   a. 125 mL   **b.** 1 L   **c.** 125 L   **d.** 125 kL

7. The combined mass of a class of 25 students is about ▦.
   a. 800 mg   **b.** 800 g   **c.** 800 kg   **d.** 8 t

8. A tea kettle holds about ▦ of water.
   a. 2 mL   **b.** 200 mL   **c.** 2 L   **d.** 200 L

9. A serving of cereal contains about ▦ of protein.
   a. 9 mg   **b.** 9 g   **c.** 90 g   **d.** 9 kg

Write the letter of the appropriate unit of measure.

10. To measure the mass of a vitamin tablet, use:
   a. liters.   **b.** kilograms.   **c.** milligrams.   **d.** millimeters.

11. To measure the capacity of an ice tray, use:
   a. kiloliters.   **b.** milliliters.   **c.** grams.   **d.** meters.

12. To measure the mass of a truckful of grain, use:
   a. kiloliters   **b.** kilometers.   **c.** grams.   **d.** tonnes.

13. To measure the capacity of a washing machine, use:
   a. liters.   **b.** kilograms.   **c.** kiloliters.   **d.** tonnes.

Estimate the capacity of: **14.** a bathtub.   **15.** a watering can.

Estimate the mass of: **16.** your best friend   **17.** your favorite car.

Mixed Applications

18. Chris bought 3.2 kg of apples for $2.56. Find the cost per kilogram.

19. Meat costs $6.73 per kg. Find the cost of 9.7 kg to the nearest cent.

20. A record mushroom of 49 kg was grown in Italy. A regular mushroom has a mass of 0.014 kg. How many regular mushrooms does it take to equal the record one?

21. *Write a problem* involving the masses of some common foods found in the grocery store. Have a classmate solve the problem.

UNDERSTANDING A CONCEPT

Converting Metric Measures

A. Bob and Karen bought 10 m of wire fence. They need 650 cm of wire fence to build a pen for their two rabbits. How many centimeters of wire fence did they buy? Did they buy enough?

You can convert from one metric unit to another by multiplying or dividing by a power of 10.

$\overbrace{\times 10}\ \overbrace{\times 10}\ \overbrace{\times 10}\ \overbrace{\times 10}\ \overbrace{\times 10}\ \overbrace{\times 10}$

kilo	hecto	deca-	unit	deci-	centi-	milli-
1,000	100	10	1	0.1	0.01	0.001

$\underbrace{\div 10}\ \underbrace{\div 10}\ \underbrace{\div 10}\ \underbrace{\div 10}\ \underbrace{\div 10}\ \underbrace{\div 10}$

Complete. **10 m = ▇ cm**

To convert from a larger unit to a smaller unit, multiply by a power of 10.

The chart shows you need to move two places to the right, so multiply by 100.

$$10 \text{ m} = (10 \times 100) \text{ cm} = 1,000 \text{ cm}$$

Since 650 cm < 1,000 cm, Bob and Karen have enough fence.

1. What is another way you could have decided if they had enough wire?

B. To convert from a smaller unit to a larger unit, divide by a power of 10.

Complete. **8.5 g = ▇ kg**

The chart shows you need to move three places to the left, so divide by 1,000.

$$8.5 \text{ g} = (8.5 \div 1,000) = 0.0085 \text{ kg}$$

2. Bob said that you can convert 8.5 grams to kilograms by multiplying by 0.001. Will you get the same answer? Why?

3. How would you convert milligrams to kilograms?

4. How would you convert 2.4 mL to liters?

TRY OUT   Write the letter of the correct answer

5. 8 mm = ▇ cm   **a.** 80   **b.** 0.08   **c.** 0.8   **d.** 800

6. 250 mL = ▇ L   **a.** 0.25   **b.** 2.5   **c.** 2,500   **d.** 250,000

7. 3.5 kg = ▇ g   **a.** 0.35   **b.** 35   **c.** 350   **d.** 3,500

8. 5.6 m = ▇ mm   **a.** 56   **b.** 560   **c.** 5,600   **d.** 56,000

PRACTICE

Complete.

9. 1 mg = ▦ g   **10.** 1 L = ▦ kL   **11.** 1 m = ▦ hm   **12.** 1 dL = ▦ kL

13. 1 kL = ▦ mL   **14.** 1 km = ▦ dam   **15.** 1 mg = ▦ kg   **16.** 1 km = ▦ cm

17. 480 cm = ▦ m   **18.** 75 mL = ▦ L   **19.** 84 cm = ▦ mm   **20.** 65 g = ▦ mg

21. 5.6 kg = ▦ g   **22.** 3.8 kL = ▦ L   **23.** 5.4 t = ▦ kg   **24.** 400 daL = ▦ kL

25. 1.2 km = ▦ cm   **26.** 9 hm = ▦ mm   **27.** 165 mL = ▦ kL   **28.** 8.3 km = ▦ cm

29. 50 cm = ▦ m   **30.** 80 mg = ▦ hg   **31.** 500 kL = ▦ L   **32.** 6.3 hm = ▦ mm

Compare. Write >, <, or =.

33. 56 cm ● 6 m   **34.** 7 kg ● 698 g   **35.** 1,500 L ● 1.5 kL

36. 0.8 t ● 90 kg   **37.** 5,999 mL ● 40 L   **38.** 536 cm ● 53.6 dm

Order the lengths from longest to shortest.

39. 3.6 m, 38 cm, 392 mm, 3 hm   **40.** 78 dam, 8,000 m, 90,000 mm, 7.6 km

Mixed Applications

Solve. Which method did you use?

ESTIMATION
MENTAL MATH
CALCULATOR
PAPER/PENCIL

41. The San Manuel mine near Tucson, Arizona, is the largest underground mine. It has over 573 km of tunnels. How many meters is this?

42. A can of frozen apple juice contains 354 mL. If you add 2 cans of water to it, about how many milliliters of juice will you make?

43. A dozen apples have a mass of 4.8 kg. What is the mass of each apple?

44. Which is the better buy: 12 oranges for $1.89 or 8 oranges for $1.35?

LOGICAL REASONING

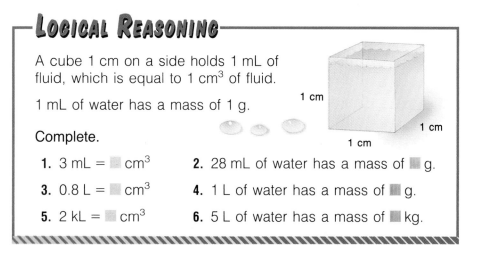

A cube 1 cm on a side holds 1 mL of fluid, which is equal to 1 cm³ of fluid.

1 mL of water has a mass of 1 g.

Complete.

1. 3 mL = ▦ cm³   **2.** 28 mL of water has a mass of ▦ g.

3. 0.8 L = ▦ cm³   **4.** 1 L of water has a mass of ▦ g.

5. 2 kL = ▦ cm³   **6.** 5 L of water has a mass of ▦ kg.

✓ UNDERSTAND
✓ PLAN
✓ TRY
  CHECK
✓ EXTEND

PROBLEM SOLVING

Strategy: Using Estimation

Since the phone company uses whole trees to make wooden telephone poles, it owns vast areas of forest. There are about 445 trees in an acre of forest. To find the number of trees tall enough to use for poles, the loggers use this formula.

Usable trees = $0.35 \times$ the number of trees

About how many acres of land would the loggers need to get enough trees for 21,200 poles?

Step 1 The loggers first underestimate the number of trees per acre.

$$0.35 \times 445 \qquad 0.3 \times 400 = 120$$

There are 120 trees per acre.

Step 2 They then overestimate the number of acres they need.

$$21,200 \div 120 \qquad 24,000 \div 120 = 200$$

The loggers estimate that they need about 200 acres to have enough trees for 21,200 poles.

1. Why do the loggers overestimate the number of acres needed?

2. The loggers want to know if 105 acres provide enough trees to make 10,500 poles. How could they estimate? Are 105 acres enough?

PRACTICE

Use estimation to solve. Did you overestimate or underestimate? Why?

3. As a paper salesperson, Bob makes about 45 phone calls a day. About 0.14 of these calls result in sales. About how many days would it take Bob to make 300 sales?

4. Some climbers hiked up a forested hillside. In order to climb 112 ft, they had to hike 300 ft. About how far would they have to hike to climb 1,920 ft?

5. A machine makes 630 ft of phone wire a minute. About 0.85 of the wire can be used for phone lines. About how many minutes would it take to create 1 mi of usable wire? (*Hint:* There are 5,280 ft in 1 mi.)

6. Hannah harvests about 320 apples from each apple tree. About 0.67 of them are good enough to sell. The rest are made into pies. Nine apples are used to make a pie. About how many trees are needed for 250 pies?

Strategies and Skills Review

Solve. Use mental math, estimation, a calculator, or paper and pencil.

7. The forest crew cleared 23 acres of land one week and twice that amount of land the next week. In the third week the crew cleared four 3-acre plots of land. How much land did the crew clear all together?

8. Lyle notices something about the last four digits of his phone number. The last digit is 3 more than the first digit. The number formed by the middle two digits is 8 times the last digit. The sum of the digits is 10. What are the last four digits in his number?

9. The phone company has 18 computer-controlled switching systems. Each system handles 850,000 calls an hour. The systems work with 97% accuracy. How many calls would not be accurately answered in a day?

10. A forest ranger watches over a circular area 20 mi in diameter from a tower in the center of the circle. He spots two fires: one 5 mi north and the other 7.5 mi east. Draw a diagram to show a straight line that the fire department could travel between the fires.

11. *Write a problem* that involves using estimation with measurement to find a solution. Ask other students to solve it.

UNDERSTANDING A CONCEPT

Mean, Median, Mode, and Range

A. The set of data below shows what six students spent on records in the last three months. Find the average amount spent.

The **mean,** or average, is one statistical measure used to describe a set of data.

Step 1 Add the amounts.

$7.50 + $8.98 + $12.50 + $12.50 + $9.48 + $8.98 = $59.94

Step 2 Divide by the number of amounts.

$59.94 ÷ 6 = $9.99

The mean of the amounts is $9.99.

B. The **median** is the middle number when data are arranged in order. When there are two middle numbers, the median is the mean of the two numbers.

Find the median of the given amounts.

$7.50 **$8.98** $8.98 $9.48 **$12.50** **$12.50**

$$\frac{\$8.98 + \$9.48}{2} = \$9.23$$

The median is $9.23.

The **mode** is the number or set of numbers that occurs most often. For the given set of data there are two modes: $8.98 and $12.50

1. Does the size of the least or the greatest number affect the mean? the median?

2. **What if** you replaced $9.48 with $8.98? What would be the mode?

3. **What if** the amounts were $7.50, $12.50, $8.98, $7.89, and $11? What would be the mode?

C. The **range** is the difference between the greatest and the least number in a set of data.

The range of the data is $12.50 − $7.50 = $5.00.

4. Which of the measures—mean, median, mode, or range—are easily found when the data are ordered from the least to the greatest?

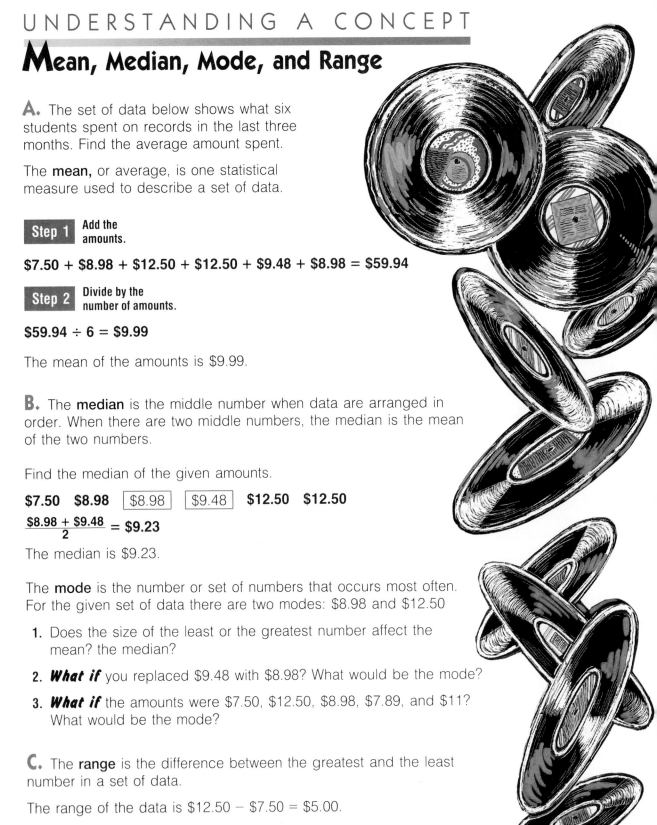

Find the mean, median, mode, and range.

5. 2.68, 3.75, 9.01, 1.66, 3.54, 8.52   **6.** $16, $18, $24, $18, $17

PRACTICE

Find the mean, median, mode, and range.

7. 20, 30, 20, 40, 50   **8.** $319, $408, $517, $206

9. 38, 45, 97, 26, 38, 97, 45, 27, 30, 45   **10.** 11.5, 19.74, 26.1, 20.2, 18, 20.2

11. $65.80, $27.95, $48.90, $65.80, $20, $116.90, $25.93

12. $1,500; $2,380; $1,500; $900; $4,640; $900

13. $125,000; $287,000; $136,000; $188,000; $201,000; $245,000

14. 0.1, 0.07, 0.1, 0.085, 0.093, 0.07, 0.091, 0.07, 0.086

15. $50,230; $50,126; $50,000; $42,500; $28,450; $50,893

16. $36,645; $51,000; $44,500; $56,000; $55,300; $56,371

Tell which of the four statistical measures is used.

17. The most popular cereal sold last week was Oats and More.

18. Half of the runners finished in 15:09 or less.

19. The prices of one brand of jeans varied by $27.80.

20. The average cost of a record is $10.72.

Critical Thinking

21. Which of the four statistical measures must always be a member of the set of data?

Mixed Applications

22. Find the mean population of the cities.

23. Write the population of São Paulo in scientific notation.

24. The population of Mexico City in 1978 was 8,299,209. By how much has its population increased?

25. Choose five cities at random. Write the populations in order from the least to the greatest.

TOP 10 CITIES IN POPULATION

Mexico City	16,000,000
São Paulo	12,600,000
Shanghai	11,900,000
Tokyo	11,600,000
Buenos Aires	9,700,000
Beijing	9,200,000
Calcutta	9,200,000
New York	9,100,000
Rio de Janeiro	9,000,000
Paris	8,500,000

Effects of Change on Data

Meg's school is having its Other Olympics. Meg's scores in the seven events she has completed are shown in the table. She has one more event to compete in. A perfect score for any single event is 10.

Changes in a set of data can affect the statistical measures—mean, median, mode, and range—used to describe the data.

MEG'S SCORES

Event	Score
Belly flops	7.0
Unicycling	9.5
Sack race	7.5
Juggling	6.5
Yo-yo tricks	10.0
Hopping and whistling	7.0
Doggie paddle	8.5
Three-legged race	—

WORKING TOGETHER

1. Record the mean, median, mode, and range of Meg's scores in the events she has completed.

2. How would the range of Meg's scores change if she scored 7.5 in the three-legged race? 6.0 in the three-legged race?

3. **What if** Meg were to score 8.0 in the three-legged race? How would it affect her mean score? Tell why.

4. Give a score for an event that would have an effect on her mean score.

5. How would Meg's median score change if she scored 7.5 in the three-legged race? 8.5 in the three-legged race?

6. **What if** Meg were to enter the three-legged race and an additional event not shown in the table? What would happen to the median if one score were above her median score and one were below her median score?

7. How would Meg's mode score change if she scored 7.0 in the three-legged race? 6.5 in the three-legged race?

8. What must be true about new data if it affects the range of the original set of data?

9. What must be true about new data if it causes the mean of the existing data to increase? to decrease?

10. What must be true about new data if it causes the median of the existing data to increase? to decrease?

11. What must be true about changes in data that cause the mode to change?

PRACTICE

Solve. Use the information in the table.

BEN'S BOWLING SCORES

Game	1	2	3	4	5	6
Score	125	135	160	125	146	149

Find the:

12. mean.   **13.** median.   **14.** mode.   **15.** range.

16. *What if* Ben had bowled 154 in game 7? How would this score change his mean?

17. *What if* Ben had bowled 140 in game 7? Which statistical measure would change? What would it change to?

18. *What if* Ben bowled 195 in game 7? Which statistical measure would not be affected?

Critical Thinking

19. Which statistical measure for a set of data would be most affected by an additional very high or very low score?

20. Which statistical measure is not likely to be affected by an additional very high or very low score?

Mixed Applications

21. Over 12 games Fred's bowling average was 140. He scored 179 in his next game. What was his new average?

22. *Write a problem* of your own that involves statistical measures and uses decimals. Solve your problem. Ask others to solve it.

DECISION MAKING

Problem Solving: Choosing a Vacation

SITUATION

The Santiago children want to send their parents on a vacation to Florida. They are considering three travel packages.

PROBLEM

Which vacation package should they choose?

DATA

Package 2

Package 1

EXPLORE the EVERGLADES

$378.00
Per Person/Double Occupancy

Includes
Round-trip airfare
Accommodations for
3 nights

Additional costs
Car rental:
$15 per day

Special conditions
Must leave on Tuesday;
better hotel rooms are
available during midweek;
additional nights are available.

Beach Bonanza

$515.00
Per Person/Double Occupancy

Includes
Round-trip airfare
Accommodations for
4 nights

Additional costs
Car rental:
$10 per day

Special conditions
Leave any day of the week;
price includes standard room;
deluxe rooms at additional
cost; additional nights are
available.

Package 3

SPACE SPECIAL

$756.00
Per Person/Double Occupancy

Includes
Round-trip airfare
Accommodations for 7 nights

Additional costs
Car rental: $145.25 per week

Special conditions
Hotel closest to space center;
better rooms are available
at a surcharge; must purchase
the entire week's package;
leave any day.

USING THE DATA

How much does the package, without car rental, cost per day for two people?

1. package 1   **2.** package 2   **3.** package 3

How much does the package, with car rental, cost per day for two people?

4. package 1   **5.** package 2   **6.** package 3

There are three Santiago children. How much would each have to pay toward the basic package (no car rental) if each pays the same amount? Round your answers to the nearest dollar.

7. package 1   **8.** package 2   **9.** package 3

MAKING DECISIONS

10. Which package should they choose to get the lowest total cost without car rental? with car rental?

11. Which package should they choose to get the lowest cost per day without car rental? with car rental?

12. Which package(s) should they choose if their parents cannot leave on a weekday?

13. Which packages(s) should they choose to get their parents better rooms?

14. *Write a list* of other factors they should consider when planning the trip.

15. Which package would you choose? Why?

Math and Social Studies

The first census in the United States was taken in 1790. There were two main reasons for that first census. The cost of the Revolutionary War had been high, and the nation had to find a way to pay its debts. It was decided that the cost would be divided among the states. In addition, the number of representatives each state sent to Congress was to be based on population.

Today the census, which is taken every ten years, gives government, business, and industry a wealth of information about the citizens of the country. The census does more than simply count heads. It allows the government to gather statistics about families, jobs, and housing that help in planning for the future.

The table below shows the total population and number of people per square mile in each of five census years.

Year	Total Population	Population Per Square Mile
1790	3,929,214	4.5
1840	17,069,453	9.8
1890	62,947,714	21.2
1940	131,697,361	55.2
1980	226,545,805	62.6

What if you want to find how many times as great as the 1790 population the 1980 population was? How can you find the answer?

Think: About how many 3,929,214s are in 226,545,805?

Round to the nearest million.
and write the short word name.   227 million ÷ 4 million

Then divide. $227 \div 4 = 56.75 \approx 57$

The 1980 population was about 57 times the 1790 population.

ACTIVITIES

1. Look up the area and population of your state for the most recent census year. Use a calculator to find the population per square mile.

2. Discuss with a group the changes in population for your state over the past hundred years. How do you expect the population to change in the future?

Computer Spreadsheet: Statistics

Mr. Lomax teaches at Valley Junior High. Some of the students in his math class want to analyze and compare their test scores on several tests. They are particularly interested in the mean, median, mode, and range of their scores. They also want to find out how well they would have to do on future tests in order to bring their averages up to a certain level.

As you have seen, spreadsheets are very useful for organizing data, performing calculations on data, and exploring what happens when the data changes. In this activity you will use the computer program THREE M to find the mean, median, mode, and range of several test scores for several students.

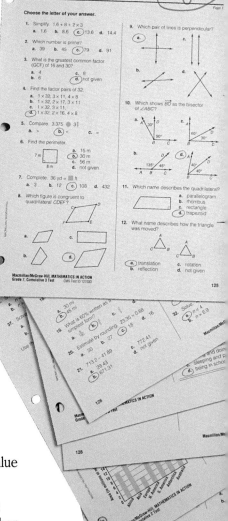

AT THE COMPUTER

The computer screen shows columns for test scores for three students.

1. On the first four tests, Beth's scores were 85, 92, 70, 85; Carl's scores were 77, 75, 88, 82; Dina's scores were 78, 86, 94, 86. Enter these values in columns B, C, and D.

2. Which student had the lowest mean score for the four tests? Which student had the greatest range in scores? What do you notice about the mean, median, and mode of Dina's four scores?

3. Can Beth bring her mean score up to 90 with the last two tests? What values should you try on the computer? Explain your reasoning.

4. Carl's score on the fifth test is 80. Does this raise or lower his mean score? How does it change his median score? Which value does not change?

5. Dina's score on the fifth test is 85 and her mean score for all six tests is 87. Experiment with different values until you find what her final test score is.

6. What is the lowest score that Carl can get on the sixth test to bring his mean score up to 82?

7. Try making up all new test scores for the students and explore questions like those above.

EXTRA PRACTICE

Mental Math: Dividing by Powers of 10, page 123

Find the quotient mentally.

1. 6,000 ÷ 1,000   **2.** 0.9 ÷ 100   **3.** 28 ÷ 10   **4.** 300.2 ÷ 10,000

5. 42.1 ÷ 1,000   **6.** 25.15 ÷ 100,000   **7.** 95 ÷ 10,000   **8.** 0.7 ÷ 1,000

9. 3,600 ÷ 100   **10.** 35.04 ÷ 1,000   **11.** 0.24 ÷ 10   **12.** 0.015 ÷ 10,000

13. 50 ÷ 100,000   **14.** 0.02 ÷ 100   **15.** 2.7 ÷ 10   **16.** 4,900 ÷ 1,000

Mental Math: Decimals and Powers of 10, page 125

Divide mentally.

1. 230 ÷ 0.1   **2.** 15 ÷ 0.01   **3.** 13 ÷ 0.001   **4.** 0.28 ÷ 0.001

5. 0.0008 ÷ 0.001   **6.** 35 ÷ 0.5   **7.** 30,000 ÷ 0.06   **8.** 2.4 ÷ 0.03

9. 0.048 ÷ 0.008   **10.** 0.077 ÷ 0.07   **11.** 100 ÷ 0.05   **12.** 25 ÷ 0.5

13. 12 ÷ 0.004   **14.** 4.2 ÷ 0.007   **15.** 1.0 ÷ 0.2   **16.** 40 ÷ 0.0008

Estimating Quotients, page 127

Estimate the quotient.

1. 631 ÷ 86   **2.** 8,243 ÷ 417   **3.** 1,557 ÷ 7.2   **4.** 198 ÷ 8.2

5. 49.2 ÷ 2.5   **6.** 19.27 ÷ 0.39   **7.** 4.12 ÷ 0.68   **8.** 9.05 ÷ 0.041

9. 3,216 ÷ 13   **10.** 65,460 ÷ 75   **11.** 618 ÷ 67   **12.** 57.84 ÷ 18

13. 77,612 ÷ 0.49   **14.** 34,701 ÷ 0.57   **15.** 926 ÷ 3.1   **16.** 2.8 ÷ 0.087

Dividing Decimals by Whole Numbers, page 129

Divide.

1. $9\overline{)20.07}$ **2.** $7\overline{)7.021}$ **3.** $15\overline{)1,127.7}$ **4.** $24\overline{)549.6}$

5. $80\overline{)24.96}$ **6.** $38\overline{)16.72}$ **7.** $42\overline{)126.525}$ **8.** $60\overline{)18.102}$

9. 1,550.372 ÷ 62   **10.** 292.668 ÷ 5.8   **11.** 0.945 ÷ 27   **12.** 0.0294 ÷ 42

13. 11.2 ÷ 200   **14.** 14.19 ÷ 300   **15.** 15.125 ÷ 250   **16.** 0.75 ÷ 150

EXTRA PRACTICE

Problem Solving: Finding Needed Information, page 131

Solve. If there is not enough information to solve, list the missing information.

1. Kareem ran the Joggers' Mile race in 4 minutes 7 seconds. Van ran the race in 4 minutes 33 seconds, and Ely finished the race 21 seconds after Kareem. Last month in the Sprinters' Mile race, Ely ran the mile in 4 minutes 38 seconds, his second best time ever. What was Ely's best time running a mile race?

2. Karen baby-sits every Friday and Saturday night at the Morrisons'. She earned $25 last week and $20 the week before. How much did Karen earn each Friday?

3. Every Monday Karen plays 5 games of volleyball. Over the last 6 weeks Karen's team has won 60% of their games. How many games have they played?

Dividing Decimals by Decimals, page 135

Divide. Use a calculator or paper and pencil.

1. $0.8)\overline{2.72}$
2. $3.6)\overline{\$14.58}$
3. $0.04)\overline{3.04}$
4. $0.06)\overline{2.1}$

5. $0.08)\overline{0.242}$
6. $0.39)\overline{\$21.06}$
7. $0.005)\overline{0.1025}$
8. $0.006)\overline{5.82}$

9. $2.52 \div 0.09$
10. $0.392 \div 0.7$
11. $6.5088 \div 3.2$
12. $0.644 \div 0.14$

13. $0.111 \div 0.15$
14. $\$28.08 \div 0.09$
15. $1.404 \div 0.45$
16. $30.135 \div 0.245$

17. $6.88098 \div 0.219$
18. $0.2884 \div 0.035$
19. $7.72005 \div 0.222$
20. $22.237 \div 3.005$

Rounding Decimal Quotients, page 137

Divide. Use a calculator or paper and pencil. Round the quotient to the nearest hundredth or cent.

1. $3.08 \div 9$
2. $67 \div 8$
3. $\$16.47 \div 7$
4. $\$17.98 \div 6$

5. $0.39 \div 15$
6. $87.63 \div 46$
7. $\$26.53 \div 14$
8. $\$17.29 \div 58$

9. $9.36 \div 2.3$
10. $0.764 \div 0.3$
11. $0.09 \div 0.62$
12. $\$156.12 \div 5.2$

13. $1.987 \div 14.2$
14. $84.52 \div 0.07$
15. $29.45 \div 0.09$
16. $\$499.67 \div 3.9$

17. $8.87 \div 0.4$
18. $0.045 \div 1.6$
19. $0.068 \div 0.5$
20. $0.05 \div 0.12$

Applying Division: Whole Numbers, Decimals **159**

EXTRA PRACTICE

Dividing Greater Numbers: Scientific Notation, page 139

Divide. Write the answer in scientific notation.

1. $\dfrac{6.0 \times 10^7}{2.0 \times 10^4}$

2. $\dfrac{5.0 \times 10^{20}}{2.0 \times 10^{15}}$

3. $\dfrac{9.0 \times 10^{17}}{5.0 \times 10^{11}}$

4. $\dfrac{3.0 \times 10^8}{4.0 \times 10^2}$

5. $\dfrac{4.0 \times 10^{12}}{8.0 \times 10^4}$

6. $\dfrac{15.0 \times 10^{45}}{3.0 \times 10^{44}}$

7. $\dfrac{8.2 \times 10^{11}}{4.1 \times 10^3}$

8. $\dfrac{9.6 \times 10^{20}}{2.4 \times 10^{13}}$

9. $\dfrac{18.0 \times 10^{10}}{6.0 \times 10^8}$

Using Multiplication and Division with Equations, page 141

Solve the equation. Check the solution.

1. $6n = 108$
2. $17n = 527$
3. $30n = 360$
4. $25n = 60$

5. $8.2n = 41$
6. $4.5n = 104.4$
7. $16.4n = 82$
8. $9.5n = 106.4$

9. $\dfrac{n}{7} = 32$
10. $\dfrac{n}{28} = 42$
11. $\dfrac{n}{12} = 27.75$
12. $\dfrac{n}{14} = 215.6$

13. $\dfrac{n}{28} = 7.75$
14. $\dfrac{n}{37} = 5.2$
15. $\dfrac{n}{0.9} = 14$
16. $\dfrac{n}{12.5} = 32.5$

Using Multiplication and Division with Inequalities, page 143

Solve the inequality. Check the solution.

1. $6n > 48$
2. $17n > 6.8$
3. $19n < 304$
4. $8n < 192.8$

5. $12n > 144$
6. $7n > 178.5$
7. $1.4n > 21.42$
8. $15n < 330$

9. $\dfrac{n}{13} > 325$
10. $\dfrac{n}{9} > 228.6$
11. $\dfrac{n}{8} < 42$
12. $\dfrac{n}{7} < 103.1$

13. $\dfrac{n}{28} < 868$
14. $\dfrac{n}{2.7} > 67.5$
15. $\dfrac{n}{12.4} < 21.2$
16. $\dfrac{n}{11.5} > 32.2$

Metric Units of Capacity and Mass, page 145

Write the letter of the best estimate.

1. mass of a horse   **a.** 500 kg   **b.** 500 g   **c.** 500 mg

2. capacity of a large pitcher   **a.** 200 mL   **b.** 20 L   **c.** 2 L

3. capacity of a teaspoon   **a.** 5 L   **b.** 500 mL   **c.** 5 mL

4. mass of an ant   **a.** 500 mg   **b.** 5 g   **c.** 5 kg

5. mass of a sports car   **a.** 200 kg   **b.** 2000 mg   **c.** 2 t

EXTRA PRACTICE

Converting Metric Measures, page 147

Complete.

1. 280 cm = ■ m
2. 55 mL = ■ L
3. 48 cm = ■ mm
4. 56 g = ■ mg
5. 6.5 kg = ■ g
6. 5 kL = ■ L
7. 26 t = ■ kg
8. 3.2 km = ■ cm
9. 5 dag = ■ g
10. 7 L = ■ kL
11. 5 L = ■ mL
12. 39 mm = ■ cm
13. 40 cm = 0.4 ■
14. 9 mg = 0.009 ■
15. 4 kL = 4,000 ■
16. 7.2 hm = 720 ■

Problem Solving: Using Estimation, page 149

Use estimation to solve Questions 1 and 2. Did you overestimate or underestimate?

1. A car leaves City A and travels 47 mi per hour. It travels for 6 hours. Will it reach City B which is 313 miles away?

2. Millie harvests 440 pumpkins every year. She sells all but 0.05 of them, which she uses to make pumpkin pie. One-half a pumpkin is used to make a pie. About how many pies will she make from her harvest?

Mean, Median, Mode, and Range, page 151

Find the mean, median, mode, and range.

1. 80; 80; 90; 70; 90
2. $400, $350, $375, $425
3. 0.15, 0.1, 0.14, 0.25, 0.2, 0.3
4. $25.80, $45.60, $38.75, $15.65, $56.85, $87.65, $67.45
5. 225,000; 350,000; 125,000; 480,000; 500,000; 480,000
6. 9, 11, 8, 12, 10, 8, 6, 9, 10, 8

Effects of Change on Data, page 153

Solve. Use the information in the table.

1. Find the mean, median, mode, and range for the data.

2. What if Jane gets 96 on test 6? How would this affect the mean?

3. What if Jane gets a 90 on test 6? What statistical measure would change? What would it change to?

JANE'S TEST SCORES

Test	1	2	3	4	5
Score	87	88	89	93	93

PRACTICE *PLUS*

KEY SKILL: Dividing Decimals by Decimals (Use after page 135.)

Level A

Copy and place the decimal point in the quotient.

1. $0.5\overline{)0.65}$ 13
2. $3.4\overline{)71.4}$ 21
3. $0.08\overline{)0.824}$ 103
4. $0.015\overline{)0.0075}$ 5

Divide.

5. $0.8\overline{)5.2}$
6. $4.2\overline{)\$8.61}$
7. $0.04\overline{)1.04}$
8. $0.06\overline{)4.92}$

9. $0.08\overline{)0.004}$
10. $\$.38\overline{)\$20.90}$
11. $0.005\overline{)0.402}$
12. $0.004\overline{)3.448}$

13. A party favor costs $.35. How many can Alicia buy with $8.75?

Level B

Copy and place the decimal point in the quotient.

14. $0.8\overline{)2.88}$ 36
15. $0.09\overline{)0.0963}$ 107
16. $0.052\overline{)0.1118}$ 215
17. $0.012\overline{)0.0003}$ 25

Divide.

18. $3.4\overline{)\$6.97}$
19. $\$.34\overline{)\$22.10}$
20. $0.008\overline{)0.644}$
21. $0.004\overline{)1.44}$

22. $0.14\overline{)0.126}$
23. $3.62\overline{)56.11}$
24. $0.34\overline{)0.3672}$
25. $3.5\overline{)\$4.76}$

26. $10.1\overline{)0.9494}$
27. $0.6\overline{)0.324}$
28. $0.019\overline{)0.0437}$
29. $7.9\overline{)8.295}$

30. $32.2 \div 0.7$
31. $0.702 \div 0.9$
32. $5.2598 \div 2.6$
33. $0.648 \div 0.12$

34. A strip of leather measures 2.5 m. How many pieces 0.25 m long can be cut from the strip?

Level C

Find the missing number.

35. $0.423 \div \blacksquare = 0.006$
36. $\blacksquare \div 0.004 = 280$
37. $0.882 \div \blacksquare = 0.14$

38. $7.506 \div \blacksquare = 3.6$
39. $0.0795 \div \blacksquare = 0.53$
40. $\$14.94 \div 0.08 = \blacksquare$

41. $0.99 \div \blacksquare = 0.45$
42. $28.91 \div 0.245 = \blacksquare$
43. $5.61 \div 0.275 = \blacksquare$

44. $\blacksquare \div 0.065 = 6.35$
45. $\blacksquare \div 0.222 = 25.5$
46. $10.528 \div \blacksquare = 3.008$

47. A stack of paper measures 5.2 cm. If each sheet is 0.0104 cm thick, how many sheets are in the stack?

Practice PLUS

KEY SKILL: **Mean, Median, Mode, and Range** (Use after page 151.)

Level A

Find the mean, median, mode, and range.

1. 30, 40, 40, 50, 60

2. $475, $125, $250, $350

3. $2,500; $1,500; $1,500; $2,500; $4,000; $3,000

4. $75.60, $68.50, $52.94, $84.76, $72.95

5. 1.2, 3.8, 1.2, 4.5, 2.3, 3.7, 1.1, 6.2

6. Jason's test scores are 90, 70, 80, 80, 90, 100. What is his mean score?

Level B

Find the mean, median, mode, and range.

7. 80, 90, 85, 100, 90

8. $429, $618, $541, $360

9. $75.80, $65.20, $50.60, $75.80, $65.20, $74.80

10. $2,500; $1,500; $800; $2,000; $3,000; $1,500; $2,200; $3,500

11. 0.3, 0.08, 0.087, 0.295, 0.07, 0.078, 0.07

12. The test scores for seven students are 80, 85, 90, 75, 85, 80, 80. What is the mode of their scores?

Level C

Find the mean, median, mode, and range.

13. $325,000; $175,000; $450,000; $425,000

14. 0.8, 0.9, 0.1, 0.1, 0.01

15. 0.4, 0.04, 0.046, 0.045, 0.4, 0.04, 0.05, 0.051

Tell which of the four statistical measures is used.

16. A store averages 1,072 customers a day.

17. Most students scored 100 on a math quiz.

18. Although the bowling scores varied by 85 points, half the group scored 100 or more.

19. The test scores for a class were 80, 90, 80, 75, 85, 65, 95, 100, 100, 80, 95, 80, 95, 80, 90. What is the median score?

CHAPTER REVIEW

LANGUAGE AND MATHEMATICS

Complete the sentence. Use the words in the chart on the right.

VOCABULARY

dividend
gram
liter
mean
median
mode

1. In the equation $8 \div 4 = 2$, the divisor is 4, the ■ is 8, and the quotient is 2. *(page 126)*

2. In a set of data, the middle number is the median, and the most frequent number is the ■. *(page 150)*

3. The basic unit of capacity in the metric system is the ■. *(page 144)*

4. In the metric system, the ■ is the basic unit of mass. *(page 144)*

5. **Write a definition** or give an example of the words you did not use from the chart.

CONCEPTS AND SKILLS

Write the letter of the best estimate. *(page 126)*

6. $35,786 \div 59$ **a.** 6   **b.** 60   **c.** 600   **d.** 60,000

7. $0.99 \div 0.25$ **a.** 0.04   **b.** 0.4   **c.** 4   **d.** 40

8. $3.089 \div 6.097$ **a.** 0.2   **b.** 0.5   **c.** 2.0   **d.** 5.0

9. $0.153 \div 3.2$ **a.** 2   **b.** 5   **c.** 0.05   **d.** 0.5

10. $407.6 \div 0.83$ **a.** 500   **b.** 50   **c.** 400   **d.** 0.5

Find the quotient. *(pages 122–125, 128, 134)*

11. $312,000 \div 500$ **12.** $0.08 \div 100$ **13.** $0.3 \div 6$

14. $0.57 \div 0.01$ **15.** $6.9 \div 0.003$ **16.** $100.5 \div 25$

17. $12,936 \div 42$ **18.** $\$4.50 \div .05$ **19.** $\$0.64 \div 0.256$

Find the quotient using scientific notation. *(page 138)*

20. $\dfrac{9.0 \times 10^3}{2.0 \times 10^1}$ **21.** $\dfrac{2.4 \times 10^6}{6.0 \times 10^2}$ **22.** $\dfrac{3.2 \times 10^5}{1.6 \times 10^5}$

Solve for *n*. *(pages 140–143)*

23. $8n = 0.4$ **24.** $4.2n = 21$ **25.** $0.1n < 10$

26. $2.3n > 2.3$ **27.** $\dfrac{n}{1.5} = 30$ **28.** $\dfrac{n}{8} < 0.4$

CHAPTER REVIEW

Use *mL*, *L*, *kL*, *mg*, *g*, or *kg* to complete the sentence. *(page 144)*

29. A math book's mass is about 1 ▨.

30. One liter is larger than 1 ▨.

Complete. *(page 146)*

31. 6,000 g = ▨ kg

32. 1.2 g = ▨ mg

33. 7.2 kL = ▨ L

34. 900 g = ▨ mg

35. 690 mL = ▨ cL

36. 5 kL = ▨ mL

Find the mean, median, mode, and range. *(page 150)*

37. 5; 25; 15; 15; 10; 32

38. $30; $42.50; $68; $201; $.75

39. 0.5; 0.25; 1; 0.75; 10

40. 0.2; 0.2; 80.8; 4.1; 50.1; 8

Critical Thinking

41. When you divide, if the divisor is rounded down and the dividend does not change, is the estimated quotient more or less than the exact quotient? *(page 126)*

42. Which basic unit in the metric system would you use to compare to pounds? quarts? fluid ounces? feet? *(page 144)*

43. Can the mean, median, and mode all be equal? *(page 150)*

44. If $n \div 4$ is a whole number, does n have to be a whole number? *(page 128)*

Mixed Applications

45. In a 6-L bottle, Luis is making a punch with 500 mL, 2 L, and 2.5 L of 3 types of juices. How many liters of punch is he making? *(page 146)*

46. Pat mowed 4 lawns in 6 hours. She was paid a total of $17. What was the mean amount she earned for the lawns? *(page 150)*

47. Matt paid $3.11 for 3 gal of gas, which he used to mow lawns. He earned $15 in 4 days. What information does he need to find the cost of gas per gallon? *(page 130)*

48. Kim's mass is twice as much as her sister's mass. Kim's mass is 80 kg. Let *s* be her sister's mass. Write an equation to show the relationship. *(pages 140, 144)*

49. The basketball receipts totaled $525 for 420 tickets. How much was each ticket? *(page 128)*

50. Five kg of seed cost $49.99. About how much is the cost per kilogram? *(page 136)*

51. A tower is more than twice as tall as the Weston Hotel. The Weston Hotel is 720 ft tall. Let the tower's height be *t* ft. Write an inequality to show the relationship. *(page 142)*

CHAPTER TEST

Choose the letter of the best estimate.

1. $49{,}029 \div 71$ **a.** 7   **b.** 70   **c.** 700   **d.** 70,000

2. $0.601 \div 0.59$ **a.** 1   **b.** 0.1   **c.** 0.01   **d.** 0.001

Find the quotient.

3. $50 \div 0.2$ **4.** $\$100 \div \$2.50$

5. $16.8 \div 0.04$ **6.** $0.06 \div 100$

Find the quotient using scientific notation.

7. $\dfrac{8.0 \times 10^3}{4.0 \times 10^3}$ **8.** $\dfrac{4.8 \times 10^7}{8.0 \times 10^3}$

Solve for n.

9. $0.4n = 8$ **10.** $2n = 0.5$

11. $6.4n > 0.64$ **12.** $\dfrac{n}{6} < 12.6$

13. $\dfrac{n}{7} < 0.35$ **14.** $\dfrac{n}{2.5} > 5$

Use *mL*, *L*, *kL*, *mg*, *g*, or *kg* to complete the sentence.

15. A baby's mass is about 3 ▦.   **16.** One liter is smaller than 1 ▦.

Complete.

17. $8 \text{ km} = $ ▦ m   **18.** $4.3 \text{ kL} = $ ▦ mL

19. $0.3 \text{ g} = $ ▦ mg   **20.** $5 \text{ mL} = $ ▦ cL

Find the mean, median, mode, and range.

21. 3; 1.5; 0.5; 6; 0.5   **22.** $20; $30; $.25; $100; $30.25; $25

Solve.

23. Harold was paid $30 for mowing 2 lawns. It took him 5 hours. How much did he earn each hour?

24. Ms. Soskis paid $44.99 for 3 kg of fertilizer. About how much did she pay per kilogram?

25. A batch of fertilizer is made with 3 ingredients weighing 0.5, 1.0, and 2.5 kg. It is mixed for 2 hours and divided equally into 4 bags. How many kilograms are in each bag?

PERPETUAL CALENDAR

John was born on July 13, 1974. What day of the week was that?

You can use the code numbers given below and follow the steps to find the day of the week for any date.

A leap year occurs every 4 years. To decide if a year is a leap year, divide by 4. If the remainder is 0, it is a leap year. For century years, divide by 400. If the remainder is 0, it is a leap year.

Leap years: 1988, 1992, 1996, 2000
Not leap years: 1700, 1900

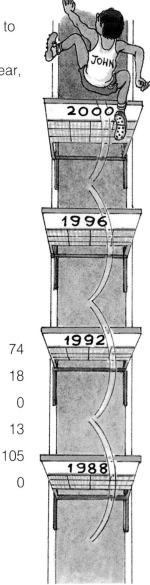

CODE NUMBERS FOR THE MONTHS

Jan. 1	Feb. 4	Mar. 4	Apr. 0	May 2	June 5
July 0	Aug. 3	Sept. 6	Oct. 1	Nov. 4	Dec. 6

LEAP YEAR CODES

Jan. 3
Feb. 0

CODE NUMBERS FOR THE DAYS

Sat. 0	Sun. 1	Mon. 2	Tues. 3	Wed. 4	Thurs. 5	Fri. 6

Step 1 Write the last two digits of the year.   74

Step 2 Divide by 4. Disregard the remainder.   18

Step 3 Write the code number for the month.   0

Step 4 Write the day of the month.   13

Step 5 Add the numbers in Steps 1–4.   105

Step 6 Divide the sum by 7. Write only the remainder.   0

The answer to Step 6 gives you the code number for the day. The code number 0 is for Saturday.

So July 13, 1974 was a Saturday.

Find the day of the week for each date. Watch for leap years.

1. Sept. 8, 1991   **2.** Jan. 1, 2000   **3.** Oct. 31, 1956

4. June 23, 1997   **5.** Apr. 1, 1969   **6.** The day you were born.

7. The date of adoption of the Declaration of Independence.

CUMULATIVE REVIEW

Choose the letter of the correct answer.

Yolanda determined that the masses of five objects in her desk drawer were 0.42, 0.085, 0.3, 0.42, and 0.38 kg.

1. Which object had the least mass?

   a. 0.085 kg   c. 0.38 kg
   b. 0.3 kg   d. not given

2. How many objects had a mass between 0 and 0.5 kg?

   a. 1   c. 4
   b. 3   d. not given

3. What was the total mass in kilograms?

   a. 6.605 kg   c. 1.605 kg
   b. 2.1 kg   d. not given

4. What was the mean of the masses?

   a. 0.321 kg   c. 1.605 kg
   b. 1.321 kg   d. not given

5. What was the median of the masses?

   a. 0.3 kg   c. 0.42 kg
   b. 0.38 kg   d. not given

6. What was the mass in grams of the 0.085-kg object?

   a. 0.000085 g   c. 850 g
   b. 8.5 g   d. not given

7. Round each mass to the nearest tenth of a kilogram and find the total mass.

   a. 1.5 kg   c. 2.4 kg
   b. 1.6 kg   d. not given

Solve for n.

8. $n - 5.4 > 3$

   a. $n > 2.4$ c. $n > 8.4$
   b. $n > 5.7$ d. not given

9. $0.16n = 8$

   a. 0.02   c. 50
   b. 0.2   d. not given

10. $\frac{n}{8} < 4.8$

    a. 6   c. 0.06
    b. 0.6   d. not given

Solve.

11. Find the circumference of a circle with $r = 0.8$ m. Use 3.14 for π.

    a. 5.024 m   c. 2.0096 m
    b. 0.5024 m   d. not given

12. Find the area of a trapezoid with $b_1 = 2.4$ m, $b_2 = 3$ m, and $h = 5$ m.

    a. 13.5 m^2 c. 36 m^2
    b. 27 m^2 d. not given

13. Find the area of a triangle with $b = 1$ ft 6 in. and $h = 4$ ft.

    a. 6 ft^2 c. 3 ft^2
    b. 5 ft 6 in.   d. not given

14. $(3.0 \times 10^3) \times (5 \times 10^3)$

    a. 1.5×10^6
    b. 1.5×10^7
    c. 1.5×10^9
    d. not given

Algebra: Equations and Formulas

CHAPTER 5

MATH CONNECTIONS: VOLUME • PROBLEM SOLVING

Napkins

200 for $ .99

Table Cloths
Paper
$2.39

Plastic
$4.89

Cups

25 for
$1.89

Plates

50 for
$2.99

Knives   Forks   Spoons

20 for $1.29

1. What information do you see in this picture?
2. How can you use the information?
3. What is the cost of place settings for 200 people seated at 20 tables covered with paper tablecloths?
4. Write a problem using this information.

UNDERSTANDING A CONCEPT

Order of Operations

A. Miranda and Bill work at a nursery. They display tomato plants in 8 rows of 9 each and marigolds in 5 rows of 6 each. How many plants do they display in all?

Miranda and Bill, write this **expression:** $8 \times 9 + 5 \times 6$.

Each of them **simplifies** the expression differently.

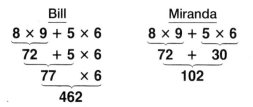

Bill	Miranda
$8 \times 9 + 5 \times 6$	$8 \times 9 + 5 \times 6$
$72\ \ + 5 \times 6$	$72\ \ +\ \ 30$
$77\ \ \ \ \times 6$	102
462	

1. How did Bill find his answer?

2. What did Miranda do differently from Bill?

So that everyone simplifies expressions in the same way, mathematicians use this **order of operations:**
  a. Multiply and divide from left to right.
  b. Add and subtract from left to right.

3. Who used the order of operations to simplify the expression?

B. To simplify an expression with parentheses or brackets, do first what is in the innermost parentheses.

Simplify: **$[34.3 - (7.8 + 24)] \times 84$**   Do the addition inside the parentheses first.
       $[34.3 - (31.8)] \times 84$ Next, do the subtraction inside the brackets.
              $2.5 \times 84 = 210$ Multiply.

4. *What if* the expression above did not have parentheses or brackets? How would you simplify it?

C. To simplify an expression with exponents, first simplify within the parentheses. Simplify quantities shown with exponents. Then follow the order of operations.

Simplify: **$[2.4 + (7 + 2)^2 - 15.2] \times 0.4$**   Begin with innermost parentheses.
       $[2.4 + (9)^2 - 15.2] \times 0.4$ Simplify the exponent.
       $[2.4 + 81 - 15.2] \times 0.4$ Simplify within the brackets.
              $68.2 \times 0.4 = 27.28$ Multiply.

5. How would you simplify $(3 + 4^2)^2$?

6. $0.5 \times 4 + 2.5 \div 5$
    a. 2.5   **c.** 0.9
    b. 2.25   **d.** 0.65

7. $25 \times [(40 + 20) \div 20]$
    a. 51   **c.** 1,001
    b. 75   **d.** 125

8. $(3 + 4) \times 5^2$
    a. 1,225   **c.** 175
    b. 529   **d.** 403

PRACTICE

What would you do first to simplify?

9. $8 \times (27 + 5)$ **10.** $4 + 4 - 8 \div 2$ **11.** $(45 - 23) \times 8 - 6^2$

Simplify.

12. $250 - 25 + 19$ **13.** $60 - 4 \times 10$ **14.** $100 + 45 \times 20 - 10$

15. $64 - (25 + 19)$ **16.** $18 \div [(6 - 3) \times 3]$ **17.** $[5.2 + (7.8 - 3)] \times 11$

18. $2 + 3^2 - 4$ **19.** $(50 + 110) \div 4^2$ **20.** $(5 + 2^2)^2$

21. $8.2 + (5 - 3)^2$ **22.** $16 - 4 \div (1 + 1)^2$ **23.** $9 - 2 + 48 \div 8$

24. $(3 + 15^2)^2$ **25.** $4 \times [6 + (8 - 5)^2]$ **26.** $7 - [(9 - 5) \times 1.2^2]$

27. $4 \times [(6 + 4) \times 15] + 64 \div 2^3$ **28.** $16.5 - [5 \times (3 + 10) - 60.7]$

Copy and place the parentheses to make the sentence true.

29. $15 + 9 \times 2 = 48$ **30.** $36 - 45 \div 9 + 27 = 4$ **31.** $76 - 40 \div 4 = 9$

32. $9 + 2 \times 3^2 - 7 = 38$ **33.** $318 - 6 + 3^2 \times 2 = 288$ **34.** $81 \div 9 \div 10 - 7 = 3$

Critical Thinking

35. Simplify $(700 \div 350) \div 50$ and $700 \div (350 \div 50)$. Compare your answers. What does this tell you about the associative property in relation to division?

36. Is subtraction associative? Give an example to support your answer.

Mixed Applications

Solve. Which method did you use?

37. Palm trees at the nursery cost $25.98 each. If Alice buys 50 trees for a hotel complex she is landscaping, how much will she spend?

38. There are gardenias in 12 rows of 8 and ivy in 15 rows of 14. Write an expression for the total number of plants. What is the number?

ESTIMATION
MENTAL MATH
CALCULATOR
PAPER/PENCIL

39. The nursery grossed $945,000 last year and $1,995,000 this year. Find the total income for the 2 years.

40. Rob has $359 for purchasing plants. If the plants cost $1.99 each, about how many can he buy?

UNDERSTANDING A CONCEPT
Variables and Formulas

A. Frank is writing a report for his science class. He reads that an ant can lift 50 times its own body weight. Frank wants to write an expression to find how heavy a load an ant can lift.

Frank realizes that the weight of an ant can vary. He uses n to represent the ant's weight. n is a **variable.** A variable is a symbol used to represent a number. He writes:

> If n = the ant's weight, then $50 \times n$ represents the weight of the load an ant can lift.

Other ways to show this are $50 \cdot n$ and $50n$.

1. Frank also reads that an anaconda snake is about 80 times as long as a thread snake. How can Frank represent the length of an anaconda snake?

B. While doing his research Frank reads many **formulas.** A formula shows a relationship between two or more quantities using more than one variable. Recall that you can evaluate a formula by substituting different numbers for the variables.

Frank finds a cricket-chirping formula to calculate temperature in degrees Fahrenheit from the number of times a cricket chirps in one minute. He makes the following table.

CRICKET-CHIRPING FORMULA: $T = \frac{n}{4} + 40$

Cricket Chirps per Minute (n)	20	40	60	80	100
Temperature in °F (T)	45	50	55	60	65

2. What can you say about the relationship between the number of cricket chirps and the temperature?

Frank wants to find the exact temperature when a cricket chirps 70 times per minute. He uses the formula.

$$T = \frac{n}{4} + 40$$
$$= \frac{70}{4} + 40$$
$$= 17.5 + 40 = 57.5$$

So when a cricket chirps 70 times per minute, the temperature is 57.5°F.

TRY OUT

Use the formula $T = \frac{n}{4} + 40$ to find T when:

3. $n = 12$.   **4.** $n = 36$.   **5.** $n = 50$.   **6.** $n = 90$.

PRACTICE

Use the formula $T = \frac{n}{4} + 40$ to complete the table.

Cricket Chirps per Minute (n)	28	48	72	94	97
Temperature in °F (T)	**7.** ▨	**8.** ▨	**9.** ▨	**10.** ▨	**11.** ▨

Use the formula to complete the table.

The formula $D = (s + s^2) \div 20$ is used to determine the approximate stopping distance for a car traveling on a dry road.

Speed in Miles per Hour (s)	15	20	35	45	50
Stopping Distance in Feet (D)	**12.** ▨	**13.** ▨	**14.** ▨	**15.** ▨	**16.** ▨

17. A car is traveling at 40 mi per hour. Will the stopping distance be longer or shorter than when it travels at 30 mi per hour?

Critical Thinking

18. Do you think the cricket-chirping formula works at all temperatures? Tell why or why not.

Mixed Applications

19. A cricket chirped 104 times in a minute. What was the temperature in degrees Fahrenheit?

20. A cricket chirped 42 times, 48 times, 46 times, 40 times, and 38 times. What is the range of its chirps?

21. Sue traveled 116 mi, 201 mi, 98.8 mi, and 122 mi in a 4-day period. How many miles did Sue average per day?

22. Make a line graph to show the results you got for Exercises 7–11 above.

UNDERSTANDING A CONCEPT

Writing Algebraic Expressions

A. Carmen has been practicing the piano for the same number of hours each week. She has decided that she will practice 4 hours more each week. How many hours will she now practice in a week?

There is not enough information to solve this problem. However, you can use an **algebraic expression** to represent the information that is given. An algebraic expression is a combination of one or more variables, numbers, and operation signs.

Let n = the number of hours Carmen practices.
Then $n + 4$ represents Carmen's new practice schedule.

1. What if Carmen decided to practice 6 hours more each week than she has been? Write an algebraic expression to represent this. Use x for the variable.

B. To **evaluate** an algebraic expression substitute a given value for the variable.

What if Carmen had been practicing 8 hours each week? If she decided to practice 4 hours more each week, how many hours would she now practice?

Write an expression. **$n + 4$**

Think: Substitute 8 for n in the expression. **$8 + 4 = 12$**

So Carmen will now practice 12 hours.

2. Evaluate the expression $n + 6$. Let $n = 8$. What can it represent?

C. The table shows some word phrases and algebraic expressions that have the same meaning.

Word Phrase	Algebraic Expression
(a) the sum of a number and 5	$n + 5$
(b) 3 less than a number	$n - 3$
(c) a number increased by 7.5	$n + 7.5$
(d) the product of 2 and a number	$2n$, $2 \times n$, or $2 \cdot n$
(e) a number divided by 3	$\frac{n}{3}$, $n \div 3$, or $\frac{1}{3}n$
(f) a number that is greater than 4	$n > 4$
(g) a number that is less than 6	$n < 6$

3. List another word phrase that can translate to the algebraic expression in (a), in (b), in (d), in (e).

TRY OUT

Write and then evaluate an algebraic expression.
Let $a = 6$ and $b = 10$.

4. 8 times a number a

5. the sum of b and 4.3

6. the quotient of a and 2

7. b decreased by 5.2

PRACTICE

Evaluate the expression. Let $c = 6$ and $d = 12$.

8. $9 - c$ **9.** $6d$ **10.** $48 \div c$ **11.** $c + 8$ **12.** $d - c$

13. $12.5c$ **14.** $\frac{c}{0.5}$ **15.** $7.6 + c$ **16.** $d - 4.1$ **17.** $1.2d - c$

18. $3.5d$ **19.** $c + d$ **20.** $\frac{d}{3}$ **21.** $2c + d$ **22.** $c - 4.2$

23. $9.1 - c$ **24.** $3.4d$ **25.** $3c - d$ **26.** $c \div d$ **27.** cd

Write and then evaluate an algebraic expression. Let $m = 8$ and $n = 14$.

28. 9 added to n

29. m decreased by 5

30. the product of m and 2.1

31. the number n divided by 7

32. 2.5 added to the number n

33. the product of m and n

34. 8 times the number m

35. 4.1 fewer than n

36. the quotient of n and 2

37. m added to n

Critical Thinking

38. Evaluate the expressions $5n + 2$ and $5(n + 2)$. Let $n = 2$.
Tell why the answers differ.

Mixed Applications

39. Kevin practiced his harmonica 3.3 hours this week, 2.5 hours last week, and 2.25 hours the week before. How many hours has he practiced in three weeks?

40. Norma jogs 2 mi farther each week than the week before. If she jogs x miles this week, write an algebraic expression to represent how far she will jog next week.

41. *What if* there were 5 hours in a day and 250 days in a year? How many hours would there be in y years?

42. Which numbers when multiplied by 7 will give a product that is greater than 49?

EXTRA Practice, page 194   Equations and Formulas   **175**

UNDERSTANDING A CONCEPT

Writing Algebraic Sentences

A. If a camel can travel 80 km per day, how long will it take the camel to travel 280 km?

You can write a word sentence to represent the situation. **Algebraic sentences** can represent word sentences. Algebraic expressions, symbols, and relation signs are used to write algebraic sentences. The "is equal to" sign tells you that the values of the sides are equivalent.

Let n = the number of days the camel will travel. 80 times the number is equal to 280.

left side		right side

80 times the number   is equal to   280 ◄——— word sentence
$\underbrace{}$ $\underbrace{}$
$80n$ =   280 ◄——— algebraic sentence

1. Write a different algebraic sentence to solve the problem.

B. Recall that you can use > and < to represent situations that are not equal. Algebraic sentences can also represent inequalities.

In 20 minutes a giant tortoise can travel more than 90 m. What is the rate of speed in meters per minute?

Let n = speed in meters per minute.

20 times the number   is greater than   90 ◄——— word sentence
$\underbrace{}$ $\underbrace{}$
$20n$ >   90 ◄——— algebraic sentence

2. What does the inequality sign tell you about the values of the sides?

3. How would replacing > with < change the meaning of the algebraic sentence above?

TRY OUT   Write an algebraic sentence.

4. A number q divided by 6 is equal to 14.

5. A number n increased by 2.5 is equal to 8.

6. 4 times a number b is less than 16.

7. A number w decreased by 3.7 is greater than 5.

PRACTICE

Complete the table.

Word Sentence	Algebraic Sentence
A number increased by 4 is equal to 9.	**8.** 
6 times a number is less than 18.	**9.**
10.	$\frac{n}{7} > 21$
11.	$24 = 8n$
7 less than a number is 6.	**12.**
13.	$n + 2 = 11$

Write an algebraic sentence.

14. A number r increased by 4 is equal to 23.

15. A number y decreased by 8.5 is equal to 14.7.

16. 35 is the product of 5 and a number w.

17. 9 times a number n is greater than 54.

18. 56 is equal to the sum of a number y and 34.

19. The quotient of a number s and 24 is less than 4.

Write as a word sentence.

20. $n + 5.2 = 11.7$

21. $\frac{x}{5} = 9$

22. $12w = 78$

23. $a - 13 = 26$

24. $y - 3 < 4$

25. $q + 7 > 10$

26. $\frac{8}{n} = 6$

27. $6t < 36$

Critical Thinking

28. Write a word sentence for this algebraic sentence: $20n \geq 65$.

29. Write an algebraic sentence for this word sentence: A number plus 7 is at most 54.

Mixed Applications

30. A spider can cover 100 m in 8 minutes and 50 seconds. A centipede can cover the same distance in 3 minutes and 25 seconds. How much faster is the time of the speedy centipede?

31. A snail can travel 100 m in 2 hours and 4 minutes. How long will it take it to go 1,000 m?

32. *Write a problem* that involves animal speeds. Ask others to solve it.

THE DAISY GAME

Logical Reasoning

A. Stan has a beautiful daisy with 9 petals. He asks Jan to play the following game with him. They will take turns picking either one petal or two petals that are next to each other. The player who picks the last petal wins.

1. Suppose Stan goes first. If he decides to pick a single petal, how many different ways can he do this? If he decides to pick a pair of petals, how many different ways can he do this? How many different first moves are possible in all?

2. Use pennies or counters to model the petals. Play the game with a partner several times. Take turns going first. Can you find a winning strategy? (*Hint:* Think about symmetry.)

3. Do you think this game is fair? Does it make a difference if you go first or second? Can one player always win? Which player?

B. Stan and Jan play the game again, this time with a daisy that has 11 petals. Jan thinks she knows how to win.

Stan goes first and picks petals 5 and 6. Then Jan picks petal 11, which is exactly opposite. The daisy looks like the bottom picture at the right. There are two equal groups of 4 petals.

After the first move Jan plays symmetrically. Whichever petals Stan takes from one group, Jan will take the opposite petals from the other group.

4. Stan picks petal 2 next. What should Jan do?

5. Stan then picks petals 3 and 4. What should Jan do?

6. Explain how the game ends. Who wins?

7. Suppose Stan's first move was to pick petal 3. What should Jan's first move have been?

8. Try playing the game several more times, using 11 and then 13 coins as petals. Alternate who goes first. Use the strategy above. Does the second player always win?

9. Suppose the game were played using an even number of petals (coins). Would this make any difference in the second player's strategy? What would change?

179

PROBLEM SOLVING

Strategy: Using Number Sense

Todd was on a bus and saw a sidewalk along a whole city block packed with people. He estimated that the block was about 300 ft long and 10 ft wide. He knew that there is room for about 25 people in a 10-ft by 10-ft room. Todd wondered, "How many people are on the block?"

UNDERSTAND

What do I know?

I know that a sidewalk about 300 ft by 10 ft is packed with people and that about 25 people can stand in a 10-ft by 10-ft room.

What do I need to find?

I need to find the number of people on the sidewalk.

PLAN

What can I do?

I can find how many 10-ft by 10-ft rooms would fit on the sidewalk. Then I need to multiply that number by 25 to estimate how many people are on the sidewalk.

TRY

Let me try my plan.

The room and the sidewalk are the same width.

Divide: $300 \div 10 = 30$

Thirty rooms fit on the sidewalk.

Multiply: $30 \times 25 = 750$

There are about 750 people on the sidewalk.

CHECK

Have I answered the question?

Yes, I have answered the question.

Does the answer make sense?

Yes, since $750 \div 25 = 30$.

EXTEND

What have I learned?

I have learned that I can use number sense to analyze the solution to some problems.

How can I apply what I have learned?

I can apply what I have learned to a similar problem. For example, I would estimate that in a crowded 200-ft by 600-ft field, there would be about 30,000 people.

PRACTICE

Use your number sense to solve the problem.

1. On the same block Todd saw a building 40 stories high. About how high in feet is the building?

A mile (about 5,200 ft) of a three-lane parkway is packed bumper to bumper with cars. No trucks or buses are allowed on the road.

2. About how many cars are on this part of the highway?

3. About how long after the first car moves will the last car begin to move?

Winona saw a stack of cases of lemonade cans on a loading dock. The stack was about 5 ft high, and there are 4 six-packs of lemonade in a case.

4. About how many cans of lemonade were on the loading dock?

5. About how many total ounces of lemonade are there in those cans?

Strategies and Skills Review

Solve. Use mental math, estimation, a calculator, or paper and pencil.

6. The wholesaler bought 52 truckloads of computers for $834,286. The next day he could have bought each truckload for $13,089. How much could he have saved on the whole order by waiting until the next day?

7. Alana was packing the truck to make a delivery in the city. All the boxes were the same size. There were 6 boxes left to pack (A, B, C, D, E, and F.) But there was room for only 4. Show the different ways she could choose to pack the boxes.

8. Draw the next two flowers in the pattern.

9. ***Write a problem*** that omits some information necessary to solve the problem. Have other students use their number sense to estimate the missing information to solve the problem.

Equations and Formulas **181**

UNDERSTANDING A CONCEPT

Solving Equations: Adding and Subtracting

A. If the Statue of Liberty were 250 ft taller, it would be as high as the Washington Monument. The Washington Monument is 555 ft tall. How high is the Statue of Liberty?

You can write an equation to solve this problem. An **equation** is a statement that two quantities are equal. To solve an equation, find the solution, or the value of the variable that makes the equation true. To do this isolate the variable using inverse operations.

Recall that addition and subtraction are **inverse operations.** To solve an addition equation, subtract the same number from both sides of the "is equal to" sign.

Let n = the height of the Statue of Liberty.
$n + 250$ = the height of the Washington Monument.

Solve. $n + 250 = 555$

Think: 250 is added to n. $n + 250 - 250 = 555 - 250$
        To isolate n, subtract 250 from both sides.

Simplify. $n = 305$

Check your answer by substituting $n + 250 = 555$
305 in the original equation. $305 + 250 \stackrel{?}{=} 555$
                                                 $555 = 555$ It checks.

So the Statute of Liberty is 305 ft high.

B. To solve a subtraction equation, add the same number to both sides of the "is equal to" sign.

Solve. $n - 4.7 = 16.1$

Think: 4.7 is subtracted from n. $n - 4.7 + 4.7 = 16.1 + 4.7$
        To isolate n, add 4.7 to both sides.

Simplify. $n = 20.8$

Check your answer by substituting $n - 4.7 = 16.1$
20.8 in the original equation. $20.8 - 4.7 \stackrel{?}{=} 16.1$
                                                $16.1 = 16.1$ It checks.

1. How would you solve the equation $m - 18 = 23$?

TRY OUT — Solve the equation. Check your solution.

2. $34 + y = 107$ **3.** $z + 1.2 = 8.4$ **4.** $x - 16 = 37$ **5.** $w - 3.8 = 4.5$

PRACTICE

Solve the equation. Check your solution.

6. $a + 12 = 22$ **7.** $64 + k = 122$ **8.** $w + 6.8 = 34$ **9.** $48.3 = r + 6.08$

10. $n - 11 = 17$ **11.** $h - 77 = 54$ **12.** $8.6 = y - 2.8$ **13.** $t - 39.2 = 15.7$

14. $p - 4.95 = 6.18$ **15.** $54 = a - 14.2$ **16.** $p + 17 = 34$ **17.** $39 = z - 17$

18. $154 = m + 18$ **19.** $14.2 = p + 3$ **20.** $48.3 = r + 6.8$ **21.** $p - 13 = 103$

22. $74 = 36 + c$ **23.** $d - 112 = 119$ **24.** $c + 3.7 = 9.2$ **25.** $y - 199 = 288.5$

26. $d - 36 = 54$ **27.** $b + 1.2 = 8.9$ **28.** $a - 46 = 80$ **29.** $m + 96 = 111$

30. $k + 18.1 = 29.6$ **31.** $f - 4.9 = 9.2$ **32.** $g - 76 = 124$ **33.** $h - 11.7 = 28.9$

Write an equation for the problem. Solve the equation.

34. A number increased by 3.7 is equal to 24.1.

35. The sum of a number and 35 is equal to 58.9.

36. Fifteen less than a number equals 101.

37. A number decreased by 35 is equal to 15.8.

38. Twenty-one added to a number is equal to 32.6.

39. Nine subtracted from a number is equal to 14.8.

Write a problem that can be solved by finding the solution of the equation.

40. $x + 23 = 41$ **41.** $z - 240 = 425$ **42.** $2.5 + n = 6$ **43.** $15 = t - 1.5$

Mixed Applications

Solve. Which method did you use? You may need to use the Databank on page 583.

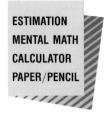

ESTIMATION
MENTAL MATH
CALCULATOR
PAPER/PENCIL

44. The Great Pyramid of Cheops is 481 ft high. It is 973 ft shorter than the Sears Tower in Chicago. How tall is the Sears Tower?

45. If a 2,550-ft tower is placed atop the 27,649-ft Mt. Everest, will it reach a height of at least 30,000 ft?

46. At 723 ft high the Peachtree Center Plaza in Atlanta is the world's tallest hotel. At 7.5 ft Manute Bol is a very tall basketball player. About how many times taller than Manute Bol is the hotel?

47. Which famous tall building in the United States is about one-half as tall as the World Trade Center in New York City?

UNDERSTANDING A CONCEPT

Solving Equations: Multiplying and Dividing

A. The world distance record for walking backward is 8,000 mi. This distance is 32 times as far as Hector has walked backward. What is Hector's record?

You can write and solve an equation for this problem. Recall that multiplication and division are inverse operations. To solve a multiplication equation, divide both sides of the equation by the same number.

Let n = the distance Hector walked backward.
  $32n$ = the world record.

Solve.
$$32n = 8,000$$

Think: 32 is multiplied by n.
  To isolate n, divide both sides by 32.
Simplify.
$$32n \div 32 = 8,000 \div 32$$
$$n = 250$$

Check your answer by substituting 250 in the original equation.
$$32n = 8,000$$
$$32 \times 250 \overset{?}{=} 8,000$$
$$8,000 = 8,000 \quad \text{It checks.}$$

So Hector's record for walking backward is 250 mi.

1. How would you solve the equation $4.6n = 92$?

B. To solve a division equation, multiply both sides of the equation by the same number.

Solve.
$$\frac{n}{12} = 18.75$$

Think: n is divided by 12.
  To isolate n, multiply both sides by 12.
Simplify.
$$\frac{n}{12} \times 12 = 18.75 \times 12$$
$$n = 225$$

Check your answer by substituting 225 in the original equation.
$$\frac{n}{12} = 18.75$$
$$\frac{225}{12} \overset{?}{=} 18.75$$
$$18.75 = 18.75 \quad \text{It checks.}$$

2. How would you solve the equation $\frac{t}{35} = 16$?

TRY OUT Solve the equation. Check your solution.

3. $6n = 45$ **4.** $4.5a = 18$ **5.** $\frac{b}{16} = 5$ **6.** $\frac{x}{2.5} = 42$

PRACTICE

Solve the equation. Check your solution.

7. $6x = 36$ **8.** $14w = 350$ **9.** $0.5d = 14$ **10.** $2.2m = 1.32$

11. $\frac{z}{4} = 8$ **12.** $19 = \frac{y}{9}$ **13.** $\frac{f}{0.2} = 8$ **14.** $\frac{k}{4} = 6.2$

15. $54q = 1{,}080$ **16.** $8n = 100$ **17.** $10s = 367$ **18.** $\frac{p}{8.5} = 22.7$

19. $17x = 357$ **20.** $\frac{t}{4} = 7.3$ **21.** $1.5c = 19.5$ **22.** $6y = 44.4$

23. $12a = 210$ **24.** $\frac{b}{16} = 23$ **25.** $\frac{m}{0.8} = 10$ **26.** $0.75t = 24$

27. $\frac{s}{4.5} = 8$ **28.** $35x = 385$ **29.** $4.5f = 54$ **30.** $\frac{m}{4} = 59$

Write an equation for the problem. Solve the equation.

31. Five times a number is equal to 65.

32. A number divided by 12 is equal to 8.5.

33. The product of a number and 46 is equal to 195.5.

34. The quotient of a number and 3.2 is equal to 18.88.

Write a problem that can be solved by finding the solution to the equation.

35. $24x = 346.8$ **36.** $\frac{p}{2.95} = 12$ **37.** $296 = 16w$ **38.** $\frac{t}{50} = 3$

Critical Thinking

39. Solving equations can be described as a process of *isolating the variable.* What do you think this means?

Mixed Applications

40. Gwen buys running shoes for $45 and shorts for $15.75. The tax is $4.56. If Gwen pays with four $20 bills, what is her change?

41. Last month Hope ran 5 km six times, 4 km five times, 3 km four times, and 6 km four times. What is the mode of this set of running times?

42. Jack ran a marathon in 2 hours 52 minutes. That is 15 minutes slower than his previous best time. What had been his best time?

43. *Write a problem* that involves writing and solving an equation. Solve your problem. Ask others to solve it.

Mixed Review

Find the answer. Which method did you use?

MENTAL MATH
CALCULATOR
PAPER/PENCIL

44. $22.75 + $8.25   **45.** 6^6

46. 3.2×0.8145

47. $1{,}695 - 1{,}205$ **48.** $3.018 \div 6$

49. $24 + 16 + 3 + 17$

Applying Equations: Volumes of Prisms

A. Armin plans to set up a display of saltwater fish in his classroom aquarium. The interior measurements of the aquarium are 50 cm by 25 cm by 30 cm. To find how much salt water Armin needs, you must know the volume of the aquarium.

The **volume** of a prism is a measure of the amount of space it takes up. Volume is measured in cubic units. The volume of a cube 1 cm on a side is 1 **cubic centimeter (cm³).**

The number of cubic centimeters in the aquarium is the number in the base times the number of layers. The area of the base is 50 × 25, or 1,250 cm². So the volume of a **rectangular prism** is the area of the base times the height.

$V = B \times h$
$= (50 \times 25) \times 30 = 1,250 \times 30 = 37,500$

The volume of the aquarium is 37,500 cm³.

1. ***What if*** the volume of another tank were 5,400 cm³ and its length and width were 20 cm and 15 cm? How would you find the height? What would be the height?

B. You can use the formula $V = B \times h$ to find the volume of any prism. Find the volume of this **triangular prism.** The top (or bottom) of a triangular prism is one of its triangular faces. Recall that the area of a triangle is one-half the product of its base and its height.

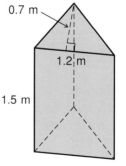

0.7 m

1.2 m

1.5 m

$V = B \times h$
$= \left(\frac{1}{2} \times 1.2 \times 0.7 \right) \times 1.5$
$= 0.63$

The volume of the triangular tank is 0.63 m³.

2. ***What if*** you knew that the volume of a triangular prism were 45 m³ and its height were 5 m? How would you find the area of the bottom? What would it be?

TRY OUT Find the volume of the prism.

3.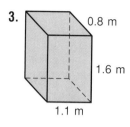
0.8 m
1.6 m
1.1 m

4.
5 cm
8 cm
5 cm

5.
12 in.
8 in.
9 in.

PRACTICE

Find the volume of the prism.

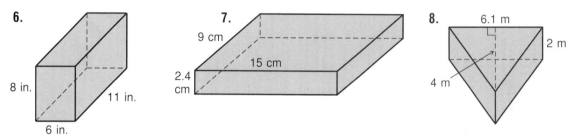

6.
8 in.
11 in.
6 in.

7.
9 cm
15 cm
2.4 cm

8.
6.1 m
2 m
4 m

9. An octagonal prism has a base with an area of 25 ft². If its height is 18 ft, what is its volume?

10. How many cubic yards of dirt were removed from a hole that is 12 ft by 9 ft by 6 ft deep?

11. The base of a mailing tube is a triangle with a 3-in. base and a height of 4.1 in. Find the volume of the tube if its length is 24 in.

12. A cubic foot of water is equal to 7.5 gal. Find the capacity of a tank in gallons if its inside measurements are 1.5 ft by 2 ft by 1 ft.

13. A tank in the science lab has an inside height of 45 cm, an inside length of 90 cm, and a volume of 202,500 cm³. Find its inside width.

14. A ton of coal occupies 35 ft³ of space. How deep is the coal in a bin that measures inside 10 ft by 7 ft if 20 t of coal are placed in the bin?

Critical Thinking

15. If the height of a rectangular prism is doubled, how is the volume of the prism affected?

16. What happens to the volume of a triangular prism if you halve both the base and the altitude of the triangular base?

Mixed Applications

17. Armin wants to spend $88.75 on fish and $33.28 on various supplies for the aquarium. If he has a budget of $150 for supplies and fish, about how much will he have left?

18. *Write a problem* using some or all of the following facts: Armin has $90 to spend on freshwater fish. Angelfish are $8.95 each, neon fish are two for $4.95, and zebra fish are $5.95 each.

PROBLEM SOLVING

Strategy: Using a Formula

A. A snail, a sloth, and a tortoise lined up at the starting line. The snail travels at 0.03 mph, the sloth travels at 0.15 mph, and the tortoise travels at 0.17 mph.

They raced for 2 hours at constant rates. How would you find the distance each animal traveled in that time?

One plan is to use the distance formula:

distance = rate × time

$$d \quad = \quad r \quad \times \quad t$$

Think: $r = 0.03$ mph and
$t = 2$ hours for the snail

$$d = 0.03 \times 2$$
$$= 0.06$$

The snail traveled 0.06 mi.

1. How far did the sloth travel? did the tortoise travel?

B. Suppose that you wanted to know how long it would take each animal to travel 1 mi. You can plan to use the distance formula in a different way.

If distance = rate × time, then
time = distance ÷ rate.

You may want to use your calculator to find the time it would take the snail to travel 1 mi.

Think: $r = 0.03$ mph
$d = 1$ mi

$$t = 1 \;\boxed{\div}\; 0.03 \;\boxed{=}\; \boxed{\textit{33.333333}}$$

It would take the snail about 33.3 hours to travel 1 mi.

2. How long would it take the sloth to travel 1 mi? How long would it take the tortoise? Round to the nearest tenth.

3. ***What if*** you wanted to find the rate of a fourth animal? Suppose you knew the distance and the time the animal took to travel that distance. How could you rewrite the distance formula to solve for rate in terms of distance and time?

PRACTICE

Use the distance formula to solve.

4. A rabbit was hopping along at a rate of 18 mph. (Rabbits can hop much faster!) At that speed how far would the rabbit travel in $1\frac{1}{2}$ hours?

5. A spider was creeping along at a rate of 1.09 mph. (That is pretty fast for a spider!) At that speed how far would the spider travel in $2\frac{1}{2}$ hours?

6. A horse ran 3 mi in 8 minutes. What was the rate of the horse in miles per hour?

7. A person was running at 13.4 mph. At that speed how long would it take the person to run 2 mi? Give your answer to the nearest hundredth.

Strategies and Skills Review

Solve. Use mental math, estimation, a calculator, or paper and pencil.

8. Danny is buying dog food for his St. Bernard. If dog food sells for $1.89 per lb, how much will 3 lb of dog food cost? Use this formula: number of pounds × unit price = total cost.

9. The number of a dog's years times 7 is comparable to the number of a human's years: $d \times 7 = h$. Use this formula to find what 5 years of a dog's life is equal to in human years.

10. Dolores is the supervisor at an animal shelter. Three bags of dog food weigh 43 lb each and another weighs 18 lb. She wants to divide the food evenly among 12 dogs. How much food does each dog receive?

11. Juanita needs 3 pieces of lumber, a total of 27 ft long, for a dog pen. The second piece has to be 4 ft longer than the first, and the third piece has to be 4 ft longer than the second. How long is each piece of lumber?

12. Fifty years ago horses moved cargo along canals that connected these towns: Erie with Dover, Port Jerry, and Sparta; Ten Mile with Port Jerry; and Dover with High Lock and Ten Mile. In how many ways could you have traveled from Port Jerry to High Lock?

13. *Write a problem* that uses a formula to find the solution. Ask other students to solve it.

DECISION MAKING

Problem Solving: Choosing Where to Hold the End-of-Year Party

SITUATION

The club members are deciding whether their end-of-year party should be in a park, or in a barn or a hall. Seventy-five people are expected.

PROBLEM

Where should they hold the end-of-year party?

DATA

	PARK	BARN	HALL
Food	Each person will bring food at a cost of about $4.00 per person.	The barn provides a cookout for $6.50 per person. All supplies are included.	The club will buy food for about $315.00 to be cooked at the hall.
Other Costs	Tablecloths, knives, forks, plates, and so on will cost about $50.00. Entry fee of $.50 per person.	Tips will cost $50.00. Parking is $3.00 per car. Twenty people have volunteered to drive.	It will cost $100.00 to rent the hall and buy party supplies.
Travel	The picnic area is about 35 miles from town. A chartered bus will cost $100.00.	The barn is just 5 miles from town. The cost of transportation is about $.10 per mile per car.	Almost everyone can walk to the hall from home.
Visitor's Report	Swimming, baseball, and other outdoor activities are available.	There is horseback riding and a hay ride available at a nominal fee.	The hall is on the first floor of a community center. It has a vinyl floor and movable lunch tables.

USING THE DATA

What is the total cost of food for the party?

1. park   **2.** barn   **3.** hall

What is the total cost of food and other costs?

4. park   **5.** barn   **6.** hall

What is the total cost per person for food and other costs? Round the answer to the nearest dollar.

7. park   **8.** barn   **9.** hall

Estimate the total cost of round-trip transportation.

10. park   **11.** barn   **12.** hall

MAKING DECISIONS

13. Which place should the club members choose to spend the least on food?

14. Which place should the members choose to spend the least on food and other costs?

15. Which place should they choose to spend the least on food, other costs, and transportation?

16. Which place should they choose to travel least?

17. Which place should they choose to get the food they want?

18. Which place should they avoid if they are concerned about rain?

19. What could they do to reduce their costs?

20. *Write a list* of other factors the club members should consider before making a decision.

21. What place would you choose? Why?

Math and Science

Archeologists can sometimes determine the date an artifact was produced because of where they found it and what they already know about that period and civilization. A more scientific method involves the **half-life** of radioactive elements. In 1900, Marie Curie discovered that some elements become radioactive and that radioactive atoms decay after a certain period of time. These elements give off rays, and they continue to do this until they have changed into a different element altogether that is not radioactive.

An element's half-life means that in a certain number of years half of that element's atoms will have changed into another element, leaving the other half unchanged. In an additional period of the same number of years, half of the remaining part will change, leaving one-fourth of the original amount.

The element Carbon-14 has a half-life of 5,700 years. This is the element that allows archeologists to date prehistoric bones by analyzing them chemically and applying their knowledge of half-life.

What if you wanted to know about how much of the original Carbon-14 would be left after 50,000 years?

Think: How many times will the element change in 50,000 years?

Divide to find the number of times the element will be halved.

$50,000 \div 5,700 = 8.771 \approx 9$

Use one-half as a factor, nine times.

$\frac{1}{2} \times \frac{1}{2} \times \frac{1}{2} \times \frac{1}{2} \times \frac{1}{2} \times \frac{1}{2} \times \frac{1}{2} \times \frac{1}{2} \times \frac{1}{2} = \frac{1}{512}$

So about $\frac{1}{512}$ of the element Carbon-14 would be left after 50,000 years.

ACTIVITIES

1. Read about the half-life of Uranium-238, which geologists use to date rocks. Write a brief report for the class.

2. Look up the mathematical meaning of *infinity*. Then find the meaning of infinity in common usage. Write two sentences, one using the mathematical meaning and the other using the common meaning.

Computer Spreadsheet: Functions

The figures below are the first three terms of a sequence. Each is built using squares that have sides measuring 1 unit. Find the perimeter of each figure and then use squares to construct the next two figures in the sequence.

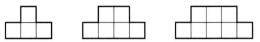

A table can be completed that shows the relationship between n, the number of the term in the sequence, and the measure of the figure's perimeter. The relationship is called a function.

A **function** is a rule for producing exactly one number from another. Functions are often written using the notation $f(n)$; this means *function of n*. For example, the function showing how many quarters are in a given number of dollars, n, would be *multiply n by 4*. This is written in function notation as $f(n) = 4n$.

You can use the computer spreadsheet program FUNCTION TABLE to find the perimeter of any term of the sequence of figures above.

AT THE COMPUTER

1. Enter the number of the first term (1) and check that your value for the perimeter of the first term is correct. Repeat the process for the next four terms of the sequence.

2. Predict the value of the perimeter of the sixth and seventh terms and then use the computer to check your prediction.

3. Look at the spreadsheet. What pattern do you notice in the value of the perimeter of consecutive terms? Check that this pattern holds true by entering any other group of consecutive terms.

4. The function for the relationship in the spreadsheet is $f(n) = an + b$. The values of a and b do not change. The value of a is the common difference between the perimeters of consecutive terms. Find the value of b, by substituting the common difference for a, and values for n and $f(n)$ from any row of the spreadsheet (for example 1 and 10). Then write the function using the values of a and b.

5. Use your function to find $f(n)$ when $n = 37$. Then use the spreadsheet to check your answer.

EXTRA PRACTICE

Order of Operations, page 171

Simplify.

1. $200 + 25 \times 30 - 20$

2. $24 \div [(7 - 3) \times 2]$

3. $[6.2 + (8.7 - 4)] \times 10$

4. $3 + 2^3 - 5$

5. $(60 + 120) \div 3^2$

6. $7.4 + (5 - 1)^2$

7. $(18 - 2) \div (1 + 1)^3$

8. $10 - 2 + 49 \div 7$

9. $(3 + 12^2)^2$

10. $3 \times [5 + (7 - 5)^2]$

11. $17 - [(8 - 5) \times 2.1^2]$

12. $3 \times [(7 + 3) \times 25] + 36 \div 2^2$

Copy and place the parentheses to make the sentence true.

13. $14 + 8 \times 2 = 44$

14. $26 - 25 \div 5 + 17 = 4$

15. $8 + 4 \times 2^2 - 7 = 65$

16. $226 - 5 + 2^3 \times 2 = 200$

17. $6 - 5 - 4 \times 2^2 = 2$

18. $3 \times 4 + 2 \div 2 = 9$

Variables and Formulas, page 173

The formula $F = \frac{9}{5}C + 32$ is used to change temperature in degrees Celsius to degrees Fahrenheit. Use the formula to complete the table.

1.

Degrees Celsius	0	10	25	30	100
Degrees Fahrenheit	**1.**	**2.**	**3.**	**4.**	**5.**

2. Is the reading in Fahrenheit more or less than one and one-half the reading in Celsius?

The formula $L = S^2 \div 18.6$ is used to determine the length of skid marks. Use the formula to complete the table.

3.

Speed (miles per hour) (S)	35	40	55	65	75
Length of skid marks (feet) (L)	**1.**	**2.**	**3.**	**4.**	**5.**

4. Is the skid mark longer when a car is traveling at 35 mi per hour or 40 mi per hour?

Writing Algebraic Expressions, page 175

Write and then evaluate an algebraic expression.

Let $a = 9$ and $b = 12$

1. *b* added to 7

2. *b* decreased by 4

3. the product of *a* and 3.2

4. *b* divided by 6

5. the sum of *b* and 3.5

6. the product of *a* and *b*

7. 6 times *a*

8. 5.1 less than *b*

9. the quotient of *b* and 3

Writing Algebraic Sentences, page 177 ·······················

Write an algebraic sentence.

1. The quotient of a number *y* and 36 is less than 9.

2. 48 is equal to the sum of a number *x* and 35.

3. 8 times a number *s* is greater than 56.

4. 25 is the product of 5 and a number *m*.

5. A number *z* decreased by 7.5 is equal to 15.1

6. A number *b* increased by 5 is equal to 17.

7. When 3 is added to a number, the sum is 12.

8. 42 is equal to 7 times a number.

9. A number divided by 8 is greater than 32.

10. 6 less than a number is 5.

11. A number divided by 37 is less than 113.

12. When 22 is added to a number, the sum is greater than 10.5.

13. 513 is greater than the sum of a number *p* and 486.

14. A number *s* decreased by 18.7 is greater than 20.

Problem–Solving Strategy: Using Number Sense, page 181 ························

Use your number sense to solve the problem.

Cases of canned vegetables are stacked up on the receiving platform at the Good Buy Supermarket. Each stack is about $5\frac{1}{2}$ ft high. Each case contains one layer of 24 small cans.

1. About how many cans of vegetables are there in one of the stacks on the receiving platform?

2. About how many total ounces of vegetables are there in those cans?

3. The receiving platform is about 32 ft wide by 48 ft deep. A case is about 1 ft wide by 1.4 ft long. About how many cases would it take to cover the platform in a single layer?

4. If each case of vegetables is about $3\frac{1}{4}$ in. high, about how many cases are in each stack?

EXTRA PRACTICE

Solving Equations: Adding and Subtracting, page 183 ·······································

Solve the equation. Check your solution.

1. $x + 15 = 32$

2. $34 + k = 112$

3. $w + 5.8 = 33.4$

4. $52.3 = r + 7.04$

5. $a - 12 = 19$

6. $n - 55 = 24$

7. $9.4 = h - 3.8$

8. $z - 29.4 = 14.8$

9. $t - 5.98 = 7.12$

10. $34 = p - 13.2$

11. $a + 18 = 36$

12. $49 = p - 27$

13. $124 = p + 17$

14. $15.8 = m + 4$

15. $37.6 = x + 7.19$

16. $q - 17 = 113$

17. $84 = c + 26$

18. $d - 76 = 116$

19. $a + 2.7 = 8.3$

20. $x - 299 = 188.5$

21. $b - 19.2 = 28.7$

22. $d + 2.3 = 9.7$

23. $a - 5.6 = 9.1$

24. $m + 18.2 = 23.7$

25. $n - 75.3 = 18.2$

26. $1.7 + p = 3.6$

27. $25.17 + 4 = z$

28. $e = 43.6 - 41.7$

29. $3 + f = 28.17$

30. $g + 5.26 = 8.73$

Solving Equations: Multiplying and Dividing, page 185 ·······························

Solve the equation. Check your solution.

1. $7y = 49$

2. $15x = 450$

3. $0.6m = 12$

4. $3.2d = 2.24$

5. $\frac{x}{5} = 7$

6. $17 = \frac{a}{8}$

7. $\frac{g}{0.5} = 7$

8. $\frac{w}{6} = 7.4$

9. $25n = 1{,}250$

10. $6q = 123$

11. $20n = 267$

12. $\frac{s}{7.5} = 34$

13. $16t = 352$

14. $\frac{x}{4} = 5.2$

15. $2.5y = 37.5$

16. $7c = 49.7$

17. $11a = 110$

18. $\frac{m}{15} = 25$

19. $\frac{b}{0.6} = 10$

20. $0.45t = 9$

21. $\frac{s}{2.5} = 12$

22. $45f = 540$

23. $3.5x = 49$

24. $\frac{m}{5} = 37$

25. $12 = 4.8a$

26. $\frac{32}{b} = 25$

27. $\frac{x}{73} = 1{,}070$

28. $66y = 1{,}815$

29. $\frac{207.9}{z} = 3.5$

30. $\frac{r}{45.2} = 212$

EXTRA PRACTICE

Applying Equations: Volumes of Prisms, page 187 ....

Find the volume.

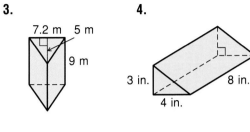

1. 8 in. 5 in. 12 in.

2. 3.2 cm 12 cm 18 cm

3. 7.2 m 5 m 9 m

4. 3 in. 8 in. 4 in.

Solve.

5. A hexagonal prism has a base with an area of 40 ft². If its height is 20 ft, what is its volume?

6. What is the volume of a rectangular prism that measures 4 in. by 8 in. by 2 in.?

7. A cubic foot of water is equal to 7.5 gal. Find the capacity of a tank in gallons if the area of the base is 35 ft² and the height is 18 ft.

8. A fish tank has a height of 18 cm, a length of 24 cm, and a volume of 5,184 cm³. What is its width?

Problem–Solving Strategy: Using a Formula, page 189 ....

Use the distance formula to solve.

1. A cheetah can run 70 mi per hour. At that speed, how far would the cheetah travel in $\frac{3}{4}$ hour?

2. An elephant was charging at a speed of 25 mi per hour. At that speed, how far would the elephant go in $\frac{1}{2}$ hour?

3. A lion ran 5 mi in 6 minutes. What was the rate of the lion in miles per hour?

4. A cat was running at 30 mi per hour. At that speed, how long would it take the cat to run 2 mi?

5. A wild turkey ran 3 mi in 12 minutes. What was the rate of the turkey in miles per hour?

6. A pig was running at 11 mi per hour. At that speed, how long would it take the pig to run 1 mi to the nearest hundredth minute?

7. A cricket hopped 25 m in 1 minute. At that rate how far will it travel in $1\frac{1}{2}$ hours?

8. A crow was flying at the rate of 16 mi per hour. At that speed how far will it travel in one day?

Equations and Formulas **197**

EXTRA PRACTICE

Practice PLUS

KEY SKILL: Solving Equations: Adding and Subtracting (Use after page 183.)

Level A

Solve the equation. Check your solution.

1. $x + 11 = 15$　　**2.** $24 + a = 58$　　**3.** $k + 16 = 34$　　**4.** $48 = w + 6$

5. $n - 13 = 18$　　**6.** $h - 55 = 34$　　**7.** $8 = y - 2$　　**8.** $t - 24 = 16$

9. $p - 5 = 6$　　**10.** $84 = a - 16$　　**11.** $p + 19 = 38$　　**12.** $49 = z - 18$

13. Ken has 47 tropical fish. This is 13 more than Paul has. How many does Paul have?

Level B

Solve the equation. Check your solution.

14. $n - 15 = 19$　　**15.** $n - 66 = 39$　　**16.** $7.4 = y + 2.7$　　**17.** $t - 29.8 = 14.9$

18. $p + 3.98 = 5.17$　　**19.** $46 = a - 17.6$　　**20.** $15 + p = 32$　　**21.** $28 = z - 19$

22. $125 = m + 17$　　**23.** $15.7 = p + 2$　　**24.** $38.4 = r + 7.09$　　**25.** $p - 17 = 102$

26. Meghan removed 2.5 gal of water from a full fish tank. There are 3.5 gal left in the tank. How much does the tank hold?

Level C

Solve the equation. Check your solution.

27. $64 = c + 46$　　**28.** $d - 86 = 112$　　**29.** $c + 2.7 = 8.2$　　**30.** $398.5 = y - 299$

31. $d - 26 = 44$　　**32.** $2.1 + b = 7.4$　　**33.** $90 = a - 56$　　**34.** $m + 76 = 91$

35. $b - 73 = 32$　　**36.** $192.7 + k = 207$　　**37.** $n + 0.6 = 2.3$　　**38.** $p = 18.7 - 4.23$

Write an equation for the problem. Solve the equation.

39. A number increased by 2.7 is equal to 27.4.

40. The sum of a number and 45 is equal to 57.8.

41. 17 less than a number equals 108.

42. A number decreased by 45 is equal to 17.9.

43. A number increased by 48.17 is equal to 553.13.

44. A number decreased by 37.93 is equal to 75.6.

45. Jane caught a fish that weighed 5.2 lb. This was 2.9 lb less than a fish Bert caught. How much did Bert's fish weigh?

KEY SKILL: Solving Equations: Multiplying and Dividing (Use after page 185.)

Level A

Solve the equation. Check your answer.

1. $5x = 30$ **2.** $16w = 48$ **3.** $5d = 15$ **4.** $4m = 28$

5. $\frac{z}{4} = 5$ **6.** $8 = \frac{y}{9}$ **7.** $\frac{t}{3} = 7$ **8.** $\frac{k}{5} = 12$

9. $24q = 120$ **10.** $7n = 196$ **11.** $\frac{s}{10} = 25$ **12.** $\frac{p}{15} = 8$

13. Sam said, "I'm thinking of a number. The number divided by 5 is 7. What is the number?

Level B

Solve the equation. Check your answer.

14. $7x = 42$ **15.** $\frac{y}{8} = 17$ **16.** $\frac{f}{0.3} = 9$ **17.** $\frac{k}{3} = 5.2$

18. $38q = 760$ **19.** $8n = 200$ **20.** $10s = 257$ **21.** $\frac{p}{7.5} = 18.4$

22. $19x = 418$ **23.** $\frac{t}{6} = 5.3$ **24.** $1.7c = 25.5$ **25.** $8y = 51.2$

26. Mike's pigs eat 16 lb of corn a day. This is 4 times as much as Ralph's pigs eat. How much do Ralph's pigs eat?

Level C

Solve the equation. Check your answer.

27. $19x = 361$ **28.** $\frac{t}{8} = 5.7$ **29.** $3.5c = 66.5$ **30.** $7y = 47.6$

31. $13a = 84.5$ **32.** $\frac{b}{14} = 19$ **33.** $\frac{m}{0.9} = 11$ **34.** $0.25t = 18$

35. $\frac{27}{a} = 3$ **36.** $13.7m = 85.351$ **37.** $\frac{s}{22.3} = 6.6$ **38.** $1.37w = 1.8769$

Write an equation for the problem. Solve the equation.

39. A number divided by 5.5 is equal to 96.

40. Forty times a number is equal to 50.

41. The product of a number and 3.5 is 49.

42. The quotient of a number and 7 is 49.

43. Jill's horses eat 1,000 lb of hay a day. This is $\frac{1}{3}$ what Pam's horses eat. How much hay do Pam's horses eat?

LANGUAGE AND MATHEMATICS

Complete the sentences. Use the words in the chart on the right.

1. The ■ of an object is measured in cubic units. *(page 186)*

2. A(n) ■ is a combination of one or more ■, numbers, and operation signs. *(page 174)*

3. To solve an equation such as $a + 2 = 17$, you can use a concept called ■. *(page 182)*

4. The ■ is a unit of volume measure. *(page 186)*

5. Write a definition or give an example of the words you did not use from the chart.

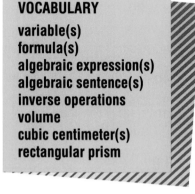

VOCABULARY

variable(s)
formula(s)
algebraic expression(s)
algebraic sentence(s)
inverse operations
volume
cubic centimeter(s)
rectangular prism

CONCEPTS AND SKILLS

Simplify. *(page 170)*

6. $6 + 1 \times 0.3$

7. $(0.1 + 0.2)^3$

8. $2.5 \div 2 \times 0.1$

9. $4 + 0.2 \div 8$

10. $5 - 0.3 \div 0.1$

11. $3 + 1.1^2$

12. $2 \times 0.1 + 4 \div 0.2$

13. $1 - 0.1 \times (2 - 0.1)$

14. $(5 \times 0.4)^2$

Evaluate the expression. Let $c = 2$ and $d = 0.5$. *(page 174)*

15. $10 + d \div 2$

16. $(c \div 4)^3$

17. $d \div d \times 5$

18. $c - 3 \times d$

19. $c \div d + 4$

20. $d + 4 \div c$

21. $3c - d$

22. $4d - c \div 2$

Write an algebraic expression. *(page 174)*

23. c decreased by d

24. 8 added to n

25. 5 fewer than k

26. x increased by 1

27. b times h

28. s squared

29. 4 more than b

30. 6 multiplied by y

31. m divided by 2

Write an algebraic sentence. *(page 176)*

32. A number c decreased by 3 is 6.

33. 8 less than a number w is 16.

34. The product of 24 and n equals 12.

35. 2 times a number n equals 9.

36. The quotient of a number c and 8 is equal to 4.

37. A number x decreased by 3 equals 9 to the second power.

38. 7 fewer than x is 3.

39. A number s is twice 5.

Solve the equation. *(pages 182, 184)*

40. $a + 18 = 34$

41. $n - 4.6 = 8.4$

42. $41 = t - 15$

43. $8x = 48$

44. $\frac{p}{5.5} = 7$

45. $13x = 247$

Find the volume *(page 186)*

46.
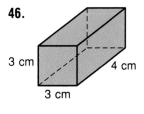
3 cm
4 cm
3 cm

47.
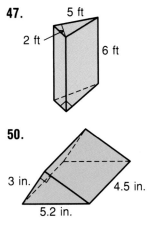
5 ft
2 ft
6 ft

48.
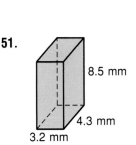
1.5 m
8.2 m
5 m

49.
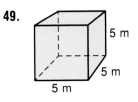
5 m
5 m
5 m

50.
3 in.
4.5 in.
5.2 in.

51.
8.5 mm
4.3 mm
3.2 mm

Solve. *(page 186)*

52. How many cubic feet of dirt were removed from a hole that is 2 feet by 2 feet by 2 feet?

53. Find the volume of an octagonal prism with a height of 10 cm and a base of 25 cm².

Critical Thinking

54. When can $5 - c = c - 5$ be true? *(page 176)*

55. When can 3 divided by x equal x divided by 3? *(page 176)*

Mixed Applications

56. The volume of a rectangular prism is 60 m³ and $h = 4$ m. What is the area of the base? *(page 186)*

57. If Erin walks 3 miles per hour, how long will it take her to walk 4.5 miles? *(page 188)*

58. If a horse travels 14 miles in 3 hours and 30 min, how far can it travel in one hour? *(page 188)*

59. To find the cost to ship a box, a company uses the formula
$$c = \$30 + \$0.02 \times m,$$
where c is the cost and m is the number of miles the package is shipped. How much would it cost to ship a box 400 miles? *(page 172)*

CHAPTER TEST

Simplify.

1. $3 + 5 \times 0.2$

2. $6 - 0.5 \div 0.1$

3. $18.9 - 2 \times (0.1 + 2.9)^2$

4. $1 \times 0.2 + 4 \div 0.5$

Evaluate the expression. Let $c = 7$ and $d = 0.1$.

5. $c - 5 \times 1.1$

6. $6 \times 3 - c \div 7$

7. $(c \div d)^2$

8. $c - 4 + d \div 2$

Write an algebraic sentence.

9. The quotient of a number b and 6 is equal to 12.

10. A number n decreased by 9 equals 3 squared.

11. 5 less than a number z is 15.

12. Twice a number x equals 8.

13. The product of 2 and a number x equals 8.

14. 4 increased by a number x is 7.

Solve the equation.

15. $x + 6.4 = 17.2$

16. $n - 14 = 20$

17. $2.6n = 52$

18. $\frac{t}{7} = 14$

Solve.

19. The base of a prism is a triangle with a 4-cm base and a 3-cm height. The height of the prism is 10 cm. Find the volume of the triangular prism.

20. Find the volume of a rectangular prism with a base of 3.2 square meters and a height of 5 m.

21. If a tortoise averages 0.15 miles per hour, how far will it go in 4 hours?

22. If Justin jogs 8 miles per hour, how long will it take him to jog 20 miles?

23. Jan walked 1 mile in 30 minutes. How many miles per hour did Jan walk?

24. How far will a truck going 32.6 miles per hour travel in 8.5 hours?

25. A car washer's daily salary is set by the formula $s = \$8.50 + \$3 \times n$, where s is the salary and n is the number of cars washed by the washer that day. How much does the car washer make on a day when he washed 12 cars?

ENRICHMENT FOR ALL

PERFECT, DEFICIENT, AND ABUNDANT NUMBERS

The ancient Greeks were fascinated by what they considered to be a mystical relationship among numbers. Their interest led to the discovery of perfect, deficient, and abundant numbers.

To find out if a number is perfect, deficient, or abundant, you must find its **proper factors.** The proper factors of a number are all the factors of a number except the number itself. For example, the proper factors of 8 are 1, 2, and 4. A number is **perfect** when the sum of all its proper factors is the number itself.

For example, 6 is a perfect number.

Think: The proper factors of 6 are 1, 2, 3.
$$1 + 2 + 3 = 6 \qquad 6 = 6$$

A number is **deficient** if the sum of all its proper factors is less than the number itself.

For example, 15 is a deficient number.

Think: The proper factors of 15 are 1, 3, 5.
$$1 + 3 + 5 = 9 \qquad 9 < 15$$

A number is **abundant** if the sum of all its proper factors is greater than the number itself.

For example, 12 is an abundant number.

Think: The proper factors of 12 are 1, 2, 3, 4, 6.
$$1 + 2 + 3 + 4 + 6 = 16 \qquad 16 > 12$$

List the numbers from 10 through 40.

1. Which of these numbers is a perfect number?

2. Which numbers are deficient numbers?

3. Which numbers are abundant numbers?

4. If a number is prime, will it be perfect, deficient, or abundant? Tell why.

5. Find the perfect number between 485 and 500. Explain why it is a perfect number.

CUMULATIVE REVIEW

Choose the letter of the correct answer.
Solve for n.

1. $n - 5.2 > 10$

   a. $n > 15.2$ **c.** $n > 4.8$
   b. $n > 6.2$ **d.** not given

2. $n + 4 = 6.5$

   a. 6.1   **c.** 10.5
   b. 6.9   **d.** not given

3. $0.8n = 4$

   a. 3.2   **c.** 5
   b. 0.5   **d.** not given

4. $\frac{n}{2} < 6.4$

   a. $n < 1.28$ **c.** $n < 12.8$
   b. $n < 3.3$ **d.** not given

5. $(3.4 \times 10^6) \times (5 \times 10^0)$

   a. 1.7×10^0 **c.** 1.7×10^7
   b. 1.7×10^6 **d.** not given

6. $(2.5 \times 10^1) \times (2 \times 10^2)$

   a. 5.0×10^3 **c.** 5.0×10^2
   b. 0.5×10^3 **d.** not given

7. A number decreased by 6 is 3. What is the number?

   a. 2   **c.** 18
   b. 3   **d.** not given

8. $4 - 0.1 \times 2$

   a. 0.2   **c.** 7.8
   b. 3.8   **d.** not given

Solve.

9. Crystal earned $5, $8.75, $4.50, $9, and $5 working on lawns. What was the mean of the amounts she earned?

   a. $32.25   **c.** $6.45
   b. $5.00   **d.** not given

10. What is the area of a circle with a diameter of 2 ft?

   a. 3.14 ft^2 **c.** 12.6 ft^2
   b. 6.28 ft^2 **d.** not given

11. What is the area of a parallelogram with a base equal to 4.5 m and a height of 4 m?

   a. 9 m^2 **c.** 8.5 m^2
   b. 18 m^2 **d.** not given

12. Find the volume of a prism with a height of 5 cm and a triangular base. The triangle has a base of 3 cm and a height of 2 cm.

   a. 10 cm^3 **c.** 30 cm^3
   b. 15 cm^3 **d.** not given

13. Find the volume of a rectangular prism with a height of 0.5 m and a base with an area of 2 m^2.

   a. 10 m^3 **c.** 100 m^3
   b. 2.5 m^3 **d.** not given

14. Harry walked 10 mi in 2 hours 30 minutes. How many miles per hour did he average?

   a. 4 mi/hour   **c.** 50 mi/hour
   b. 5 mi/hour   **d.** not given

Patterns and Number Theory

CHAPTER 6

MATH CONNECTION: PROBLEM SOLVING

POLLUTION ABATEMENT AND CONTROL EXPENDITURES		
Type of Pollution	1985 Amount (millions of dollars)	Percent Paid by Government
Air	33,177	1.4
Water	28,121	31.7
Solid Waste	12,985	31.2
TOTAL	74,283	18.1

1. What information do you see in this picture?
2. How can you use the information?
3. How many more millions of dollars were spent on air pollution than on water pollution in 1985?
4. Write a problem using the information.

DEVELOPING A CONCEPT

Sequences

A. A newspaper ran a contest challenging readers to find number patterns. The following number patterns appeared in Monday's edition.

A: 32.6, 31.2, 29.8, 28.4, . . .   **B:** 18, 28, 23, 33, 28, . . .

WORKING TOGETHER

1. Look at **A.** Find the rule. List the next three numbers.

2. Look at **B.** Tell how it differs from **A.** List the next three numbers.

Lists of numbers such as **A** and **B** are called sequences. A **sequence** is an ordered set of numbers. Each number in a sequence is called a **term.** To show that a sequence continues indefinitely, write . . .

3. Look at sequence **C:** 12, 15, 18, . . . What is the rule for this sequence? List the next three terms.

B. The sequence 2, 5, 8, 11, . . . is an arithmetic sequence. An **arithmetic sequence** is a sequence generated by adding or subtracting the same number repeatedly.

4. Which of the sequences, **A, B,** and **C,** are arithmetic sequences?

The 1st and 4th terms of an arithmetic sequence are 8 and 26. Find the rule used to generate this sequence.

Since the terms of the sequence are increasing, the rule is to add.

Think: A number is added to 8 three times to get 26.
Since $26 - 8 = 18$, divide 18 by 3. $18 \div 3 = 6$.

1st	2nd	3rd	4th
8	■	■	26

The rule to generate the sequence is to add 6.

5. Find the 2nd and 3rd terms of this sequence to check the rule.

SHARING IDEAS

6. If the first 3 terms of a sequence are 11, 13, 15, what are the 4th and 5th terms?

7. What is the rule used to generate the sequence where the 1st and 4th terms are 10 and 34?

8. What is the rule used to generate the sequence where the 1st and 4th terms are 75 and 60?

PRACTICE

The first three terms of an arithmetic sequence are given. What is the rule? Find the next two terms.

9. 0, 4, 8, . . .   **10.** 10, 8, 6, . . .   **11.** 29, 27, 25, . . .

12. 3, 11, 19, . . .   **13.** 21, 25, 29, . . .   **14.** 75, 70, 65, . . .

15. 90, 81, 72, . . .   **16.** 100, 94, 88, . . .   **17.** 100, 200, 300, . . .

18. 150, 125, 100, . . .   **19.** 200, 189, 178, . . .   **20.** 295, 270, 245, . . .

21. 0.1, 0.8, 1.5, . . .   **22.** 1.1, 3.3, 5.5, . . .   **23.** 2.5, 4.5, 6.5, . . .

24. 9.0, 8.8, 8.6, . . .   **25.** 47.5, 45, 42.5, . . .   **26.** 53, 58.5, 64, . . .

27. 61.0, 54.5, 48.0, . . .   **28.** 51.0, 57.9, 64.8, . . .   **29.** 2.25, 2.5, 2.75, . . .

What is the rule used to generate the arithmetic sequence?

30. The 1st and 5th terms are 1 and 21.   **31.** The 1st and 5th terms are 45 and 21.

32. The 1st and 6th terms are 28 and 48.   **33.** The 1st and 6th terms are 93 and 53.

Critical Thinking

Is the statement *true, sometimes true,* or *false*? Give examples to support your answer.

34. If the first term in an arithmetic sequence is an even number, each of the other terms will be even.

35. If the difference between two consecutive terms in an arithmetic sequence is even, the terms in the sequence are always even.

Mixed Applications

36. Write an algebraic sentence for this: A number increased by 16 is equal to 54.

37. Write and solve the equation for this: A number decreased by 14 is equal to 85.

38. Make up your own arithmetic sequence using only even numbers. Have others find the rule and write the next three terms.

39. ***Write a problem*** involving an arithmetic sequence using only odd numbers. Have others find the rule and write the next three terms.

Mixed Review

MENTAL MATH
CALCULATOR
PAPER/PENCIL

Find the answer. Which method did you use?

40. $6.24 × 3.5   **41.** 4.8 × 0.25   **42.** 5.25 × 0.028

43. 427 ÷ 0.7   **44.** 17.76 ÷ 24   **45.** $51.60 ÷ 40

Sums of Sequences

A. Alison started a part-time lawn service business. She kept a record of the number of lawns she mowed each week.

Week 1	Week 2	Week 3	Week 4	Week 5	Week 6
3	5	7	9	11	13

1. Do the numbers 3, 5, 7, 9, 11, 13 form an arithmetic sequence? Why or why not?

Alison wants to find the total number of lawns she has mowed. You can find the sum of an arithmetic sequence by grouping the terms into pairs of addends.

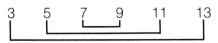

2. How many pairs of addends are there?

3. Compare the sum of each pair. What do you notice?

4. How can you use multiplication to find the total number of lawns Alison mowed? Find the total.

B. Now look at these sequences.

A: 40, 60, 80, 100, 120, 140   **B:** 4, 6, 8, 10, 12

5. Is sequence **A** an arithmetic sequence? Is sequence **B**? Why?

6. How many terms are there in sequence **A**? in sequence **B**?

7. How many pairs of addends are there in sequence **A**? in sequence **B**? What happened in sequence **B**?

8. What is the sum of each pair in sequence **A**? in sequence **B**?

9. What is the sum of sequence **A**? of sequence **B**?

SHARING IDEAS

10. What happened when you used the pair method to find the sum of sequence **B**? How did you adjust the method to account for this difference?

11. How would you find the rule used to generate the sequence 1, 5, 9, 13, 17? What is the rule?

12. What is the sum of the sequence?

PRACTICE

Find the sum of the sequence.

13. 8, 9, 10, 11, 12, 13

14. 8, 9, 10, 11, 12

15. 2.5, 3.5, 4.5, 5.5, 6.5, 7.5

16. 2.5, 3.5, 4.5, 5.5, 6.5

17. 50, 51, 52, 53, 54

18. 3, 7, 11, 15, 19, 23

19. 2, 4, 6, 8, 10, 12, 14, 16

20. 11, 22, 33, 44, 55, 66, 77

21. 15.25, 18.25, 21.25, 24.25

22. 0.5, 2.0, 3.5, 5.0, 6.5, 8.0, 9.5

23. the first six even numbers

24. the first five even numbers

25. the first seven odd numbers

26. the first ten odd numbers

27. 1, 2, 3, 4, 5, . . . , 50

28. 1, 2, 3, 4, 5, . . . , 100

Critical Thinking

29. Experiment with a sequence having an odd number of terms, such as 8, 9, 10, 11, 12. Is there a faster way to find its sum using only multiplication? How?

Mixed Applications

30. Marge mowed lawns on 5 weekends. Each weekend she mowed 2 lawns more than on the previous one. She mowed 2 lawns on the 1st weekend. How many did she mow in all?

31. Carole spends $35.85 on lawn chemicals, $22.00 for a sprayer, and $15.40 for trimmers. How much change does she receive from a $100 bill?

32. Rita mows 3.5 times as many lawns as Rick. If Rick mows 50 lawns, how many lawns does Rita mow?

33. *Write a problem* that involves finding the sum of an arithmetic sequence. Ask others to solve it.

CHALLENGE

The sequence 2, 4, 8, 16, 32 is a geometric sequence. A **geometric sequence** is a sequence generated by multiplying or dividing by the same number repeatedly. The rule for this sequence is to multiply by 2.

What is the rule used to generate the sequence? Is the sequence *arithmetic, geometric,* or *neither*?

1. 1, 6, 11, 16, 21

2. 3, 12, 48, 192

3. 162, 54, 18, 6, 2

4. 100, 90, 95, 85, 90

Patterns and Number Theory **209**

PROBLEM SOLVING

Strategy: Finding a Pattern

The highway authority wants to determine the number of lanes that should be open during the weekday morning rush hour.

Make a plan.

The highway authority uses rounded numbers to keep track of the number of cars arriving at the toll plaza from 6 A.M. to 7 A.M. on a weekday morning. They look at the data to try to find a pattern to predict how many cars would arrive between 7:20 and 9:00 A.M. The number of cars at each interval will determine the number of lanes that should be open at each time.

Try the plan.

Time	6:00	6:20	6:40	7:00	7:20	7:40	8:00	8:20	8:40	9:00
Number of Cars	500	1,000	1,500	2,000						

1. What is the difference between the number of cars at 6:20 A.M. and the number at 6:00 A.M.?

2. What is the difference between the number of cars at 6:40 A.M. and the number at 6:20 A.M.?

3. Does the pattern continue for 7:00 A.M.? What is the pattern?

4. Complete the pattern for 7:20 A.M. through 9:00 A.M.

About how many times as great is the number of cars at 9:00 A.M. as the number of cars at:

5. 6:00 A.M.?

6. 7:20 A.M.?

What if two lanes were open at 6:00 A.M.? About how many lanes should be open at:

7. 7:20 A.M.?

8. 9:00 A.M.?

9. How might the traffic patterns be different for a Saturday?

PRACTICE

Find the pattern and solve.

10. One toll plaza has the following number of toll collectors each hour, starting at midnight: 1, 2, 4, 7, and 11. If the pattern continues, how many toll collectors would you expect the plaza to have for each of the next 3 hours?

11. The tulip arrangements at each toll booth have the following pattern. If the pattern continues, what should the next two arrangements look like?

12. In an attempt to beautify the parkways, the highway authority placed the four murals shown below at a toll plaza. If the pattern continues, what might a fifth mural look like?

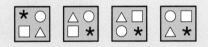

13. The highway authority was comparing the number of cars for every bus at the toll plaza during the weekday rush hour. At 5 A.M. there were 12 cars for every 1 bus; at 6 A.M., 9 cars; at 7 A.M., 15 cars; and at 8 A.M., 12 cars. If the pattern continues, how many cars for every bus could they expect at 9 A.M.? at 10 A.M.?

Strategies and Skills Review

Solve. Use mental math, estimation, a calculator, or paper and pencil.

14. What number from 1 through 4 is naturally preferred by most people? Ask 20 friends to name a digit from 1 through 4. Show your results on a bar graph.

15. Janna earned a total of $210 over 3 days as a toll plaza survey taker. Each day she earned twice as much as she did on the previous day. How much did she earn each day?

16. Sound travels about 1,100 ft per second. Ellis was looking out his car window when he saw the lightning strike. He checked his watch and heard the thunder 9 seconds later. About how far away was the lightning?

17. The state is preparing its yearly budget. Over the last four years the income from all bridge toll plazas has been $8.4 million, $9 million, $10.2 million, and $12.6 million. Use this pattern to estimate the income for next year.

18. Elyssa was planning a car trip. She knew that she would make 6 stops. She took 15- and 18-minute stops on her last trip. Estimate the total time of the stops. Did you over- or underestimate the time?

19. ***Write a problem*** that uses a pattern to solve it. Solve your problem. Ask other students to solve it.

UNDERSTANDING A CONCEPT

Mental Math: Divisibility

A. Matt and Carol are in charge of calling 234 students to encourage them to participate in the bikeathon. Nine people will do the phoning. Can each of the nine people call the same number of students?

Recall that one number is **divisible** by another if the remainder is 0 when you divide.

Carol uses her calculator to divide and finds that 234 is divisible by 9.

 234 ÷ **9** = 26.

Matt remembers the divisibility test for 9. Mentally he adds the digits of 234: $2 + 3 + 4 = 9$. Since 9 is divisible by 9, the number 234 is divisible by 9.

Each phoner can call the same number of students.

Recall the rules for divisibility.

A number is divisible by:	
2 if the ones digit is 0, 2, 4, 6, or 8.	3 if the sum of the digits is divisible by 3.
4 if the number formed by the last two digits is divisible by 4.	5 if the ones digit is 0 or 5.
6 if the number is divisible by 2 and by 3.	8 if the number formed by the last three digits is divisible by 8.
9 if the sum of the digits is divisible by 9.	10 if the ones digit is 0.

B. Recall that a number is divisible by a second number if that number is a **factor** of the first number. Any whole number, except 0, is divisible by each of its factors.

Find the factors of 24.

$24 \div 1 = 24$	$24 \div 3 = 8$	$24 \div 6 = 4$	$24 \div 12 = 2$
$24 \div 2 = 12$	$24 \div 4 = 6$	$24 \div 8 = 3$	$24 \div 24 = 1$

So the factors of 24 are 1, 2, 3, 4, 6, 8, 12, and 24. The **factor pairs** are 1×24, 2×12, 3×8, and 4×6.

1. Do you have to do eight divisions as shown above to find the eight factors of 24? Why or why not?

2. Use the divisibility rules to find the factor pairs of 40.

T<small>RY OUT</small> Write the letter or letters of the correct answer.

3. 128 is divisible by: **a.** 5.   **b.** 3.   **c.** 6.   **d.** 4.

4. 837 is divisible by: **a.** 3.   **b.** 5.   **c.** 9.   **d.** 10.

5. Which is a factor pair of 78?   **a.** 7×8 **b.** 2×39 **c.** 3×25 **d.** 6×13

6. Which is a factor pair of 54?   **a.** 3×18 **b.** 5×4 **c.** 6×8 **d.** 6×9

P<small>RACTICE</small>

Complete the table. Write *yes* or *no*.

Number	Divisible by: 2?	3?	4?	5?	6?	8?	9?	10?
225	No.	**7.** ▨	**8.** ▨	**9.** ▨	**10.** ▨	**11.** ▨	**12.** ▨	**13.** ▨
420	**14.** ▨	**15.** ▨	**16.** ▨	Yes.	**17.** ▨	**18.** ▨	**19.** ▨	**20.** ▨
945	**21.** ▨	**22.** ▨	**23.** ▨	**24.** ▨	**25.** ▨	**26.** ▨	**27.** ▨	No.
160	**28.** ▨	No.	**29.** ▨	**30.** ▨	**31.** ▨	**32.** ▨	**33.** ▨	**34.** ▨
352	**35.** ▨	**36.** ▨	**37.** ▨	**38.** ▨	**39.** ▨	Yes.	**40.** ▨	**41.** ▨
10,648	Yes.	**42.** ▨	**43.** ▨	**44.** ▨	**45.** ▨	**46.** ▨	**47.** ▨	**48.** ▨
2,907	**49.** ▨	**50.** ▨	No.	**51.** ▨	**52.** ▨	No.	**53.** ▨	**54.** ▨
1,368	**55.** ▨	**56.** ▨	Yes.	**57.** ▨	**58.** ▨	**59.** ▨	Yes.	**60.** ▨

Find the factor pairs for the number.

61. 48   **62.** 100   **63.** 55   **64.** 96   **65.** 19   **66.** 81

Critical Thinking

67. Does every number have an even number of factors? Tell why or why not.

68. Write a divisibility rule for 20. Test to see that it works.

Mixed Applications

69. Jerry found out that last year the school budget was $3.82 million and this year the budget is $4.6 million. How much more is the budget this year?

70. The students in Ellen's class study about 384 hours a year. What are reasonable factor pairs of hours per day and days per year that each student studies?

71. Wanda recorded these high and low temperatures in degrees Fahrenheit for the school week. Make a double-line graph to show the data.

	Mon.	Tues.	Wed.	Thurs.	Fri.
High	85	92	75	78	90
Low	55	60	45	58	60

UNDERSTANDING A CONCEPT

Primes and Prime Factorization

A. A whole number greater than 1 that has exactly two factors, 1 and the number itself, is a **prime** number. The number 79 is a prime number. A whole number greater than 1 that has more than 2 factors is a **composite** number. The number 6 is a composite number. It has factors 1, 2, 3, and 6.

The numbers 0 and 1 are neither prime nor composite.

B. Every composite number is a product of prime factors. This product of prime factors is the **prime factorization** of the number.

Find the prime factorization of 120. You can use a **factor tree.**

Step 1	Express the number as a product of two numbers.

Step 2	Continue to express each number as a product of two numbers until only prime factors remain.

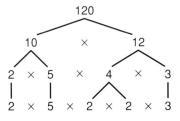

C. You can also use division to find the prime factors.

Step 1	Divide the number by a prime number.

$$\frac{60}{2)120}$$

Step 2	Continue to divide the quotients by prime factors until the quotient is 1.

$$\frac{30}{2)60} \quad \frac{15}{2)30} \quad \frac{5}{3)15} \quad \frac{1}{5)5}$$

The prime factorization of 120 is $2 \times 2 \times 2 \times 3 \times 5$.

You can use exponents to write the prime factorization of 120 as $2^3 \times 3 \times 5$.

1. Make a factor tree for 120. Start with 4×30. What do you find?

If the prime factorizations of two whole numbers contain no common factor, the numbers are **relatively prime.**

$18 = 2 \times 3^2 \qquad 35 = 5 \times 7$

2. Are 18 and 35 relatively prime? Are 24 and 108?

TRY OUT

3. Is 59 prime or composite?

4. What is the prime factorization of 360?

PRACTICE

Tell whether the number is *prime* or *composite*.

5. 45   **6.** 83   **7.** 51   **8.** 151   **9.** 63   **10.** 473

Find the prime factorization of the number. Write the answer using exponents.

11. 48   **12.** 90   **13.** 82   **14.** 104   **15.** 408   **16.** 189

17. 200   **18.** 360   **19.** 275   **20.** 352   **21.** 490   **22.** 1,408

Tell whether the pair is relatively prime. Write *yes* or *no.*

23. 25, 36   **24.** 18, 500   **25.** 150, 231   **26.** 189, 220

27. 17, 595   **28.** 90, 641   **29.** 102, 729   **30.** 5,400; 2,694

Twin primes are two prime numbers that differ by 2.

Is the given number one of a pair of twin primes? If yes, give the other prime in the pair. If not, write *no.*

31. 31   **32.** 41   **33.** 47   **34.** 97   **35.** 103   **36.** 977

Critical Thinking

37. Are two prime numbers relatively prime? Do numbers have to be prime in order to be relatively prime? Give examples to support your answer.

38. Is the product of two prime numbers a prime number? Give examples to support your answer.

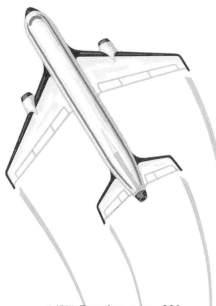

Mixed Applications

Solve. Which method did you use? You may need to use the Databank on page 582.

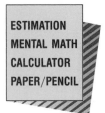

ESTIMATION
MENTAL MATH
CALCULATOR
PAPER/PENCIL

39. The wingspan of a Boeing 747 is a little more than half the length of a football field. About how long is the wingspan in feet?

40. A mechanic for one airline makes $18.83 per hour. How much does the mechanic earn for a 40-hour workweek?

41. A company purchases 25 planes for $2.8 million each. How much does it spend in all?

PROBLEM SOLVING

Strategy: Making an Organized List

The Space Center still has not announced the final crew for the flight to Mars scheduled for October. The crew will be chosen from this list of astronauts.

Crew List
Amann, E.
Crockett, K.
Roskoff, M.
Stendel, D.
Zoll, E.

How many possible choices does the Space Center have for a three-person crew?

Make a plan.

The supervisor uses the initials of the last names of the astronauts to list the possible crews. He wants to include all the possibilities, with no repeats.

Try the plan.

Here is how he starts his list: ACR
ACS
ACZ

1. List the other crews that could have Amann as a member. How many are there?

2. Look at the list of crews you have so far. List the other crews that could have Crockett as a member. How many are there?

3. Look at the list of crews you have so far. List the other crews that could have Roskoff as a member. How many are there?

4. Are there any other crews that could have Stendel or Zoll as a member? Why or why not?

5. How many different choices are there for three-member crews?

6. **What if** a sixth astronaut, T. Dexter, joined the training? List the additional three-person crews that could be formed. How many are there?

7. How many three-member crews could be formed with six astronauts?

8. **What if** two of the six astronauts, Amann and Crockett, dropped out of the training? List the three-person crews that could be formed.

9. How many three-member crews could be formed with four astronauts?

PRACTICE

Make an organized list and solve.

10. Four people, Alice, Bea, Carey, and Doug, are standing up on a shuttle bus. What are all the possible pairs who could occupy the two empty seats?

11. Dolores, Elvin, Fred, Gregg, Harry, and Inez are on the Astros basketball team. What are all the possible five-person teams they could form?

12. The airline offers 6 tapes for listening: classical, country, jazz, new wave, pop, and rock. Shamir has enough time to listen to four tapes. List the different combinations of the six tapes he could listen to.

13. For a shuttle launching there are five balloons at a concession stand: Moon, rocket, astronaut, flag, and Earth. List all the selections of two balloons that a child could make. How many are there?

Strategies and Skills Review

Solve. Use mental math, estimation, a calculator, or paper and pencil.

14. You are walking down a corridor at an airport and notice these gate numbers:

4   10   18   ■   40

What is the missing gate number?

15. While waiting for a flight, Les buys 6 lunches for his family. Lunches cost about $3.65 each. Should he over- or underestimate the total cost of the lunches? What is the total cost?

16. The *Faster-Than-Sound Spaceship* traveled 52,000 mi in 3 hours. Each hour it traveled 3 times as fast as the previous hour. How fast did it travel each hour?

17. Tomas, Urik, Vicka, and Yvonne are astronauts who have just landed on the Moon. Only three of them can walk on the Moon at one time. What are all the possible ways they can do this?

18. Two astronauts orbiting Earth traveled at a rate of 15,250 mph for 2 hours. Use the distance formula to find the distance they traveled.

19. *Write a problem* that involves making an organized list to solve. Ask other students to solve it.

Logical Reasoning

A. Captain Jack spent much of his life sailing the high seas, and he often talks about his adventures.

He tells a story about a large fish he once caught. This fish weighed 100 pounds plus one-third of its weight. How much did the fish weigh?

1. Suppose the fish weighed 120 pounds. Then what is one-third of its weight? Does it weigh 100 pounds plus one-third of its weight?

2. Do you think the fish weighed more or less than 100 pounds? Why? Keep trying different weights until you find the one that works.

B. Captain Jack said the crew always watched for whales when the ship was sailing in Alaskan waters. He described one whale as follows.

The whale's head was 5 feet long.
The whale's tail was as long as its head, plus half the length of its body.
The whale's body was as long as its head and tail together.

How long was the whale?

3. The whale's body must be longer than 10 feet. Why?

4. Suppose the whale's body was 15 feet long. Then how long would the tail be? Would the tail equal the length of the head plus half the length of the body?

5. Keep trying different lengths for the body until you find the one that works. What is the body length?

6. How long was the whale?

C. Captain Jack said, "My ship is really old." "How old is it?" asked his niece Carrie. Captain Jack answered her this way:

"My ship is twice as old as its boiler was when the ship was as old as the boiler is now. The sum of their ages is presently 49 years."

Carrie figured out the ages of the ship and the boiler. Can you?

7. If the ship is 30 years old, then how old is the boiler? Why?

8. Use your answer from question 7. How many years ago would the ship have been as old as the boiler is now? How old would the boiler have been then? So, if the ship is 30 years old, is it twice as old as the boiler was then?

9. Start again with a different guess for the present age of the ship. See if your guess works. Keep trying until you find the correct age. How old is the ship? How old is the boiler?

UNDERSTANDING A CONCEPT

Greatest Common Factor

A. Eliot has 18 rosebushes and 42 azalea bushes. He wants to plant them in groups that have the same number of bushes but only one type of plant. What is the greatest number of bushes that Eliot can plant in each group?

Eliot thinks that since he wants to divide the bushes into equal groups, he can use factors to help. He thinks of the factors of 18 and 42.

Factors of 18: 1, 2, 3, 6, 9, 18
Factors of 42: 1, 2, 3, 6, 7, 14, 21, 42

1. Which factors do 18 and 42 have in common?

2. What is the greatest factor 18 and 42 have in common?

The greatest whole number that is a factor of two or more whole numbers is the **greatest common factor (GCF)** of the numbers.

The GCF of 18 and 42 is 6.

3. How many rosebushes should Eliot plant in each group?

4. How many azalea bushes should Eliot plant in each group?

B. You can also use prime factorization to find the GCF of numbers.

Find the GCF of 63 and 108.

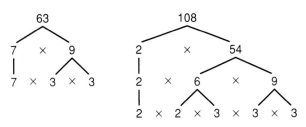

Pair up the common factors.

63: $3 \times 3 \times 7$

108: $2 \times 2 \times 3 \times 3 \times 3$

The GCF of 63 and 108 is equal to 3×3, or 9.

5. Find the GCF of 48 and 36.

6. **What if** you had to find the GCF of 9 and 18 and the GCF of 134 and 206? Which method would you use for each? Why?

T RY OUT Write the letter of the correct answer.

7. Find the GCF of 28 and 63.   **a.** 4   **b.** 7   **c.** 3   **d.** 9

8. Find the GCF of 125 and 500.   **a.** 125   **b.** 5   **c.** 500   **d.** 25

P RACTICE

Find the GCF of the numbers.

9. 45, 72	**10.** 18, 24	**11.** 25, 55	**12.** 24, 56	**13.** 75, 150
14. 28, 48	**15.** 50, 75	**16.** 90, 48	**17.** 100, 60	**18.** 200, 700
19. 16, 30	**20.** 21, 42	**21.** 27, 48	**22.** 48, 60	**23.** 30, 145
24. 110, 770	**25.** 63, 88	**26.** 54, 81	**27.** 80, 32	**28.** 200; 1,450
29. 16, 24, 64	**30.** 15, 18, 24	**31.** 24, 48, 30	**32.** 75, 32, 40	
33. 36, 42, 54	**34.** 21, 35, 42	**35.** 18, 81, 45	**36.** 240, 510, 630	

Critical Thinking

37. If the greatest common factor of two numbers is one of the numbers, what is true about the numbers?

Mixed Applications

Use the table for Problems 38–41.

38. About how many kilometers of roads are there in the five countries all together?

39. How many more kilometers of roads does France have than the Soviet Union?

40. The United States has 288,072 km of railroad tracks. About how many times as many kilometers of roads does the United States have?

41. *Write a problem* using the data in the table. Solve your problem. Ask others to solve it.

ROADS

Country	Kilometers
United States	6,365,590
Canada	3,002,000
France	1,502,000
Brazil	1,411,936
Soviet Union	1,408,800

Mixed Review

Solve. Which method did you use?

MENTAL MATH
CALCULATOR
PAPER/PENCIL

42. 48.4×0.25

43. $8.63 + 2.37$

44. $(8 \times 10^8) \times (4 \times 10^4)$

45. $\begin{array}{r} 1,782 \\ \times\ 6.75 \end{array}$

46. $\begin{array}{r} \$101,853 \\ -\ 92,957 \end{array}$

47. $\dfrac{9 \times 10^{12}}{4 \times 10^3}$

UNDERSTANDING A CONCEPT

Least Common Multiple

A. Two runners start from the same point, at the same time, on a cross-country course. Joan takes 8 minutes to go once around the course, and Karen takes 12 minutes. If they keep running, in how many minutes will Joan and Karen be together again at the starting point?

Recall that you can find a **multiple** of a number by multiplying the number by 0, 1, 2, 3, ...

Multiples of 8: 0, 8, 16, 24, 32, 40, 48, 56, . . .
Multiples of 12: 0, 12, 24, 36, 48, 60, 72, 84, . . .

1. What are the common multiples of 8 and 12?

The **least common multiple (LCM)** of two numbers is the smallest nonzero multiple of both numbers. The LCM of 8 and 12 is 24.

It will be 24 minutes before Joan and Karen are together again at the start of the track.

B. You can also use prime factorization to find the LCM.

Find the LCM of 8 and 12.

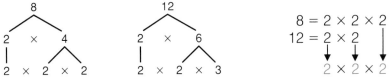

$$8 = 2 \times 2 \times 2$$
$$12 = 2 \times 2 \quad | \times 3$$
$$2 \times 2 \times 2 \times 3$$

The LCM of 8 and 12 is equal to $2 \times 2 \times 2 \times 3 = 24$.

2. One way to find the LCM of two numbers is to multiply the prime factors of the first number by the prime factors of the second number that are *not* factors of the first number. Test this procedure with five different pairs of numbers. Does it always work?

3. How could you find the LCM of 8 and 12 mentally?

TRY OUT   Write the letter of the correct answer.

4. Find the LCM of 9 and 15.   **a.** 135   **b.** 15   **c.** 45   **d.** 3

5. Find the LCM of 45 and 54.   **a.** 2,430   **b.** 9   **c.** 270   **d.** 405

PRACTICE

Find the LCM of the numbers.

6. 8, 10   **7.** 15, 20   **8.** 10, 15   **9.** 12, 18   **10.** 20, 30

11. 25, 30   **12.** 8, 9   **13.** 10, 13   **14.** 24, 48   **15.** 50, 100

16. 35, 21   **17.** 17, 10   **18.** 22, 33   **19.** 54, 81   **20.** 121, 55

21. 60, 90, 120   **22.** 45, 100, 200   **23.** 15, 40, 50   **24.** 80, 100, 140

Critical Thinking

25. Give an example of when the LCM of two numbers is the same as the product of the two numbers.

Mixed Applications

26. In 1980 Eric Heiden set a speed-skating record of 38.03 seconds in the 500-m race. If he could maintain that pace, how long would it take him to skate 2,000 m?

27. While in training for a race, one athlete ran 2.2 hours each day. How many hours would he run in a year if he trained for 6 days each week?

28. In 1984 Carl Lewis of the United States jumped 28 ft $\frac{1}{4}$ in. in the long jump. In 1896 Ellery Clark, also of the United States, jumped 20 ft $\frac{3}{4}$ in. How much farther than Ellery Clark did Carl Lewis jump?

29. A speed skater circles an oval rink in 60 seconds. Another skater circles the rink in 75 seconds. If they start at the same point, after how many seconds would they be together at the starting point again?

LOGICAL REASONING

An interesting relationship exists between the GCF and LCM of two numbers.

Find the prime factorization of 15 and 20.

$15 = 3 \times 5$ GCF: 5
$20 = 2 \times 2 \times 5$ LCM: $2 \times 2 \times 3 \times 5 = 60$

1. Find the product of 15 and 20.

2. Find the product of the GCF and LCM.

3. What do you notice about the answers in Problems 1 and 2?

The product of two numbers is equal to the product of their GCF and LCM.

4. Do you think this relationship is always true? Test it with the following six pairs of numbers: 4 and 14; 55 and 25; 45 and 75; 27 and 36; 42 and 70; 1,001 and 6,006.

DECISION MAKING

Problem Solving: Choosing a Science Project to Demonstrate

SITUATION

Students in the science club work with elementary school students. They want to demonstrate a science experiment about pollution. They must choose from three experiments.

PROBLEM

Which experiment should they demonstrate?

DATA

Experiment 3
Water Pollution

Equipment
An aquarium, 2 styrofoam cups, a can of motor oil, eye dropper, strainer, water

Procedure:
Fill the aquarium almost full with water. Float the styrofoam cups on top. Every half hour (for at least 6 hours) have a student add one drop of oil to the water. Let it stay overnight.
Check the cups for traces of pollution. Strain the water and observe the pollution.

Experiment 1
Soil Pollution

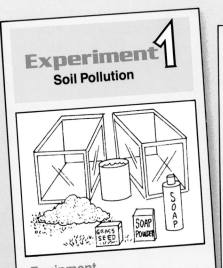

Equipment
Two small aquariums, potting soil, grass seeds, soap powder, liquid soap, water

Procedure:
Fill the bottom of each aquarium with 3 in. of soil. Label one aquarium EXPERIMENT and thoroughly mix the liquid soap and soap powder into the soil. Sprinkle the grass seeds on top and mix gently into the soil. Add one cup of water. Label the other aquarium CONTROL. Sprinkle the grass seed on top and mix gently into the soil.
Observe and record the grass growth for several weeks.

Experiment 2
Biodegradable Materials

Equipment
A small shovel, styrofoam cup, small plastic bottle, strips of newspaper, apple core, orange peel, water, camera

Procedure:
Dig a hole outside about 1 ft deep. Place the materials listed above (excluding the shovel and camera) in the hole. Sprinkle water in and around the hole. Re-cover with dirt and mark the spot. Return once a month to uncover the hole and observe how each of the items decays. Take pictures to keep a record.

Pollution Experiments

USING THE DATA

Predict what will happen when students conduct the experiment.

1. Experiment 1: Soil Pollution

2. Experiment 2: Biodegradable Materials

3. Experiment 3: Water Pollution

Explain why the experiment will turn out as you predicted.

4. Experiment 1: Soil Pollution

5. Experiment 2: Biodegradable Materials

6. Experiment 3: Water Pollution

MAKING DECISIONS

7. Which experiment will take the longest?

8. Which experiment will have the most predictable results?

9. Which experiment(s) should they choose for students to do at home?

10. Describe another experiment to teach about pollution.

11. **Write a list** of other factors they should consider when choosing an experiment.

12. Which experiment would you choose? Why?

Math and Music

When a cellist draws the bow across a string, the string vibrates. The listener hears not only the note that is played but also traces of several other tones. This is because the string vibrates simultaneously as a whole and in sections of its entire length. The basic note that sounds is called the *fundamental*. The notes that sound with the fundamental are called *overtones*.

The series of overtones a fundamental produces is called the *harmonic series*. Each instrument is different in terms of which overtone is strongest. These differences are what give each instrument its unique sound.

Look at the musical notation at the right. It shows the harmonic series up to the eighth overtone of the lower A in the bass clef. The frequency of vibration of each note in the series is given in vibrations per second.

What if you want to find the pattern of the frequencies of the harmonic series? What is the relationship of each overtone to the fundamental A?

Think: Look at the way the frequencies increase. Is there a pattern?

Fundamental: 110
1st harmonic: $220 = 110 + 110$ or 2×110
2nd harmonic: $330 = 220 + 110$ or 3×110

Add 110 to a term to find the next term or multiply 110 by 1, 2, 3, and so on.

Harmonic Series

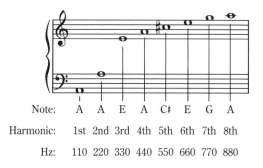

Note:	A	A	E	A	C♯	E	G	A
Harmonic:	1st	2nd	3rd	4th	5th	6th	7th	8th
Hz:	110	220	330	440	550	660	770	880

ACTIVITIES

1. Middle C has a frequency of 262 vibrations per second. Find the frequency of the 8th overtone.

2. Partially fill a narrow-necked bottle with water. Blow across the mouth so that your breath is split by the opposite rim. When you can produce a tone, try blowing harder to get an overtone. This is called overblowing. Is the overtone higher or lower?

Computer Exploration: Star Polygons

In this lesson you will explore an interesting relationship that lets you create stars based on commands that form regular polygons.

AT THE COMPUTER

1. Enter REPEAT 5 [FD 50 RT 72]. What figure is drawn?

2. Enter REPEAT 5 [FD 50 RT 144]. What figure is drawn?

3. How are the two sets of commands similar? How are they different?

4. The commands REPEAT 6 [FD 50 RT 60] will draw a hexagon. What commands might you use to draw a six-pointed star? Try it. Did it work? What was drawn on the screen?

5. To draw a regular polygon using Logo, the turn angle can be found by dividing 360° by the number of sides. For example, to draw an octagon, the turn angle would be 360° ÷ 8, or 45°. Enter the procedure below. It allows you to explore the effect of using multiples of the turn angle of any regular polygon.

    TO PICTURE :MULTIPLIER :SIDES
    REPEAT :SIDES [FD 50 RT (:MULTIPLIER $*$ 360/:SIDES)]
    END

6. To draw the figure in Problem 1, enter PICTURE 1 5. What should you enter to draw the figure in Problem 2?

7. Experiment with the values for MULTIPLIER and SIDES that represent the unshaded boxes in the table at the right. If a pair of values produces a star with as many points as the value of SIDES, write "Y" in the table. Otherwise write "N." The results obtained from Problems 1–4 have already been entered.

		SIDES				
MULTIPLIER		5	6	7	8	9	10
1		N	N				
2		Y	N				
3							
4							

8. Look for a pattern in the table. List the pairs of values of MULTIPLIER and SIDES for which "Y" appeared? What relationship do these pairs of values share?

9. Note that for each box in the table the value of MULTIPLIER is less than half the value of SIDES. Experiment with larger values of MULTIPLIER. Describe what happened.

EXTRA PRACTICE

Sequences, page 207

The first three terms of an arithmetic sequence are given. What is the rule? Find the next two terms.

1. 0, 5, 10 . . .

2. 30, 25, 20 . . .

3. 38, 47, 56 . . .

4. 74, 71, 68 . . .

5. 100, 95, 90 . . .

6. 0.8, 1.0, 1.2 . . .

7. 32, 36, 40 . . .

8. 2.1, 1.8, 1.5 . . .

9. 45, 41.5, 38 . . .

10. 285, 260, 235 . . .

11. 58.5, 54, 49.5 . . .

12. 1.2, 9, 16.8 . . .

13. 100, 300, 500 . . .

14. 150, 135, 120 . . .

15. 51.2, 59.9, 68.6 . . .

16. 4, 107, 210 . . .

17. 26, 25.3, 24.6 . . .

18. 87, 84.4, 81.8 . . .

19. 7, 24, 41 . . .

20. 28, 59, 90 . . .

21. 533, 519.8, 506.6 . . .

What is the rule used to generate the arithmetic sequence?

22. The 1st and 6th terms are 3 and 33.

23. The 1st and 5th terms are 65 and 37.

24. The 1st and 6th terms are 34 and 49.

25. The 1st and 6th terms are 83 and 58.

26. The 1st and 5th terms are 103 and 75.

27. The 1st and 7th terms are 21 and 51.

28. The 1st and 8th terms are 7 and 35.

29. The 1st and 9th terms are 12 and 84.

30. The 1st and 7th terms are 152 and 68.

31. The 1st and 5th terms are 83 and 75.

Sums of Sequences, page 209

Find the sum of the sequence.

1. 7, 8, 9, 10, 11, 12, 13, 14

2. 15, 16, 17, 18, 19, 20

3. 1.5, 2.5, 3.5, 4.5, 5.5, 6.5

4. 1.5, 2.5, 3.5, 4.5, 5.5

5. 40, 41, 42, 43, 44

6. 2, 7, 12, 17, 22, 27

7. 3, 5, 7, 9, 11, 13, 15, 17

8. 7, 14, 21, 28, 35, 42, 49

9. 8.75, 10.75, 12.75, 14.75

10. 0.5, 1.0, 1.5, 2.0, 2.5, 3.0, 3.5

11. the first eight even numbers

12. the first six odd numbers

13. 1, 2, 3, 4, 5, . . . , 60

14. 1, 2, 3, 4, 5, . . . , 25

15. The next five odd numbers greater than 12

16. The next six even numbers less than 33

Problem-Solving Strategy: Finding a Pattern, page 211

Find the pattern and solve.

1. Denise and her brother Sheldon opened a roadside farmer's market on Route 101 at their parents' farm. On opening day, Monday, they had 10 customers. On Tuesday they had 18 customers, and on Wednesday 26 customers came by. At this rate, how many customers can they expect on Friday?

2. Before deciding on a location for their market, Sheldon and Denise studied the traffic patterns on Route 101. From 6 A.M. to 7 A.M., 95 cars passed. Between 7 A.M. and 8 A.M., 80 cars passed, and 65 cars went by between 8 A.M. and 9 A.M. If the pattern continues, how many cars passed between 10 A.M. and 11 A.M.?

3. Denise weighed her newborn pig every other day. The first day, the pig weighed 35 lb. At the next weighings, the pig weighed 38, 41, 44, and 47 lb. At this rate of gain, after how many more days will the pig weigh more than 100 lb?

4. Suspecting that someone might be stealing from the chicken coop, Sheldon counted eggs every morning. The first day, he counted 21; thereafter the counts were 18, 20, 17, 19, 16, 18, 15, and 17. At this rate, how many eggs will Sheldon find on the 38th day?

5. Sheldon and Denise take turns baling hay. Sheldon bales on Mondays, Wednesdays and Fridays; Denise bales on the other days except Sunday, when they both rest. The first day of baling is a Monday, and they count their total bales at the end of each day. The totals at the end of each day for the first week are 7, 15, 22, 30, 37, and 45. On what day of the week will their total reach 60 bales?

Mental Math: Divisibility and Factors, page 213

Write *yes* or *no*.

Number	Divisible by:							
	2?	3?	4?	5?	6?	8?	9?	10?
345	1.	2.	3.	4.	5.	6.	7.	8.
810	9.	10.	11.	12.	13.	14.	15.	16.
1,035	17.	18.	19.	20.	21.	22.	23.	24.
480	25.	26.	27.	28.	29.	30.	31.	32.
488	33.	34.	35.	36.	37.	38.	39.	40.
20,628	41.	42.	43.	44.	45.	46.	47.	48.
9,801	49.	50.	51.	52.	53.	54.	55.	56.
8,964	57.	58.	59.	60.	61.	62.	63.	64.
17,028	65.	66.	67.	68.	69.	70.	71.	72.

EXTRA PRACTICE

Primes and Prime Factorization, page 215

Tell whether the number is prime or composite.

1. 57   **2.** 37   **3.** 29   **4.** 121   **5.** 197   **6.** 91

7. 17   **8.** 1,003   **9.** 1,007   **10.** 23   **11.** 33   **12.** 31

Find the prime factorization of the number. Write the answer using exponents.

13. 60   **14.** 56   **15.** 58   **16.** 176   **17.** 208   **18.** 567

19. 300   **20.** 198   **21.** 325   **22.** 448   **23.** 360   **24.** 2,816

Is the pair relatively prime? Write *yes* or *no*.

25. 3 and 17   **26.** 48 and 75   **27.** 16 and 35   **28.** 11 and 18

29. 28 and 56   **30.** 170 and 510   **31.** 200 and 300   **32.** 4,800 and 2,495

Problem–Solving Strategy: Making an Organized List, page 217

Make an organized list and solve.

1. Alice, Jason, Paul, and Rita are going to a basketball game. The tickets are for seats in row 12. In how many different ways could they sit in the seats?

2. Malcolm has a hot-air balloon. Only three people can go up for a ride at one time. Josef, Dom, and Karen want to take a ride. What are all the possible ways they can do this?

3. Matt wants to participate in three activities at school this year. He is interested in football, chess, basketball, and art. He definitely wants to join the chess team. List all the different combinations of activities in which Matt could take part.

4. Sonia is arranging cut-glass animals in a row on the mantelpiece. She has an owl, a seal, a duck, and a bird. Sonia always places the owl on the left. In how many different ways could she arrange the glass animals?

5. Ria sells five kinds of soup at the Soup 'N Bread Stop where she works. The soups are lentil, carrot, avocado, barley, and spinach. She has tasted lentil and two other soups. List all the different combinations of soups Ria could have tried.

6. Hank buys a six-shelf bookcase at a garage sale. He has four different color rolls of shelving paper. The colors are blue, green, yellow, and red. He wants to use three colors. List all the possible combinations Hank could use.

EXTRA PRACTICE

Greatest Common Factor, page 221

Find the GCF of the numbers.

1. 45, 60	**2.** 20, 28	**3.** 18, 48	**4.** 45, 75
5. 42, 105	**6.** 15, 70	**7.** 28, 42	**8.** 200, 80
9. 300, 800	**10.** 72, 132	**11.** 26, 52	**12.** 25, 65
13. 51, 68	**14.** 60, 185	**15.** 50, 175	**16.** 44, 77
17. 48, 108	**18.** 70, 56	**19.** 90, 27	**20.** 180, 1,200
21. 8, 20	**22.** 15, 25	**23.** 9, 48	**24.** 14, 42
25. 45, 99	**26.** 24, 40, 56	**27.** 21, 27, 33	**28.** 25, 35, 45
29. 71, 13, 19	**30.** 36, 45, 81	**31.** 200, 240, 360	**32.** 14, 49, 63
33. 32, 48, 128	**34.** 24, 48, 16	**35.** 20, 30, 50	**36.** 80, 16, 20
37. 40, 10, 12	**38.** 54, 108, 135	**39.** 39, 65, 91	**40.** 1,000, 3,000, 5,000
41. 51, 153, 85	**42.** 30, 84, 54	**43.** 66, 99, 165	**44.** 260, 520, 455

Least Common Multiple, page 223

Find the LCM of the numbers.

1. 6, 8	**2.** 4, 6	**3.** 8, 11	**4.** 9, 12
5. 14, 21	**6.** 15, 35	**7.** 6, 9	**8.** 8, 12
9. 6, 10	**10.** 20, 25	**11.** 12, 20	**12.** 32, 48
13. 24, 28	**14.** 25, 125	**15.** 4, 14	**16.** 21, 49
17. 15, 12	**18.** 14, 35	**19.** 16, 32	**20.** 24, 30
21. 15, 25	**22.** 9, 20	**23.** 14, 42	**24.** 9, 48
25. 7, 13	**26.** 3, 4, 6	**27.** 2, 4, 16	**28.** 8, 16, 20
29. 3, 12, 36	**30.** 24, 36, 144	**31.** 20, 64, 80	**32.** 15, 18, 10
33. 16, 32, 96	**34.** 36, 124, 18	**35.** 24, 40, 60	**36.** 45, 90, 180
37. 18, 72, 90	**38.** 53, 106, 212	**39.** 13, 2, 6	**40.** 34, 17, 204
41. 23, 184, 69	**42.** 7, 2, 6	**43.** 3, 8, 5	**44.** 2, 3, 17

Practice PLUS

KEY SKILL: Greatest Common Factor (Use after page 221.)

Level A

Find the GCF of the numbers.

1. 25, 35   **2.** 24, 36   **3.** 18, 45   **4.** 18, 21   **5.** 14, 21

6. 28, 36   **7.** 16, 32   **8.** 48, 64   **9.** 35, 49   **10.** 60, 70

11. 22, 66   **12.** 80, 100   **13.** 150, 200   **14.** 64, 75   **15.** 12, 18

16. 20, 32   **17.** 36, 48   **18.** 500, 700   **19.** 27, 81   **20.** 91, 221

21. A jewelry maker made 25 necklaces and 35 bracelets. He wants to make packages of necklaces and packages of bracelets and put the same number of items in each package and not have any left over. How many should he put in each package?

Level B

Find the GCF of the numbers.

22. 36, 54   **23.** 14, 63   **24.** 24, 64   **25.** 18, 25   **26.** 48, 60

27. 300, 500   **28.** 44, 88   **29.** 600, 800   **30.** 16, 52   **31.** 30, 65

32. 40, 100   **33.** 100, 175   **34.** 120, 300   **35.** 36, 72   **36.** 42, 63

37. 24, 32, 56   **38.** 27, 45, 72   **39.** 12, 28, 40   **40.** 15, 45, 70

41. A jewelry maker made 4 silver rings and 6 gold rings. She wants to package them in groups of equal size of the same type. How many should she put in each package?

Level C

Find the GCF of the numbers.

42. 48, 54   **43.** 42, 63   **44.** 64, 88   **45.** 63, 108   **46.** 60, 132

47. 54, 90   **48.** 280, 440   **49.** 90, 210   **50.** 300, 700   **51.** 45, 60

52. 100, 121   **53.** 150, 375   **54.** 240, 600   **55.** 18, 54   **56.** 84, 108

57. 40, 48, 64   **58.** 55, 80, 95   **59.** 39, 45, 48   **60.** 32, 48, 80

61. A jewelry maker made 12 pairs of emerald earrings, 15 pairs of ruby earrings, and 18 pairs of diamond earrings. He wants to package them in groups of equal size of the same type. How many should he put in each package?

Practice PLUS

KEY SKILL: Least Common Multiple (Use after page 223.)

Level A

Find the LCM of the numbers.

1. 8, 6   **2.** 7, 9   **3.** 5, 12   **4.** 5, 25   **5.** 6, 10

6. 3, 5   **7.** 4, 16   **8.** 4, 9   **9.** 16, 24   **10.** 7, 5

11. 15, 20   **12.** 5, 45   **13.** 10, 12   **14.** 16, 32   **15.** 10, 15

16. 8, 20   **17.** 3, 11   **18.** 20, 25   **19.** 6, 30   **20.** 7, 12

21. Lenny bought the same number of pens as pencils. Pens come in packages of 3. Pencils come in packages of 4. What is the least of each he could have bought?

Level B

Find the LCM of the numbers.

22. 30, 40   **23.** 6, 25   **24.** 18, 20   **25.** 7, 12   **26.** 25, 15

27. 16, 6   **28.** 15, 24   **29.** 9, 15   **30.** 18, 27   **31.** 22, 55

32. 8, 14   **33.** 7, 25   **34.** 125, 25   **35.** 60, 24   **36.** 40, 24

37. 40, 60, 80   **38.** 30, 100, 200   **39.** 50, 60, 100

40. 15, 60, 90   **41.** 5, 12, 120   **42.** 8, 14, 20

43. Barbara wants to buy the same number of paper plates as paper cups. Plates come in packages of 10 and cups come in packages of 12. What is the least number of each she should buy?

Level C

Find the LCM of the numbers.

44. 15, 50   **45.** 42, 54   **46.** 28, 42   **47.** 30, 16   **48.** 18, 81

49. 30, 63   **50.** 18, 24   **51.** 20, 38   **52.** 21, 33   **53.** 16, 80

54. 63, 42   **55.** 45, 72   **56.** 14, 70   **57.** 64, 40   **58.** 25, 60

59. 15, 25, 30   **60.** 50, 80, 200   **61.** 30, 80, 100

62. 25, 40, 60   **63.** 11, 44, 132   **64.** 7, 15, 17

65. George makes lanyard key chains. Every 6th key chain has red in it. Every 8th key chain has white in it. How often does a key chain have both red and white in it?

CHAPTER REVIEW

LANGUAGE AND MATHEMATICS

Complete the sentence. Use the words in the chart on the right.

1. Seven and one are the only two factors of 7, so 7 is a ▓. *(page 214)*

2. Whole numbers that have more than two different factors are ▓. *(page 214)*

3. Five is the greatest factor of both 10 and 15, so 5 is called their ▓. *(page 220)*

4. Thirty is the smallest multiple of 5 and 6, so 30 is called their ▓. *(page 222)*

5. ***Write a definition*** or give an example of the words you did not use from the chart.

> **VOCABULARY**
>
> **prime number**
> **composite number**
> **prime factorization**
> **relatively prime number**
> **greatest common factor (GCF)**
> **least common multiple (LCM)**

CONCEPTS AND SKILLS

State whether the number is *prime* or *composite*. *(page 214)*

6. 75	**7.** 187	**8.** 819
9. 210	**10.** 79	**11.** 441

Find the prime factorization. *(page 214)*

12. 56	**13.** 88	**14.** 28
15. 375	**16.** 153	**17.** 180

Find the factor pairs. *(page 212)*

18. 168	**19.** 225	**20.** 490
21. 12	**22.** 20	**23.** 50
24. 37	**25.** 66	**26.** 43

Find the GCF. *(page 220)*

27. 9, 27	**28.** 18, 30	**29.** 6, 15
30. 25, 50	**31.** 24, 36	**32.** 100, 150
33. 16, 36	**34.** 14, 49	**35.** 225, 300

List the first three multiples. *(page 222)*

36. 6	**37.** 10	**38.** 7	**39.** 13

Find the LCM. *(page 222)*

40. 8, 12

41. 21, 42

42. 13, 5

43. 8, 18

44. 9, 15

45. 22, 40

46. 100, 10

47. 55, 44

48. 6 and 20

49. 5 and 14

50. 18 and 48

51. 15 and 36

Critical Thinking

52. Is the product of two composite numbers always a composite number? *(page 214)*

53. Is the sum of two prime numbers always a prime number? *(page 214)*

54. If a number n is the GCF of numbers m and n, is m divided by n always a whole number? *(page 220)*

55. If the product of numbers x and y is the LCM of x and y, can x and y have a common factor? *(page 222)*

Mixed Applications

56. Andy and Liza are in a pizza-eating contest. It takes Andy 6 minutes and Liza 8 minutes to eat a slice of pizza. They both begin at the same time and continue to eat. After how long will they both start to eat a slice of pizza again at the same time? *(page 222)*

57. Ms. Hobbs has 15 boys and 18 girls in her class. She wants to divide the boys and girls into groups of equal sizes. Each group is to contain only boys or only girls. What is the greatest number of students she can have in one group? *(page 220)*

58. Loren was studying the meaning of new words. After the first day he had 15 words left to learn. After the second day he had 12 words left to learn. The next day he had 9 words left. At that rate, how many days will it take him to learn all the words? *(page 210)*

59. Daisy begins taking piano lessons. Each day she plans to practice 10 minutes more than she practiced the previous day. On the first day she plans to practice 20 minutes. How long does she plan to practice on the fourth day? *(page 210)*

60. Elly was studying new words for a spelling bee. The first day she studied 10 new words. The next three days she studied 15, 20, and then 25 new words. If she continues this sequence, how many words will she have studied in all after five days? *(page 208)*

61. Victor was increasing the number of chin-ups he did each day. He started with 5 the first day. The next three days he did 7, 9, and 11. At that rate, how many will he do on the sixth day? *(page 208)*

CHAPTER TEST

State whether the number is *prime* or *composite*.

1. 47   **2.** 99   **3.** 572   **4.** 101

Find the prime factorization.

5. 60   **6.** 141   **7.** 625

Find the factor pairs.

8. 36   **9.** 57   **10.** 75   **11.** 89

Find the GCF.

12. 24, 8   **13.** 28, 14   **14.** 125, 75   **15.** 18, 72

16. 6, 35   **17.** 12, 42   **18.** 45, 75   **19.** 36, 54

Find the LCM.

20. 12, 9   **21.** 7, 17   **22.** 125, 100   **23.** 24, 30

24. 10, 14   **25.** 22, 6   **26.** 27, 25   **27.** 15, 12

Find the sum of the sequence.

28. 12, 24, 36, 48, 60, 72   **29.** 1.5, 2.0, 2.5, 3.0, 3.5

Solve.

30. Kerry and Cassie are writing their list of spelling words over and over again. It takes Kerry 2 minutes to write all the words, and it takes Cassie 3 minutes. They both start writing the list at the same time. How long will it be before they both begin the list again at the same time?

31. Cal has 12 blue blocks and 8 red blocks. He wants to make stacks of blocks with the same number of blocks in each stack. He does not want to mix blue and red blocks in a stack. What is the greatest number of blocks he can put into each stack?

32. Kelly was practicing making baskets. The first day she practiced until she made 10 baskets. The next three days she practiced until she made 14, 18, and 22 baskets. If she continues that pattern, how many baskets will she have made on the sixth day?

33. Jess is learning to type. He is practicing typing the letters r, t, y, and u. Make a list of the different ways he can type the 4 letters with the u first.

PASCAL'S TRIANGLE

A ball is rolled down chutes from the top of the frame to the intersections. If the ball moves only down, along how many different paths can it travel from the top of the frame to the intersection marked X?

The diagrams show all the paths that are possible.

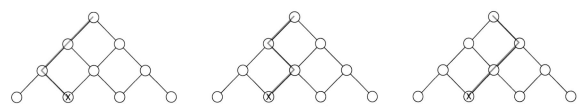

The ball can travel along three different paths.

Now find the number of paths a ball can travel from the top to *each* intersection. Copy the diagram at the right on a sheet of paper. Write the number of different paths to each intersection in the circle at the intersection.

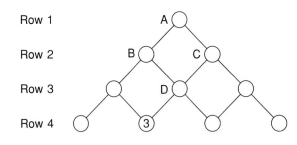

Row 1
Row 2
Row 3
Row 4

A
B   C
D
3

Look for number patterns in your diagram.

1. Start at intersection A. Follow the path to the left. What do you notice about the numbers on this path?

2. Start at intersection C. Follow the path to the left. What is the difference between these numbers?

3. Add up the numbers in each row. What do you notice?

4. ***What if*** there were a fifth row? What would you expect the sum of the numbers in this row to be?

5. Make the fifth row and the sixth row in the diagram.

The numbers in the diagram form a triangle that is known as **Pascal's triangle.** Blaise Pascal was a French mathematician and philosopher who studied this triangle in the 17th century. The triangle can be used to solve many problems in mathematics.

6. What other patterns can you find in Pascal's triangle?

CUMULATIVE REVIEW

Choose the letter of the correct answer.

1. $(2.5 \times 10^3) \times (5 \times 10^4)$

   a. 1.25×10^7

   b. 1.25×10^8

   c. 1.25×10^{12}

   d. not given

2. $\frac{6.2 \times 10^5}{2.0 \times 10^3}$

   a. 3.1×10^2 c. 3.1×10^{15}

   b. 3.1×10^8 d. not given

3. Solve for n: $\frac{n}{0.7} > 3.5$

   a. $n > 0.5$ c. $n > 24.5$

   b. $n > 5.0$ d. not given

4. Six objects weighed 1.5, 2.6, 3.5, 1, 3.5, and 0.5 oz. What was the mean of their weights?

   a. 2.1 oz   c. 12.6 oz

   b. 2.6 oz   d. not given

5. Six less than a number is 3. What is the number?

   a. 3   c. 9

   b. 6   d. not given

6. $1 + 3.2 \times 5$

   a. 21   c. 17

   b. 16.5   d. not given

7. Find the volume of a rectangular prism with a base 4 m by 0.5 m and a height of 6 m.

   a. 12 m³   c. 6 m³

   b. 10.5 m³   d. not given

8. What is the area of a circle with a diameter of 6 ft? Use 3.14 for π.

   a. 18.84 ft²   c. 113.04 ft²

   b. 37.68 ft²   d. not given

9. A car traveled 110 mi in 2 hours. How many mi per hour did the car average?

   a. 220 mi per hour

   b. 55 mi per hour

   c. 50 mi per hour

   d. not given

10. What is the prime factorization of 36?

    a. 4×9 c. 1×36

    b. 6×6 d. not given

11. What is the GCF of 8 and 12?

    a. 4   c. 96

    b. 24   d. not given

12. What is the LCM of 15 and 10?

    a. 5   c. 150

    b. 30   d. not given

13. What is the next number in the sequence 6, 12, 18, 24, . . . ?

    a. 28   c. 36

    b. 30   d. not given

14. How many factors does a prime number have?

    a. 0   c. 2

    b. 1   d. not given

Fractions: Addition and Subtraction

CHAPTER 7

MATH CONNECTIONS: ALGEBRA • PROBLEM SOLVING

EVENING SCHEDULE

7:00 – 7:30   News
7:30 – 8:00   Quiz Time
8:00 – 9:00   Detective
               Story
9:00 – 10:00   Space:
               2100 A.D.

1. What information do you see in this picture?

2. How can you use the information?

3. What fraction of the evening programming is devoted to Quiz Time and Detective Story?

4. Write a problem using the information.

239

UNDERSTANDING A CONCEPT

Equivalent Fractions

A. What part of the diamond is yellow?

$\frac{9}{12}$ of the diamond is yellow.

What part of the set of shapes is circles?

$\frac{6}{8}$ of the set is circles.

A **fraction** names part of a whole or part of a set.

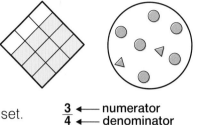

$\frac{3}{4}$ ← numerator
← denominator

B. Equivalent fractions name the same number. You can find equivalent fractions by multiplying or by dividing the numerator and the denominator by the same nonzero number.

$$\frac{3}{4} = \frac{3 \times 2}{4 \times 2} = \frac{6}{8} \qquad \frac{9}{12} = \frac{9 \div 3}{12 \div 3} = \frac{3}{4}$$

$\frac{6}{8}$ and $\frac{9}{12}$ are equivalent to $\frac{3}{4}$.

1. Is $\frac{15}{16}$ equivalent to $\frac{3}{4}$? Why or why not?

Find the value of n to make $\frac{3}{5}$ equivalent to $\frac{n}{20}$.

$\frac{3}{5} = \frac{n}{20}$ **Think:** $5 \times 4 = 20$. Multiply the numerator and the denominator by 4.

$$\frac{3}{5} = \frac{3 \times 4}{5 \times 4} = \frac{12}{20}$$

So $n = 12$.

2. To make $\frac{24}{27}$ equivalent to $\frac{8}{n}$, what would you do to the terms 24 and 27 to find n? What is the value of n?

C. A fraction is in **simplest form** if the numerator and the denominator have no common factors other than 1.

Write $\frac{24}{60}$ in simplest form.

Method 1	**Method 2**
Use repeated divisions.	Divide the numerator and the denominator by their greatest common factor.

$$\frac{24}{60} = \frac{24 \div 2}{60 \div 2} = \frac{12}{30} \qquad \textbf{\textit{Think:}}\ \text{The GCF of 24 and 60 is 12.}$$

$$\frac{12}{30} = \frac{12 \div 6}{30 \div 6} = \frac{2}{5} \qquad \frac{24}{60} = \frac{24 \div 12}{60 \div 12} = \frac{2}{5}$$

So $\frac{24}{60}$ simplifies to $\frac{2}{5}$.

TRY OUT

3. Find three equivalent fractions for $\frac{3}{8}$.

4. Find n. $\frac{6}{9} = \frac{n}{27}$.

5. Write $\frac{45}{75}$ in simplest form.

6. Write $\frac{21}{27}$ in simplest form.

PRACTICE

Find three fractions equivalent to the given fraction.

7. $\frac{1}{2}$

8. $\frac{3}{5}$

9. $\frac{4}{7}$

10. $\frac{2}{3}$

11. $\frac{5}{8}$

12. $\frac{2}{9}$

13. $\frac{8}{9}$

14. $\frac{5}{11}$

15. $\frac{7}{12}$

16. $\frac{1}{15}$

17. $\frac{20}{30}$

18. $\frac{7}{100}$

Find n.

19. $\frac{3}{5} = \frac{n}{15}$

20. $\frac{5}{6} = \frac{n}{24}$

21. $\frac{2}{3} = \frac{n}{36}$

22. $\frac{8}{15} = \frac{n}{60}$

23. $\frac{56}{64} = \frac{n}{8}$

24. $\frac{36}{99} = \frac{n}{11}$

25. $\frac{30}{45} = \frac{n}{3}$

26. $\frac{49}{70} = \frac{n}{10}$

27. $\frac{16}{24} = \frac{4}{n}$

28. $\frac{7}{12} = \frac{21}{n}$

29. $\frac{1}{5} = \frac{30}{n}$

30. $\frac{25}{25} = \frac{10}{n}$

Write the fraction in simplest form.

31. $\frac{3}{9}$

32. $\frac{5}{10}$

33. $\frac{8}{12}$

34. $\frac{15}{18}$

35. $\frac{12}{20}$

36. $\frac{16}{24}$

37. $\frac{48}{80}$

38. $\frac{10}{50}$

39. $\frac{36}{42}$

40. $\frac{42}{49}$

41. $\frac{63}{90}$

42. $\frac{24}{32}$

43. $\frac{25}{40}$

44. $\frac{45}{60}$

45. $\frac{15}{15}$

46. $\frac{100}{350}$

47. $\frac{180}{210}$

48. $\frac{0}{20}$

Mixed Applications

Solve. You may need to use the Databank on page 584.

49. Neptune revolves around the Sun once every 165 years. Its rotation on its axis takes 16 hours. How many rotations on its axis does Neptune make in one revolution around the Sun? (*Remember:* 1 year = 365 days.)

50. About how many times as great is the mass of Jupiter as that of Earth?

51. The mean distance from the Sun to Mars is 141.5 million mi. Saturn is about 886 million mi from the Sun. About how much farther from the Sun is Saturn than Mars?

UNDERSTANDING A CONCEPT

Mixed Numbers and Improper Fractions

A. Jason is making muffins. The recipe calls for $2\frac{1}{3}$ c flour. The measuring cup he uses can hold only $\frac{1}{3}$ c. How many measuring cups should he use?

You can count the number of thirds in $2\frac{1}{3}$.

$2\frac{1}{3} = 1 \qquad + 1 \qquad + \frac{1}{3}$

3 thirds + 3 thirds + 1 third = 7 thirds

A **mixed number** is the sum of a whole number and a fraction. An **improper fraction** is a fraction with a numerator that is greater than or equal to the denominator.

The mixed number $2\frac{1}{3}$ can be renamed as an improper fraction by writing the sum, 7, over the denominator, 3: $2\frac{1}{3} = \frac{7}{3}$.

Here is a shortcut method for renaming a mixed number as a fraction.

Step 1	**Step 2**
Multiply the whole number by the denominator.	**Add the numerator.**
$2\frac{1}{3} \quad 2 \times 3 = 6$	$2\frac{1}{3} \quad 6 + 1 = 7$

There are 7 thirds in $2\frac{1}{3}$.

Jason should use 7 measuring cups.

1. Describe how to rename $6\frac{2}{5}$ as an improper fraction.

2. Why can you express 5 as $\frac{5}{1}$? In what other ways can you express 5 as an improper fraction?

B. You can rename an improper fraction as a mixed number.

Rename $\frac{13}{4}$ as a mixed number.

Since $\frac{13}{4}$ means $13 \div 4$, you can divide.

$$\begin{array}{r} 3\,\text{R}1 \\ 4\overline{)13} \\ \underline{12} \\ 1 \end{array} \longrightarrow 3\frac{1}{4} \quad \text{Write the remainder over the divisor.}$$

So $\frac{13}{4} = 3\frac{1}{4}$.

Rename as a mixed number or as an improper fraction in simplest form.

3. $\frac{32}{6}$ **4.** $\frac{192}{56}$ **5.** $4\frac{5}{9}$ **6.** $8\frac{5}{8}$

PRACTICE

Rename as an improper fraction in simplest form.

7. $4\frac{2}{3}$ **8.** $2\frac{3}{8}$ **9.** $11\frac{1}{4}$ **10.** $3\frac{5}{9}$ **11.** $8\frac{6}{11}$ **12.** $5\frac{2}{3}$

13. $6\frac{3}{4}$ **14.** $4\frac{6}{7}$ **15.** $8\frac{7}{12}$ **16.** $3\frac{5}{8}$ **17.** $33\frac{1}{2}$ **18.** $10\frac{3}{5}$

19. $7\frac{11}{12}$ **20.** $5\frac{63}{100}$ **21.** $5\frac{5}{9}$ **22.** $2\frac{4}{15}$ **23.** $8\frac{7}{10}$ **24.** $10\frac{17}{20}$

Rename as a whole number or as a mixed number in simplest form.

25. $\frac{3}{2}$ **26.** $\frac{8}{6}$ **27.** $\frac{15}{4}$ **28.** $\frac{20}{8}$ **29.** $\frac{15}{11}$ **30.** $\frac{24}{7}$

31. $\frac{35}{9}$ **32.** $\frac{28}{10}$ **33.** $\frac{45}{12}$ **34.** $\frac{52}{8}$ **35.** $\frac{52}{13}$ **36.** $\frac{100}{21}$

37. $\frac{40}{12}$ **38.** $\frac{37}{18}$ **39.** $\frac{79}{10}$ **40.** $\frac{126}{25}$ **41.** $\frac{711}{100}$ **42.** $\frac{205}{50}$

43. 13 halves   **44.** 24 sevenths   **45.** 18 eighths   **46.** 45 twelfths

Mixed Applications

Solve.

47. A bakery uses $\frac{473}{4}$ bags of flour in one week. Express this fraction as a mixed number.

48. The bakery charges $.50 for each muffin it sells. How much does it make from the sale of 42 muffins?

49. One year the bakery's sales were $78,399. The next year the sales were $82,000. By about how much did sales increase the second year?

50. The bakery earned $128.80 on bread one day. If bread sells for $1.15 per loaf, how many loaves did the bakery sell?

Mixed Review ▨▨▨▨▨▨▨▨▨▨▨▨▨▨▨▨▨▨▨▨▨▨▨▨▨▨▨▨▨▨▨▨▨

Find the answer. Which method did you use?

**MENTAL MATH
CALCULATOR
PAPER/PENCIL**

51. $\frac{9.0 \times 10^{15}}{3.0 \times 10^5}$

52.
$$\begin{array}{r} 8.5 \\ -\ 6.023 \end{array}$$

53.
$$\begin{array}{r} \$11.50 \\ \times\ \ \ 0.08 \end{array}$$

54.
$$\begin{array}{r} 8,654.32 \\ +\ 7,986.007 \end{array}$$

55. $3 + n = 7$

56. $3 + n < 7$

UNDERSTANDING A CONCEPT

Fractions, Mixed Numbers, and Decimals

A. Elisa is a wildlife biologist studying the behavior of seals in Alaska. She examined 25 seals and found that $\frac{8}{25}$ of them were marked with red tags. How can she record this fraction as a decimal?

Since 25 is a factor of 100, Elisa first wrote an equivalent fraction for $\frac{8}{25}$ with a denominator of 100. Then she renamed it as a decimal.

$$\frac{8}{25} = \frac{8 \times 4}{25 \times 4} = \frac{32}{100} = 0.32$$

Elisa recorded the fraction as 0.32.

1. How would you rename $5\frac{3}{4}$ as a decimal?

You can use an equivalent fraction with denominator 1,000 to rename a fraction as a decimal.

$$\frac{7}{8} = \frac{7 \times 125}{8 \times 125} = \frac{875}{1,000} = 0.875$$

B. You can also rename decimals as fractions.

Rename 30.625 as a fraction in simplest form.

Think: $0.625 = \frac{625}{1,000}$

$$0.625 = \frac{625 \div 125}{1,000 \div 125} = \frac{5}{8}$$

So $30.625 = 30\frac{5}{8}$.

2. How would you rename 5.45 as a fraction in simplest form?

To rename a decimal as a fraction, make the decimal a numerator with a denominator of 10, 100, or 1,000 and then simplify.

3. How would you rename 21.4 as a fraction in simplest form?

TRY OUT Write the letter of the correct answer.

Rename as a decimal.

4. $\frac{3}{8}$ **a.** 125 **b.** $\frac{375}{1,000}$ **c.** 0.38 **d.** 0.375

Rename the decimal as a fraction or as a mixed number in simplest form.

5. 0.05 **a.** $\frac{5}{10}$ **b.** $\frac{1}{2}$ **c.** $\frac{1}{20}$ **d.** $\frac{1}{200}$

PRACTICE

Rename the fraction or the mixed number as a decimal.

6. $\frac{1}{2}$ **7.** $\frac{3}{5}$ **8.** $8\frac{3}{4}$ **9.** $16\frac{9}{10}$ **10.** $25\frac{13}{100}$ **11.** $\frac{18}{50}$

12. $11\frac{4}{5}$ **13.** $3\frac{9}{20}$ **14.** $\frac{21}{25}$ **15.** $12\frac{7}{50}$ **16.** $100\frac{11}{20}$ **17.** $9\frac{19}{25}$

18. $3\frac{5}{8}$ **19.** $10\frac{7}{8}$ **20.** $5\frac{7}{40}$ **21.** $11\frac{3}{125}$ **22.** $4\frac{89}{250}$ **23.** $2\frac{17}{500}$

Rename the decimal as a fraction or as a mixed number in simplest form.

24. 0.7   **25.** 0.27   **26.** 0.03   **27.** 0.5   **28.** 0.05   **29.** 0.25

30. 0.16   **31.** 0.45   **32.** 3.125   **33.** 6.64   **34.** 7.24   **35.** 50.8

36. 29.625   **37.** 5.375   **38.** 0.33   **39.** 23.75   **40.** 4.005   **41.** 9.025

Critical Thinking

42. Could you use Elisa's method for renaming $\frac{2}{3}$ as a decimal? Why or why not?

Mixed Applications

43. If 18 scientists marked 4,885 bears, about how many bears did each scientist mark?

44. Ely found that $\frac{3}{10}$ of the bears were marked. How can he record this fraction as a decimal?

45. One year a university sent 18 researchers to the Arctic Circle. Each received a salary of $18,500. What was the total amount paid in salaries?

46. A team of biologists is studying deer in a square region with a side that measures 250 ft. What is the area of the region?

CHALLENGE

Fractions can be paired with points on a number line. This number line is scaled in fourths, which means that the distance between two whole numbers is divided into four equal parts.

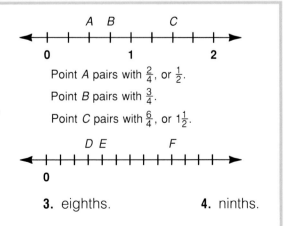

Point *A* pairs with $\frac{2}{4}$, or $\frac{1}{2}$.

Point *B* pairs with $\frac{3}{4}$.

Point *C* pairs with $\frac{6}{4}$, or $1\frac{1}{2}$.

Give the fractions or mixed numbers in simplest form for points *D*, *E*, and *F* if the number line is scaled in:

1. fourths.   **2.** sixths.   **3.** eighths.   **4.** ninths.

UNDERSTANDING A CONCEPT

Terminating and Repeating Decimals

A. An environmental scientist wants to compare the amount of lead impurities in various pipes. One pipe weighing 20 kg contains 3 kg of lead. In the pipes, 3 kg of 20 kg is lead.

You can express this as a fraction, $\frac{3}{20}$.

Rename $\frac{3}{20}$ as a decimal.

Recall that one way to rename a fraction as a decimal is to find an equivalent fraction with a denominator of 10; 100; or 1,000. You can also rename a fraction as a decimal by division.

Calculator

3 ⊡ 20 ⊟ | 0.15 |

Paper and Pencil

$$
\begin{array}{r}
0.15 \\
20\overline{)3.00} \\
2\,0 \\
\hline
1\,00 \\
1\,00 \\
\hline
0 \ \longleftarrow \text{The remainder is zero.}
\end{array}
$$

You can write any fraction in the form $\frac{a}{b}$, where $b \neq 0$, as a decimal. The decimal 0.15 is a **terminating decimal** because the remainder is zero when you divide.

1. Rename $\frac{3}{20}$ as a decimal by finding an equivalent fraction. Did you get the same answer?

B. Sometimes when you divide, the remainder is not zero.

Rename $\frac{1}{11}$ as a decimal.

Calculator

1 ⊡ 11 ⊟ | 0.0909090 |

Paper and Pencil

$$
\begin{array}{r}
0.0909 \longleftarrow \\
11\overline{)1.0000} \\
99 \\
\hline
100 \\
99 \\
\hline
1 \longleftarrow
\end{array}
$$

The digits 0 and 9 repeat forever.

The remainder will never be zero.

So $\frac{1}{11} = 0.0909\ldots$ or $0.\overline{09}$. The bar shows that the digit or digits repeat. So $0.\overline{09}$ is a **repeating decimal.**

2. Rename $\frac{1}{6}$ as a decimal. Use a bar to show the repeating decimal. Which digits repeat?

Rename as a decimal. Use a bar to show
a repeating decimal.

3. $\frac{1}{5}$ **4.** $3\frac{1}{4}$ **5.** $\frac{3}{8}$ **6.** $\frac{5}{11}$ **7.** $\frac{7}{12}$ **8.** $2\frac{2}{3}$

PRACTICE

Rename as a decimal. Use a bar to show a repeating decimal.

9. $\frac{3}{4}$ **10.** $\frac{13}{20}$ **11.** $\frac{7}{50}$ **12.** $\frac{5}{8}$ **13.** $\frac{33}{48}$ **14.** $\frac{1}{16}$

15. $\frac{6}{9}$ **16.** $\frac{8}{9}$ **17.** $\frac{1}{3}$ **18.** $\frac{5}{12}$ **19.** $\frac{2}{11}$ **20.** $\frac{10}{11}$

21. $5\frac{1}{2}$ **22.** $6\frac{1}{8}$ **23.** $1\frac{3}{16}$ **24.** $1\frac{5}{6}$ **25.** $3\frac{3}{40}$ **26.** $8\frac{7}{25}$

27. $\frac{3}{16}$ **28.** $\frac{7}{9}$ **29.** $\frac{10}{25}$ **30.** $\frac{3}{11}$ **31.** $\frac{7}{8}$ **32.** $\frac{1}{9}$

33. $\frac{1}{12}$ **34.** $\frac{7}{40}$ **35.** $\frac{9}{11}$ **36.** $1\frac{1}{6}$ **37.** $3\frac{2}{9}$ **38.** $4\frac{7}{8}$

Critical Thinking

Is the statement *always true, sometimes true,* or *never true?* Give
examples to support your answer.

39. A terminating decimal is less than 1.

40. A decimal that does not terminate has a remainder of zero.

Mixed Applications

41. A pipe that weighs 15 kg has a lead content
of 3 kg. Rename $\frac{3}{15}$ as a decimal.

42. One pipe has a lead content of 0.035.
Another pipe has a lead content of
0.35. Which pipe has more lead?

43. One pipe is 19.5 m long. How many
sections of pipe can be made from this
piece if each section is 1.5 m long?

44. Pipe connectors cost $2.79 each.
Estimate the cost of 150 connectors.

UNDERSTANDING A CONCEPT
Ordering Mixed Numbers and Decimals

A. Craig and Sally are doing a report on natural and synthetic gems for their science class. Craig learned that the world's largest natural emerald is 18.35 carats. Sally read in a magazine article about a synthetic emerald that is $18\frac{3}{8}$ carats. Which is larger, the natural emerald or the synthetic one?

You can compare 18.35 and $18\frac{3}{8}$ using fractions or decimals.

Fractions	Decimals
$18\frac{3}{8} = 18\frac{15}{40}$	$18\frac{3}{8} = 18\frac{375}{1,000} = 18.375$
$18.35 = 18\frac{35}{100} = 18\frac{7}{20} = 18\frac{14}{40}$	18.35
$18\frac{15}{40} > 18\frac{14}{40}$, so $18\frac{3}{8} > 18.35$.	$18.375 > 18.35$, so $18\frac{3}{8} > 18.35$.

The synthetic emerald is larger.

1. Which is greater, $3\frac{3}{4}$ or 3.8? Which method did you use? Why?

B. Often you can compare decimals and fractions mentally.

Order these numbers from greatest to least: 0.5, $\frac{5}{16}$, and $0.\overline{5}$.

Look at the decimals. Since $0.\overline{5} = 0.555 \ldots$, $0.\overline{5} > 0.5$.

Look at the fraction. Since $0.5 = \frac{1}{2}$ and $\frac{5}{16} < \frac{1}{2}$, $0.5 > \frac{5}{16}$.

The numbers in order from greatest to least are $0.\overline{5}$, 0.5, and $\frac{5}{16}$.

2. Which is greater, 35.45 or $35\frac{3}{8}$? How do you know?

TRY OUT Write the letter of the correct answer. Order the numbers from greatest to least.

3. $25\frac{1}{2}$, $25\frac{3}{4}$, 25.55

    a. $25\frac{3}{4}$, 25.55, $25\frac{1}{2}$

    b. 25.55, $25\frac{1}{2}$, $25\frac{3}{4}$

    c. $25\frac{1}{2}$, 25.55, $25\frac{3}{4}$

    d. $25\frac{3}{4}$, $25\frac{1}{2}$, 25.55

4. 0.06, $0.0\overline{6}$, $\frac{3}{5}$

    a. $\frac{3}{5}$, 0.06, $0.0\overline{6}$

    b. 0.06, $0.0\overline{6}$, $\frac{3}{5}$

    c. $\frac{3}{5}$, $0.0\overline{6}$, 0.06

    d. $0.0\overline{6}$, $\frac{3}{5}$, 0.06

5. $11\frac{7}{12}$, 11.59, $11\frac{1}{2}$

    a. $11\frac{7}{12}$, 11.59, $11\frac{1}{2}$

    b. $11\frac{1}{2}$, 11.59, $11\frac{7}{12}$

    c. 11.59, $11\frac{7}{12}$, $11\frac{1}{2}$

    d. $11\frac{1}{2}$, $11\frac{7}{12}$, 11.59

PRACTICE

Which is greater?

6. $\frac{3}{4}$, $\frac{2}{3}$

7. 0.8, $0.\overline{8}$

8. $\frac{3}{5}$, $\frac{14}{25}$

9. 0.666, $\frac{2}{3}$

10. $5\frac{3}{4}$, 5.8

11. $2\frac{7}{9}$, $2\frac{4}{5}$

12. $8\frac{1}{3}$, $8\frac{2}{7}$

13. 13.325, $13\frac{3}{8}$

Write in order from greatest to least.

14. 4.078, 4.708, 4.78

15. $2\frac{1}{2}$, 2.499, $2.\overline{5}$

16. $4\frac{6}{8}$, 4.8, $4\frac{6}{9}$

17. $\frac{3}{4}$, $\frac{5}{7}$, 0.777

18. $\frac{4}{5}$, $0.\overline{8}$, 0.95

19. $\frac{9}{10}$, $\frac{2}{3}$, $\frac{13}{15}$

20. $11\frac{1}{40}$, $11\frac{3}{1,600}$, 11.02

21. 8.555, $8\frac{5}{9}$, 8.5

22. 0.68, 0.678, $\frac{11}{16}$

23. $4\frac{4}{5}$, $4\frac{5}{6}$, 4.4

24. $1\frac{7}{8}$, 1.8, 1.08

25. $2\frac{5}{6}$, 2.66, $2\frac{2}{3}$

26. $6\frac{2}{3}$, 6.6, 6.7, $6\frac{4}{7}$

27. 0.3, 0.33, $\frac{1}{2}$, $\frac{1}{3}$

28. 1.749, $1\frac{3}{4}$, $\frac{37}{20}$, $\frac{5}{3}$

Compare. Write >, <, or =.

29. $\frac{6}{13}$ ● $\frac{8}{13}$

30. $\frac{90}{50}$ ● 1.45

31. $7\frac{1}{3}$ ● 7.3

32. $\frac{3}{5}$ ● $\frac{2}{3}$

33. 7.63 ● $7\frac{2}{3}$

34. $\frac{7}{8}$ ● $\frac{6}{7}$

35. $\frac{9}{4}$ ● 2.25

36. $\frac{12}{7}$ ● $1\frac{2}{7}$

37. $\frac{19}{20}$ ● $\frac{9}{10}$

38. 6.45 ● $6\frac{4}{7}$

39. $\frac{2}{3}$ ● $\frac{6}{9}$

40. $\frac{11}{8}$ ● 1.5

Critical Thinking

41. Which is greater, $\frac{7}{6}$ or $\frac{7}{5}$? $\frac{9}{5}$ or $\frac{9}{14}$? How can you compare fractions with the same numerator and different denominators?

42. Which is greater, $\frac{3}{5}$ or $\frac{4}{5}$? How can you compare fractions with the same denominator but different numerators?

Mixed Applications

Solve. Which method did you use?

43. A 4.5-carat diamond was sold for $399 per carat. For how much did the diamond sell?

44. The largest diamond in the world is 3,106 carats. Using the fact that 1 carat is equivalent to 200 mg, find the weight of the diamond in grams.

45. A Russian prince once purchased a 199-carat diamond for $450,000. About how much did the prince spend per carat?

46. *Write a problem* that involves comparing two decimals and a fraction. Solve your problem. Ask others to solve it.

ESTIMATION
MENTAL MATH
CALCULATOR
PAPER/PENCIL

PROBLEM SOLVING

Strategy: Solving a Simpler Problem

A. Lee is a mathemagician. As part of his act he asks a person to call out any number from 1 through 10. Then he asks this person to name a power of the number from 1st through 99th. He can tell the ones digit in the answer almost instantly. What will Lee say is the ones digit in 9^{37}?

Make a plan.

Look at lesser powers of 9. Find a pattern that you can use for greater powers of 9.

Try the plan.

$9^1 = 9$ $\qquad$ $9^2 = 81$ $\qquad$ $9^3 = 729$ $\qquad$ $9^4 = 6,561$ $\qquad$ $9^5 = 59,049$

1. Look at the ones digit in each power. What pattern do you see?

2. **What if** you know that the power is an even number? What will be the ones digit?

Lee will say the ones digit in 9^{37} is 9.

B. Stacey wants Lee to name the ones digit in 7^{21}.

Make a plan.

Look at lesser powers of 7. Find a pattern that you can use for greater powers of 7.

Try the plan.

$7^1 = \qquad 7$	$7^2 = \qquad 49$	$7^3 = \qquad 343$	$7^4 = \qquad 2,401$
$7^5 = 16,807$	$7^6 = 117,649$	$7^7 = 823,543$	$7^8 = 5,764,801$

3. Look at the ones digit in each power. What pattern do you see?

4. Into which position in the cycle does the exponent 21 fall? Why?

5. What will Lee say is the ones digit in 7^{21}?

6. What is the ones digit in 7^{18}? Why?

7. What is the ones digit in 7^{52}?

8. Calculate the following powers of 8.
   $8^1 = \blacksquare$ $8^2 = \blacksquare$ $8^3 = \blacksquare$ $8^4 = \blacksquare$ $8^5 = \blacksquare$ $8^6 = \blacksquare$ $8^7 = \blacksquare$ $8^8 = \blacksquare$

9. What pattern do you see?

10. What is the ones digit in 8^{83}? Why?

PRACTICE

Use a simpler problem to solve.

11. You want to try Lee's mathemagic tricks. Calculate the first six powers of 2. Describe the pattern you find. How could you use the pattern to find the ones digit in 2^{19}?

12. You know the patterns for powers of 2, 7, 8, and 9. Find the patterns for the powers of 3 and 4. How could you use these patterns in your act?

13. The receipts from the mathemagic show are locked in the school safe. The 3-digit combination is the power of a number and ends in 9. What is the combination?

14. The crowd in the auditorium started with one person and doubled every minute. After how many minutes would there be 16,384 people? How can you find the answer using patterns?

Strategies and Skills Review

Solve. Use mental math, estimation, a calculator, or paper and pencil.

15. Lee is driving 140 mi to his next show. Last time he averaged 55 mph. Should he over- or underestimate how long it will take him to get to the show this time? What is his estimate?

16. Lee describes a tree in his act. The tree starts with 1 branch. In one week that branch grows 2 branches. In the second week those branches each grow 2 branches. At the end of four weeks, how many branches does the tree have?

17. A person who made up a combination to a safe in the magic shop liked patterns. What is the missing number in the combination?
3 12 31 ▉ 99

18. Lee did a total of 45 tricks in 3 consecutive shows. For each show he performed 7 fewer tricks than in the previous show. How many tricks did he do in each show?

19. There are 4 magic assistants. They shared equally the $60 they earned. Two other shows each brought them $16, which they also shared. How much did each assistant earn?

20. *Write a problem* that requires solving a simpler pattern problem to find a solution. Ask others to solve it.

COLLECTOR'S *Thoughts*

Estimating

A. The world's largest bottle cap collection contains 38,750 bottle caps.

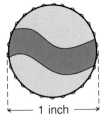

The average bottle cap is 1 inch in diameter.

1 inch

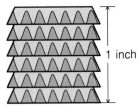

1 inch

A stack of 6 bottle caps is 1 inch high.

Use a calculator to help you solve these problems.

1. Suppose you wanted to display the entire bottle cap collection. Do you think all the bottle caps could fit on the back wall of your classroom? Why or why not?

2. Suppose your bulletin board is 18 inches wide. What length (rounded to the nearest tenth of a foot) of bulletin board would you need to display the entire collection? What assumptions did you make to find an answer?

3. Imagine that you stacked the entire collection. How high would the stack reach (to the nearest tenth of a foot)?

4. Design a box large enough to contain the entire collection. What would the dimensions be (rounded to the nearest inch)? Explain your reasoning.

5. What if you wanted the box to be in the shape of a cube? What dimensions would you use?

B. Many people collect and trade baseball cards. In fact, a man in New Jersey has collected 1 million baseball cards.

The dimensions of a baseball card are 2.5 × 3.5 in.

6. If the whole collection were spread out on a baseball field, how many square inches would the collection cover? To the nearest whole number, how many square feet is that?

7. Suppose you laid the cards out end to end. How many inches long would the line be? How many feet (to the nearest foot)? Is that more or less than 50 miles? How many miles more or less?

8. How many feet can you walk in 10 seconds? Experiment to find out. At that rate, how many seconds would it take you to walk the entire length of your baseball card road? How many minutes is that (to the nearest minute)? If you walked 8 hours a day, would it take you more or less than a week? Explain.

9. Suppose the collector decided to sell the cards for $.15 each. How much money (in dollars) would he get?

10. Suppose the collector decided to give the cards away at the rate of 250 per day. How many days would it take to give away the entire collection? If the giveaway started on January 1, 1991, in what year would it end?

11. How could you determine the weight of the whole collection if all you had was a postage scale?

12. Do you collect anything? Make up some questions about your collection. Ask a friend to solve them.

UNDERSTANDING A CONCEPT

Estimating Sums and Differences

A. A highway crew was painting center lines on a highway. In the first hour, they painted $12\frac{3}{4}$ miles of center lines. In the second hour, they painted $12\frac{1}{5}$ miles. About how many miles of center lines did the crew paint on the highway in the two-hour period?

Estimate $12\frac{3}{4} + 12\frac{1}{5}$.

Here are two ways to estimate the sum:

Rounding to the Nearest Whole Number

$12\frac{3}{4} \longrightarrow \quad 13$ **Think:** $\frac{3}{4} > \frac{1}{2}$ Round up.

$+ 12\frac{1}{5} \longrightarrow + 12$ $\frac{1}{5} < \frac{1}{2}$ Round down.

$\overline{ 25}$

Front-End Estimation

$12\frac{3}{4}$ **Think:** Use the whole-number part.

$+ 12\frac{1}{5}$

$\overline{ 24}$

The crew painted about 24 or 25 miles of center lines.

1. How can you adjust the front-end estimate to make it closer to the exact sum?

B. You can also use the rounding and front-end methods to estimate differences.

Estimate: $12\frac{1}{8} - 8\frac{2}{3}$.

Rounding to the Nearest Whole Number

$12\frac{1}{8} \longrightarrow \quad 12$

$- 8\frac{2}{3} \longrightarrow - 9$

$\overline{ 3}$

Front-End Estimation

$12\frac{1}{8}$

$- 8\frac{2}{3}$

$\overline{ 4}$

2. Is the exact answer greater than or less than the front-end estimate of 4? How can you tell?

TRY OUT

Estimate by rounding.

3. $12\frac{2}{9} + \frac{9}{10} + 18\frac{1}{4}$ **4.** $15\frac{11}{12} - 10\frac{1}{8}$ **5.** $17\frac{3}{8} + 13\frac{1}{4}$

Estimate by using the front digits.

6. $7\frac{3}{5} + 8\frac{5}{6} + \frac{5}{12}$ **7.** $25\frac{3}{10} - 10\frac{8}{9}$ **8.** $17\frac{7}{9} - 9\frac{1}{3}$

PRACTICE

Estimate by rounding.

9. $1\frac{1}{2} + 3\frac{2}{3}$

10. $7\frac{11}{12} + 5\frac{4}{15} + 9\frac{7}{10}$

11. $51\frac{5}{18} + \frac{7}{8} + 27\frac{3}{20}$

12. $16\frac{7}{12} - 8\frac{1}{3}$

13. $19\frac{2}{7} - 11\frac{8}{9}$

14. $40\frac{1}{5} - 20\frac{7}{9}$

Estimate by using the front digits.

15. $8\frac{4}{2} + 6\frac{1}{3}$

16. $17\frac{2}{3} + \frac{7}{12} + 9\frac{1}{8}$

17. $8\frac{2}{5} + \frac{11}{12} + 12\frac{13}{16}$

18. $18\frac{5}{6} - 9\frac{3}{10}$

19. $5\frac{7}{8} - \frac{3}{16}$

20. $42\frac{1}{5} - 29\frac{7}{12}$

Estimate.

21. $4\frac{1}{8} + 11\frac{6}{7} + \frac{5}{9}$

22. $15\frac{4}{11} - 12\frac{7}{9}$

23. $16\frac{9}{13} + 20\frac{2}{5} + \frac{5}{6}$

24. $3\frac{5}{9} + 8\frac{7}{12} + 3\frac{5}{6}$

25. $7\frac{1}{11} - 2\frac{5}{8}$

26. $9\frac{7}{8} - \frac{5}{6}$

27. $4\frac{2}{5} + 6\frac{5}{6} + 10\frac{3}{8}$

28. $15\frac{7}{9} + \frac{11}{12} + \frac{3}{10}$

29. $16\frac{5}{8} - 9\frac{1}{2}$

Estimate to compare. Write > or <.

30. $4\frac{6}{7} + 1\frac{8}{9} + \frac{2}{5}$ ● 6

31. $9\frac{11}{12} - 2\frac{12}{13}$ ● 6

32. $78\frac{47}{50} - 20\frac{1}{20}$ ● 60

Critical Thinking

33. When rounding a fraction to one or zero, the first step is to determine whether the fraction is greater than, equal to, or less than one-half. How would you round a fraction to one, one-half, or zero?

Mixed Applications

Solve. Did you find an estimate or exact answer?

34. Sandra worked on a highway construction crew for 12 weeks. If she made $12.88 per hour and worked 40 hours a week each week, how much did she earn?

35. A contractor bid $3.8 million to resurface and widen 25 miles of road. How much per mile would it cost to resurface and widen the road?

36. The painting crew had $53\frac{2}{3}$ mi of center lines to paint. If they completed $24\frac{2}{9}$ mi, did they finish at least half of the painting?

37. A contractor is fined $3,400 per day for each day that a job runs beyond the promised finish date. If a job runs 18 days late, about how much money will the contractor be fined?

Adding and Subtracting Fractions

A. Alexa works part-time in a model shop. She worked $\frac{3}{5}$ hour on Monday making a model plane. On Tuesday she worked $\frac{5}{6}$ hour. How many hours did she work in all on the model?

Add: $\frac{3}{5} + \frac{5}{6}$

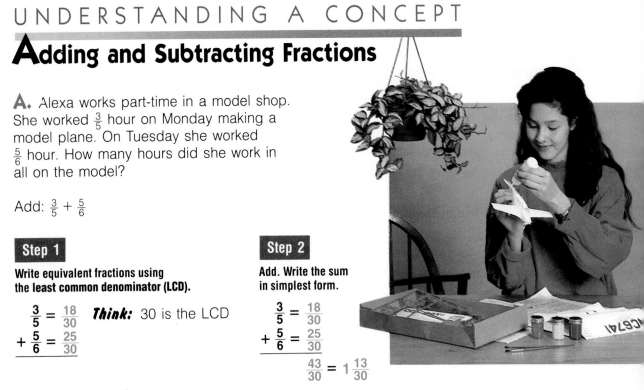

Step 1

Write equivalent fractions using the least common denominator (LCD).

$\frac{3}{5} = \frac{18}{30}$ **Think:** 30 is the LCD

$+ \frac{5}{6} = \frac{25}{30}$

Step 2

Add. Write the sum in simplest form.

$\frac{3}{5} = \frac{18}{30}$

$+ \frac{5}{6} = \frac{25}{30}$

$\frac{43}{30} = 1\frac{13}{30}$

Alexa worked $1\frac{13}{30}$ hours.

1. Do you need to use the LCD to write equivalent fractions? What is the advantage of using the LCD?

2. **What if** you wanted to find $\frac{7}{8} + \frac{3}{5} + \frac{1}{8} + \frac{2}{5}$? How could you find the sum mentally?

B. You can subtract fractions using the least common denominator.

Subtract: $\frac{2}{3} - \frac{3}{8}$

Step 1

Write equivalent fractions using the least common denominator.

$\frac{2}{3} = \frac{16}{24}$

$- \frac{3}{8} = \frac{9}{24}$

Step 2

Subtract. Write the difference in in simplest form if necessary.

$\frac{2}{3} = \frac{16}{24}$

$- \frac{3}{8} = \frac{9}{24}$

$\frac{7}{24}$

So $\frac{2}{3} - \frac{3}{8} = \frac{7}{24}$.

TRY OUT   Find the sum or difference in simplest form.

3. $\frac{1}{2} + \frac{1}{3}$

4. $\frac{11}{12} + \frac{3}{8}$

5. $\frac{5}{6} - \frac{1}{2}$

6. $\frac{3}{4} - \frac{3}{5}$

PRACTICE

Add or subtract. Write the answer in simplest form.

7. $\dfrac{1}{5}$
   $+\dfrac{3}{5}$

8. $\dfrac{4}{7}$
   $+\dfrac{2}{7}$

9. $\dfrac{5}{9}$
   $+\dfrac{1}{3}$

10. $\dfrac{6}{7}$
    $+\dfrac{3}{14}$

11. $\dfrac{7}{12}$
    $+\dfrac{5}{6}$

12. $\dfrac{11}{12}$
    $-\dfrac{7}{12}$

13. $\dfrac{5}{6}$
    $-\dfrac{1}{6}$

14. $\dfrac{7}{8}$
    $-\dfrac{1}{8}$

15. $\dfrac{7}{8}$
    $-\dfrac{3}{4}$

16. $\dfrac{9}{16}$
    $-\dfrac{3}{8}$

17. $\dfrac{3}{4}$
    $+\dfrac{2}{3}$

18. $\dfrac{7}{8}$
    $-\dfrac{1}{5}$

19. $\dfrac{7}{12}$
    $-\dfrac{2}{9}$

20. $\dfrac{11}{15}$
    $+\dfrac{3}{4}$

21. $\dfrac{5}{7}$
    $+\dfrac{7}{9}$

22. $\dfrac{24}{25}$
    $-\dfrac{3}{5}$

23. $\dfrac{17}{20}$
    $-\dfrac{3}{8}$

24. $\dfrac{7}{10}$
    $+\dfrac{2}{3}$

25. $\dfrac{3}{8}$
    $+\dfrac{8}{15}$

26. $\dfrac{11}{12}$
    $+\dfrac{13}{20}$

27. $\dfrac{5}{9}-\dfrac{1}{8}$

28. $\dfrac{3}{5}+\dfrac{2}{3}+\dfrac{1}{2}$

29. $\left(\dfrac{4}{9}+\dfrac{1}{6}\right)-\dfrac{11}{18}$

30. $\left(\dfrac{5}{8}+\dfrac{1}{2}\right)-\dfrac{7}{12}$

Critical Thinking

31. Can you find three fractions such that two of them are less than $\dfrac{1}{4}$ and the sum of all three is greater than 1? greater than $1\dfrac{1}{2}$? If yes, give examples.

32. Can you find three fractions such that the sum of each pair is less than $\dfrac{1}{2}$ and the sum of all three is greater than 1? If yes, give an example.

Mixed Applications

Solve. Which method did you use?

ESTIMATION
MENTAL MATH
CALCULATOR
PAPER/PENCIL

33. Shirley bought landscaping materials and some track at a train shop. The total cost of her purchase was $124.16. If her rectangular train board measures 4 ft by 8 ft, how much per square foot did she spend?

34. Ed could purchase five cars for his model train for $8.99, $12.75, $8.25, $10.50, and $14.88. He could purchase kits for $4.99 each and make the cars himself. How much would he save by purchasing the kits?

35. Bert is building a model plane. A rectangular piece of the model measures $\dfrac{7}{8}$ in. by $\dfrac{2}{3}$ in. What is the perimeter of the piece?

36. Carla bought 4 new models to add to her collection. She paid $5.99 for each. About how much did she spend in all?

Fractions: Addition and Subtraction   **257**

UNDERSTANDING A CONCEPT

Adding and Subtracting Mixed Numbers

A. Three students in a woodworking class made an antique-style rolltop desk. They made the body of the desk $22\frac{7}{8}$ in. high, and they made the legs $6\frac{1}{2}$ in. high. How high is the desk?

You can add to find the total.

Add: $22\frac{7}{8} + 6\frac{1}{2}$

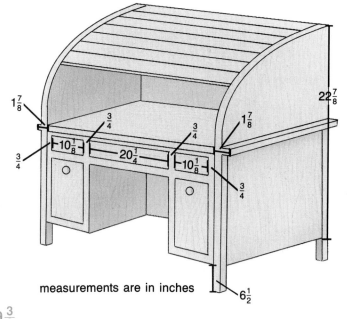

measurements are in inches

Step 1	**Step 2**
Write equivalent fractions using the least common denominator.	Add the fractions. Add the whole numbers. Write the sum in simplest form.

$$22\frac{7}{8} = 22\frac{7}{8}$$
$$+\ 6\frac{1}{2} = \ 6\frac{4}{8}$$

$$22\frac{7}{8} = 22\frac{7}{8}$$
$$+\ 6\frac{1}{2} = \ 6\frac{4}{8}$$
$$28\frac{11}{8} = 29\frac{3}{8}$$

The desk is $29\frac{3}{8}$ in. high.

1. Compare your estimate with the answer. Does your estimate make the answer seem reasonable?

2. **What if** you wanted to find $6\frac{3}{8} + 2\frac{1}{2} + 8\frac{1}{8}$? How could you find the sum mentally?

B. You can also subtract mixed numbers using the least common denominator.

Subtract: $22\frac{7}{8} - 18\frac{2}{3}$

Step 1	**Step 2**
Write equivalent fractions using the least common denominator.	Subtract the fractions. Subtract the whole numbers. Write the difference in simplest form.

$$22\frac{7}{8} = 22\frac{21}{24}$$
$$-\ 18\frac{2}{3} = 18\frac{16}{24}$$

$$22\frac{7}{8} = 22\frac{21}{24}$$
$$-\ 18\frac{2}{3} = 18\frac{16}{24}$$
$$4\frac{5}{24}$$

So $22\frac{7}{8} - 18\frac{2}{3} = 4\frac{5}{24}$.

3. $5\frac{3}{5} + 8\frac{2}{3}$ **4.** $7\frac{5}{7} + 8\frac{2}{7}$ **5.** $17\frac{3}{4} - 9\frac{3}{8}$ **6.** $14\frac{2}{3} - 5\frac{1}{2}$

PRACTICE

Add or subtract. Write the answer in simplest form.

7. $\begin{array}{r} 6\frac{5}{16} \\ +\ 3\frac{7}{16} \\ \hline \end{array}$ **8.** $\begin{array}{r} 1\frac{1}{2} \\ +\ 9\frac{3}{8} \\ \hline \end{array}$ **9.** $\begin{array}{r} 12\frac{3}{5} \\ +\ 7\frac{3}{4} \\ \hline \end{array}$ **10.** $\begin{array}{r} 12\frac{1}{4} \\ +\ 5\frac{2}{3} \\ \hline \end{array}$ **11.** $\begin{array}{r} 16\frac{9}{10} \\ +\ 13\frac{5}{8} \\ \hline \end{array}$

12. $\begin{array}{r} 8\frac{5}{9} \\ -\ 4\frac{2}{9} \\ \hline \end{array}$ **13.** $\begin{array}{r} 9\frac{3}{4} \\ -\ 1\frac{1}{4} \\ \hline \end{array}$ **14.** $\begin{array}{r} 14\frac{7}{8} \\ -\ 3\frac{2}{3} \\ \hline \end{array}$ **15.** $\begin{array}{r} 16\frac{3}{8} \\ -\ 8\frac{1}{8} \\ \hline \end{array}$ **16.** $\begin{array}{r} 21\frac{11}{12} \\ -\ 3\frac{1}{4} \\ \hline \end{array}$

17. $\begin{array}{r} 27\frac{1}{2} \\ +\ 21\frac{7}{12} \\ \hline \end{array}$ **18.** $\begin{array}{r} 12\frac{1}{3} \\ -\ 8\frac{1}{5} \\ \hline \end{array}$ **19.** $\begin{array}{r} 15\frac{7}{12} \\ -\ 12\frac{3}{8} \\ \hline \end{array}$ **20.** $\begin{array}{r} 21\frac{5}{6} \\ +\ 4\frac{1}{4} \\ \hline \end{array}$ **21.** $\begin{array}{r} 27\frac{9}{10} \\ -\ 20\frac{3}{4} \\ \hline \end{array}$

22. $12\frac{2}{5} - 9\frac{1}{3}$ **23.** $21\frac{7}{8} + 13\frac{3}{5}$ **24.** $20\frac{3}{5} - 12\frac{7}{16}$

25. $6\frac{1}{4} + 3\frac{3}{8} + 1\frac{7}{16}$ **26.** $\left(12\frac{3}{4} - 8\frac{1}{6}\right) + 2\frac{1}{2}$ **27.** $\left(8\frac{7}{10} + 6\frac{1}{2}\right) - 3\frac{1}{5}$

Show how you can add the numbers mentally.

28. $6\frac{1}{2} + 3\frac{3}{4} + 7\frac{1}{2} + 8\frac{2}{3} + 1\frac{1}{4}$ **29.** $4\frac{3}{8} + 7\frac{1}{4} + 2\frac{1}{8} + 6\frac{1}{2} + 7\frac{1}{4}$

Mixed Applications

30. Find the total width of the antique-style rolltop desk the students made on page 258.

31. Bob spent $198.45 on materials to make a table. If he sold the table for $600, how much profit did he make?

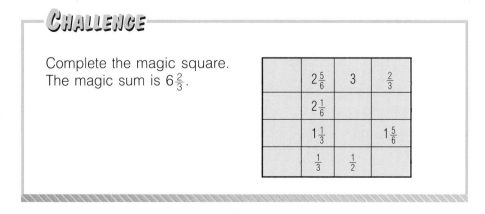

CHALLENGE

Complete the magic square.
The magic sum is $6\frac{2}{3}$.

$2\frac{5}{6}$	3	$\frac{2}{3}$
$2\frac{1}{6}$		
$1\frac{1}{3}$		$1\frac{5}{6}$
$\frac{1}{3}$	$\frac{1}{2}$	

UNDERSTANDING A CONCEPT

Renaming Before Subtracting

A. Sue kept track of the value of her ABS stock. One day the high for one share of the stock was $40 and the low was $38\frac{5}{8}$. By how much did the price of a share change that day?

You can subtract to find the answer.

Subtract: $40 - \$38\frac{5}{8}$

Step 1	Step 2
Rename the whole number as a mixed number.	**Subtract the fractions. Subtract the whole numbers. Write the difference in simplest form.**
$\$40 = \$39\frac{8}{8}$ $- \$38\frac{5}{8} = \$38\frac{5}{8}$	$\$40 = \$39\frac{8}{8}$ $- \$38\frac{5}{8} = \$38\frac{5}{8}$ $\$1\frac{3}{8}$

The stock price changed by $\$1\frac{3}{8}$ during that day.

1. Why did you need to rename $40 in Step 1?

B. Sometimes you need to rename twice when subtracting mixed numbers.

Subtract: $38\frac{5}{8} - 36\frac{3}{4}$

Step 1	Step 2	Step 3
Write equivalent fractions using the least common denominator.	**Rename if necessary.**	**Subtract the fractions. Subtract the whole numbers. Write the difference in simplest form.**
$38\frac{5}{8} = 38\frac{5}{8}$ $- 36\frac{3}{4} = 36\frac{6}{8}$	$38\frac{5}{8} = 38\frac{5}{8} = 37\frac{13}{8}$ $- 36\frac{3}{4} = 36\frac{6}{8} = 36\frac{6}{8}$	$38\frac{5}{8} = 38\frac{5}{8} = 37\frac{13}{8}$ $- 36\frac{3}{4} = 36\frac{6}{8} = 36\frac{6}{8}$ $1\frac{7}{8}$

So $38\frac{5}{8} - 36\frac{3}{4} = 1\frac{7}{8}$.

2. Why did you need to rename $38\frac{5}{8}$ in Step 2? Tell how you renamed it.

3. How would you rename $38\frac{1}{2}$ so that you could subtract $36\frac{3}{4}$ from it?

Find the difference in simplest form.

4. $25 - 18\frac{5}{6}$ **5.** $100 - 56\frac{3}{4}$ **6.** $20\frac{1}{4} - 5\frac{5}{6}$ **7.** $15\frac{1}{8} - 10\frac{2}{5}$

PRACTICE

Write the answer in simplest form.

8. 8
$\underline{-\ 7\frac{3}{10}}$

9. 13
$\underline{-\ 11\frac{11}{12}}$

10. 6
$\underline{-\ 3\frac{9}{10}}$

11. 19
$\underline{-\ 14\frac{3}{4}}$

12. 49
$\underline{-\ 18\frac{1}{6}}$

13. $7\frac{1}{2}$
$\underline{-\ 3\frac{4}{5}}$

14. $15\frac{1}{6}$
$\underline{-\ 8\frac{5}{12}}$

15. $15\frac{1}{4}$
$\underline{-\ 11\frac{7}{16}}$

16. $27\frac{3}{7}$
$\underline{-\ 12\frac{13}{14}}$

17. $21\frac{1}{2}$
$\underline{-\ 18\frac{5}{6}}$

18. 20
$\underline{-\ 14\frac{3}{11}}$

19. $28\frac{1}{2}$
$\underline{-\ 17\frac{3}{5}}$

20. $15\frac{1}{6}$
$\underline{-\ 14\frac{3}{10}}$

21. 35
$\underline{-\ 16\frac{73}{100}}$

22. $56\frac{2}{3}$
$\underline{-\ 18\frac{7}{8}}$

23. $19\frac{2}{3} - 15\frac{7}{8}$ **24.** $23 - 15\frac{5}{7}$ **25.** $29 - 18\frac{11}{12}$

26. $\left(56 - 24\frac{3}{5}\right) - 7\frac{1}{2}$ **27.** $\left(28\frac{1}{2} - 19\frac{7}{12}\right) - 7\frac{1}{6}$ **28.** $60 - \left(5\frac{1}{4} - 3\frac{5}{6}\right)$

Critical Thinking

29. Malcolm found $40 - 8\frac{3}{7}$ mentally by thinking $(40 - 9) + \frac{4}{7} = 31 + \frac{4}{7} = 31\frac{4}{7}$. Was he correct? Why or why not? Will his method always work?

Mixed Applications

Solve.

30. Eleanor bought stock in a mining company at $\$16\frac{7}{8}$ per share. She sold the stock at $\$20\frac{1}{4}$. How much profit per share did Eleanor make on the sale?

31. Mario recorded the closing price of one stock on Monday through Friday: $\$26\frac{5}{8}$, $\$27\frac{1}{2}$, $\$28$, $\$25\frac{1}{4}$, and $\$26\frac{1}{8}$. Make a line graph to show the closing prices.

Mixed Review

Find the answer. Which method did you use?

MENTAL MATH
CALCULATOR
PAPER/PENCIL

32. 3.4×1.09 **33.** 0.5×3.402 **34.** 23.8×3.25

35. $(8 \times 10^8) \times (4 \times 10^6)$ **36.** $0.008 \times 25,000$ **37.** 8.02×21.6

38. $2.5 \times \$3.88$ **39.** 500×0.0016 **40.** 0.25×12.36

UNDERSTANDING A CONCEPT

Solving Equations: Adding and Subtracting Fractions

A. Keith and George were hiking along the $8\frac{1}{2}$-mi trail to Worthewalk Pond. They eventually reached a trail marker showing that the pond was still $5\frac{3}{4}$ mi away. How far had they hiked?

You can find how far they hiked by writing and solving an equation. Recall that to solve an equation you must isolate the variable using inverse operations. You can solve an addition equation by subtracting the same number from both sides of the equation.

Let n = how far they hiked.

$n + 5\frac{3}{4}$ = the total distance.

Solve.

$$n + 5\frac{3}{4} = 8\frac{1}{2}$$

Think: $5\frac{3}{4}$ is added to n.
To isolate n, subtract $5\frac{3}{4}$ from both sides.

$$n + 5\frac{3}{4} - 5\frac{3}{4} = 8\frac{1}{2} - 5\frac{3}{4}$$

Simplify.

$$n = 2\frac{3}{4}$$

Check your answer by substituting $2\frac{3}{4}$ in the original equation.

$$n + 5\frac{3}{4} = 8\frac{1}{2}$$

$$2\frac{3}{4} + 5\frac{3}{4} \overset{?}{=} 8\frac{1}{2}$$

$$8\frac{1}{2} = 8\frac{1}{2} \quad \text{It checks.}$$

The boys had hiked $2\frac{3}{4}$ mi.

B. You can solve a subtraction equation by adding the same number to each side of the equation.

Solve.

$$n - 1\frac{1}{4} = 5\frac{1}{8}$$

Think: $1\frac{1}{4}$ is subtracted from n.
To isolate n, add $1\frac{1}{4}$ to both sides.

$$n - 1\frac{1}{4} + 1\frac{1}{4} = 5\frac{1}{8} + 1\frac{1}{4}$$

Simplify.

$$n = 6\frac{3}{8}$$

Check your answer by substituting $6\frac{3}{8}$ in the original equation.

$$n - 1\frac{1}{4} = 5\frac{1}{8}$$

$$6\frac{3}{8} - 1\frac{1}{4} \overset{?}{=} 5\frac{1}{8}$$

$$5\frac{1}{8} = 5\frac{1}{8} \quad \text{It checks.}$$

TRY OUT Solve the equation. Check your solution.

1. $n + \frac{1}{3} = \frac{5}{6}$

2. $n + \frac{2}{5} = 1\frac{1}{2}$

3. $n - \frac{1}{5} = \frac{3}{10}$

4. $n - 2\frac{2}{3} = 5\frac{1}{4}$

PRACTICE

Solve the equation. Check your solution.

5. $n + \frac{1}{6} = \frac{2}{3}$

6. $n + \frac{1}{3} = \frac{7}{8}$

7. $n + \frac{3}{4} = 3$

8. $n + 2\frac{4}{5} = 4\frac{1}{3}$

9. $n - \frac{1}{4} = \frac{1}{8}$

10. $n - \frac{5}{6} = \frac{3}{4}$

11. $n - 1\frac{3}{4} = 4$

12. $n - 5\frac{7}{8} = 2\frac{1}{6}$

13. $n - \frac{3}{4} = 8\frac{1}{2}$

14. $n + \frac{5}{8} = 2$

15. $n - 2 = \frac{3}{5}$

16. $n - \frac{1}{2} = 12\frac{3}{4}$

17. $n - 1\frac{1}{6} = \frac{2}{3}$

18. $n + \frac{1}{5} = 7\frac{1}{10}$

19. $n + 11\frac{3}{8} = 14\frac{5}{8}$

20. $n + 4 = 5\frac{1}{3}$

21. $n - 1\frac{1}{2} = \frac{1}{3}$

22. $n + \frac{2}{5} = \frac{7}{8}$

23. $n - \frac{1}{5} = \frac{2}{3}$

24. $n - 1\frac{1}{5} = \frac{3}{4}$

Write an equation for the problem. Solve the equation.

25. The sum of a number and $\frac{1}{2}$ is equal to 3. Find the number.

26. When $\frac{3}{4}$ is subtracted from a number, the result is $1\frac{1}{2}$. Find the number.

27. When $\frac{1}{5}$ is added to a number, the sum is $2\frac{3}{10}$. Find the number.

28. If 5 is subtracted from a number, the result is $1\frac{2}{3}$. What is the number?

Write a problem that can be solved by finding the solution of the equation.

29. $n - \frac{3}{4} = \frac{3}{8}$

30. $n + \frac{2}{3} = 5$

31. $n - 1\frac{1}{2} = 6\frac{1}{4}$

32. $n + 6\frac{2}{3} = 8\frac{13}{15}$

Critical Thinking

Without solving, decide if n is greater than or is less than 1.

33. $n + \frac{2}{3} = 2$

34. $n - \frac{5}{6} = \frac{1}{3}$

35. $n + 2\frac{1}{5} = 3\frac{1}{10}$

36. $n - \frac{5}{6} = \frac{1}{24}$

Mixed Applications

37. Sally has walked a certain distance. If she walks $1\frac{3}{4}$ mi more, she will have walked $4\frac{1}{4}$ mi. How far has she walked?

38. Fred caught fish that weighed $2\frac{1}{2}$ lb, $3\frac{1}{4}$ lb, $1\frac{7}{8}$ lb, and $2\frac{1}{8}$ lb. Estimate the weight of his entire catch.

Mixed Review

Find the answer. Which method did you use?

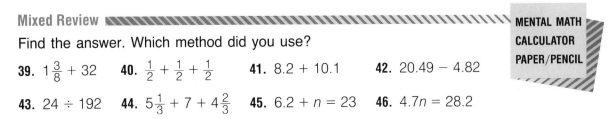

MENTAL MATH
CALCULATOR
PAPER/PENCIL

39. $1\frac{3}{8} + 32$

40. $\frac{1}{2} + \frac{1}{2} + \frac{1}{2}$

41. $8.2 + 10.1$

42. $20.49 - 4.82$

43. $24 \div 192$

44. $5\frac{1}{3} + 7 + 4\frac{2}{3}$

45. $6.2 + n = 23$

46. $4.7n = 28.2$

Fractions: Addition and Subtraction **263**

PROBLEM SOLVING

Strategy: Using Different Strategies

Suppose that you are the coach of a baseball team. The team members have red uniforms and blue uniforms. They play 3 games. In how many different ways can you as coach choose which uniform should be worn for each game?

Plan your strategy.

You realize that at least two different strategies can be used to solve this problem. You can draw a diagram, or you can make an organized list.

Try your plan.

Diagram

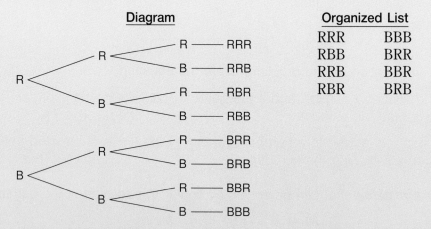

Organized List

RRR	BBB
RBB	BRR
RRB	BBR
RBR	BRB

Both the diagram and the list show that you have eight ways to choose uniforms for the games.

1. Which strategy would you use to solve the problem? Why?

2. **What if** the team members could not wear the same color uniforms twice in a row? In how many ways do you as coach now have to choose the uniforms?

3. **What if** the team members had to wear the same color uniform for all three games? In how many ways do you now have to choose uniforms?

PRACTICE

Use different strategies to solve.

4. Either Sally or Monica plays second base for the team. The team members play 3 games. In how many different ways can the manager choose who will start for the 3 games?

5. Rick can take 1 of 3 trains to the stadium—the L train, the M train, or the N train. There are 4 games. In how many different ways can Rick choose to take a train to the 4 games?

6. The manager of the team chooses 3 players (A, B, and C) to bat first, second, and third. In how many ways can she assign these players to the first 3 places in the batting order?

7. Lyle can sell either popcorn or juice at each game. There are 4 games. In how many different ways can he choose what to sell for the 4 games?

Strategies and Skills Review

Solve. Use mental math, estimation, a calculator, or paper and pencil.

8. The team members are traveling in the team bus. They cover 1,152 mi in 6 days. Then they travel 732 mi in 4 days. They end up traveling 371 mi on the last day. About how far did they travel each day?

9. A pitcher throws a curve and a fast ball. The members of the other team are trying to predict his pitches. They notice this pattern: CFCCFFCFCC. What would they predict his next 5 pitches to be?

10. The last time uniforms cost $3.65 each to be cleaned. The manager has to get all 18 uniforms cleaned. How should she overestimate or underestimate the total cost?

11. Fred is getting ready to ride his horse. He can ride bareback, with a Western saddle, or with an English saddle. He can use blinders on the horse or leave them off. He can use a blanket or leave it off. How many possible combinations of equipment is that?

12. Sound travels 1,100 ft in 1 second. Juana is sitting 550 ft away from home plate. About how long after the ball hits the bat will she hear the sound?

13. ***Write a problem*** that can be solved using two different strategies. Ask other students to solve it.

COOPERATIVE LEARNING

DECISION MAKING

Problem Solving: Planning a Cable TV Show

SITUATION

The school puts on a 20-minute cable TV show every Monday morning. They have four 5-minute segments. Usually, they tape the segments in advance. Students can suggest topics they would like to have on the schedule. Then the production crew has to decide which suggestions to use for each show. Rita, Leon, and Sylvia recommended these schedules.

PROBLEM

Which schedule should the production crew use?

DATA

Cable TV SUBJECT: Planning for Today's Show

SCHEDULE

	RITA	LEON	SYLVIA
8:00–8:05	THE PRESIDENT SPEAKS–Student council president on upcoming events	MUSIC–Video of one of the top ten songs for the past week	SPORTS SCENE– Announcements of sports events for the week
8:05–8:10	THE PRINCIPAL IDEA– Interview with the principal about important school issues	SCHOOL NEWS–Student reporter presents school events (not sports) in a news format.	TALENT SEARCH– Performances by students with an emphasis on music and humor
8:10–8:15	SPORTS TALK–5 coaches talk for 1 minute each about their teams and upcoming games.	FUN FIVE–Students produce humorous skit about some aspect of school life.	LIVE CAM–Crew with live camera goes into classrooms and asks students for their opinions.
8:15–8:20	REVIEWS–Student reporters review movies, places to eat, and so on.	SPORTS NEWS–Student reporter presents school sports in a news format.	OUR OPINION– Students' points of view on important issues

USING THE DATA

What fraction of each schedule is devoted to sports?

1. Rita's Schedule   **2.** Leon's Schedule   **3.** Sylvia's Schedule

What fraction of each schedule is devoted to music or performance?

4. Rita's Schedule   **5.** Leon's Schedule   **6.** Sylvia's Schedule

What fraction of each schedule is devoted to interviews?

7. Rita's Schedule   **8.** Leon's Schedule   **9.** Sylvia's Schedule

MAKING DECISIONS

10. Which schedule should they choose to have the most music or performance?

11. Which schedule looks as if it would be the easiest to produce? Why?

12. Which schedule looks as if it would be the most difficult to produce? Why?

13. *What if* the producers decide they want performances by students? Which schedule should they avoid?

14. Which schedule would you choose? Why?

15. Would you change the order of the schedule? If so, show how.

16. *Write a list* of other factors the producers should consider.

17. Draw up your own schedule. Explain why you chose each segment.

Math and Music

A note in music lasts for a specific number of beats. This number may include a fraction.

Half note (♩) two beats   Quarter note (♩) one beat

Eighth note (♪) $\frac{1}{2}$ beat   Sixteenth note (♬) $\frac{1}{4}$ beat

A *dot* after a note lengthens the note by half its value. For example, ♩. is equal to three beats. A *tie* (⌣) adds the value of the notes together.

Some notes are emphasized more than the others. In the song above, these *accents* (>) fall between the beats. This is called *syncopation*.

The meter signature of $\frac{4}{4}$ means there are four beats in each measure.

What if you clap on each beat of the song? What syllables are sung on the beats in measure 2?

Think: On beat 1 is the syllable *Jer-*. The syllable *i-* comes after beat 1 and continues into the first half of beat 2. The syllable *-cho* comes after beat 2 and continues through beats 3 and 4.

ACTIVITIES

1. Work with a partner. Copy the song. Below each note write its length. Check the answers by addition. Each measure should equal 4 beats.

2. Circle the note or notes in measure 1 that add up to one beat. Find the length of the accented notes.

Computer Exploration: Fractions and Decimals

It is easy to determine whether fractions such as $\frac{2}{3}$, $\frac{1}{9}$, or $\frac{3}{5}$ are terminating or repeating decimals. Can the same thing be said of fractions such as $\frac{13}{97}$ or $\frac{11}{2,048}$?

You can use the computer program FRACTIONS UNLIMITED to explore fractions and their decimal equivalents. The program will display the decimal equivalent for any fraction, showing up to 200 digits to the right of the decimal point.

AT THE COMPUTER

First find the decimal equivalent for the fractions $\frac{1}{3}$, $\frac{1}{4}$, $\frac{13}{5}$, and $\frac{235}{11}$ using paper and pencil or a calculator. Then run the program for each of these fractions to see how it works.

1. Are the fractions $\frac{13}{97}$ and $\frac{11}{2,048}$ repeating or terminating decimals? Could you have determined this using a calculator only? Why or why not? Try out several other fractions of your own. (Do not use fractions with denominators greater than 175 for this part of the activity.) Keep track of which ones terminate and which ones repeat.

2. Examine the fractions $\frac{1}{9}$, $\frac{1}{99}$, and $\frac{1}{999}$. Describe the pattern in the way their decimals repeat. Predict what $\frac{1}{9,999}$ will look like as a decimal. Then check your prediction.

3. Examine the fractions $\frac{3}{9}$ and $\frac{37}{99}$. Predict what $\frac{7}{9}$ and $\frac{46}{99}$ will look like as decimals. Then check your predictions.

4. Repeat what you did in Problem 2 using the fractions $\frac{1}{11}$, $\frac{1}{101}$, and $\frac{1}{1,001}$. Make your prediction for $\frac{1}{10,001}$ and then check it.

5. Find a fraction whose denominator is less than 97 and has a repeating section greater than 20 digits long.

6. Examine the fractions $\frac{1}{2}$, $\frac{1}{3}$, $\frac{1}{4}$, $\frac{1}{5}$, . . . , $\frac{1}{98}$, $\frac{1}{99}$, $\frac{1}{100}$. Keep track of which decimals repeat and which terminate. Do you see any pattern or possible rule to explain which ones terminate? If so, test your pattern or rule with some other fractions.

Fractions: Addition and Subtraction **269**

EXTRA PRACTICE

Equivalent Fractions, page 241

Find three fractions equivalent to the given fraction.

1. $\frac{7}{9}$
2. $\frac{5}{7}$
3. $\frac{4}{5}$
4. $\frac{1}{3}$
5. $\frac{30}{40}$
6. $\frac{9}{100}$

Find the missing number.

7. $\frac{2}{5} = \frac{n}{25}$
8. $\frac{6}{15} = \frac{n}{45}$
9. $\frac{49}{56} = \frac{n}{8}$
10. $\frac{36}{48} = \frac{3}{n}$
11. $\frac{48}{80} = \frac{n}{5}$

12. $\frac{9}{16} = \frac{27}{n}$
13. $\frac{1}{6} = \frac{20}{n}$
14. $\frac{6}{6} = \frac{n}{8}$
15. $\frac{8}{14} = \frac{40}{n}$
16. $\frac{7}{8} = \frac{n}{32}$

Write the fraction in simplest form.

17. $\frac{6}{9}$
18. $\frac{9}{18}$
19. $\frac{15}{20}$
20. $\frac{18}{24}$
21. $\frac{25}{30}$
22. $\frac{30}{90}$

23. $\frac{64}{80}$
24. $\frac{81}{90}$
25. $\frac{21}{21}$
26. $\frac{75}{100}$
27. $\frac{125}{250}$
28. $\frac{160}{280}$

Mixed Numbers and Improper Fractions, page 243

Rename as an improper fraction in simplest form.

1. $8\frac{2}{3}$
2. $5\frac{7}{8}$
3. $12\frac{1}{4}$
4. $2\frac{5}{9}$
5. $4\frac{8}{11}$
6. $3\frac{5}{7}$

7. $5\frac{11}{12}$
8. $24\frac{1}{2}$
9. $11\frac{3}{5}$
10. $4\frac{53}{100}$
11. $3\frac{4}{15}$
12. $7\frac{9}{10}$

Rename as a whole number or as a mixed number in simplest form.

13. $\frac{5}{2}$
14. $\frac{9}{6}$
15. $\frac{17}{4}$
16. $\frac{26}{8}$
17. $\frac{25}{11}$
18. $\frac{29}{7}$

19. $\frac{42}{9}$
20. $\frac{36}{10}$
21. $\frac{54}{12}$
22. $\frac{130}{25}$
23. $\frac{195}{50}$
24. $\frac{875}{100}$

Fractions, Mixed Numbers, and Decimals, page 245

Rename the fraction or the mixed number as a decimal.

1. $5\frac{1}{2}$
2. $2\frac{3}{5}$
3. $\frac{3}{4}$
4. $6\frac{7}{10}$
5. $\frac{19}{25}$
6. $30\frac{17}{20}$

7. $13\frac{3}{50}$
8. $4\frac{7}{8}$
9. $7\frac{9}{10}$
10. $8\frac{59}{250}$
11. $3\frac{21}{500}$
12. $19\frac{2}{125}$

Rename the decimal as a fraction or as a mixed number in simplest form.

13. 0.9
14. 0.37
15. 3.5
16. 0.65
17. 8.75
18. 4.84

19. 35.125
20. 0.4
21. 16.875
22. 0.73
23. 6.015
24. 11.075

EXTRA PRACTICE

Terminating and Repeating Decimals, page 247

Rename as a decimal. Use a bar to show a repeating decimal.

1. $\frac{7}{20}$
2. $\frac{3}{50}$
3. $\frac{7}{8}$
4. $\frac{9}{48}$
5. $\frac{5}{16}$

6. $\frac{7}{9}$
7. $\frac{1}{4}$
8. $\frac{4}{9}$
9. $3\frac{1}{6}$
10. $\frac{11}{12}$

11. $\frac{4}{11}$
12. $\frac{8}{11}$
13. $6\frac{1}{2}$
14. $4\frac{5}{8}$
15. $2\frac{7}{16}$

16. $\frac{5}{6}$
17. $2\frac{7}{40}$
18. $8\frac{9}{25}$
19. $\frac{9}{16}$
20. $\frac{7}{12}$

21. $\frac{11}{40}$
22. $\frac{7}{11}$
23. $5\frac{1}{3}$
24. $9\frac{3}{8}$
25. $3\frac{4}{7}$

26. $17\frac{2}{3}$
27. $6\frac{7}{12}$
28. $5\frac{3}{4}$
29. $10\frac{1}{3}$
30. $\frac{5}{11}$

Ordering Mixed Numbers and Decimals, page 249

Write in order from greatest to least.

1. 5.017, 5.71, 5.701
2. $\frac{2}{3}, \frac{5}{8}, 0.633$
3. $\frac{3}{4}, 0.76, 0.85$
4. $\frac{5}{6}, \frac{3}{4}, \frac{11}{15}$

5. $6\frac{5}{9}, 6.6, 6.65, 6\frac{5}{8}$
6. $7\frac{4}{5}, 7\frac{7}{9}, 7.78, 7\frac{5}{7}$
7. $0.1, 0.11, \frac{1}{9}, \frac{1}{8}$
8. $\frac{47}{10}, 4.751, 4\frac{4}{5}, \frac{33}{7}$

9. $3.2, 3\frac{1}{3}, 3.3, 3\frac{2}{5}$
10. $\frac{1}{17}, 0.17, 0.7, \frac{2}{7}$
11. $\frac{9}{11}, 0.911, 0.\overline{9}, 1.9$
12. $2\frac{4}{7}, 2.\overline{6}, 2.6, 2.67$

Compare. Write $>$, $<$, or $=$.

13. $\frac{5}{11} \bullet \frac{7}{11}$
14. $\frac{40}{25} \bullet 1.65$
15. $5\frac{2}{3} \bullet 5.6$
16. $\frac{4}{5} \bullet \frac{3}{4}$
17. $\frac{17}{30} \bullet \frac{8}{15}$

18. $8.45 \bullet 8\frac{4}{9}$
19. $\frac{3}{4} \bullet \frac{9}{12}$
20. $\frac{17}{6} \bullet 2.8\overline{3}$
21. $\frac{8}{5} \bullet \frac{8}{7}$
22. $7\frac{5}{7} \bullet 7.71$

23. $\frac{13}{17} \bullet \frac{15}{19}$
24. $11.6 \bullet 11.\overline{6}$
25. $1\frac{2}{7} \bullet 1.3$
26. $\frac{2}{7} \bullet \frac{1}{4}$
27. $\frac{1}{4} \bullet 0.253$

Problem—Solving Strategy: Solving a Simpler Problem, page 251

Use a simpler problem to solve.

1. In its first year Brett's apple orchard had 3 trees that yielded fruit. In the following years the number of trees that yielded fruit tripled. After how many years would Brett have 729 trees yielding fruit?

2. Doreen collected the receipts from the charity fashion show. She locked the receipts in her safe. The 6-digit combination to the safe is the power of a number and ends in 1. What is the combination?

EXTRA PRACTICE

Estimating Sums and Differences, page 255

Estimate.

1. $2\frac{1}{5} + 4\frac{5}{6}$

2. $3\frac{13}{15} + 5\frac{5}{12} + 8\frac{9}{10}$

3. $82\frac{9}{20} + \frac{4}{5} + 34\frac{7}{25}$

4. $18\frac{5}{6} - 9\frac{1}{4}$

5. $17\frac{4}{9} - 12\frac{6}{7}$

6. $30\frac{1}{6} - 10\frac{6}{7}$

7. $9\frac{1}{4} + 5\frac{1}{3}$

8. $15\frac{4}{5} + \frac{7}{15} + 8\frac{1}{4}$

9. $7\frac{2}{3} + \frac{5}{12} + 13\frac{15}{16}$

10. $16\frac{2}{3} - 7\frac{3}{10}$

11. $4\frac{11}{16} - \frac{3}{8}$

12. $33\frac{1}{6} - 19\frac{11}{12}$

13. $5\frac{1}{6} + 9\frac{7}{8} + \frac{5}{9}$

14. $12\frac{3}{7} - 8\frac{7}{8}$

15. $18\frac{6}{13} + 20\frac{4}{5} + \frac{1}{6}$

16. $4\frac{3}{5} + 7\frac{11}{20} + 3\frac{2}{3}$

Adding and Subtracting Fractions, page 257

Add or subtract. Write the answer in simplest form.

1. $\frac{1}{7}$ $+ \frac{5}{7}$

2. $\frac{1}{6}$ $+ \frac{3}{6}$

3. $\frac{1}{6}$ $+ \frac{2}{3}$

4. $\frac{4}{5}$ $+ \frac{3}{4}$

5. $\frac{5}{12} + \frac{2}{3}$

6. $\frac{7}{8} - \frac{5}{8}$

7. $\frac{8}{9} - \frac{5}{9}$

8. $\frac{9}{12} - \frac{3}{12}$

9. $\frac{5}{8} - \frac{1}{3}$

10. $\frac{11}{16} - \frac{5}{8}$

11. $\frac{5}{6} + \frac{3}{4}$

12. $\frac{5}{6} - \frac{2}{5}$

13. $\frac{7}{12} - \frac{3}{12}$

14. $\frac{11}{15} + \frac{5}{6}$

15. $\frac{6}{7} + \frac{5}{8}$

16. $\frac{21}{25} - \frac{2}{5}$

17. $\frac{9}{10} - \frac{5}{8}$

18. $\frac{7}{20} + \frac{2}{3}$

19. $\frac{5}{8} + \frac{7}{15}$

20. $\frac{11}{15} + \frac{17}{20}$

Adding and Subtracting Mixed Numbers, page 259

Add or subtract. Write the answer in simplest form.

1. $8\frac{3}{5} + \frac{2}{5}$

2. $5\frac{2}{3} + 3\frac{3}{4}$

3. $12\frac{7}{8} + 4\frac{1}{4}$

4. $13\frac{1}{2} + 4\frac{3}{5}$

5. $15\frac{5}{6} + 12\frac{1}{8}$

6. $8\frac{9}{16} - 2\frac{5}{16}$

7. $9\frac{5}{6} - 4\frac{1}{6}$

8. $13\frac{9}{10} - 2\frac{3}{10}$

9. $11\frac{3}{8} - 7\frac{1}{5}$

10. $16\frac{5}{12} - 9\frac{3}{8}$

11. $13\frac{3}{8} - 8\frac{1}{6}$

12. $21\frac{1}{3} + 5\frac{7}{24}$

13. $22\frac{3}{4} + 19\frac{1}{8}$

14. $18\frac{3}{4} - 9\frac{3}{10}$

15. $14\frac{11}{12} - 7\frac{1}{6}$

16. $22\frac{8}{9} + 26\frac{2}{3}$

17. $15\frac{5}{9} - 8\frac{1}{2}$

18. $43\frac{5}{6} + \frac{1}{8}$

19. $15\frac{1}{5} + 12\frac{3}{5}$

20. $16\frac{5}{6} - 7\frac{1}{4}$

Renaming Before Subtracting, page 261

Subtract. Write the answer in simplest form.

1. 8
   $- 3\frac{2}{3}$

2. 15
   $- 11\frac{5}{12}$

3. 7
   $- 4\frac{7}{10}$

4. $16\frac{1}{4}$
   $- 12\frac{5}{8}$

5. $39\frac{1}{6} - 16\frac{2}{3}$

6. $19 - 10\frac{7}{15}$

7. $37\frac{1}{3} - 15\frac{4}{5}$

8. $14\frac{3}{8} - 12\frac{5}{6}$

9. $45\frac{2}{5} - 17\frac{5}{6}$

10. $58 - 19\frac{17}{20}$

11. $18\frac{5}{6} - 16\frac{3}{4}$

12. $\left(22 - 16\frac{7}{9}\right)$

13. $27 - \left(18\frac{3}{10} - 7\frac{4}{5}\right)$

14. $50 - \left(5\frac{5}{14} - 3\frac{6}{7}\right)$

15. $25\frac{1}{6} - \left(12\frac{2}{9} - 6\frac{3}{4}\right)$

16. $30 - 16\frac{8}{11}$

17. $38\frac{1}{3} - 19\frac{7}{8}$

18. $45\frac{1}{2} - 29\frac{3}{4}$

19. $50\frac{2}{7} - 27\frac{11}{14}$

20. $35\frac{1}{2} - 24\frac{4}{5}$

Solving Equations: Adding and Subtracting Fractions, page 263

Solve the equation. Check your solution.

1. $n + \frac{1}{4} = \frac{5}{8}$

2. $n - \frac{1}{3} = \frac{7}{8}$

3. $n - 1\frac{5}{6} = 36$

4. $n + 2\frac{3}{4} = 5\frac{1}{6}$

5. $n - \frac{5}{8} = 7\frac{1}{2}$

6. $n + \frac{3}{4} = 3$

7. $n + \frac{1}{6} = 5\frac{5}{12}$

8. $n - 3 = \frac{4}{7}$

9. $n + \frac{1}{5} = 5\frac{1}{3}$

10. $n + \frac{3}{5} = \frac{5}{6}$

11. $n - \frac{2}{3} = 12\frac{1}{2}$

12. $n - 1\frac{1}{5} = \frac{9}{10}$

13. $n - 1\frac{2}{5} = \frac{7}{15}$

14. $n + \frac{2}{5} = \frac{7}{8}$

15. $n - 1\frac{2}{3} = \frac{5}{6}$

16. $n + 10\frac{5}{7} = 14\frac{2}{7}$

Problem–Solving Strategy: Using Different Strategies, page 265

Use different strategies to solve.

1. Jason can take either Buster or K.C. to 4 dog shows. In how many different ways can Jason choose who will go to the 4 shows?

2. Fifi can wear her red jeweled collar, her silver studded collar, or her braided leather collar at each dog show. In how many different ways can Fifi appear at the 2 dog shows?

3. Dusty, Lucky, and Sparky will win first-, second-, and third-place ribbons. In how many ways can these dogs place first, second, and third?

4. Bo can do one of 4 tricks in his class at the show: Rollover, Sit, Laydown, Handshake. There are 3 classes. In how many different ways can Bo do tricks in the 3 classes?

Practice PLUS

KEY SKILL: Terminating and Repeating Decimals (Use after page 247.)

Level A

Rename as a decimal. Use a bar to show a repeating decimal.

1. $\frac{4}{5}$
2. $\frac{6}{10}$
3. $\frac{7}{20}$
4. $\frac{1}{8}$
5. $\frac{7}{40}$

6. $\frac{5}{16}$
7. $\frac{1}{11}$
8. $\frac{2}{9}$
9. $\frac{5}{9}$
10. $\frac{7}{12}$

11. $\frac{1}{12}$
12. $\frac{2}{11}$
13. $3\frac{1}{4}$
14. $1\frac{3}{4}$
15. $2\frac{5}{6}$

16. $1\frac{9}{50}$
17. $2\frac{5}{8}$
18. $3\frac{1}{2}$
19. $3\frac{7}{8}$
20. $2\frac{2}{3}$

21. Karen and Steve spent $\frac{1}{10}$ of the time reading the map for the scavenger hunt. Write $\frac{1}{10}$ as a decimal.

Level B

Rename as a decimal. Use a bar to show a repeating decimal.

22. $\frac{2}{3}$
23. $\frac{3}{25}$
24. $\frac{16}{50}$
25. $\frac{9}{20}$
26. $\frac{11}{40}$

27. $\frac{3}{16}$
28. $1\frac{10}{50}$
29. $3\frac{2}{30}$
30. $4\frac{10}{11}$
31. $2\frac{9}{15}$

32. $6\frac{7}{9}$
33. $1\frac{1}{33}$
34. $\frac{7}{15}$
35. $\frac{8}{9}$
36. $\frac{17}{18}$

37. $\frac{28}{45}$
38. $\frac{11}{12}$
39. $\frac{3}{22}$
40. $2\frac{2}{11}$
41. $5\frac{15}{16}$

42. Jerry and Nancy spent $\frac{3}{20}$ of the time on the scavenger hunt finding the first item. Rename $\frac{3}{20}$ as a decimal.

Level C

Rename as a decimal. Use a bar to show a repeating decimal.

43. $\frac{7}{20}$
44. $\frac{5}{6}$
45. $\frac{1}{7}$
46. $\frac{5}{24}$
47. $\frac{8}{9}$

48. $\frac{5}{11}$
49. $\frac{29}{48}$
50. $\frac{13}{16}$
51. $1\frac{1}{15}$
52. $4\frac{5}{33}$

53. $3\frac{6}{7}$
54. $\frac{7}{22}$
55. $\frac{37}{45}$
56. $\frac{17}{30}$
57. $2\frac{7}{21}$

58. $\frac{11}{15}$
59. $5\frac{4}{7}$
60. $\frac{17}{80}$
61. $4\frac{2}{3}$
62. $8\frac{3}{7}$

63. Bill and Sarah spent $\frac{2}{15}$ of the time on the scavenger hunt finding the last item. Rename $\frac{2}{15}$ as a decimal.

KEY SKILL: Adding and Subtracting Mixed Numbers (Use after page 259.)

Level A

Add or subtract. Write the answer in simplest form.

1. $6\frac{1}{8} + 2\frac{5}{8}$

2. $7\frac{4}{15} + 1\frac{2}{15}$

3. $4\frac{3}{4} + 5\frac{3}{4}$

4. $13\frac{1}{2} + 4\frac{3}{4}$

5. $15\frac{1}{2} + 13\frac{1}{3}$

6. $9\frac{5}{8} - 5\frac{1}{8}$

7. $8\frac{9}{10} - 1\frac{5}{10}$

8. $12\frac{2}{3} - 7\frac{1}{3}$

9. $14\frac{3}{4} - 8\frac{1}{2}$

10. $21\frac{4}{5} - 8\frac{3}{5}$

11. $17\frac{1}{2} + 12\frac{5}{6}$

12. $12\frac{7}{10} - 3\frac{1}{2}$

13. $22\frac{2}{3} + 3\frac{5}{6}$

14. $15\frac{11}{12} - 11\frac{1}{6}$

15. $28\frac{2}{3} - 20\frac{1}{9}$

16. $7\frac{3}{8} + 6\frac{3}{4}$

17. A share of stock was selling for $9\frac{3}{4}$. It dropped $1\frac{1}{8}$. What is the cost of one share now?

Level B

Add or subtract. Write the answer in simplest form.

18. $4\frac{1}{6} + 5\frac{2}{3}$

19. $17\frac{3}{5} - 9\frac{7}{10}$

20. $13\frac{3}{8} + 5\frac{3}{4}$

21. $16\frac{2}{3} - 7\frac{5}{9}$

22. $17\frac{2}{7} + 12\frac{13}{14}$

23. $10\frac{1}{2} - 6\frac{3}{4}$

24. $12\frac{7}{8} - 3\frac{3}{4}$

25. $22\frac{10}{13} + 5\frac{19}{26}$

26. $41\frac{3}{11} + \frac{17}{22}$

27. $11\frac{1}{8} - 8\frac{3}{4}$

28. $8\frac{3}{10} + 5\frac{3}{5}$

29. $27\frac{9}{10} - 18\frac{2}{5}$

30. $15\frac{3}{4} - 7\frac{11}{12}$

31. $23\frac{1}{2} + 9\frac{3}{4}$

32. $14\frac{7}{8} - 9\frac{1}{2}$

33. $13\frac{15}{16} - 8\frac{3}{4}$

34. Yesterday a stock closed $27\frac{3}{4}$. Today it closed $1\frac{7}{8}$ higher. What is the price now?

Level C

Add or subtract. Write the answer in simplest form.

35. $5\frac{7}{8} + 19\frac{1}{5}$

36. $2\frac{5}{6} + 8\frac{3}{4}$

37. $12\frac{3}{8} - 7\frac{4}{5}$

38. $15\frac{5}{6} - 6\frac{7}{9}$

39. $19\frac{1}{2} + 4\frac{5}{7}$

40. $25\frac{9}{10} - 17\frac{3}{4}$

41. $22\frac{1}{9} - 16\frac{5}{6}$

42. $27\frac{2}{9} + 6\frac{1}{4}$

43. $15\frac{3}{5} + 18\frac{2}{7}$

44. $20\frac{3}{7} - 11\frac{4}{5}$

45. $7\frac{1}{3} - 3\frac{2}{11}$

46. $8\frac{1}{15} - 3\frac{2}{3}$

47. $7\frac{4}{9} + 3\frac{7}{12} + 2\frac{1}{6}$

48. $\left(12\frac{5}{6} - 2\frac{2}{5}\right) + 16\frac{2}{15}$

49. $\left(14\frac{5}{6} - 7\frac{1}{4}\right) + 3\frac{3}{8}$

50. $\left(7\frac{1}{2} + 5\frac{1}{7}\right) - 3\frac{5}{14}$

51. $\left(3\frac{2}{3} - 1\frac{1}{7}\right) - \frac{4}{21}$

52. $\left(16\frac{3}{8} - 5\frac{3}{4}\right) - 1\frac{15}{16}$

53. A share of stock was selling for $25\frac{1}{4}$. Yesterday the price rose $2\frac{5}{8}$. Today it closed $1\frac{1}{2}$ lower. What is the price of the stock now?

CHAPTER REVIEW

LANGUAGE AND MATHEMATICS

Complete the sentences. Use the words in the chart on the right.

1. The sum of a whole number and a fraction is a(n) ▪. *(page 242)*

2. A fraction in which the numerator is greater than the denominator is a(n) ▪. *(page 242)*

3. When adding 2 fractions, the least common multiple of the denominators is the ▪. *(page 256)*

4. In writing a fraction as a decimal, if there is no remainder when you divide, it is a(n) ▪. *(page 246)*

5. ***Write a definition*** or give an example of the words you did not use from the chart.

CONCEPTS AND SKILLS

Find the value of *n*. *(page 240)*

6. $\frac{2}{5} = \frac{n}{25}$

7. $\frac{2}{3} = \frac{n}{12}$

8. $\frac{7}{8} = \frac{n}{56}$

9. $\frac{3}{4} = \frac{n}{100}$

Find the missing number. *(pages 240, 242)*

10. $\frac{9}{11} = \frac{27}{\blacksquare}$

11. $\frac{15}{20} = \frac{\blacksquare}{4}$

12. $10\frac{2}{7} = \frac{\blacksquare}{7}$

13. $8\frac{3}{4} = \frac{\blacksquare}{4}$

Rename as a whole number or as a mixed number in simplest form. *(page 242)*

14. $\frac{19}{4}$

15. $\frac{78}{10}$

16. $\frac{22}{6}$

17. $\frac{375}{25}$

Rename as a decimal. *(pages 244, 246)*

18. $\frac{3}{10}$

19. $\frac{2}{5}$

20. $\frac{1}{3}$

21. $\frac{5}{9}$

Rename as a fraction or mixed number in simplest form. *(page 244)*

22. 0.13

23. 0.65

24. 8.56

25. 4.056

Which is greater? *(page 248)*

26. $\frac{2}{5}, \frac{1}{3}$

27. 0.6, $0.\overline{6}$

28. $5\frac{5}{8}$, 5.5

29. 1.125, $1\frac{2}{9}$

Find the sum or difference in simplest form. *(pages 256, 258, 260)*

30. $\frac{3}{5} - \frac{2}{25}$

31. $\frac{2}{9} + \frac{2}{6}$

32. $6\frac{3}{4} + 7\frac{5}{6}$

33. $6 - \frac{2}{9}$

First round the numbers to the nearest whole number, and then find the sum or difference. *(page 254)*

34. $24\frac{11}{12} + 5\frac{8}{9} + \frac{5}{6}$

35. $45\frac{2}{7} - 40\frac{1}{3}$

36. $2\frac{5}{8} - \frac{2}{9}$

Write in order from greatest to least. *(page 248)*

37. $\frac{2}{7}$, 0.26, $0.\overline{3}$

38. $1\frac{7}{13}$, 1.5, $\frac{22}{13}$

39. $\frac{6}{3}$, $1\frac{2}{3}$, 1.68

Solve the equation. Check your solutions. *(page 262)*

40. $n - 3 = 5\frac{1}{7}$

41. $n + 2\frac{3}{4} = 5\frac{1}{8}$

42. $n + 9\frac{1}{2} = 9\frac{3}{4}$

43. $n - \frac{5}{12} = 2\frac{7}{8}$

44. $n - \frac{3}{8} = 4$

45. $n - 3\frac{1}{5} = 2\frac{3}{4}$

46. $n + 3\frac{2}{3} = 5\frac{2}{7}$

47. $n - 6\frac{2}{3} = 1\frac{3}{4}$

Complete with a whole number. *(page 264)*

48. 360 h = ▇ min

49. 96 h = ▇ d

50. 12 y = ▇ mo

51. 8 min 40 s = ▇ sec

52. 367 min = ▇ h ▇ min

53. 29 h = ▇ d ▇ h

Critical Thinking

54. Can you add two fractions by renaming them with a common denominator that is greater than the LCM? *(page 256)*

55. If two mixed numbers in simplest form are added, and the sum is a whole number, what is the sum of the fractional parts of the numbers? *(page 258)*

56. Al found $100 - 24\frac{2}{9}$ by thinking $(100 - 25) + \frac{7}{9} = 75 + \frac{7}{9} = 75\frac{7}{9}$. Was he correct? *(page 260)*

Mixed Applications

57. Jaye caught fish that weighed $2\frac{1}{4}$ lb, $4\frac{5}{8}$ lb, and $3\frac{1}{2}$ lb. Estimate the total weight of the fish Jaye caught. *(page 254)*

58. Greg lives 4 mi from the beach and $2\frac{1}{4}$ mi from the school. How much farther does he live from the beach than from the school? *(page 260)*

59. The Drama Club is putting on a play for three nights. Either Susan or Norm can take tickets at the door. In how many ways can they arrange who will take the tickets? *(page 264)*

60. The receipts from ticket sales are kept in a safe. The combination is a 4-digit number that is a power of a number and ends in 1. What could the combination be? *(page 250)*

61. After another $\frac{2}{5}$ hours Rejo will have worked for 3 hours. How many hours has he worked already? *(page 263)*

62. Les jogged $\frac{9}{10}$ mi to the park, $\frac{3}{10}$ mi to the school, and $\frac{1}{2}$ mi home. How far did Les jog in all? *(page 256)*

CHAPTER TEST

Estimate the sum or difference by rounding to the nearest whole number.

1. $13\frac{18}{19} + 3\frac{7}{9} + \frac{4}{5}$ **2.** $34\frac{3}{5} - 12\frac{1}{6}$ **3.** $4\frac{6}{13} - \frac{2}{9}$

Find the sum or difference in simplest form.

4. $\frac{3}{4}$ $-\frac{7}{20}$ **5.** $\frac{5}{8}$ $+\frac{11}{12}$ **6.** $8\frac{1}{2}$ $-\frac{3}{4}$ **7.** $1\frac{1}{6}$ $+2\frac{2}{3}$ **8.** 7 $-4\frac{2}{3}$

Solve for n. Write the solution in simplest form.

9. $n + \frac{3}{7} = \frac{5}{7}$ **10.** $n + \frac{2}{3} = 8$ **11.** $n - \frac{1}{2} = \frac{4}{9}$

12. $n - 4 = 7\frac{3}{7}$ **13.** $n + 1\frac{2}{3} = 6\frac{1}{3}$ **14.** $n - 3\frac{5}{8} = 9\frac{7}{12}$

Rename the fraction or mixed number as a decimal.

15. $1\frac{7}{8}$ **16.** $\frac{14}{25}$ **17.** $6\frac{7}{200}$

Order from least to greatest.

18. $7.249, \frac{57}{8}, \frac{29}{4}, 7\frac{3}{8}$ **19.** $16.\overline{6}, 16\frac{9}{13}, 16.66, 16\frac{7}{12}$

Solve.

20. Sara knows that a certain 5-digit number is a power of 7 and that its ones digit also is 7. What is the number?

21. The crowd at the stadium started with one person and doubled every minute. How many minutes before the 65,536 seats were filled?

22. Either Sasha or Nicole will be the starting hitter in each of 4 games of a tournament. In how many ways can they start the games?

23. Lee batted 3 times in the game. He likes to use 3 types of bats. In how many ways could Lee have chosen to use the bats?

24. Miguel may order one type of snack before each game. In how many ways can Miguel choose to order 1 of 3 types of snacks before 2 games?

25. Debby knows that the missing digit in the combination to the safe is the same as the ones digit of 9^{52}. What is the missing digit?

ENRICHMENT FOR ALL

PARADOXES

A mouse stands 1 ft from his hole in the wall. The mouse then moves halfway to the hole. Now he is $\frac{1}{2}$ ft from the hole. He moves half the distance to the hole again. This move leaves him $\frac{1}{4}$ ft from the hole.

Every time the mouse moves, he covers half the distance to the hole.

Copy the table below on a sheet of paper. Write a fraction to show how close to the hole the mouse would be after each move.

Move	1	2	3	4	5	6	7	8
Distance to the Hole	$\frac{1}{2}$ ft	$\frac{1}{4}$ ft	**1.** ▓ ft	**2.** ▓ ft	**3.** ▓ ft	**4.** ▓ ft	**5.** ▓ ft	**6.** ▓ ft

Look for a pattern in your table. After two moves, the mouse is $\frac{1}{2 \times 2}$ ft from the hole.

7. After three moves, is the mouse $\frac{1}{2 \times 2 \times 2}$ ft from the hole?

8. How can you rewrite $2 \times 2 \times 2$ using exponents?

9. After four moves, is the mouse $\frac{1}{2^4}$ ft from the hole?

10. Use exponents to express the mouse's distance from the hole after five moves.

11. What pattern do you see? Does this pattern work for six moves? seven moves?

12. Write a formula to show the mouse's distance to the hole after n moves. Check to see that this formula works for $n = 8$.

13. If the mouse kept moving like this, would he ever reach the hole? Why or why not?

14. Would it make sense to say that, because of this, the mouse could never reach the hole? Why?

15. **_Write a story_** like that of the mouse about something getting closer and closer but never reaching its goal.

CUMULATIVE REVIEW

Choose the letter of the correct answer.

1. $\frac{3.5 \times 10^6}{7.0 \times 10^2}$

   a. 5.0×10^3 **c.** 5.0×10^8
   b. 5.0×10^4 **d.** not given

2. Five objects weigh 0.4, 1.6, 2, 3.1, and 8 oz. What is the mean of their weights?

   a. 6.1 oz   **c.** 3.02 oz
   b. 3.2 oz   **d.** not given

3. Twenty-five fewer than a number x is 25. What is the number?

   a. 0   **c.** 100
   b. 25   **d.** not given

4. $8 + 0.2 \times 0.3$

   a. 2.46   **c.** 8.6
   b. 8.06   **d.** not given

5. A car traveled 55 miles per hour for 5 hours. How far did the car travel?

   a. 11 mi   **c.** 275 mi
   b. 50 mi   **d.** not given

6. Find the prime factorization of 18.

   a. 2×3^2 **c.** 2×9
   b. $2^3 \times 3$ **d.** not given

7. What is the GCF of 6 and 12?

   a. 3   **c.** 72
   b. 12   **d.** not given

8. What is the LCM of 6 and 10?

   a. 2   **c.** 60
   b. 30   **d.** not given

9. What is the next number in the sequence 9, 13, 17, 21, . . . ?

   a. 23
   b. 25
   c. 27
   d. not given

10. Solve for n: $n + \frac{2}{3} = 5\frac{3}{8}$

    a. $6\frac{1}{24}$ **c.** $5\frac{1}{5}$
    b. $4\frac{17}{24}$ **d.** not given

11. Solve for n: $n - 8\frac{4}{5} = \frac{3}{10}$

    a. $1\frac{1}{10}$ **c.** $9\frac{1}{10}$
    b. $8\frac{1}{5}$ **d.** not given

12. Solve for n: $n + \frac{6}{7} = 9$

    a. $9\frac{6}{7}$ **c.** $8\frac{1}{7}$
    b. $8\frac{4}{7}$ **d.** not given

Solve.

13. What is the ones digit in 8^{23}?

    a. 2   **c.** 6
    b. 4   **d.** 8

14. Arbor City started by planting one tree and tripled the number it planted every week. How many weeks before the number of trees planted would reach 2,187?

    a. 6 weeks
    b. 7 weeks
    c. 8 weeks
    d. not given

CHAPTER 8

Fractions: Multiplication and Division

MATH CONNECTIONS: ALGEBRA • CUSTOMARY MEASUREMENT • PROBLEM SOLVING

CARPET PRICES
per square yard

Short Pile	$ 4.99
Soft Pile	$ 6.99
Stain Resistant	$ 8.99
Stain Free	$13.99

1. What information do you see in this picture?
2. How can you use the information?
3. If a room measures 25 yd², about how much will the least expensive carpet cost?
4. Write a problem using the information.

UNDERSTANDING A CONCEPT

Multiplying Fractions

A. Hillsboro has a very strict building code. Because of this code a developer can build on only $\frac{2}{3}$ of a $\frac{3}{4}$-acre lot and must use the rest for landscaping. How much of this lot can the developer use for building?

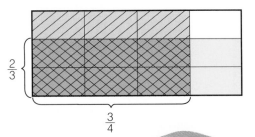

Multiply: $\frac{2}{3} \times \frac{3}{4}$

Step 1	Step 2
Multiply the numerators. Multiply the denominators.	Write the answer in simplest form.
$\frac{2}{3} \times \frac{3}{4} = \frac{6}{12}$	$\frac{6 \div 6}{12 \div 6} = \frac{1}{2}$

The developer can use $\frac{1}{2}$ acre of this lot for building.

1. **What if** there are 9 acres of land and $\frac{2}{5}$ of the land can be used? How many acres can be used?

B. Sometimes you can simplify before you multiply.

Multiply: $8 \times \frac{3}{4}$

Step 1	Step 2	Step 3
Rename the whole number as an improper fraction.	Divide a numerator and a denominator by a common factor.	Multiply the numerators. Multiply the denominators. Write the answer in simplest form.
$8 \times \frac{3}{4} = \frac{8}{1} \times \frac{3}{4}$	$\frac{\overset{2}{\cancel{8}}}{1} \times \frac{3}{\underset{1}{\cancel{4}}}$	$\frac{\overset{2}{\cancel{8}}}{1} \times \frac{3}{\underset{1}{\cancel{4}}} = \frac{6}{1} = 6$
	Think: $4 \div 4 = 1$ $8 \div 4 = 2$	

C. Two numbers whose product is 1 are **reciprocals.**

$$\frac{1}{3} \times \frac{3}{1} = 1 \qquad \frac{3}{5} \times \frac{5}{3} = 1 \qquad 2\frac{1}{2} \times \frac{2}{5} = \frac{5}{2} \times \frac{2}{5} = 1$$

$\frac{1}{3}$ and $\frac{3}{1}$ or 3, $\frac{3}{5}$ and $\frac{5}{3}$ or $1\frac{2}{3}$, $2\frac{1}{2}$ and $\frac{2}{5}$ are reciprocals. 0 has no reciprocal.

To find the reciprocal of a number, interchange the numerator and denominator of its fraction.

TRY OUT

What is the product in simplest form?

2. $\frac{3}{8} \times \frac{14}{15}$

3. $\frac{7}{12} \times 18$

4. $\frac{4}{5} \times \frac{5}{12}$

Find the reciprocal.

5. $\frac{2}{3}$

6. 12

7. $2\frac{1}{3}$

PRACTICE

Multiply. Write the answer in simplest form. Do as many as you can mentally.

8. $\frac{1}{2} \times \frac{3}{5}$

9. $\frac{2}{3} \times 15$

10. $\frac{4}{5} \times 25$

11. $\frac{5}{9} \times 36$

12. $\frac{8}{9} \times \frac{7}{12}$

13. $\frac{3}{5} \times \frac{20}{27}$

14. $\frac{10}{21} \times \frac{7}{20}$

15. $\frac{5}{8} \times \frac{12}{25}$

16. $\frac{9}{16} \times \frac{20}{21}$

17. $\frac{13}{36} \times \frac{21}{26}$

18. $\frac{9}{10} \times \frac{5}{6}$

19. $24 \times \frac{5}{6}$

20. $\frac{4}{5} \times \frac{12}{20}$

21. $4 \times \frac{5}{8}$

22. $\frac{3}{4} \times \frac{8}{15}$

23. $\frac{8}{11} \times 77$

24. $\frac{3}{4} \times \frac{5}{6}$

25. $\frac{2}{3} \times \frac{7}{8}$

26. $\frac{5}{12} \times \frac{8}{15}$

27. $\frac{9}{13} \times 78$

28. $\frac{3}{4} \times \frac{5}{18}$

29. $\frac{9}{14} \times \frac{28}{33}$

30. $\frac{5}{7} \times 49$

31. $\frac{1}{2} \times \frac{5}{6} \times \frac{4}{5}$

32. $\frac{3}{5} \times \frac{4}{7} \times \frac{0}{8}$

Find the reciprocal.

33. $\frac{1}{5}$

34. $\frac{1}{2}$

35. $\frac{2}{3}$

36. 7

37. $3\frac{1}{2}$

38. $1\frac{1}{6}$

39. $\frac{8}{5}$

40. 4

41. $2\frac{3}{5}$

42. $\frac{7}{6}$

43. $\frac{8}{9}$

44. $\frac{10}{3}$

45. Find the product of $\frac{3}{7}$ and $\frac{21}{25}$.

46. Find the product of $\frac{2}{9}$, $\frac{24}{25}$, and $\frac{15}{18}$.

Critical Thinking

47. Can the product of two proper fractions be greater than 1? Why or why not? Give examples to support your answer.

48. What is the reciprocal of a whole number? What number is its own reciprocal?

Mixed Applications

49. A contractor plans to build on $\frac{3}{5}$ of a 15-acre lot. How much acreage does the contractor plan to use for buildings?

50. Erin, a real estate agent, sold houses priced at $49,000; $85,000; $74,500; $12,200; and $53,000. Find the mean price of the houses.

51. Brian sold $\frac{1}{2}$ of a 16-acre plot. He then sold $\frac{2}{3}$ of the remaining piece. How much of the 16 acres remained unsold?

UNDERSTANDING A CONCEPT

Multiplying Fractions by Mixed Numbers

A. Sharon and Ted are helping to clean up a $3\frac{3}{4}$ mi stretch of the river bank near their school. They have completed about $\frac{2}{3}$ of the job. About how many miles have they completed?

You can estimate to find the answer.

Estimate: $\frac{2}{3} \times 3\frac{3}{4}$

Think: Change the mixed number to a whole number that is divisible by the denominator of the fraction.

$$\frac{2}{3} \times 3\frac{3}{4}$$

$$\frac{2}{\underset{1}{3}} \times \overset{1}{3} = 2$$

Sharon and Ted have completed about 2 mi.

1. What is the advantage of changing $3\frac{3}{4}$ to 3 instead of to 4?

B. You can multiply to find the exact answer.

Multiply: $\frac{2}{3} \times 3\frac{3}{4}$

Step 1	Step 2	Step 3
Rename the mixed number as an improper fraction.	Divide a numerator and a denominator by a common factor.	Multiply the fractions.
$\frac{2}{3} \times 3\frac{3}{4} = \frac{2}{3} \times \frac{15}{4}$	$\frac{2}{3} \times \frac{\overset{5}{\cancel{15}}}{\underset{2}{\cancel{4}}}$ (with $\frac{\overset{1}{2}}{3}$)	$\frac{\overset{1}{2}}{\underset{1}{3}} \times \frac{\overset{5}{\cancel{15}}}{\underset{2}{\cancel{4}}} = \frac{5}{2} = 2\frac{1}{2}$

Sharon and Ted have cleaned up $2\frac{1}{2}$ mi of riverbank.

2. Why is the estimate less than the exact answer?

TRY OUT Estimate. Then find the answer in simplest form.

3. $\frac{1}{8} \times 14\frac{2}{5}$ **4.** $\frac{3}{4} \times 15\frac{1}{3}$ **5.** $11\frac{3}{7} \times \frac{3}{5}$ **6.** $\frac{8}{9} \times 10\frac{1}{4}$

PRACTICE

Estimate.

7. $3\frac{7}{8} \times \frac{3}{4}$

8. $\frac{5}{6} \times 25\frac{2}{3}$

9. $\frac{3}{5} \times 27\frac{1}{2}$

10. $\frac{5}{9} \times 16\frac{4}{5}$

11. $20\frac{1}{5} \times \frac{3}{7}$

12. $25\frac{3}{5} \times \frac{2}{9}$

13. $\frac{9}{10} \times 28\frac{2}{3}$

14. $\frac{7}{8} \times 82\frac{3}{5}$

Multiply. Write the answer in simplest form.

15. $\frac{3}{4} \times 1\frac{7}{9}$

16. $\frac{2}{3} \times 2\frac{1}{4}$

17. $\frac{7}{9} \times 5\frac{1}{4}$

18. $1\frac{11}{12} \times 4\frac{4}{5}$

19. $\frac{11}{14} \times 6\frac{6}{11}$

20. $\frac{5}{6} \times 3\frac{7}{10}$

21. $2\frac{8}{9} \times \frac{3}{13}$

22. $\frac{1}{4} \times 11\frac{1}{3}$

23. $\frac{3}{7} \times 12\frac{4}{7}$

24. $25\frac{1}{3} \times \frac{5}{8}$

25. $17\frac{3}{7} \times \frac{3}{4}$

26. $4\frac{2}{3} \times \frac{4}{5}$

27. $\frac{5}{8} \times 3\frac{3}{4}$

28. $\frac{3}{10} \times 2\frac{1}{6}$

29. $6 \times 2\frac{3}{16} \times \frac{4}{5}$

30. $3\frac{1}{7} \times \frac{9}{16} \times \frac{7}{8}$

31. Find the product of $\frac{9}{16}$ and $4\frac{5}{6}$.

32. Find the product of $6\frac{1}{4}$ and $\frac{2}{25}$.

Critical Thinking

33. When you multiply a fraction by a mixed number, is your answer always greater than 1? If no, give an example to support your answer.

Mixed Applications

Solve. Which method did you use?

34. A hiking trail covers $4\frac{1}{2}$ mi. Three groups of students working on a clean-up project agree to clean up $\frac{1}{3}$ of the trail. How many miles will each group clean up?

35. In one state officials estimated that they clean up 28.5 T of trash a year. How many tons of trash do they clean up every month, to the nearest tenth of a ton?

36. Aluminum is selling for $.48 per lb. If students collect 250 lb, about how much will they make?

ESTIMATION
MENTAL MATH
CALCULATOR
PAPER/PENCIL

LOGICAL REASONING

An automobile race takes place on a circular track. The total number of cars in the race is $\frac{1}{3}$ of the number of cars in front of the maroon car, added to $\frac{3}{4}$ of the number of cars behind the maroon car. What is the total number of cars in the automobile race?

UNDERSTANDING A CONCEPT

Multiplying Mixed Numbers

A. When training for a marathon, Kristin runs at a pace of $6\frac{3}{4}$ mi per hour. If she runs $1\frac{2}{3}$ hours each day, how far does she run per day?

Estimate: $1\frac{2}{3} \times 6\frac{3}{4}$

Round each factor to the nearest whole number.

$$1\frac{2}{3} \times 6\frac{3}{4}$$

Think: $2 \quad \times 7 \quad = 14$

Kristin runs about 14 mi per day.

1. Will the exact answer be greater than or less than 14? Why?

B. You can multiply to find the exact answer.

Multiply: $1\frac{2}{3} \times 6\frac{3}{4}$

Step 1	Step 2	Step 3
Rename the mixed numbers as improper fractions.	**Divide a numerator and a denominator by a common factor.**	**Multiply the fractions. Write the answer in simplest form.**
$1\frac{2}{3} \times 6\frac{3}{4} = \frac{5}{3} \times \frac{27}{4}$	$\frac{5}{3} \times \frac{\overset{9}{27}}{4}$	$\frac{5}{\underset{1}{3}} \times \frac{\overset{9}{27}}{4} = \frac{45}{4} = 11\frac{1}{4}$

Kristin runs $11\frac{1}{4}$ mi per day.

TRY **OUT** Estimate. Then multiply to find the exact answer in simplest form.

2. $1\frac{1}{4} \times 3\frac{2}{3}$ **3.** $7\frac{5}{6} \times 4\frac{4}{5}$ **4.** $3\frac{3}{5} \times 1\frac{5}{6}$ **5.** $8\frac{1}{3} \times 1\frac{3}{5}$

PRACTICE

Estimate.

6. $2\frac{4}{5} \times 8\frac{1}{2}$ **7.** $7\frac{3}{8} \times 3\frac{1}{5}$ **8.** $7\frac{6}{11} \times 8\frac{4}{5}$ **9.** $5\frac{2}{9} \times 11\frac{7}{10}$

10. $7\frac{2}{3} \times 9\frac{1}{2}$ **11.** $5\frac{3}{5} \times 6\frac{7}{8}$ **12.** $6\frac{9}{10} \times 8\frac{7}{8}$ **13.** $4\frac{1}{3} \times 11\frac{4}{5}$

Multiply. Write the answer in simplest form.

14. $2\frac{1}{2} \times 3\frac{1}{3}$ **15.** $2\frac{5}{6} \times 1\frac{3}{5}$ **16.** $1\frac{1}{5} \times 2\frac{1}{6}$ **17.** $2\frac{2}{5} \times 1\frac{3}{4}$

18. $3\frac{2}{3} \times 2\frac{1}{11}$ **19.** $6\frac{3}{4} \times 3\frac{2}{9}$ **20.** $3\frac{3}{4} \times 2\frac{2}{5}$ **21.** $4\frac{4}{5} \times 5\frac{7}{8}$

22. $2\frac{7}{8} \times 1\frac{3}{5}$ **23.** $4\frac{5}{7} \times 4\frac{2}{3}$ **24.** $5\frac{1}{3} \times \frac{3}{5} \times 2\frac{1}{2}$ **25.** $\left(2\frac{1}{2} + \frac{3}{4}\right) \times \left(3\frac{2}{3} - \frac{5}{6}\right)$

26. Find the product of $1\frac{5}{8}$ and $3\frac{1}{3}$.   **27.** Find the product of $12\frac{7}{8}$ and 3.5.

Estimate to compare. Write $>$ or $<$.

28. $5\frac{1}{8} \times 4\frac{1}{3} \bullet 20$ **29.** $6\frac{2}{3} \times 5\frac{1}{2} \bullet 42$ **30.** $3\frac{1}{8} \times 5\frac{1}{3} \bullet 20$

Mixed Applications

31. Tom bought a bicycle for $455.98, a helmet for $55.25, and cycling shorts for $19.95. How much did he spend in all for the three items?

32. Steve knows that cross-country skiing burns 610 calories per hour. If he skis for $4\frac{1}{2}$ hours before lunch and $1\frac{1}{4}$ hours afterward, how many calories does he burn?

33. Carla likes to go swimming at her local pool. She swims 40 laps every day. If each lap is 25 m, how far does Carla swim every day?

34. Cathy runs a mile in $8\frac{1}{2}$ minutes. At that rate, how long does it take her to run $3\frac{3}{4}$ mi?

MENTAL MATH

You can use the distributive property to multiply by mixed numbers mentally.

$$5\frac{3}{4} \times 16 = \left(5 + \frac{3}{4}\right) \times 16 = (5 \times 16) + \left(\frac{3}{4} \times 16\right)$$
$$= 80 + 12$$
$$= 92$$

Multiply.

1. $3\frac{1}{2} \times 12$ **2.** $7\frac{2}{3} \times 12$ **3.** $12\frac{3}{5} \times 10$ **4.** $6\frac{5}{8} \times 40$

PROBLEM SOLVING

Strategy: Solving a Simpler Problem

During a reception at the Algoral Embassy, the Chief of Protocol noticed that there were 8 people in the room who did not know one another. The chief would have to arrange a handshake among all these people. How many handshakes is that? How could she keep track of these handshakes?

Plan the strategy.

The chief plans to first solve a simpler problem. She will determine how many handshakes there would be among 5 people.

Try the plan.

The chief draws five dots on a piece of paper.
Then she draws lines to connect all the dots.

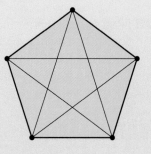

1. How can you use the diagram to determine the number of handshakes among 5 people?

2. How many handshakes would there be among 5 people?

3. Use a diagram to determine how many handshakes there would be among 6 people; among 7 people.

4. What pattern do you notice in the answers to problems 2 and 3?

5. How many handshakes does the chief have to arrange for? How did you determine the answer?

PRACTICE

Solve by using a simpler problem.

6. The entrance wall to the embassy has 10 quivers of arrows. The first quiver has 1 arrow, the second has 2 arrows, and so on up to 10 arrows. Could the embassy personnel put the arrows into 2 piles with the same number of arrows in each pile?

7. The King of Algoral was visiting the embassy. People brought the king 100 boxes of coins. The first box had 1 coin, the second box had 2 coins, and so on. Could the king divide the coins evenly among 2 strongboxes? Why or why not?

8. The chandelier at the reception consisted of four globes suspended from two spots on the ceiling. The globes were all connected with wires to one another and to the spots on the ceiling. How many wires is that?

9. One night the embassy had a very large reception. The Chief of Protocol had to arrange a handshake among each of 10 people. How many handshakes was that?

Strategies and Skills Review

Solve. Use mental math, estimation, a calculator, or paper and pencil.

10. One day 30 buses with 48 people in each bus visited the embassy. Fifty cars arrived: thirteen each held 1 person, eight each held 2, three each held 3, twenty-two each held 4, and four each held 5. Twelve people came on foot. How many people visited the embassy that day?

11. Five members of the Embassy staff went on a biking trip. During the first hour they traveled 10 miles. During each of the next 5 hours they traveled $\frac{1}{2}$ mile less than they did the previous hour. How many miles did they travel in all?

12. The embassy has a total of 72 rooms. The windows in each room measure 4 ft by 8 ft. There are either 2 or 3 doors in a room. There are just as many windows as doors. Can you find the number of windows in the embassy?

13. Is it possible to walk through each door on one floor of your house or apartment once and only once? Draw a diagram to find out.

14. There were 4 tour guides at the embassy—Jim, Olga, Maureen, and Will. A team of 2 guides had to be on duty at all times. How many possible teams of 2 tour guides are there?

15. *Write a problem* that involves solving a simpler problem. Ask other students to solve it.

DEVELOPING A CONCEPT

Dividing Fractions: Using Common Denominators

A. You can use fraction strips to find $\frac{7}{8} \div \frac{1}{8}$.

1. How can you use fraction strips to show $\frac{7}{8}$? to show $\frac{1}{8}$?

2. How many $\frac{1}{8}$s are there in $\frac{7}{8}$? What is $\frac{7}{8} \div \frac{1}{8}$?

3. Use fraction strips to find each quotient.

   a. $\frac{5}{6} \div \frac{1}{6}$ **b.** $\frac{5}{12} \div \frac{1}{12}$ **c.** $4 \div \frac{1}{2}$ **d.** $2 \div \frac{1}{3}$

B. You can also divide fractions by using equivalent fractions.

Divide: $\frac{1}{2} \div \frac{1}{4}$

Step 1	**Step 2**
Rename the numbers with a common denominator.	**Divide the numerators.**
$\frac{1}{2} \div \frac{1}{4} = \frac{2}{4} \div \frac{1}{4}$	$\frac{2}{4} \div \frac{1}{4}$
Think: $\frac{1}{2} = \frac{2}{4}$	***Think:*** $2 \div 1 = 2$
So $\frac{1}{2} \div \frac{1}{4} = 2$.	

4. Use equivalent fractions to find each quotient.

   a. $\frac{5}{6} \div \frac{1}{12}$ **b.** $\frac{3}{5} \div \frac{1}{10}$ **c.** $\frac{3}{4} \div \frac{1}{8}$ **d.** $6 \div \frac{3}{4}$

C. Sometimes you do not get a whole number as a quotient.

Divide: $\frac{3}{8} \div \frac{3}{4}$

Step 1	**Step 2**
Rename the numbers with a common denominator.	**Divide the numerators.**
$\frac{3}{8} \div \frac{3}{4} = \frac{3}{8} \div \frac{6}{8}$	$\frac{3}{8} \div \frac{6}{8}$
Think: $\frac{3}{4} = \frac{6}{8}$	***Think:*** $3 \div 6 = \frac{3}{6} = \frac{1}{2}$
So $\frac{3}{8} \div \frac{3}{4} = \frac{1}{2}$.	

5. Find each quotient.

   a. $\frac{3}{4} \div \frac{7}{8}$ **b.** $\frac{1}{5} \div \frac{2}{3}$ **c.** $\frac{3}{7} \div \frac{3}{5}$ **d.** $\frac{2}{3} \div \frac{3}{4}$

SHARING IDEAS

6. How would you use the method in B to find $\frac{7}{8} \div \frac{3}{4}$?

7. What was your answer?

8. Was this the same answer other students got?

PRACTICE

Divide.

9. $\frac{2}{3} \div \frac{1}{3}$

10. $\frac{4}{5} \div \frac{1}{5}$

11. $\frac{5}{8} \div \frac{1}{8}$

12. $\frac{7}{9} \div \frac{1}{9}$

13. $\frac{9}{10} \div \frac{1}{10}$

14. $\frac{1}{3} \div \frac{1}{6}$

15. $\frac{1}{4} \div \frac{1}{8}$

16. $\frac{1}{5} \div \frac{1}{10}$

17. $\frac{1}{2} \div \frac{1}{6}$

18. $\frac{1}{6} \div \frac{1}{12}$

19. $3 \div \frac{1}{2}$

20. $8 \div \frac{2}{3}$

21. $9 \div \frac{3}{4}$

22. $6 \div \frac{1}{3}$

23. $5 \div \frac{5}{8}$

24. $\frac{1}{3} \div \frac{1}{9}$

25. $\frac{5}{6} \div \frac{1}{12}$

26. $\frac{2}{3} \div \frac{2}{9}$

27. $\frac{5}{6} \div \frac{5}{12}$

28. $\frac{3}{5} \div \frac{3}{10}$

29. $\frac{1}{6} \div \frac{1}{3}$

30. $\frac{1}{10} \div \frac{2}{5}$

31. $\frac{3}{8} \div \frac{3}{4}$

32. $\frac{4}{5} \div \frac{3}{10}$

33. $\frac{7}{8} \div \frac{1}{2}$

34. $\frac{2}{3} \div 3$

35. $\frac{5}{6} \div 4$

36. $\frac{1}{3} \div 3$

37. $12 \div \frac{2}{3}$

38. $4 \div \frac{3}{5}$

39. $\frac{1}{3} \div \frac{2}{3}$

40. $5 \div \frac{1}{4}$

41. $\frac{2}{5} \div \frac{3}{10}$

42. $\frac{2}{3} \div \frac{5}{6}$

43. $\frac{5}{6} \div \frac{1}{2}$

44. $\frac{5}{6} \div \frac{2}{3}$

45. $\frac{4}{7} \div \frac{1}{7}$

46. $4 \div \frac{1}{3}$

47. $\frac{3}{4} \div \frac{1}{2}$

48. $\frac{3}{4} \div \frac{1}{12}$

49. $\frac{1}{2} \div \frac{4}{5}$

50. $\frac{1}{7} \div \frac{3}{10}$

51. $\frac{2}{3} \div \frac{2}{5}$

52. $\frac{3}{4} \div \frac{1}{6}$

53. $\frac{5}{8} \div \frac{1}{3}$

Critical Thinking

54. What can you say about a quotient when you divide a whole number by a fraction less than 1? Give examples to support your answer.

55. What can you say about a quotient when you divide a fraction less than 1 by a fraction less than 1? Give examples to support your answer.

Mixed Applications

Solve. You may need to use the Databank on page 584.

56. Jill earns $240 as a waitress. She saves $\frac{2}{3}$ of her salary. How much does she spend?

57. There are 88 students in the seventh grade. About $\frac{1}{3}$ have been to a local pizza place. About how many students have been there?

58. How many cups of dry ingredients do you need for 24 servings of tapioca pudding?

59. How many cups of tapioca do you need for 4 servings of pudding?

Dividing Fractions: Using Reciprocals

A. You can use a number line and patterns to help you divide by a fraction.

Divide: $6 \div \frac{1}{4}$

The number line shows that there are twenty-four $\frac{1}{4}$s in 6.

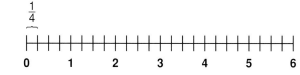

Look at these division and multiplication patterns.

$6 \div \frac{1}{4} = 24$ $6 \times 4 = 24$

$3 \div \frac{1}{4} = 12$ $3 \times 4 = 12$

$2 \div \frac{1}{4} = 8$ $2 \times 4 = 8$

↑——— reciprocals ———↑

Notice that dividing by a fraction is the same as multiplying by its reciprocal.

So $6 \div \frac{1}{4} = 6 \times 4 = 24$.

1. Use reciprocals to find $6 \div \frac{3}{4}$. Use the number line to check your answer.

B. You can also use reciprocals to divide a fraction by a fraction.

Divide: $\frac{7}{9} \div \frac{2}{3}$

Step 1

Multiply by the reciprocal of the divisor.

$\frac{7}{9} \div \frac{2}{3} = \frac{7}{9} \times \frac{3}{2} = \frac{7}{\overset{3}{\cancel{9}}} \times \frac{\overset{1}{\cancel{3}}}{2} = \frac{7}{6}$

So $\frac{7}{9} \div \frac{2}{3} = 1\frac{1}{6}$.

Step 2

Write the answer in simplest form.

$\frac{7}{6} = 1\frac{1}{6}$

2. How would you use reciprocals to find $\frac{6}{11} \div 3$? What is the quotient? (*Hint:* The reciprocal of 3 is $\frac{1}{3}$.)

TRY OUT   Write the letter of the correct answer.

3. $12 \div \frac{3}{4}$ **a.** 9   **b.** 16   **c.** $\frac{1}{9}$ **d.** $\frac{1}{16}$

4. $\frac{2}{3} \div \frac{5}{6}$ **a.** $\frac{4}{5}$ **b.** $1\frac{4}{9}$ **c.** $1\frac{1}{4}$ **d.** $\frac{5}{9}$

5. $\frac{9}{10} \div 6$ **a.** $5\frac{2}{5}$ **b.** $\frac{5}{27}$ **c.** $6\frac{2}{3}$ **d.** $\frac{3}{20}$

6. $\frac{5}{8} \div \frac{5}{12}$ **a.** $\frac{25}{96}$ **b.** $\frac{60}{40}$ **c.** $1\frac{1}{2}$ **d.** $\frac{2}{3}$

PRACTICE

Divide. Write the answer in simplest form.

7. $10 \div \frac{5}{8}$ **8.** $12 \div \frac{3}{5}$ **9.** $2 \div \frac{4}{9}$ **10.** $35 \div \frac{7}{11}$ **11.** $4 \div \frac{11}{12}$

12. $\frac{2}{3} \div \frac{1}{6}$ **13.** $\frac{3}{4} \div \frac{7}{8}$ **14.** $\frac{13}{18} \div \frac{5}{9}$ **15.** $\frac{5}{7} \div \frac{2}{7}$ **16.** $\frac{11}{12} \div \frac{5}{6}$

17. $\frac{3}{4} \div 12$ **18.** $\frac{2}{7} \div \frac{1}{2}$ **19.** $\frac{6}{17} \div 3$ **20.** $\frac{7}{9} \div 21$ **21.** $\frac{3}{8} \div \frac{1}{4}$

22. $\frac{10}{21} \div \frac{5}{21}$ **23.** $\frac{6}{7} \div \frac{4}{5}$ **24.** $\frac{1}{6} \div \frac{11}{12}$ **25.** $16 \div \frac{3}{4}$ **26.** $\frac{25}{31} \div 10$

27. $\frac{9}{16} \div \frac{3}{4}$ **28.** $\frac{7}{12} \div 35$ **29.** $\frac{8}{9} \div 6$ **30.** $18 \div \frac{3}{11}$ **31.** $75 \div \frac{10}{11}$

32. $2 \div \frac{5}{6}$ **33.** $\frac{3}{5} \div \frac{5}{3}$ **34.** $\frac{8}{15} \div 4$ **35.** $\frac{5}{9} \div \frac{3}{5}$ **36.** $6 \div \frac{2}{5}$

37. $\frac{3}{4} \div \frac{3}{8}$ **38.** $24 \div \frac{8}{15}$ **39.** $\frac{5}{8} \div \frac{1}{2}$ **40.** $\frac{2}{5} \div \frac{5}{8}$ **41.** $\frac{1}{4} \div \frac{9}{10}$

Critical Thinking

42. Will the answer to $12 \div \frac{2}{3}$ be greater than 12 or less than 12? Why?

43. Which answer will be greater: $\frac{5}{6} \div \frac{1}{3}$ or $\frac{5}{6} \div 3$? Why?

Mixed Applications

Solve.

44. Lou worked at a nursery part-time one summer. He had $\frac{5}{6}$ lb of seed to put in 10 packages. How much seed could he put in each package?

45. Janet worked at Fabrics and More. She earned $4.35 per hour. One week she earned $165.30. How many hours did she work?

46. Chris worked at an animal shelter one Saturday. She was paid double her hourly wage of $4.55. How much did she earn for 6.5 hours?

47. Sun Li planned to work for 12 weeks one summer at $105 per week. About how much could she earn for the summer?

Mixed Review

Find the answer. Which method did you use?

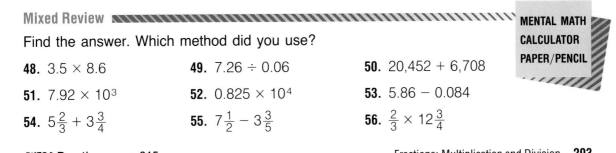

MENTAL MATH
CALCULATOR
PAPER/PENCIL

48. 3.5×8.6 **49.** $7.26 \div 0.06$ **50.** $20,452 + 6,708$

51. 7.92×10^3 **52.** 0.825×10^4 **53.** $5.86 - 0.084$

54. $5\frac{2}{3} + 3\frac{3}{4}$ **55.** $7\frac{1}{2} - 3\frac{3}{5}$ **56.** $\frac{2}{3} \times 12\frac{3}{4}$

FRACTION REACTIONS

Using Number Concepts

A. How good is your "fraction reaction"? Try each problem. The more stars a problem has, the harder it is.

1. A bottle of perfume is one-tenth full. It has $2\frac{1}{2}$ ounces of perfume in it. What is the capacity of the bottle?

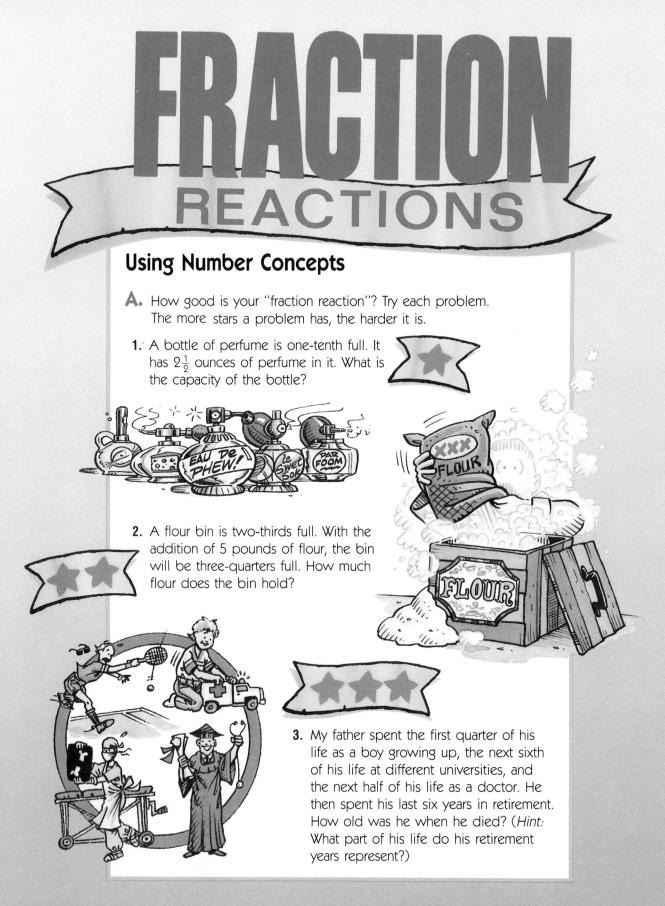

2. A flour bin is two-thirds full. With the addition of 5 pounds of flour, the bin will be three-quarters full. How much flour does the bin hold?

3. My father spent the first quarter of his life as a boy growing up, the next sixth of his life at different universities, and the next half of his life as a doctor. He then spent his last six years in retirement. How old was he when he died? (*Hint:* What part of his life do his retirement years represent?)

4. Each morning, Kathy walks to school at a steady rate. At one-third of the way she passes a bakery, and halfway to school she passes a bookstore. At the bakery, her watch says 7:50, and at the bookstore it says 7:55. At what time does Kathy arrive at her school?

B. By now you are warmed up and ready for a 5-star problem. Good luck.

5. You have a glass of juice in front of you, and you drink one-sixth of it. Then you pour as much water into the glass as you drank of juice. You drink one-third of this mixture and, again, you pour as much water into the glass as you drank of the mixture. Now you drink one-half of the contents of the glass and, for the last time, you fill the glass up with water. When this is done, you drink the whole glass.

Can you tell if you drank more water or more juice, and how much did you drink of each?

Here are some hints if you need them:

- After you filled the glass with water the first time, what part of the mixture was water and what part was juice?

- Then how much of the part that was water did you drink? How much of the part that was juice did you drink?

- How much was left of each?

Continue to reason this way until you solve the problem.

UNDERSTANDING A CONCEPT

Dividing Mixed Numbers

A. Jared is a meteorologist. His records show that the usual rainfall for a 6-month period in Danville is $5\frac{3}{5}$ in. What is the average rainfall per month?

You can divide to find the exact answer.

Divide: $5\frac{3}{5} \div 6$

Step 1	**Step 2**
Rename both numbers as improper fractions.	Multiply by the reciprocal of the divisor.
$5\frac{3}{5} \div 6 = \frac{28}{5} \div \frac{6}{1}$	$\frac{28}{5} \div \frac{6}{1} = \frac{28}{5} \times \frac{1}{6} = \frac{\overset{14}{28}}{5} \times \frac{1}{\underset{3}{6}} = \frac{14}{15}$

The average amount of rainfall per month is $\frac{14}{15}$ in.

1. Is $\frac{14}{15}$ in. a reasonable answer? Why?

B. You can also divide a mixed number by a fraction.

Divide: $3\frac{2}{5} \div \frac{2}{3}$

2. Will the answer be greater than 1 or less than 1? Why?

3. Will the answer be greater than 3 or less than 3? Why?

Step 1	**Step 2**
Rename the mixed number as an improper fraction.	Multiply by the reciprocal of the divisor. Write the answer in simplest form.
$3\frac{2}{5} \div \frac{2}{3} = \frac{17}{5} \div \frac{2}{3}$	$\frac{17}{5} \div \frac{2}{3} = \frac{17}{5} \times \frac{3}{2} = \frac{51}{10} = 5\frac{1}{10}$

So $3\frac{2}{5} \div \frac{2}{3} = 5\frac{1}{10}$.

4. Find $6\frac{2}{5} \div \frac{1}{3}$ and $6\frac{2}{5} \div \frac{1}{2}$.

5. How you would divide a number by a fraction with a numerator of 1?

RY OUT Write the letter of the correct answer.

6. $7\frac{1}{2} \div \frac{3}{8}$ **a.** 20   **b.** $2\frac{13}{16}$ **c.** $\frac{16}{45}$ **d.** $\frac{1}{20}$

7. $15\frac{5}{8} \div 25$ **a.** $1\frac{3}{5}$ **b.** $\frac{5}{8}$ **c.** $390\frac{5}{8}$ **d.** $\frac{8}{3,125}$

8. $6\frac{6}{7} \div \frac{4}{7}$ **a.** $3\frac{45}{49}$ **b.** $\frac{49}{192}$ **c.** $\frac{1}{12}$ **d.** 12

PRACTICE

Divide. Write the answer in simplest form.

9. $6\frac{2}{3} \div 5$

10. $8\frac{1}{2} \div 4$

11. $11\frac{2}{5} \div 19$

12. $6\frac{1}{4} \div 5$

13. $3\frac{1}{2} \div \frac{3}{8}$

14. $2\frac{3}{4} \div \frac{3}{8}$

15. $3\frac{1}{5} \div \frac{2}{15}$

16. $5\frac{1}{4} \div \frac{7}{12}$

17. $1\frac{5}{6} \div \frac{5}{6}$

18. $3\frac{1}{3} \div 5$

19. $1\frac{7}{8} \div \frac{3}{4}$

20. $5\frac{5}{7} \div 10$

21. $2\frac{6}{7} \div 5$

22. $5\frac{3}{5} \div \frac{7}{10}$

23. $7\frac{4}{5} \div \frac{3}{20}$

24. $9\frac{3}{8} \div \frac{15}{28}$

25. $20\frac{2}{3} \div 4$

26. $24\frac{1}{2} \div 14$

27. $7\frac{3}{8} \div 19$

28. $3\frac{5}{9} \div \frac{2}{3}$

29. $3\frac{1}{10} \div \frac{3}{5}$

30. $3\frac{3}{5} \div 6$

31. $5\frac{1}{7} \div \frac{3}{4}$

32. $6\frac{3}{4} \div 9$

33. $4\frac{2}{7} \div \frac{5}{7}$

34. $2\frac{5}{8} \div \frac{3}{4}$

35. $5\frac{2}{5} \div 9$

36. $50 \div \frac{1}{10}$

Find the answer in simplest form.

37. $\left(\frac{1}{2} + \frac{3}{4}\right) \div \frac{2}{3}$

38. $\left(\frac{5}{8} \div \frac{3}{4}\right) + \left(\frac{1}{2} \div \frac{3}{4}\right)$

39. $\left(\frac{3}{4} \div \frac{1}{2}\right) - \left(\frac{3}{5} \div \frac{1}{2}\right)$

40. $3\frac{3}{5} \div \left(\frac{3}{4} \times \frac{2}{5}\right)$

41. $\left(\frac{5}{6} + \frac{1}{3}\right) \div 4$

42. $2\frac{2}{5} \div \left(6\frac{2}{7} \div 6\frac{2}{7}\right) \div \frac{4}{15}$

Mixed Applications

Solve. You may need to use the Databank on page 585.

43. One year Harrisville received $33\frac{3}{4}$ in. of rain. What was the average monthly rainfall?

44. Find the number of centimeters of snow that fell per hour in Alaska during the record 24-hour snowfall.

45. The high temperatures in Tucson one week were 85°, 92°, 98°, 104°, 104°, 101°, and 93°. For the same dates one year ago, the temperatures were 78°, 80°, 81°, 65°, 68°, 72°, and 80°. Make a double–bar graph to show these temperatures.

46. Find the average of each group of temperatures in Problem 45. Round your answers to the nearest tenth.

Mixed Review

Find the answer. Which method did you use?

MENTAL MATH
CALCULATOR
PAPER/PENCIL

47.
$$\begin{array}{r} 18.02 \\ \times\ \ \ 1.4 \\ \hline \end{array}$$

48.
$$\begin{array}{r} 20,000 \\ \times\ \ \ 4.82 \\ \hline \end{array}$$

49.
$$\begin{array}{r} \$8,745.60 \\ -\ \ \ 982.80 \\ \hline \end{array}$$

50. $\dfrac{4.84 \times 10^5}{2 \times 10^2}$

51. $21\frac{2}{3} + 18\frac{5}{6}$

52. $12\frac{7}{10} - 8\frac{3}{4}$

53. $1\frac{4}{5} \times 5$

54. $3.2\overline{)20.32}$

UNDERSTANDING A CONCEPT

Mixed Number Divisors

A. Sara is a surveyor. She needs to divide a 13-acre plot of land into lots for houses. Each lot will have $1\frac{5}{8}$ acres. About how many lots will there be?

Estimate: $13 \div 1\frac{5}{8}$

Round the divisor to the nearest whole number. Then use compatible numbers.

$$13 \div 1\frac{5}{8}$$
$$\downarrow \quad \downarrow$$

Think: $14 \div 2 = 7$

There will be about 7 lots for new houses.

1. Estimate $10\frac{1}{4} \div 3\frac{5}{6}$. Is there more than one possible estimate? Why?

B. You can divide to find the exact answer.

Divide: $13 \div 1\frac{5}{8}$

Step 1	Step 2
Rename both numbers as improper fractions.	**Multiply by the reciprocal of the divisor. Write the answer in simplest form.**

$$13 \div 1\frac{5}{8} = \frac{13}{1} \div \frac{13}{8} \qquad \frac{13}{1} \div \frac{13}{8} = \frac{13}{1} \times \frac{8}{13} = \frac{\overset{1}{\cancel{13}}}{1} \times \frac{8}{\underset{1}{\cancel{13}}} = \frac{8}{1} = 8$$

There will be exactly 8 lots for new houses.

2. How would you estimate $\frac{3}{4} \div 7\frac{1}{2}$? What is the exact answer?

C. You can also divide a mixed number by a mixed number.

Divide: $4\frac{1}{5} \div 3\frac{3}{4}$

Step 1	Step 2
Rename the mixed numbers as improper fractions.	**Multiply by the reciprocal of the divisor. Write the answer in simplest form.**

$$4\frac{1}{5} \div 3\frac{3}{4} = \frac{21}{5} \div \frac{15}{4} \qquad \frac{21}{5} \div \frac{15}{4} = \frac{21}{5} \times \frac{4}{15} = \frac{\overset{7}{\cancel{21}}}{5} \times \frac{4}{\underset{5}{\cancel{15}}} = \frac{28}{25} = 1\frac{3}{25}$$

TRY OUT
Estimate. Then find the quotient.

3. $25 \div 3\frac{1}{3}$

4. $\frac{7}{8} \div 5\frac{1}{4}$

5. $10\frac{1}{2} \div 4\frac{4}{5}$

6. $1\frac{9}{10} \div 3\frac{4}{5}$

PRACTICE

Estimate.

7. $2\frac{5}{7} \div 1\frac{1}{3}$

8. $5\frac{1}{4} \div 7\frac{3}{4}$

9. $6\frac{2}{5} \div 2\frac{4}{5}$

10. $9\frac{3}{4} \div 1\frac{1}{2}$

11. $4\frac{1}{6} \div 2\frac{1}{3}$

12. $12 \div 3\frac{1}{3}$

13. $\frac{7}{8} \div 7\frac{1}{5}$

14. $5\frac{2}{3} \div 1\frac{5}{9}$

Find the quotient. Write the answer in simplest form.

15. $12 \div 1\frac{1}{5}$

16. $16 \div 2\frac{1}{3}$

17. $18 \div 1\frac{5}{7}$

18. $20 \div 7\frac{1}{2}$

19. $3\frac{3}{4} \div 2\frac{1}{2}$

20. $1\frac{1}{5} \div 2\frac{1}{2}$

21. $2\frac{2}{3} \div 2\frac{1}{4}$

22. $1\frac{5}{6} \div 1\frac{1}{10}$

23. $1\frac{3}{4} \div 1\frac{1}{4}$

24. $\frac{5}{9} \div 4\frac{1}{6}$

25. $27 \div 2\frac{4}{7}$

26. $6\frac{2}{3} \div 1\frac{1}{9}$

27. $3\frac{2}{3} \div 9\frac{1}{6}$

28. $25 \div 2\frac{1}{2}$

29. $12\frac{3}{5} \div 2\frac{7}{10}$

30. $\frac{7}{12} \div 2\frac{3}{4}$

31. $5 \div 2\frac{6}{7}$

32. $10\frac{5}{6} \div 4\frac{1}{3}$

33. $\frac{8}{15} \div 1\frac{1}{3}$

34. $18 \div 2\frac{13}{16}$

35. $9\frac{1}{2} \div 9\frac{1}{2}$

36. $6\frac{3}{4} \div 1\frac{1}{8}$

37. $5\frac{1}{7} \div 2\frac{2}{5}$

38. $2\frac{2}{3} \div 8$

Estimate. Find the quotients less than 1.

39. $2\frac{6}{7} \div 5$

40. $10\frac{5}{6} \div 4\frac{1}{3}$

41. $\frac{8}{15} \div 1\frac{1}{3}$

42. $6\frac{1}{2} \div 8\frac{2}{3}$

43. $\frac{5}{12} \div 3\frac{3}{4}$

44. $2\frac{1}{5} \div \frac{4}{5}$

45. $3\frac{3}{5} \div 1\frac{4}{5}$

46. $1 \div 2\frac{2}{5}$

Mixed Applications

47. A surveying team surveys 20 city blocks in $2\frac{1}{2}$ hours. How many blocks does the team survey per hour?

48. Garrick is surveying a piece of land that measures 400 yd by 375 yd. What is the area of the land?

49. A busy city street is 30.9 ft wide. The city wants to add two more lanes, each 10.75 ft wide, to the street. How wide will the street be then?

50. **Write a problem** using the following information. Surveying costs for a big project are $2,398.50 per day. Solve your problem. Ask others to solve it.

Mixed Review

Find the answer. Which method did you use?

51. 5.86×0.084

52. $732 \div 40$

53. $5.37 + 22.8$

54. $n \div 3 = 24$

55. $n \times 5 = 60$

56. $n + 1,400 = 1,500$

MENTAL MATH
CALCULATOR
PAPER/PENCIL

UNDERSTANDING A CONCEPT

Solving Equations: Multiplying and Dividing Fractions

A. Mr. Willis made a down payment of $\frac{2}{5}$ of the cost of new fencing. If his down payment was $1,800, what was the total cost?

You can find the total cost by writing and solving an equation.

You can solve a multiplication equation by dividing both sides of the equation by the same number.

Let n = the total cost of the fencing.
$\frac{2}{5} \times n$ = the down payment

Solve.

$$\frac{2}{5} \times n = 1{,}800$$

Think: n is multiplied by $\frac{2}{5}$.
To isolate n, divide both sides by $\frac{2}{5}$.
Use the reciprocal of $\frac{2}{5}$.

$$\frac{2}{5} \times n \div \frac{2}{5} = 1{,}800 \div \frac{2}{5}$$

$$\frac{2}{5} \times n \times \frac{5}{2} = 1{,}800 \times \frac{5}{2}$$

Simplify.

$$\frac{\overset{1}{\cancel{2}}}{\underset{1}{\cancel{5}}} \times n \times \frac{\overset{1}{\cancel{5}}}{\underset{1}{\cancel{2}}} = \frac{\overset{900}{\cancel{1{,}800}}}{1} \times \frac{5}{2}$$

$$n = 4{,}500$$

Check your answer by substituting 4,500 in the original equation.

$$\frac{2}{5} \times n = 1{,}800$$

$$\frac{2}{5} \times 4{,}500 \overset{?}{=} 1{,}800$$

$$1{,}800 = 1{,}800 \quad \text{It checks.}$$

The total cost of the new fencing was $4,500.

B. You can solve a division equation by multiplying both sides of the equation by the same number.

Solve.

$$n \div \frac{2}{3} = 9$$

Think: n is divided by $\frac{2}{3}$.
To isolate n, multiply both sides by $\frac{2}{3}$.
Use the reciprocal of $\frac{2}{3}$.

$$n \div \frac{2}{3} \times \frac{2}{3} = 9 \times \frac{2}{3}$$

$$n \times \frac{3}{2} \times \frac{2}{3} = \frac{9}{1} \times \frac{2}{3}$$

Simplify.

$$n \times \frac{\overset{1}{\cancel{3}}}{\underset{1}{\cancel{2}}} \times \frac{\overset{1}{\cancel{2}}}{\underset{1}{\cancel{3}}} = \frac{\overset{3}{\cancel{9}}}{1} \times \frac{2}{\underset{1}{\cancel{3}}}$$

$$n = 6$$

Check your answer by substituting 6 in the original equation.

$$n \div \frac{2}{3} = 9$$

$$6 \div \frac{2}{3} \overset{?}{=} 9$$

$$9 = 9 \quad \text{It checks.}$$

TRY OUT   Solve the equation. Check your solution.

1. $\frac{3}{4}n = 9$

2. $2\frac{1}{2}n = 20$

3. $15 = n \div \frac{5}{3}$

4. $\frac{n}{8} = 1\frac{3}{4}$

PRACTICE

Solve the equation. Check your solution. Do as many as you can mentally.

5. $\frac{1}{2}n = 4$

6. $12 = \frac{1}{3}n$

7. $\frac{2}{3}n = 10$

8. $\frac{5}{6}n = 35$

9. $1\frac{1}{2}n = 18$

10. $52 = 3\frac{1}{4}n$

11. $5\frac{4}{5}n = 580$

12. $1\frac{1}{6}n = \frac{2}{3}$

13. $\frac{n}{2} = \frac{1}{2}$

14. $\frac{3}{8} = \frac{n}{4}$

15. $\frac{n}{2} = 4\frac{1}{2}$

16. $\frac{n}{4} = 3\frac{1}{4}$

17. $n \div \frac{1}{2} = 36$

18. $n \div \frac{1}{4} = 8$

19. $n \div \frac{2}{5} = 10$

20. $n \div \frac{3}{4} = 18$

21. $\frac{3}{5}n = 1$

22. $\frac{2}{3}n = 14$

23. $2\frac{2}{3} = \frac{n}{6}$

24. $1\frac{1}{3}n = 20$

25. $\frac{4}{5}n = 16$

26. $1\frac{1}{3}n = \frac{1}{2}$

27. $\frac{2}{3}n = 6$

28. $\frac{1}{4} = \frac{n}{4}$

29. $\frac{n}{5} = 1\frac{1}{3}$

30. $2\frac{1}{5} = \frac{n}{4}$

31. $\frac{2}{3}n = 13$

32. $\frac{1}{3}n = \frac{2}{5}$

Write an equation for the problem. Solve the equation.

33. A number divided by $\frac{1}{2}$ is equal to 5.

34. A number divided by $\frac{2}{3}$ is equal to 9.

35. A number multiplied by $\frac{1}{2}$ is equal to 10.

36. A number multiplied by $\frac{3}{4}$ is equal to 8.

37. A number divided by $\frac{3}{4}$ is equal to $2\frac{1}{2}$.

38. A number multiplied by $1\frac{1}{4}$ is equal to $2\frac{1}{2}$.

Mixed Applications

Solve. Which method did you use?

39. Two-thirds of 12 livestock ranches in western Colorado raise the same breed of cattle. How many of the ranches raise the same breed of cattle?

40. Patsy has a 36-ft roll of barbed wire in the storage shed. She needs to cut it into strips that are $2\frac{1}{4}$ ft long. How many strips can she make from the barbed wire?

41. Gus cooks chili dogs at the rodeo. He always plans that each person eats 2. If 2,658 people have bought tickets, about how many chili dogs should Gus make?

42. Charlene spent $4,228.84 on feed for livestock on her farm. Three-fourths of the feed is for the sheep. How much did it cost her to feed the sheep?

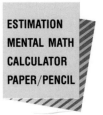

ESTIMATION
MENTAL MATH
CALCULATOR
PAPER/PENCIL

UNDERSTANDING A CONCEPT

Customary Units of Measure

A. You can use an inch ruler to measure lengths, such as a paintbrush.

The length of the paintbrush is $5\frac{0}{2}$ in. to the nearest $\frac{1}{2}$ in.

1. What is the length of the paintbrush to the nearest $\frac{1}{4}$ in.? the nearest $\frac{1}{8}$ in.? the nearest $\frac{1}{16}$ in.?

- The distance from the knuckle on your thumb to your fingertip is about 1 in.

- The width of a desk drawer is about 1 ft.

- A baseball bat is about 1 yd long.

- It takes about 6 minutes to bike 1 mi.

B. Recall that capacity is the amount a container can hold.

- A coffee measure holds about 1 fl oz.

- A baby's bottle holds about 1 c.

- A large container of mayonnaise holds about 1 qt.

- The largest container of milk sold in a store holds 1 gal.

C. Customary units of weight include ounces, pounds, and tons.

- A pencil weighs about 1 oz.

- The weight of a box of raisins is 1 lb.

- The weight of a car is about 1 T.

TRY OUT   Find the answer.

Measure the line segment to the nearest:

2. $\frac{1}{2}$ in.

3. $\frac{1}{4}$ in.

Which unit would you use to measure:

4. the diameter of a kitchen pipe?

5. the capacity of a hot-water heater?

PRACTICE

Measure the line segments.

A |———————————————————————————————| B

C |———————————————————————————| D

What is the length of $\overline{AB}$ to the nearest:

6. $\frac{1}{16}$ in.?　　　**7.** $\frac{1}{8}$ in.?　　　**8.** $\frac{1}{4}$ in.?　　　**9.** $\frac{1}{2}$ in.?

What is the length of $\overline{CD}$ to the nearest:

10. $\frac{1}{16}$ in.?　　　**11.** $\frac{1}{8}$ in.?　　　**12.** $\frac{1}{4}$ in.?　　　**13.** $\frac{1}{2}$ in.?

Complete. Write the most appropriate unit of measure.

14. A piece of fabric is 4 ▨ long.

15. The speed of a car is 35 ▨ per hour

16. A bridge can support a truck weighing at most 10 ▨.

17. A glass of juice holds about 10 ▨.

18. A container of vitamins weighs 3 ▨.

Write the letter of the best estimate.

19. the height of a door	**a.** 7 ft	**b.** 7 in.	**c.** 7 yd
20. the weight of a carton of books	**a.** 50 oz	**b.** 50 lb	**c.** 50 T
21. the capacity of a washing machine	**a.** 20 gal	**b.** 20 fl oz	**c.** 20 qt
22. the length of a field	**a.** 100 in.	**b.** 100 yd	**c.** 100 mi
23. the weight of a jar of honey	**a.** 24 oz	**b.** 24 fl oz	**c.** 24 lb
24. the capacity of a frying pan	**a.** 3 oz	**b.** 3 qt	**c.** 3 c

Estimate.

25. the height of your desk

26. the weight of a chicken

27. the capacity of a bathtub

28. the weight of your leg

29. the length of a newborn baby

30. the volume of a yogurt container

Mixed Applications

31. Sally bought 4 gerbils at $4.99 each and a cage for $15.50. How much did she spend in all?

32. ***Write a problem*** involving units of measure. Solve your problem. Ask others to solve it.

UNDERSTANDING A CONCEPT

Converting Customary Units

A. The table shows some commonly used customary units of length, capacity, and weight.

Length	Capacity	Weight
1 ft = 12 in.	1 c = 8 fl oz	1 lb = 16 oz
1 yd = 3 ft	1 pt = 2 c	1 T = 2,000 lb
1 mi = 1,760 yd	1 qt = 2 pt	
1 mi = 5,280 ft	1 gal = 4 qt	

To convert from a larger unit to a smaller unit, multiply.

$$3\frac{1}{2} \text{ qt} = \blacksquare \text{ pt}$$

Think: 1 qt = 2 pt

$$3\frac{1}{2} \text{ qt} = \left(3\frac{1}{2} \times 2\right) \text{ pt}$$
$$= 7 \text{ pt}$$

To convert from a smaller unit to a larger unit, divide.

$$22 \text{ oz} = \blacksquare \text{ lb}$$

Think: 16 oz = 1 lb

$$22 \text{ oz} = (22 \div 16) \text{ lb}$$
$$= 1\frac{3}{8} \text{ lb}$$

1. How would you find the number of yards in 3 mi 200 yd? What is your answer?

2. How would you find the number of tons and pounds in 3,145 lb? What is your answer?

B. You can add, subtract, or multiply measures.

```
  3 ft 6 in.
  6 ft 7 in.
+ 7 ft 5 in.
────────────
 16 ft 18 in. = 17 ft 6 in.,
                or 17½ ft
```

```
   8   5
   9 gal 1 qt
 − 5 gal 2 qt
────────────
   3 gal 3 qt, or 3¾ qt
```

```
   5 T 500 lb
 ×        9
────────────
 45 T 4,500 lb = 47 T 500 lb,
                 or 47¼ T
```

Think: 16 ft 18 in.
  = 16 ft + 1 ft 6 in.
  = 17 ft 6 in.

Think: 9 gal 1 qt
  = 8 gal 4 qt + 1 qt
  = 8 gal 5 qt

Think: 45 T 4,500 lb
  = 45 T + 2 T 500 lb
  = 47 T 500 lb

3. Write how you renamed:
   a. 18 in. as 1 ft 6 in.
   b. 9 gal 1 qt as 8 gal 5 qt.
   c. 4,500 lb as 2 T 500 lb.
   d. 17 ft 6 in. as $17\frac{1}{2}$ ft.
   e. 3 gal 3 qt as $3\frac{3}{4}$ gal.
   f. 47 T 500 lb as $47\frac{1}{4}$ T.

TRY OUT   Find the answer.

4. $8\frac{1}{2}$ gal = $\blacksquare$ pt

5. 34 oz = $\blacksquare$ c

6.   4 yd   4 in.
   − 2 yd 10 in.

7.   10 qt 2 c
   ×   6

PRACTICE

Complete.

8. 10 ft = ▧ in.   **9.** $\frac{1}{2}$ gal = ▧ fl oz   **10.** $4\frac{1}{4}$ lb = ▧ oz   **11.** 48 ft = ▧ yd

12. 88 fl oz = ▧ pt   **13.** 7,000 lb = ▧ T   **14.** 9,328 yd = ▧ mi   **15.** 1,500 lb = ▧ T

16. $6\frac{1}{2}$ gal = ▧ pt   **17.** 2.5 pt = ▧ c   **18.** 2.1 mi = ▧ yd   **19.** 12 oz = ▧ lb

20. 8 ft 9 in. = ▧ in.   **21.** 12 lb 9 oz = ▧ oz   **22.** 15 pt 8 fl oz = ▧ fl oz

23. 9 qt = ▧ gal ▧ qt   **24.** 3,599 lb = ▧ T ▧ lb   **25.** 266 in. = ▧ yd ▧ ft ▧ in.

26. 2.5 mi = 4,400 ▧   **27.** 11 yd = 396 ▧   **28.** 880 oz = 55 ▧   **29.** 19 pt = $9\frac{1}{2}$ ▧

Add, subtract, or multiply.

30.   8 ft 9 in.
    2 ft 4 in.
 + 5 ft 5 in.

31.   2 yd
    9 yd 2 ft
 + 10 yd 1 ft

32.   6 gal 3 qt
    1 gal
 + 4 gal 3 qt

33.   1 T 900 lb
    3 T 850 lb
 + 6 T 950 lb

34.   8 ft 3 in.
 − 3 ft 7 in.

35.   12 gal 2 qt
 − 7 gal 3 qt

36.   8 c 4 fl oz
 − 7 c 7 fl oz

37.   10 T 200 lb
 − 5 T 800 lb

38.   2 mi 500 yd
 ×   6

39.   10 yd 2 ft
 ×   8

40.   4 c 6 oz
 ×   5

41.   3 T 400 lb
 ×   10

42.   1 yd 2 ft 10 in.
    2 yd 1 ft   8 in.
 +   2 ft 10 in.

43.   7 pt 1 c 6 fl oz
 − 2 pt 1 c 7 fl oz

44.   2 mi 500 yd 2 ft
 ×   5

You can also divide with customary measures.

$$\begin{array}{r} 3\ \text{ft} \\ 2\overline{)7\ \text{ft}\ 6\ \text{in.}} \\ -\ 6\ \text{ft} \\ \hline 1\ \text{ft} \end{array}$$

$$\begin{array}{r} 3\ \text{ft}\ 9\ \text{in.} \\ 2\overline{)7\ \text{ft}\ 6\ \text{in.}} \\ -\ 6\ \text{ft} \\ \hline 1\ \text{ft}\ 6\ \text{in.} \end{array}$$

Think: 1 ft 6 in. = 18 in.
18 in. ÷ 2 = 9 in.

Divide.

45. 3$\overline{)14\ \text{ft}\ 6\ \text{in.}}$ **46.** 5$\overline{)23\ \text{ft}\ 9\ \text{in.}}$ **47.** 8$\overline{)30\ \text{ft}\ 8\ \text{in.}}$

Mixed Applications

48. A bowling ball weighs 256 oz, and a soccer ball weighs 15 oz. About how many soccer balls would it take to weigh as much as the bowling ball?

49. Sally bought 8 cans of juice at $.79 each and 1 package of paper at $1.19. How much did she spend in all?

PROBLEM SOLVING

Strategy: Working Backward

A detective is trying to figure out a sticky problem. Someone has stolen a truckload of honey. There are 156 gal in the truck when the detective finds it.

The original driver had been in the truck the whole time. He was able to give the detective the following information. The robbers first emptied half the contents of the truck at a honey company. Then they added 12 gal of honey obtained from a warehouse. They had just dropped off another 15 gal at a restaurant when they were found. How much honey was in the truck when the robbers stole it?

Plan a strategy.

The detective begins with what she knows and works backward.

Try the plan.

- There are 156 gal in the truck when she finds it.   **156**

- 15 gal were dropped off at a restaurant just before this.

  Think: There were 15 more gallons than 156 gal.   **156 + 15**

- 12 gal were added from a warehouse.

  Think: There were 12 less than (156 + 15) gal.   **156 + 15 − 12**

- Half the contents were emptied at a honey company.

  Think: Since (156 + 15 − 12) gal were left, then double this amount was in the truck at the start.   **(156 + 15 − 12) × 2**

1. How many gallons of honey were in the truck at the time of the robbery?

2. ***What if*** the robbers had emptied out $\frac{3}{4}$ of the contents at the honey company? Then how much would have been in the truck to begin with?

PRACTICE

Work backward to solve.

3. The Sweet Honey Company has a coded time lock. To remember the code, the employees say: "CODE plus fifteen, minus nine, divide by two, add six, is equal to twenty-eight." What is the code for the time lock?

4. At 4:00 P.M. the Sweet Honey Company blimp was at 2,000 ft. During the previous hour it had dropped 1,000 ft. The hour before that it had doubled its height. How high was the balloon at 2:00 P.M.?

5. The streets in a town were numbered 1–200 going uptown. The detective was tracing the movement of a criminal. She had traced him to 109 Street. To get there the fugitive had traveled uptown 15 blocks. Before that he traveled downtown 6 blocks. He had gotten there by traveling uptown 10 blocks from his starting place. What street did he start on?

6. The Sweet Honey truck driver had $612.50 at the end of the route. At his last stop he collected $81.40. Before that he collected a total of $453.60. He paid $2.50 in tolls. How much did he begin with?

Strategies and Skills Review

Solve. Use mental math, estimation, a calculator, or paper and pencil.

7. The Sweet Honey Company operates most efficiently if there is at least one employee for every 4,500 lb of honey sold in one week. The company makes $.23 on each pound it sells. Last week the company made $287,000. How many employees should the company be employing?

8. At 4:00 P.M. the store had 240 bottles of honey on the shelf. Between 3:00 and 4:00 the store workers doubled the number of bottles. Between 2:00 and 3:00 the store sold 100 bottles. Between 1:00 and 2:00 the workers added 50 bottles. Between 12:00 and 1:00 the store sold half the bottles it had. How many bottles were on the shelf at 12:00 noon?

9. A detective is trying to find out the license plate number of a car. The plate has three digits. A person remembers that each digit is double the preceding digit and that the sum is 14. What is the license number?

10. *Write a problem* that could be solved by working backward. Solve the problem and ask other students to solve it.

DEVELOPING A CONCEPT

Mental Math: Scaling Up and Down

A. A scale drawing is a reduced or enlarged drawing of an actual object. The **scale** is the relationship between the lengths or distances in the drawing and the actual lengths or distances.

A road map uses the scale $\frac{1}{4}$ in. = 25 mi. On the map Houston and San Antonio are 2 in. apart. What is the actual driving distance between the two cities?

You can solve this problem mentally by **scaling up.**

Think: Keep doubling.

$\frac{1}{4}$ **in. = 25 mi**

$\frac{1}{2}$ **in. = 50 mi** ⌐× 2

1 in. = 100 mi ⌐× 2

2 in. = 200 mi ⌐× 2

The actual driving distance between the two cities is 200 mi.

1. What is the actual distance between two cities that are 4 in. apart on the map? that are $\frac{1}{8}$ in. apart on the map?

2. Dallas is about 250 mi from Houston. Using the same scale, how many inches apart would these two cities be on a map? Explain your answer.

B. Mr. Juarez owns an auto body shop. Two strips of chrome cost $32. How much do 25 strips cost?

You can solve this problem mentally by **scaling down and up.**

Think: Multiply and divide.

2 strips = $32

1 strip = $16 ⌐÷ 2

5 strips = $80 ⌐× 5

25 strips = $400 ⌐× 5

The cost of the 25 strips is $400.

3. Solve this problem again by using scaling with different numbers. Did you get the same answer? Why or why not?

TRY OUT

Solve by scaling up and/or down.

4. A road map uses the scale 1 in. = 60 mi. What is the actual distance between two cities that are $\frac{1}{4}$ in. apart on the map?

5. Two cities are 150 mi apart. What is the distance between the cities on a map that uses the scale 1 in. = 50 mi?

6. One gallon of car paint costs \$60. What is the cost of $2\frac{1}{2}$ gal?

7. One gallon of gasoline costs \$1.20. How many gallons can you buy for \$24?

PRACTICE

Solve by scaling up and/or down. Solve as many as you can mentally.

8. 2 hubcaps for \$60
50 hubcaps for ■

9. 8 tires for \$220
2 tires for ■

10. 4 gal for \$8
3 gal for ■

11. $\frac{1}{2}$ in. = 40 mi
$1\frac{1}{2}$ in. = ■ mi

12. 1 in. = 20 mi
$\frac{1}{4}$ in. = ■ mi

13. 1 in. = 60 mi
$\frac{3}{4}$ in. = ■ mi

14. Two-fifths of the cost is \$2,000. Find the total cost.

15. One and one-half of the cost is \$4,500. Find the total cost.

Solve. Use the scale $\frac{1}{2}$ in. = 60 mi.

16. How far apart are two cities that are 2 in. apart on the map?

17. Two cities are 360 mi apart. What is their map distance?

18. How far apart are two cities that are $\frac{1}{8}$ in. apart on the map?

19. How far apart are two cities that are $1\frac{1}{4}$ in. apart on the map?

Critical Thinking

20. What are some of the factors you might consider when scaling up and/or down to solve a problem mentally?

Mixed Applications

21. Cities A and B are $1\frac{3}{4}$ in. apart on the map. Cities C and D are 225 mi apart. The scale on the map is 1 in. = 120 mi. Which pair of cities is closer? How much closer?

22. Ron drove round-trip between two cities that are 125.8 mi apart. How many miles did he drive in all?

23. Mr. Juarez charged a customer \$21.75, \$25, \$58.50, and \$37.50 for parts. If the labor cost was \$41.75, estimate the total bill.

24. ***Write a problem*** involving scaling up or scaling down. Solve your problem. Ask others to solve it.

EXTRA **Practice, page 317**

DECISION MAKING

Problem Solving: Choosing and Buying Carpeting

SITUATION

Dolores and her father want to buy new wall-to-wall carpeting for their living room.

PROBLEM

How much will the new carpeting cost? What type should they buy?

DATA

Their living room measures $24\frac{3}{4}$ ft by 12 ft.

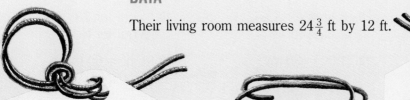

Type: _Short Pile_
Cost per sq. yard: _$4.99_
Features: _Sturdy carpet_

Cleaning: _Clean every 4 months_
Cost: _$45.00_
Colors: _Four basic colors_
Buyer's Notes: _Not luxurious; pile very short_

Type: _Stain Resistant_
Cost per sq. yard: _$8.99_
Features: _Good quality carpet that resists most stains_

Cleaning: _Clean once a year_
Cost: _$45.00_
Colors: _Sixteen colors available_
Buyer's Notes: _Softest, with long, thick pile_

Type: _Stain Free_
Cost per sq. yard: _$12.99_
Features: _Top quality carpet that will not stain_

Cleaning: _Vacuum only; never needs cleaning_
Cost:
Colors: _Comes in 16 colors_
Buyer's Notes: _Longest, thickest pile; stain-free treatment causes stiffness_

USING THE DATA

How much will it cost to carpet the living room with:

1. short pile?   **2.** stain resistant?   **3.** stain free?

How much will it cost to clean the carpet each year?

4. short pile   **5.** stain resistant   **6.** stain free

What would be the total cost of buying and cleaning the carpet at the end of three years?

7. short pile   **8.** stain resistant   **9.** stain free

MAKING DECISIONS

10. Which carpet should Dolores and her father choose to get the lowest purchase price?

11. Which carpet should they choose to get the lowest cost of purchase and cleaning after 1 year? after 3 years?

12. How can they reduce the cost of cleaning the short pile carpet?

13. Which carpet should they avoid if they want to select from a variety of colors?

14. Which carpet should they choose to get the softest pile?

15. *Write a list* of other factors they should consider.

16. Which carpet(s) would you buy for the living room? Why?

Math and Science

In some ways, the human body can be thought of as a gigantic plumbing system. Fluids move through the body continually. Without this complex system of moving fluids, the body could not survive. An adult has about 60,000 miles of arteries and veins circulating about 5 quarts of blood. About half of this blood is water. Even bones are one-fourth to one-third water.

The human body seems to be made of solid flesh and bones. You can feel bumps and bruises. Bones can break. However, you might be surprised to know that the human body is three-fifths water.

What if you could remove all the water from a 200-pound adult? How much would the adult weigh?

Think: The body is three-fifths water. Find three-fifths of 200 and subtract the product from 200: $\frac{3}{5} \times 200 = 120$; $200 - 120 = 80$. The adult would weigh 80 pounds.

ACTIVITIES

1. In a small group, guess the weights of four of your favorite stars in entertainment or sports. Calculate the amount of pounds left if water were removed from each star's weight. Combine the information into a chart, giving weight, water, and pounds left after water is removed. Find the mean, median, and mode for the group.

2. Read about the make-up of blood. Find out about plasma, red cells, white cells, and platelets. Share your findings.

Calculator: School Records

Cassandra keeps track of records and unusual data for the seventh grade at Lincoln School. The record for throwing a softball the farthest is 135.5 feet. How far is that in inches? in yards?

1 foot = 12 inches 135.5 ⊠ 12 ⊟ ☐ $1626.$

3 yards = 1 foot 135.5 ⊟ 3 ⊟ 45.166666

The record is 1,626 inches and $45.1\overline{6}$ or $45\frac{1}{6}$ yards.

USING THE CALCULATOR

Use your calculator to find other ways to record some of Cassandra's data.

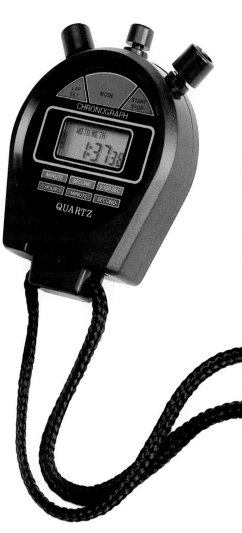

1. The record for running 600 yards is 1 minute 38 seconds. How long is that in seconds? in hours?

2. Sam Snailberg holds the school record for the mile run: 5.25 minutes. How long is that in seconds? in hours?

3. The school record for the standing broad jump is 7.5 feet How many inches is that?

4. In 1989, Sue Springer broke the running long jump record by leaping 16.6 feet. How far is that in inches?

5. The school record for pumpkin lifting is 41.14 pounds. How heavy was that record-breaking pumpkin in ounces? Hans, who holds the record, said that the pumpkin weighed a ton. How many tons did it actually weigh?

6. Some Lincoln School students have had part-time jobs. Ronald Slump had the best-paying job on record. He earned $6.75 per hour in his uncle's computer store. At that rate of pay, how much does Ronald earn in an 8-hour day? in a full 5-day work week? in an entire year?

If you looked through Cassandra's files, you might find additional interesting or unusual records. Think about what some of them might be. Write them down and ask others to convert them to other customary measurements.

EXTRA PRACTICE

Multiplying Fractions, page 283

Multiply. Write the answer in simplest form.

1. $\frac{1}{3} \times \frac{2}{5}$ 2. $\frac{3}{4} \times 16$ 3. $\frac{3}{5} \times 20$ 4. $\frac{5}{7} \times 28$ 5. $\frac{2}{3} \times \frac{5}{12}$

6. $\frac{4}{5} \times \frac{15}{20}$ 7. $\frac{5}{24} \times \frac{8}{25}$ 8. $\frac{10}{27} \times \frac{9}{20}$ 9. $\frac{7}{16} \times \frac{24}{28}$ 10. $\frac{11}{15} \times \frac{25}{44}$

11. $\frac{7}{10} \times \frac{5}{9}$ 12. $32 \times \frac{7}{8}$ 13. $\frac{3}{5} \times \frac{4}{15}$ 14. $6 \times \frac{11}{18}$ 15. $\frac{9}{5} \times \frac{15}{18}$

16. $\frac{2}{3} \times \frac{5}{8}$ 17. $\frac{7}{16} \times \frac{32}{35}$ 18. $\frac{8}{9} \times 48$ 19. $\frac{1}{3} \times \frac{3}{4} \times \frac{16}{21}$ 20. $\frac{4}{5} \times \frac{6}{7} \times \frac{35}{48}$

Multiplying Fractions by Mixed Numbers, page 285

Estimate.

1. $5\frac{3}{4} \times \frac{2}{3}$ 2. $\frac{7}{8} \times 23\frac{5}{6}$ 3. $\frac{1}{2} \times 19\frac{4}{5}$ 4. $\frac{4}{7} \times 12\frac{8}{9}$ 5. $29\frac{1}{5} \times \frac{1}{6}$

Multiply. Write the answer in simplest form.

6. $\frac{3}{5} \times 2\frac{1}{7}$ 7. $\frac{2}{3} \times 6\frac{3}{4}$ 8. $6\frac{2}{3} \times \frac{3}{5}$ 9. $\frac{7}{9} \times 1\frac{1}{3}$ 10. $\frac{5}{16} \times 1\frac{3}{5}$

11. $\frac{7}{15} \times 4\frac{2}{7}$ 12. $\frac{3}{4} \times 2\frac{1}{2}$ 13. $\frac{3}{5} \times 2\frac{2}{3}$ 14. $\frac{9}{16} \times 6\frac{2}{3}$ 15. $\frac{10}{21} \times 2\frac{4}{5}$

16. $\frac{3}{8} \times 1\frac{1}{9}$ 17. $\frac{5}{8} \times 1\frac{5}{7}$ 18. $\frac{2}{3} \times 1\frac{2}{9}$ 19. $\frac{8}{9} \times 1\frac{1}{2}$ 20. $\frac{5}{8} \times 3\frac{1}{5}$

Multiplying Mixed Numbers, page 287

Estimate.

1. $3\frac{5}{8} \times 6\frac{1}{2}$ 2. $8\frac{1}{4} \times 2\frac{1}{5}$ 3. $7\frac{5}{9} \times 4\frac{4}{5}$ 4. $5\frac{1}{6} \times 10\frac{4}{5}$ 5. $7\frac{3}{4} \times 5\frac{7}{8}$

Multiply. Write the answer in simplest form.

6. $9\frac{1}{3} \times 2\frac{1}{4}$ 7. $2\frac{2}{9} \times 4\frac{1}{2}$ 8. $4\frac{2}{3} \times 2\frac{1}{6}$ 9. $2\frac{5}{8} \times 5\frac{1}{4}$ 10. $7\frac{2}{3} \times 9\frac{1}{3}$

11. $2\frac{5}{8} \times 9\frac{1}{3}$ 12. $2\frac{1}{12} \times 4\frac{4}{5}$ 13. $2\frac{2}{5} \times 4\frac{5}{6}$ 14. $7\frac{3}{4} \times 1\frac{1}{2}$ 15. $6\frac{2}{3} \times 5\frac{1}{4}$

16. $3\frac{1}{2} \times 5\frac{1}{4}$ 17. $3\frac{1}{5} \times 6\frac{2}{3}$ 18. $2\frac{6}{13} \times 1\frac{5}{8}$ 19. $3\frac{1}{5} \times \frac{5}{8} \times 2\frac{2}{3}$ 20. $\frac{3}{8} \times 1\frac{5}{6} \times 2\frac{1}{2}$

21. $\left(2\frac{1}{2} + \frac{5}{6}\right) \times \left(3\frac{1}{2} - \frac{7}{8}\right)$ 22. $\left(\frac{7}{8} + 1\frac{3}{4}\right) \times \left(1\frac{3}{8} + 4\frac{1}{2}\right)$ 23. $\left(3\frac{3}{5} - \frac{3}{4}\right) \times \left(1\frac{3}{10} - \frac{1}{2}\right)$

Problem—Solving Strategy: Solving a Simpler Problem, page 289 ·

Think of a similar problem. Then solve the problem.

1. In the annual Briar Wood Bowling Tournament held every May, 6 teams play for the county championship. The teams play each other 3 times. How many games are played? How many championship games were played between May 1982 and December 1986?

2. Due to the popularity of the bowling tournament, the league director added 10 rows of seating. Each row had 2 more seats than the row in front of it and none had an even number of seats. There were a total of 300 seats added. How many seats were in each row?

Dividing Fractions: Using Common Denominators, page 291 ·

Divide.

1. $\frac{5}{6} \div \frac{1}{6}$

2. $\frac{7}{10} \div \frac{1}{10}$

3. $\frac{2}{3} \div \frac{1}{6}$

4. $\frac{3}{4} \div \frac{1}{8}$

5. $\frac{2}{5} \div \frac{1}{10}$

6. $4 \div \frac{2}{7}$

7. $7 \div \frac{1}{3}$

8. $9 \div \frac{1}{2}$

9. $6 \div \frac{3}{4}$

10. $8 \div \frac{2}{3}$

11. $\frac{2}{7} \div \frac{2}{14}$

12. $\frac{3}{5} \div \frac{3}{10}$

13. $\frac{5}{8} \div \frac{5}{16}$

14. $\frac{1}{4} \div 3$

15. $\frac{6}{9} \div 6$

16. $\frac{1}{4} \div \frac{1}{2}$

17. $\frac{3}{8} \div \frac{1}{3}$

18. $\frac{3}{4} \div \frac{3}{5}$

19. $\frac{1}{2} \div \frac{2}{3}$

20. $\frac{7}{8} \div \frac{1}{2}$

21. $\frac{3}{8} \div \frac{3}{4}$

22. $\frac{4}{5} \div \frac{2}{3}$

23. $\frac{7}{8} \div \frac{1}{4}$

24. $\frac{1}{3} \div \frac{1}{2}$

25. $\frac{13}{16} \div \frac{7}{8}$

Dividing Fractions: Using Reciprocals, page 293 ·

Divide. Write the answer in simplest form.

1. $8 \div \frac{2}{3}$

2. $6 \div \frac{3}{4}$

3. $4 \div \frac{2}{9}$

4. $14 \div \frac{7}{15}$

5. $5 \div \frac{6}{7}$

6. $\frac{2}{5} \div 8$

7. $\frac{3}{8} \div \frac{1}{3}$

8. $\frac{4}{15} \div 8$

9. $\frac{9}{10} \div 5$

10. $\frac{7}{8} \div \frac{1}{4}$

11. $\frac{8}{15} \div \frac{4}{15}$

12. $\frac{5}{7} \div \frac{3}{5}$

13. $\frac{1}{6} \div \frac{7}{18}$

14. $12 \div \frac{2}{3}$

15. $\frac{9}{11} \div 15$

16. $\frac{10}{15} \div \frac{2}{5}$

17. $\frac{11}{12} \div 22$

18. $\frac{2}{3} \div 6$

19. $24 \div \frac{8}{15}$

20. $55 \div \frac{10}{11}$

21. $39 \div \frac{13}{17}$

22. $72 \div \frac{8}{9}$

23. $12 \div \frac{4}{5}$

24. $5 \div \frac{3}{8}$

25. $21 \div \frac{7}{8}$

EXTRA PRACTICE

Dividing Mixed Numbers, page 297

Divide. Write the answer in simplest form.

1. $2\frac{1}{2} \div \frac{3}{4}$ **2.** $1\frac{3}{7} \div 5$ **3.** $6\frac{2}{3} \div 20$ **4.** $8\frac{8}{9} \div 10$ **5.** $8\frac{4}{7} \div 15$

6. $4\frac{1}{2} \div 6$ **7.** $8\frac{1}{8} \div \frac{5}{16}$ **8.** $5\frac{3}{5} \div \frac{3}{10}$ **9.** $3\frac{3}{7} \div \frac{14}{15}$ **10.** $3\frac{7}{9} \div \frac{14}{15}$

11. $7\frac{1}{5} \div \frac{3}{4}$ **12.** $2\frac{4}{5} \div 7$ **13.** $2\frac{5}{8} \div 7$ **14.** $3\frac{3}{4} \div \frac{10}{23}$ **15.** $1\frac{1}{3} \div \frac{8}{15}$

Mixed Number Divisors, page 299

Find the quotient. Write the answer in simplest form.

1. $1\frac{4}{5} \div 2\frac{7}{10}$ **2.** $6\frac{7}{8} \div 2\frac{1}{2}$ **3.** $2\frac{4}{5} \div 1\frac{1}{3}$ **4.** $3\frac{2}{3} \div 1\frac{2}{9}$ **5.** $2\frac{5}{6} \div 2\frac{1}{2}$

6. $1\frac{1}{8} \div 1\frac{1}{16}$ **7.** $3\frac{3}{4} \div 1\frac{1}{8}$ **8.** $9\frac{1}{5} \div 2\frac{7}{10}$ **9.** $7\frac{2}{7} \div 3\frac{3}{14}$ **10.** $10\frac{2}{3} \div 2\frac{1}{6}$

11. $9\frac{2}{7} \div 1\frac{1}{4}$ **12.** $8\frac{1}{4} \div 3\frac{6}{7}$ **13.** $8\frac{3}{4} \div 2\frac{3}{4}$ **14.** $10\frac{3}{4} \div 5\frac{1}{8}$ **15.** $12\frac{3}{8} \div 6\frac{3}{5}$

Solve Equations: Multiplying and Dividing Fractions, page 301

Solve the equation. Check your solution. Do as many as you can mentally.

1. $\frac{1}{4}n = 5$ **2.** $15 = \frac{2}{3}n$ **3.** $\frac{3}{4}n = 6$ **4.** $\frac{1}{6}n = 7$ **5.** $2\frac{1}{2}n = 5$

6. $45 = 3\frac{3}{4}n$ **7.** $4\frac{3}{5}n = 230$ **8.** $1\frac{1}{3}n = \frac{1}{2}$ **9.** $\frac{n}{3} = \frac{2}{3}$ **10.** $\frac{7}{12} = \frac{n}{4}$

11. $5\frac{1}{3} = \frac{n}{3}$ **12.** $\frac{n}{5} = 2\frac{1}{5}$ **13.** $n \div \frac{1}{3} = 27$ **14.** $n \div \frac{1}{5} = 10$ **15.** $n \div \frac{3}{4} = 12$

Customary Units of Measure, page 303

Complete. Write the most appropriate unit of measure.

1. The height of a person is 4 ■.

2. The shipping weight of a blouse is 4 ■.

3. The speed of the bicycle is 15 ■ per hour.

4. The capacity of a swimming pool is 30,000 ■.

5. An elephant weighs 1 ■.

6. The length of a football field is 100 ■.

7. A pitcher holds about 32 ■.

8. The width of a piece of paper is $8\frac{1}{2}$ ■.

Converting Customary Units, page 305

Complete.

1. $\frac{1}{2}$ pt = ■ fl oz
2. $3\frac{1}{2}$ lb = ■ oz
3. 40 fl oz = ■ pt
4. 9,000 lb = ■ T

5. 6,160 yd = ■ mi
6. 1,000 lb = ■ T
7. $7\frac{1}{2}$ gal = ■ pt
8. 3.5 pt = ■ c

9. 7 ft 5 in. = ■ in.
10. 15 lb 8 oz = ■ oz
11. 12 pt 6 fl oz = ■ fl oz

12. 12 yd 1 ft 7 in. = ■ in.
13. 5 gal 3 qt 1 pt = ■ pt
14. 700 ft = ■ yd ■ ft

15. 11 qt = ■ gal ■ qt
16. 4,879 lb = ■ T ■ lb
17. 345 in. = ■ yd ■ ft ■ in.

18. 10 yd = 360 ■
19. 560 oz = 35 ■
20. 24 pt = 3 ■

Problem–Solving Strategy: Working Backward, page 307

Work backward to solve.

1. Idget, a poodle, gained $\frac{1}{4}$ lb, lost $1\frac{3}{4}$ lb, and then gained $3\frac{1}{2}$ lb. He now weighs 38 lb. How much did Idget weigh at the start?

2. Jenna wrote checks for $35.98, $25.07, $68.95, and $18.98. She then had a balance of $249.17. With how much did she start?

3. School starts at 8:00 A.M. It takes Jason 15 minutes to get to school and 35 minutes to get ready and have breakfast. What time should he get up?

4. The Sports Club has decided to have a "dog wash" and charge $3 per dog. They can wash 3 dogs at a time. Each dog takes $5\frac{1}{2}$ minutes to bathe and $4\frac{1}{2}$ minutes to dry. How long will it take them to make $200?

Mental Math: Scaling Up and Down, page 309

Solve by scaling up and/or down. Solve as many as you can mentally.

1. 2 shirts for $40
40 shirts for ■

2. 6 blouses for $90
2 blouses for ■

3. 5 skirts for $100
4 skirts for ■

4. 8 ties for $44
5 ties for ■

5. $\frac{1}{2}$ in. = 30 mi
$2\frac{1}{2}$ in. = ■ mi

6. $\frac{1}{4}$ in. = 20 mi
$1\frac{1}{2}$ in. = ■ mi

7. 1 in. = 40 mi
$\frac{1}{8}$ in. = ■ mi

8. 1 in. = 120 mi
$\frac{3}{8}$ in. = ■ mi

9. $\frac{3}{4}$ of the cost is $300. Find the total cost.

10. $\frac{2}{5}$ of the cost is $40. Find the total cost.

PRACTICE PLUS

KEY SKILL: Multiplying Mixed Numbers (Use after page 287.)

Level A

Estimate. Then multiply. Write the answer in simplest form.

1. $2\frac{1}{4} \times 2\frac{1}{5}$

2. $1\frac{1}{4} \times 3\frac{1}{9}$

3. $2\frac{1}{3} \times 1\frac{1}{5}$

4. $2\frac{2}{3} \times 3\frac{3}{4}$

5. $6\frac{2}{3} \times 5\frac{1}{4}$

6. $1\frac{3}{4} \times 1\frac{1}{2}$

7. $1\frac{4}{5} \times 2\frac{2}{9}$

8. $2\frac{1}{2} \times 3\frac{1}{5}$

9. $2\frac{1}{4} \times 3\frac{1}{3}$

10. $2\frac{1}{4} \times 5\frac{2}{3}$

11. $1\frac{1}{2} \times 3\frac{1}{6}$

12. $2\frac{1}{3} \times 1\frac{3}{4}$

13. $1\frac{7}{8} \times 3\frac{1}{5}$

14. $2\frac{4}{5} \times 2\frac{1}{2}$

15. $1\frac{2}{5} \times 3\frac{1}{8}$

16. $3\frac{3}{8} \times 5\frac{3}{7}$

17. Shena can type $8\frac{1}{2}$ pages in an hour. How many pages of manuscript can she type in $2\frac{2}{3}$ hour?

Level B

Estimate. Then multiply. Write the answer in simplest form.

18. $2\frac{5}{6} \times 4\frac{1}{2}$

19. $4\frac{2}{5} \times 1\frac{7}{8}$

20. $2\frac{2}{11} \times 1\frac{3}{8}$

21. $1\frac{1}{3} \times 2\frac{1}{4}$

22. $3\frac{3}{8} \times 4\frac{2}{3}$

23. $1\frac{2}{3} \times 3\frac{2}{5}$

24. $1\frac{5}{8} \times 6\frac{2}{9}$

25. $3\frac{3}{8} \times 2\frac{1}{6}$

26. $8\frac{1}{6} \times 1\frac{6}{7}$

27. $4\frac{1}{5} \times 3\frac{4}{7}$

28. $6\frac{1}{4} \times 4\frac{1}{2}$

29. $4\frac{2}{3} \times 6\frac{1}{7}$

30. $8\frac{1}{3} \times 2\frac{1}{10}$

31. $3\frac{3}{8} \times 1\frac{5}{7}$

32. $2\frac{2}{3} \times 3\frac{3}{7}$

33. $5\frac{7}{8} \times 2\frac{2}{5}$

34. Alice worked $6\frac{3}{4}$ hours on Thursday. On Friday she worked $1\frac{2}{3}$ times as much. How many hours did she work on Friday?

Level C

Estimate. Then multiply. Write the answer in simplest form.

35. $5\frac{2}{5} \times 12\frac{1}{2}$

36. $3\frac{1}{9} \times 1\frac{1}{14}$

37. $6\frac{1}{2} \times 3\frac{1}{3}$

38. $3\frac{1}{8} \times 1\frac{1}{4}$

39. $6\frac{3}{5} \times 2\frac{5}{9}$

40. $8\frac{5}{9} \times 2\frac{3}{7}$

41. $1\frac{1}{11} \times 3\frac{3}{10}$

42. $4\frac{1}{6} \times 2\frac{7}{10}$

43. $1\frac{1}{3} \times 4\frac{2}{5}$

44. $5\frac{3}{5} \times 3\frac{4}{7}$

45. $7\frac{3}{5} \times 2\frac{1}{2}$

46. $2\frac{7}{9} \times 5\frac{4}{5}$

47. $\left(2\frac{1}{8} + 3\frac{1}{4}\right) \times \left(3\frac{3}{5} - 2\frac{1}{10}\right)$

48. $\left(6\frac{7}{8} - 1\frac{3}{4}\right) \times \left(8\frac{2}{3} + 2\frac{4}{9}\right)$

49. $\left(3\frac{3}{8} - 2\frac{11}{16}\right) \times \left(3\frac{4}{5} - 1\frac{2}{3}\right)$

50. $\left(7\frac{11}{15} - 4\frac{4}{5}\right) \times \left(10\frac{2}{9} - 8\frac{5}{7}\right)$

51. Larry earned $32.40 on Monday. He earned $1\frac{1}{2}$ as much on Tuesday. How much did he earn on Tuesday?

KEY SKILL: Mixed Number Divisors (Use after page 299.)

Level A

Estimate. Then find the quotient. Write the answer in simplest form.

1. $10 \div 1\frac{1}{4}$ **2.** $14 \div 2\frac{1}{3}$ **3.** $4 \div 2\frac{2}{9}$ **4.** $8 \div 2\frac{1}{2}$

5. $9 \div 4\frac{1}{2}$ **6.** $12\frac{1}{2} \div 2\frac{1}{2}$ **7.** $7\frac{1}{2} \div 3\frac{1}{3}$ **8.** $3\frac{8}{9} \div 1\frac{1}{4}$

9. $2\frac{4}{5} \div 1\frac{1}{5}$ **10.** $4\frac{1}{6} \div 1\frac{1}{9}$ **11.** $\frac{2}{3} \div 1\frac{1}{5}$ **12.** $\frac{8}{9} \div 1\frac{1}{3}$

13. $\frac{1}{2} \div 1\frac{1}{8}$ **14.** $\frac{4}{5} \div 1\frac{1}{2}$ **15.** $\frac{3}{4} \div 2\frac{1}{2}$ **16.** $7 \div 8\frac{3}{4}$

17. Morty has $8\frac{3}{4}$ cans of cat food. He feeds his cat $1\frac{1}{4}$ cans each day. How many days will the food last?

Level B

Estimate. Then find the quotient. Write the answer in simplest form.

18. $3 \div 2\frac{2}{11}$ **19.** $3\frac{1}{3} \div 3\frac{1}{9}$ **20.** $\frac{10}{21} \div 1\frac{1}{3}$ **21.** $10 \div 2\frac{2}{9}$

22. $24 \div 2\frac{2}{5}$ **23.** $4\frac{3}{4} \div 1\frac{1}{2}$ **24.** $\frac{3}{20} \div 3\frac{3}{4}$ **25.** $\frac{1}{4} \div 4\frac{1}{2}$

26. $8\frac{4}{5} \div 2\frac{3}{4}$ **27.** $18 \div 4\frac{1}{2}$ **28.** $\frac{3}{4} \div 7\frac{1}{5}$ **29.** $15 \div 3\frac{4}{7}$

30. $17\frac{1}{2} \div 8\frac{1}{3}$ **31.** $11\frac{5}{8} \div 1\frac{1}{2}$ **32.** $\frac{1}{2} \div 4\frac{1}{2}$ **33.** $\frac{1}{3} \div 5\frac{1}{2}$

34. Maggie has $16\frac{1}{2}$ lb of dog food. She feeds her dogs $5\frac{1}{2}$ lb each day. How many days will the food last?

Level C

Estimate. Then find the quotient. Write the answer in simplest form.

35. $10\frac{1}{9} \div 2\frac{1}{6}$ **36.** $21 \div 9\frac{1}{3}$ **37.** $35 \div 6\frac{2}{3}$ **38.** $\frac{14}{15} \div 1\frac{1}{9}$

39. $15\frac{3}{4} \div 4\frac{2}{3}$ **40.** $11\frac{5}{32} \div 5\frac{1}{4}$ **41.** $\frac{9}{10} \div 1\frac{1}{5}$ **42.** $36 \div 4\frac{4}{5}$

43. $\frac{2}{3} \div 3\frac{5}{9}$ **44.** $28\frac{2}{3} \div 6\frac{1}{7}$ **45.** $12 \div 2\frac{4}{7}$ **46.** $6 \div 3\frac{1}{5}$

47. $\frac{5}{16} \div 8\frac{1}{8}$ **48.** $\frac{5}{6} \div 13\frac{1}{3}$ **49.** $11\frac{3}{5} \div 4\frac{5}{6}$ **50.** $3\frac{5}{8} \div \frac{11}{27}$

51. $\left(\frac{3}{16} + \frac{9}{10}\right) \div 6$ **52.** $8\frac{3}{5} \div \left(4\frac{2}{3} - 2\frac{1}{2}\right)$ **53.** $\left(1\frac{3}{8} \times 2\frac{4}{5}\right) \div \frac{3}{4}$

54. Jeanne has $24.50 for lunch money. She spends $1\frac{3}{4}$ dollars a day for lunch. How many days will the money last?

CHAPTER REVIEW

LANGUAGE AND MATHEMATICS

Complete the sentences. Use the words in the chart on the right.

VOCABULARY
reciprocal(s)
length
capacity
weight
scale drawing
scale

1. Cup, pint, quart, and gallon are customary measurement units of ▓. *(page 302)*

2. Ounce, pound and ton are customary measurement units of ▓. *(page 302)*

3. The product of ▓ always equals one. *(page 292)*

4. A ▓ is a reduced or enlarged drawing of an object. *(page 308)*

5. ***Write a definition*** or give an example of the words you did not use from the chart.

CONCEPTS AND SKILLS

Find the reciprocal. *(page 282)*

6. $\frac{1}{3}$ **7.** $\frac{6}{17}$ **8.** $\frac{8}{35}$ **9.** $2\frac{2}{5}$ **10.** $6\frac{1}{2}$

Choose the best estimate. *(pages 284, 286, 298)*

11. $2 \times 14\frac{1}{2}$
     a. 14   **b.** 30   **c.** 17   **d.** 7

12. $6\frac{3}{4} \times 2\frac{2}{5}$
     a. 8   **b.** 10   **c.** 12   **d.** 14

13. $1\frac{8}{9} \times 1\frac{8}{9}$
     a. 1   **b.** 2   **c.** 4   **d.** 8

14. $12\frac{3}{8} \div 4\frac{1}{9}$
     a. 3   **b.** 4   **c.** 8   **d.** 48

Find the product in simplest form. *(pages 282, 284, 286)*

15. $\frac{4}{5} \times \frac{5}{10}$ **16.** $6 \times \frac{2}{3}$ **17.** $\frac{6}{7} \times 2\frac{1}{4}$

18. $4\frac{6}{7} \times 9\frac{3}{8}$ **19.** $4\frac{2}{3} \times 7\frac{1}{2} \times \frac{1}{5}$ **20.** $6\frac{2}{5} \times 3\frac{3}{4} \times \frac{1}{9}$

Find the quotient in simplest form. *(pages 290, 292, 296, 298)*

21. $\frac{4}{3} \div \frac{2}{3}$ **22.** $\frac{6}{7} \div \frac{2}{21}$ **23.** $\frac{11}{15} \div 2$ **24.** $5\frac{3}{4} \div 5$

25. $3\frac{1}{6} \div \frac{7}{12}$ **26.** $6\frac{1}{2} \div 1\frac{1}{2}$ **27.** $\left(\frac{1}{2} \times \frac{1}{5}\right) \div \frac{1}{8}$ **28.** $6\frac{2}{3} \div \left(\frac{5}{6} \times \frac{6}{7}\right)$

Solve for *n*. *(page 300)*

29. $\frac{5}{6}n = 1$ **30.** $2\frac{1}{2}n = 20$ **31.** $n \div \frac{4}{5} = 50$ **32.** $\frac{2}{3}n = 18$

33. $\frac{1}{6}n = 24$ **34.** $\frac{2}{7}n = 3$ **35.** $15 = n \div \frac{3}{5}$ **36.** $20 = n \div \frac{1}{4}$

Complete. Write in., ft, yd, mi, c, qt, gal, oz, lb, or ton. *(page 302)*

37. The width of a book is about 8 ▨.

38. A hamburger weighs about 3 ▨.

39. The weight of a man's shoe is about 1 ▨.

40. The height of a wall in a room is about 3 ▨.

Measure to the nearest $\frac{1}{16}$ in. *(page 302)*

41. ———————————————————

42. ———————————————

Complete. *(page 304)*

43. 16 pt = ▨ gal

44. $2\frac{3}{4}$ lb = ▨ oz

45. 8 ft = ▨ yd ▨ ft

46. $12\frac{1}{4}$ ft = ▨ in.

Compute. *(page 304)*

47. 6 ft 4 in.
        2 ft 7 in.
     + 3 ft 9 in.

48. 9 gal 2 qt
     − 5 gal 3 qt

49. 20 yd 2 ft
          × 6

50. 4$\overline{)13\text{ ft 4 in.}}$

Complete the scales. *(page 308)*

51. 1 in. = 60 mi
        3 in. = ▨ mi

52. $1\frac{1}{2}$ in. = 20 mi
        15 in. = ▨ mi

53. $\frac{3}{4}$ in. = 12 ft
        6 in. = ▨ ft

Critical Thinking

Write **yes** or **no**. Give an example to support your answer.

54. If x is greater than one, is the product of x and $\frac{1}{2}$ always greater than one? *(page 284)*

55. Is the product of two mixed numbers always greater than one? *(page 286)*

56. Dividing a number by the reciprocal of x is the same as multiplying by x. *(page 292)*

57. A number x is greater than y and y is greater than one. Is x divided by y always greater than one? *(page 298)*

Mixed Applications

58. A company ended the day with 500 jars of honey. It had sold 150 jars during the day and it had made 300 jars. How many jars did it have when the day started? *(page 306)*

59. Arno's dog eats a case of 12 cans of dog food in one week. How many cans does he eat in a year? *(page 288)*

60. A hotel rents its 200 rooms for $21.50 a night on weekends and $32.00 a night during the week. During a busy week when all the rooms are full, how much money will it take in? *(page 280)*

Fractions: Multiplication and Division **321**

CHAPTER REVIEW

CHAPTER TEST

Choose the best estimate.

1. $\frac{3}{4} \times 12\frac{1}{5}$ **a.** 9   **b.** 12   **c.** 16   **d.** 36

2. $18\frac{1}{2} \div 1\frac{2}{3}$ **a.** 10   **b.** 15   **c.** 25   **d.** 6

Find the product in simplest form.

3. $\frac{6}{7} \times \frac{3}{4}$ 4. $7 \times \frac{5}{6}$ 5. $7\frac{1}{5} \times 5\frac{3}{4}$

Find the quotient in simplest form.

6. $\frac{6}{7} \div \frac{2}{3}$ 7. $3\frac{1}{2} \div 4$ 8. $6\frac{2}{5} \div 8\frac{1}{4}$

Measure the following lines. Write the answer to the nearest $\frac{1}{16}$ in.

9. _____   10. _____

11. _____

Solve for *n*.

12. $\frac{2}{3}n = 8$ 13. $18 = \frac{1}{5}n$ 14. $n \div \frac{1}{3} = 24$ 15. $n \div \frac{3}{5} = 15$

Complete with a whole number.

16. 8 gal = ■ pt   17. $12\frac{1}{2}$ ft = ■ in.   18. $2\frac{1}{4}$ lb = ■ oz

Use scaling up or down to solve.

19. $\frac{1}{2}$ in. = 10 mi
    1 in. = ■ mi

20. 1 in. = 30 mi
    $\frac{1}{3}$ in. = ■ mi

21. 1 in. = 64 mi
    $\frac{3}{4}$ in. = ■ mi

Solve.

22. The Communication's Director at the Pentagon wants to install telephone lines that connect every corner office to all the other corner offices. If there are 3 office floors in the building, how many lines will have to be installed?

23. Through erosion a seaside cliff is washing away at the rate of 18 in. a year. In 7,000 years how much of the cliff will have washed away? Give the answer in the most appropriate unit of measure, to the nearest 50 yds.

24. A bakery ended a day with 250 clean shirts. Fifty employees used one shirt each and 30 used two shirts each. The laundry sent 100 clean shirts at noon. How many clean shirts did they have at the start of the day?

25. The average height of the players on the Hillcrest basketball team is 72 ■ or 6 ■.

CHAPTER TEST

RENAMING REPEATING DECIMALS AS FRACTIONS

Every decimal that repeats can be renamed as a fraction. The bar over a digit or digits shows that the digit or digits repeat.

$0.\overline{3} = 0.333\ldots$ $0.\overline{63} = 0.6363\ldots$ $0.\overline{074} = 0.074074\ldots$

Follow the steps to rename $0.\overline{3}$, $0.\overline{63}$, and $0.\overline{074}$ as fractions.

	$0.\overline{3}$	$0.\overline{63}$	$0.\overline{074}$
Step 1 Move the decimal point to make the repeating digit(s) a whole number.	$0.3 \to 3$	$0.63 \to 63$	$0.074 \to 74$
Step 2 Count the number of decimal places you moved. Use this number as an exponent for 10 and multiply.	$10^1 = 10$	$10^2 = 100$	$10^3 = 1{,}000$
Step 3 Subtract 1 from the product in Step 2.	$10 - 1 = 9$	$100 - 1 = 99$	$1{,}000 - 1 = 999$
Step 4 Divide the number in Step 1 by the answer in Step 3.	$\frac{3}{9} = \frac{1}{3}$	$\frac{63}{99} = \frac{7}{11}$	$\frac{74}{999} = \frac{2}{27}$
Step 5 Write the fraction.	$0.\overline{3} = \frac{1}{3}$	$0.\overline{63} = \frac{7}{11}$	$0.\overline{074} = \frac{2}{27}$

Rename the repeating decimal as a fraction.

1. $0.\overline{6}$ **2.** $0.\overline{2}$ **3.** $0.\overline{27}$

4. $0.\overline{296}$ **5.** $0.\overline{342}$ **6.** $0.\overline{142857}$

7. Can you explain why this method works?

CUMULATIVE REVIEW

Choose the letter of the correct answer.

1. Twice a number x is 5. What is the number?

    a. 2.5
    b. 10
    c. 25
    d. not given

2. $6 - 0.4 \times 0.3$

    a. 0.06
    b. 0.6
    c. 4.8
    d. not given

3. Find the prime factorization of 36.

    a. 1×36
    b. 6×6
    c. 9×4
    d. not given

4. What is the LCM of 9 and 6?

    a. 3   **c.** 54
    b. 18   **d.** not given

5. What is the GCF of 3 and 18?

    a. 3
    b. 18
    c. 54
    d. not given

6. $(3.2 \times 10^5) \times (1.5 \times 10^3)$

    a. 4.8×10^7
    b. 4.8×10^8
    c. 4.8×10^9
    d. not given

7. Solve for n: $n - \frac{2}{3} = 6\frac{3}{4}$

    a. $1\frac{5}{12}$ **c.** $7\frac{5}{12}$
    b. $6\frac{5}{7}$ **d.** not given

8. Solve for n: 6 ft 2 in. = n in.

    a. 8
    b. 62
    c. 74
    d. not given

9. Solve for n: $n + 2\frac{3}{4} = 3\frac{1}{2}$

    a. $\frac{3}{4}$ **c.** $2\frac{1}{4}$
    b. $1\frac{1}{4}$ **d.** not given

10. Solve for n: $n + 3 = 5\frac{7}{9}$

    a. $8\frac{7}{9}$ **c.** $2\frac{4}{9}$
    b. $2\frac{1}{3}$ **d.** not given

11. First round to the nearest whole numbers, and then find the product of $2\frac{1}{9} \times 14\frac{7}{9}$.

    a. 15
    b. 28
    c. 30
    d. not given

12. $3 \times \frac{5}{6}$

    a. $\frac{15}{18}$ **c.** $3\frac{5}{6}$
    b. $2\frac{1}{2}$ **d.** not given

13. $2\frac{3}{5} \times \frac{1}{5}$

    a. $\frac{13}{25}$ **c.** $2\frac{3}{5}$
    b. $2\frac{3}{25}$ **d.** not given

14. $3 \div \frac{1}{4}$

    a. $\frac{1}{12}$ **c.** 12
    b. $\frac{3}{4}$ **d.** not given

Geometry

MATH CONNECTION: PROBLEM SOLVING

Your City is serving you!

RENOVATION PROJECT

Federal Funds	$12,320,060
State Funds	$ 4,823,560
City Funds	$ 1,834,262

8,400 apartments refurbished

14.6 acres of park land

10 art wall murals

---

1. What information do you see in this picture?

2. How can you use the information?

3. About how much more comes from federal funds than from state and city funds combined?

4. Write a problem using the information.

Lines and Angles

The world around you contains many examples of geometric ideas.

Figure	Definition	Symbol	Read
• A	A **point** is a position in space.	A	point A
ℓ, A, B	A **line** is a continuous straight set of points with no endpoints. It extends infinitely in both directions.	$\overleftrightarrow{AB}$, $\overleftrightarrow{BA}$, or ℓ	line AB, line BA, or line ℓ
F, G	A **line segment** is part of a line that has two endpoints.	$\overline{FG}$ or $\overline{GF}$	line segment FG or line segment GF
P	A **plane** is a flat surface that extends infinitely in all directions.	plane P	plane P
C, B	A **ray** is part of a line that has one endpoint and continues infinitely in one direction.	$\overrightarrow{BC}$	ray BC
A, B, 1, C	An **angle** is formed by two rays with a common endpoint called the **vertex**.	∠ABC, ∠CBA, ∠B, or ∠1	angle ABC, angle CBA, angle B, or angle 1

TRY **OUT**   Name and write the symbol for the figure.

1. R — S

2. G — E — O

3. S — T

4. P — Q

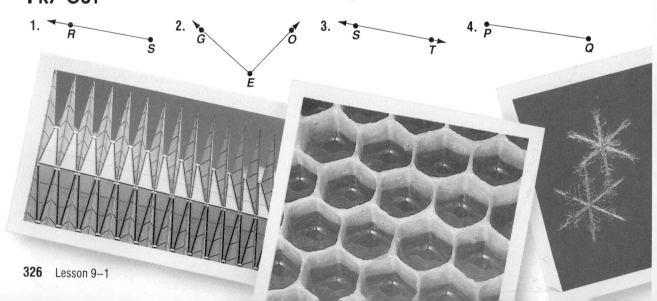

PRACTICE

Name and write the symbol for the figure.

5. • *M*

6.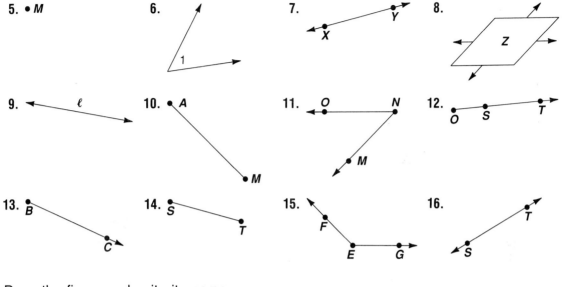

7.

8.

9. *ℓ*

10. • *A*

11. *O* — *N*

12. *O* *S* *T*

13. *B* *C*

14. *S* *T*

15. *F* *E* *G*

16. *T* *S*

Draw the figure and write its name.

17. ∠*A*   18. $\overline{RS}$ 19. $\overrightarrow{TU}$ 20. $\overleftrightarrow{MN}$ 21. ∠*MOP*   22. ∠3

Use the figure at the right for Problems 23–25.

23. Name all the line segments that have *C* as an endpoint.

24. Name all the rays shown.

25. Name three different angles that have a vertex at *A*.

Mixed Applications

26. The city of Masonville has 23 sanitation workers and pays them each $446 per week. What is the total amount the city spends per year for these salaries?

27. The city spends 0.33 of its $2.4 million budget on health and human services. How much of its budget does the city spend on health and human services?

28. The city spent $4,444,800 improving 2.4 mi of roadway. How much did the city spend per mile?

UNDERSTANDING A CONCEPT

Measuring Angles

A. Angles can be classified according to their measures in degrees (°).

A **right angle** measures 90°.

An **acute angle** measures less than 90°.

An **obtuse angle** measures greater than 90° and less than 180°.

A **straight angle** measures 180°.

B. You can use a protractor to measure angles.

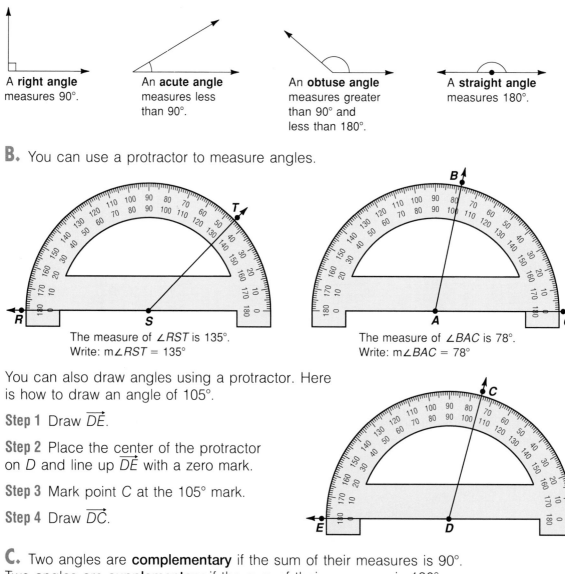

The measure of ∠RST is 135°.
Write: m∠RST = 135°

The measure of ∠BAC is 78°.
Write: m∠BAC = 78°

You can also draw angles using a protractor. Here is how to draw an angle of 105°.

Step 1 Draw $\overrightarrow{DE}$.

Step 2 Place the center of the protractor on D and line up $\overrightarrow{DE}$ with a zero mark.

Step 3 Mark point C at the 105° mark.

Step 4 Draw $\overrightarrow{DC}$.

C. Two angles are **complementary** if the sum of their measures is 90°. Two angles are **supplementary** if the sum of their measures is 180°.

1. What is the measure of the complement of 55°? the supplement of 55°?

TRY OUT

2. What is m∠ABC? What type of angle is ∠ABC?

3. What is the supplement of m∠ABC?

4. What is the complement of a 30° angle?

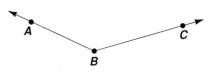

PRACTICE

Estimate the measure of the angle. Classify the angle as *acute, obtuse, right,* or *straight.* Then measure the angle using a protractor.

5.

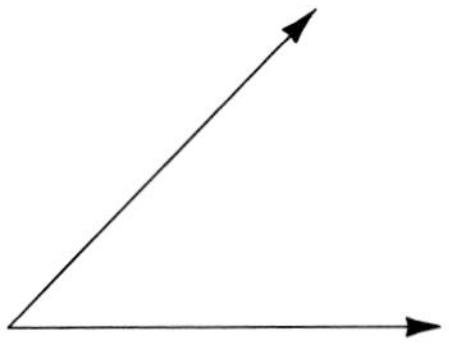

6.

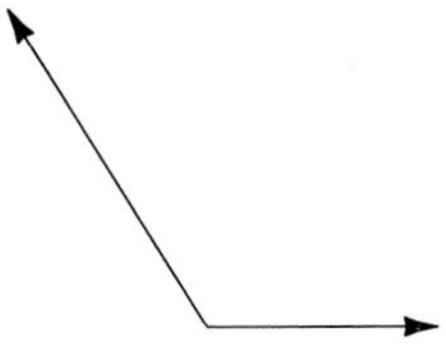

7.

8.

9.

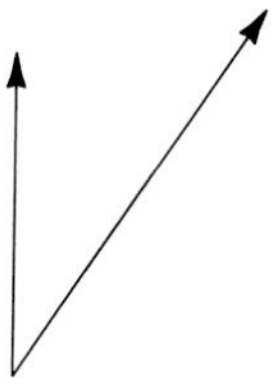

10.

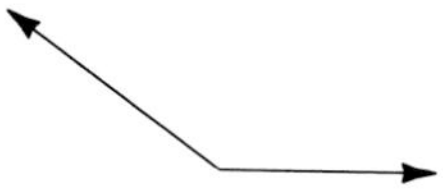

11.

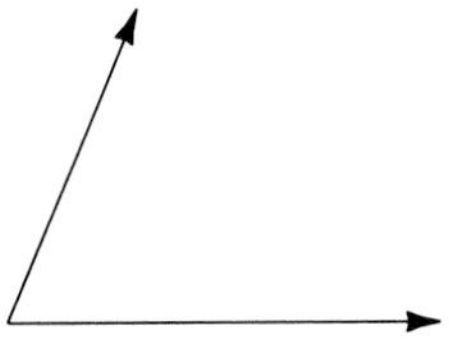

12.

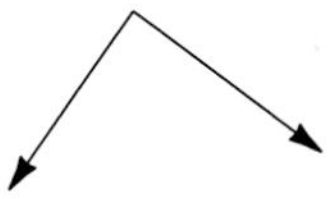

Draw an angle with the given measure.

13. 45° **14.** 95° **15.** 158° **16.** 24° **17.** 90° **18.** 132°

Find the complement of the angle with the given measure.

19. 45° **20.** 25° **21.** 54° **22.** 10° **23.** 88° **24.** 13°

Find the supplement of the angle with the given measure.

25. 150° **26.** 25° **27.** 90° **28.** 110° **29.** 82° **30.** 173°

Critical Thinking

31. What type of angle is the supplement of an acute angle?

32. How can you find the supplement of an angle if you know its complement?

Mixed Applications

33. An angle on a piece of tile is 54° and is placed in one corner of a square. What should be the measure of the angle on another piece of tile to complete the square corner?

34. Jon built a table in $8\frac{1}{2}$ hours. If he wanted to earn $12.50 per hour for his time and his materials cost $48.75, how much should he charge for the table?

35. Betty spent $188.50 on materials for 6 bookshelves. How much did she spend per shelf, to the nearest cent?

36. For a project, Lou had a triangular piece of wood with a base of 45 in. and a height of 19 in. Find the area of the wood.

UNDERSTANDING A CONCEPT

Construct Congruent Segments and Angles

A. A drafter conveys an architect's ideas through precise drawings. Often a drafter must draw congruent figures.

Recall that **congruent** figures are figures that have the same size and shape. Congruent line segments have the same length. Congruent angles have the same measure.

You can use a compass and a straightedge to construct a line segment congruent to $\overline{AB}$.

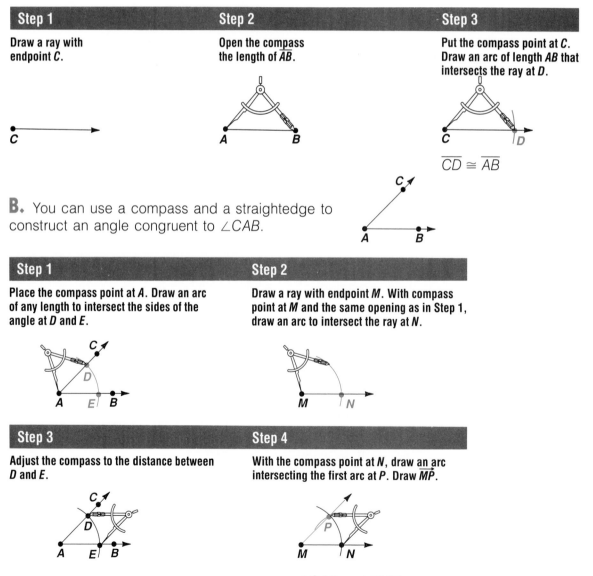

Step 1	Step 2	Step 3
Draw a ray with endpoint *C*.	Open the compass the length of $\overline{AB}$.	Put the compass point at *C*. Draw an arc of length *AB* that intersects the ray at *D*.

$$\overline{CD} \cong \overline{AB}$$

B. You can use a compass and a straightedge to construct an angle congruent to $\angle CAB$.

Step 1	Step 2
Place the compass point at *A*. Draw an arc of any length to intersect the sides of the angle at *D* and *E*.	Draw a ray with endpoint *M*. With compass point at *M* and the same opening as in Step 1, draw an arc to intersect the ray at *N*.

Step 3	Step 4
Adjust the compass to the distance between *D* and *E*.	With the compass point at *N*, draw an arc intersecting the first arc at *P*. Draw $\overrightarrow{MP}$.

$$\angle CAB \cong \angle PMN$$

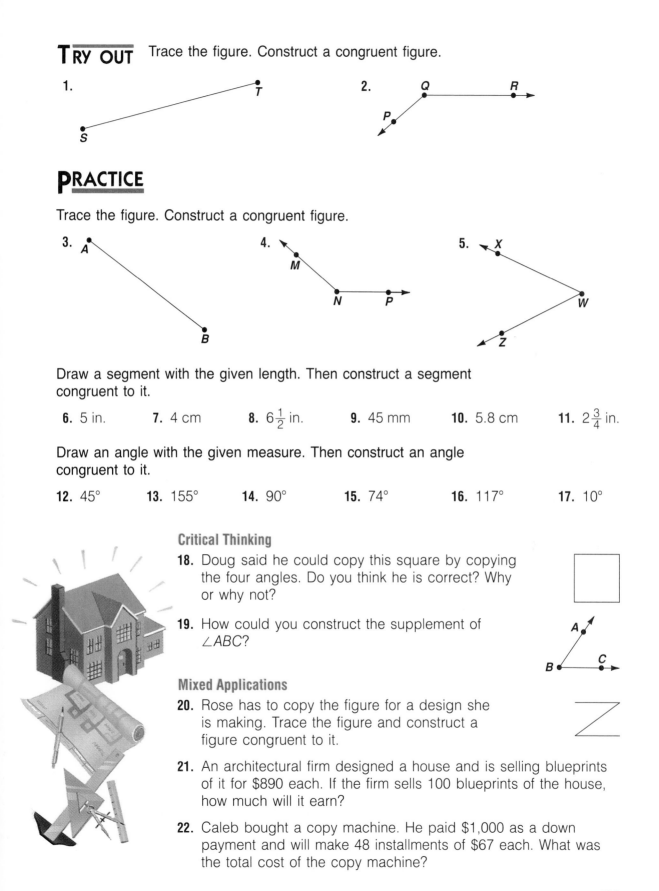

Trace the figure. Construct a congruent figure.

1.

T

S

2.

Q R

P

PRACTICE

Trace the figure. Construct a congruent figure.

3.

A

B

4.

M

N P

5.

X

W

Z

Draw a segment with the given length. Then construct a segment congruent to it.

6. 5 in.   **7.** 4 cm   **8.** $6\frac{1}{2}$ in.   **9.** 45 mm   **10.** 5.8 cm   **11.** $2\frac{3}{4}$ in.

Draw an angle with the given measure. Then construct an angle congruent to it.

12. 45°   **13.** 155°   **14.** 90°   **15.** 74°   **16.** 117°   **17.** 10°

Critical Thinking

18. Doug said he could copy this square by copying the four angles. Do you think he is correct? Why or why not?

19. How could you construct the supplement of $\angle ABC$?

A

B C

Mixed Applications

20. Rose has to copy the figure for a design she is making. Trace the figure and construct a figure congruent to it.

21. An architectural firm designed a house and is selling blueprints of it for $890 each. If the firm sells 100 blueprints of the house, how much will it earn?

22. Caleb bought a copy machine. He paid $1,000 as a down payment and will make 48 installments of $67 each. What was the total cost of the copy machine?

Lines: Intersecting, Perpendicular, Parallel

A. Two lines that cross at a point are **intersecting lines.** In the figure at the right, $\overleftrightarrow{AB}$ intersects $\overleftrightarrow{CD}$ at E.

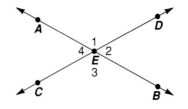

When two lines intersect, they form **vertical angles.** ∠1 and ∠3 are vertical angles. Vertical angles are congruent. So ∠1 ≅ ∠3.

1. Write ∠1 ≅ ∠3 using letters for the angles. Why is it easier to use numbers?

2. Name another pair of vertical angles in the figure.

Two angles having a common side and a common vertex and lying on opposite sides of their common side are **adjacent angles.** ∠1 and ∠2 are adjacent angles.

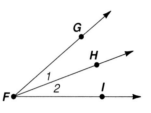

Sometimes lines that intersect form right angles. These lines are **perpendicular.** In the figure at the right, $\overleftrightarrow{JK}$ is perpendicular to $\overleftrightarrow{LM}$. Write: $\overleftrightarrow{JK} \perp \overleftrightarrow{LM}$

3. Name a pair of vertical angles and a pair of adjacent angles in the figure.

B. Two lines in the same plane that do not intersect are **parallel lines.** In the figure at the right, $\overleftrightarrow{OP}$ is parallel to $\overleftrightarrow{QR}$. Write: $\overleftrightarrow{OP} \parallel \overleftrightarrow{QR}$

Notice that $\overleftrightarrow{XY}$ intersects $\overleftrightarrow{OP}$ and $\overleftrightarrow{QR}$. $\overleftrightarrow{XY}$ is a **transversal.** When a transversal intersects a pair of parallel lines, it forms eight angles. ∠1 and ∠5 are **corresponding angles.** Corresponding angles are congruent.

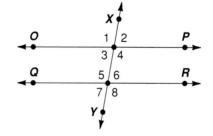

4. Which angle corresponds to ∠2? to ∠7? to ∠4?

TRY **OUT** Use the figure to answer the questions.

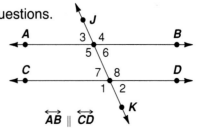

5. Complete. ∠2 and ∠▨ are vertical angles.

6. Which angles are adjacent to ∠3?

7. Which angle corresponds to ∠1?

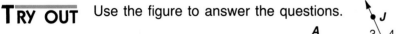

PRACTICE

Use the figure to answer the questions.

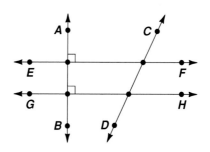

8. Which two lines will intersect?

9. Which two lines are perpendicular to $\overleftrightarrow{AB}$?

10. Name a pair of parallel lines.

Identify the pair of angles as *vertical, adjacent,* or *corresponding.*

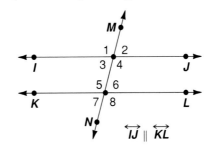

11. $\angle 4$ and $\angle 3$ **12.** $\angle 6$ and $\angle 8$

13. $\angle 1$ and $\angle 5$ **14.** $\angle 2$ and $\angle 4$

15. $\angle 2$ and $\angle 6$ **16.** $\angle 5$ and $\angle 8$

17. *What if* the measure of $\angle 2$ is 75°? What are the measures of the other angles?

Critical Thinking

Is the statement *always, sometimes,* or *never* true? If *sometimes,* give examples to support your answer.

18. Intersecting lines are perpendicular.

19. Adjacent angles are supplementary.

20. Angles adjacent to the same angle are congruent.

21. Angles adjacent to corresponding angles are congruent.

Mixed Applications

Solve.

22. A 6-in. by 4-in. picture is enlarged so that its longer side measures 18 in. What is the length of the shorter side of the enlargement?

23. The area of a rectangular room is 281.025 ft². If the length is 22.5 ft, what is the width of the room?

Mixed Review

MENTAL MATH
CALCULATOR
PAPER/PENCIL

Find the answer. Which method did you use?

24. $12\frac{1}{2} + 15$ **25.** $17 - 10\frac{4}{5}$ **26.** $1\frac{1}{2} \times 1\frac{1}{2}$ **27.** $3\frac{1}{3} \div \frac{1}{2}$

28. $2.6 + 5.4$ **29.** $64 - 24.5$ **30.** 88.03×2.47 **31.** $21 \div 1.5$

32. 42% of 200   **33.** 1.5% of 32   **34.** 25.2×34.8 **35.** $19 + [24 - (6 + 12)]$

Construct Perpendicular and Parallel Lines

A. Marjorie is an engineer for the city. She is drawing a plan for a subdivision. When laying out the streets, she needs to construct a line perpendicular to $\overleftrightarrow{AB}$ at C. You can use a compass and a straightedge to construct a line perpendicular to a given line through a point on the given line.

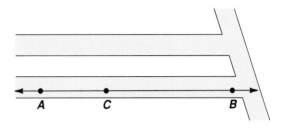

Step 1	Step 2	Step 3
Place the compass point at *C*. Using the same radius, mark two arcs intersecting $\overleftrightarrow{AB}$ at *E* and *F*.	Set the compass at a larger opening than in Step 1. With the compass point at *E* and then at *F*, draw arcs that intersect at *G*.	Draw $\overleftrightarrow{GC}$, a line perpendicular to $\overleftrightarrow{AB}$ through point *C*. $\overleftrightarrow{GC} \perp \overleftrightarrow{AB}$

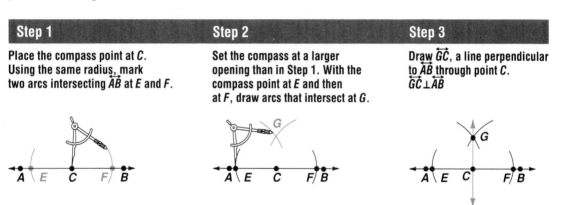

1. What is m∠*ACG* and m∠*BCG*? How do you know?

B. You can construct a line parallel to a given line by constructing perpendicular lines.

Step 1	Step 2
Choose a point *C* on $\overleftrightarrow{AB}$ and construct a line perpendicular to $\overleftrightarrow{AB}$ through point *C*. Label the line $\overleftrightarrow{CD}$.	Construct $\overleftrightarrow{ED}$ perpendicular to $\overleftrightarrow{CD}$ through point *D*. $\overleftrightarrow{ED}$, which you constructed, is parallel to $\overleftrightarrow{AB}$. $\overleftrightarrow{ED} \parallel \overleftrightarrow{AB}$

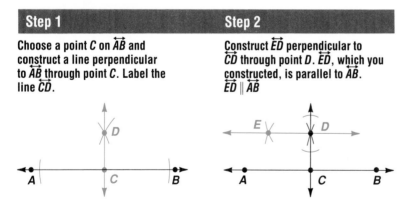

2. How could you construct a pair of parallel lines through a given line.

TRY **OUT** Draw $\overleftrightarrow{XY}$. Construct:

3. a line perpendicular to $\overleftrightarrow{XY}$.

4. a line parallel to $\overleftrightarrow{XY}$.

PRACTICE

Trace the line. Draw a line perpendicular to it through the given point.

5.
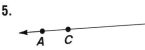

6.
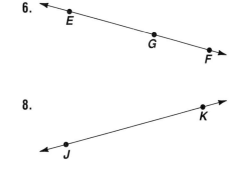

Trace the line. Draw a line parallel to it.

7.

8.

Draw $\overleftrightarrow{RS}$ containing point *T*. Construct:

9. $\overleftrightarrow{WT}$ perpendicular to $\overleftrightarrow{RS}$ through *T*.

10. $\overleftrightarrow{WZ}$ perpendicular to $\overleftrightarrow{WT}$ through *W*.

11. Draw a line segment 5 cm long. Construct a square using the line segment as one of the sides.

12. Construct a right triangle with 3-in. and 4-in. legs.

13. Construct a rectangle with 5-cm and 8-cm sides.

Mixed Applications

Solve. You may need to use the Databank on page 582.

14. On her plan Roberta wants to draw a street that is parallel to Elm Street, which she has represented by $\overleftrightarrow{AB}$. Trace $\overleftrightarrow{AB}$ and construct a line to represent such a street.

15. The Johnson Construction Company built 4 houses at a cost of $98,000 each and 3 houses at a cost of $112,000 each. What was the total cost to the company of building the houses?

16. One real estate developer has a 25-acre plot of land. She has applied for permission to divide the plot into $\frac{5}{8}$-acre lots. How many lots will the developer have?

17. Love Company is constructing 4 doubles tennis courts for the Sports School. How many square feet of clay does the company need?

EXTRA Practice, page 363

PROBLEM SOLVING

✓ UNDERSTAND
✓ PLAN
✓ TRY
✓ CHECK
✓ EXTEND

Strategies Review

Use these problem-solving strategies to solve the problems.

Remember that some problems can be solved using more than one strategy.

- Conducting an Experiment
- Using Estimation
- Guess, Test, and Revise
- Solving a Multistep Problem
- Drawing a Diagram
- Finding Needed Information

- Using Number Sense
- Finding a Pattern
- Making an Organized List
- Solving a Simpler Problem
- Using a Formula
- Working Backward

Solve. Tell which strategy you used.

1. A bicyclist rode 100 mi in 3 days. The ride on the middle day was 8 mi shorter than the ride on the first day. The last day's ride was 14 mi longer than the second day's ride. How far did the bicyclist ride each day?

2. Tourists visiting a museum are standing in a 12-ft by 12-ft room that is 8 ft high. A pendulum hangs down 7 ft from the center of the ceiling. If it is swung at full force, will it strike the ceiling or the wall? Why?

3. Four friends deliver *Travel Guide Magazine* each week. They earn $.85 per customer per month. Two have routes with 78 papers. One has a route with 92 papers, and one has a route with 54 papers. What is the total the friends make in one month?

4. The explorers notice piles of rocks encircling campfires. Each pile in the circle has a certain number of stones. One pile of stones is missing. The piles of stones are arranged 1, 4, 13, 40, ▉, 364. How many stones are probably in this missing pile?

5. There are 3 parts for a crowd scene in the school play. Five people are trying out for these parts. What are the possible ways the director can choose among the 5 people to fill the parts?

6. Ancient records show that a triangular wall was built with an area of 780 ft². The records also show that the wall was 30 ft high. What was the base of the triangular wall?

7. It is a custom in some foreign countries that before business begins, each person exchanges gifts with every other person at the business meeting. If 12 people are at such a meeting, how many gifts will they exchange? How many exchanges of gifts will there be?

8. A retired couple plan to visit 3 countries per week on a 7-week tour around the world. Their lodgings in each country average $110 per person, and airfare is $1,420 per person. What is the combined cost of lodgings and airfare for the couple?

9. A climber went up an 8,900-ft mountain. She covered the distance in 3 days. She climbed 2,900 ft less on the second day than on the first day. The last day she climbed 1,200 ft more than on the second day. How far did she climb each day?

10. While vacationing, the members of a family visit an amusement park. They watch 5 trained porpoises put on shows each hour. Only 2 porpoises are used in each show. What are the possible teams of porpoises?

11. The Livingston family is visiting relatives who live on a large farm. The relatives have a big circular field around which is a road 9.4 mi long. Jenny and Bill decide to drive a tractor straight from the road to the center of the field. About how many miles will their drive be?

12. Place different objects in paper bags. Have students try to identify them without looking into the bags. Record and interpret your results.

13. The map shows how towns are connected by rivers. How many different ways can you travel between Armonk and Edgartown if the river between Beaumont and Delano is too shallow to travel? List them.

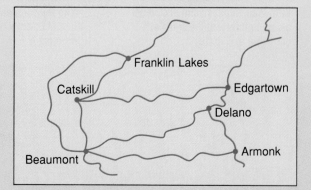

UNDERSTANDING A CONCEPT

Construct Segment and Angle Bisectors

A. A new airport is to be located at an equal distance from the cities of Bensen and Tuckersville shown on the line segment on the map. In order to find a possible location for the airport, the engineers needed to construct the **perpendicular bisector** of the line segment that connects the two cities.

You can use a compass and a straightedge to construct the perpendicular bisector of a line segment. Draw $\overline{BT}$, where B represents Bensen and T represents Tuckersville.

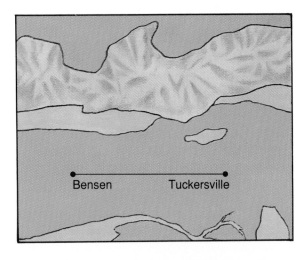

Step 1	Step 2	Step 3
Open your compass to greater than half the length of $\overline{BT}$. Place the compass point at point B. Draw an arc.	With the compass point at T and the same opening, draw another arc to intersect the first one at C and D.	Draw $\overleftrightarrow{CD}$, the perpendicular bisector of $\overline{BT}$. F is the midpoint of $\overline{BT}$.

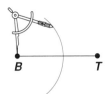 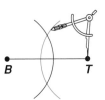 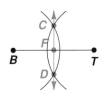

1. How can you use your compass to show that $\overline{BF} \cong \overline{FT}$?

B. You can also use a compass and a straightedge to construct an **angle bisector**.

Step 1	Step 2	Step 3
With the compass point at C, draw an arc to intersect the sides of the angle at D and E.	With the compass point at D and then at E, draw two arcs to intersect at F.	Draw $\overrightarrow{CF}$, the bisector of $\angle ACB$.

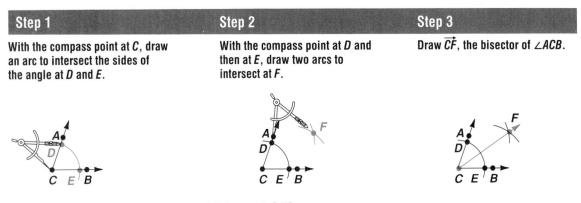

2. How can you show that $\angle ACF \cong \angle BCF$?

Trace the figure. Construct:

3. the perpendicular bisector.

4. the angle bisector.

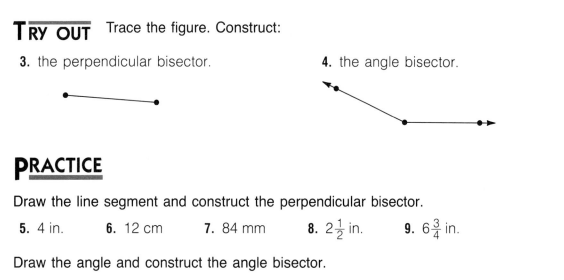

PRACTICE

Draw the line segment and construct the perpendicular bisector.

5. 4 in.   **6.** 12 cm   **7.** 84 mm   **8.** $2\frac{1}{2}$ in.   **9.** $6\frac{3}{4}$ in.

Draw the angle and construct the angle bisector.

10. 90°   **11.** 120°   **12.** 95°   **13.** 36°   **14.** 158°

Solve.

15. Draw a line segment 6 in. long. Construct the perpendicular bisector of the line segment and then construct the perpendicular bisectors of the halves. What is the length of each segment formed?

16. Draw a 130° angle. Construct the angle bisector and then construct the angle bisector of each of the new angles. What is the measure of each new angle formed?

Critical Thinking

17. Must line segment bisectors always be perpendicular to the original line? Give examples to support your answer.

Mixed Applications

18. At a busy airport one plane lands every minute. At this rate how many planes land in a 24-hour period?

19. One week 129,500 people left from the Bentonville Airport. About how many people left per day?

20. Under an airline's family plan, a family of 4 can purchase tickets for $\frac{2}{3}$ the cost of one full-fare ticket. If a full-fare ticket is $684, how much are 4 tickets under the family plan?

Mixed Review ▨▨▨▨▨▨▨▨▨▨▨▨▨▨▨▨▨▨▨▨▨▨▨▨▨▨▨▨▨▨▨▨

Find the answer. Which method did you use?

MENTAL MATH
CALCULATOR
PAPER/PENCIL

21. $2.1\overline{)8.4}$ **22.** $0.50742 - 0.0999$ **23.** 0.015×6.5

24. $0.0327 + 0.83$ **25.** $0.3982 \div 0.055$ **26.** 0.01×0.0027

UNDERSTANDING A CONCEPT

Triangles

A. One advance in technology that makes the construction of very tall buildings possible is the use of braces in the shapes of triangles.

You can classify triangles according to the measures of their angles.

right triangle
one right angle

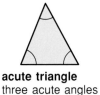

acute triangle
three acute angles

obtuse triangle
one obtuse angle

Triangles can also be classified according to the lengths of their sides. On the figures below slash marks indicate congruent sides.

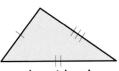

scalene triangle
no congruent sides

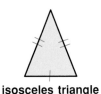

isosceles triangle
at least two
congruent sides

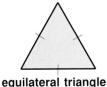

equilateral triangle
three congruent sides

1. Draw each triangle on dot paper. Describe the method you used.
   a. acute   **b.** scalene   **c.** obtuse   **d.** isosceles   **e.** right

2. You can also classify triangles by their angles and sides. Draw the triangle on dot paper.
   a. right isosceles   **b.** right scalene   **c.** acute isosceles   **d.** obtuse scalene

B. In a triangle the sum of the measures of the angles is 180°. If you know the measures of two angles, you can find the measure of the third.

Find the m∠P in △PQR.

Think: m∠P + m∠Q + m∠R = 180
                  n + 88 + 35 = 180
                         n + 123 = 180
                                  n = 57

So m∠P = 57°.

3. In △ABC, m∠A = 46° and m∠B = 90°. What is the m∠C?

4. Are the acute angles of a right triangle always complementary? Why?

Find the measure of the missing angle. Classify the
triangle in two ways.

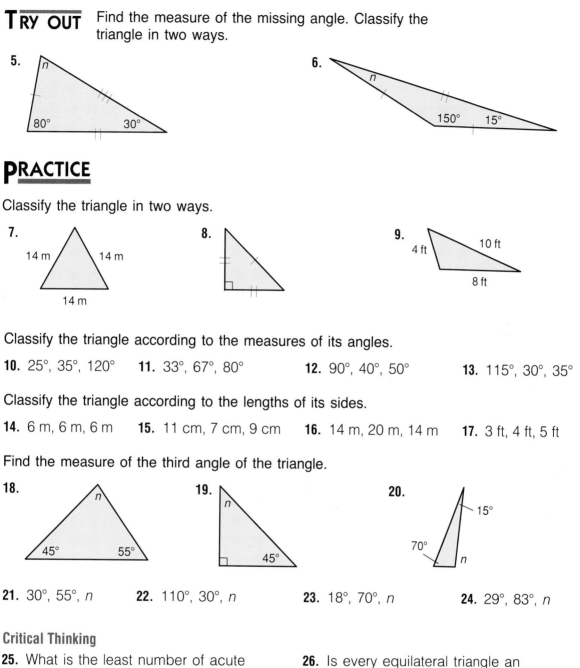

5.

6.

PRACTICE

Classify the triangle in two ways.

7.

8.

9.

Classify the triangle according to the measures of its angles.

10. 25°, 35°, 120°   **11.** 33°, 67°, 80°   **12.** 90°, 40°, 50°   **13.** 115°, 30°, 35°

Classify the triangle according to the lengths of its sides.

14. 6 m, 6 m, 6 m   **15.** 11 cm, 7 cm, 9 cm   **16.** 14 m, 20 m, 14 m   **17.** 3 ft, 4 ft, 5 ft

Find the measure of the third angle of the triangle.

18.

19.

20.

21. 30°, 55°, n **22.** 110°, 30°, n **23.** 18°, 70°, n **24.** 29°, 83°, n

Critical Thinking

25. What is the least number of acute
angles that are possible in a triangle?
the greatest number of obtuse angles?

26. Is every equilateral triangle an
isosceles triangle? an acute triangle?
Why or why not?

Mixed Applications

27. Each of one pair of vertical angles
formed by the intersection of two
roads measures 45°. What is the
measure of each of the other pair of
vertical angles?

28. ***Write a problem*** involving the
measure of the missing angle of a
triangle. Solve your problem. Then
ask others to solve it.

Visual Reasoning

A. If you start with a large square,

you can cut it into 4 smaller squares,

or into 6 smaller squares.

You can cut a square into 10 smaller squares this way,

or this way.

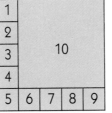

1. Make copies of the large, uncut square above. Find ways to cut the squares into each of the following numbers of smaller squares: 7, 8, 9, 11, 12, 13, 14, 15, 16.

2. Can you find more than one way to cut the squares for some numbers? Which numbers?

3. For which numbers can you cut the square into equal-sized smaller squares?

B. Suppose you have a square display case with 16 compartments. Arranged in the case are 10 mounted butterflies, as shown at the right.

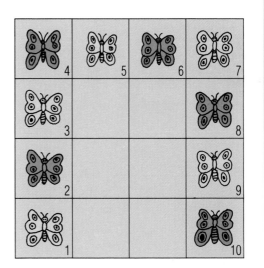

You want to rearrange the display as follows:

- There is to be an even number of butterflies in each row, in each column, and along the two diagonals of the square.

- The butterfly at the bottom right-hand corner (number 10) is very delicate and is not to be moved.

- Only 4 of the other butterflies may be moved.

4. How can you rearrange the original display by moving only 2 butterflies? Use arrows to show how the butterflies were moved.

5. Suppose you wanted to rearrange the original display by moving exactly 4 butterflies (with the same conditions above). Show how you could do this.

UNDERSTANDING A CONCEPT
Polygons

A **polygon** is a closed plane figure formed by line segments. A polygon is often named according to the number of sides. In a **regular polygon** all sides and all angles are congruent.

1. What type of triangle is a regular polygon? Why?

Some quadrilaterals have special names.

Polygon	Number of Sides
triangle	3
quadrilateral	4
pentagon	5
hexagon	6
heptagon	7
octagon	8
nonagon	9
decagon	10

Quadrilateral	Description
trapezoid	a quadrilateral with exactly one pair of parallel sides
parallelogram	a quadrilateral with opposite sides parallel and congruent and opposite angles congruent
rhombus	a parallelogram with four congruent sides
rectangle	a parallelogram with four right angles
square	a rectangle with four congruent sides

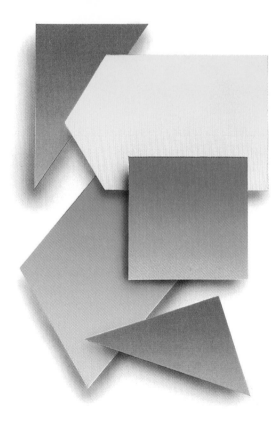

A **diagonal** is a line segment other than a side that joins any two vertices of a polygon. $\overline{AC}$ is a diagonal of quadrilateral *ABCD*. The diagonal divides the quadrilateral into two triangles.

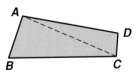

2. Use a ruler to draw any quadrilateral. Choose a vertex. From the vertex, draw a diagonal. What figures have you formed?

3. Recall the sum of the angles of a triangle. What is the sum of the angles of a quadrilateral? Why?

T̲RY̲ OUT

4. Draw a trapezoid, a parallelogram, a rhombus, a rectangle, and a square. Label each figure *ABCD*. Name the congruent sides and angles of each figure. Name the parallel sides of each figure.

5. Draw a pentagon. Label it *ABCDE*. What is the sum of the measures of the angles? How did you find the sum?

P̲RACTICE

Classify the quadrilateral.

6. 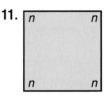 **7.** 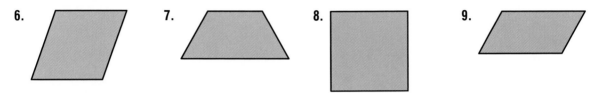 **8.** **9.**

Find the missing measure. Use what you know about quadrilaterals.

10. 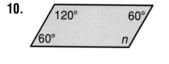 **11.** **12.**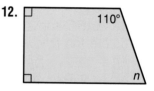

Copy and complete the table.

Polygon	Diagonals from One Vertex	Number of Triangles	Sum of the Measures of the Angles
quadrilateral	**13.** ▨	**14.** ▨	**15.** ▨
pentagon	**16.** ▨	**17.** ▨	**18.** ▨
hexagon	**19.** ▨	**20.** ▨	**21.** ▨
octagon	**22.** ▨	**23.** ▨	**24.** ▨

25. What patterns do you see in the table? Use these patterns to find the sum of the measures of the angles in a decagon.

Critical Thinking

Is the statement *always, sometimes,* or *never* true. If *sometimes,* give examples to support your answer.

26. A square is a rhombus.

27. A rhombus is a regular polygon.

28. A trapezoid is a parallelogram.

29. An isosceles triangle is a regular polygon.

DEVELOPING A CONCEPT

REASONING

Congruence and Similarity

A. The drawing is by the artist M. C. Escher. Notice that if you cut out two salamanders and place one on top of the other, one would fit over the other exactly. The salamanders are congruent. **Congruent figures** have the same size and shape.

In the figures below, triangle *ABC* is congruent to triangle *DEF*.

Write: $\triangle ABC \cong \triangle DEF$.

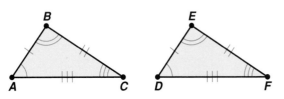

1. Trace $\triangle ABC$ and $\triangle DEF$. Use a ruler and a protractor to complete the following.
   a. $\overline{AB} = \blacksquare$ cm $\overline{DE} = \blacksquare$ cm
   b. $\overline{BC} = \blacksquare$ cm $\overline{EF} = \blacksquare$ cm
   c. $\overline{AC} = \blacksquare$ cm $\overline{DF} = \blacksquare$ cm
   d. $m\angle A = \blacksquare$ $m\angle D = \blacksquare$
   e. $m\angle B = \blacksquare$ $m\angle E = \blacksquare$
   f. $m\angle C = \blacksquare$ $m\angle F = \blacksquare$

In congruent figures the corresponding sides are congruent and the corresponding angles are congruent. In $\triangle ABC$ and $\triangle DEF$, $\overline{AB}$ corresponds to $\overline{DE}$. Write: $\overline{AB} \longleftrightarrow \overline{DE}$.

2. What are the other pairs of corresponding sides? of corresponding angles?

B. Look at the Escher drawing. Notice that the figures are the same shape but not necessarily the same size. **Similar figures** have the same shape but not necessarily the same size.

Triangle *GHI* is similar to triangle *JKL*.

Write: $\triangle GHI \sim \triangle JKL$.

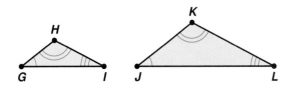

3. What are the corresponding sides of △GHI and △JKL? the corresponding angles?

4. What can you conclude about the corresponding sides of these similar figures? about the corresponding angles?

5. Did you reach the same conclusions as other students?

PRACTICE

Identify the pair of figures as *congruent, similar,* or *neither.*

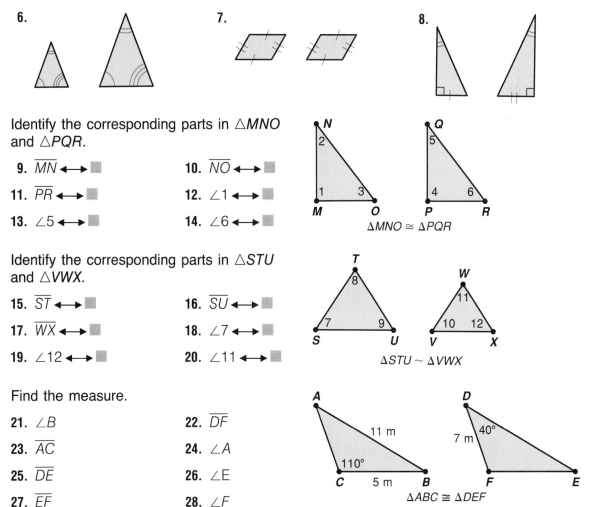

6.

7.

8.

Identify the corresponding parts in △MNO and △PQR.

9. $\overline{MN}$ ⟷ ▨

10. $\overline{NO}$ ⟷ ▨

11. $\overline{PR}$ ⟷ ▨

12. ∠1 ⟷ ▨

13. ∠5 ⟷ ▨

14. ∠6 ⟷ ▨

△MNO ≅ △PQR

Identify the corresponding parts in △STU and △VWX.

15. $\overline{ST}$ ⟷ ▨

16. $\overline{SU}$ ⟷ ▨

17. $\overline{WX}$ ⟷ ▨

18. ∠7 ⟷ ▨

19. ∠12 ⟷ ▨

20. ∠11 ⟷ ▨

△STU ~ △VWX

Find the measure.

21. ∠B

22. $\overline{DF}$

23. $\overline{AC}$

24. ∠A

25. $\overline{DE}$

26. ∠E

27. $\overline{EF}$

28. ∠F

△ABC ≅ △DEF

Critical Thinking

29. Are all similar figures congruent? Why or why not?

30. Are all congruent figures similar? Why or why not?

UNDERSTANDING A CONCEPT

Symmetry and Reflections

A. This triangle is **symmetric** about the dotted line. If it is folded along the dotted line, each half of the figure fits exactly over the other. The dotted line is called a **line of symmetry.**

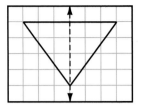

A figure can have no lines of symmetry, one line of symmetry, or many lines of symmetry.

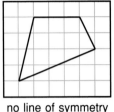
no line of symmetry

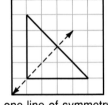
one line of symmetry

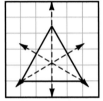
three lines of symmetry

1. How many lines of symmetry does a square have?

2. How many lines of symmetry does a circle have?

B. Look at triangles *A* and *B*. Each triangle is a mirror image, or a **reflection,** of the other. The dashed line is a line of symmetry. It is the "mirror" in which the given figures are reflected.

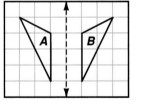

3. Are figures *A* and *B* congruent? Why or why not?

4. Trace triangle *C* and the line of symmetry on graph paper. Draw its reflection, triangle *D*. How did you do it? Compare your method with the methods others used.

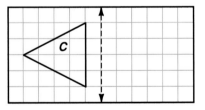

TRY OUT Trace the figure and the dashed line on graph paper. Draw its reflection about the dashed line.

5.
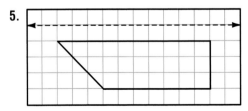

6.
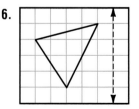

PRACTICE

Is the dashed line a line of symmetry?

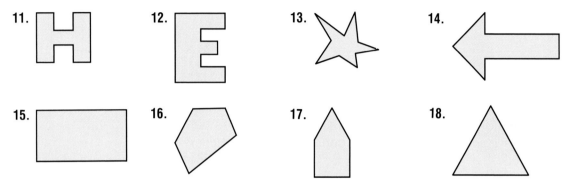

7. 8. 9. 10.

How many lines of symmetry does the figure have?

11. 12. 13. 14.

15. 16. 17. 18.

Trace the figure and the dashed line on graph paper. Draw its reflection about the dashed line.

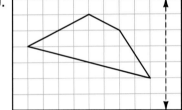

19.

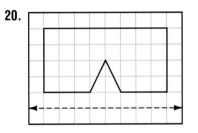

20.

Critical Thinking

21. Draw an equilateral triangle, a square, and a regular pentagon. Then draw as many lines of symmetry as you can for each figure. What do you notice? Use what you discover to predict the number of lines of symmetry for any regular polygon.

Mixed Applications

22. The base of a triangular road sign measures 7 m, and its height is 6 m. What is the area of the sign?

23. Isabel entered a contest to design an ad for a new car. She submitted 3 of her 24 ads. What fraction of her work in simplest form did she submit?

24. Billy looks at his watch in the mirror and sees that the time is 7:00. What is the actual time?

25. Carrie drove 325 mi at an average rate of 50 mi per hour. About how many hours did she drive?

UNDERSTANDING A CONCEPT

Translations and Rotations

A. When a figure slides to a new position without turning, the movement is called a **translation.** In the figures at the right, notice the difference between a translation and a reflection. A reflection image of △ABC is △DEF. A translation image of △ABC is △GHI.

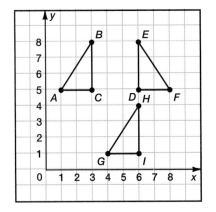

1. What are the coordinates of the vertices of △ABC? of △GHI?

2. Which vertex in △GHI corresponds to point A in △ABC?

3. How do the coordinates of point A compare to the corresponding point in the translation image? Will the same relationship be true for the other corresponding points? Why or why not?

B. When a figure is turned at a given angle about a point, the movement is called a **rotation.** If △ABC is rotated $\frac{1}{4}$ turn in a clockwise direction, the new position would be Position 1 as shown on the grid on the right. The origin (0, 0) is the center of rotation.

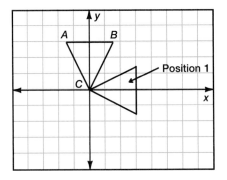

4. Trace △ABC on graph paper. Rotate △ABC $\frac{1}{2}$ turn clockwise. Label this Position 2.

5. Trace △ABC on graph paper. Rotate △ABC 1 turn. Label it Position 3. Now rotate △ABC 2 turns and 3 turns. What do you notice?

TRY OUT

6. Which point is the translation image of G?

   a. H   **c.** K
   b. J   **d.** L

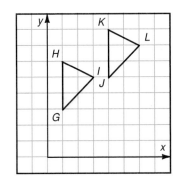

7. Which triangle is a $\frac{1}{2}$-turn rotation of △RST?

   a. 1   **c.** 3
   b. 2   **d.** 4

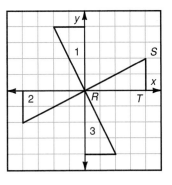

PRACTICE

Use the drawing for Problems 8–9.

8 Which point is a translation image of K? of L? of M?

9. Give the coordinates of each point and name its translation image with its coordinates. Describe the translation.

Use graph paper for Problems 10–13.

10. Draw △ABC with vertices A (1, 2), B (1, 5), and C (3, 3). Draw a translation image described by right 1, up 2.

11. Draw △ABC again. Draw a translation image described by right 3, down 1.

12. Draw △PQR with vertices P (0, 0), Q (0, 5), and R (5, 5). Draw a $\frac{1}{2}$-turn clockwise rotation of the figure about the vertex P.

13. Draw △PQR again. Draw a $\frac{1}{2}$-turn clockwise rotation of the figure about the vertex R.

Critical Thinking

14. Slide arrow $\overrightarrow{XY}$ shows the direction and distance of a translation. Predict what will happen if you measure the distance between corresponding vertices. Use a ruler to verify your prediction.

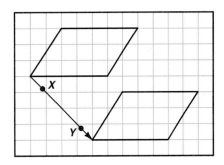

15. What clockwise rotation of a figure is equivalent to a $\frac{3}{4}$-turn counterclockwise rotation?

Mixed Applications   Solve. You may need to use the Databank on page 585.

16. Alani bought 3 lamps on sale. They were marked $\frac{1}{5}$ off the list price. If each lamp originally was listed for $165, how much did Alani pay for the three lamps?

17. Alberto bought a rectangular rug for his 20-ft by 18-ft living room. When he centered it on the floor, 72 ft² of floor space remained uncovered. What are the dimensions of the rug?

18. Warren's dresser is centered along one wall in his room. He plans to slide it 2 ft to the right. Will the movement be a reflection, a translation, or a rotation?

19. Consider the world's largest dome and the world's widest street. Would the dome fit within the street? Why or why not?

UNDERSTAND
✓ PLAN
  ✓ TRY
    CHECK
      ✓ EXTEND

PROBLEM SOLVING

Strategy: Using Spatial Thinking

A **tessellation** is a tiling of an area in which repetitions of the same shape or shapes completely cover the area without overlapping.

In what ways can you form a tessellation within a hexagonal area?

Make a plan.

Examine several kinds of tessellations.

Try the plan.

Each of these hexagons has been tessellated with various shapes.

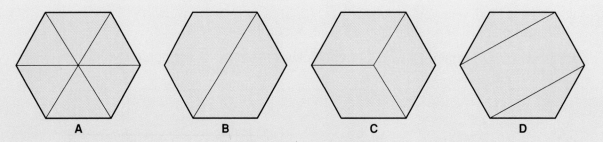

A   B   C   D

A has been tessellated with 6 equilateral triangles.
B has been tessellated with 2 trapezoids.
C has been tessellated with 3 rhombuses.
D has been tessellated with 2 triangles and a rectangle.

1. Look at each figure. What basic shape was used to make the tessellation?

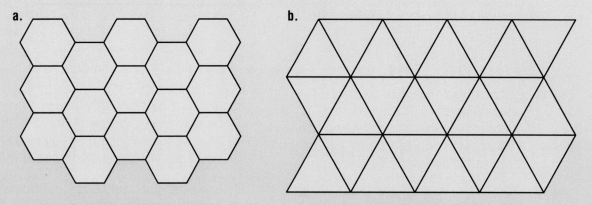

a.   b.

2. What do you notice about the lengths of the sides of the shapes used to make each tessellation in Problem 1?

PRACTICE

What basic shapes are used in the tessellation?

3.

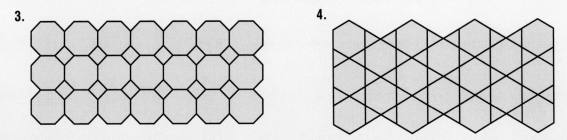

4.

Trace each figure. Can it be used to form a tessellation? Write *yes* or *no*.

5.

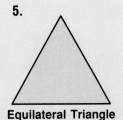

Equilateral Triangle

6.

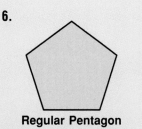

Regular Pentagon

7.

Square

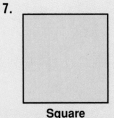

Strategies and Skills Review

Solve. Use mental math, estimation, a calculator, or paper and pencil. You may need to use the Databank on page 582.

8. Phyllis had diamond and half-diamond tiles to put down in her hallway. Show how she could use these together to tile the hall.

9. Franco had rectangular bricks to build a garden wall. Show how he could use 3 different brick designs to build the wall.

10. Elaine measured a bike course at 7.8 mi. For 15 days she rode once around the course. For 5 days she rode one-half of the course. She rode one-third of the course for 3 days. How many miles did she ride in all?

11. It takes about 18 minutes to travel by subway in Washington, D.C., from Dupont Circle to Eastern Market. About how long would it take to travel from Dupont Circle to Gallery Place by subway?

12. You are at Dupont Circle in Washington, D.C. Show the different ways you can travel to the Pentagon without leaving the subway.

13. *Write a problem* in which you want an area to be tessellated with specified shapes. Have another student tessellate the area.

Geometry **353**

Pythagorean Theorem

Annie's uncle is building a ramp from a storage bay in his warehouse to the ground. The bay is 5 ft high, and he wants the ramp to extend 12 ft from the bay. What length of wood does Annie's uncle need for the ramp?

WORKING TOGETHER

You can solve the problem by exploring the relationship between the sides of a right triangle.

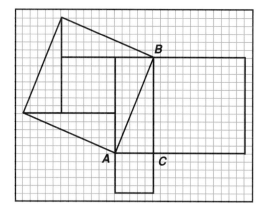

$\triangle ABC$ represents the problem. $\overline{AB}$, the side opposite the right angle, is the **hypotenuse.** $\overline{AC}$ and $\overline{BC}$ are the **legs.** A square has been drawn on each of its sides.

1. What is the length of $\overline{AC}$? of $\overline{BC}$?

2. What is the area of the square with side $\overline{AC}$? with side $\overline{BC}$?

3. How can you find the area of the square with side $\overline{AB}$? What is its area?

4. What is the length of side $\overline{AB}$? How do you know? What length of wood does Annie's uncle need?

SHARING IDEAS

5. Trace and cut out the 3, 4, 5 right triangle shown. Show that the area of the square with side *c* is the sum of the areas of the squares with sides *a* and *b*. Compare your methods.

6. The Greek mathematician Pythagoras proved that in every right triangle there is a special relationship between the areas of the squares on the legs of the triangle and the area of the square on the hypotenuse: $a^2 + b^2 = c^2$. Think about what you have discovered. In your own words write a description of this special relationship.

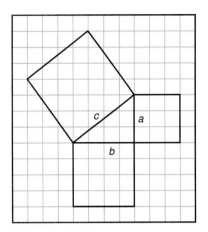

ON YOUR OWN

Show that the Pythagorean Theorem works for the triangle.

7.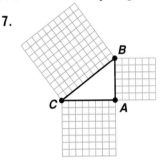

8.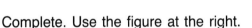

Complete. Use the figure at the right.

9. The area of a square with side $\overline{DE}$ is ▨.

10. The area of a square with side $\overline{DF}$ is ▨.

11. The sum of the areas of the squares on sides $\overline{DE}$ and $\overline{DF}$ is ▨.

12. The area of a square with side $\overline{EF}$ is ▨.

Is the triangle a right triangle?

13. 8 mm, 15 mm, 17 mm   **14.** 5 ft, 7 ft, 11 ft   **15.** 7 km, 24 km, 25 km

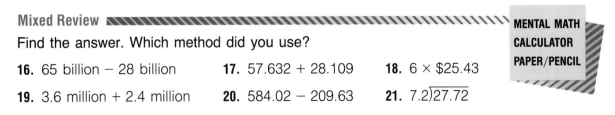

Mixed Review

Find the answer. Which method did you use?

16. 65 billion − 28 billion   **17.** 57.632 + 28.109   **18.** 6 × $25.43

19. 3.6 million + 2.4 million   **20.** 584.02 − 209.63   **21.** 7.2$\overline{)27.72}$

MENTAL MATH
CALCULATOR
PAPER/PENCIL

DEVELOPING A CONCEPT

Square Roots

A. Carmine has been hired to paint a giant chessboard on the sidewalk in the town park. The area of the board will be 16 ft². A chessboard has the shape of a square. What will be the length of each side of the square?

Carmine knows that he can find the area of the square by multiplying the length of one side by itself: $A = s \times s = s^2$. If the area of the square is 16, then Carmine must find the number whose square is 16, or the **square root** of 16. This is written $\sqrt{16}$.

1. Use graph paper to make a square with an area of 16 square units. Explain how you made the square.

2. What is the length of a side of a square with an area of 16 square units?

3. What is the square root of 16 ($\sqrt{16}$)?

4. How can you check your answer?

You can also find $\sqrt{16}$ by using a square root table. To use the table, first find 16 in the column labeled n.

5. What is the number in the column labeled $\sqrt{n}$ to the right of 16?

6. Use the square root table to find $\sqrt{17}$.

SQUARES AND SQUARE ROOTS

n	n^2	$\sqrt{n}$	n	n^2	$\sqrt{n}$
1	1	1.000	16	256	4.000
2	4	1.414	17	289	4.123
3	9	1.732	18	324	4.243
4	16	2.000	19	361	4.359
5	25	2.236	20	400	4.472
6	36	2.449	21	441	4.583
7	49	2.646	22	484	4.690
8	64	2.828	23	529	4.796
9	81	3.000	24	576	4.899
10	100	3.162	25	625	5.000
11	121	3.317	26	676	5.099
12	144	3.464	27	729	5.196
13	169	3.606	28	784	5.292
14	196	3.742	29	841	5.385
15	225	3.873	30	900	5.477

B. The number 16 is called a **perfect square** because its square root is a whole number, 4.

7. Use the square root table to find the first five perfect squares.

SHARING IDEAS

8. How would you use graph paper to find $\sqrt{49}$? What is $\sqrt{49}$?

9. Did you get the same answer as the other students?

PRACTICE

Find the square root.

10. $\sqrt{1}$ **11.** $\sqrt{4}$ **12.** $\sqrt{9}$ **13.** $\sqrt{25}$ **14.** $\sqrt{36}$

15. $\sqrt{49}$ **16.** $\sqrt{64}$ **17.** $\sqrt{81}$ **18.** $\sqrt{100}$ **19.** $\sqrt{121}$

20. $\sqrt{144}$ **21.** $\sqrt{225}$ **22.** $\sqrt{7}$ **23.** $\sqrt{12}$ **24.** $\sqrt{18}$

25. $\sqrt{24}$ **26.** $\sqrt{29}$ **27.** $\sqrt{30}$ **28.** $\sqrt{13}$ **29.** $\sqrt{23}$

Is the number a perfect square?

30. 10 **31.** 25 **32.** 40 **33.** 42 **34.** 81

Mixed Applications

35. Forty players entered the park's teen competition. Half of the players were under 18 years old, and a fourth of those were under 15. How many players were under 15 years old?

36. A bicyclist rides up a 17-ft ramp in the park to a height of 8 ft. The base of this triangle is 15 ft. Is this a right triangle?

37. The area of a square playground in the town park is 81 m². What are the dimensions of the playground?

38. *Write a problem* involving square root and the area of a square surface. Solve your problem. Ask others to solve it.

CALCULATOR

You can also use your calculator to find the square root of a number.

Find $\sqrt{169}$ this way: 169 $\boxed{\sqrt{x}}$ $\boxed{\textit{13.}}$

You can check your answer in either of two ways.

13 $\boxed{\times}$ 13 $\boxed{=}$ $\boxed{\textit{169.}}$ or 13 $\boxed{x^2}$ $\boxed{\textit{169.}}$

Find the square root using a calculator.

1. $\sqrt{16}$ **2.** $\sqrt{25}$ **3.** $\sqrt{81}$ **4.** $\sqrt{225}$ **5.** $\sqrt{415}$ **6.** $\sqrt{500}$

DECISION MAKING

Problem Solving: Planning a Wall Mural

SITUATION

The city of Clinton is doing extensive improvements on its buildings and parks. As part of the project, the Garfield School art classes have volunteered to paint a wall mural. The students held a contest to choose a design for the mural. They have narrowed the choices down to three.

PROBLEM

Which mural should the students paint?

DATA

Town Scene: 12 ft wide by $4\frac{1}{4}$ ft high; very colorful; will require 7 qts of regular paint plus 6 qts of special paint.

School Scene: $5\frac{1}{2}$ ft wide by $8\frac{1}{4}$ ft high; not many colors used; will require 7 qts of regular paint.

Park Scene: 10 ft wide by $5\frac{1}{2}$ ft high; very colorful; will require 7 qts of regular paint plus 4 qts of special paint.

Paints cost $7.25 per qt for standard colors and $8.35 per qt for special colors.

USING THE DATA

How many square feet would the mural occupy?

1. School   **2.** Park   **3.** Town

Nine artists will share the work equally. About how many square feet of the mural will each artist paint?

4. School   **5.** Park   **6.** Town

How high will the top of the mural be if the base is 2 feet off the ground?

7. School   **8.** Park   **9.** Town

How much would it cost to paint the mural?

10. School   **11.** Park   **12.** Town

MAKING DECISIONS

13. Which mural might be the most difficult to paint? the easiest? Why?

14. Which mural should the students choose to have the most people working at one time? Why?

15. Which mural should they choose if they have very little time in which to meet the deadline? Why?

16. *What if* the city cannot pay for the paint, but the students have $75 in the treasury allotted for art projects? Which mural should the students choose in order to stay within the allotted $75?

17. *Write a list* of other factors the students should consider.

18. Which mural would you choose to paint? Why?

Math and Science

Many shapes in nature are geometrical. One of the most interesting and beautiful shapes in nature is the spiral. In the head of a simple daisy, there are two opposite sets of rotating spirals made by individual flowerets. Pine cones also have alternate spirals, five going in one direction and eight in the other. Bumps on pineapples alternate with eight spiraling in one direction and thirteen in the other.

The numbers in alternating spirals in nature fit a pattern called the *Fibonacci* sequence. It is named for Leonardo "Fibonacci" da Pisa, an Italian mathematician of the late twelfth and early thirteenth centuries.

In this sequence of numbers, starting with two 1s, the next number is always produced by adding the last two numbers.

The sequence begins: 1, 1, 2, 3, 5, 8, ...

You can see how it works: $1 + 1 = 2$ (1, 1, 2); $1 + 2 = 3$ (1, 1, 2, 3); $2 + 3 = 5$ (1, 1, 2, 3, 5); and so on.

What if there are 21 spirals going in one direction in a daisy, and in the other direction, the number of spirals is the next number in the Fibonacci sequence? Find the number of spirals in the other direction.

Think: Each number in the sequence is produced by adding the preceding two numbers. The pattern given so far is 1, 1, 2, 3, 5, 8.
Continuing the pattern:

(5 + 8) 13; (8 + 13) 21; (13 + 21) 34.

There are 34 spirals in the other direction.

ACTIVITIES

1. Find out about the geometrical shape in a honeycomb. Why is it the best shape for the purpose?

2. Learn about other geometrical shapes in nature. Prepare a bulletin board with pictures and captions that explain the geometrical shape involved.

Computer Exploration: Symmetry

When can simple Logo drawings be changed into interesting, symmetric shapes? In the following activity, you will find out.

AT THE COMPUTER

Enter the following procedures.

TO SQUANGLE	TO WHATSIT
FD 80 RT 130	FD 50 RT 50
FD 40 RT 125	FD 60 RT 90
FD 60 RT 15	FD 30 RT 100
END	END

1. Run the first procedure by entering SQUANGLE. What do you think will be displayed if the SQUANGLE procedure is repeated many times? Test your idea by entering REPEAT 8 [SQUANGLE]. What happened?

2. Clear the screen. Run the second procedure by entering WHATSIT. Then use the REPEAT command to form 20 repetitions of WHATSIT. What commands did you enter? What appeared on the screen?

3. To produce a repeating pattern, the turtle must return to its original heading (direction) and position. In the SQUANGLE procedure the total measure of the right turns is $130° + 125° + 15°$, or $270°$. How many degrees must the turtle continue to turn to the right to be at its original heading?

4. How many degrees must the turtle continue to turn to the right to be at its original heading after the SQUANGLE procedure is entered twice? three times? four times?

5. How many repetitions of the SQUANGLE procedure are needed to return the turtle to its original heading?

6. What is the relationship between the number of degrees in a full rotation ($360°$) and the answers to Problems 3 and 5?

7. What commands will produce 1 complete pattern using the WHATSIT procedure? Explain.

8. The SQUANGLE figure has 4-fold symmetry. What type of symmetry does the WHATSIT procedure have? Suppose you want a figure with 9-fold symmetry? What should be the total rotation for the procedure?

9. Write a procedure that will show 9-fold symmetry. Use the computer to check your work.

EXTRA PRACTICE

Lines and Angles, page 327 ....

Name and write the symbol for the figure.

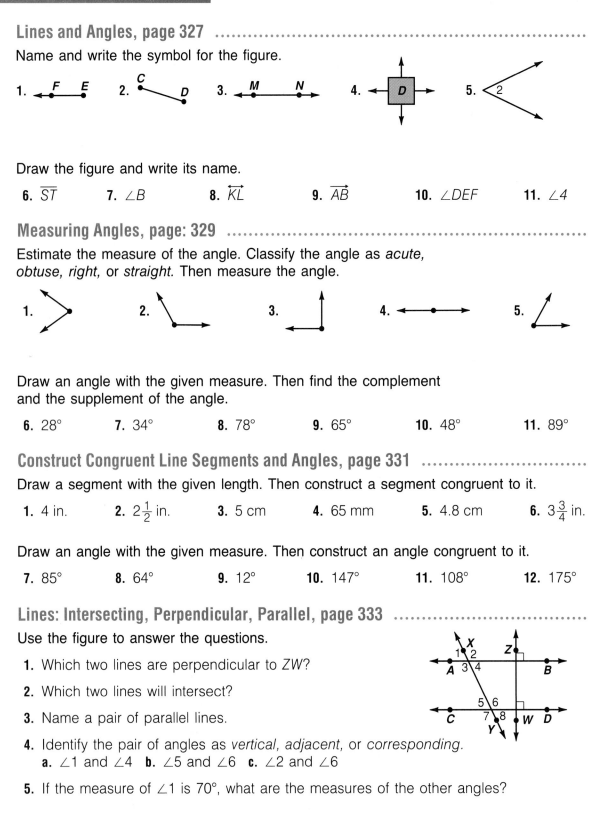

1. F E 2. C D 3. M N 4. D 5. 2

Draw the figure and write its name.

6. $\overline{ST}$ **7.** $\angle B$ **8.** $\overleftrightarrow{KL}$ **9.** $\overrightarrow{AB}$ **10.** $\angle DEF$ **11.** $\angle 4$

Measuring Angles, page: 329 ....

Estimate the measure of the angle. Classify the angle as *acute, obtuse, right,* or *straight.* Then measure the angle.

1. 2. 3. 4. 5.

Draw an angle with the given measure. Then find the complement and the supplement of the angle.

6. 28° **7.** 34° **8.** 78° **9.** 65° **10.** 48° **11.** 89°

Construct Congruent Line Segments and Angles, page 331 ....

Draw a segment with the given length. Then construct a segment congruent to it.

1. 4 in. **2.** $2\frac{1}{2}$ in. **3.** 5 cm **4.** 65 mm **5.** 4.8 cm **6.** $3\frac{3}{4}$ in.

Draw an angle with the given measure. Then construct an angle congruent to it.

7. 85° **8.** 64° **9.** 12° **10.** 147° **11.** 108° **12.** 175°

Lines: Intersecting, Perpendicular, Parallel, page 333 ....

Use the figure to answer the questions.

1. Which two lines are perpendicular to *ZW*?

2. Which two lines will intersect?

3. Name a pair of parallel lines.

4. Identify the pair of angles as *vertical, adjacent,* or *corresponding.*
  a. $\angle 1$ and $\angle 4$ **b.** $\angle 5$ and $\angle 6$ **c.** $\angle 2$ and $\angle 6$

5. If the measure of $\angle 1$ is 70°, what are the measures of the other angles?

EXTRA PRACTICE

Construct Perpendicular and Parallel Lines, page 335 ....

Trace the line. Draw a line perpendicular to it through the given point.

Trace the line. Draw a line parallel to it.

1.

2.

3.

4.

Draw $\overleftrightarrow{JK}$ containing point L. Construct:

5. $\overleftrightarrow{RL}$ perpendicular to $\overleftrightarrow{JK}$ through L.

6. $\overleftrightarrow{RM}$ perpendicular to $\overleftrightarrow{RL}$ through L.

Construct:

7. a right triangle with 6-cm and 8-cm legs.

8. a rectangle with 2-in. and 4-in. sides.

Problem Solving: Strategies Review, page 337 ....
Solve. Tell which strategy you used.

1. Melissa paid $9.70 for taxi fare from her home to the tennis courts, including a $1 tip. Maxi Taxi charges $1.90 for the first mile plus $.20 for each additional $\frac{1}{5}$ mile. How many miles is Melissa's home from the tennis court?

2. There are 24 students in a class. Ten play tennis, 9 ski, and 12 swim. Three play tennis and swim. Four ski and swim. None can do all three. How many only play tennis? only ski? only swim?

3. In a tennis tournament there are 16 entries. Two contestants compete at a time. The loser is eliminated. How many games will be played before there is a tournament winner?

4. Tennis balls are placed so that there is 1 in the top layer, 3 in the second layer, 6 in the third layer, and 10 in the fourth layer. How many are in the fifth layer?

Construct Segment and Angle Bisectors, page 339 ....

Draw the line segment and construct the perpendicular bisector.

1. 5 in.   **2.** 11 cm   **3.** 75 mm   **4.** $1\frac{1}{2}$ in.   **5.** $7\frac{3}{4}$ in.   **6.** 57 mm

Draw the angle and construct the angle bisector.

7. 140°   **8.** 80°   **9.** 48°   **10.** 125°   **11.** 164°   **12.** 32°

EXTRA PRACTICE

Triangles, page 341

Classify the triangle in two ways.

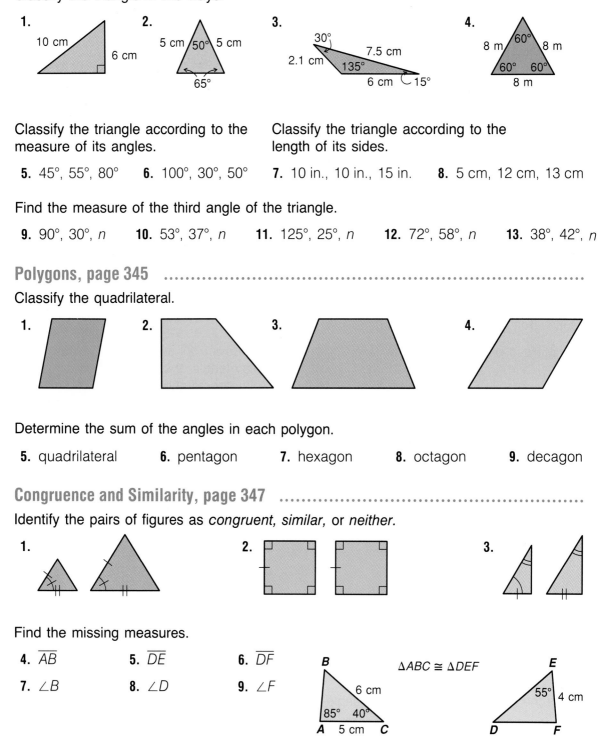

1. 10 cm, 6 cm

2. 5 cm, 50°, 5 cm, 65°

3. 30°, 7.5 cm, 2.1 cm, 135°, 6 cm, 15°

4. 60°, 8 m, 8 m, 60°, 60°, 8 m

Classify the triangle according to the measure of its angles.

Classify the triangle according to the length of its sides.

5. 45°, 55°, 80°   **6.** 100°, 30°, 50°   **7.** 10 in., 10 in., 15 in.   **8.** 5 cm, 12 cm, 13 cm

Find the measure of the third angle of the triangle.

9. 90°, 30°, *n*   **10.** 53°, 37°, *n*   **11.** 125°, 25°, *n*   **12.** 72°, 58°, *n*   **13.** 38°, 42°, *n*

Polygons, page 345

Classify the quadrilateral.

1.   **2.**   **3.**   **4.**

Determine the sum of the angles in each polygon.

5. quadrilateral   **6.** pentagon   **7.** hexagon   **8.** octagon   **9.** decagon

Congruence and Similarity, page 347

Identify the pairs of figures as *congruent, similar,* or *neither.*

1.   **2.**   **3.**

Find the missing measures.

4. $\overline{AB}$ **5.** $\overline{DE}$ **6.** $\overline{DF}$

7. $\angle B$ **8.** $\angle D$ **9.** $\angle F$

$\triangle ABC \cong \triangle DEF$

B, 6 cm, 85°, 40°, A, 5 cm, C

E, 55°, 4 cm, D, F

EXTRA PRACTICE

Symmetry and Reflections, page 349

How many lines of symmetry
does the figure have?

Trace the figure and the dashed
line on graph paper. Draw its reflection.

1. 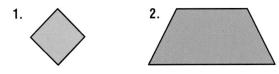   **2.**

3.   **4.**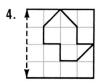

Translations and Rotations, page 351

Use the drawing for Problems 1 and 2.

1. Which point is a translation image of
A? of B? of C? of D?

2. Give the coordinates of each point.
Name its translation image with its
coordinates. Describe the translation.

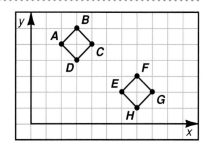

Use graph paper for Problems 3 and 4.

3. Draw triangle ABC with vertices A (2, 2), B (4, 4),
C (4, 2). Draw a $\frac{1}{2}$ turn counterclockwise rotation
of the figure about the vertex A.

4. Draw triangle ABC again. Draw a $\frac{1}{2}$ turn clockwise
rotation of the figure about the vertex C.

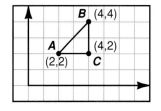

Problem–Solving Strategy: Using Spatial Thinking, page 353

Solve.

1. Marian is using mats shaped like
triangles to cover a rectangular-
shaped dining table. Show two
possible designs she could make.

2. Leo is using vinyl tiles to cover his
kitchen floor. The tiles are shaped
like squares and rectangles. Show
two different designs that Leo could
make.

Square Roots, page 357

Find the square root.

1. $\sqrt{169}$ **2.** $\sqrt{256}$ **3.** $\sqrt{361}$ **4.** $\sqrt{2}$ **5.** $\sqrt{8}$ **6.** $\sqrt{28}$

Is the number a perfect square? Write *yes* or *no*.

7. 38   **8.** 360   **9.** 400   **10.** 576   **11.** 800   **12.** 841

KEY SKILL: Lines and Angles (Use after page 327.)

Level A

Name and write the symbol for the figure.

1. •*N*

2.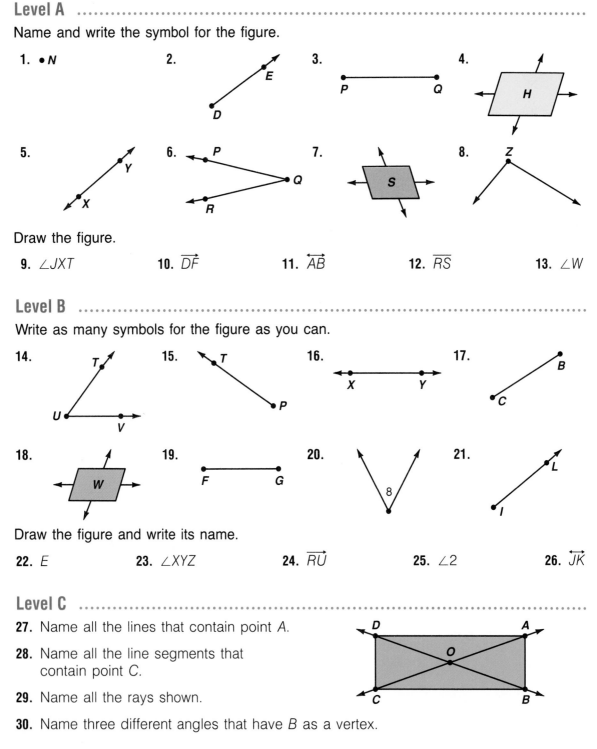
E
D

3.
•—————————•
P   *Q*

4.
H

5.
Y
X

6. *P*
Q
R

7.
S

8. *Z*

Draw the figure.

9. ∠*JXT*   **10.** $\overrightarrow{DF}$ **11.** $\overleftrightarrow{AB}$ **12.** $\overline{RS}$ **13.** ∠*W*

Level B

Write as many symbols for the figure as you can.

14.
T
U   *V*

15.
T
P

16.
X   *Y*

17.
•*B*
C

18.
W

19.
•——————•
F   *G*

20.
8

21.
L
I

Draw the figure and write its name.

22. *E*   **23.** ∠*XYZ*   **24.** $\overrightarrow{RU}$ **25.** ∠2   **26.** $\overleftrightarrow{JK}$

Level C

27. Name all the lines that contain point *A*.

28. Name all the line segments that contain point *C*.

29. Name all the rays shown.

30. Name three different angles that have *B* as a vertex.

D   *A*
O
C   *B*

KEY SKILL: Translations and Rotations (Use after page 351.)

Level A

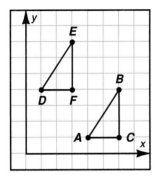

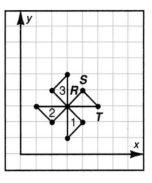

1. Which point is a translation image of *A*? of *B*? of *C*?

2. Give the coordinates of each point of △*ABC* and name its translation image with its coordinates. Describe the translation.

3. Which triangle is a $\frac{1}{2}$-turn rotation of △*RST*?

Level B

Use graph paper for Questions 4–5.

4. Draw △*ABC* with vertices *A*(3, 2), *B*(3, 5), *C*(5, 2). Draw a translation image described by left 3, up 4.

5. Draw △*ABC* again. Draw a $\frac{1}{2}$-turn clockwise rotation of the figure about the vertex *C*.

6. Tim has a bookcase centered on one wall. He has decided to move it to exactly the same place on the opposite wall. Will the move be a reflection, rotation, or a translation?

Level C

Use graph paper for Questions 7–8.

7. Draw △*DEF* with vertices *D*(3, 2), *E*(3, 5), *F*(5, 2). Draw a translation image described by right 3, down 1.

8. Draw △*DEF* again. Draw a $\frac{1}{4}$-turn counterclockwise rotation of the figure about the vertex *D*.

9. Jim is moving his television 90° from a point marked by his favorite chair so he has a better view of it. Will the move be a reflection, rotation, or a translation?

CHAPTER REVIEW

LANGUAGE AND MATHEMATICS

Complete the sentences. Use the words in the chart on the right.

1. An angle with a measure equal to 90° is a(n) ▪.
   (page 328)

2. A line that divides an angle into 2 angles with the same measure is a(n) ▪. *(page 338)*

3. When a figure is turned about a point, the movement is a(n) ▪. *(page 350)*

4. Lines that never intersect are ▪. *(page 332)*

5. **Write a definition** or give an example of the words you did not use from the chart.

VOCABULARY

right angle
perpendicular lines
parallel lines
angle bisector
rhombus
reflection
rotation

CONCEPTS AND SKILLS

Classify the angle as *acute, obtuse, right,* or *straight.* Then measure the angle using a protractor. *(page 328)*

6. ∠ACE
7. ∠BCE
8. ∠ACD
9. ∠1

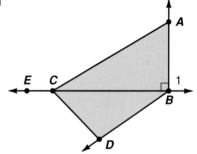

10. In the figure, name the line segments with *D* as an endpoint. *(page 326)*

11. Draw an angle with a measure of 116°. *(page 328)*

12. Construct an angle congruent to the angle of Exercise 8. *(page 330)*

Identify the pair of lines as *parallel, perpendicular* or *neither.* *(page 332)*

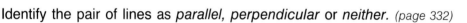

Identify the pair of figures as *congruent, similar* or *neither.* *(page 346)*

Name the polygon. *(page 344)*

Trace the figure and draw all possible lines of symmetry. *(page 348)*

Classify the triangle according to the measures of its angles and according to the lengths of its sides. *(page 340)*

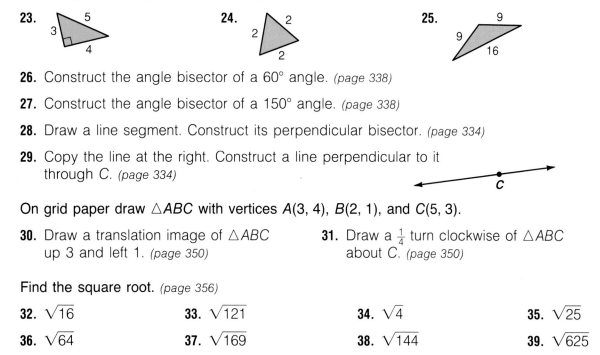

23.   5
    3 ⌐
       4

24.   2
    2
       2

25.   9
    9
       16

26. Construct the angle bisector of a 60° angle. *(page 338)*

27. Construct the angle bisector of a 150° angle. *(page 338)*

28. Draw a line segment. Construct its perpendicular bisector. *(page 334)*

29. Copy the line at the right. Construct a line perpendicular to it through *C*. *(page 334)*

On grid paper draw △*ABC* with vertices *A*(3, 4), *B*(2, 1), and *C*(5, 3).

30. Draw a translation image of △*ABC* up 3 and left 1. *(page 350)*

31. Draw a $\frac{1}{4}$ turn clockwise of △*ABC* about *C*. *(page 350)*

Find the square root. *(page 356)*

32. $\sqrt{16}$ **33.** $\sqrt{121}$ **34.** $\sqrt{4}$ **35.** $\sqrt{25}$

36. $\sqrt{64}$ **37.** $\sqrt{169}$ **38.** $\sqrt{144}$ **39.** $\sqrt{625}$

Critical Thinking

For Questions 40–43, write **yes** or **no**. Then give an example.

40. Are all triangles with 2 sides measuring 3 cm and 4 cm congruent? *(page 346)*

41. Is the sum of the measures of 2 acute angles always greater than 90°? *(page 328)*

42. Are all triangles with a 50° and a 60° angle similar? *(page 346)*

43. Is every angle either obtuse or acute? *(page 328)*

44. A figure was translated right 2 units and up 3 units and then rotated $\frac{1}{4}$ turn clockwise. What translation and rotation would return it to its original position? *(page 350)*

Mixed Applications

45. Calvin rearranged the objects in his room. He switched all objects on the north wall with the objects on the south wall. Is this a reflection, translation, or rotation of the original arrangement? *(pages 348, 350)*

46. Streets A and B intersect at a 45° angle. Street C is parallel to street A. What are the measures of the two supplementary angles formed by the intersection of streets B and C? *(page 332)*

CHAPTER TEST

Trace each figure and draw all possible lines of symmetry.

1. E

2.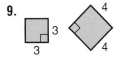

List all names for each polygon.

3.

4.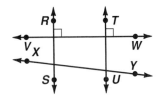

Classify each triangle according to the lengths of its sides.

5.

6. 6 4 9

Classify each type of angle.

7.

8.

In Items 9 and 10, classify the figures as *congruent, similar,* or *neither.*

9. 3 3 / 4 4

10.

11. In the figure at the right, which two lines are perpendicular to $\overleftrightarrow{VW}$?

12. In the figure, name a pair of parallel lines.

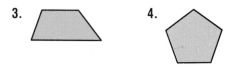

R ● T
V X W
S U Y

13. Construct the angle bisector of a 40° angle.

14. Construct the angle bisector of a 170° angle.

15. Draw line segment $\overline{AB}$. Construct its perpendicular bisector.

On graph paper draw $\triangle ABC$ with vertices $A(2, 5)$, $B(3, 2)$, and $C(5, 3)$.

16. Draw a translation image of $\triangle ABC$, up 2 and right 3.

17. Draw a $\frac{1}{2}$ turn counterclockwise rotation of $\triangle ABC$ about C.

Find the square root. You can refer to the table on page 356.

18. $\sqrt{81}$ **19.** $\sqrt{225}$ **20.** $\sqrt{8}$ **21.** $\sqrt{49}$ **22.** $\sqrt{29}$ **23.** $\sqrt{400}$

24. Mr. Dekker moved all of the chairs in his classroom forward 2 feet. Is the new arrangement a reflection, translation, or rotation of the original arrangement?

25. Streets A and B are parallel. Street C is perpendicular to Streets A and B. Street D is parallel to Street C. Is it possible for Street D to intersect Street A? B? C?

CONSTRUCTING TRIANGLES

Suppose that you know that a triangle has a base of 5 cm and a height of 4 cm. One of the other sides is 4.5 cm long. Use your compass and straightedge to construct the triangle. Follow the steps below.

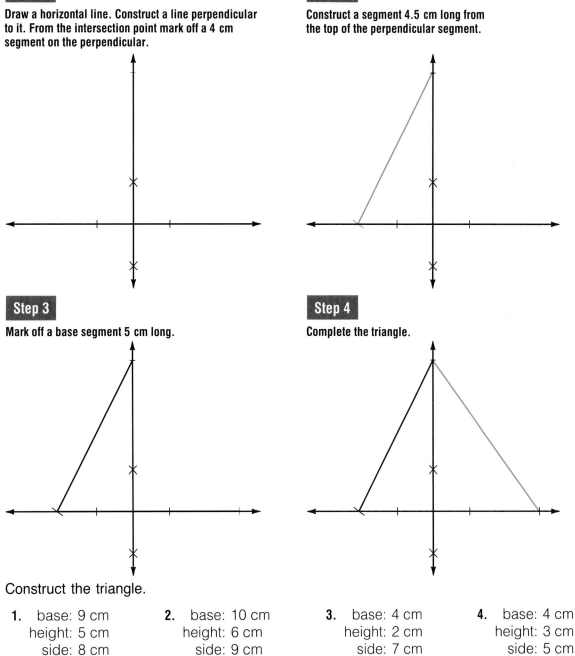

Step 1

Draw a horizontal line. Construct a line perpendicular to it. From the intersection point mark off a 4 cm segment on the perpendicular.

Step 2

Construct a segment 4.5 cm long from the top of the perpendicular segment.

Step 3

Mark off a base segment 5 cm long.

Step 4

Complete the triangle.

Construct the triangle.

1. base: 9 cm
    height: 5 cm
    side: 8 cm

2. base: 10 cm
    height: 6 cm
    side: 9 cm

3. base: 4 cm
    height: 2 cm
    side: 7 cm

4. base: 4 cm
    height: 3 cm
    side: 5 cm

CUMULATIVE REVIEW

Choose the letter of the correct answer.

1. What is the GCF of 10 and 12?

   a. 2   **c.** 120
   b. 60   **d.** not given

2. What is the LCM of 6 and 9?

   a. 3   **c.** 54
   b. 36   **d.** not given

3. Solve for n: $n - 1 = 5\frac{2}{3}$

   a. $5\frac{1}{3}$ **c.** $6\frac{2}{3}$
   b. $4\frac{2}{3}$ **d.** not given

4. Solve for n: $n + \frac{3}{4} = 6\frac{1}{2}$

   a. $5\frac{3}{4}$ **c.** $7\frac{1}{4}$
   b. $6\frac{1}{4}$ **d.** not given

5. Solve for n: $n - 2\frac{5}{7} = 5\frac{1}{2}$

   a. $1\frac{3}{14}$ **c.** $8\frac{3}{14}$
   b. $2\frac{4}{5}$ **d.** not given

6. First round to the nearest whole numbers and then find the product of $5\frac{1}{6} \times 4\frac{7}{8}$.

   a. 20   **c.** 30
   b. 24   **d.** not given

7. $\frac{2}{9} \times 6$

   a. $\frac{12}{54}$ **c.** $6\frac{2}{9}$
   b. $1\frac{1}{3}$ **d.** not given

8. $2\frac{1}{3} \div \frac{2}{3}$

   a. $2\frac{2}{9}$ **c.** $3\frac{1}{2}$
   b. $2\frac{2}{3}$ **d.** not given

9. $15 \div \frac{3}{5}$

   a. $\frac{5}{3}$ **c.** 25
   b. 9   **d.** not given

10. What is the square root of 25?

   a. 5   **c.** 625
   b. 50   **d.** not given

11. Complete: All ■ are similar.

   a. squares
   b. rhombuses
   c. rectangles
   d. not given

12. What kind of angle is shown?

   a. acute   **c.** right
   b. obtuse   **d.** not given

13. What kind of triangle is shown?

   a. obtuse   **c.** scalene
   b. isoceles   **d.** not given

14. What kind of quadrilateral is shown?

   a. square   **c.** parallelogram
   b. rhombus   **d.** not given

Ratio, Proportion, and Percent

MATH CONNECTIONS: ALGEBRA • GEOMETRY • PROBLEM SOLVING

(newspaper in photo)

VIDEO NEWS

CLASSIFIED

NATIONAL VCR SALES

NUMBER OF UNITS
1,000,000
900,000
800,000
700,000
600,000
500,000
400,000
300,000
200,000
100,000

October   November   December
MONTH

1. What information do you see in this picture?
2. How can you use the information?
3. About how many million units were sold during the three month period?
4. Write a problem using the information.

UNDERSTANDING A CONCEPT

Ratios and Equal Ratios

A. The museum has a new display which includes three plant-eating dinosaurs and two meat-eating dinosaurs. The ratio of plant-eating dinosaurs to meat-eating dinosaurs is 3 to 2.

A **ratio** is used to compare two quantities. The numbers 3 and 2 are called the **terms** of the ratio. The ratio may be written in three ways: 3:2 or $\frac{3}{2}$ or 3 to 2.

1. What is the ratio of plant-eating dinosaurs to all the dinosaurs shown? Write the ratio in three ways.

B. Equal ratios make the same comparison.

You can find equal ratios by multiplying **(scaling up)** or dividing **(scaling down)** both terms of a ratio by the same nonzero number.

$$\overset{\times 2}{\overset{\frown}{\frac{2}{5}}} \overset{\times 2}{= \overset{\frown}{\frac{4}{10}}} = \frac{8}{20} \qquad \overset{\div 2}{\overset{\frown}{\frac{12}{18}}} \overset{\div 3}{= \overset{\frown}{\frac{6}{9}}} = \frac{2}{3}$$

2. Which ratios are in simplest form?

3. How would you write the ratio 1.5 to 4.5 in simplest form?

TRY OUT Write the letter of the correct answer. What is the ratio in simplest form?

10 fish	9 amphibians	8 reptiles

4. reptiles to amphibians
  a. 9 to 8   **b.** 9 to 10   **c.** 8 to 9   **d.** 8 to 10

5. fish to reptiles
  a. $\frac{5}{4}$ **b.** $\frac{10}{9}$ **c.** $\frac{4}{5}$ **d.** $\frac{9}{10}$

6. amphibians to all animals
  a. 1:2   **b.** 1:3   **c.** 4:5   **d.** 5:4

7. all animals to fish
  a. $\frac{27}{10}$ **b.** 10:27   **c.** 19 to 10   **d.** $\frac{19}{8}$

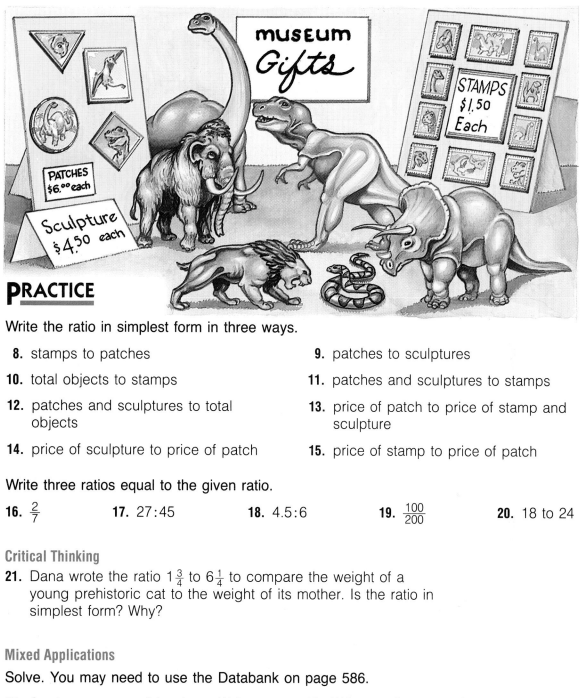

PRACTICE

Write the ratio in simplest form in three ways.

8. stamps to patches

9. patches to sculptures

10. total objects to stamps

11. patches and sculptures to stamps

12. patches and sculptures to total objects

13. price of patch to price of stamp and sculpture

14. price of sculpture to price of patch

15. price of stamp to price of patch

Write three ratios equal to the given ratio.

16. $\frac{2}{7}$

17. $27:45$

18. $4.5:6$

19. $\frac{100}{200}$

20. 18 to 24

Critical Thinking

21. Dana wrote the ratio $1\frac{3}{4}$ to $6\frac{1}{4}$ to compare the weight of a young prehistoric cat to the weight of its mother. Is the ratio in simplest form? Why?

Mixed Applications

Solve. You may need to use the Databank on page 586.

22. Apatosaurus was 24 m long. Write a ratio comparing the length of apatosaurus to that of comptosaurus, which was 4.8 m long.

23. Write a ratio comparing the length of tyrannosaurus rex to that of megalosaurus.

24. Tyrannosaurus rex lived from 130 million to 65 million years ago. For how many years did this species live? Write your answer in standard form.

25. Stegosaurus was 25 ft long. How many times as long as a 3.5-ft-long dog was stegosaurus? (Round your answer to the nearest tenth.)

UNDERSTANDING A CONCEPT

Using Rates: Mental Math

A. The Milsteins rented a car at the rate of $27.50 per day. They rented the car for 8 days. How much did they pay?

One way to find the answer mentally is by scaling up.

$27.50 for 1 day $27.50 for 1 day

■ for 8 days $55.00 for 2 days

                          $110.00 for 4 days

                          $220.00 for 8 days

$\left.\right\} \times 2$ $\left.\right\} \times 2$ $\left.\right\} \times 2$

The Milsteins paid $220.00 for the rental car.

1. How much would the Milsteins pay for 16 days?

B. The Wilsons' rental car used 8 gal of gasoline on a 240-mi trip. How many miles does the car go on 1 gal of gasoline?

Gasoline mileage can be written as a rate, $\frac{\text{number of mi}}{\text{number of gal}}$. A **rate** is a ratio that compares different kinds of units. When the second term of a rate is 1, the rate is a **unit rate.**

Sometimes you can find the unit rate mentally by scaling down.

240 mi uses 8 gal   240 mi ⟶ 8 gal

■ mi uses 1 gal   120 mi ⟶ 4 gal

                     60 mi ⟶ 2 gal

                     30 mi ⟶ 1 gal

$\left.\right\} \div 2$ $\left.\right\} \div 2$ $\left.\right\} \div 2$

The Wilsons' car went 30 mi on 1 gal of gasoline, or 30 mi per gal.

2. How can you find the unit rate by dividing one time?

C. Rent-a-Rattler charges $56 per week for a rental car. The Chung family needs a car for 10 days. What will the car cost them?

Step 1

Find the unit rate by scaling down.

$56 for 7 days

$8 for 1 day

$\left.\right\} \div 7$

Step 2

Find the 10-day cost by scaling up.

$8 for 1 day

$80 for 10 days

$\left.\right\} \times 10$

The Chung family will pay $80 for the 10-day rental.

3. What is the cost of a 4-day rental? a 16-day rental?

TRY OUT Write the letter of the correct answer.

4. The gas tank of Clyde's car holds 16 gal. He can drive the car 400 mi without refueling. What is his gas mileage in miles per gallon (mpg)?

a. 8 mpg **b.** 384 mpg **c.** 16 mpg **d.** 25 mpg

5. Van's Van charges $32.50 to rent a van for 2 days. What is the cost to rent a van for 3 days?

a. $4.87 **b.** $48.75 **c.** $16.25 **d.** $42.50

PRACTICE

Use mental math to find the unit rate. Write the answer as a fraction.

6. 160 km in 2 hours   **7.** 40 mi in 4 hours   **8.** 280 mi in 8 hours

9. 180 km on 6 gal   **10.** 320 km on 8 gal   **11.** $64 for 16 days

12. 165 mi in 3 hours   **13.** $72 for 8 days   **14.** 156 mi on 12 gal

Solve. Use mental math.

15. 150 mi using 3 gal
How many miles on 1 gal?

16. 270 mi using 9 gal
How many miles on 1 gal?

17. $25 for 1 day
How much for 4 days?

18. 22.5 mi using 1 gal
How many miles on 4 gal?

19. 140 mi using 7 gal
How many miles on 10 gal?

20. $124 for 8 weeks
How much for 2 weeks?

21. $65 for 5 days
How much for 3 days?

22. $2,100 for 3 months
How much for 7 months?

Mixed Applications

23. Victoria bought 6 road maps for $27.90. What did each cost?

24. The cost for a weekly car rental is $84. What would it cost to rent a car for 12 days?

25. It is 275 km from Macville to Kaneville. Flo has driven $\frac{2}{5}$ of the way. How much farther does she have to go?

26. Sandy bought oil for $1.10, gas for $10.75, washer fluid for $1.49, and dry gas for $.79. Estimate the total cost.

Mixed Review

Find the answer. Which method did you use?

MENTAL MATH
CALCULATOR
PAPER/PENCIL

27. 0.7×42 **28.** $\$2.95 + \$4.87$ **29.** $\frac{3}{8} \times 48$ **30.** $34.07 - 8.6$

31. $80 \div 0.5$ **32.** $\frac{2}{3} + 1\frac{1}{2} + 4\frac{5}{6}$ **33.** $\frac{8}{9} \div \frac{4}{5}$ **34.** $1.7 + 23.8 + 4.5$

UNDERSTANDING A CONCEPT

Solving Proportions

A. Mark wants to buy a new bicycle that costs $240. He earns $30 in 4 hours mowing lawns. How many hours will Mark have to work in order to earn enough money to buy the bicycle?

Mark writes a proportion to help find the answer. A **proportion** is an equation that states that two ratios are equal.

Let n represent the number of hours worked to earn $240.

$$\text{hours worked} \rightarrow \frac{4}{30} = \frac{n}{240} \leftarrow \text{hours worked}$$
$$\text{earnings} \rightarrow \qquad\qquad \leftarrow \text{earnings}$$

To solve the proportion mentally, Mark finds equal ratios by scaling up.

$$\frac{4}{30} = \frac{n}{240} \qquad \textit{Think: } 240 = 30 \times 8 \qquad \frac{4}{30} = \frac{4 \times 8}{30 \times 8} = \frac{32}{240}$$

Mark will have to work 32 hours to earn $240.

1. Are there other ways you could have scaled up to solve the proportion?

B. If two ratios are equal, then their **cross products** are equal. You can use cross products to check if two ratios are equal.

In the proportion $\frac{4}{30} = \frac{32}{240}$, the cross products are **4 × 240** and **30 × 32.**

2. Find 4 × 240 and 30 × 32. Are the two products the same? Are $\frac{4}{30}$ and $\frac{32}{240}$ equal ratios?

C. You can also use cross products to solve a proportion.

Solve the proportion.	$\frac{2}{5} = \frac{5}{n}$
Find the cross products.	$2 \times n = 5 \times 5$
Solve for n.	$2n = 25$
Think: Divide both sides by 2.	$\frac{2n}{2} = \frac{25}{2}$
	$n = 12\frac{1}{2}$

3. How can you check that the solution is correct?

4. Why would the above proportion not be easy to solve by scaling up?

5. *What if* you wanted to solve $\frac{n}{7} = \frac{24}{48}$? How would writing $\frac{24}{48}$ in simplest form make the problem easier?

TRY OUT   Solve the proportion. Check your solution.

6. $\frac{5}{n} = \frac{20}{24}$

7. $\frac{7}{9} = \frac{n}{54}$

8. $\frac{3}{2} = \frac{16}{n}$

9. $\frac{n}{2.1} = \frac{30}{12.6}$

PRACTICE

Are the ratios equal? Write = or ≠.

10. $\frac{3}{4} \bullet \frac{6}{8}$

11. $\frac{8}{5} \bullet \frac{20}{15}$

12. $\frac{7}{8} \bullet \frac{21}{24}$

13. $\frac{12}{16} \bullet \frac{8}{12}$

14. $\frac{5}{6} \bullet \frac{25}{36}$

15. $\frac{9}{4} \bullet \frac{21}{14}$

16. $\frac{4}{7} \bullet \frac{10}{17.5}$

17. $\frac{10}{16} \bullet \frac{15}{24}$

18. $\frac{60}{70} \bullet \frac{70}{60}$

19. $\frac{2}{3} \bullet \frac{88}{132}$

Solve the proportion. Do as many as you can mentally.

20. $\frac{1}{5} = \frac{n}{15}$

21. $\frac{4}{7} = \frac{26}{n}$

22. $\frac{n}{27} = \frac{5}{9}$

23. $\frac{2}{n} = \frac{1}{11}$

24. $\frac{8}{6} = \frac{n}{24}$

25. $\frac{n}{9} = \frac{25}{50}$

26. $\frac{8}{n} = \frac{10}{2}$

27. $\frac{3}{10} = \frac{n}{7}$

28. $\frac{3}{5} = \frac{n}{8}$

29. $\frac{9}{15} = \frac{n}{18}$

30. $\frac{5.5}{2.2} = \frac{11}{n}$

31. $\frac{3}{10} = \frac{1.5}{n}$

32. $\frac{6}{1.2} = \frac{n}{4.8}$

33. $\frac{3}{n} = \frac{4}{6}$

34. $\frac{n}{3.6} = \frac{25}{100}$

35. $\frac{14}{8} = \frac{n}{100}$

36. $\frac{16}{11} = \frac{96}{n}$

37. $\frac{5}{4} = \frac{1.25}{n}$

38. $\frac{4}{n} = \frac{8}{2.75}$

39. $\frac{2.5}{n} = \frac{12.5}{40}$

40. $\frac{7}{n} = \frac{1.4}{2.8}$

41. $\frac{3}{n} = \frac{35}{14}$

42. $\frac{3.4}{34} = \frac{0.21}{n}$

43. $\frac{1.3}{n} = \frac{6.5}{15}$

44. $\frac{3}{7} = \frac{n}{5}$

Critical Thinking

45. Given that $\frac{1}{2} = \frac{3}{6}$, write three other proportions using the numbers 1, 2, 3, and 6.

Mixed Applications

46. Ivan worked 8 hours one holiday and was paid time and a half. If his hourly wage was $4.88, how much did he earn?

47. Roberta earned $1,413.60 one summer. If she worked 20 hours a week for 12 weeks, how much did she earn per hour?

48. Sally mows lawns on weekends. She mowed 4 lawns in 6 hours. At that rate how long will it take her to mow 6 lawns?

49. **Write a problem** involving a proportion. Solve your problem. Ask others to solve it.

Mixed Review

Find the answer. Which method did you use?

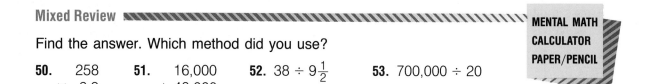

50. $\begin{array}{r} 258 \\ \times\ 3.9 \\ \hline \end{array}$

51. $\begin{array}{r} 16,000 \\ +\ 48,000 \\ \hline \end{array}$

52. $38 \div 9\frac{1}{2}$

53. $700,000 \div 20$

MENTAL MATH
CALCULATOR
PAPER/PENCIL

54. $5\frac{1}{2} \times 3\frac{2}{3}$

55. 0.065×0.4

56. $12.68 + 5.32$

57. $34.57 - 9.98$

UNDERSTANDING A CONCEPT

Scale Drawings and Similar Figures

A. Greg is an architect designing a new racquet club. The scale drawing shows one of the courts. The length of the back wall on the drawing is 1 in. What is the actual length?

You can write and solve a proportion to solve the problem.

Think: The scale is 0.5 in. = 10 ft.

Let n = the length of the back wall in feet.

length in drawing (in.) → $\dfrac{0.5}{10} = \dfrac{1}{n}$ ← length in drawing (in.)
actual length (ft) →   ← actual length (ft)

Solve the proportion mentally.

Think: $0.5 \times 2 = 1$ $\dfrac{0.5}{10} = \dfrac{0.5 \times 2}{10 \times 2} = \dfrac{1}{20}$

$$n = 20$$

The back wall is 20 ft long.

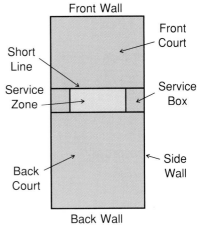

Front Wall

Front Court

Short Line

Service Zone

Service Box

Back Court

Side Wall

Back Wall
Scale: 0.5 in. = 10 ft

1. The width of the service box is 5 ft. What is the width in the scale drawing?

2. **What if** Greg had made a second drawing of the racquetball court using the scale 1 in. = 10 ft? How would each of the lengths have compared with those in the first drawing?

B. The scale drawings and the actual objects they represent are examples of similar figures. Corresponding sides of similar figures are in proportion. The sign of the racquet club and the card are similar figures. What is the height of the card?

Let n = height of card. Write a proportion.

width of sign → $\dfrac{18}{3} = \dfrac{12}{n}$ ← height of sign
width of card →   ← height of card

Cross multiply to solve. $18 \times n = 3 \times 12$
$$18n = 36$$
$$n = 2$$

The card is 2 in. high.

12 in.

JOIN THE RACQUET CLUB

18 in.

n

3 in.

3. What is the ratio of the height of the sign to its width? What is the ratio of the height of the card to its width? What do you notice about the two ratios?

TRY OUT Solve for *n*.

4. Scale: 1 cm = 4 m
Drawing: 5 cm
Actual: *n*

5. Scale: 2 in. = 5 mi
Drawing: 6.5 in.
Actual: *n*

6.
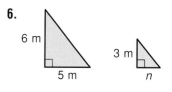

PRACTICE

Solve for *n*.

7. Scale: 1 cm = 3 km
Drawing: 6 cm
Actual: *n*

8. Scale: 3 in. = 5 ft
Drawing: 9 in.
Actual: *n*

9. Scale: 1 cm = 5 m
Drawing: 4 cm
Actual: *n*

10. Scale: 0.5 in. = 5 ft
Drawing: 2 in.
Actual: *n*

11. Scale: 0.5 cm = 4 m
Drawing: 4 cm
Actual: *n*

12. Scale: 2 in. = 14 mi
Drawing: 9.5 in.
Actual: *n*

13. Scale: 2.5 cm = 6 m
Drawing: *n*
Actual: 18 m

14. Scale: 2 cm = 15 km
Drawing: *n*
Actual: 75 km

15. Scale: 2 cm = 7.5 m
Drawing: *n*
Actual: 30 m

16. Scale: 0.5 in. represents 25 mi.
If the drawing shows 4 in., the actual
length is *n* mi.

17. Scale: 1.5 cm represents 4 m.
If the drawing shows *n* cm, the actual
length is 16 m.

Solve for *n* for the pair of similar figures.

18.
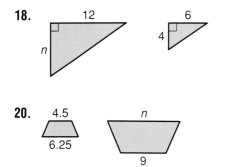

19.
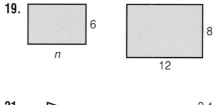

20.

21.
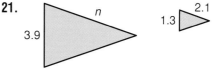

Mixed Applications

Solve. You may need to use the Databank on page 582.

22. Eugene made a model of a football field using the scale
1 in. = 4 ft. What are the dimensions of Eugene's model?

23. Make a scale drawing of a football field using a scale different
from the one Eugene used.

24. The distance from Morrisville to Lanesburg is 315 mi. Jake has
driven $\frac{2}{3}$ of the way. How far does he have to go?

EXTRA Practice, page 409

Ratio, Proportion, and Percent **381**

✓ UNDERSTAND
✓ PLAN
✓ TRY
CHECK
✓ EXTEND

PROBLEM SOLVING

Strategy: Using Proportions

Bob and Janine want to make carrot cake for a class party. They got this recipe from a book of recipes for healthful snacks.

Carrot Cake

1 cup vegetable oil
2 cups grated carrots
1 cup brown sugar
3 tbs. honey
4 eggs beaten
2 tsp. baking soda
2 cups flour
2½ tsp. cinnamon
Combine first five ingredients and mix well.
Add combined soda, flour and cinnamon.
Bake in a greased and floured 13 inch by
9 inch pan at 325° for 40 to 45 minutes.
Serves 12.

Bob and Janine want to bake enough carrot cake to serve 66 people. How many cups of flour do they need? They plan to use a proportion to solve the problem.

Write and solve a proportion.

cups of flour ⟶ $\dfrac{2}{12} = \dfrac{x}{66}$ ⟵ cups of flour
people served ⟶ $\phantom{\dfrac{2}{12}}$ ⟵ people served

$$12x = 2 \times 66$$
$$x = 11$$

Bob and Janine need 11 c of flour.

Show how much of the ingredient they need to serve 66 people.

1. oil
2. carrots
3. brown sugar
4. honey

5. eggs
6. baking soda
7. cinnamon

8. **What if** they wished to use 30 eggs? How much of each ingredient would they need?

Applesauce Cake

2/3 cup margarine
1 cup sugar
2 tsp. baking soda
1½ cups unsweetened hot applesauce

2 cups flour
1 cup raisins

Pour melted shortening into hot applesauce. Add sugar. Sift flour, baking soda, and cinnamon. Add raisins. If desired, add cinnamon, nuts, and wheatgerm to taste. Bake in a greased 9 inch by 13 inch pan at 375° for 1 hour or in two 8 inch pans for 25 minutes and have one to freeze.

PRACTICE

Use a proportion to solve. Round to the nearest tenth.

9. Carmen and Luigi decided to make applesauce cake. They had 4 c of applesauce they wished to use in the cake. How much of each ingredient would they need?

10. *What if* Carmen and Luigi had only 1 c of applesauce, how much of each ingredient would they need?

Strategies and Skills Review

Solve. Use mental math, estimation, a calculator, or paper and pencil.

11. One cook made 12 cookies that weighed 4 oz each. Another batch of 8 cookies weighed 6.5 oz each. Another cook made 1 cookie that weighed 7.5 oz. How many ounces of cookies is that all together?

12. The town was 100 years old. The bakers made a huge birthday cake and put a 2-ft candle in its center. The candle's shadow is 5 ft long. A statue of the founder casts a shadow 20 ft long. How tall is the statue?

13. Ann separated a box of cookies into two groups. Next, she separated each group into two more groups, and then repeated this process six more times. How many groups of cookies did she form?

14. A bakery donates 1.5% of its baked goods to the poor. The bakers make about 2 T of goods per week. About how many weeks will it take to donate 1,000 lb of baked goods?

15. During a shortage a loaf of bread got very expensive. Here is what happened to its price in the first 4 weeks: $.50, $1.00, $3.00, $12.00. If this pattern continues, what will prices be in the next 2 weeks?

16. *Write a problem* that could be solved by using a proportion. Have another student solve the problem.

Ratio, Proportion, and Percent **383**

Watch Things Grow

Investigating Patterns

A. At different times, the United States Treasury has issued paper money with the following values:

Suppose you take these three values and form a sequence:

Notice that the ratios of pairs of successive terms are the same, in this case 1:2.

1. What is the next term of this sequence? Is it a paper-money value? Are any other terms in this sequence paper-money values?

2. Use only the values of the money shown above. How many different sequences can you form containing three or more terms such that the ratios for pairs of successive terms are the same?

3. Did you find at least one sequence using the $2 bill? If not, try again.

4. Compare and discuss your findings with other students.

B. Fred Factor, communications director for The Outdoor Club, has set up a system designed to rapidly inform club members of important announcements. Fred wrote the names and telephone numbers of all club members on lists, each containing 5 names and numbers. He kept one list for himself and distributed the other lists to club members. When an important announcement must be rapidly communicated to the club members, Fred makes telephone calls to the 5 members on his list and tells them the message. Then each member who receives a call relays the message by telephone to the 5 members on his or her list. This process continues until all the members on all the lists have been called.

5. How many calls does Fred make to pass on a message?

6. If all the members called by Fred call all the people on their lists, how many additional calls will be made?

7. If all the additional members called in Problem 6 then call all the people on their lists, how many calls will they make? What pattern do you notice? How many calls will have been made in all?

8. Suppose one of the people Fred called lost his or her list and could not make any calls. How many club members would be called if everyone else who was called made all their calls?

9. Another club uses a similar system, with each list showing 6 names and numbers. If it takes three "complete rounds" for a message to be relayed, how many calls are made in the third round? How many calls are made in all?

UNDERSTANDING A CONCEPT

Percent

A. One hundred pets are entered in the National Pet Singing Contest. In the first round of the competition, 17 out of the 100 pets refused to make a sound. How can you express this ratio as a percent?

A **percent** is a ratio that compares a number to 100. *Percent* means "per hundred."

17 out of 100 = 17:100 = $\frac{17}{100}$ = 17%

So 17% did not make a sound.

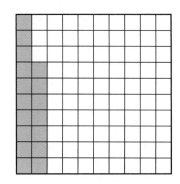

1. What percent of the pets did sing a song?

B. You can use equal ratios to rename a fraction with a denominator of 10 or 1,000 as a percent.

Rename $\frac{9}{10}$ as a percent.

Think: Scale up by 10.

$\frac{9}{10} = \frac{9 \times 10}{10 \times 10} = \frac{90}{100} = 90\%$

Rename $\frac{50}{1,000}$ as a percent.

Think: Scale down by 10.

$\frac{50}{1,000} = \frac{50 \div 10}{1,000 \div 10} = \frac{5.0}{100} = 5\%$

2 How would you rename $\frac{55}{1,000}$ as a percent?

TRY OUT Rename as a percent.

3. 9 out of 100   **4.** 6:100   **5.** $\frac{60}{100}$ **6.** $\frac{44}{1,000}$

PRACTICE

What percent of the grid is shaded?

7. **8.** **9.**

Rename as a percent.

10. 7 out of 100   **11.** 70 out of 100   **12.** 65 out of 100   **13.** 23 out of 100

14. 6:100   **15.** 3:100   **16.** 14:100   **17.** 87:100   **18.** $\frac{40}{100}$ **19.** $\frac{95}{100}$

20. $\frac{55}{100}$ **21.** $\frac{59}{100}$ **22.** $\frac{1}{10}$ **23.** $\frac{3}{10}$ **24.** $\frac{5}{10}$ **25.** $\frac{7}{10}$

26. $\frac{36}{1,000}$ **27.** $\frac{89}{1,000}$ **28.** $\frac{95}{100}$ **29.** $\frac{7}{1,000}$ **30.** $\frac{54}{1,000}$ **31.** $\frac{900}{1,000}$

Compare. Write >, <, or =.

32. $\frac{9}{10}$ ● 80%   **33.** $\frac{76}{1,000}$ ● 76%   **34.** 60% ● $\frac{60}{100}$ **35.** $\frac{36}{100}$ ● 63%

One dollar is equal to 100 cents. What percent of a dollar is the amount?

36. $.15   **37.** 29¢   **38.** $.88   **39.** 7¢   **40.** $.09   **41.** 11¢

42. 5 nickels   **43.** 2 quarters and a nickel   **44.** 1 quarter, 2 dimes, and a nickel

KNEEDEEP

Mixed Applications

45. Twenty-three birds and 8 cats entered the contest. What is the ratio of cats to birds?

46. Four out of 10 pets at the contest will return next year. What percent will return?

47. On a map with a scale of 1 in. = 4 mi, the theater is 3 in. from the hotel. What is the actual distance?

48. *Write a problem* that involves renaming a fraction as a percent. Solve your problem. Ask others to solve it.

Decimals and Percents

A. Shana surveyed the students in her class and found that 0.65 of them watch a daily television news report and that 0.4 of them listen to a daily radio news report. What percent of the students watch a television news report? What percent of them listen to a radio news report?

One way to rename a decimal as a percent is to rename the decimal as a fraction with a denominator of 100 and then rename the fraction as a percent.

Think: $0.65 = 65$ hundredths $= \frac{65}{100} = 65\%$

$0.4 = 4$ tenths $= \frac{4}{10} = \frac{40}{100} = 40\%$

So 65% of the students in Shana's class watch a TV news report, and 40% of them listen to a radio news report.

1. What percent is 0.048 equivalent to?

B. You can use a shortcut to rename a decimal as a percent.

Think: Move the decimal point two places to the right, and write the percent sign.

$0.54 \longrightarrow 0.5\,4 \longrightarrow 54\%$

$0.6 \longrightarrow 0.6\,0 \longrightarrow 60\%$

$0.037 \longrightarrow 0.0\,3\,7 \longrightarrow 3.7\%$

C. You can also use a shortcut to rename a percent as a decimal.

Think: Move the decimal point two places to the left, and omit the percent sign.

$48\% \longrightarrow 4\,8.\% \longrightarrow 0.48$

$8.2\% \longrightarrow 0\,8.2\% \longrightarrow 0.082$

$16.75\% \longrightarrow 1\,6.7\,5\% \longrightarrow 0.1675$

TRY OUT

Rename as a percent.

2. 0.28　　　**3.** 0.62　　　**4.** 0.9　　　**5.** 0.01　　　**6.** 0.535

Rename as a decimal.

7. 34%　　　**8.** 75%　　　**9.** 50%　　　**10.** 6%　　　**11.** 82.4%

PRACTICE

Rename as a decimal.

12. 43% **13.** 29% **14.** 55% **15.** 38% **16.** 40% **17.** 2%

18. 4% **19.** 9% **20.** 12% **21.** 25.9% **22.** 18.8% **23.** 90.4%

24. thirty-three and one-half percent **25.** twenty and two-fifths percent

Rename as a percent.

26. 0.35 **27.** 0.94 **28.** 0.28 **29.** 0.13 **30.** 0.66 **31.** 0.9

32. 0.03 **33.** 0.07 **34.** 0.04 **35.** 0.355 **36.** 0.045 **37.** 0.503

38. seventeen hundredths **39.** ninety-eight thousandths

Mixed Applications

40. In another class survey Rob found that 0.44 of the students go to at least two movies per month. Rename this decimal as a percent.

41. Kevin surveyed 50 students at random and found that the tallest was $70\frac{1}{2}$ in. and the shortest was $49\frac{7}{8}$ in. Find the difference between the two heights.

42. Tamborah made a table to show the results of a survey of the students in her class regarding their favorite foods. Make a bar graph to show the results of Tamborah's survey.

FAVORITE FOODS SURVEY

Food	Number of Students
Pizza	20
Hamburger	15
Chicken	8
Taco	14
None of these	3

43. In a class survey 48 students said they walk to school each day. This is $1\frac{1}{2}$ times the number who come by bus. How many come by bus?

CHALLENGE

Estimate what percent is shaded.

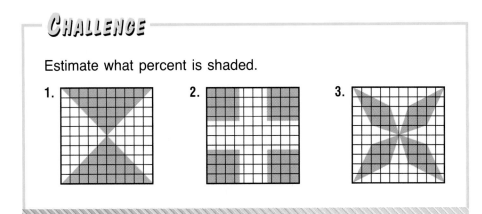

1. 2. 3.

UNDERSTANDING A CONCEPT

Fractions and Percents

A. In the last 20 Olympic Games, $\frac{3}{4}$ of the records set in the 400-m dash were under 49 seconds. What percent is this?

Here are two methods you can use to rename a fraction as a percent:

Method 1	Method 2
Divide. Rename the decimal as a percent.	**Write an equivalent fraction with a denominator of 100.**

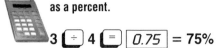

$3 \boxed{\div} 4 \boxed{=} \boxed{0.75} = 75\%$ 　　　　 $\frac{3}{4} = \frac{3 \times 25}{4 \times 25} = \frac{75}{100} = 75\%$

So 75% of the records set in the 400-m dash were under 49 seconds.

1. Rename $\frac{1}{8}$ as a percent. Which method did you use? Why?

B. When division results in a repeating decimal, rename the decimal as a mixed number.

$\frac{5}{6} = 5 \boxed{\div} 6 \boxed{=} \boxed{0.8333333} \longrightarrow 83.\overline{3}\% \text{ or } 83\frac{1}{3}\%$

C. You can rename a percent as a fraction.

Use 100 as the denominator and write the fraction in simplest form.

Rename 45% as a fraction. 　　　　 Rename $16\frac{2}{3}\%$ as a fraction.

$$45\% = \frac{45}{100} = \frac{45 \div 5}{100 \div 5} = \frac{9}{20}$$

$$16\frac{2}{3}\% = \frac{16\frac{2}{3}}{100} = 16\frac{2}{3} \div 100$$
$$= 16\frac{2}{3} \times \frac{1}{100}$$
$$= \frac{50}{3} \times \frac{1}{100} = \frac{1}{6}$$

2. How would you rename 48.2% as a fraction in simplest form?

TRY OUT

Rename as a percent.

3. $\frac{8}{25}$ **4.** $\frac{1}{6}$ **5.** $\frac{3}{8}$ **6.** $\frac{4}{5}$

Rename as a fraction in simplest form.

7. 45%   **8.** $41\frac{2}{3}\%$ **9.** 54.4%   **10.** 16.5%

PRACTICE

Rename as a percent.

11. $\frac{2}{5}$ **12.** $\frac{1}{4}$ **13.** $\frac{7}{10}$ **14.** $\frac{3}{5}$ **15.** $\frac{1}{10}$ **16.** $\frac{5}{8}$

17. $\frac{7}{9}$ **18.** $\frac{2}{7}$ **19.** $\frac{7}{12}$ **20.** $\frac{11}{15}$ **21.** $\frac{63}{200}$ **22.** $\frac{3}{80}$

Rename as a fraction.

23. 25%   **24.** 40%   **25.** 50%   **26.** 90%   **27.** 20%   **28.** 54%

29. $8\frac{1}{3}\%$ **30.** $66\frac{2}{3}\%$ **31.** $62\frac{1}{2}\%$ **32.** $33\frac{1}{3}\%$ **33.** 29.6%   **34.** 31.5%

Copy and complete the table.

	Fraction	Decimal	Percent
35.	$\frac{7}{100}$	■	■
36.	■	0.12	■
37.	■	■	30%
38.	■	0.8	■
39.	$\frac{9}{25}$	■	■

	Fraction	Decimal	Percent
40.	■	0.05	■
41.	$\frac{3}{8}$	■	■
42.	■	■	88%
43.	■	0.625	■
44.	■	■	$55\frac{5}{9}\%$

Mixed Applications

Solve. Which method did you use?

45. In a recent Olympic Games, the United States won $\frac{2}{3}$ as many gold medals as the Soviet Union. Rename the fraction as a percent.

46. During the 1988 Olympic Games, there were 1,750 minutes of TV commercials. If the price of a 1-minute commercial was $620,000, about how much revenue was raised from commercials?

47. Four people each ran 100 m in the 400-m relay. The team won a gold medal with a total time of 37.83 seconds. What was the average time of each person to the nearest hundredth second?

> ESTIMATION
> MENTAL MATH
> CALCULATOR
> PAPER/PENCIL

Percents Greater Than 100 and Less Than 1

A. The secretary of a 400-member club called the airline to find out if one of its planes would hold the entire club. He was told that a jumbo jet would hold 120% of them. Will the entire club fit on the plane?

You can use a model to show percents greater than 100%.

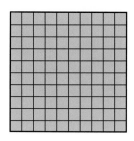

1. How does the model show 120%?

2. Using the model, explain what 120% means.

You can also write 120% as a decimal or as a fraction or mixed number.

$$120\% \longrightarrow 120. \longrightarrow 1.20 = 1.2 \qquad 120\% = \frac{120}{100} = \frac{6}{5} \longrightarrow 1\frac{1}{5}$$

The entire club will fit on the plane. There will also be extra space.

3. Draw models for 110% and 250%. Rename each as a decimal and as a fraction.

4. Rename 1.85, $1\frac{1}{2}$, and 3 as a percent.

B. You can use a model to show percents less than 1%.

5. This model shows $\frac{1}{2}$%. What does $\frac{1}{2}$% mean?

You can also rename $\frac{1}{2}$% as a decimal or as a fraction.

$$\frac{1}{2}\% = 0.5\% \longrightarrow 00.5 \longrightarrow 0.005$$

$$\frac{1}{2}\% = \frac{\frac{1}{2}}{100} = \frac{1}{2} \div 100 = \frac{1}{2} \times \frac{1}{100} = \frac{1}{200}$$

6. Draw a model for 0.25%.

7. Rename:
  a. $\frac{3}{4}$% as a decimal and as a fraction.
  b. 0.7% as a fraction.
  c. 0.004 and $\frac{1}{250}$ as a percent.
  d. $\frac{1}{125}$ as a percent.

SHARING IDEAS

8. Which is greater, 5 or 500%? $\frac{1}{5}$% or $\frac{1}{5}$?

9. How can you rename 225% as a decimal using a calculator?

10. How can you rename $\frac{1}{4}$% as a decimal using a calculator?

PRACTICE

Rename as a decimal.

11. 175%   **12.** 120%   **13.** 185%   **14.** 250%   **15.** 225%   **16.** 300%

17. 134%   **18.** 240%   **19.** $\frac{1}{4}$%   **20.** $\frac{2}{5}$%   **21.** $\frac{1}{8}$%   **22.** $\frac{7}{10}$%

23. 0.6%   **24.** 0.9%   **25.** 0.8%   **26.** 0.55%   **27.** 0.73%   **28.** 0.16%

Rename as a fraction or as a mixed number.

29. 110%   **30.** 140%   **31.** 220%   **32.** 180%   **33.** 350%   **34.** 912%

35. 0.6%   **36.** 0.4%   **37.** 0.25%   **38.** 0.85%   **39.** 0.12%   **40.** 0.55%

Rename as a percent.

41. 0.7   **42.** 1.6   **43.** 4.32   **44.** $1\frac{3}{5}$ **45.** $1\frac{2}{5}$ **46.** $2\frac{3}{8}$

47. 0.075   **48.** 0.004   **49.** 0.317   **50.** $\frac{1}{4}$ **51.** $\frac{1}{500}$ **52.** $\frac{1}{25}$

Write in order from greatest to least.

53. 1.6, 0.3%, 165%, 0.004, $\frac{1}{200}$

54. 178%, $1\frac{7}{8}$, 0.007, 0.8%, $\frac{1}{100}$

The table shows the sizes of some groups flying overseas and the seating capacity of the airplanes in which they are flying.

Group	Membership	Seating Capacity of Chartered Plane
Dentists	300	150
Jugglers	15	600
Mimes	600	500
Scientists	500	550

55. What percent of the capacity of the plane do the dentists make up?

56. What percent of the capacity of the plane do the jugglers make up?

57. What percent of the capacity of the plane do the mimes make up?

58. Write a percent that shows how the seating capacity of the plane compares with the size of the group of scientists.

Mixed Applications

Solve. Which method did you use?

ESTIMATION
MENTAL MATH
CALCULATOR
PAPER/PENCIL

59. A tour bus has 60 seats. Seventy-five people signed up for the tour. By what percent was the tour overbooked?

60. Over a three-day period, 175, 92, and 125 planes departed. How many planes departed?

61. A new exhibit opened at the city museum. It will run for one full week. The curator expects 50,000 visitors to see the exhibit. About how many people will see it each day?

Percent of a Number

There is going to be a performance of Japanese Bunraku puppetry at an 80-seat theater. Twenty-five percent of the seats have been sold in advance. How many tickets have been sold in advance?

WORKING TOGETHER

You can use graph paper to model the 80-seat theater.
In your model let each box represent one seat.

1. How many boxes are in the grid?

2. What percent of the boxes are shaded?

3. How many boxes are shaded?

4. What is 25% of 80?

5. How many tickets were sold in advance?

Here is one way you can model the problem.

Step 1 Cut a 10-by-10 grid out of graph paper.

Step 2 Cut off two rows of boxes.

Step 3 Shade $\frac{1}{4}$ of the boxes.

25 parts out of 100 is the same as 20 parts out of 80.

25% of 80 = 20

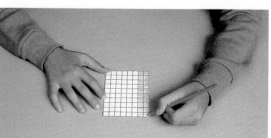

SHARING IDEAS

6. What happens to the percent of a number as the percent increases?

7. For which percents is the percent of a number less than the original number?

ON YOUR OWN

Write the letter of the correct answer.

8. 40% of 25   **a.** 10   **b.** 25   **c.** 40

9. 125% of 60   **a.** 45   **b.** 60   **c.** 75

10. 50% of 300   **a.** 30   **b.** 150   **c.** 300

11. 25% of 48   **a.** 12   **b.** 48   **c.** 60

12. 100% of 35   **a.** 5   **b.** 35   **c.** 50

Look at the percents in the box. Suppose that you used each to find a percent of 25.

7%	135%	72%
230%	68%	9%
11%	155%	89%

13. Which percents would give you an answer greater than 25? less than 25?

14. What did you notice? Would this be true of any number?

Percent of a Number: Mental Math and Estimation

A. On an average day Joel's intake of calories from food is about 2,500. Protein makes up 20% of these calories. How many calories does Joel get from the protein in his food on an average day?

To solve this problem find 20% of 2,500.

1. What fraction is equivalent to 20%?

2. How can you use this fraction to find 20% of 2,500? What is 20% of 2,500?

3. How many calories of protein are in Joel's food?

Other commonly used percents are often renamed as their fractional equivalents to solve problems mentally.

4. Look at the chart at the right. What other percents can you add to it?

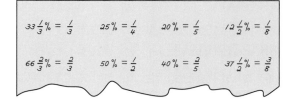

$33\frac{1}{3}\% = \frac{1}{3}$ $25\% = \frac{1}{4}$ $20\% = \frac{1}{5}$ $12\frac{1}{2}\% = \frac{1}{8}$

$66\frac{2}{3}\% = \frac{2}{3}$ $50\% = \frac{1}{2}$ $40\% = \frac{2}{5}$ $37\frac{1}{2}\% = \frac{3}{8}$

B. You can also use percent-fraction equivalents to estimate the percent of a number mentally.

Estimate: 34% of 59

Think: 34% is about $33\frac{1}{3}\%$

$33\frac{1}{3}\% = \frac{1}{3}$

59 is about 60

$\frac{1}{3} \times \overset{20}{\cancel{60}} = 20$

So 34% of 59 is about 20.

5. **What if** you estimate by using the fractional equivalent for 30% instead of $33\frac{1}{3}\%$? What is your estimate?

6. Which estimate is closer to the exact answer? Why?

SHARING IDEAS

7. If you know 10% of a number, how can you find 1% of it? 20% of it? 40% of it? 100% of it?

8. If you know 100% of a number, how can you find 150% of it? 200% of it?

9. If you know 10% of a number, how can you find 5% of it? How can you use this to find 15% of the number?

PRACTICE

Find the percent of the number mentally.

10. 50% of 20   **11.** 5% of 40   **12.** 20% of 2,000   **13.** 15% of 400

14. $33\frac{1}{3}$% of 6,000   **15.** $66\frac{2}{3}$% of 24   **16.** $12\frac{1}{2}$% of 8,000   **17.** 25% of 10,000

18. 100% of 270   **19.** 140% of 15   **20.** 150% of 620   **21.** 200% of 99

Estimate the percent of the number.

22. 48% of 201   **23.** 73% of 392   **24.** 21% of 51   **25.** 23% of 2,019

26. 151% of 1,000   **27.** 198% of 4,068   **28.** 224% of 5,023   **29.** 148% of 6,000

30. 9.86% of 31   **31.** 19.6% of 1,004   **32.** 76.5% of 47   **33.** 23.8% of 84

34. Is 50% of 40 the same as 40% of 50? Explain. Try this with other pairs of numbers. What do you find? How can you use this to find 18% of $66\frac{2}{3}$?

Mixed Applications

35. Both Kevin and Julie ate lunches containing about 800 calories. Kevin's lunch was 40% carbohydrates, and Julie's was $\frac{1}{2}$ carbohydrates. Whose lunch contained more carbohydrates?

36. The school cafeteria serves hot and cold lunches. Two-thirds of the students who eat lunch there buy hot lunches. If 273 students bought school lunches today, how many ordered a cold lunch?

37. A Deluxe Burger at Mindy's has 606 calories. Blanca ate about $33\frac{1}{3}$% of hers. About how many calories were in the portion she ate?

38. *Write a problem* that uses estimation with percents. Give the problem to other students to solve.

Mixed Review

Write the fraction or mixed number as a decimal.

39. $\frac{5}{8}$ **40.** $3\frac{1}{6}$ **41.** $\frac{2}{5}$ **42.** $2\frac{1}{4}$ **43.** $5\frac{7}{8}$

Write the decimal as a fraction or mixed number.

44. 0.65   **45.** 2.75   **46.** 1.4   **47.** 0.025   **48.** $6.\overline{3}$

Complete.

49. 0.438 m = ▨ cm   **50.** 7.2 cm = ▨ mm   **51.** 3.5 kg = ▨ g

52. 4 ft 5 in. = ▨ in.   **53.** 195 min = ▨ h   **54.** $2\frac{3}{4}$ c = ▨ fl oz

Percent of a Number: Using Equations and Proportions

A. A seventh-grade class is having a Trivia Olympics Night. The students need to prepare 175 questions, of which 20% will be about sports. How many questions will be about sports?

You can use an equation to find the percent of a number.

Let n = the number of questions about sports.

$n = 20\%$ of 175

Solve: $n = 20\%$ of 175

You can solve the equation in either of two ways.

Using a fraction equivalent	**Using a decimal equivalent**
20% of 175 = _n_	**20% of 175 = _n_**
$\frac{1}{5} \times 175 = n$	$0.2 \times 175 = n$
$\frac{175}{5} = n$	$35 = n$
$35 = n$	

There will be 35 questions about sports.

1. Is 35 a reasonable answer? Why?

B. You can also use a proportion to find the percent of a number.
Find 20% of 175.

Write a proportion.

Let n = the number you are looking for.

Think: $20\% = \frac{20}{100}$

$$\overset{\frown{\text{part}}}{\underset{\smile{\text{whole}}}{\frac{20}{100} = \frac{n}{175}}}$$

Solve the proportion using cross products.

$100 \times n = 20 \times 175$

$100n = 3{,}500$

$n = 35$

TRY OUT Write the letter of the correct answer.

2. 6% of 85   **a.** 4.8   **b.** 5.1   **c.** 48   **d.** 51

3. 63% of 30   **a.** 1.89   **b.** 9.3   **c.** 18.9   **d.** 93

4. 127.5% of 144   **a.** 39.6   **b.** 41.9   **c.** 183.6   **d.** 185.9

5. $\frac{1}{2}$% of 400   **a.** 2   **b.** 20   **c.** 200   **d.** 402

PRACTICE

Find the percent of the number. Use an equation or a proportion.

6. 31% of $64   **7.** 25% of 32   **8.** 50% of 23   **9.** $75\frac{1}{2}$% of 120

10. 150% of $40   **11.** $33\frac{1}{3}$% of 150   **12.** 7.4% of 180   **13.** $\frac{1}{3}$% of 75

14. $5\frac{1}{4}$% of $20   **15.** 90% of 130   **16.** 0.6% of 24   **17.** $\frac{3}{4}$% of 80

18. Find $66\frac{2}{3}$% of 33.   **19.** Find $83\frac{1}{2}$% of 500.   **20.** Find 188% of 24.4.

21. What is 30% of 4,000?   **22.** What number is 1% of 7.5?

Find the percent of the number.

23. 300% of 45   **24.** 0.5% of 125   **25.** 6.8% of 220   **26.** 44% of 440

27. $4\frac{1}{4}$% of 200   **28.** $\frac{2}{3}$% of 1,500   **29.** 200% of 35.5   **30.** 7.5% of 10

Estimate. Do only those problems that have an answer greater than 25.

31. 82% of 50   **32.** 120% of 20   **33.** 78% of 140   **34.** $\frac{1}{4}$% of 100

Critical Thinking

35. Choose the answer that will make the statement true: 80% of a number is equal to 40% of (half, twice) that number. Give reasons for your choice.

Mixed Applications

36. Of the 450 people in the audience at Trivia Night, 4% were teachers. How many people in the audience were not teachers?

37. Trivia Night began at 7:30 P.M. and ended at 10:18 P.M. How long did Trivia Night last?

38. If each question that was used on Trivia Night took an average of 1.5 minutes to ask and to answer, what is the total number of questions that could be asked during the night?

39. Students wrote 375 questions for Trivia Night. They chose only 175 of them. Write a fraction for the questions they chose. Rename the fraction as a percent.

Exploring Proportions and Percents

A. Of the week's top 20 television shows, 7 are on the WEYE network. What percent of the shows are on the network?

WORKING TOGETHER

Divide a 10-by-10 grid into 20 equal sections. Shade 7 sections.

1. What fractional part of the grid is shaded?

2. How many unit squares are in the whole grid?

3. How many unit squares are shaded?

4. What percent of the whole grid is shaded?

5. What percent of the top 20 shows are on WEYE?

Here is a way you can model the problem.

Step 1 Divide a 10-by-10 grid into 20 equal sections.

Step 2 Shade 7 out of the 20 sections.

7 parts out of 20 is the same as 35 parts out of 100.

$\frac{7}{20} = \frac{35}{100} = 35\%$

B. Three actors on the leading television show had never appeared on television before. If the 3 actors make up 25% of the cast, how many actors are in the cast?

Draw a 10-by-10 grid. Shade 25% of the grid.

6. If the shaded area represents 3 actors, what does the whole grid represent?

7. How many actors are in the whole cast?

Here is a way to model the problem.

Cut out a 10-by-10 grid and shade 25% of it.

If 25% of the whole grid is 3, then $\frac{1}{4}$ of the whole grid is 3.

The whole grid is 4×3, or 12.

SHARING IDEAS

8. What proportion could you have used to solve the problem in section A?

9. What proportion could you have used to solve the problem in section B?

ON YOUR OWN

Solve by modeling the problem.

10. Of the 8 new songs written for a movie, Don wrote 6. What percent of the songs did he write?

11. Four of the season's new television shows are sitcoms. If this is 25% of the new shows, how many new shows are there?

12. Eight new employees have been hired for the lighting staff. If this is 10% of the staff, how many employees are on the lighting staff?

13. Of the 10 new offices, 7 are decorated. What percent of the offices are decorated? not decorated?

PROBLEM SOLVING

Checking for a Reasonable Answer

It is boom time in a mining town. A newspaper reporter is writing a story about 10 miners who have set up a camp outside town. Each week for the next 3 weeks, the number of miners in the camp will multiply by 9. How many miners will be in the camp after 4 weeks?

The reporter said 360 people would be in the camp after 4 weeks. How can you check that this answer is reasonable? One way is to use estimation.

Think: The 9 times increase in the number of miners is close to a 10 times increase. There were 10 miners to start with.

There should be close to $10 \times 10 \times 10 \times 10$, or 10,000, miners in the camp after 4 weeks.

Since 360 is *not* close to 10,000, 360 is *not* a reasonable answer. The exact answer is $10 \times 9 \times 9 \times 9$, or 7,290, miners after 4 weeks.

1. What mistake do you think the reporter made in arriving at the answer of 360?

2. **What if** 50 miners had set up the camp the first week? How many would there have been in the camp after 4 weeks?

PRACTICE

Solve. Determine whether the answer given is reasonable. If it is not, find the correct answer.

3. In the first week a mine tunnel was expanded to 8 ft. Then its length was multiplied by $7\frac{1}{2}$ times each week for 2 weeks. About how long was the mine tunnel at the end of 3 weeks? Answer: 124 ft

4. The miners were loading trucks. In the first truck they loaded 50 lb of ore. In each of the next 3 trucks the weight was tripled. How many pounds of ore was loaded into the fourth truck? Answer: 1,350 lb

5. A mining town has a population of 17,000, of which 9% are miners. If the mining company lays off 10% of these miners, how many miners are still employed? Answer: 680 miners

6. A miner earned $500 in overtime pay one week. During each of the next 4 weeks, he earned $\frac{4}{5}$ as much as the previous week's overtime pay. How much overtime pay did he earn in the last week? Answer: $100

Strategies and Skills Review

Solve. Use mental math, estimation, a calculator, or paper and pencil.

7. A prospector digging in a mine gets 12 wagonloads of ore that yield 4 oz of gold per wagonload. Another miner gets 6.5 oz out of each of 8 wagonloads. A third miner gets 7.5 oz of gold panning in the stream. How much gold is that all together?

8. The cost of mining tools has risen sharply. Over the last four months the costs were as follows: January, $.75; February, $.85; March, $1.03; April, $1.35. If this pattern continues, what will mining tools cost in May?

9. On Sunday morning a mine had 2 tunnels. During each day each tunnel was extended into 2 other tunnels. If each section is 15 ft, how many tunnels will there be on Tuesday night?

10. Ron put a 3-ft stake in the ground to mark the location of his mine site. Its shadow is 5 ft long. The shadow of a tree is 20 ft long. About how tall is the tree?

11. One mine yields 2.5% of its ore as gold. The miners extract about 6 T of ore a day. About how many days would it take to mine 2,000 lb of gold?

12. **_Write a problem_** and give an unreasonable answer. Share your problem with other students and have them determine if your answer is reasonable.

DECISION MAKING

Problem Solving: Choosing a VCR

SITUATION

The TV production club plans to buy a videocassette recorder. They researched several models and have chosen three models that would suit their needs.

PROBLEM

Which VCR should the production club choose?

DATA

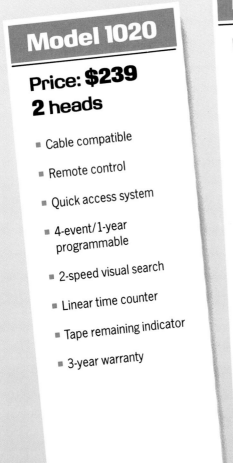

Model 1020

Price: **$239**
2 heads

- Cable compatible
- Remote control
- Quick access system
- 4-event/1-year programmable
- 2-speed visual search
- Linear time counter
- Tape remaining indicator
- 3-year warranty

Model 2030

Price: **$329**
4 heads

- 89-channel cable compatible
- Remote control
- Quick access system
- 2-event/14-day programmable
- 2-speed visual search
- Linear time counter
- Tape remaining indicator
- Variable slow motion
- VHS index search system
- On-screen program display
- 2-year warranty

Model 5040

Price: **$439**
4 heads

- 122-channel cable compatible
- Remote control
- Quick access system
- 4-event/14-day programmable
- GOTO visual search
- Linear time counter
- Tape remaining indicator
- HQ PRO image-enhancing circuitry
- 10-key random-access tuning
- On-screen programming
- 1-year warranty

USING THE DATA

What is the total cost of each VCR if there is a 7% sales tax?

1. Model 1020

2. Model 2030

3. Model 5040

The store gives a 10% discount to schools. What is the cost of each VCR for a school?

4. Model 1020

5. Model 2030

6. Model 5040

Schools don't have to pay sales tax. How much less will the school pay than the original price plus tax?

7. Model 1020

8. Model 2030

9. Model 5040

MAKING DECISIONS

10. Which VCR should the production crew choose in order to spend the least?

11. Which should they choose to get the easiest to operate? Why?

12. Which should they choose to have the least problems with repairs?

13. *What if* the store is offering a 15% discount on Model 5040. Which VCR should the production crew choose in order to spend the least?

14. Which VCR should they choose to get the best possible picture?

15. Which model should they choose if they want to be able to program it over the summer vacation?

16. Why might they prefer model 2030 or 5040 over model 1020?

17. *Write a list* of other factors they should consider.

18. Which VCR would you choose? Why?

Math and the Arts

An astounding sculpture draws tourists to Mount Rushmore, South Dakota. Carved into the 5,725-ft (1,745-m) granite mountain are likenesses of George Washington, Thomas Jefferson, Abraham Lincoln, and Theodore Roosevelt. Each face is about 60 ft (18 m) from chin to forehead. This is to the scale of a person 465 ft (142 m) high.

The work was designed by the American sculptor Gutzon Borglum (1867–1941). Drilling for the first face, that of George Washington, was begun in 1924 and unveiled to the public in 1930, although still not complete. The final face was completed in October of 1941, six months after Borglum died.

The sculptor could not start such a mammoth piece of art by simply chipping away at the side of the mountain. Rough models were made first. The scale used was an inch to the foot (1 in. = 1 ft). A team of workmen carefully transferred the measurements to the mountain and began blasting and drilling and chipping. In all, 500,000 tons of stone were removed by dynamite.

What if the distinctive mole on Lincoln's face measured $1\frac{1}{3}$ inches on the model? What size would it be on the finished mountain carving?

Think: The scale used is 1 in. = 1 ft. Because 1 ft = 12 in., multiply $1\frac{1}{3}$ by 12. The mole on the mountain is 16 in.

ACTIVITIES

1. Work with a partner. Measure each other's heads, including the face, and make scale drawings. You may use graph paper and any scale that allows you to draw the entire figure on one page.

2. Read more about the construction of the faces on Mount Rushmore. Share your findings with the class.

Computer Spreadsheet: Compound Interest

When a person deposits money in a savings account, the bank pays *interest* for the use of the money. The interest is a percent of the amount of money in the account. The amount of money deposited is called the *principal,* and the percent of the principal that the bank will pay each year is called the *rate of interest.*

Banks pay interest not only on the original principal, but also on interest that has been earned during the period of deposit. This is called *compound interest.* For example, if you deposit $1,000 at an annual rate of interest of 6%, at the end of the year your account will hold a total of $1,060 ($1,000 plus $60 interest). The next year, the interest will be calculated on the total amount of $1,060. Compound interest can be calculated using a complicated formula, or by consulting special tables. Computer programs are also used to calculate compound interest.

You can use the computer spreadsheet program COMPOUND INTEREST to find out how a savings account in which you deposit $100 can grow in size over a period of time.

AT THE COMPUTER

1. Enter $100 as the principal in column A. Enter 10% as the rate of interest in column B and 1 year as the period of deposit in column C. The computer will calculate the amount of interest that you earn after 1 year. Now find the total interest earned after 2 years, at the same rate of interest. Subtract to find the amount of interest earned during the second year. Why is more interest earned during the second year than during the first?

2. When the total interest reaches $100 or more, you have doubled the size of your account. How many years do you think it would take to double your money at an annual rate of 15%? Enter 15% in column B and your estimate of the period of time in column C. Is the total interest close to $100? Change your entry in column C until you find the least time it would take to earn more than $100 in interest.

3. Enter several different annual rates of interest between 3% and 20%. Experiment to find the least period of time to double your money at those rates.

4. If the total interest earned is $200 or more, you have tripled the size of your savings account. What is the lowest rate of interest that would allow you to triple your money in 10 years?

EXTRA PRACTICE

Ratios and Equal Ratios, page 375

Write the ratio in simplest form in three ways.

1. total objects to pencils   **2.** crayons to total objects

3. pens to crayons   **4.** crayons to pens and pencils

> 5 pencils
> 7 pens
> 8 crayons

Write three ratios equal to the given ratio.

5. $\frac{2}{5}$ **6.** 9:12   **7.** 3.9:9   **8.** $\frac{50}{150}$ **9.** 16:48

Which ratio is not equal to the others?

10. 18:6; 12:3; 21:7   **11.** $\frac{4}{7}, \frac{12}{21}, \frac{13}{22}, \frac{16}{28}$ **12.** $\frac{8}{12}, \frac{4}{6}, \frac{16}{24}, \frac{6}{10}$

Using Rates: Mental Math, page 377

Use mental math to find the unit rate. Write the answer as a fraction.

1. 320 km in 4 hours   **2.** 120 mi in 3 hours   **3.** 360 mi in 9 hours

4. $84 for 7 days   **5.** 210 mi on 7 gal   **6.** 360 km on 8 gal

Solve. Use mental math.

7. 160 mi using 8 gal
How many miles on 1 gal?

8. $32 for 1 day
How much for 5 days?

9. $900 for 3 weeks
How much for 10 weeks?

10. 28.5 mi using 1 gal
How many miles on 8 gal?

Solving Proportions, page 379

Are the ratios equal? Write = or ≠.

1. $\frac{3}{5}$ ● $\frac{6}{10}$ **2.** $\frac{9}{4}$ ● $\frac{14}{9}$ **3.** $\frac{11}{14}$ ● $\frac{9}{12}$ **4.** $\frac{12}{18}$ ● $\frac{2}{3}$ **5.** $\frac{4}{7}$ ● $\frac{20}{35}$

Solve the proportion. Do as many as you can mentally.

6. $\frac{2}{3} = \frac{n}{12}$ **7.** $\frac{5}{9} = \frac{30}{n}$ **8.** $\frac{n}{24} = \frac{7}{4}$ **9.** $\frac{3}{n} = \frac{1}{9}$ **10.** $\frac{12}{8} = \frac{n}{18}$

11. $\frac{n}{11} = \frac{14}{28}$ **12.** $\frac{3}{n} = \frac{6}{5}$ **13.** $\frac{5}{3} = \frac{n}{2}$ **14.** $\frac{7}{21} = \frac{1}{n}$ **15.** $\frac{5}{n} = \frac{25}{4}$

16. $\frac{135}{10} = \frac{n}{22}$ **17.** $\frac{19}{15} = \frac{152}{n}$ **18.** $\frac{n}{1.5} = \frac{4}{6}$ **19.** $\frac{10}{n} = \frac{8}{1}$ **20.** $\frac{3.6}{7.2} = \frac{10}{n}$

21. $\frac{1.8}{18} = \frac{0.17}{n}$ **22.** $\frac{2.1}{n} = \frac{8.4}{15}$ **23.** $\frac{n}{26.6} = \frac{7}{13.3}$ **24.** $\frac{5}{8} = \frac{n}{5}$ **25.** $\frac{n}{1} = \frac{23}{3}$

EXTRA PRACTICE

Scale Drawings and Similar Figures, page 381 ·····························

Solve for *n*.

1. scale: 1 cm = 5 km
drawing: 7 cm
actual: *n*

2. scale: 5 in. = 9 ft
drawing: 20 in.
actual: *n*

3. scale: 1 cm = 12 m
drawing: 9 cm
actual: *n*

4. scale: 0.5 in. = 8 ft
drawing: 3 in.
actual: *n*

5. scale: 0.5 cm = 3 mi
drawing: 6 cm
actual: *n*

6. scale: 3 in. = 15 mi
drawing: 10.5 in.
actual: *n*

7. scale: 2 cm = 11 km
drawing: 7.5 cm
actual: *n*

8. scale: 3 cm = 8.5 m
drawing: 12 cm
actual: *n*

9. scale: 4 in. = 7.5 km
drawing: 8 in.
actual: *n*

10. scale: 2 in. = 10 mi
drawing: 7.5 in.
actual: *n*

11. scale: 1.5 cm = 10 km
drawing: 18 cm
actual: *n*

12. scale: 2.5 cm = 100 mi
drawing: 12.5 cm
actual: *n*

Problem–Solving Strategy: Using Proportions, page 383 ····················

Use a proportion to solve.

1. The ratio of pineapple juice to orange juice is 3 to 5. There are 10 quarts of orange juice. How many quarts are there of pineapple juice?

2. For every 3 swimcaps sold, a department store sold 15 swimsuits. The store sold 7 swimcaps. How many swimsuits were sold?

Percent, page 387 ···

Rename as a percent.

1. 9 out of 100

2. 36 out of 100

3. 7:100

4. 82:100

5. $\frac{63}{100}$

6. $\frac{9}{10}$

7. $\frac{46}{1,000}$

8. $\frac{3}{1,000}$

Compare. Write >, <, or =.

9. $\frac{7}{10}$ ● 60%

10. $\frac{88}{1,000}$ ● 88%

11. 90% ● $\frac{90}{100}$

12. $\frac{41}{100}$ ● 41.2%

One dollar is equal to 100 cents. What percent of a dollar is the amount?

13. $.12

14. 38¢

15. $.94

16. 4¢

17. $.03

18. 17¢

EXTRA PRACTICE

Decimals and Percents, page 389

Rename as a decimal.

1. 31% **2.** 19% **3.** 6% **4.** 50% **5.** 5% **6.** 3%

7. 1% **8.** 72.1% **9.** 30.2% **10.** 68.4% **11.** 20.5% **12.** 49.9%

13. forty-five and one-half percent **14.** fifty and three-fifths percent

Rename as a percent.

15. 0.47 **16.** 0.82 **17.** 0.16 **18.** 0.25 **19.** 0.92 **20.** 0.7

21. 0.08 **22.** 0.02 **23.** 0.05 **24.** 0.417 **25.** 0.036 **26.** 0.706

27. eleven hundredths **28.** seventy-six thousandths **29.** 7 hundredths

Fractions and Percents, page 391

Rename as a fraction and decimal.

1. 10% **2.** 60% **3.** 46% **4.** 40% **5.** 35% **6.** 80%

7. $66\frac{2}{3}\%$ **8.** $12\frac{1}{2}\%$ **9.** $8\frac{1}{6}\%$ **10.** $11\frac{1}{9}\%$ **11.** $83\frac{1}{3}\%$ **12.** $44\frac{4}{9}\%$

Rename as a percent.

13. $\frac{2}{5}$ **14.** $\frac{1}{4}$ **15.** $\frac{9}{10}$ **16.** $\frac{2}{9}$ **17.** $\frac{51}{200}$ **18.** $\frac{1}{80}$

19. 0.18 **20.** 0.6 **21.** 0.08 **22.** 0.785 **23.** 0.16 **24.** 0.5

Percents Greater Than 100 and Less Than 1, page 393

Rename as a decimal.

1. 140% **2.** 400% **3.** $\frac{3}{4}\%$ **4.** $\frac{3}{8}\%$ **5.** 0.7% **6.** 0.18%

Rename as a fraction or as a mixed number.

7. 120% **8.** 260% **9.** 815% **10.** 0.8% **11.** 0.45% **12.** 0.92%

Rename as a percent.

13. 0.4 **14.** 2.8 **15.** 5.85 **16.** $6\frac{1}{2}$ **17.** $4\frac{3}{5}$ **18.** $2\frac{5}{8}$

19. 0.035 **20.** 0.007 **21.** 0.528 **22.** $\frac{3}{4}$ **23.** $\frac{1}{400}$ **24.** $\frac{1}{50}$

EXTRA PRACTICE

Percent of a Number: Mental Math and Estimation, page 397

Find the percent of the number mentally.

1. 50% of 80 **2.** 5% of 20 **3.** 100% of 212 **4.** 18% of 300

5. 300% of 6 **6.** $\frac{1}{4}$% of 10,000 **7.** 25% of 16,000 **8.** $6\frac{1}{4}$% of 1,000

Estimate the percent of the number.

9. 74% of 198 **10.** 11% of 62 **11.** 24% of 1,012 **12.** 149% of 2,000

13. 226% of 1,015 **14.** 9.92% of 42 **15.** 19.9% of 502 **16.** 24.6% of 98

Percent of a Number: Using Equations and Proportions, page 399

Find the percent of the number. Use an equation or a proportion.

1. 25% of 64 **2.** 75% of 80 **3.** 24% of 90 **4.** 250% of 30

5. 2% of 12.6 **6.** $6\frac{1}{4}$% of 40 **7.** 0.8% of 32 **8.** $\frac{1}{4}$% of 120

Find the percent of the number.

9. 200% of 65 **10.** 0.3% of 155 **11.** 9.5% of 320 **12.** 32% of 320

13. $2\frac{1}{2}$% of 400 **14.** $\frac{1}{3}$% of 2,700 **15.** 400% of 15.5 **16.** 9.6% of 10

Problem Solving: Checking for a Reasonable Answer, page 403

Solve. Check that your answer is reasonable.

1. In the first week a mine tunnel was extended to 11 ft. Its length was multiplied 5 times each week for 3 weeks. About how long was the mine tunnel at the end of 4 weeks?

2. Two thousand pounds of coal is waiting to be unloaded. Every hour the load is diminished to $\frac{1}{5}$ of its weight. How much does the load weigh after 2 hours?

Solve. Determine whether the answer given is reasonable. If it is not, find the correct answer.

3. A mining town has a population of 21,000, of which 11% are miners. If the mining company lays off 4% of these miners, about how many are still employed? Answer: about 2,000 miners

4. The mine camp has 20,000 cans of corn. Each day the miners eat $\frac{1}{10}$ of the numbers of cans of corn. How many are left after 3 days? Answer: 2 cans

Practice PLUS

KEY SKILL: Fractions and Percents (Use after page 391.)

Level A

Rename as a fraction and decimal.

1. 75% **2.** 30% **3.** 15% **4.** 5% **5.** 8% **6.** $2\frac{1}{2}$%

Rename as a percent.

7. $\frac{4}{5}$ **8.** $\frac{9}{20}$ **9.** $\frac{3}{10}$ **10.** $\frac{7}{20}$ **11.** $\frac{9}{25}$ **12.** $\frac{1}{25}$

13. $\frac{1}{50}$ **14.** $\frac{1}{100}$ **15.** $\frac{3}{20}$ **16.** $\frac{3}{25}$ **17.** $\frac{7}{10}$ **18.** $\frac{1}{40}$

19. In a recent poll $\frac{1}{2}$ of the students named pizza as their favorite food. Rename the fraction as a percent.

Level B

Rename as a fraction and decimal.

20. 85% **21.** 95% **22.** 65% **23.** $37\frac{1}{2}$% **24.** $28\frac{4}{7}$% **25.** $77\frac{7}{9}$%

26. $33\frac{1}{3}$% **27.** $68\frac{3}{4}$% **28.** $62\frac{1}{2}$% **29.** $87\frac{1}{2}$% **30.** $13\frac{1}{3}$% **31.** $38.\overline{8}$%

Rename as a percent.

32. $\frac{8}{10}$ **33.** $\frac{3}{8}$ **34.** $\frac{22}{25}$ **35.** $\frac{5}{7}$ **36.** $\frac{2}{9}$ **37.** $\frac{1}{15}$

38. $\frac{11}{16}$ **39.** $\frac{3}{9}$ **40.** $\frac{1}{75}$ **41.** $\frac{90}{100}$ **42.** $\frac{6}{45}$ **43.** $\frac{3}{15}$

44. In a recent poll $\frac{13}{20}$ of the people surveyed watched Monday Night Football. Rename the fraction as a percent.

Level C

Rename as a fraction and decimal.

45. $58\frac{1}{3}$% **46.** $20\frac{5}{6}$% **47.** $55\frac{5}{9}$% **48.** $41\frac{2}{3}$% **49.** $3\frac{3}{4}$% **50.** $73\frac{1}{3}$%

51. $56\frac{2}{3}$% **52.** 15% **53.** 16% **54.** $53\frac{1}{3}$% **55.** $87\frac{1}{2}$% **56.** 3%

Rename as a percent.

57. $\frac{8}{9}$ **58.** $\frac{3}{7}$ **59.** $\frac{5}{12}$ **60.** $\frac{7}{15}$ **61.** $\frac{49}{200}$ **62.** $\frac{7}{80}$

63. $\frac{5}{8}$ **64.** $\frac{4}{30}$ **65.** $\frac{17}{80}$ **66.** $\frac{19}{40}$ **67.** $\frac{53}{80}$ **68.** $\frac{57}{60}$

69. In a recent poll 6 out of 7 people surveyed chose Brand A over Brand B. What percent chose Brand A?

KEY SKILL: Percent of a Number: Using Equations and Proportions

(Use after page 399.)

Level A

Find the percent of the number. Use an equation or a proportion.

1. 25% of 36 **2.** 50% of 30 **3.** 75% of 60 **4.** 20% of 55

5. 10% of 85 **6.** 150% of 40 **7.** 200% of 120 **8.** 30% of 50

9. 40% of 90 **10.** 65% of 120 **11.** 85% of 180 **12.** 21% of 200

13. Of the 400 people in the audience 75% were under 12. How many were under 12?

Level B

Find the percent of the number. Use an equation or a proportion.

14. 37% of 400 **15.** 58% of 42 **16.** 86% of 106 **17.** 95% of 180

18. $45\frac{1}{2}$% of 78 **19.** $2\frac{1}{4}$% of 124 **20.** 0.8% of 6 **21.** 300% of $2

22. $\frac{1}{2}$% of 50 **23.** 8.5% of 100 **24.** $66\frac{2}{3}$% of 66 **25.** $6\frac{1}{4}$% of $80

Estimate. Do only those that have an answer greater than 50.

26. 6% of 910 **27.** 35% of 88 **28.** 17% of 350 **29.** 28% of 430

30. Of the 350 people who attended a Beethoven Concert, 60% were over 65 years of age. How many were over 65?

Level C

Find the percent of the number. Use an equation or a proportion.

31. 68% of 145 **32.** 47% of 120 **33.** $6\frac{1}{2}$% of 40 **34.** $6\frac{3}{4}$% of $12

35. 10.5% of 54 **36.** 110% of 160 **37.** 250% of 500 **38.** $\frac{1}{8}$% of 125

39. $\frac{2}{3}$% of 17 **40.** 4.6% of 93 **41.** 113% of 23 **42.** 12% of 1,050

Estimate. Do only those that have an answer greater than 25.

43. $\frac{1}{8}$% of 203 **44.** 180% of 15 **45.** $\frac{1}{6}$% of 1,800 **46.** 250% of 17.5

47. 13% of 320 **48.** 80% of 30 **49.** 320% of 7 **50.** 42% of 65

51. Of the 240 VCR types you have $12\frac{1}{2}$% of them are comedies. How many are comedies?

CHAPTER REVIEW

LANGUAGE AND MATHEMATICS

Complete the sentences. Use the words in the chart on the right.

1. An equation stating that two ratios are equal is a ▨.
   (page 378)

2. A ▨ is a ratio that compares a number to 100. *(page 386)*

3. A ▨ is a ▨ that compares different kinds of units. *(page 376)*

4. ***Write a definition*** or give an example of the word you
   did not use from the chart.

> **VOCABULARY**
> ratio
> rate
> proportion
> cross-product
> percent

CONCEPTS AND SKILLS

Write the ratio in simplest form in two ways. *(page 374)*

5. 4 to 14	**6.** 12 to 8	**7.** 100:10	**8.** 6:81	**9.** $\frac{21}{45}$

Solve for *n*. *(pages 376, 378, 380)*

10. $\frac{3}{8} = \frac{12}{n}$ **11.** $\frac{8}{2.4} = \frac{n}{1.2}$ **12.** $15 for 1 day   **13.** $175 for 4 tires
                                                                n for 5 days   *n* for 2 tires

14. scale: 1 cm = 10 km   **15.** scale: 1 in. = 100 mi   **16.** scale: 1 cm = ▨ m
        drawing: 2 cm   drawing: *n*   drawing: 14 cm
        actual: *n*   actual: 75 mi   actual: 168 m

Copy and complete the table. Write in simplest form. *(pages 388, 390, 392)*

	Fraction	Decimal	Percent		Fraction	Decimal	Percent
17.	$\frac{2}{100}$	▨	▨	**18.**	$\frac{90}{1000}$	▨	▨
19.	▨	0.05	▨	**20.**	▨	▨	4.5%
21.	▨	0.3	▨	**22.**	▨	4.67	▨
23.	▨	▨	20%	**24.**	▨	▨	0.4%

Find the unit rate. Use mental math. *(page 376)*

25. 300 mi in 6 hours   **26.** 300 mi on five gal   **27.** 8 muffins in 4 hours

Rename as a percent. *(page 388)*

28. $\frac{60}{1000}$ **29.** 23 out of 100   **30.** $\frac{7}{10}$ **31.** 64 out of 100

32. 0.225   **33.** 0.014   **34.** 50 out of 200   **35.** 4 thousandths

Compare. *(page 386)*

36. $\frac{9}{10}$ ● 80% **37.** $\frac{32}{1000}$ ● 32% **38.** $\frac{4}{100}$ ● 4% **39.** $\frac{65}{100}$ ● 6%

Rename as a decimal. *(page 388)*

40. 22% **41.** 60% **42.** $33\frac{1}{3}$% **43.** 80% **44.** 100%

Find the percent of the number. *(page 398)*

45. 75% of 12 **46.** 150% of 5 **47.** $66\frac{2}{3}$% of 36 **48.** 110% of 80

The two figures are similar. Solve for *n*. *(page 380)*

49. **50.** **51.**

Rename as a fraction. *(page 390)*

52. $33\frac{1}{3}$% **53.** 75% **54.** 20% **55.** 9% **56.** $66\frac{2}{3}$%

Write in order from greatest to least. *(page 392)*

57. 2.7, 0.2%, 140%, 0.005, $\frac{1}{100}$ **58.** 125%, $1\frac{2}{5}$, 0.006, 0.2%, $\frac{1}{200}$

Critical Thinking

59. Twenty-five percent of a number is *y*. What is 50% of the number? *(page 396)*

60. One percent of a number is *y*. What is 100% of the number? *(page 396)*

Mixed Applications

61. A coat that regularly costs $35.89 is on sale for $33\frac{1}{3}$% off. Which is the most reasonable estimate of the sale price? *(page 402)*
  a. $10 **b.** $12 **c.** $24 **d.** $33

62. A mining company has 60 miners. Fifteen percent of the miners have a son who is a miner. How many miners have sons who are miners? *(page 400)*

63. To make a triple batch of pudding, how much molasses is used? *(page 382)*

64. To make a half batch of pudding, how much flour and sugar are used? *(page 382)*

A Partial Recipe for Pudding

2 cups flour
$\frac{1}{2}$ cup sugar
$\frac{2}{3}$ cup molasses

CHAPTER TEST

Use the information below to write each ratio in simplest form.

| 3 horses | 9 goats | 4 cows | 8 sheep |

1. goats to cows

2. horses to goats

3. cows to all animals

4. all animals to sheep

Solve for *n*.

5. $\frac{4}{5} = \frac{20}{n}$

6. $\frac{3}{1.4} = \frac{n}{0.7}$

7. $\frac{n}{7} = \frac{7}{10}$

8. 76 mi on 5 gal
  n mi on 1 gal

9. scale: 1 cm = 100 km
  drawing: 20 cm
  actual: *n*

10. scale: 2 in. = 50 mi
  drawing: *n*
  actual: 75 mi

Copy and complete the table. Write each fraction in simplest form.

	Fraction	Decimal	Percent
11.	$\frac{3}{50}$	▪	▪
12.	▪	▪	80%
13.	▪	0.031	▪
14.	$\frac{430}{1000}$	▪	▪
15.	▪	7.2	▪
16.	▪	▪	12%

Find the percent of the number.

17. 25% of 20

18. 30% of 9

19. 175% of 16

20. $33\frac{1}{3}$% of 120

21. This pair of figures is similar. Solve for *n*.

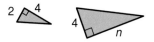

What percent of a dollar is each amount?

22. $.25

23. 30 cents

24. A briefcase that regularly sells for $29.99 is on sale for 10% off. Which is the most reasonable estimate of the sale price?

  a. $3 **c.** $27
  b. $19 **d.** $29

25. A recipe calls for $\frac{2}{3}$ of a cup of milk to make a batch of cookies. How much milk should Tony use to make 4 batches?

GOLDEN RATIO

The **Golden Ratio** has been studied by mathematicians for over a thousand years. The ratio appears in nature, architecture, mathematics, and so on. The ratio is about 1:1.6. A **golden rectangle** is a rectangle that has a $\frac{\text{length}}{\text{width}}$ ratio of about $\frac{1.6}{1}$. A golden rectangle is considered very pleasing to the eye.

Use graph paper, a ruler, and a compass to construct a golden rectangle.

Step 1 Draw ray AB and square $ABCD$.

Step 2 Mark the midpoint, M, of $\overrightarrow{AB}$, so $\overline{AM} \cong \overline{MB}$.

Step 3 With your compass at M, and $\overrightarrow{MC}$ as a radius, draw an arc intersecting $\overrightarrow{AB}$ at E.

Step 4 Draw $\overline{EF}$ and complete the rectangle $AEFD$.

Step 5 Measure $\overline{AE}$ and $\overline{AD}$.

Step 6 Use a calculator to find $\frac{\overline{AE}}{\overline{AD}}$. Give your answer as a decimal to the nearest hundredth.

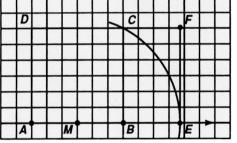

Use a ruler to measure the length and width of several rectangular objects.

1. Record the dimensions in a table.

2. Find the $\frac{\text{length}}{\text{width}}$ ratio of the objects. How many golden rectangles did you find?

3. The first two terms of the **Fibonacci Sequence** are 1, and each succeeding term is the sum of the previous two terms. So the sequence is: 1, 1, 2, 3, 5, 8, 13, 21, 34, . . . Use your calculator to find out how the Golden Ratio is related to the Fibonacci Sequence.

4. A five-pointed star constructed inside a regular pentagon uses a Golden Ratio. Find the ratio in this figure.

5. Research the Golden Ratio and the Fibonnacci Sequence. How many other examples of the Golden Ratio can you find in nature, art, architecture, and so on.

Choose the letter of the correct answer.

1. Solve for n: $n + \frac{2}{3} = 5\frac{1}{3}$

  a. $4\frac{2}{3}$ **c.** 6

  b. $5\frac{2}{3}$ **d.** not given

2. Solve for n: $n - \frac{3}{5} = \frac{2}{9}$

  a. $\frac{1}{4}$ **c.** $\frac{37}{45}$

  b. $\frac{5}{14}$ **d.** not given

3. Solve for n: $\frac{n}{6} = \frac{3}{4}$

  a. 2   **c.** 18

  b. 4.5   **d.** not given

4. $3 \times \frac{5}{6}$

  a. $\frac{15}{18}$ **c.** $3\frac{5}{6}$

  b. $2\frac{1}{2}$ **d.** not given

5. $\frac{4}{5} \div \frac{2}{5}$

  a. 2   **c.** $\frac{2}{5}$

  b. $\frac{8}{25}$ **d.** not given

6. $2\frac{1}{4} \times 3$

  a. $\frac{3}{4}$ **c.** $6\frac{3}{4}$

  b. $2\frac{3}{4}$ **d.** not given

7. What is the square root of 100?

  a. 50   **c.** 1,000

  b. 200   **d.** not given

8. What kind of angle is this?

  a. obtuse   **c.** acute

  b. straight   **d.** not given

9. What kind of triangle is this?

  a. equilateral   **c.** scalene

  b. obtuse   **d.** not given

10. What kind of quadrilateral is this?

  a. parallelogram   **c.** square

  b. rectangle   **d.** not given

11. What percent equals $\frac{2}{50}$?

  a. 2%

  b. 25%

  c. 40%

  d. not given

12. What percent equals 0.3?

  a. 3%   **c.** $33\frac{1}{3}$%

  b. 30%   **d.** not given

13. What is 25% of 50?

  a. 20   **c.** 125

  b. 25   **d.** not given

Solve.

14. A map scale sets 1 cm = 10 km. What is the actual distance between two towns that are 3.5 cm apart on the map?

  a. 0.35 km   **c.** 350 km

  b. 35 km   **d.** not given

Statistics

MATH CONNECTION: PROBLEM SOLVING

TYPE OF ACCOUNT	INTEREST RATE
Investment Checking	5% calculated daily on balance over $500
Savings	5.00%
60 day CD	8.75%
120 day CD	9.42%

1. What information do you see in this picture?

2. How can you use the information?

3. How much interest is earned on an Investment Checking account with an average daily balance of $486.55?

4. Write a problem using the information.

419

DEVELOPING A CONCEPT

Reading and Interpreting Histograms

Jody is the manager at Duds for Dudes, which is open from 9 A.M. to 9 P.M. She wants to find the time of day when the greatest number of customers arrive. One day she kept track of the number of customers entering the store and recorded the results in a frequency table.

WORKING TOGETHER

1. What do the intervals have in common?

2. What other intervals might Jody have chosen?

3. **What if** she chose the intervals 9:00–12:59, 1:00–4:59, and 5:00–8:59? How would the table change? What are the advantages and disadvantages of using these intervals?

DUDS FOR DUDES CUSTOMERS

Time Interval	Frequency
9:00–10:59	59
11:00–12:59	90
1:00–2:59	70
3:00–4:59	78
5:00–6:59	35
7:00–8:59	65

Jody made a histogram. A **histogram** is a graph that shows the frequency distribution of grouped data.

Look at the graph she made.

4. What information is given on the vertical axis? on the horizontal axis?

5. What determines the bar heights?

6. During which interval did the greatest number of customers come into the store?

7. What is the range of the frequencies?

8. During which interval was the number of customers entering less than 50?

9. About what percent of the customers enter the store from 9:00 to 4:59?

10. If Jody can open her store for only six hours a day, what hours should she choose?

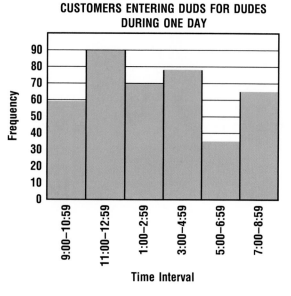

CUSTOMERS ENTERING DUDS FOR DUDES DURING ONE DAY

SHARING IDEAS

11. How does a histogram display the information in a frequency table?

12. What are some conclusions that Jody can make by using her histogram?

13. Describe how to make a histogram given a frequency table.

PRACTICE

Use the histogram at the right to answer Problems 14–18.

14. During which interval did the greatest number of shoppers arrive?

15. During which interval did the least number of shoppers arrive?

16. During which interval(s) was the number of entering cars greater than 90?

17. What is the range of the frequencies?

18. During which six-hour period did more than 50% of the shoppers come to the mall?

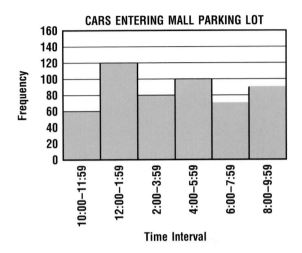

CARS ENTERING MALL PARKING LOT

Use the histogram at the right to answer Problems 19–23.

19. From which age group does the greatest number of Claude's customers come?

20. From which age group does the least number of Claude's customers come?

21. What is the range of the frequencies?

22. What does the histogram tell you about the kinds of clothes Claude probably sells?

23. Predict what the graph would look like if it were extended to include customers over 35.

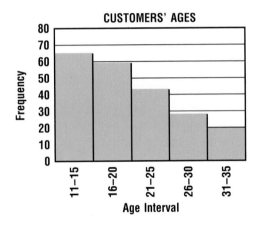

CUSTOMERS' AGES

Make a histogram using the data.

24. The table at the right shows the number of dresses, by price range, that Bean Pole Clothing sells.

BEAN POLE DRESSES

Price Interval	$20–$29	$30–$39	$40–$49	$50–$59	$60–$69
Frequency	12	17	22	36	41

Mixed Applications

25. Two hundred fifty people shopped at Dan's. Sixty percent were men. How many were men?

26. The six bars of a histogram show frequencies from 24 to 66. What is the range of the frequencies?

DEVELOPING A CONCEPT

Reading and Interpreting Circle Graphs

A circle graph shows how a whole is divided into its parts. The circle graph at the right shows the projected populations of various towns of a county in the year 2000.

PROJECTED POPULATION IN 2000
TOTAL PROJECTION: 2,000,000

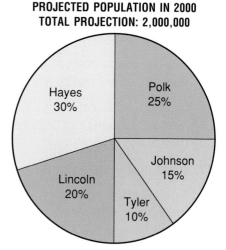

WORKING TOGETHER

1. Into how many towns is the county divided?

2. Which town should have the greatest population in the year 2000? Which town should have the least population?

3. What is the sum of all the percents shown in the graph? What does the graph represent?

4. Which town is projected to have one-quarter of the population?

5. Which two towns combined are projected to have half the population?

Here are two ways you can use to find the projected population of the town of Hayes.

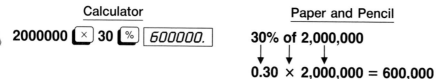

Calculator	Paper and Pencil
2000000 $\times$ 30 % **600000.**	30% of 2,000,000
	$0.30 \times 2,000,000 = 600,000$

6. What is the projected population of Lincoln? of Johnson?

7. Which two towns are projected to have a combined population of 500,000?

8. How many more people are projected to be in Polk than in Tyler?

SHARING IDEAS

9. Can you use different calculations to find the projected populations?

10. **What if** the actual population of the town of Polk had been 1,000,000 instead of 500,000? How would this have affected the total population? What percent of the total population would have been in the town of Polk?

11. **What if** you wanted to show how a population has changed over a period of time? Would you use a circle graph? Why or why not?

PRACTICE

Use the circle graph at the right to answer Problems 12–17.

12. Which city had the least population in the year 1000?

13. Which city had a population about twice the population of Kyoto, Japan?

14. What was the population of Córdoba, Spain, in the year 1000?

15. What was the population of Kaifeng, China, in the year 1000?

16. Which two cities together had a population of about 900,000?

17. Find the approximate population of Kyoto in the year 1000.

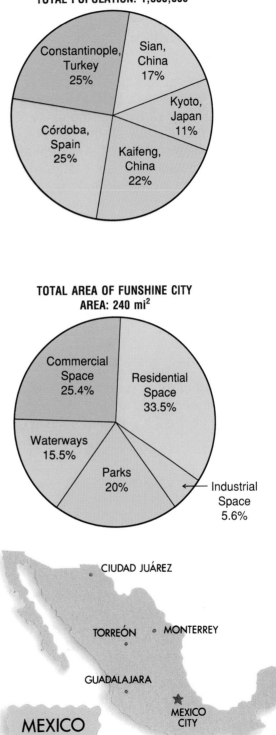

WORLD'S LARGEST URBAN AREAS IN THE YEAR 1000
TOTAL POPULATION: 1,800,000

- Constantinople, Turkey 25%
- Sian, China 17%
- Kyoto, Japan 11%
- Kaifeng, China 22%
- Córdoba, Spain 25%

Use the circle graph at the right to answer Problems 18–22.

18. Which area takes up the greatest space?

19. Which area takes up the least space?

20. What is the total area of the parks?

21. What is the total area of the residential space?

22. What is the approximate area of the commercial space?

TOTAL AREA OF FUNSHINE CITY
AREA: 240 mi^2

- Commercial Space 25.4%
- Residential Space 33.5%
- Waterways 15.5%
- Parks 20%
- Industrial Space 5.6%

Mixed Applications

23. The population of a town is now 122% of what it was five years ago. If the population was 6,100 five years ago, what is it today?

24. It is projected that in the year 2000 the total population of the world's five largest urban areas will be 126,500,000. It is also projected that the population of Mexico City will represent 25% of that total. What is its projected population?

CIUDAD JUÁREZ

TORREÓN · MONTERREY

GUADALAJARA

MEXICO CITY ★

MEXICO

DEVELOPING A CONCEPT

Making Circle Graphs

Two hundred students sign up for after-school clubs. Each student can join only one club. You can use the information in the table to make a circle graph.

Each region of a circle graph is called a sector. A **sector** is formed by a **central angle,** an angle whose vertex is the center of the circle. The size of each sector depends on the percent, which determines the measure of the central angle. Recall that the total degree measure of the central angles in a circle is 360°.

CLUB MEMBERSHIP

Club	Enrollment	Percent
Drama	18	9
Band	10	5
Sports	90	45
Chess	12	6
Computer	40	20
Newspaper	30	15
Total	200	100

WORKING TOGETHER

Before you draw a circle graph, you must find the measure of each central angle. Here is how to find the central angle for the Drama sector.

Think: 9% of 360° = 0.09 × 360° = 32.4°, or about 32°

1. Find the measure to the nearest degree of each of the other central angles. Is the sum of the angles 360°?

2. Use a compass to draw a circle large enough in which to write. Mark the center with a dot. Use a protractor to draw each central angle. Label each part of the circle graph. What did you include?

Tamara made this circle graph.

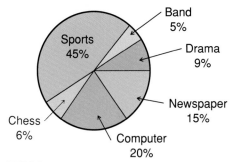

SHARING IDEAS

3. How is your graph the same as Tamara's graph? How is it different?

4. Did all of your central angles fit within the circle? If not, what does this tell you?

5. **What if** all the Chess Club members joined the Drama Club instead? What steps would you use to make a new circle graph?

PRACTICE

Use the data to make a circle graph.

6.

TEAM MEMBERSHIP

Team	Members	Percent
Track	12	10
Tennis	12	10
Football	30	25
Basketball	12	10
Baseball	24	20
Swimming	30	25
Total	120	100

7.

CLUB MEMBERSHIP

Club	Enrollment	Percent
Stargazers	20	20
Archaeology	8	8
Cooking	12	12
Dance	28	28
Orchestra	32	32
Total	100	100

Solve.

8. While playing basketball in gym class, 35% of the students missed no foul shots, 30.5% missed 1 foul shot, 25% missed 2 foul shots, and 9.5% missed 3 foul shots. Make a circle graph to show the results of the foul shooting by the gym class.

9. ***Write a summary*** of the results you get from making a circle graph about a subject of your choice. Before you draw the graph predict the results your graph will show. Then collect the data and make the graph.

Critical Thinking

10. Why is the size of the circle you use to represent the data unimportant?

11. Which percents of 360 are you able to find using mental math? Why?

Mixed Review

Find the answer. Which method did you use?

12. Find 42% of 200.

13. $1\frac{1}{2} \times 1\frac{1}{2}$

14. 88.03×2.47

15. $0.7 + 0.6 + 0.4$

16. $\frac{5}{12} \times \frac{8}{15}$

17. $0.68\overline{)0.051}$

18. Divide 21 by 1.5.

19. Find 5.5% of $12.

20. What percent of 360 is 120?

PROBLEM SOLVING

Strategy: Making a Graph

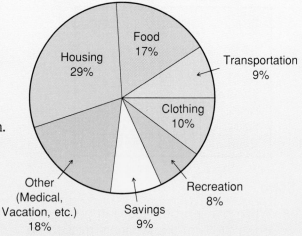

The members of the Castillo family use this circle graph to show their monthly budget. The Castillos decide they would like to contribute to their two children's college education. However, to do so means saving an additional $192 of their money each month.

Presently they take home a total of $2,400 a month.

The Castillos ask themselves the following questions to understand their situation better.

1. How much do the Castillos presently spend each month on housing?

2. How much do they reserve for savings each month?

3. Which categories can they probably not change?

4. Which categories can they change?

Make a plan.

The Castillos decide to deduct $192 from the categories that can be changed.

5. Which categories would you deduct from? By what amounts?

Try the plan.

The Castillos decide to reduce the amount they spend on clothing by $24 per month, on recreation by $72 per month, and on other expenses by $96 per month.

6. Draw a circle graph showing the changes in percents of the Castillos' new budget. Is the sum of the percents equal to 100%?

What if the Castillos' total take-home pay goes up to $2,800 a month, and the amount spent on housing is $812, on savings is $308, and on other expenses is $518?

7. Draw a circle graph to show the new percent for savings, other expenses, and housing. What is the remaining percent that they can distribute to the other categories?

8. Complete the graph to show how you would distribute the rest of their income.

9. How much do the Castillos now spend on each of the other categories?

Practice

Solve. Make or use a circle graph.

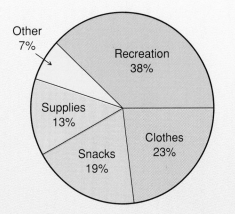

10. Delores receives a $12 per week allowance. Use the circle graph to find how much she spends on each category.

11. **What if** Delores received $75 per month? How much would she spend per week on each category? (Assume 1 month = 4 weeks.)

12. Redraw the circle graph to show what Delores' budget would look like if she spent $5.52 on recreation, $3 on clothes, $2.16 on snacks, and $.60 on supplies each week out of the original $12 allowance.

13. A town is deciding how to spend its budget of $32,000,000. The main costs are schools, police, sanitation, recreation, and roads. Draw a circle graph to show how you would distribute the money. Explain your choices.

Strategies and Skills Review

Solve. Use mental math, estimation, a calculator, or paper and pencil.

14. The Castillos saved $2,000 for a vacation. They plan to spend their money this way: travel, $540; lodging, $600; food, $380; souvenirs, $200; sightseeing, $220; miscellaneous, $260. Draw a circle graph to show what percent they plan to spend on each category.

15. On Friday the Castillos had $83 left from their food budget. On Thursday they spent half of the remaining money. On Wednesday they spent $46. On Tuesday they received an $8 refund. On Monday they spent $26. How much money did they start with?

16. The Castillos spent $144 on clothes. A pair of pants cost $24 more than a pair of shoes. A coat was twice as expensive as the pants. How much did each item cost?

17. The Castillos noticed that their housing costs went up 22% a year. Their costs were $500 per month the first year. What were the monthly costs after 4 years?

18. **Write a problem** that involves making and using a circle graph to find the answer. Have another student solve the problem.

ZOO STORIES

Logical Reasoning

A. The Albyville Zoo has a series of numbered animal cages (each cage has a door) arranged like this:

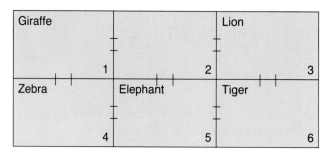

Note that cage 2 is empty. One day the zoo keeper decides that the lion and the tiger should change cages. However, the zoo keeper warns that while the animals are being moved, no two animals can ever be in the same cage at the same time. The other animals do not have to return to their original cages, as long as the lion and tiger are switched. So, for example, the elephant could be moved into cage 2, then the tiger could be moved to cage 5, the lion to cage 6, and so on.

Of course, the animals do not like being moved around, so the zoo workers want to accomplish the switch in as few moves as possible.

1. Make a copy of the cages on a sheet of paper. Use slips of paper with an animal name written on each. Move the slips around until you find a way to switch the lion and the tiger. Try it several times until you think you have found the shortest solution.

2. Find a method of recording your solution. Then compare your solutions with others. Did anyone find a shorter way?

B. One morning zoo workers find the zebra outside of its cage. Somebody must have neglected to shut the cage door properly. Who could it have been?

The four zoo workers, one of whom was the careless one, said the following:

Bob: Carol left the door open.

Carol: Eddie did it.

Donna: I didn't do it.

Eddie: Carol lied when she said I did it.

If only one is telling the truth, who left the door open?

3. Can Bob be the *only one* telling the truth? If he is, then who did it? Would Donna's and Eddie's statements be true or false? What does this mean?

4. Can Carol be the only one telling the truth? Explain.

5. Who was the only person telling the truth? How do you know? Who left the door open?

6. Suppose only one of the people was *lying*. Then who would be lying and who would be the guilty one?

DEVELOPING A CONCEPT

Representing Data

Hugh uses statistics in his store, Hugh's Shoes, to determine which shoes to stock. He finds out who his customers are and which shoes they like. Since his computer draws graphs, he uses graphs to interpret the information he collects.

Recall that, depending on the relationship you want to show among data, you may use any of the following graphs.

- A *line graph* is useful for showing changes over a period of time.

- A *bar graph* is useful for showing comparisons of several quantities.

- A *histogram* is useful for showing the frequency of grouped or rounded data.

- A *circle graph* is useful for showing how a whole quantity is divided into parts.

WORKING TOGETHER

For the situation, make a table and a graph.

1. To identify the ages of his customers, Hugh found the percent of them who were under 8, 10%; who were 8–11, 20%; who were 12–15, 30%; who were 16–19, 16%; who were 20–23, 9%; and who were over 23, 15%. He served a total of 500 customers during the two-week period he collected the data.

2. Over a two-week period, Hugh kept a record of sales to compare the popularity of these five athletic shoes: black nylon, 37; red with Velcro, 82; white leather, 65; yellow with reflectors, 22; and green with air inserts, 34. The total sales for the two-week period was 240 athletic shoes.

3. For two weeks Hugh charted the daily sales for his latest athletic shoe, a purple nylon high-top with side pockets, rearview mirrors, wings, and helium inserts. For the two-week period he obtained these sales figures: 5, 7, 6, 12, 8, 13, 14, 19, 24, 23, 26, and 26.

SHARING IDEAS

Use the tables and graphs in Problems 1–3 to answer the question.

4. Which type of graph best displays each situation?

5. What conclusions about the data can you draw from each graph?

PRACTICE

Solve.

6. You want to compare sales of four items during the same period of time. What kind of graph should you use? Why?

7. You want to compare the quantities of different items that make up the stock in your clothing store. What kind of graph should you use? Why?

Make a table to record the data. Then draw a graph.

8. A local telephone company wanted to find the time breakdown of calls made. On a particular weekday it surveyed 100 customers. The company computed the following percents: 12 midnight–6 A.M., 10%; 6 A.M.–12 noon, 25%; 12 noon–6 P.M., 45%; and 6 P.M.–12 midnight, 20%.

9. The same telephone company surveyed the same 100 customers. It tallied the number of calls the customers made and came up with the following number of calls: Sunday, 400; Monday, 175; Tuesday, 200; Wednesday, 225; Thursday, 150; Friday, 250; and Saturday, 450.

Tell why the graph is not the best choice to display the data. Give a better choice.

10. a circle graph to show the increase in the sales of Air-Jackson tennis shoes over a six-month period

11. a line graph to show the percent of shoes sold in several categories

12. a histogram to compare last year's total sales with this year's total sales

Mixed Applications

13. Forty-two percent of the 150 squash shoes were squashed in their boxes. How many were squashed?

14. What kind of graph would you use to show the number of new shoe stores opening each month over a two-year period?

Mixed Review

Find the answer. Which method did you use?

MENTAL MATH
CALCULATOR
PAPER/PENCIL

15. $\frac{2}{3} + \frac{4}{5}$

16. $\frac{7}{8} - \frac{2}{3}$

17. $1\frac{1}{2} \times 3\frac{1}{2}$

18. $6 \div \frac{1}{2}$

19. $5.8 + 2 + 8$

20. $24 - 9.6$

21. 0.17×4.53

22. $66 \div 3.3$

23. $20\% \times 100$

Misleading Statistics

A. Look at the bars on the graph. It appears that females live more than three times as long as males in each country.

Use the scale on the graph to find the difference in life expectancies in each country:

United States: 78 − 71 = 7 years
Canada: 78.9 − 71.9 = 7 years
Austria: 77.2 − 70.1 = 7.1 years
France: 78.4 − 70.4 = 8 years
Australia: 78.7 − 72.6 = 6.1 years

In each country females live only about 7 years more than males, not nearly three times as long.

1. Why is the graph misleading?

2. How could you change the graph to give a clearer representation of the situation?

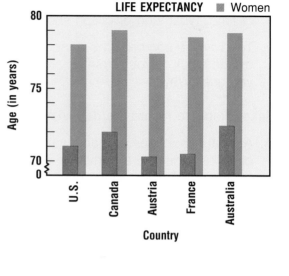

LIFE EXPECTANCY
■ Men
■ Women

Age (in years)
80
75
70
0

U.S. Canada Austria France Australia
Country

B. When you look at the graph, it appears that whole milk contains three to four times as much fat. But, using the scale on the graph, you find that there are 8 grams of fat in whole milk and 5 grams in 2% milk.

Think: $\frac{8}{5}$, or about $1\frac{1}{2}$

There is about $1\frac{1}{2}$ times as much fat in whole milk as in 2% milk.

3. How could you show this data in a more informative way?

FAT CONTENT OF 1 C. MILK

Fat (grams)
8
4
0

Whole Milk   2% Milk
Kinds

4. From the graph, about how many times as long as a $1 bill does a $20 bill appear to last?

5. About how many times as long as a $1 bill does a $20 actually last?

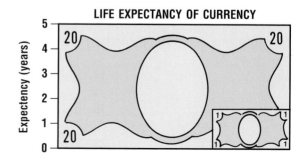

LIFE EXPECTANCY OF CURRENCY

Expectancy (years)
5
4
3
2
1
0

20   20

20

PRACTICE

The graph at the right shows the rate of unemployment in a city.

6. What was the percent of unemployed people in January?

7. What was the percent of unemployed people in June?

8. By how much did the unemployment rate actually change?

9. What appears to be true about the unemployment rate according to the graph?

11. What appears to be true about the unemployment rate in Problem 10?

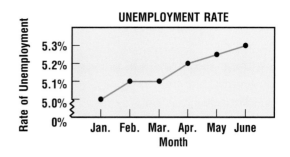

10. Redraw the graph using the numbers 1.0, 1.5, 2.0, 2.5, . . . , 5.5 on the vertical scale.

12. Which graph, the one above or the one you drew in Problem 10, presents the data more clearly? Why?

A magazine published the graph at the right to show how its number of subscriptions had increased.

13. Use the graph to find how many times the subscriptions appear to have increased.

14. Find the approximate increase in the number of subscriptions from 1989 until 1991.

15. How is the graph misleading?

16. How could you change the graph to give a clearer representation of the situation?

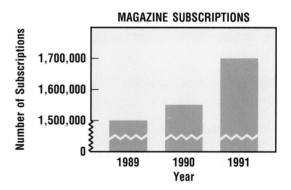

Critical Thinking

17. The manager at a bike store wants to recommend to the owner that he stop buying Turtle bikes. Which graph might he use to make his case?

18. A sales representative of Turtle bikes wants to convince the owner to continue to buy its bikes. Which graph might she use to make her case?

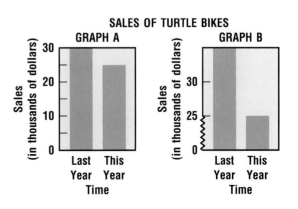

Making Stem-and-Leaf Plots

Another way to organize data is to use a **stem-and-leaf plot.** The stem-and-leaf plot at the right shows the heights, in stories, of the 25 tallest buildings in Houston, Texas.

HOUSTON'S TALLEST BUILDINGS

stems		leaves
3		4,5,6,6
4		0,0,1,2,4,4,5,7,7,7
5		0,0,0,2,3,4,5,6
6		4
7		1,5

3|4 represents
34 stories

1. The stems are the tens digits of the data. What do the leaves represent?

2. What are the least and the greatest values of the data? How are the values represented in the plot?

3. How many buildings have 47 stories? 36 stories?

WORKING TOGETHER

Here are the steps for making a stem-and-leaf plot.

Step 1 Find the least value and the greatest value of the data.

Step 2 Use the values in Step 1 to choose appropriate stem values. On graph paper write the stem values vertically with a line to the right.

Step 3 Separate each value of the data into a stem and a leaf. Then place the leaves on the plot to the right of a stem in order from the least to the greatest.

Step 4 Next to the plot, write an explanation of the stems and leaves.

Step 5 Write a title above the plot.

4. Use the steps to make a stem-and-leaf plot of the table showing Boston's tallest buildings.

BOSTON'S TALLEST BUILDINGS

Building	Stories	Building	Stories
John Hancock Tower	60	New England Merchant Bank	40
Prudential Center	52	U.S. Custom House	32
Boston Co. Building	41	John Hancock Building	26
Federal Reserve Building	32	State Street Bank	34
International Place	46	One Hundred Summer Street	30
First National Bank	37	McCormack Building	33
One Financial Center	46	Keystone Funds	22
Shawmut Bank	38	Saltonstall Office Building	32
Exchange Place	39	Devonshire	22
Sixty State Street	38	Harbor Towers	40
One Post Office Square	40	Westin Hotel	40
One Beacon Street	40	Federal Center	28

SHARING IDEAS

5. Use your stem-and-leaf plot to find the mode and the median of the data.

6. Why is it easy to find these statistical measures using the plot?

7. What are the advantages of using a stem-and-leaf plot instead of a bar graph? the disadvantages?

ON YOUR OWN

Make a stem-and-leaf plot for the set of data. Then describe the data.

8. Here are the heights, in stories, of the 25 tallest buildings in Los Angeles: 73, 62, 53, 55, 52, 52, 48, 42, 42, 44, 42, 41, 36, 36, 36, 32, 28, 34, 32, 31, 33, 27, 28, 31, and 26.

9. These are the enrollments for 20 seventh-grade classes in one school district: 37, 21, 24, 28, 16, 29, 33, 35, 41, 28, 34, 29, 22, 17, 23, 19, 25, 30, 22, and 21.

10. Collect data on a topic that interests you. Make a stem-and-leaf plot. Then summarize the information in a paragraph.

EXPLORING A CONCEPT

Making Box-and-Whisker Plots

The students in Ms. Poe's seventh-grade class took a national reading test and obtained the following scores:

5.8, 7.6, 7.4, 6.5, 5.9, 9.8, 9.6, 5.5, 8.1, 7.7, 6.5, 7.4, 6.6, 5.1, 8.1, 11.3, 6.3, 7.2, 7.9, 8.3, 6.7

One way to display the results of the test is to use a **box-and-whisker plot.** A box-and-whisker plot displays the median values. Recall that the median is the middle value in a set of data.

WORKING TOGETHER

Here are the steps for making a box-and-whisker plot.

Step 1 Write the data in order from the least to the greatest.

5.1, 5.5, 5.8, 5.9, 6.3, 6.5, 6.5, 6.6, 6.7, 7.2, 7.4, 7.4, 7.6, 7.7, 7.9, 8.1, 8.1, 8.3, 9.6, 9.8, 11.3

Step 2 Find the median of the data.
The median score on the test is 7.4.

Step 3 Find the median for the lower half of the data.
The median score for the lower half of the test scores is 6.4.

Step 4 Find the median for the upper half of the data.
The median score for the upper half of the test scores is 8.1.

Step 5 Find the lower extreme.   The lowest test score is 5.1.

Step 6 Find the upper extreme.   The greatest test score is 11.3.

Step 7 Mark the five numbers on a number line. Draw a line segment above the number line from 5.1 to 11.3. Then draw vertical segments at the three medians, 6.4, 7.4, and 8.1. Connect the endpoints at the tops and bottoms of the segments to make boxes.

Step 8 Write the title of the graph.

Here is the box-and-whisker plot for the reading test scores for the seventh-grade class.

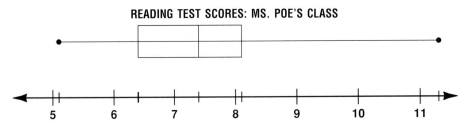

READING TEST SCORES: MS. POE'S CLASS

1. How do you find the median for the lower half of the test scores?

2. How do you find the median for the upper half of the test scores?

Mr. Whitman's students received these reading test scores:

7.2, 9.5, 10.3, 6.8, 4.8, 5.2, 5.6, 8.0, 9.1, 11.6,
7.6, 8.5, 6.1, 5.7, 7.1, 8.8, 8.2, 7.9, and 7.4.

Here is the box-and-whisker plot for these scores.

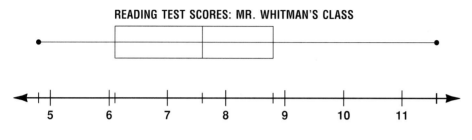

READING TEST SCORES: MR. WHITMAN'S CLASS

3. Compare the box-and-whisker plots. What do you notice about the overall size of the boxes? How do the extremes compare?

4. What do the two box-and-whisker plots tell you about the national reading test scores for the students in Ms. Poe's and Mr. Whitman's classes?

SHARING IDEAS

5. What does the distance between extremes tell you about the spread of values within a set of data?

6. What are the advantages of a box-and-whisker plot?

7. What are the disadvantages of a box-and-whisker plot?

ON YOUR OWN

Make a box-and-whisker plot.

8. Ms. Keller's class rated the job performance of the town's mayor. The lowest possible rating was 0 and the highest possible rating was 50. Here is a list of the ratings: 24, 25, 27, 28, 30, 30, 35, 37, 15, 14, 13, 15, 11, 15, 22, 20, 21, 22, 23, 6, 8, 10, 22, 3, and 10.

9. Here are the job performance ratings given by the students in Mr. Toon's class: 17, 34, 34, 19, 24, 28, 37, 16, 30, 21, 22, 39, 44, 28, 19, 20, 42, 37, 25, 21, and 29.

10. ***Write a paragraph*** that compares two box-and-whisker plots. To do this, collect two sets of data on the same topic and make the two plots.

UNDERSTAND
✓ PLAN
  ✓ TRY
    CHECK
  ✓ EXTEND

PROBLEM SOLVING

Strategy: Drawing a Venn Diagram

At the Roosevelt School the director of the dramatics club was auditioning seventh graders for a musical production. On the actors' list were 15 names, on the musicians' list were 12 names, and on the singers' list were 18 names.

The director noticed that several students' names appeared on more than one list.

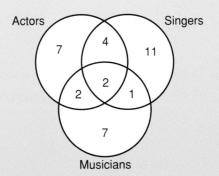

- 2 were on all three lists.

- 3 were on both the musicians' and singers' lists.

- 4 were on both the actors' and musicians' lists.

- 6 were on both the actors' and singers' lists.

The director scratched her head and thought, "How many students are there all together?"

Make a plan.

One way to solve this problem is to draw a Venn diagram.

Try the plan.

The director knew that 2 students were on all 3 lists. She wrote 2 in the part common to all 3 circles. She looked at the parts of the musicians' and the singers' circles that overlapped. From the list she knew that the number here had to be 3. So she put 1 in the place where only the singers' and musicians' circles overlapped.

1. Why did the director put a 4 where only the actors' and singers' circles overlapped?

2. Why did she put a 2 where only the actors' and musicians' circles overlapped?

3. How many students are just actors? just musicians? just singers?

4. How many students auditioned all together?

5. **What if** there were 20 students on the actors' list, 30 on the musicians' list, and 40 on the singers' list and all other information were the same? Redraw the Venn diagram to find how many students auditioned all together.

PRACTICE

Draw a Venn diagram to solve the problem.

6. Look at the original lists of students who auditioned for the musical. What if the number of students on the actors' list was 22, the number on both the actors' list and musicians' list was 9, and all other information remained the same? How many different students would have auditioned all together?

7. There are 100 people in a large musical production. 25 wear tweed suits, 30 sing a solo, 6 wear boots and sing a solo, 7 wear boots and tweed suits, 8 wear tweed suits and sing a solo, and 3 wear boots and tweed suits and sing a solo. How many just wear boots?

8. In a play an English tea merchant receives 60 trunks of tea from India. There are 3 brands. 15 trunks contain Brand B, 5 contain Brand A and Brand B, and 2 contain Brand B and Brand C. None contains all 3 brands. How many trunks contain just Brand B?

9. In his mathemagicianal show Lee asks the audience, "How many of the first ten nonzero multiples of each number, 8, 9, and 12, are shared by the other numbers?"

Strategies and Skills Review

Solve. Use mental math, estimation, a calculator, or paper and pencil. You may need to use the Databank on page 583.

10. Sara and Roy took a bus to see the opening night of *La Traviata* in St. Paul, Minnesota. The bus traveled 14.5 mi in 45 minutes. At what speed, to the nearest mph, did the bus travel? If the bus gets 3 mi to the gallon, how much would the gas for this trip cost?

11. The Witty Players perform 2 shows per year. They have a choice of 3 locations: Oakland, Riverine, and Croton Falls. What are all the possible combinations of locations where they could perform the 2 shows?

12. Students belong to 3 school clubs. 6 belong to just the Chess Club, 4 belong to just the Dance Club, 2 belong to just the Games Club, and 3 belong to all 3 clubs. 8 belong to both the Chess Club and the Games Club. 7 belong to both the Chess Club and the Dance Club. How many are in the Chess Club?

13. **Write a problem** that uses the Drawing a Venn Diagram strategy to find the answer. Solve the problem. Give it to other students to solve.

ECISION MAKING

Problem Solving: Choosing a Budget

SITUATION

A group of students is discussing budgets. Each one of them has to decide how to budget his or her allowance. They agree on three sample budgets from which to choose. They may select the same budgets.

PROBLEM

Which budget should each student choose?

DATA

	BUDGET A	BUDGET B	BUDGET C
Records and Tapes	6%	12%	11%
Movies and Social Events	16%	35%	20%
Food	9%	18%	10%
Clothes	36%	9%	45%
Savings	6%	6%	3%
Miscellaneous	27%	20%	11%

Lynne: Earns $25 every week babysitting; has to buy her own clothes; loves to go to the movies; wants to save money for a special trip.

Dawn: Has an allowance of $12.50 every week; her parents buy her clothes; likes to buy records and tapes.

John: Has an allowance of $10.00 every week; earns about $75.00 every month doing occasional odd jobs like washing windows, cleaning out attics, yardwork, etc; must buy own clothes; likes to go horseback riding whenever he has enough money.

USING THE DATA

How much money does each student have available every month?
(Assume 1 mo. = 4 wks)

1. Lynne   **2.** Dawn   **3.** John

How much could each student spend on records and tapes on each
budget in a month?

4. Budget A   **5.** Budget B   **6.** Budget C

How much could each student save in a month on each budget?

7. Budget A   **8.** Budget B   **9.** Budget C

How much would each student have to spend in each of these categories
on budget B in a month?

10. Clothes   **11.** Movies and Social Events   **12.** Miscellaneous

MAKING DECISIONS

13. Which budget should Lynne and John not consider? Why?

14. Which budget or budgets would allow Lynne the most savings?

15. Which budget would allow John the most money for horseback riding?

16. Which budget allows Dawn the most money to spend on records and
tapes? movies and social events? food?

17. Which budget would probably be best for Dawn to choose? Why?

18. Which budget should Lynne choose? should John choose? Why?

19. *Write a list* of other expenses students should consider when
setting up a budget.

20. Which budget would you choose? Why?

Math and Social Studies

You may have heard that people live longer now than they used to. That's true, but how much longer?

Life expectancy is the number of years that a group of people of a certain age may expect to live. It is based on statistics of the number of people of the same age who were living in various years. The table below shows that the life expectancy at birth (age 0) in the years 1900–1902 in the United States was 48.23 years. In that same period, 1900–1902, the life expectancy of a 10-year-old was an *additional* 50.59 years, or 60.59 years in all.

The Granger Collection

LIFE EXPECTANCY IN THE UNITED STATES

Period	Age (in years)				
	0	10	20	50	80
1900–1902	48.23	50.59	42.19	20.76	5.10
1985	71.9	62.9	53.3	25.8	6.8

What if you compare age groups 0 and 10? In which age group is there a greater percent increase in life expectancy?

Think: Subtract to find the amount of increase.

Then, divide to find the percent of increase.

For Age 0: $71.9 - 48.23 = 23.67$
$23.67 \div 48.23 = 0.4907 \approx 49\%$

For Age 10: $62.9 - 50.59 = 12.31$
$12.31 \div 50.59 = 0.2433 \approx 24\%$

There is a greater percent increase for age group 0.

ACTIVITIES

1. Work with a partner. Use the figures above to make a line graph showing the same information. You may want to use an almanac to include figures for additional time periods. Write five questions that can be answered using your graph.

2. Look in an almanac or newspaper for other information that is reported in statistics. Choose one that interests you and prepare a report. Draw as many valid conclusions as you can.

Computer Graphing: Circle Graphs

A circle graph is used to show how each part of a whole compares to the other parts and also to the whole itself. You can create a circle graph from data by finding how each quantity should compare to a 360° central angle of a circle and then using a protractor to construct the sectors. Another way is to simply enter each quantity into a computer graph program, and let it perform the calculations and construction for you. For this activity you will use the computer program CIRCLE POWER.

The table below shows the monthly expenses of a small travel agency.

MONTHLY EXPENSES

Office rental	$1,946
Employee salaries	$4,192
Advertising	$2,350
Utilities	$594
Other	$782

Use the table as data for the circle-graph program on the computer.

AT THE COMPUTER

1. Enter each amount in the correct column on the computer screen, and instruct the program to create the circle graph. Which two expenses together account for more than the employee salaries?

2. Write down the percents for each sector of the graph. How do you think each would change if the company had spent an additional $1,000 on advertising?

3. Enter the new advertising amount in the correct column on the computer screen, and have the program redraw the circle graph. How do the percents compare with your predictions?

4. One month the company decides that it should allocate only 18% of its expenses to advertising. Dollar amounts for the other four expense categories will not change. Predict the advertising expense that will be 18% of the total expenses.

5. Check your prediction by having the program redraw the graph using the new figure. Try various figures in the advertising column until the circle graph shows that it accounts for 18% of the total expenses.

EXTRA PRACTICE

Reading and Interpreting Histograms, page 421

Use the histogram below to answer the questions.

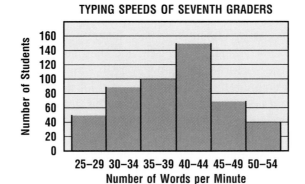

TYPING SPEEDS OF SEVENTH GRADERS

1. In which interval did the greatest number of students type?

2. In which interval did the least number of students type?

3. How many students type 35 or more words per minute?

4. What is the range of frequencies?

5. Between which two intervals do 50% of the students type?

Reading and Interpreting Circle Graphs, page 423

The circle graph shows the results of a survey of 200 students.

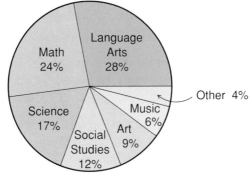

WHAT IS YOUR FAVORITE SUBJECT?

1. Which subject was twice as popular as social studies?

2. How many students chose language arts as their favorite subject?

3. How many students chose science as their favorite subject?

4. About half the students chose which two subjects?

5. If 1,000 students were surveyed, how many would you expect would choose art or music as their favorite subject?

Making Circle Graphs, page 425

Use the data to make a circle graph.

1. THE HARRISONS' MONTHLY BUDGET

Item	Amount	Percent
Rent	$800	25%
Food	$400	$12\frac{1}{2}$%
Utilities	$320	10%
Savings	$480	15%
Clothes	$256	10%
Education	$640	20%
Miscellaneous	$208	$7\frac{1}{2}$%
Total	$3,200	100%

2.

Class	Members	Percent
7th	400	$33\frac{1}{3}$%
8th	180	15%
9th	180	15%
10th	150	$12\frac{1}{2}$%
11th	200	$16\frac{2}{3}$%
12th	90	$7\frac{1}{2}$%
Total	1,200	100%

3. Mr. Brown plants 40% of his farm with corn, 30% with soybeans, 20% with oats, and 10% is grass for hay. Make a circle graph to show the part of Mr. Brown's farm used for each crop.

Problem–Solving Strategy: Making and Using a Graph, page 427

Solve.

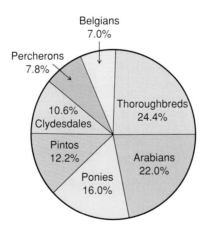

1. The Brandon horse farm has seven different breeds of horses. They have 500 horses at the farm. Use the circle graph to find how many horses they have of each breed.

2. *What if* there were twice as many pintos, half as many Thoroughbreds, 7 more Clydesdales, 4 less ponies, 5 less Belgians, 11 more Percherons, and 9 fewer Arabians? How many would there be of each breed? Redraw the circle graph to show how many of each breed there are now.

EXTRA PRACTICE

Representing Data, page 431

1. You want to compare the heights of the six tallest buildings in the world. What kind of graph should you use?

2. You want to compare the average monthly precipitation in Honolulu, Hawaii, and San Antonio, Texas. What kind of graph should you use?

Make a table to record the data. Then draw a graph.

3. A group of students made a survey of favorite colors of 200 preschoolers. They computed the percents: red, 35%; blue, 25%; yellow, 15%; green, 5%; orange, 10%; purple, 10%.

4. Another group of students took the results of the survey of preschoolers' color preferences. They tallied the results by the number of students that chose each color: red, 70; blue, 50; yellow, 30; green, 10; orange, 20; purple, 20.

Misleading Statistics, page 433

The Work 4 Us company published these graphs to show how its wages have increased.

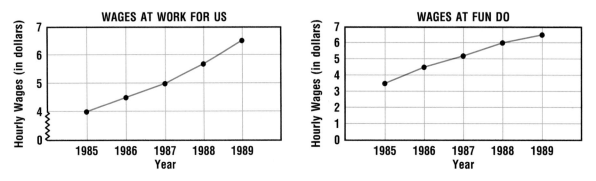

1. From the graph, which company's wages show a greater increase over the years?

2. Find the approximate increase in wages for both companies.

3. How is the graph misleading?

4. How are the graphs different?

5. How could you change the graphs to give a clearer representation of the situation?

EXTRA PRACTICE

Problem–Solving Strategy: Drawing a Venn Diagram, page 439 ....

Draw a Venn diagram to solve.

1. Some students play two musical instruments.
30 play piano.
20 play guitar.
10 play both guitar and piano.
How many students in all play these two instruments?

2. A group of adults are teachers and parents.
20 are parents.
25 are teachers.
15 are both teachers and parents.
How many adults in all are teachers and parents?

3. A group of games can be played by two and four players.
10 can be played by two players.
14 can be played by four players.
10 can be played by only four players.
How many can be played by two or four players?

4. Some students can do two dives.
6 can do a triple somersault.
2 can do both a triple somersault and jackknife.
14 can do a jackknife.
How many can do only a jackknife?

5. Students surveyed enjoy two types of music.
30 enjoy rock.
15 enjoy country.
10 enjoy only country.
How many enjoy only rock?

6. Students travel to school in three ways.
34 ride the bus, 26 walk, 23 ride in a car.
3 travel all three ways.
7 walk or ride in a car.
6 walk or ride a bus.
How many only walk to school?

7. Students surveyed enjoy three activities.
10 enjoy just plays.
25 enjoy just movies.
12 enjoy just concerts.
2 enjoy all three.
3 enjoy both plays and concerts.
3 enjoy movies and concerts.
How many students enjoy concerts?

8. Students play three sports.
10 swim.
9 play baseball.
8 play basketball.
1 plays all three.
2 swim and play baseball.
2 swim and play basketball.
How many only swim?

9. Students belong to three musical groups.
40 belong to the orchestra.
60 belong to the marching band.
10 belong to orchestra and jazz band.
10 belong to marching band and orchestra.
10 belong to all three.
How many only belong to the orchestra?

10. Students are in three school clubs.
7 only belong to the drama club.
6 only belong to the art club.
2 belong to all three clubs.
8 only belong to the games club.
11 belong to drama and art.
17 belong to games and drama club.
How many belong to the drama club?

KEY SKILL: Reading and Interpreting Circle Graphs (Use after page 423.)

Level A

Use the circle graph at the right to answer the questions.

1. What is Ralph's computer used most for?

2. What is Ralph's computer used least for?

3. In 10 hours, how many minutes are used for each task?

4. Which task does Ralph do 3 times as much as he plays computer games?

Level B

Use the circle graph at the right to answer the questions.

The seventh grade voted where to go on a field trip.

5. What place was the most popular?

6. What place was the least popular?

7. If there are 400 seventh graders, how many voted for each place?

8. Which activity was 3 times as popular as the zoo?

Level C

Use the circle graph at the right to answer the questions.

9. Which ocean takes up the greatest space?

10. Which ocean takes up the least space?

11. What is the total area of each ocean to the nearest million square miles?

12. Which two oceans together take up about 50% of the world's water?

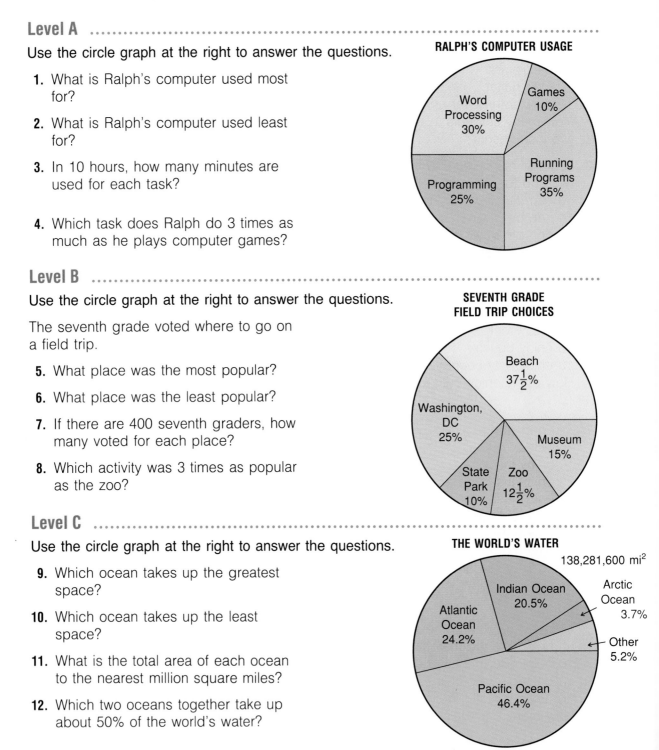

RALPH'S COMPUTER USAGE

- Word Processing 30%
- Games 10%
- Running Programs 35%
- Programming 25%

SEVENTH GRADE FIELD TRIP CHOICES

- Beach $37\frac{1}{2}$%
- Washington, DC 25%
- Museum 15%
- State Park 10%
- Zoo $12\frac{1}{2}$%

THE WORLD'S WATER

138,281,600 mi²

- Indian Ocean 20.5%
- Arctic Ocean 3.7%
- Atlantic Ocean 24.2%
- Other 5.2%
- Pacific Ocean 46.4%

KEY SKILL: Misleading Statistics (Use after page 433.)

Level A

The graph at the right shows Tim's test scores in math.

1. How much did Tim's test scores improve?

2. What appears to be true about the test scores according to the graph?

3. Redraw the graph using an appropriate scale to give a clearer representation of the situation?

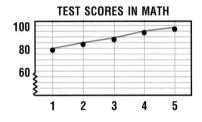

TEST SCORES IN MATH

Level B

The graph shows the profits of Magazines R Us.

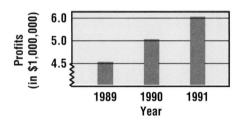

4. How much did the company's profits increase from 1989 to 1991?

5. How much do the profits appear to have increased according to the graph?

6. Redraw the graph using an appropriate scale.

Level C

The graph at the right shows the oil production of oil field A.

7. How much did the oil production at oil field A increase from 1989 to 1990?

8. How much does it appear to have increased?

9. Redraw the graph to correctly show how the oil production increases from one year to the next.

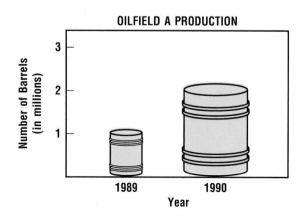

OILFIELD A PRODUCTION

CHAPTER REVIEW

LANGUAGE AND MATHEMATICS

Complete the sentences. Use the words in the chart on the right.

VOCABULARY
histogram
circle graph
sector
central angle

1. A bar graph that shows the frequency distribution of grouped data is a ■. *(page 420)*

2. A ■ shows how a whole is divided into its parts. *(page 422)*

3. An angle whose vertex is the center of a circle is a ■. *(page 424)*

4. *Write a definition* or give an example of the word you did not use from the chart.

CONCEPTS AND SKILLS

This histogram shows the number of customers at a diner during one weekend. *(page 420)*

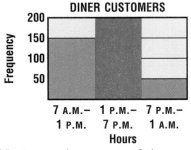

DINER CUSTOMERS

5. How many customers were at the diner that weekend?

6. In which hours did the diner have the most customers?

7. In which hours did the diner have the fewest customers?

8. What was the range of the number of customers?

9. How many more customers came between 1 P.M. and 7 P.M. than between 7 P.M. and 10 P.M.?

This histogram shows the number of TVs one store sold by price. *(page 432)*

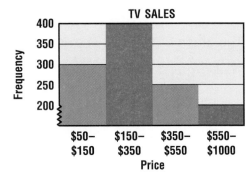

TV SALES

10. Which price range sold the least?

11. How many TVs were sold at the store altogether?

12. How many more TVs were sold in the $150–$350 price range than in the $550–$1,000 price range?

13. What is the ratio of the number of $150–$350 sales to $50–$150 sales?

14. To the nearest percent, what percent of the sales were $350–$550 TVs?

15. How many times as tall is the $150–$350 bar compared to the $550–$1,000 bar?

Critical Thinking

Use the histogram for Exercises 10–15 to answer Exercises 16–18. *(page 432)*

16. Do the heights of the bars show the actual relationships between the numbers of sales for the price ranges?

17. If the scale started at 0, how many times as tall would the $150–$350 bar be compared to the $550–$1,000 bar?

18. How does this histogram make the sales on $550–$1,000 TVs appear relatively small?

Mixed Applications

This circle graph shows Lida's budget. *(page 422)*

19. For which item does she budget most?

20. For which item does she budget least?

21. Which 3 items total just half of her budget?

22. For which 2 items does she budget the same percent?

23. Which 2 items account for just $\frac{1}{5}$ of her budget?

24. How much more is the savings percent than the food percent?

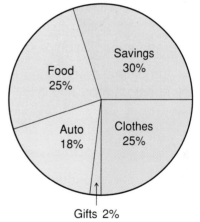

LIDA'S BUDGET

Gifts 2%

25. What fraction of her budget does she spend on gifts?

26. If she earns $45.50, how much of it does she save?

27. If she earns $82, how much of it does she spend on gifts?

28. Lida cut her food budget to 20%. If she earned $80, how many dollars were cut from her food budget?

29. Lida earned $80. How much money did she budget for gifts and clothes combined?

30. Make a circle graph to show the composition of the earth's crust. *(page 424)*

Element	Percent
Oxygen	47%
Silicon	28%
Aluminum	8%
Other	17%

CHAPTER TEST

Use the histogram to answer questions 1–10.

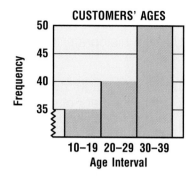

CUSTOMERS' AGES

1. What is the range of the frequencies?

2. Which interval has the fewest customers?

3. How many customers are ages 30 to 39?

4. How many customers are ages 10 to 29?

5. How many customers are shown in all?

6. What percent of the customers are ages 30 to 39?

7. What fraction of the customers are ages 20 to 29?

8. How many more customers are ages 30 to 39 than 20 to 29?

9. How many times as tall is the bar for ages 30 to 39 as the bar for ages 20 to 29?

10. Why is the histogram misleading?

This circle graph shows Sandy's budget.

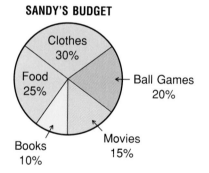

SANDY'S BUDGET

11. What is the difference between the percent spent on food and on movies?

12. Which two items total half her budget?

13. What fraction of her budget does she spend on clothes?

14. If she earns $24.80, how much does she spend on movies?

15. If she earns $50, how much does she spend on books?

The proceeds from the annual school fair were distributed as shown in the table.

Activity	Percent of Proceeds
Clubs	5%
Yearbook	25%
Athletics	40%
Newspaper	?
Total	100%

16. What percent of the proceeds was allocated to the school newspaper?

17. What is the main visual advantage of a circle graph?

18. In a circle graph, how many degrees would be required by the yearbook?

19. Make a circle graph to show the allocation of funds from the school fair.

20. In a Venn Diagram showing three intersecting circles, what does the part common to all these circles represent?

ESTIMATING WILDLIFE POPULATIONS

The Fish and Wildlife Association wants to know how many birds there are in a wildlife refuge.

It is impossible to count the exact number of birds. Some are always in flight. Others are hidden in trees. Therefore, the Fish and Wildlife Association needs to *estimate* the number of birds. The members decide to use the method described below.

First, they put up huge nets across regions where birds usually fly. (The nets trap the birds but do not harm them.) The nets are then taken down and tags are put around the birds' legs.

They trap 3,000 birds the first time.

A few weeks later, they put the nets up again. This time, they find the percent of trapped birds that have tags.

18% of the trapped birds have tags on their legs.

Based on this data, they assume that they are trapping only 0.18 of all the birds. They write and solve a proportion to estimate the total number of birds.

$$\frac{18}{100} = \frac{3,000}{x}$$
$$18x = 300,000$$
$$x = 16,666.\overline{6}$$

The Association estimates that there are about 17,000 birds in the refuge.

Solve the problem.

1. One day 85 deer from a park were caught, tagged, and released. Several weeks later 9% of the deer caught in a day had tags. Estimate the deer population in the park.

2. One year the Wildlife Service in the park caught, tagged, and released 192 bears. The following year 45% of the bears that were caught had tags. Estimate the bear population in the park.

CUMULATIVE REVIEW

Choose the letter of the correct answer.

1. $\frac{3}{5} \times 4$

   a. $\frac{3}{20}$ c. $2\frac{2}{5}$

   b. $\frac{12}{20}$ d. not given

2. $\frac{2}{5} \div \frac{2}{5}$

   a. $\frac{1}{5}$ c. $\frac{4}{5}$

   b. $\frac{2}{5}$ d. not given

3. Find the square root of 25.

   a. 5   c. 225
   b. 25   d. not given

4. Which type of angle has a measure between 0 and 90 degrees?

   a. obtuse   c. scalene
   b. acute   d. not given

5. In what type of triangle do all sides have the same measure?

   a. scalene   c. isosceles
   b. obtuse   d. not given

6. Solve for n: $\frac{4}{n} = \frac{10}{7.5}$

   a. 3   c. 40
   b. 30   d. not given

7. A map scale sets 1 in. = 20 mi. If two places are 5 mi apart, how far apart are they on the map?

   a. $\frac{1}{4}$ in.   c. 100 in.
   b. 4 in.   d. not given

8. What fraction equals 30%?

   a. $\frac{3}{100}$ c. $\frac{1}{3}$

   b. $\frac{10}{3}$ d. not given

9. What percent equals $\frac{5}{2}$?

   a. 2.5%   c. 250%
   b. 40%   d. not given

This circle graph shows the number of pieces of chicken in a deluxe basket.

CHICKEN PIECES IN A DELUXE BASKET

10. How many pieces are in the basket?
    a. 10   c. 100
    b. 20   d. not given

11. What is the difference between the number of legs and the number of wings?
    a. 3   c. 13
    b. 5   d. not given

12. What percent of the pieces are backs?
    a. 2%   c. 20%
    b. 10%   d. not given

13. What fraction of the pieces are thighs?

    a. $\frac{1}{5}$ c. $\frac{1}{2}$

    b. $\frac{1}{4}$ d. not given

14. The legs and thighs together make up what percent of the pieces?
    a. 5%   c. 75%
    b. 15%   d. not given

Measurement: Surface Area and Volume

MATH CONNECTIONS: ALGEBRA • PROBLEM SOLVING

REGIONAL THEATER TROUPE

Shakespearean Festival

Tues. – Thur. 7:30 P.M.	$15.00
Fri. & Sat. 7:30 P.M.	$20.00
Sun. Matinee 2:00 P.M.	$12.50

SCRIPT

1. What information do you see in this picture?
2. How can you use the information?
3. How much could a family of four save by going to the Sunday matinee instead of the Saturday night show?
4. Write a problem using the information.

A. Geometric figures whose vertices lie in more than one plane are **space figures.** Space figures whose faces are polygons are **polyhedrons.** Two faces of a polyhedron intersect at an edge.

These polyhedrons are **prisms.** Recall that a prism has two parallel bases that are congruent polygons and that the other faces are parallelograms. A prism might not always sit on its base.

Triangular Prism **Rectangular Prism** **Pentagonal Prism**

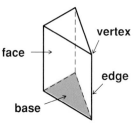 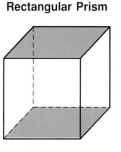 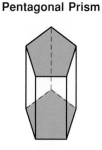

These polyhedrons are **pyramids.** Recall that a pyramid has a polygon as a base and that the other faces are triangles. The base is always opposite the vertex.

Triangular Pyramid **Rectangular Pyramid** **Hexagonal Pyramid**

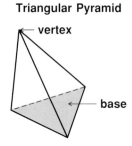 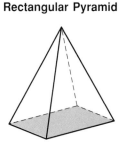 

B. A polyhedron can be unfolded into a two-dimensional pattern. The pattern at the right will form a cube when folded along the dashed lines.

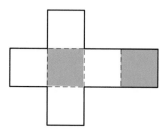

1. Model a cube using the pattern shown. Draw other patterns that will form a cube.

2. Use the connecting geometric shapes to model:
   a. a triangular prism.
   b. a triangular pyramid.

3. Describe what you see when you view each figure you made in Problem 2 from the top, from the side, from the bottom.

456 Lesson 12–1

C. You can use isometric dot paper to draw some prisms.

| Step 1 | Draw the bases. Label the bases. |

| Step 2 | Connect the corresponding vertices. Dashed lines are used for the hidden edges. |

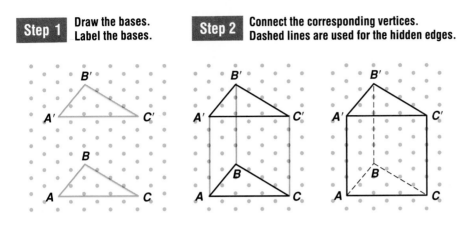

4. Draw a hexagonal prism on isometric dot paper.

WORKING TOGETHER

5. What do prisms and pyramids have in common?

6. How do they differ?

7. Why is a cube a rectangular prism? a square prism?

8. Look around the classroom. Find ordinary objects that are examples of prisms and pyramids. Make a table of the examples you find for each figure.

D. These are also called space figures.

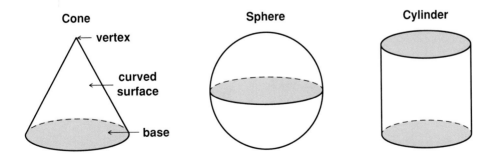

9. Why are these space figures not polyhedrons?

10. Look around the classroom. Find ordinary objects that are examples of cones, spheres, and cylinders. Make a table of the examples you find for each figure. Then make a combined list for all the students in the class.

11. Compare your patterns in Problem 1 with those of other students. Make a list of all the examples on the chalkboard.

12. Were there any patterns that did not work? What can you conclude?

13. How can you determine which face is the base of a prism?

14. Compare your answers to Problem 8. Make a list of all the examples the class found.

PRACTICE

Identify the space figure.

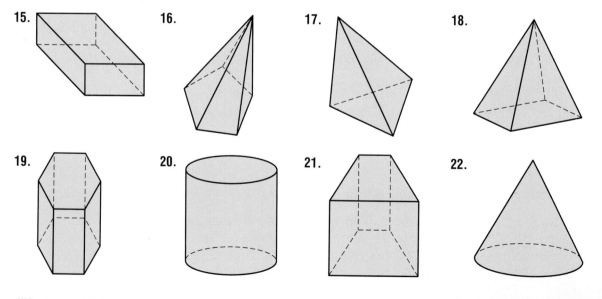

15.   **16.**   **17.**   **18.**

19.   **20.**   **21.**   **22.**

Complete the table.

Space Figure	Shape of the Base	Shape of the Faces	Number of Faces
Triangular prism	23.	24.	25.
Triangular pyramid	26.	27.	28.
Rectangular prism	29.	30.	31.
Rectangular pyramid	32.	33.	34.
Cube	35.	36.	37.
Hexagonal prism	38.	39.	40.

Use isometric dot paper to draw:

41. a pentagonal prism.   **42.** an octagonal prism.

What polyhedron will be formed when you fold the pattern?

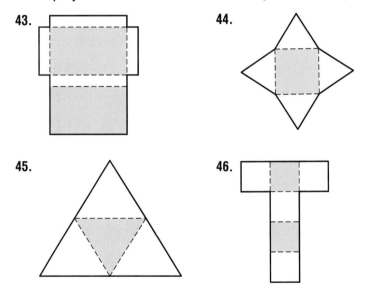

43.   **44.**

45.   **46.**

Identify the space figure from the view given. Give all possible answers from the list given. Assume the figure is sitting on a base.

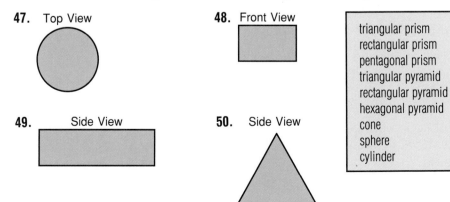

47. Top View   **48.** Front View

triangular prism
rectangular prism
pentagonal prism
triangular pyramid
rectangular pyramid
hexagonal pyramid
cone
sphere
cylinder

49. Side View   **50.** Side View

DEVELOPING A CONCEPT

Surface Area: Prisms

Penelope has a box that she uses to hold her collection of picture postcards. The box is a rectangular prism. She wants to cover the entire outside of the box with paper. What is the surface area of the box?

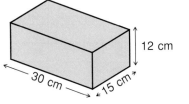

12 cm
30 cm
15 cm

WORKING TOGETHER

The box is a rectangular prism. Its surface area is the sum of the areas of its faces. Look at the pattern.

1. How many faces does it have?

2. What is the area of each face?

3. What is the surface area of the box?

30 cm

Back — 12 cm

Side | Bottom | Side — 15 cm

Front — 12 cm

Top

Compare the method of finding the area of each individual face with the following method.

Think: Area of top and bottom: $2 \times (30 \times 15) = 900$
Area of front and back: $2 \times (30 \times 12) = 720$
Area of two sides: $2 \times (15 \times 12) = 360$

$900 \text{ cm}^2 + 720 \text{ cm}^2 + 360 \text{ cm}^2 = 1{,}980 \text{ cm}^2$

The box has a surface area of $1{,}980 \text{ cm}^2$.

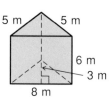

SHARING IDEAS

4. How are the two methods the same? How are they different?

5. What important property of rectangular prisms does the second method use? How does it make the computation easier?

What if you were asked to find the surface area of this triangular prism to the nearest whole number?

6. How many faces does it have?

7. How many pairs of congruent faces does it have? How does this help you find the surface area?

8. What is the surface area to the nearest whole number?

5 m   5 m
6 m
3 m
8 m

PRACTICE

Find the surface area. Use a calculator or paper and pencil.

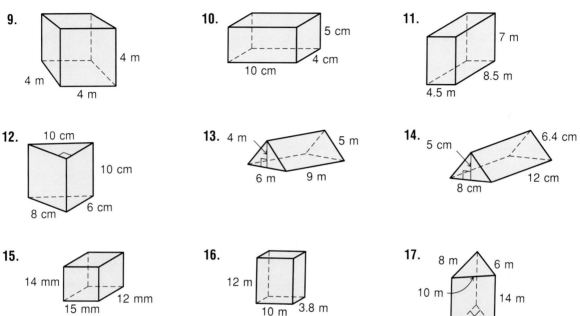

9.

4 m
4 m
4 m

10.

5 cm
10 cm
4 cm

11.

7 m
8.5 m
4.5 m

12.

10 cm
10 cm
8 cm
6 cm

13.

4 m
5 m
6 m
9 m

14.

5 cm
6.4 cm
8 cm
12 cm

15.

14 mm
15 mm
12 mm

16.

12 m
10 m
3.8 m

17.

8 m
6 m
10 m
14 m

Critical Thinking

18. How would the surface area of a cube change if the length were doubled? were tripled?

Mixed Applications

19. A dog is tied to a pole with a leash that is 3 m long. What is the area in which he can move? Use 3.14 for π.

20. A rectangular room is 4.5 m wide and twice as long. What is the area of a rug that covers the floor completely?

21. An apartment has an area of 700 m². Carla is covering 40% of it with carpet. How much carpet will she need?

22. A stereo speaker is a prism. It is 0.5 m wide, 0.3 m deep, and 1 m high. Jack wants to paint it black. What is the area of the faces that will show?

Mixed Review

Find the answer. Which method did you use?

MENTAL MATH
CALCULATOR
PAPER/PENCIL

23. $105.64 \div 1.9$

24. 56.12×0.87

25. $1.5 \times 2 \times 0.5$

26. 50% of 200

27. 45.5% of 25

28. $11\frac{1}{2} + 10\frac{1}{4} + 23$

UNDERSTANDING A CONCEPT

Surface Area: Pyramids

The local leadership of a small town commissioned the sculptor Dietmar to sculpt a giant upside-down square pyramid in honor of the town's centennial. What is the surface area of the pyramid?

6 m

6 m

4 m

CENTENNIAL DEDICATION

Look at the pattern of the square pyramid. The pyramid has four congruent triangular faces and a square base.

Think: Area of triangular faces: $4 \times (\frac{1}{2} \times 6 \times 4) = 48$
Area of base: $6 \times 6 = 36$

$48 \text{ m}^2 + 36 \text{ m}^2 = 84 \text{ m}^2$

The square pyramid has a surface area of 84 m².

4 m

6 m

6 m

(top)

1. Compare the procedures for finding the surface areas of pyramids and prisms. How are they the same? How are they different?

TRY OUT   Find the surface area. Use a calculator or paper and pencil.

2.

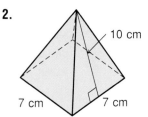

10 cm

7 cm   7 cm

3.

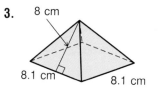

8 cm

8.1 cm   8.1 cm

4.

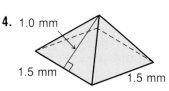

1.0 mm

1.5 mm   1.5 mm

PRACTICE

Find the surface area. Use a calculator or paper and pencil.

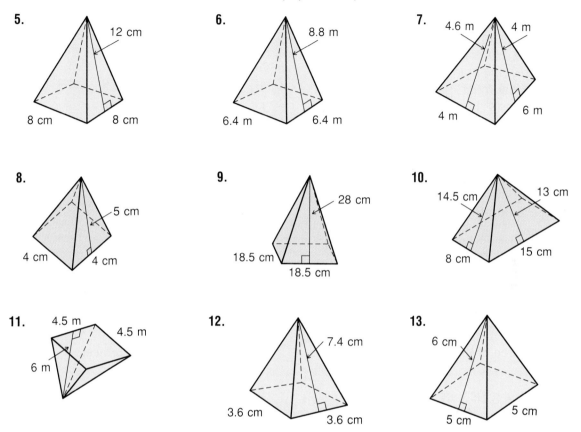

5. 12 cm, 8 cm, 8 cm

6. 8.8 m, 6.4 m, 6.4 m

7. 4.6 m, 4 m, 4 m, 6 m

8. 5 cm, 4 cm, 4 cm

9. 28 cm, 18.5 cm, 18.5 cm

10. 14.5 cm, 13 cm, 8 cm, 15 cm

11. 4.5 m, 4.5 m, 6 m

12. 7.4 cm, 3.6 cm, 3.6 cm

13. 6 cm, 5 cm, 5 cm

Critical Thinking

14. *What if* the length of a side of a square pyramid were doubled and the height of each triangular face were doubled? How would the surface area change?

Mixed Applications

15. Tar paper for roofing costs $7 per m². What is the cost of covering the two triangular faces of a roof if each face measures 8 m by 6 m high?

16. A building brick that has the shape of a rectangular prism has a length of 8 in., a width of 6 in., and a height of 5.5 in. What is the total surface area of the brick?

17. A hollow, glass square pyramid has been constructed in the courtyard. How much glass was used in the construction if the base measures 20 m on a side and each face has a height of 16 m?

18. *Write a problem* about the surface area of a pyramid. Solve the problem. Then ask others to solve it.

UNDERSTANDING A CONCEPT

Surface Area: Cylinders

Sam is an artist who is making a sculpture using many soup cans of the same size. He is covering each can completely, including the top and the bottom. How much paper does he need for each can?

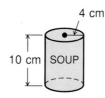

A soup can is a cylinder. Recall that a cylinder is a space figure with two congruent circular bases and a curved surface.

You can find the surface area of a cylinder by adding the areas of the circular bases and the area of the curved surface.

When the curved surface of a cylinder is opened up, it has the shape of a rectangle. The width of the rectangle is the height of the can. The length of the rectangle is the circumference of the circular base.

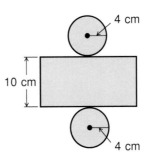

Area of the circular bases:

$A = \pi r^2$ Use 3.14 for π.

$A \approx 3.14 \times 4^2$

$A \approx 50.24$

There are two bases. $2 \times 50.24 = 100.48$

The area of the two circular bases is approximately 100.48 cm².

Area of the curved surface:

$A = Bh$

$A = 2\pi rh$

$A \approx (2 \times 3.14 \times 4) \times 10$

$A \approx 251.2$

The area of the curved surface is approximately 251.2 cm².

Surface area of the can:

Surface area = 100.48 + 251.2 = 351.68

The can has a surface area of 352 cm² to the nearest whole number.

TRY OUT Find the surface area. Use 3.14 for π. Use a calculator or paper and pencil.

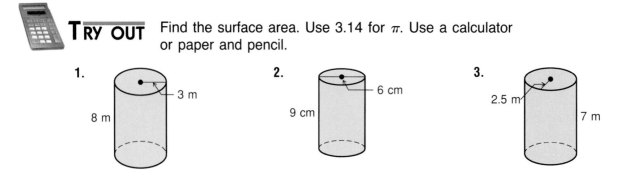

1. 3 m, 8 m

2. 6 cm, 9 cm

3. 2.5 m, 7 m

PRACTICE

Find the surface area of the cylinder. Use 3.14 for π. Use a calculator
or paper and pencil.

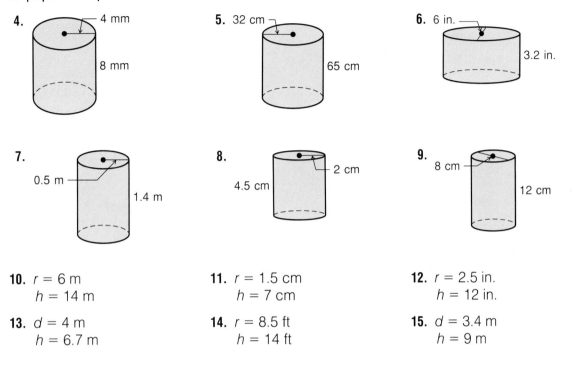

4. 4 mm / 8 mm

5. 32 cm / 65 cm

6. 6 in. / 3.2 in.

7. 0.5 m / 1.4 m

8. 2 cm / 4.5 cm

9. 8 cm / 12 cm

10. $r = 6$ m
$h = 14$ m

11. $r = 1.5$ cm
$h = 7$ cm

12. $r = 2.5$ in.
$h = 12$ in.

13. $d = 4$ m
$h = 6.7$ m

14. $r = 8.5$ ft
$h = 14$ ft

15. $d = 3.4$ m
$h = 9$ m

Critical Thinking

16. Which do you think would cause a greater change in the surface
area of a cylinder—doubling the height or doubling the radius of
the base? Tell why.

Mixed Applications

Solve. Which method did you use?

17. A giant green cube is the sensation of the new art exhibit. What
is its surface area if each side measures 5 m?

18. A box containing Elena's collection of ceramic skunks is 8 in.
long, 6 in. wide, and 5 in. high. Elena wants to cover 25% of it
with self-sticking shelf paper. How much paper will she need?

19. For a fund-raising dinner honoring the fiftieth anniversary of the
modern art museum, 80% of those invited came. How many did
not attend if 5,000 people were invited?

20. The area of the curved surface of a metal cylindrical sculpture is
approximately 62.8 m². The base has an area of approximately
12.5 m². How much sheet metal to the nearest whole number
was needed to make it?

ESTIMATION
MENTAL MATH
CALCULATOR
PAPER/PENCIL

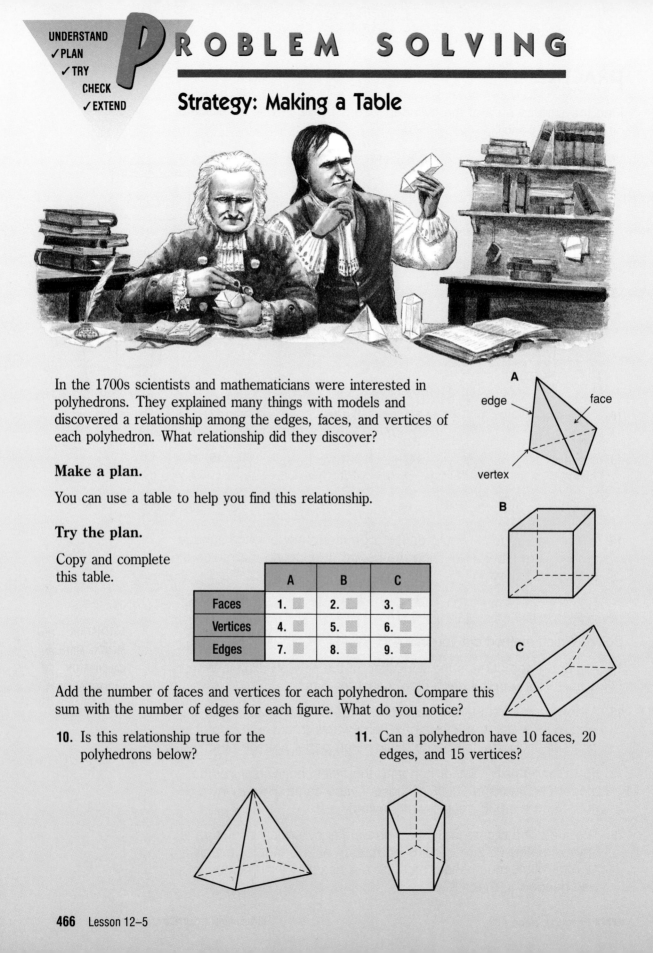

PROBLEM SOLVING

Strategy: Making a Table

In the 1700s scientists and mathematicians were interested in polyhedrons. They explained many things with models and discovered a relationship among the edges, faces, and vertices of each polyhedron. What relationship did they discover?

A

edge   face

vertex

Make a plan.

You can use a table to help you find this relationship.

B

Try the plan.

Copy and complete this table.

	A	B	C
Faces	1.	2.	3.
Vertices	4.	5.	6.
Edges	7.	8.	9.

C

Add the number of faces and vertices for each polyhedron. Compare this sum with the number of edges for each figure. What do you notice?

10. Is this relationship true for the polyhedrons below?

11. Can a polyhedron have 10 faces, 20 edges, and 15 vertices?

Make a table to solve the problem.

Here is a situation that describes what can happen when a bus comes to a bus stop.

- If nobody is waiting for the bus, only one thing can happen. No one will get on.

- If one person is waiting for the bus, two things can happen. The person will either get on or not get on.

- If two people are waiting for the bus, four things can happen. They both will get on, only the first person will get on, only the second person will get on, or no one will get on.

How many things can happen if 6 people are waiting for the bus?

Use the table to complete the pattern.

12. What pattern do you see in the table?

13. How could you use the top row of numbers as exponents to get the bottom row?

0	1	2	3	4	5	6
1	2	4	8			

Strategies and Skills Review

Solve. Use mental math, estimation, a calculator, or paper and pencil.

14. Mr. Abate is a curator of a museum. He just received a shipment of three murals which he has to arrange on a wall. He labeled the murals A, B, and C. List all the different ways Mr. Abate can arrange the murals.

15. Draw a circle. Choose two points on the circle and connect them. You form 2 regions. Choose a third point and connect it with the other points. You form 4 regions. Continue the pattern to complete the table.

Points	2	3	4	5	6
Regions	2	4			

16. If a scientist works 60 hours one week, how many hours does she devote to writing reports? What if she spends 15 hours writing reports in one 60-hour week? Show how she might redistribute her time in percents.

17. *Write a problem* that requires making a table to find a solution. Solve your problem. Ask others to solve it.

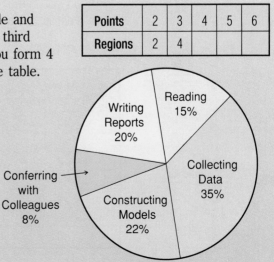

SOME THINGS Change,

Visual Reasoning

A. Suppose you have 10 separate unit cubes. Then the total volume is 10 cubic units, and the total surface area is 60 square units.

If you arrange the cubes in a shape like this, then the volume is still 10 cubic units, but now the surface area is only 36 square units (convince yourself this is true by counting faces).

For each problem below, assume that all the cubes are stacked to form a single shape (no loose cubes allowed).

1. How can you arrange 10 cubes to get a surface area of 34 square units? Draw a sketch.

2. What is the greatest possible surface area you can get with 10 cubes? Sketch the arrangement.

3. How can you arrange the 10 cubes to get the least possible surface area? What is this area?

4. Experiment with some cubes. Copy and complete the table below.

Volume (Number of Cubes)	Greatest Possible Surface Area	Least Possible Surface Area
10		
11		
12		
13		
14		
15		
16		

SOME Don't

B. Look at your table and think about the different arrangements you made.

5. What arrangement always has the greatest possible surface area for a given number of cubes?

6. Since volume (*V*) equals the number of unit cubes, what is the relationship between *V* and the greatest possible surface area? Write a formula.

7. Use your formula. What is the greatest possible surface area for 125 unit cubes? If the greatest possible surface area of a shape made from a certain set of cubes is 614 square units, what is the volume of the shape?

8. What arrangement or general shape seems to have the least possible surface area for a given volume?

9. What is the least possible surface area for a volume of 27 cubic units? 64 cubic units? 125 cubic units?

10. Suppose you wanted to make a 3-dimensional cardboard shape with a volume of 1,000 cubic centimeters. What dimensions would give the required volume using the least amount of cardboard?

11. Consider this: Biologists have found that an animal's surface area is an important factor in its regulation of body temperature. Why do you think that snakes are long and thin? Why do you think that some furry animals curl up in a ball when they hibernate?

UNDERSTANDING A CONCEPT

Volume: **Cylinders**

After Amy broke the handle of her
favorite mug, she decided to use the
mug as a planter. The inside of the mug
is 7 cm high and has a diameter of 6 cm.
How much dirt will it hold?

Amy needs to find the volume of the mug. Recall
that **volume** is a measurement of the number of
cubic units needed to fill the region of space.

The mug is a cylinder. You can find the volume of a
cylinder the same way you found the volume of a prism.

Volume of a prism: $V = Bh$ Volume of a cylinder: $V = Bh = \pi r^2 h$

Amy substituted the dimensions of the
mug in the formula.
$V = \pi r^2 h$ Use 3.14 for π.

Think: $d = 6$ cm, so $r = 3$ cm

$V \approx (3.14 \times 3 \times 3) \times 7$
$V \approx 197.82$

The volume of the mug is 198 cm³ to the nearest cubic centimeter.

1. If you know the volume and the radius of the base of a cylinder,
how can you find the height?

TRY OUT   Find the volume. Use 3.14 for π. Use a calculator
or paper and pencil.

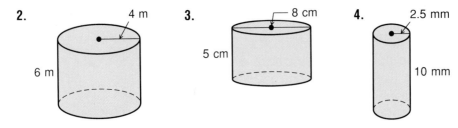

2.   4 m   6 m

3.   8 cm   5 cm

4.   2.5 mm   10 mm

PRACTICE

Find the volume of the cylinder. Use 3.14 for π. Use a calculator or paper and pencil.

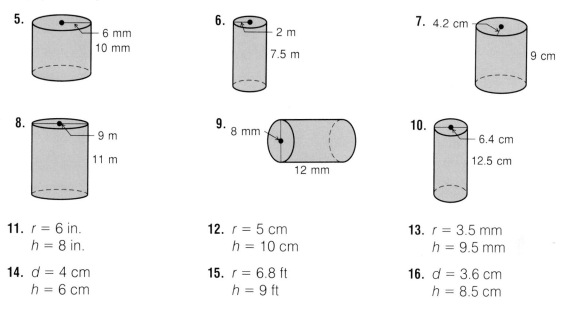

5. 6 mm / 10 mm

6. 2 m / 7.5 m

7. 4.2 cm / 9 cm

8. 9 m / 11 m

9. 8 mm / 12 mm

10. 6.4 cm / 12.5 cm

11. $r = 6$ in.
$h = 8$ in.

12. $r = 5$ cm
$h = 10$ cm

13. $r = 3.5$ mm
$h = 9.5$ mm

14. $d = 4$ cm
$h = 6$ cm

15. $r = 6.8$ ft
$h = 9$ ft

16. $d = 3.6$ cm
$h = 8.5$ cm

Find the height of the cylinder.

17. $V \approx 549.5$ m³, $r = 5$ m

18. $V \approx 282.6$ cm³, $r = 3$ cm

Find the volume of the figure. Use 3.14 for π.

19. 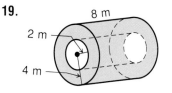 8 m / 2 m / 4 m

20. 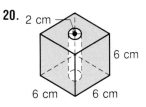 2 cm / 6 cm / 6 cm / 6 cm

Critical Thinking

21. How would the volume of a cylinder be affected if the radius of its base were doubled?

22. A cylinder and a prism are the same height. Their bases have the same area. Do they have the same volume? Why or why not?

Mixed Review
Find the answer. Which method did you use?

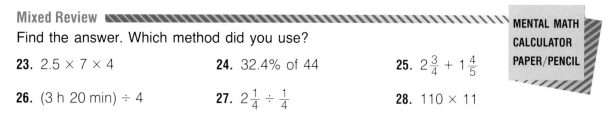
MENTAL MATH
CALCULATOR
PAPER/PENCIL

23. $2.5 \times 7 \times 4$

24. 32.4% of 44

25. $2\frac{3}{4} + 1\frac{4}{5}$

26. (3 h 20 min) ÷ 4

27. $2\frac{1}{4} \div \frac{1}{4}$

28. 110×11

DEVELOPING A CONCEPT

Volume: Pyramids

You can use what you know about the volume of a prism to find the volume of a pyramid.

WORKING TOGETHER

You can use a model to find the volume of a pyramid. You will need construction paper, a ruler, tape, and centimeter cubes.

Use a pattern like this one to make a cube with no top. The length of each side of your cube should be 5 cm.

Use a pattern like this one to make a pyramid with a square base. The base is open.

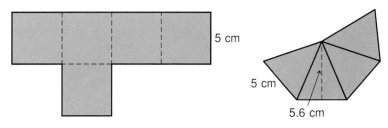

5 cm

5 cm

5.6 cm

1. Fill the cube with centimeter cubes. Record the number it takes to fill the cube completely.

2. Using the same number of centimeter cubes, how many times can you fill the pyramid? Describe what you discover. Recall that the formula for the volume of a prism is $V = Bh$.

3. What relationship do you discover between the volume of a cube and the volume of a pyramid with the same base and height?

4. Use the formula for the volume of a prism to write a formula for the volume of a pyramid.

SHARING IDEAS

5. Compare your results with the following results. Did you get the same formula?

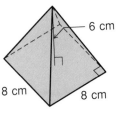

6 cm

8 cm   8 cm

A pyramid with the same base and height as a prism will have a volume that is $\frac{1}{3}$ the volume of the prism: $V = \frac{1}{3} Bh$.

6. What is the volume of this pyramid? Round your answer to the nearest whole number.

7. How can you find the height of a pyramid if you know the volume and the area of the base?

PRACTICE

Find the volume of the pyramid. Use a calculator or paper and pencil.

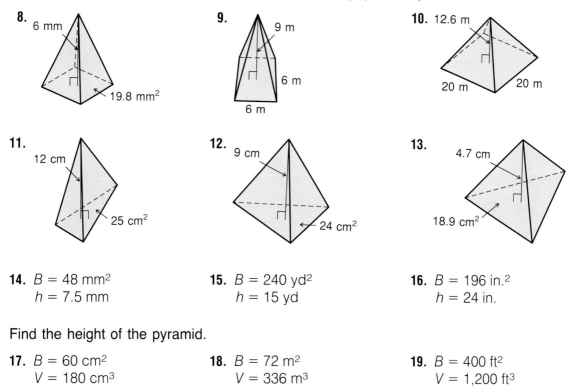

8. 6 mm   19.8 mm²

9. 9 m   6 m   6 m

10. 12.6 m   20 m   20 m

11. 12 cm   25 cm²

12. 9 cm   24 cm²

13. 4.7 cm   18.9 cm²

14. $B = 48$ mm²
     $h = 7.5$ mm

15. $B = 240$ yd²
     $h = 15$ yd

16. $B = 196$ in.²
     $h = 24$ in.

Find the height of the pyramid.

17. $B = 60$ cm²
     $V = 180$ cm³

18. $B = 72$ m²
     $V = 336$ m³

19. $B = 400$ ft²
     $V = 1,200$ ft³

Mixed Applications

Solve. You may need to use the Databank on page 586.

20. A room in a museum is 6 m high. Its rectangular floor has an area of 98 m². If each visitor needs at least 12 m³ of air, how many visitors, at most, should be in the room?

21. An exhibit at the museum will be displayed in a room that is 25 ft wide and 38 ft long. What is the area of the floor of the room?

22. Before the exhibit is set up, the floor will have to be refinished at a cost of $30 per ft². What will the refinishing job cost?

23. The pyramid of Cheops has a volume of approximately 2,601,900 m³. What is its approximate height in meters?

DEVELOPING A CONCEPT
Volume: Cones

You can use what you know about the volume of a cylinder to find the volume of a cone.

WORKING TOGETHER

You can use a model to find the volume of a cone. You will need scissors, tape, construction paper, a centimeter ruler, and centimeter cubes.

Follow these steps to make a cylinder and a cone.

Step 1 Cut a piece of typing paper in half.

Step 2 Make a cylinder with a height of approximately 10 cm and a diameter of approximately 7 cm.

Step 3 With another half of the paper, make a cone with approximately the same height and diameter.

1. Fill the cylinder with centimeter cubes. Record the approximate number it takes to fill the cylinder completely.

2. Using the same number of centimeter cubes, how many times can you fill the cone? Record the results.

Recall that the formula for finding the volume of a cylinder is $V = Bh$ or $V = \pi r^2 h$.

3. What relationship do you discover between the volume of a cylinder and the volume of a cone with the same base and height?

4. Use the formula for the volume of a cylinder to write the formula for the volume of a cone.

SHARING IDEAS

5. Compare your results with the following results. Did you get the same formula?

A cone with the same base and height as a cylinder will have a volume that is $\frac{1}{3}$ the volume of the cylinder: $V = \frac{1}{3} \pi r^2 h$.

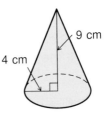

6. What is the volume of this cone? Use 3.14 for π. Round the answer to the nearest whole number.

PRACTICE

Find the volume of the cone. Use 3.14 for π. Use a calculator or paper and pencil.

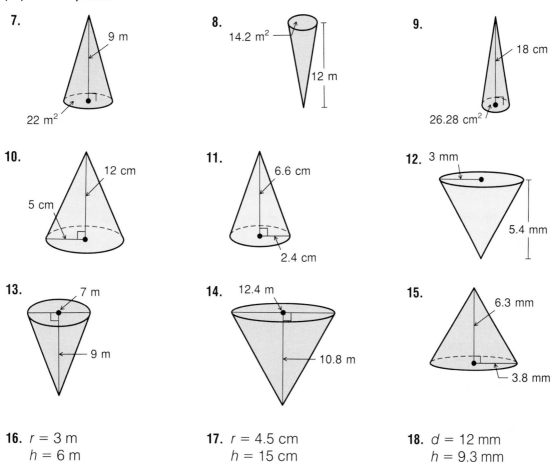

7. 9 m, 22 m²

8. 14.2 m², 12 m

9. 18 cm, 26.28 cm²

10. 12 cm, 5 cm

11. 6.6 cm, 2.4 cm

12. 3 mm, 5.4 mm

13. 7 m, 9 m

14. 12.4 m, 10.8 m

15. 6.3 mm, 3.8 mm

16. $r = 3$ m
$h = 6$ m

17. $r = 4.5$ cm
$h = 15$ cm

18. $d = 12$ mm
$h = 9.3$ mm

Critical Thinking

19. Describe the relationship between cones and pyramids that have equal heights and bases with equal areas.

20. What would happen to the volume of a cone if the radius were doubled? if the height were doubled?

Mixed Applications

21. Darryl's closet is 1 m wide, 2 m high, and 1.5 m deep. What is the volume of his closet?

22. A circular rug with a diameter of 3 m is on a rectangular floor that measures 10 m by 6 m. What area is not covered by the rug?

23. ***Write a problem*** involving the volume of a cone. Solve it. Then ask others to solve it.

PROBLEM SOLVING

Strategy: Making a Physical Model

Roseanna is an industrial designer whose specialty is designing containers. She is designing a box in which each top flap is a different color—either red, yellow, blue, or green. How can the top flaps be folded so that the top of the box will not open.

Make a plan.

Roseanna decided to make a physical model. She constructed a cardboard box with top flaps of red, yellow, blue, and green as shown below. Then she tried to find a way to overlap the top flaps so that they would stay in place.

Try the plan.

Roseanna found a way. It is represented by the diagram on the right.

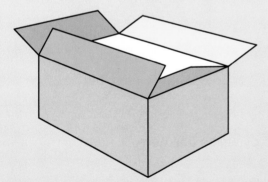

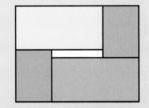

1. Use a box as a model and copy Roseanna's method. If you do not have a box, use four rectangular pieces of colored construction paper to represent the top flaps.

2. There is one other way to fold the flaps so that the top will not open. Use your model to find it. Draw a diagram to represent your answer.

3. What if the top flaps did not have to stay in place? Use your model to find as many ways as possible to close the box top. Draw a diagram to represent each way.

PRACTICE

Solve the problem by using a model.

4. Roseanna is designing a pattern for a box to contain rolled documents, such as posters or maps. When the pattern is folded, it will form a triangular prism. Make a model of this pattern. Then test it by cutting it out and folding it.

5. Roseanna decided to make another pattern for a box to contain rolled documents. This time the pattern will fold into a triangular prism that has three triangular flaps of different colors on each end. Then the purchaser can fold the flaps on top of each other and leave exposed the color he or she likes best. Make a model of this pattern.

6. An architect has designed a room in the shape of a rectangular prism. The front and back walls of the room are squares, and the two side walls are rectangles. A window will be placed in the front wall in one of three places shown below. Describe a model you can make to determine the window placement that will maximize the amount of midafternoon sunlight entering the room.

Strategies and Skills Review

Solve. Use mental math, estimation, a calculator, or paper and pencil.

7. Architects take many precautions against fire in their designs. This graph shows the causes of fire in one year. If there were 925,000 fires, how many were caused by heating equipment? by children playing?

8. Engineers are making a model of the lobby of a building. They want to cover a rectangular floor with a pattern of regular hexagons and equilateral triangles. Draw part of the design.

9. *Write a problem* that you can solve by making a model. Solve the problem. Ask others to solve it.

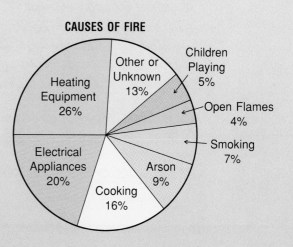

CAUSES OF FIRE

- Heating Equipment 26%
- Other or Unknown 13%
- Children Playing 5%
- Open Flames 4%
- Smoking 7%
- Arson 9%
- Cooking 16%
- Electrical Appliances 20%

DECISION MAKING

Problem Solving: Choosing a Drama Club Outing

SITUATION

The Drama Club must decide where to go on their club outing. They have narrowed down their options to three possibilities.

PROBLEM

Which club outing should the Drama Club choose?

DATA

Local Theater Group: We can see this season's play for free. The club will then donate 2⅓ hours every Friday for 10 weeks to help prepare for the next production. We will help with costumes, props, scenery, and make-up. Bus fare from the school to the theater is $.50 per person. We can each get a free ride home from the theater.

Regional Theater Troupe: Tickets are $12.50 per person. The bus will cost $123.95. After the play the club has been invited to go backstage to meet the cast and ask questions. There is the possibility of inviting the troupe members to speak at future Drama Club meetings.

Broadway Play: A Broadway cast is on tour from New York City. Tickets will cost $20.00 per person. The bus will cost $166.50.

We are proud to announce there are 37 members in the Drama Club.

USING THE DATA

1. How much will bus fare cost the Drama Club if each member takes the bus from school to the local theater for 10 weeks?

How much is bus fare per person for the club outing?

2. Local Theater Group   3. Regional Theater Troupe   4. Broadway Play

How much is the club outing, including ticket price and bus fare, per person?

5. Local Theater Group   6. Regional Theater Troupe   7. Broadway Play

MAKING DECISIONS

8. Which outing should the Drama Club choose to spend the least money? the most money?

9. Which outing should the Drama Club choose to learn the most about play production? Why?

10. Which outing should they choose in order to make contacts with possible future club speakers?

11. Why might the club choose the Broadway Play over the other two outings?

12. What advantage would the Regional Theater Troupe outing have over the Local Theater Group outing?

13. What advantage would the Local Theater Group outing have over the Regional Theater Troupe outing?

14. **Write a list** of other factors the Drama Club should consider when choosing a club outing.

15. Which club outing would you choose? Why?

Math and Social Studies

When a king died in ancient Egypt, his people placed his body in a tomb befitting a ruler. For hundreds of years these tombs were in the form of a pyramid.

The Great Pyramid is the largest of three built during the period from 2613 to 2494 B.C. It is estimated that 2,300,000 blocks of stone, averaging $2\frac{1}{2}$ tons each, were used to construct the pyramid.

The length of each side of the square base of the Great Pyramid is about 775 feet. The original height was 481 feet, although that has crumbled to about 451 feet.

The length of each side of the base of the middle pyramid is about 707 feet. Its original height was 471 feet. The length of each side of the base of the third pyramid is about 356 feet. Its original height was 218 feet.

What if you want to find the difference between the original volume of the largest and the smallest of the three pyramids?

Think: Use the formula $V = \frac{1}{3}Bh$ to find the volume of each pyramid.

Volume of Great Pyramid $= \frac{1}{3}(775)^2\ 481$
$$= \frac{1}{3}(600,625)\ 481 \approx 96,300,206 \text{ ft}^3$$

Volume of smallest pyramid $= \frac{1}{3}(356)^2\ 218$
$$= \frac{1}{3}(126,736)\ 218 \approx 9,209,483 \text{ ft}^3$$

$96,300,206 - 9,209,483 = 87,090,723$

The difference between the volume of the largest and smallest pyramid is about $87,090,723$ ft^3.

ACTIVITIES

1. Work with a partner. Find the volume of the middle pyramid. Then look in reference books for the base and height measurements of other pyramids. Calculate their volumes. Prepare a chart showing the name, location, and measurements of several pyramids.

2. Read about the custom of burial in pyramids or other tombs in ancient Egypt. You may want to read about King Tutankhamen. Share the information with your class.

Calculator: Volume of a Cone

The piece of paper shown has a radius of 10 centimeters. It is curled to form a cone. What is the volume of the cone formed when the radius of the base is 6 centimeters?

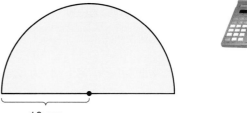

10 cm

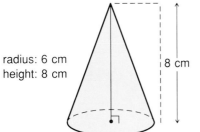

radius: 6 cm
height: 8 cm

8 cm

$$V = \frac{1}{3}\pi r^2 h$$

1 $\div$ 3 $\times$ 3.14 $\times$ 36 $\times$ 8 $=$

301.43997

To the nearest cubic centimeter, the volume is 301 cm³.

USING THE CALCULATOR

Cut out a paper circle with a radius of 10 centimeters. Cut the circle along one radius. You can curl the paper to form cones of different sizes.

Copy and complete a table like the one below. Use your calculator to compute each volume. Predict which one will have the greatest volume.

Radius of the base	Height	Volume
0 cm	10 cm	0 cm³
2 cm		
4 cm		
6 cm	8 cm	301 cm
8 cm		
10 cm	0 cm	0 cm³

1. What happens to the height as the radius increases?

2. What happens to the lateral area as the radius increases?

3. Examine your results. Which cone has the greatest volume? Which have the least volumes?

4. First estimate, then find the volume of the cones with bases having radii of 7 cm and 9 cm.

EXTRA PRACTICE

Spatial Visualization, page 459

Use isometric dot paper to draw:

1. a rectangular pyramid.

2. a triangular prism.

What polyhedron will be formed when you fold the pattern?

3.

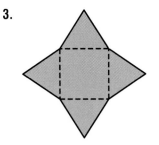

4.

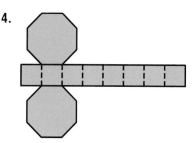

Surface Area: Prisms, page 461

Find the surface area. Use a calculator or paper and pencil.

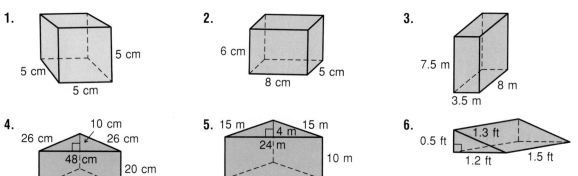

1. 5 cm, 5 cm, 5 cm, 5 cm

2. 6 cm, 8 cm, 5 cm

3. 7.5 m, 8 m, 3.5 m

4. 10 cm, 26 cm, 26 cm, 48 cm, 20 cm

5. 15 m, 4 m, 15 m, 24 m, 10 m

6. 0.5 ft, 1.3 ft, 1.2 ft, 1.5 ft

Surface Area: Pyramids, page 463

Find the surface area. Use a calculator or paper and pencil.

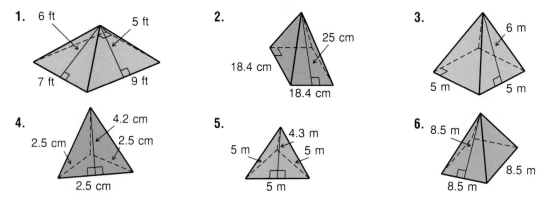

1. 6 ft, 5 ft, 7 ft, 9 ft

2. 25 cm, 18.4 cm, 18.4 cm

3. 6 m, 5 m, 5 m

4. 4.2 cm, 2.5 cm, 2.5 cm, 2.5 cm

5. 4.3 m, 5 m, 5 m, 5 m

6. 8.5 m, 8.5 m, 8.5 m

Surface Area: Cylinders, page 465 ···

Find the surface area of the cylinder. Use 3.14 for π. Use a calculator or paper and pencil.

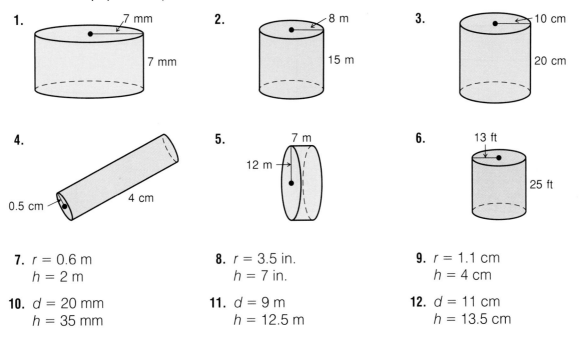

1. 7 mm / 7 mm

2. 8 m / 15 m

3. 10 cm / 20 cm

4. 0.5 cm / 4 cm

5. 7 m / 12 m

6. 13 ft / 25 ft

7. $r = 0.6$ m
$h = 2$ m

8. $r = 3.5$ in.
$h = 7$ in.

9. $r = 1.1$ cm
$h = 4$ cm

10. $d = 20$ mm
$h = 35$ mm

11. $d = 9$ m
$h = 12.5$ m

12. $d = 11$ cm
$h = 13.5$ cm

Problem–Solving Strategy: Making a Table, page 467 ·····························

Make a table to solve the problem.

Here is a situation that describes what can happen when a car stops at an intersection.

- If one car stops, it can go left (L), right (R), or straight (S).

- If two cars stop, there are nine possibilities: LL, LR, LS, RR, RS, RL, SS, SR, SL.

1. How many possibilities are there if six cars stop at an intersection? Use the table to complete the pattern.

1	2	3	4	5	6
3	9	27			

2. What pattern do you see in the table?

3. How could you use the top row of numbers as exponents to get the bottom row?

EXTRA PRACTICE

Volume: Cylinders, page 471

Find the volume of the cylinder. Use 3.14 for π. Use a calculator or paper and pencil.

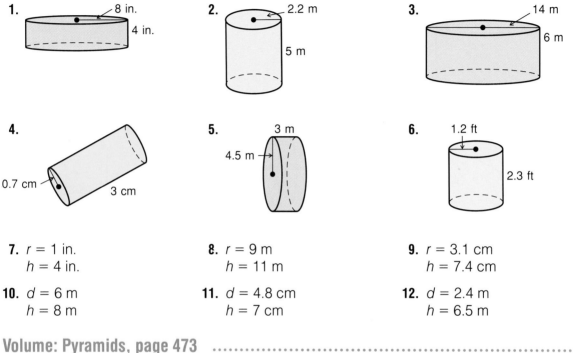

1. 8 in. 4 in.

2. 2.2 m 5 m

3. 14 m 6 m

4. 0.7 cm 3 cm

5. 3 m 4.5 m

6. 1.2 ft 2.3 ft

7. $r = 1$ in.
$h = 4$ in.

8. $r = 9$ m
$h = 11$ m

9. $r = 3.1$ cm
$h = 7.4$ cm

10. $d = 6$ m
$h = 8$ m

11. $d = 4.8$ cm
$h = 7$ cm

12. $d = 2.4$ m
$h = 6.5$ m

Volume: Pyramids, page 473

Find the volume of the pyramid. Use a calculator or paper and pencil.

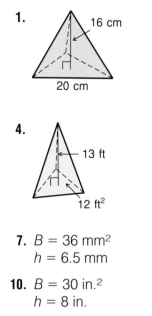

1. 16 cm 20 cm

2. 9 m 5 m 5 m

3. 13.8 cm 10 cm 10 cm

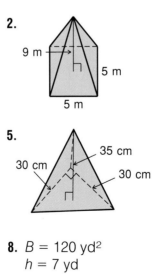

4. 13 ft 12 ft^2

5. 35 cm 30 cm 30 cm

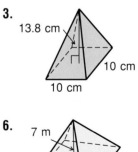

6. 7 m 10 m 9 m

7. $B = 36$ mm^2
$h = 6.5$ mm

8. $B = 120$ yd^2
$h = 7$ yd

9. $B = 200$ in.^{2}
$h = 12$ in.

10. $B = 30$ in.^{2}
$h = 8$ in.

11. $B = 64$ cm^2
$h = 6$ cm

12. $B = 168$ in.^{2}
$h = 22$ in.

EXTRA PRACTICE

Volume: Cones, page 475

Find the volume of the cone. Use 3.14 for π. Use a calculator or paper and pencil.

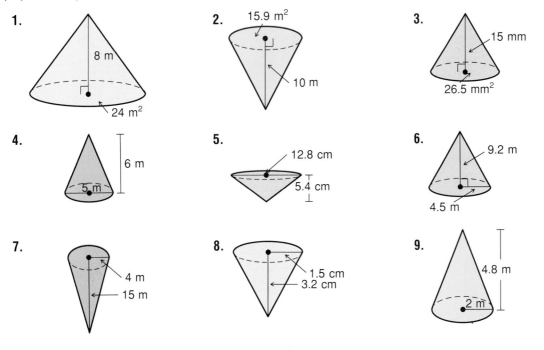

1. 8 m, 24 m²

2. 15.9 m², 10 m

3. 15 mm, 26.5 mm²

4. 6 m, 5 m

5. 12.8 cm, 5.4 cm

6. 9.2 m, 4.5 m

7. 4 m, 15 m

8. 1.5 cm, 3.2 cm

9. 4.8 m, 2 m

Problem–Solving Strategy: Making a Model, page 477

Solve by using a model.

1. A glass ornament is 6 cm long and has a diameter of 3.8 cm. A strip of cardboard 6 cm wide and 12 cm long will be used to box the ornament. A plastic top and bottom will be used. What shape boxes can be used?

2. A cube ornament has a tree and snowflake on opposite sides. A wreath and candle are also on opposite sides. A reindeer and snowman are on the other two sides. The side with the candle touches the sides with the tree, the snowflake, the reindeer, and the snowman. Which sides does the side with the reindeer touch?

3. Diane wants to be able to fold a sheet of foil paper into an octahedron, an eight-sided figure with triangular faces. What will the pattern look like?

4. Joshua makes ornaments from used greeting cards. He cuts the cards into 8-in. by 1-in. strips. He then folds the strips into a cube. How does he fold the strips?

Measurement: Surface Area and Volume **485**

EXTRA PRACTICE

Practice PLUS

KEY SKILL: Surface Area: Prisms (Use after page 461.)

Level A

Find the surface area. Use a calculator or paper and pencil.

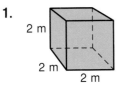
1. 2 m, 2 m, 2 m

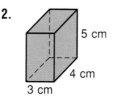
2. 5 cm, 4 cm, 3 cm

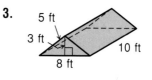
3. 5 ft, 3 ft, 8 ft, 10 ft

4. Ken wants to glue vinyl to the sides of a ring box that measures 3 cm by 3 cm by 3 cm. How much vinyl does he need?

5. A refrigerator carton measures 6 ft by 6 ft by 6 ft. What is its surface area?

Level B

Find the surface area. Use a calculator or paper and pencil.

6. 4 m, 6 m, 2.5 m

7. 5 ft, 3 ft, 4 ft, 12 ft

8. 10 m, 10 m, 5 m, 20 m, 17.2 m

9. Anna is making a box for valentines. She wants to glue red velvet to the sides. If the box measures 15 in. by 12 in. by 10 in., how much red velvet does she need?

10. A rectangular storage bin is 12 ft wide, 21 ft deep, and 9 ft high. How many square yards of padded fabric will it take to line the bin?

Level C

Find the surface area. Use a calculator or paper and pencil.

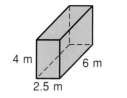
11. 6.5 m, 4.5 m, 5.5 m

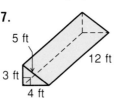
12. 9.2 ft, 11.1 ft, 10 ft, 12.5 ft

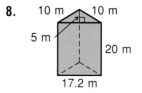
13. 3.4 cm, 6.5 cm, 8 cm, 11 cm

14. Adam is making a pup tent with a floor from canvas. The door is an equilateral triangle with sides of 3 ft and a height of 2.5 feet. The floor is 5.5 ft long?

15. A triangular drinking straw has an opening 0.5 cm × 0.5 cm × 0.5 cm and a length 22 cm. What is the surface area of the straw?

KEY SKILL: Volume: Cylinders (Use after page 471.)

Level A ....

Find the volume of the cylinder. Use 3.14 for π. Use a calculator or
paper and pencil.

1.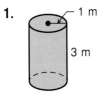
1 m
3 m

2.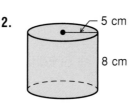
5 cm
8 cm

3.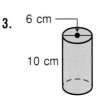
6 cm
10 cm

4. A water tank has a radius of 2 m and a height of 6 m. What is the volume of the tank?

5. A soup can has a height of 12 cm and a diameter of 8 cm. What is its volume?

Level B ....

Find the volume of the cylinder. Use 3.14 for π. Use a calculator or
paper and pencil.

6.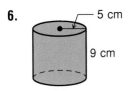
5 cm
9 cm

7.
1.5 in.
6 in.

8.
2.4 m
6.5 m

9. A glass shaped like a cylinder has a radius 3.2 cm and a height of 14 cm. What is the volume of the glass?

10. A new pencil has a radius of 40 mm and a length of 20 cm. What is its volume?

Level C ....

Find the volume of the figure. Use 3.14 for π. Use a calculator or
paper and pencil.

11.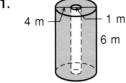
4 m
1 m
6 m

12.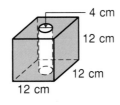
4 cm
12 cm
12 cm
12 cm

13.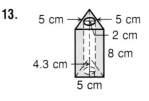
5 cm
5 cm
2 cm
8 cm
4.3 cm
5 cm

14. The radius of a cylindrical tank is 2.5 ft. Its volume is approximately 235.5 ft. What is its height?

15. A diameter of a film cannister is 30 cm. It has a volume of 2,826 cm³. What is its height?

CHAPTER REVIEW

LANGUAGE AND MATHEMATICS

Complete the sentences. Use the words in the chart on the right.

1. A ▨ is a polyhedron with 2 congruent, parallel bases and with other faces that are all parallelograms. *(page 456)*

2. A ▨ is a polyhedron with a polygon as a base and with triangles that have a common vertex as its other faces. *(page 456)*

3. A space figure that has pentagons for all of its faces is an example of a ▨. *(page 456)*

4. ***Write a definition*** or give an example of the words you did not use from the chart.

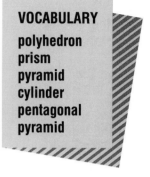

VOCABULARY

polyhedron
prism
pyramid
cylinder
pentagonal
pyramid

CONCEPTS AND SKILLS

Sketch the indicated figure. *(pages 456, 460, 462, 464, 470, 474)*

5. rectangular pyramid   **6.** triangular prism   **7.** cone   **8.** cylinder

Find the surface area. *(pages 460, 462, 464)*

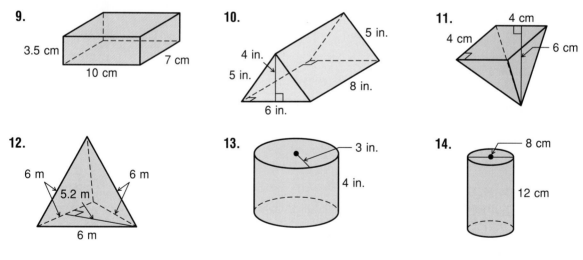

9. 3.5 cm, 10 cm, 7 cm

10. 5 in., 4 in., 5 in., 8 in., 6 in.

11. 4 cm, 4 cm, 6 cm

12. 6 m, 6 m, 5.2 m, 6 m

13. 3 in., 4 in.

14. 8 cm, 12 cm

Find the volume. *(pages 470, 472, 474)*

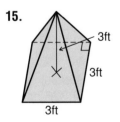

15. 3ft, 3ft, 3ft

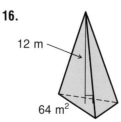

16. 12 m, 64 m²

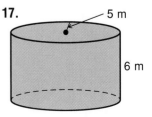

17. 5 m, 6 m

18.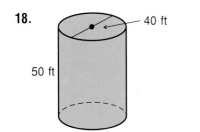
40 ft
50 ft

19.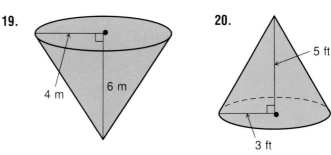
4 m
6 m

20.
5 ft
3 ft

CRITICAL THINKING

21. What is the minimum number of faces of a pyramid? *(page 456)*

22. What is the minimum number of faces of a prism? *(page 456)*

23. If the height of a cylinder is tripled, how does the volume change? *(page 470)*

24. If each edge of a cube is halved, how does the surface area change? *(page 460)*

25. If the diameter of a cone is halved, how does the volume change? *(page 474)*

26. If a polyhedron has n faces and n vertices, how many edges does it have? *(page 466)*

MIXED APPLICATIONS

27. A square box measures 2 ft by 2 ft by 2 ft. The back, top, and bottom are not exposed. What is the area of the exposed faces? *(page 460)*

28. What is the size of the rectangle formed by the visible part of a label on a can that has a radius of 5 in. and a height of 6 in.? *(page 464)*

29. What is the area of a base of a cylinder that has a volume of 24 m³ and a height of 4 m? *(page 470)*

30. What is the length of an edge of a cube that has a surface area of 600 ft³? *(page 460)*

31. The surface area of a triangular pyramid is 20 m². If all the faces are the same size, what is the area of one face? *(page 462)*

32. What is the surface area of a rectangular prism that has a base that measures 5 m by 5 m and a height of 6 m? *(page 460)*

33. If a polyhedron has 7 faces and 15 edges, how many vertices does it have? *(page 466)*

34. If a polyhedron has 7 faces and 7 vertices, how many edges does it have? *(page 466)*

35. If a polyhedron has 4 faces and 9 edges, how many vertices does it have? *(page 466)*

36. If a polyhedron has 8 edges and 5 vertices, how many faces does it have? *(page 466)*

37. How many faces, edges, and vertices does a cube have? *(page 466)*

38. How many faces, edges, and vertices does a triangular prism have? *(page 466)*

CHAPTER TEST

1. How many faces does a hexagonal prism have?

2. How many faces does a rectangular pyramid have?

3. What is the shape of the base of a cylinder?

4. What shape are the sides of a rectangular pyramid?

5. Sketch a triangular pyramid.

6. Sketch a rectangular prism.

Find the surface area.

7.
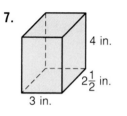
4 in.
$2\frac{1}{2}$ in.
3 in.

8.
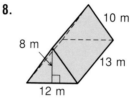
10 m
8 m
13 m
12 m

9.
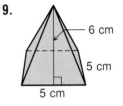
6 cm
5 cm
5 cm

10.
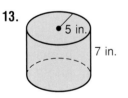
3.6 m
3 m
3 m

11.
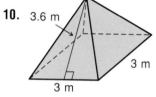
15 cm
20 cm

12.
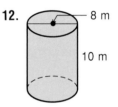
8 m
10 m

Find the volume.

13.
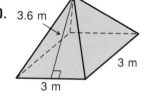
5 in.
7 in.

14.
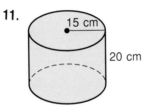
8 m
18 m²

15.
6 ft
4 ft

16. Pyramid
   length: 5.6 m
   width: 5.6 m
   height: 9 m

17. Cone
   radius: 5 ft
   height: 6.3 ft

18. Cylinder
   diameter: 12 cm
   height: 15 cm

19. What is the pattern in the table?

1	2	3	4	5
0	3	8	15	24

20. Draw a pattern that when cut and folded will form a rectangular prism.

EXPLORING THE LATERAL AREA OF A CONE

The base of the cone is a circle with a radius (R). The **slant height** (H) is the distance from the edge of the base to the top of the cone. The cone's **lateral area** is the area of its curved surface. To find the lateral area of a cone, use this formula:

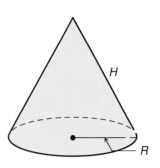

Lateral Area $(LA) = \pi R H$

1. In one cone $R = 2$ cm and $H = 4$ cm. What is the lateral area? Use 3.14 for π.

Conduct this experiment.

Cut out a semicircle from a piece of paper.

Fold the semicircle into a cone. Tape together the two line segments labeled H.

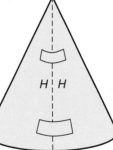

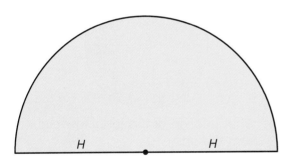

You know that the formula for the area of a circle is $A = \pi r^2$.

2. What is the formula for the area of a semicircle?

3. How could you use the formula for the semicircle to find the lateral area of the cone?

4. **What if** the radius of the semicircle were 4 cm? What would be the lateral area of the cone if the radius of the base were 2 cm?

5. Is the radius of the semicircle the same length as the slant height of the cone?

6. Rewrite the formula for the lateral area of the cone. This time write r (for the radius of a semicircle) in place of H.

7. The **surface area** of the cone is the sum of the lateral area and the area of the base. What is a formula for the surface area?

8. Find the surface area of a cone if $R = 3$ cm, $r = 5$ cm.

CUMULATIVE REVIEW

Choose the letter of the correct answer.

1. Find the square root of 400.

   a. 20   **c.** 1,600
   b. 200   **d.** not given

2. Which type of triangle has exactly 2 sides with the same measure?

   a. obtuse   **c.** equilateral
   b. scalene   **d.** not given

3. Solve for n: $\frac{n}{3} = \frac{6}{1.5}$

   a. 2   **c.** 18
   b. 12   **d.** not given

4. What is the distance between two points 10 cm apart on a map with scale 1 cm = 5 km?

   a. 0.1 km   **c.** 10 km
   b. 0.5 km   **d.** not given

5. What decimal equals 125%?

   a. 1.25   **c.** 125
   b. 12.5   **d.** not given

6. How many faces does a triangular pyramid have, including the base?

   a. 3   **c.** 5
   b. 4   **d.** not given

7. If a polyhedron has 4 faces and 7 edges, how many vertices does it have?

   a. 1   **c.** 5
   b. 3   **d.** not given

8. What is the surface area of a cube with one side 2.5 m long?

   a. 6.25 m²   **c.** 37.5 m²
   b. 15.625 m² **d.** not given

9. What is the volume of a cone with a radius of 10 m and a height of 12 m?

   a. 100π m³   **c.** $1{,}200\pi$ m³
   b. 400π m³   **d.** not given

10. The diameter of a cylinder is 3 cm and the height is 2 cm. What is the volume?

   a. 4.5π cm³   **c.** 18π cm³
   b. 6π cm³   **d.** not given

This graph appeared in a pizza parlor.

PIZZA SUPREME TOPPINGS BY WEIGHT

11. What fraction of the topping weight is from the onion?

   a. $\frac{1}{100}$ **c.** $\frac{100}{10}$
   b. $\frac{1}{10}$ **d.** not given

12. Cheese and onion are what percent of the topping weight?

   a. 6%   **c.** 60%
   b. 40%   **d.** not given

13. If the toppings weigh 16 oz, how much does the meat weigh?

   a. 3.2 oz   **c.** 8 oz
   b. 4 oz   **d.** not given

14. What is the ratio of the onion to the mushroom?

   a. 1:20   **c.** 20:10
   b. 1:30   **d.** not given

Probability

CHAPTER 13

MATH CONNECTION: PROBLEM SOLVING

VOTE TODAY

MONDAY'S POLL

How would you rate
the candidates' responses
to the issues?

Excellent	38%
Good	20%
Fair	14%
Poor	17%
No Opinion	11%

★ BALLOT BOX

1. What information do you see in this picture?
2. How can you use the information?
3. Were most students satisfied with the candidates' responses to the issues?
4. Write a problem using the information.

493

Modeling an Experiment

Ellen and her brother, John, must decide who takes out the garbage. Ellen suggests that they roll a number cube, numbered from 1 through 6. If the outcome is 3 or greater, John takes out the garbage. If the outcome is less than 3, Ellen takes it out. Who do you think is more likely to take out the garbage?

WORKING TOGETHER

1. You can use a number cube to model the experiment. Roll the number cube 30 times. Record the results in a table like this one.

Outcome	Tally
3 or greater	
less than 3	

2. According to your experiment, who is more likely to take out the garbage?

3. Are the results what you expected? Why or why not?

4. Since there are six numbers on the number cube, there are six possible outcomes. How many outcomes favor Ellen?

John realizes that it is likely that he will be taking out the garbage if he takes Ellen's offer. He makes a counteroffer with the same rule. This time, however, he suggests that they use this spinner.

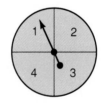

5. Why is this a fair method to decide which one will take out the garbage?

6. Do you think the results will change if the spinner is spun more than once? Spin it 30 times. Tally your results in a table.

7. According to your experiment, who is more likely to take out the garbage?

SHARING IDEAS

8. Make a table of the total class results for the two experiments. Are the results what you expected?

9. Do you think you would get the same results if you were to repeat each experiment 100 times? Why?

10. How could Ellen change her offer to make it fair?

11. Make up your own experiment that will produce fair or equally likely results.

PRACTICE

List the possible outcomes for the experiment.

12. Spin the spinner.

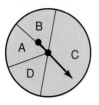

13. Pick a card.

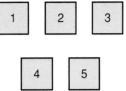

Tell whether you think the outcomes described are *equally likely* or *not equally likely*. If they are not equally likely, tell which one is most likely.

14. Toss a coin.
Possible outcomes: heads, tails

15. Roll a number cube with faces numbered 1, 2, 3, 4, 5, and 6.
Possible outcomes: 1, 2, 3, 4, 5, 6

16. Spin the spinner.
Possible outcomes: A, B, C, D

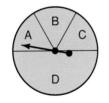

17. Spin the spinner.
Possible outcomes: red, white, blue

18. Pick a card.
Possible outcomes: 1, 2

19. Pick a card.
Possible outcomes: 1, 2, 3, 4, 5

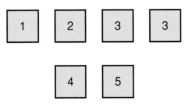

Probability of Simple Events

A. Winona is going to pick a card from the five cards without looking. This is choosing a card at **random.** The set of all possible outcomes is called the **sample space.** The sample space for Winona's experiment is 1, 2, 3, 4, 5. Any part of the sample space is called an **event.** One event for this experiment is picking a 4. An event can be one or more outcomes or no outcome.

If all events are equally likely, you can find the chance, or **probability,** that an event will occur by using the following ratio.

Probability (event) $= \dfrac{\text{number of favorable outcomes}}{\text{number of possible outcomes}}$

Winona wants to find the probability of picking a 4.

$$P(4) = \tfrac{1}{5}$$

The probability of picking a 4 is $\tfrac{1}{5}$.

Probability can also be expressed as a decimal or as a percent.

So $P(4) = \tfrac{1}{5}$ or 0.2 or 20%.

1. What is P(even number)? P(odd number)? Write each as a ratio.

2. **What if** a sixth card, labeled 6, were included among the cards? What would be P(even number)? Write the answer as a ratio in simplest form.

B. Look at the spinner at the right. Are all the events equally likely?

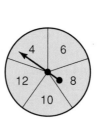

What is P(even number)?

Think: All five numbers are even.

P(even number) $= \tfrac{5}{5}$, or 1

What is P(odd number)?

Think: None of the numbers are odd.

P(odd) $= \tfrac{0}{5}$, or 0

The probability of an event that is **certain** is 1. The probability of an event that is **impossible** is 0.

3. Using the same spinner, find P(multiples of 2) and P(not an even number).

TRY OUT   A number cube with faces labeled 1 through 6 is rolled.

4. List the sample space.

What is the probability of the outcome?

5. $P(3)$ **6.** P(number less than 5)   **7.** $P(7)$ **8.** P(number less than 10)

PRACTICE

List the sample space for the experiment.

9. tossing a quarter   **10.** drawing a ball from the box

   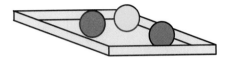

The spinner is spun once. Write the probability as a ratio.

11. $P(5)$ **12.** P(not 4)

13. P(even number)   **14.** P(odd number)

15. $P(7)$ **16.** P(number less than 7)

One card is picked at random. Write the probability as a ratio and as a decimal.

| 1 | 2 | 3 | 4 | 4 |

17. $P(2)$ **18.** $P(4)$

19. P(not 4)   **20.** P(number less than 3)

One marble is picked at random. Write the probability as a percent.

21. P(red)   **22.** P(yellow)

23. P(not green)   **24.** P(silver)

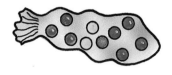

Critical Thinking
25. Tell why the probability of an event that is neither certain nor impossible must be between 0 and 1.

Mixed Applications
26. There are 24 players on the baseball team. Six of the 24 players are outfielders. What is the probability that a player on the team is an outfielder?

27. A spinner in a game consists of eight equal sections numbered 1 through 8. To win a game a player needs to spin a 5, 6, or 7. Is it a fair game? Why or why not?

UNDERSTANDING A CONCEPT

Probability of Mutually Exclusive Events

Lucille will win a prize if she can answer one question correctly. She knows that of the nine questions she could be asked, one is about history, two are about architecture, four are about science, and two are about mathematics. What is the probability Lucille will be asked either a history *or* an architecture question?

To find the probability, look at the sample space.

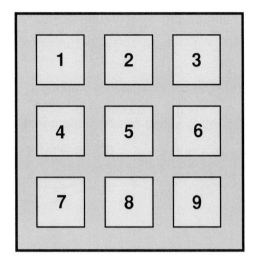

H	A	A	S	S

S	S	M	M

The probability of history is $\frac{1}{9}$.

The probability of architecture is $\frac{2}{9}$.

$P(\text{history}) = \frac{1}{9}$ $P(\text{architecture}) = \frac{2}{9}$

$P(\text{history or architecture}) = \frac{3}{9}$ or $\frac{1}{3}$

Since Lucille can be asked only one question, she cannot be asked both a history and an architecture question. This is an example of **mutually exclusive events.** The two events cannot occur at the same time.

If A and B are mutually exclusive events, $P(A \text{ or } B) = P(A) + P(B)$.

1. Find $P(M \text{ or } S)$.

TRY OUT   The spinner is spun once. Write the probability as a ratio.

2. $P(2 \text{ or } 4)$

3. $P(\text{even or } 5)$

4. $P(1 \text{ or } 2 \text{ or } 3)$

PRACTICE

A number cube with faces labeled 1 through 6 is rolled. Write the probability as a ratio.

5. *P*(6 *or* 4)

6. *P*(odd *or* even)

7. *P*(0 *or* 8)

8. *P*(7 *or* multiple of 2)

One card is picked at random. Write the probability as a ratio.

9. *P*(1 *or* 5)

10. *P*(1 *or* 5 *or* 9)

11. *P*(5 *or* multiple of 3)

12. *P*(3 *or* not 3)

Spin the spinner once. Write the probability as a ratio.

13. *P*(red *or* yellow)

14. *P*(red *or* yellow *or* blue)

15. *P*(red *or* not red)

16. *P*(blue *or* purple)

A letter is picked at random. Write the probability as a ratio, as a decimal, and as a percent.

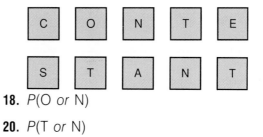

17. *P*(C *or* E)

18. *P*(O *or* N)

19. *P*(T *or* A *or* E)

20. *P*(T *or* N)

21. *P*(N *or* not N)

22. *P*(C *or* O *or* N *or* T *or* S *or* E)

Critical Thinking

A spinner has ten equal sections labeled 2 through 11. Is the event mutually exclusive? If not, tell why.

23. a 2 *or* a prime number

24. a 2 *or* an even number

25. a multiple of 4 *or* an odd number

26. a number less than 6 *or* a number greater than 3

27. a factor of 8 *or* a factor of 15

Experimental Probability: Using Random Digits

The students in Abernathy's seventh-grade class designed a method of collecting the results of rolling a number cube without really rolling the cube. They wanted to find out the number of times an even number would result from 200 rolls of the cube.

WORKING TOGETHER

The students found that to simulate the rolling of the number cube, they could use a **table of random digits.**

**TABLE OF RANDOM DIGITS FROM 1 TO 6
TO SIMULATE 200 ROLLS OF A NUMBER CUBE**

4	4	3	5	4	1	5	3	5	2	2	1	4	4	1	1	6	3	4	6
3	5	1	3	3	1	5	5	3	4	4	5	1	4	4	3	4	5	3	2
6	4	6	1	3	2	3	6	3	5	4	6	6	1	5	1	2	4	3	4
1	3	6	3	3	6	5	5	3	5	4	6	2	5	2	2	1	5	2	3
4	1	6	5	4	5	4	2	1	2	1	5	3	1	6	6	6	3	2	4
5	4	4	6	1	1	4	4	1	5	4	2	5	6	4	6	5	3	3	4
4	2	4	1	6	3	2	2	5	2	4	3	1	4	4	6	2	3	3	2
6	1	6	6	4	6	6	2	3	1	4	6	4	4	2	5	3	3	3	1
2	6	2	4	6	5	2	4	6	4	2	3	5	6	5	5	5	4	6	5
6	6	5	4	5	1	2	4	1	2	1	2	5	5	1	2	6	5	3	4

1. Count the number of times an even digit appears in the table.

2. What is the ratio of the number of even digits to the total number of digits?

The ratio you just found is called the **experimental ratio,** or **experimental probability.**

SHARING IDEAS

3. You know from the probability formula that the **theoretical probability** of rolling an even number is $\frac{1}{2}$. How does this compare with your experimental probability?

4. What is the theoretical probability of rolling a 4? What is the experimental probability? How do they compare?

5. What if the class wanted to find the ratio of the number of odd numbers to the total number of digits? How could they find it without counting? What is the ratio?

PRACTICE

Find the experimental probability of rolling each of the following. Use the table of random digits from 1 to 6 on page 500.

6. a number less than 3

7. a number greater than 5

8. a prime number

9. an even number less than 5

The following table of random digits from 0 to 9 simulates 200 spins of the spinner at the right.

1	6	8	7	7	0	4	4	1	9	7	5	9	3	9	9	5	5	6	7
7	6	4	3	1	7	5	4	0	7	5	5	7	6	2	4	1	4	0	3
5	9	2	6	9	3	8	7	9	3	4	4	7	2	2	7	6	7	9	2
5	4	1	4	6	1	3	2	5	8	1	0	0	1	7	5	9	6	5	7
4	1	3	8	9	4	1	8	5	1	8	1	9	5	6	6	8	3	2	0
3	2	5	1	1	2	5	8	4	1	5	3	4	6	9	3	2	4	8	7
2	4	1	9	8	4	7	5	4	7	8	3	0	4	3	4	6	8	0	6
6	6	7	7	8	2	8	3	8	4	0	3	9	0	7	4	1	1	3	2
0	2	0	0	6	1	5	4	1	3	8	0	3	6	6	9	6	9	8	8
3	9	1	5	4	5	0	4	4	2	9	9	0	4	6	9	1	4	5	8

Find the experimental probability of spinning each of the following.

10. 5

11. 0

12. an odd number

13. an odd number less than 4

14. a prime number

15. a number less than 4

Mixed Applications

Solve. Which method did you use?

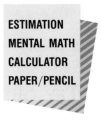

ESTIMATION
MENTAL MATH
CALCULATOR
PAPER/PENCIL

16. Half of the 12 members of the outdoors club were on the camping trip. A third of those on the trip got poison ivy. How many of the campers did not get poison ivy?

17. Elaine went swimming for 6 hours. The sun block she put on lasts 1.5 hours. For what percent of her swimming time was Elaine protected from the sun?

18. Duane bought a tent for camping. The area of the floor of Duane's tent is 48 ft². His sleeping bag measures $5\frac{1}{2}$ ft by $2\frac{1}{2}$ ft. How much floor space is left in the tent once Duane places his sleeping bag on the floor?

19. On last year's camping trip, it rained on 2 of every 5 days. If the weather this year is expected to be the same as it was last year, how many days of rain can the campers expect on this year's 20-day excursion?

UNDERSTANDING A CONCEPT

Statistics and Probability: Making Predictions

A. Jim's Clothing Store has a special offer for the summer months. Every customer who buys a pair of jeans gets to spin the spinner at the right. If the spinner lands on a 2, 7, or 9, the customer gets a free belt. About how many belts will Jim give away if 200 customers spin the spinner?

You can predict the number of times that a favorable outcome will occur by multiplying its probability by the number of attempts.

P(favorable outcome) × number of attempts = $\frac{3}{10}$ × 200 = 60

Jim can expect to give away 60 belts.

1. How can you solve this problem using proportion?

B. The weather department predicted a 50% chance of rain for each day in the month of April. Weather forecasters make their predictions based on past records. In the past it has rained 50% of the days when the atmospheric conditions have been like those expected in April.

2. Use the weather department's statistic from past records to predict the number of days it will rain in April.

TRY OUT

3. Use the jar at the right. Predict the number of times you would pick a red marble in 200 tries.

4. Predict the number of times you would expect to pick a green marble from the jar in 150 tries.

5. The weather forecast is for 40% chance of above 60°F temperatures for the month of November. How many days will the temperature probably be above 60°F?

PRACTICE

You shuffle these five cards, place them face down, and then pick one. You do this 25 times, always replacing the card you have picked.

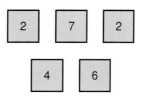

How many times can you expect to choose:

6. a 7? **7.** a 4? **8.** a 2?

You roll a number cube 50 times. About how many times can you expect to roll:

9. a 4? **10.** a 3 or a 5? **11.** a number less than 4?

You guess every answer on a 40-question multiple-choice questionnaire. About how many correct answers can you expect to get if each of the questions has:

12. 4 choices? **13.** 3 choices? **14.** 5 choices?

15. A store owner predicts that she will sell 75% of the summer merchandise before July 15. If she started the summer with 300 bathing suits, how many will she probably sell before the deadline of July 15?

16. If the store owner started the summer with 500 bathing suits, how many will she probably not sell by July 15?

Mixed Applications

Solve. You may need to use the Databank on page 586.

17. You take a 25-question multiple-choice test. Each question has 3 answer choices. The test is written in a language that you do not know. About how many questions can you expect to answer correctly?

18. Darnell answered 20 questions correctly on a 25-question multiple-choice test. How many questions can he expect to answer correctly on a 75-question multiple-choice test? Assume that the tests are similar.

19. Nico and Kara are among 20 students who took a test. The tests were collected, shuffled, then passed back to the students for grading. What is the probability that either Nico or Kara gets his or her own test back to grade?

20. Predict the number of correct responses for the boys and girls in this year's class if Mrs. Cole gives a 50-question test.

PROBLEM SOLVING

Strategy: Conducting a Simulation

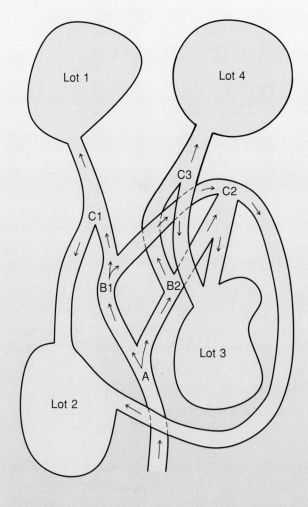

The diagram shows the roads that lead to the stadium parking lots.

At each point where a road splits, a car is just as likely to go left or right.

Make a plan.

To simulate traffic flow, flip a coin at each point. If the coin comes up *heads,* the car moves left. If the coin comes up *tails,* the car moves right.

Predict the percent of the cars that will end up at the lot.

1. Lot 1   **2.** Lot 2   **3.** Lot 3   **4.** Lot 4

Try the plan.

Do the simulation for 24 cars by flipping a coin. List the number and percent of the cars that end up at the parking lot.

5. Lot 1   **6.** Lot 2   **7.** Lot 3   **8.** Lot 4

9. Could you use this simulation to predict the way the cars would park in the lots? Why or why not?

10. *What if* the road from B2 to C2 were closed? How would this affect which lots the cars parked in?

PRACTICE

Do a simulation to solve the problem.

11. Wind direction measured in degrees in one location can be simulated by tossing 2 number cubes with faces numbered 1 to 6. Multiply the sum on the cubes by 30 to find the wind direction. Toss the cubes 30 times. Which wind direction in degrees occurs most often? Why do you think this is so?

12. Three safety switches control the lights in the parking lot. They must all be off to shut down the power. The action of switches can be simulated by tossing 3 pennies. Tails means off. Do a simulation by tossing 3 pennies 25 times. What percent of the time would the power be shut down?

13. Look at the diagram showing the roads to the parking lots. What if Lot 2 were closed and the roads leading to it from C1 and C2 were blocked off? Predict the percent of cars that would go to the remaining parking lots. Do a simulation for 20 cars by flipping a coin.

14. The ball on the string can be blown left or right from pole to pole. Flip a coin. Heads means right, tails means left. Do ten trials. Keep flipping until the ball moves all the way right or left. What percent of the time did the ball end up left?

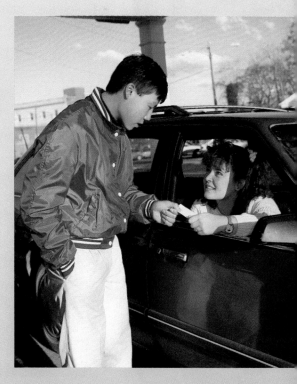

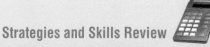

Strategies and Skills Review

Solve. Use mental math, estimation, a calculator, or paper and pencil.

15. A person is making up a test. Each item has 6 choices. Only one is correct. The first 12 correct answers are 1, 6, 4, 3, 1, 1, 5, 2, 4, 2, 3, and 6. Roll a number cube with faces numbered 1 to 6 twelve times to see how often a person would get the correct answer by guessing.

16. A company ships boxes in vans, trucks, and railroad cars.

> Rail car   2,050 boxes
> Truck   480 boxes
> Van   24 boxes

On one day the supervisor sent out 12 rail cars, 42 trucks, and 14 vans. How many boxes is that?

17. Six parking lot attendants were on standby in case they were needed. They always went out in teams of 2. What are the possible teams that could be formed from these 6 attendants?

18. *Write a problem* that uses a simulation to find a solution. Solve the problem. Ask others to solve it.

Experimenting and Predicting

A. Suppose your friend asks you to play the following game.

You both start with 10,000 points. You will roll two number cubes. If the sum of the two numbers you roll is a 7 or a 10, you get 500 of your friend's points. If you roll anything else, you give your friend 100 of your points. The winner is the player with more points after 20 rolls.

Do you want to play this game by these rules? Do you think one player has an advantage and, if so, which player?

Try an experiment.

1. Roll two number cubes 20 times. Record the results in a table like the one below.

NUMBER OF TIMES YOU GET THE SUM

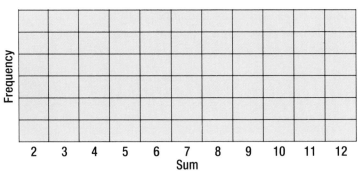

2. Use the results from your table to compute the following.

   Points you win = (total number of 7s and 10s) × 500
   Points your friend wins = (total number of other throws) × 100

3. Based on your experiment, who will come out ahead?

B. Here is another way you can analyze this game.

4. Copy and complete the table of sums at the right. How many different rolls are there in all?

5. How many ways can you get each sum?

Complete the table below.

+	1	2	3	4	5	6
1						
2						
3						
4						
5						
6						

Sum	2	3	4	5	6	7	8	9	10	11	12
Number of Ways											

Based on the tables you made, compute the following probabilities.

6. $P(7)$

7. $P(10)$

8. $P(7 \text{ or } 10)$

9. $P(\text{anything else})$

Then in 20 rolls the number of times you can expect to win is $P(7 \text{ or } 10) \times 20$, and the number of times you can expect to lose is $P(\text{anything else}) \times 20$. Therefore,

Points you win = $P(7 \text{ or } 10) \times 20 \times 500$
Points your friend wins = $P(\text{anything else}) \times 20 \times 100$

10. Compute the point values above. Who comes out ahead, you or your friend? What will the final score be? Explain.

11. Suppose that the rules of the game change. You lose 200 points if you do not roll a 7 or a 10. Who comes out ahead now?

DEVELOPING A CONCEPT

Representing Outcomes

Miyoko's brother is buying a car. He is deciding between a sedan and a hatchback and whether the car should be red, gray, or blue.

1. What orderly method can you use to find all the possible outcomes?

One way to find all the outcomes is to use a **tree diagram.**

Step 1 Choose a letter to represent each type of car.

Step 2 Choose a letter to represent each color.

Step 3 Draw a branch for each outcome.

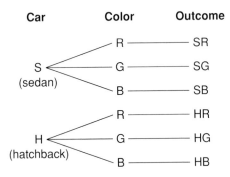

Car	Color	Outcome
	R	SR
S (sedan)	G	SG
	B	SB
	R	HR
H (hatchback)	G	HG
	B	HB

For each type of car, there are three color choices.

2. How many outcomes are possible?

3. What outcome is represented by SG? by HB?

Another way to find all the outcomes is to use a table.

	Red (R)	Gray (G)	Blue (B)
Sedan (S)	SR	SG	SB
Hatchback (H)	HR	HG	HB

SHARING IDEAS

4. **What if** Miyoko's brother is also deciding whether to get a sunroof? Use both methods to find all possible outcomes.

5. How many possible outcomes are there? How does the choice of the sunroof affect the original number of outcomes?

6. What are the advantages and the disadvantages of each method?

PRACTICE

Use a tree diagram or a table to list all the possible outcomes. How many are there?

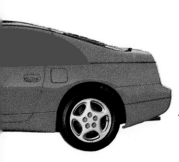

7. a car model that comes in gray or beige and can have 2 or 4 doors

8. a 2-door, 4-door, or hatchback car that comes with a choice of air conditioning, a sunroof, or a tape deck

9. a car that is available as a sedan or as a station wagon, with a choice of the color red, green, blue, or pink

10. bicycles that can have 3, 5, or 10 speeds and can be red, black, white, or gold

Mixed Applications

11. The restaurant across the street from the car dealership offers sandwiches made with wheat, oat, or bran bread filled with either cheese, tuna, or egg salad. What kinds of sandwiches are possible there?

12. Five salespeople—Don, Donna, Dan, Danielle, and Dorothy—are awaiting Randy as she enters the car showroom. What is the probability that Don or Dorothy will wait on her?

13. A car that regularly sells for $15,500 is discounted 20%. What is the amount of the discount?

14. *Write a problem* that involves finding outcomes. Find the solution. Ask others to solve the problem.

Mixed Review

Find the answer. Which method did you use?

MENTAL MATH
CALCULATOR
PAPER/PENCIL

15. 4.35×0.06

16. $\frac{1}{2} \times \frac{3}{8}$

17. 20% of 555

18. 25% of 40% of 40

19. $4^2 + 3^4$

20. $3\frac{1}{2} - 1\frac{5}{6}$

CHALLENGE

The graph at the right shows the distribution of a city's cars by age groups. If a car is chosen at random, what is the probability that it is 8 years old or less?

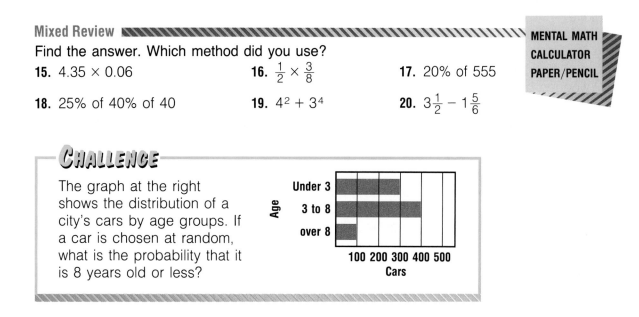

UNDERSTANDING A CONCEPT

Probability of Independent Events

A. Mario plays baseball for Stowe Middle School. In his home he has a box containing a wooden bat and an aluminum bat. His duffle bag contains a catcher's glove, a pitcher's glove, and an outfielder's glove. He grabs a bat and a glove at random. What is the probability that he takes a wooden bat *and* an outfielder's glove?

You can use a table to find all the possible outcomes.

<table>
<tr><th colspan="4">GLOVES</th></tr>
<tr><th></th><th>Catcher's
(C)</th><th>Pitcher's
(P)</th><th>Outfielder's
(O)</th></tr>
<tr><td>Aluminum
(A)</td><td>AC</td><td>AP</td><td>AO</td></tr>
<tr><td>Wood
(W)</td><td>WC</td><td>WP</td><td>WO</td></tr>
</table>

BATS

There are 6 outcomes.

A wooden bat with an outfielder's glove is 1 out of 6 outcomes. So P(wooden bat *and* outfielder's glove) $= \frac{1}{6}$.

1. What other method can you use to find the possible outcomes?

B. Choosing a bat and a glove are **independent events.** The choice of a bat does not affect the choice of a glove.

Notice in the table that the P(wooden bat) $= \frac{1}{2}$, and the P(outfielder's glove) $= \frac{1}{3}$. Since the P(wooden bat *and* outfielder's glove) $= \frac{1}{6}$, you can find the probability of independent events.

$$P(A \text{ and } B) = P(A) \times P(B)$$

P(wooden bat *and* outfielder's glove) $= P$(wooden bat) $\times P$(outfielder's glove)

2. Write a multiplication sentence to show the probability of choosing at random the aluminum bat but not the pitcher's glove.

TRY OUT Write the probability as a ratio.

A coin is tossed and a number cube with faces labeled 1 through 6 is rolled.

3. P(H *and* 2) **4.** P(T *and* 6) **5.** P(T *and* 1)

6. P(H *and* odd number) **7.** P(T *and* not 5) **8.** P(H *and* not 3)

PRACTICE

Two number cubes with faces labeled 1 through 6 are rolled.

9. Make a table of all the possible sums when both cubes are rolled.

Find the probability.

10. P(a sum of 2)   **11.** P(a sum of 12)   **12.** P(a sum of 8)   **13.** P(a sum of 7)

Three coins are tossed.

14. Draw a tree diagram to find all the possible outcomes.

Find the probability.

15. P(at least two heads)   **16.** P(exactly two heads)   **17.** P(more than 2 tails)

18. P(all alike)   **19.** P(just two alike)   **20.** P(all tails)

Each spinner at the right is spun once. Find the probability.

21. P(1 *and* red)

22. P(2 *and* green)

23. P(even number *and* striped color)

24. P(odd number *and* striped color)

25. P(4, blue)

26. P(a number, a color)

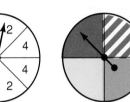

The first spinner is spun three times. Find the probability.

27. P(three 4s)   **28.** P(three 2s)   **29.** P(no 2s)   **30.** P(a sum of 16)

Critical Thinking

31. A student tossed a coin 10 times and got 10 heads. She said, "I will definitely get tails on the next toss." Is she right? Why or why not? What is the probability of her throwing a tails on the next throw?

Mixed Applications

32. The baseball team raised $43.88, $54.29, and $88.34 at three bake sales. They needed $200 for equipment. Did they make the goal? If not, about how much more money did they need?

33. There were 200 students playing baseball one spring. Of these, 15 were on the Rockets team. What percent of the students were on the Rockets team?

EXPLORING A CONCEPT

Dependent Events

Ted's red running shoes and brown loafers were by his bed. His dog spotted the shoes at the foot of Ted's bed. He ran in and out of Ted's room twice, each time with one shoe in his mouth. What is the probability that Spot scampered off with two red running shoes?

WORKING TOGETHER

You can perform an experiment to find the probability. Use four index cards.

Step 1 Mark two cards with a red *R* to represent the running shoes and two with a brown *B* to represent the loafers.

Step 2 Shuffle the four cards and place them facedown on the desk. Now turn up one card and note its color mentally.

Step 3 Return the card to the pile, shuffle it, and pick another card.

1. Were both cards red, both brown, or one red and one brown?

2. Turn another card, remember its color, return it to the pile, shuffle, and pick another card. What combination did you get?

Do this experiment a total of 30 times and record the results in a frequency table that lists all possibilities for picking two cards from this deck of four cards. Use RR to indicate two reds, BB for two browns, and RB for one red and one brown.

3. What did you notice? Did you pick two reds more than half the time, about half the time, or less than half the time?

4. Were your results what you expected? Explain.

Now try another experiment. Use the same four cards. This time, pick *two* cards at a time and record the results before returning the cards to the pile and shuffling. Repeat 30 times.

5. Did you pick two reds more times or fewer times than you did in the first experiment?

6. Describe the results of both experiments. Were they what you expected?

7. In which experiment is the picking of the second card *affected* by the picking of the first card? How is it affected?

8. Recall that independent events are events that have no influence on one another. Which experiment is independent?

9. The problem about the dog and the shoes requires finding the probability of a **dependent event.** Use what you have discovered to write a definition for dependent events.

ON YOUR OWN

Are the events *dependent* or *independent?* Tell why.

10. There are five marbles in a bag. You reach in and take one out. You replace it and remove another marble.

11. You and the captain of the opposing softball team are choosing players from a group to be on your teams. The other captain chose Connie. Now it is your pick.

12. It is dark. You reach into your drawer for socks, hoping to get a matching pair. You take one sock out. You hold it in your other hand and reach into the drawer again.

13. You pick a numbered card from a deck of numbered cards, replace it, and draw another card.

14. You toss a coin twice.

15. Nine cards, each with a letter from the word *PINEAPPLE* on it, are in a shoe box. Attempting to pick two vowels, you pick a card at random, do not replace it, then pick another card.

DEVELOPING A CONCEPT

Probability of Dependent Events

A box contains the four cards below. You pick a card without looking. Without replacing the first card, you pick a second card.

| W | O | R | M |

What is the probability of picking R and then picking M?

You can use a tree diagram to show all possible outcomes.

There are 12 possible outcomes. One of the outcomes is RM, so the $P(R, \text{then } M) = \frac{1}{12}$.

SHARING IDEAS

1. How many possible choices are there for the first pick?

2. What is the $P(R)$?

3. Given the first pick is R, how many possible choices of letters are there for the second draw?

4. What is the $P(M$ on the second draw)?

5. Compare the probabilities of $P(R)$, $P(M$ on the second draw), and $P(R, \text{then } M)$. Write a rule for finding the probability of two dependent events.

PRACTICE

A box contains 2 blue marbles and 2 yellow marbles. You pick a marble. Without replacing it, you pick another marble. Write the probability.

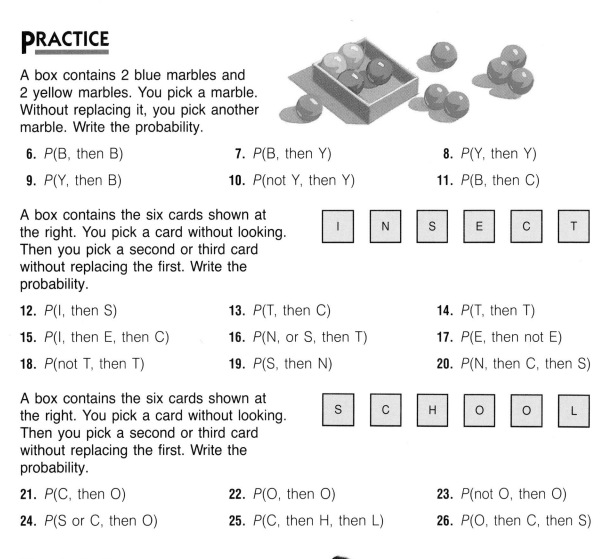

6. P(B, then B)

7. P(B, then Y)

8. P(Y, then Y)

9. P(Y, then B)

10. P(not Y, then Y)

11. P(B, then C)

A box contains the six cards shown at the right. You pick a card without looking. Then you pick a second or third card without replacing the first. Write the probability.

| I | N | S | E | C | T |

12. P(I, then S)

13. P(T, then C)

14. P(T, then T)

15. P(I, then E, then C)

16. P(N, or S, then T)

17. P(E, then not E)

18. P(not T, then T)

19. P(S, then N)

20. P(N, then C, then S)

A box contains the six cards shown at the right. You pick a card without looking. Then you pick a second or third card without replacing the first. Write the probability.

| S | C | H | O | O | L |

21. P(C, then O)

22. P(O, then O)

23. P(not O, then O)

24. P(S or C, then O)

25. P(C, then H, then L)

26. P(O, then C, then S)

Mixed Applications

27. Cheryl is shopping for shirts. She is deciding whether to buy a green, blue, or gray shirt and whether it should have long or short sleeves. How many outcomes are possible?

28. Bill's friend is buying him a T-shirt. He told her to choose red, blue, white, pink, or orange. What is the probability she will choose a pink shirt or an orange shirt?

29. Todd has to decide between blue, red, and tan shoes and between white, green, and gray socks. What is the probability he will choose tan shoes and red socks?

PROBLEM SOLVING

Strategy: Using More Than One Strategy

Lou wrote down how many people are in each of his three classes.
Math class: 15 people
English class: 16 people
Science class: 19 people

- 5 people are in all 3 of his classes.

- 13 people are in just 2 of his classes.

- Of the 13 there are 3 more in the English and science classes than in the math and English classes.

- There are 4 fewer in the English and science classes than in the math and science classes.

How many people are in just one of his classes?

Make a plan.

Often you may need to use two strategies to solve a problem. First for each pair of classes he finds the number of people in just those 2 classes using the Guess and Check strategy. Then for each class he finds the number of people in just that class using the Make a Diagram strategy.

Try the plan.

First Lou uses the Guess and Check strategy.

Math and English—1; English and Science—4; Math and Science—8
Check: 4 is 3 more than 1; 4 is 4 less than 8; 1 + 4 + 8 = 13

Then Lou uses the information to make a Venn Diagram.

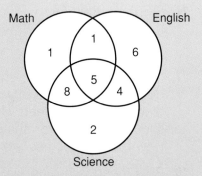

1. Check that the numbers of people in each class in the diagram are the same as the numbers in Lou's original list.

2. How many people are in just his math class? just his English class? just his science class?

3. How many people are just in one of his classes?

4. **What if** 4 of the 8 people who are in both Lou's math and science classes are transferred into another science class? Redraw the diagram to reflect this new information.

PRACTICE

Use more than one strategy to solve the problem.

5. A total of 17 high school runners raced over 3 days. There were 2 more runners on the second day than on the first day. There were twice as many, less 1 on the third day than on the second day. In how many ways could the runners on the first day have finished first, second, and third?

6. The number of students taking an after-school journalism class has been twice the number on the school newspaper. Over the last 5 years, the number of students on the paper has grown from 3 to 5 to 8 to 12 to 17. How many students would you expect to take the journalism class in the next 2 years?

7. On his homework, Charlie spends 3 minutes reading a page in his history text. He spends twice that time on a math problem, and 2 minutes more than 6 times that time writing a poem. For tonight's homework Charlie has to read 10 pages of history, do 10 math problems, and write 2 poems. How much time will Charlie spend on his homework tonight?

8. Students are enrolled for the following classes: 30 take woodworking (W), 11 take metal shop (M), and 19 take art (A). Four are in all 3 classes. Seven are in just 2 of the classes. There are twice as many in W and M than in M and A. There are 2 more in W and A than in W and M. How many are just taking woodworking?

Strategies and Skills Review

Solve. Use mental math, estimation, a calculator, or paper and pencil.

9. In class a teacher used a piece of paper to simulate how many different people a person could effectively supervise. She folded it repeatedly in half in the same direction. Each fold means one person. How many folds could you make with one piece of paper? What does it mean?

10. The mathematics teacher was going to give a test. He told the class, "The date of the test is the middle of 3 digits. The first digit is 7 more than the middle digit. The last digit is 3 times the middle digit. The sum of the digits is 47." On what date is the test?

11. On the first day of practice, 100 students came out for the team. Each day for 6 days, 5% of the original group quit. How many members were there on the 7th day?

12. **_Write a problem_** for which you must use two different strategies to solve it. Solve your problem. Then ask others to solve it.

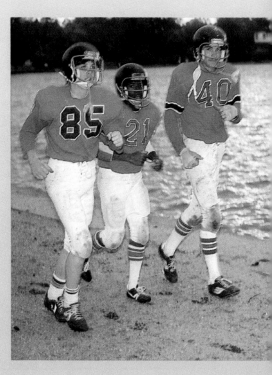

DEVELOPING A CONCEPT

Counting Outcomes: Permutations

Alex, Bonita, and Carol are going to the movies. They want to sit together in the same row. How many different seating orders are possible?

Bonita uses a tree diagram to find the different possible seating arrangements.

There are 6 possible arrangements.

An ordered arrangement of people or objects is a **permutation.**

Carol realizes that she can use multiplication to find the number of possible arrangements.

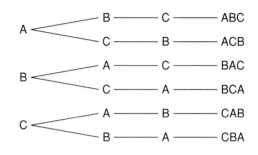

| 1st seat | 2nd seat | 3rd seat |

3 choices × 2 choices left × 1 left over = 6

Another way to express 3 × 2 × 1 is to use **factorial notation** and write 3! This is read as "three factorial."

SHARING IDEAS

1. In how many ways can four friends sit next to one another in a row at the movies? Which method did you use? Why?

2. What do you think 4! means? 5!?

PRACTICE

Solve.

3. In how many different orders can three people stand in a line for a movie?

4. Five teams were in a three-legged race. In how many different orders can they finish?

5. Using the digits 1 through 6, how many different 6-digit numbers can you form without repeating a digit in a number?

6. How many arrangements of letters are possible using the letters A, B, D, and E?

7. What is the probability that a random arrangement of the letters in Problem 6 will form the word BEAD?

8. You and seven friends are about to enter a relay race. In how many different ways can you arrange the running order? Give your answer using factorial notation.

9. Nine players are on your softball team. How many batting orders are possible? Give your answer using factorial notation.

Mixed Applications

Solve. Which method did you use?

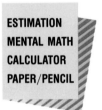

ESTIMATION
MENTAL MATH
CALCULATOR
PAPER/PENCIL

10. Gina took a 40-question movie quiz. Each question was worth the same number of points. She got 25 correct answers. Give her test score as a percent.

11. Roberto is deciding which of 20 movies to see. He rejects 20% of them, because his friend has seen them already. He rejects 4 others because the show times are inconvenient. How many movies are left to choose from?

12. Krista saw three movies last week. The running times for the movies were 2 hours 10 minutes, 100 minutes, and 130 minutes. What is the mean running time for the movies?

13. Denise got these test scores: 86, 92, 74, and 88. What is her mean score for the tests? What must she get on the next test to maintain that average?

Mixed Review

Solve. Which method did you use?

14. $\frac{3}{8} \times \frac{4}{5}$

15. 25% of 440

16. 88.9 + 21.1

17. $21 \div \frac{3}{4}$

18. 4.004 ÷ 1,000

19. 58% of 58

EXTRA Practice, page 529; Practice *PLUS*, page 531

E X P L O R I N G   A   C O N C E P T

Counting Outcomes: Combinations

A. Meg has been asked to exhibit some of her paintings in the art show. From four of her paintings, she will submit two for exhibit. How many selections of the two paintings are possible?

WORKING TOGETHER

Label four index cards A, B, C, and D to represent each painting. Use them to make a list of possible outcomes of two paintings from four paintings.

1. How many outcomes are possible?

Here is Meg's list of possible outcomes: AB, AC, AD, BA, BC, BD, CA, CB, CD, DA, DB, DC.

Recall that when you count permutations, the order of the objects matters. Choosing the arrangement AB is not the same as choosing the arrangement BA.

2. In Meg's situation, is choosing painting A and then choosing painting B the same as choosing B and then A? Which selection would be the same as the selection CD? as the selection DA?

3. Which ordered pairs can Meg eliminate from her list? How many choices are left?

A selection of objects from a set *without regard to order* of selection is a **combination** of the objects.

4. How many combinations of paintings are possible when selecting two paintings out of a set of four?

B. Bo plans to submit three of the four paintings he made for exhibition in the art show. How many selections of three paintings are possible?

5. Find the number of permutations of three objects from four objects. List them using *A*, *B*, *C*, and *D* to represent the paintings.

6. List the combinations. How many combinations of three of his paintings can Bo submit?

SHARING IDEAS

If the given situation represents a permutation, reword it to represent a combination. If it represents a combination, reword it to represent a permutation.

7. The art gallery received ten new paintings. The curator selected five of them to display.

8. Six people are on line to buy tickets for the museum. Wendell is wondering in how many ways they could be on line.

9. Twenty artists are competing for first place and second place in a competition. Suki is computing the possible orders in which they can finish.

10. Art students are asked to write a report on the works of any three of a group of seven painters.

ON YOUR OWN

Does the situation represent a *permutation* or a *combination?* Find the answer.

11. How many selections of three books from five books are possible?

12. Six students entered the limerick competition. How many orders of finish are possible?

13. Five artists applied for grants. Four will get them. In how many ways can the grants be given?

14. Five museum visitors lined up at the water fountain. How many different arrangements of people could there be in this line?

15. A team of two students will represent each school in the debating contest. Six students at the Calhoun School are competing for this honor. How many two-member teams from this school are possible?

16. How many different selections of five essay topics are possible from a list of six topics?

DECISION MAKING

Problem Solving: Choosing a Candidate

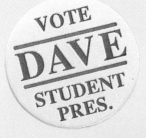

SITUATION

Toni, Dave, and Ramon are candidates for class president. Sandy would like to run too, but she is not sure of her chances of winning. Her friends took a poll of the students to find out.

PROBLEM

Should Sandy run for class president?

DATA

Three questions were asked of 150 students. Here are the results.
   A. Do you agree with the candidate's stand on student issues?
   B. Do you think the candidate would be a good president?
   C. If the election were held today, for which candidate would you vote?

		Toni	Dave	Ramon	Sandy
A.	Yes	75	100	87	90
	No	60	35	55	54
	Undecided	15	15	8	6
B.	Yes	55	105	90	87
	No	80	39	48	48
	Undecided	15	6	12	15
C.		21	45	39	36

USING THE DATA

What fraction of the students chose *yes* to question A for the candidate? What percent is that?

1. Toni **2.** Dave **3.** Ramon **4.** Sandy

What fraction of the students chose *yes* to question B for the candidate? What percent is that?

5. Toni **6.** Dave **7.** Ramon **8.** Sandy

What percent of the students said they would vote for the candidate?

9. Toni **10.** Dave **11.** Ramon **12.** Sandy

13. How many undecided votes are there for question C? If the undecided students voted for Sandy, how many votes would she get?

What if there are three basic stands being presented in this election—Toni's stand, Dave's stand, and Ramon and Sandy's stand. What percent of the votes goes for each stand?

14. Toni **15.** Dave **16.** Ramon and Sandy

MAKING DECISIONS

17. Which candidate has the highest percentage of votes in the poll?

18. Which candidate has the higher percentage of votes in the poll, Ramon or Sandy? by what percentage?

19. ***What if*** all of the students vote their present choice and all undecided students choose a candidate? Can Sandy win the election?

20. Can Sandy possibly win the election? Why or why not?

21. Should Sandy run for office? Why or why not?

22. ***Write a list*** of other factors Sandy should consider in deciding whether or not to run for office.

23. Would you run for office if you were Sandy? Why or why not?

Math and Social Studies

Rates for life insurance are based on the life expectancy of different groups of people. For example, a female nonsmoker has a longer life expectancy than a male nonsmoker of the same age. The probability is that she will live longer; therefore she will pay insurance premiums for more years. She is a better risk for the insurance company.

The table below shows some typical annual premiums, or payments per year, for various groups for a $100,000 life insurance policy.

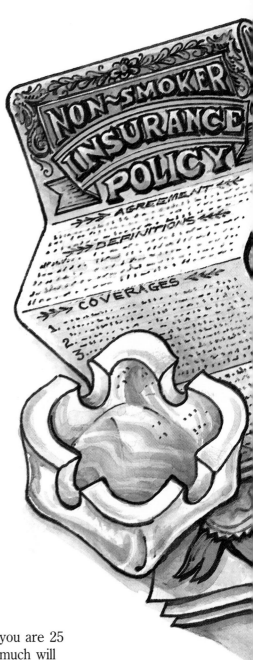

LIFE INSURANCE ANNUAL PREMIUM

	Age 25	Age 45	Age 55	Age 65
Nonsmoker				
Male	$132	$249	$542	$1,504
Female	$103	$179	$370	$ 995
Smoker				
Male	$235	$454	$950	$2,449
Female	$169	$312	$636	$1,609

What if a 45-year-old male stops smoking? Assuming his premium will stay at the figure given until age 55, how much money will he save over the next 10 years?

Think: $454   – $249   = $205
             ↑   ↑
         Premium   Premium
           for   for
         smokers   nonsmokers

10 × $205 = $2,050

He will save $2,050 in insurance premiums over 10 years.

ACTIVITIES

1. Work with a partner. Use the rates on the chart. Assume you are 25 years old. You buy an insurance policy for $100,000. How much will you have spent by age 64?

2. Look for newspaper and magazine articles about automobile and health insurance costs. Display your clippings on a bulletin board.

Computer Simulation: Dependent Probability

Suppose you reach into a bag containing 6 red marbles and 4 blue marbles and pick two. What is the probability that both marbles will be the same color? If you conduct the experiment 15 times, how many times do you think you will pick two marbles of the same color?

Recall that picking two marbles without replacing the first one is an example of a dependent event. To find the probability that the two selected marbles are the same color, find the sum of the probability of picking 2 red marbles and the probability of picking 2 blue marbles.

$$P(\text{2 red marbles}) = \frac{6}{10} \times \frac{5}{9} = \frac{1}{3}$$

$$P(\text{2 blue marbles}) = \frac{4}{10} \times \frac{3}{9} = \frac{2}{15}$$

$$P(\text{same color}) = \frac{1}{3} + \frac{2}{15} = \frac{7}{15}$$

The probability of picking either 2 red marbles or 2 blue marbles is $\frac{7}{15}$. Therefore, for every 15 selections, you would expect 7 favorable outcomes—pairs of marbles of the same color.

You can use the computer simulation program RANDOM PICK to simulate picking the marbles from the bag. It will conduct the experiment in trials of 200 selections and keep track of the results. You can use the program to test your predictions about different combinations of marbles.

AT THE COMPUTER

1. List all the possible combinations of 10 red and blue marbles that contain at least one of each color. Which combination do you think will give the greatest number of favorable outcomes?

2. Enter 1 red and 9 blue marbles as the marble combination for the first trial of 200 selections. Predict the number of favorable outcomes. Have the program conduct the simulation. How does the number the computer found compare with your prediction?

3. Predict whether the number of favorable outcomes for 2 red and 8 blue marbles will be higher or lower than for 1 red marble and 9 blue marbles. Compare the program's outcome with your prediction.

4. Run the program using all the other combinations on your list. Which combination gave the greatest number of favorable outcomes? How did this compare with your prediction in Problem 1?

5. Study the results of each trial. Were any similar? Explain.

EXTRA PRACTICE

Modeling an Experiment, page 495 ··

Tell whether you think the outcomes described are equally likely to
happen or not equally likely to happen. If they are not equally likely
to happen, tell which is most likely.

1. Pick a card.

Possible outcomes:
1 2 3 4 5 6

2. Spin the spinner.

Possible outcomes:
+ − × =

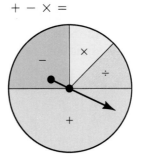

3. Choose a cube.

Possible outcomes:
red, blue, yellow,
green

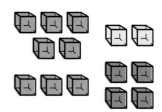

Probability of Simple Events, page 497 ··

List the sample space for the experiment.

1. A marble is picked from a bag.

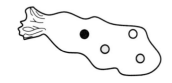

2. A card is picked at random.

1 2 3 4 5 6 7

Spin the spinner once. Write the probability
as a ratio, a decimal, and a percent.

3. $P(2)$

4. $P(1)$

5. $P(\text{not } 1)$

6. $P(\text{odd number})$

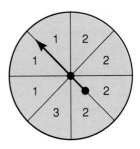

Probability of Mutually Exclusive Events, page 499 ····································

A letter is picked at random. Write the probability as a ratio, a
decimal, and a percent.   G E O M E T R Y

1. $P(G)$

2. $P(E)$

3. $P(E \text{ or } O)$

4. $P(M \text{ or } T)$

5. $P(E, R, \text{ or } Y)$

6. $P(M \text{ or not } M)$

7. $P(G, E, O, M, \text{ or } T)$

8. $P(T, R, \text{ or } Y)$

EXTRA PRACTICE

Experimental Probability: Using Random Digits, page 501 ·······························

Find the theoretical probability. Then find the experimental probability using the Table of Random Digits. Use at least 100 random digits.

1. Val's car keys could be in one of 7 places. She wants to find the keys in the first place she looks.

2. Bob has a penny, nickel, a dime, a quarter, a 50¢ piece, and a silver dollar in his pocket. He needs a nickel for the parking meter.

3. Find the experimental probability for Problems 1 and 2. Use numbered cards or a spinner to find the experimental probability. How do these results compare with the answer you found with the Table of Random Digits?

Statistics and Probability: Making Predictions, page 503 ·······························

1. A store allows every customer to spin for a discount. Out of 200 customers, how many would you expect to get:
   a. 10%?   **b.** 20%?   **c.** 30%?   **d.** 40%?

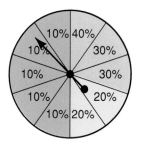

2. You guess every answer on a 50-question multiple-choice questionnaire. About how many correct answers can you expect to get if each of the questions has:
   a. 2 choices?   **b.** 3 choices?   **c.** 4 choices?   **d.** 5 choices?

Problem–Solving Strategy: Conducting a Simulation, page 505 ·······················

Do a simulation to solve.

1. A race is to begin at the south easternmost intersection. Where does the race start?

2. How many blocks is the race?

3. Jim is at 4th and Ridge. He is 3 blocks ahead of George and 2 blocks behind Marcia. Where are George and Marcia?

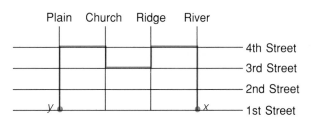

EXTRA PRACTICE

Representing Outcomes, page 509 ·

Use a tree diagram or a table to list all the possible outcomes. How many are there?

1. an outfit from 4 pairs of pants and 5 shirts

2. a dentist appointment for 3:30 P.M., 4:00 P.M., 4:30 P.M. on April 1 or 2

3. a notebook that comes in red, black, blue, white, or green with 1-in. or 2-in. rings

4. a sandwich with tuna, chicken, beef, or ham filling on rye, white, or whole wheat

Probability of Independent Events, page 511 ·

Each spinner is spun once.

1. Draw a tree diagram to find all the possible outcomes.

Find the probability.

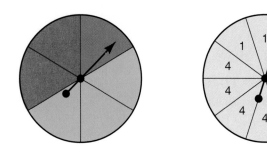

2. *P*(red and 1)   **3.** *P*(blue and 2)   **4.** *P*(green and 3)

5. *P*(red and 2)   **6.** *P*(red and 3)   **7.** *P*(blue and 1)

8. *P*(red and 4)   **9.** *P*(blue and 3)   **10.** *P*(green and 1)

11. *P*(green and 2)   **12.** *P*(blue and 4)   **13.** *P*(green and 4)

Probability of Dependent Events, page 515 ·

A box contains the 5 cards shown. You pick a card without looking. Then you pick a second card without replacing the first. Write the probability. H E L L O

1. *P*(H, then E)   **2.** *P*(L, then L)   **3.** *P*(not L, then L)

4. *P*(H or E, then L)   **5.** *P*(H, then E, then L)   **6.** *P*(O, then L, then H)

EXTRA PRACTICE

Problem–Solving Strategy: Using Different Strategies, page 517

Use different strategies to solve.

1. Ellen buys a skirt and a scarf. Her bill is $40.50. If she spent $24.50 more for the skirt than the scarf, how much did each item cost?

2. Alex took a taxi to the airport. The rate was $4.00 for the first mile and $.20 for each additional $\frac{1}{6}$ of a mile, or part thereof. The ride cost $16.80. How many miles did he travel?

3. The children at Coldspring Camp are enrolled in the following activities: 20 in swimming (S), 7 in canoeing (C), and 13 in tennis (T). Two are in all 3 classes. Eight are in just 2 of the classes. There are twice as many in S and C as in C and T. There are 3 more in S and T than in S and C. How many are enrolled just in swimming?

4. The number of adults taking a computer class at the local high school has been twice the number taking art. Over the last 4 years, the number taking art has grown from 2 to 5 to 9 to 14. How many adults would you expect to enroll in the computer class over the next 3 years?

5. Last summer, Eric caught 23 fish, each a different species. In July he caught three times as many fish as he did in June, plus one. In August, he caught twice as many as he did in July. If he caught a rainbow trout in July, what is the probability that it was the third fish he caught that month.

Counting Outcomes: Permutations, page 519

1. In how many different ways can you award first, second, and third prize in a contest among 6 people?

2. In how many ways can you order 4 swimmers in 4 lanes?

3. How many arrangements of letters are possible using the letters A B E K?

4. What is the probability that a random arrangement of the letters in Problem 3 will form the word BAKE?

5. In how many ways can you fill the jobs of lifeguard and swimming instructor from 5 applicants?

6. In how many orders can the 5 job applicants in Problem 5 be interviewed?

PRACTICE *PLUS*

KEY SKILL: Probability of Independent Events (Use after page 511.)

Level A

A number cube with faces 1 through 6 and a cube with 3 red sides, 2 blue sides, and 1 yellow side are rolled.

1. Make a tree diagram or table to find all the possible outcomes.

Find the probability.

2. P(1 and red)

3. P(2 and blue)

4. P(a number and red)

5. P(even number and blue)

6. P(odd number and yellow)

7. P(number less than 4 and red)

8. The track team has a choice of red or white uniforms and Fast Track, Winner, or Number One sneakers. How many possible outfits are there?

Level B

Each spinner at the right is spun once. Find the probability.

9. P(1 and red)

10. P(1 and blue)

11. P(2 and yellow)

12. P(2 and green)

13. P(3 and red)

14. P(3 and yellow)

15. P(4 and blue)

16. P(4 and green)

17. P(1 and orange)

18. A baseball player has a choice of 3 bats and 3 gloves. How many different combinations of bats and gloves are there?

Level C

The spinner is spun three times. Find the probability.

19. P(3 reds)

20. P(3 blues)

21. P(3 yellows)

22. P(no red)

23. P(red or yellow and 2 blues)

24. P(red and blue and yellow)

25. P(red and blue and green)

26. P(red, blue or yellow, green)

27. The basketball team has a choice of red or white shirts; black, red, or white shorts; and striped, dotted, or solid socks. How many possible uniforms are there?

PRACTICE PLUS

KEY SKILL: Counting Outcomes: Permutations (Use after page 519.)

Level A
Solve.

1. In how many ways can 3 friends sit next to one another in a row?

2. In how many ways can 4 dogs line up in a dog show?

3. Using the digits 1 through 5, how many different 5-digit numbers can you form without repeating a digit in the number?

4. How many arrangements of letters are possible using the letters *A, E, S, T.*

Level B
Solve.

5. Four teams are in a relay race. How many different orders of finish are possible?

6. Using the digits 1 through 7, how many different 7-digit numbers can you form without repeating a digit in a number?

7. How many arrangements of letters are possible using the letters *A, E, M, T?*

8. What is the probability that a random arrangement of the letters in Problem 7 will form the word *TEAM.*

9. What is the probability that a random arrangement of the same letters will form either *TEAM, TAME, MEAT* or *MATE*?

Level C
Solve.

10. You and 8 friends are going to stand in line at a movie theater. In how many different ways can you stand in line for the movie?

11. Using digits 1 through 8, how many different 8-digit numbers can you form without repeating a digit?

12. How many arrangements of letters are possible using the letters *A, E, K, R, S, T?*

13. What is the probability that a random arrangement of the letters in Problem 12 will form the word *SKATER*?

CHAPTER REVIEW

LANGUAGE AND MATHEMATICS

Complete the sentences. Use the words in the chart on the right.

1. If the outcome of one event is influenced by another, they are ■. *(page 512)*

2. If the outcome of one event is *not* influenced by another, they are ■. *(page 510)*

3. If 2 events cannot happen together then they are ■. *(page 498)*

4. Arrangements that are ordered are ■. *(page 518)*

5. **Write a definition** or give an example of the words you did not use from the chart.

> **VOCABULARY**
>
> events
> mutually exclusive events
> tree diagrams
> independent events
> dependent events
> permutations

CONCEPTS AND SKILLS

A cube with faces labeled 1-6 is rolled once. Express these probabilities in fraction form or as a whole number. *(page 496)*

6. $P(4)$

7. $P(\text{multiple of } 3)$

8. $P(\text{number less than } 6)$

9. $P(\text{factor of } 6)$

10. $P(\text{number greater than } 7)$

11. $P(\text{prime number})$

Julia tossed a coin. Express these probabilities in decimal and percent form. *(pages 496, 510)*

12. $P(\text{one head})$ on one toss

13. $P(2 \text{ tails})$ after 2 tosses

14. $P(\text{exactly 2 tails})$ after 3 tosses

15. $P(\text{at least 1 head})$ after 3 tosses

A box contains 7 red, 8 blue, and 5 yellow marbles. One marble is drawn at random. Express these probabilities in decimal form and in percent form. *(pages 496, 498)*

16. $P(\text{blue})$

17. $P(\text{not red})$

18. $P(\text{blue } or \text{ red})$

19. $P(\text{red, blue } or \text{ yellow})$

Each letter in the word "MULTIPLY" is written on a card and the cards are placed face down. One card is drawn at random and then, without the card being replaced, a second card is drawn. Express these probabilities in fraction form. *(pages 496, 498, 514)*

20. $P(L)$ on first draw

21. $P(M, T, or Y)$ on the first draw

22. $P(U, \text{ then not } I)$

23. $P(M or U, \text{ then } T)$

The eight cards of Exercises 20–23 are shuffled and a card is chosen. Then the card is placed back with the others. If this procedure is performed 400 times, how many times can you expect to choose these letters? *(page 502)*

24. an *M*

25. an *L*

26. *T* or *P* or *Y*

27. any letter except *U* or *I*

28. If the probability of rain is 20% on a day in June, on how many June days would you expect rain? *(page 502)*

29. If the probability of snow is $\frac{1}{3}$ on a day in January, on how many January days would you expect snow? *(page 502)*

Solve. *(page 518)*

30. In how many different orders can 3 boys finish in a 3-boy race?

31. In how many ways can you order the letters *M*, *A*, *T*, and *H*?

32. In how many different orders can 5 different belts be worn, one a day, in 5 days?

33. In how many ways can 3 baseball players play first, second, and third base?

Critical Thinking

A bandmaster has a choice of either red or blue for new hats and a choice of a red, white, or blue sash for new uniforms. She randomly chooses one color for the hat and one for the sash.

34. Are the choices independent or dependent events? *(page 512)*

35. Are choosing a red hat and a red sash mutually exclusive? *(page 498)*

36. Is a list of the possible outcomes without regard to order a permutation or combination? *(pages 518, 520)*

37. If she also has a 3rd choice of hat color, by how many events does the sample space increase? *(pages 496, 510)*

Mixed Applications

38. The probability of an event is $\frac{2}{7}$. The number of possible outcomes must be a multiple of what prime number? *(page 496)*

39. The probability of an event is 60%. The number of favorable outcomes must be a multiple of what prime number? *(page 496)*

40. The probability of an event is $\frac{3}{4}$. The number of favorable outcomes is what percent of the number of possible outcomes? *(page 496)*

41. The probability of an event is 0.25. What is the minimum number of events that can be in the sample space? *(page 496)*

CHAPTER TEST

A cube with faces labeled 1–6 is rolled once. Express these probabilities in fraction form or as a whole number.

1. $P(2)$

2. $P(1 \text{ or } 5)$

3. $P(\text{a multiple of } 6)$

4. $P(\text{a factor of } 4)$

5. $P(\text{number} > 1)$

6. $P(\text{number} < 7)$

Jerry tossed a coin. Express these probabilities in decimal and percent form.

7. $P(2 \text{ heads})$ after 2 tosses

8. $P(\text{at least } 1 \text{ tail})$ after 3 tosses

A box contains 1 red, 1 blue, 1 green, and 2 yellow marbles. One marble is drawn at random. If you put the marble back each time and draw a total of 40 times, how many times could you expect to choose these colors?

9. red

10. yellow

11. red, blue, *or* green

12. a color other than red

Without the first marble being replaced, a second marble is drawn. Express these probabilities in decimal and percent form.

13. $P(\text{blue, then red})$

14. $P(\text{blue, not yellow})$

15. $P(\text{yellow, then yellow})$

16. $P(\text{blue, then blue})$

17. $P(\text{red, then green})$

18. $P(\text{red } or \text{ green, then yellow})$

Solve.

19. If the probability of fog is $\frac{1}{6}$ on a day in April how many days would you expect fog in April?

20. In how many ways can you order 5 posters in a row?

21. In how many different orders can a person eat 3 desserts?

22. In how many different orders can 6 people stand in a line?

23. In how many different orders can 4 people run on a relay team?

24. With every apple you buy from the Cooking Club you get a token with the letter B, C, K, or O. When you have all the tokens needed to spell the name of the prize, you get a cookbook. Predict how many apples you will have to buy to get the prize.

25. The tandem bicycle riding club has 8 members. How many different teams of 2 riders each can be formed from the 8 members?

ENRICHMENT FOR ALL

BUFFON'S NEEDLE PROBLEM

Count Buffon created an experiment using probability to find the value of π. To recreate the experiment, you will need a piece of plain paper, 10 toothpicks cut to 1 in. in length, and a ruler. Then, follow these steps.

Step 1 Draw at least five parallel lines on the piece of paper. The lines should be 2 in. apart. Make the lines at least 8 in. long.

Step 2 Drop the 10 toothpicks from a height of about 1 ft. Record the number of toothpicks that touch one of the lines.

Step 3 Repeat Step 2 nine more times. Each time record the number of toothpicks that touch one of the lines.

Step 4 Find the total number of times a toothpick touched a line during the 10 trials.

Step 5 Write the following ratio for your experiment.

$$\frac{\text{TOTAL NUMBER OF TOOTHPICKS THAT TOUCHED A LINE}}{\text{TOTAL NUMBER OF TOOTHPICKS DROPPED}}$$

Step 6 Find the reciprocal of your ratio. Then find the value of the reciprocal by dividing the numerator by the denominator.

1. What ratio did you write in Step 5?

2. What is the reciprocal of your ratio? the value of the reciprocal?

3. Compare your value to the value of π, 3.14. Is it close?

4. Repeat the experiment again. Did you get a value that is closer to the value of π?

CUMULATIVE REVIEW

Choose the letter of the correct answer.

1. Solve for n: $\frac{4}{n} = \frac{10}{8}$
   a. 2
   c. 20
   b. 5
   d. not given

2. Complete. 250% = ■
   a. 2.5
   c. 250
   b. 25
   d. not given

3. How many faces does a rectangular pyramid have?
   a. 4
   c. 6
   b. 5
   d. not given

4. What is the surface area of a cube with one side 3 in. long?
   a. 9 in.^{2}
   c. 54 in.^{2}
   b. 27 in.^{2}
   d. not given

This graph shows Gina's budget.

GINA'S BUDGET

5. How much more does she budget for records than for games?
   a. 0.1%
   c. 40%
   b. 10%
   d. not given

6. What is the ratio of the amount budgeted for books to the amount budgeted for games?
   a. 8:3
   c. 40:55
   b. 4:15
   d. not given

7. If she earns $60, how much does she spend on games?
   a. $0.90
   c. $6.00
   b. $4.00
   d. not given

8. What is the volume of a cylinder with a diameter of 10 cm and a height of 2.5 cm?
   a. 12.5π cm^3
   c. 62.5π cm^3
   b. 25π cm^3
   d. not given

9. What is the volume of a rectangular pyramid with a base of 3 ft by 3 ft and a height of 4 ft?
   a. 12 ft^3
   c. 36 ft^3
   b. 24 ft^3
   d. not given

10. In how many different orders can 3 people stand in a line?
    a. 3
    c. 9
    b. 6
    d. not given

A jar contains 1 red, 2 blue, and 2 green marbles. One is drawn at random, and then, without the first marble being replaced, a second marble is drawn.

11. What is P(red) on the first draw?
    a. 1:10
    c. 1:2
    b. 1:4
    d. not given

12. What is P(red or blue) on the first draw?
    a. 3%
    c. 60%
    b. 30%
    d. not given

13. What is P(blue, then red)?
    a. 0.04
    c. 0.6
    b. 0.1
    d. not given

14. If the marble is replaced and one is drawn 50 times, how many times can you expect to draw green?
    a. 2
    c. 20
    b. 10
    d. not given

Algebra: Integers and Coordinate Graphing

CHAPTER 14

MATH CONNECTIONS: GEOMETRY • PROBLEM SOLVING

5.3 mi   4.9 mi

8.7 mi

1. What information do you see in this picture?

2. How can you use the information?

3. All 3 routes lead to Stoney Point. If Sean bikes there by the blue route and returns by the green route, how far will he have traveled?

4. Write a problem using the information.

Comparing and Ordering Integers

A. The highest temperature in the world, 136°F, was recorded in Libya in 1922. The lowest temperature recorded was in Antarctica in 1983, when it was 129° below zero on the Fahrenheit scale.

The **integers** are the numbers:

. . . , $^-5$, $^-4$, $^-3$, $^-2$, $^-1$, 0, $^+1$, $^+2$, $^+3$, $^+4$, $^+5$, . . .

Integers greater than zero are **positive integers,** for example, $^+136$°F. Integers less than zero are **negative integers,** for example, $^-129$°F.

Integers can be shown on a number line.

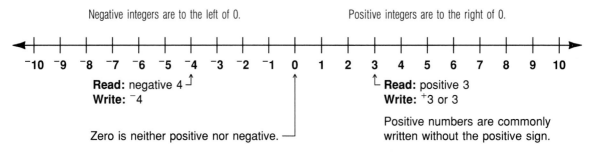

Negative integers are to the left of 0.   Positive integers are to the right of 0.

Read: negative 4
Write: $^-4$

Zero is neither positive nor negative.

Read: positive 3
Write: $^+3$ or 3

Positive numbers are commonly written without the positive sign.

B. The **absolute value** of an integer is the distance that the number is from zero. You can use the number line to help you find absolute value.

The absolute value of 3 is 3.   **Write:** $|3| = 3$
The absolute value of $^-8$ is 8.   **Write:** $|^-8| = 8$

C. The **opposite** of an integer is the number that is the same distance from zero in the opposite direction. Each integer has an opposite.

What is the opposite of $^-3$?

Look on the number line. The number that is the same distance from 0 as $^-3$ but in the opposite direction is 3. The opposite of $^-3$ is 3.

  1. What is the opposite of 10?

D. You can use the number line to compare two integers. Which is greater, $^-10$ or $^-5$? The integer that is farther to the right is greater.

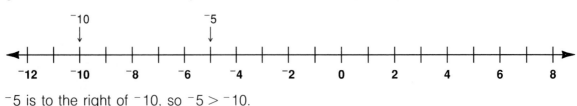

$^-5$ is to the right of $^-10$, so $^-5 > ^-10$.

TRY OUT

Find the absolute value of the integer. Then write the opposite of the integer.

2. ⁻7   **3.** 16   **4.** ⁻22   **5.** 14   **6.** ⁻13

Compare. Write >, <, or =.

7. ⁻7 ● ⁻5   **8.** ⁻8 ● 4   **9.** 5 ● ⁻5   **10.** ⁻12 ● ⁻24   **11.** ⁻17 ● ⁻17

PRACTICE

Write an integer to describe the situation.

12. a temperature 14° above zero   **13.** a loss of $45

14. a loss of 13 yd   **15.** a gain in altitude of 200 m

Find the absolute value of the integer.

16. |⁻4| **17.** |⁻15| **18.** |9| **19.** |⁻22| **20.** |18| **21.** |⁻523|

Write the opposite of the integer.

22. 7   **23.** ⁻12   **24.** ⁻8   **25.** 13   **26.** ⁻30   **27.** ⁻278

Compare. Write >, <, or =.

28. 8 ● 3   **29.** 13 ● 27   **30.** ⁻6 ● ⁻9   **31.** ⁻34 ● ⁻23

32. 9 ● ⁻4   **33.** 25 ● ⁻11   **34.** ⁻34 ● 14   **35.** ⁻35 ● 41

Write the integers in order from least to greatest.

36. ⁻3, 8, ⁻12   **37.** 2, ⁻4, ⁻10

38. ⁻9, ⁻14, 8   **39.** ⁻456, 456, ⁻460

40. ⁻4, ⁻6, 3, ⁻9, 0   **41.** 6, ⁻20, ⁻16, 20, 21, ⁻1

Critical Thinking

42. What is the opposite of zero?

43. Is the absolute value of an integer ever negative? Why or why not?

Mixed Applications

44. The high temperature in Fargo one day was ⁻14°F. The same day the high temperature in Harrisburg was ⁻8°F. In which city was it warmer?

45. The high temperatures in Hilo for five days were 85°F, 88°F, 93°F, 98°F, and 84°F. Find the average high temperature.

EXPLORING A CONCEPT

Adding Integers with Counters

Bob is a running back on his school's football team. In two attempts he gained 3 yd and lost 7 yd. What was his total running yardage for the two attempts?

WORKING TOGETHER

You can use two-color counters to model gains and losses. Let a yellow counter represent a gain of 1 yd. Let a red counter represent a loss of 1 yd.

gain of 1 yd   loss of 1 yd

A gain of 1 yd and a loss of 1 yd are opposites, so one *cancels* the other.

1. Using counters, how would you represent a gain of 3 yd? a loss of 7 yd?

2. Pair the counters. What counters are left?

3. What do these counters represent?

4. What is Bob's total gain or loss?

Here is one way you can use two-color counters to model the problem.

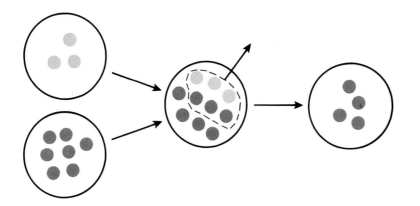

Bob had a total loss of 4 yd.

5. **What if** on his next play he had lost 5 yd? Use two-color counters to find the total gain or loss for the three plays.

6. **What if** on his final play he had gained 15 yd? Use two-color counters to find the total gain or loss for the four plays.

7. When will the sum of two integers be zero?

8. When will the sum of two integers be negative?

9. When will the sum of two integers be positive?

10. What other methods can you use to model addition of integers?

ON YOUR OWN

Add, using two-color counters. Write a number sentence to show what you did.

11. On two running plays Sean gained 6 yd and lost 3 yd. What was his total gain or loss?

12. On three running plays Duane gained 4 yd, lost 6 yd, and then gained 3 yd. What was his total gain or loss?

13. On four running plays Ralph lost 2 yd, gained 5 yd, gained 9 yd, and lost 6 yd. What was his total gain or loss?

14. On his first running play Arnold lost 7 yd. Then he caught a pass for a gain of 6 yd. What was his total gain or loss?

15. Manuel gained 12 yd on his first carry. On his next two carries he lost 2 yd and 4 yd. What was his total gain or loss?

DEVELOPING A CONCEPT

Adding Integers

Professor Huntly, an archeologist, found a city that is partly above and partly below sea level. He found a vase that was 2 ft above sea level and a bowl that was 5 ft higher. How far above or below sea level was the bowl?

WORKING TOGETHER

You can use a number line to add integers.

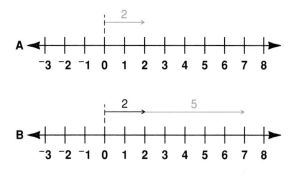

1. What does the blue arrow represent above number line A? above number line B?

2. Find the sum.

3. Write a number sentence to describe the situation.

4. How far above or below sea level was the bowl?

These number lines show other examples of adding integers.

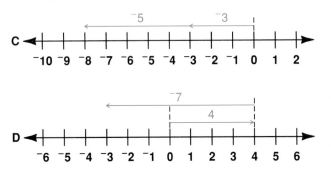

5. Write a number sentence to describe the addition on number line C.

6. Write a number sentence to describe the addition on number line D.

7. Draw a number line to model each addition. Then write a number sentence.

   a. 7 + 4 **b.** 2 + 3 **c.** ⁻4 + ⁻9

   d. ⁻4 + ⁻3 **e.** 6 + ⁻8 **f.** 9 + ⁻1

   g. ⁻3 + 5 **h.** ⁻7 + 2 **i.** 6 + ⁻6

What pattern did you notice when you added:

8. two positive integers?

9. two negative integers?

10. a positive integer and a negative integer?

Write a rule for adding:

11. two positive integers.

12. two negative integers.

13. a positive integer and a negative integer.

PRACTICE

Is the sum *positive, negative,* or *zero*?

14. 3 + 12

15. ⁻6 + ⁻14

16. 8 + ⁻7

17. ⁻9 + 9

18. 4 + 1

19. 8 + ⁻11

20. ⁻12 + ⁻12

21. ⁻6 + 14

Add. Use the number line to check.

22. 6 + 12

23. 9 + 4

24. ⁻3 + ⁻8

25. ⁻4 + ⁻6

26. 3 + ⁻7

27. ⁻8 + 6

28. ⁻5 + 5

29. ⁻7 + 9

30. 8 + ⁻18

31. ⁻2 + 5

32. 27 + 6

33. 0 + ⁻14

34. 16 + ⁻5

35. 9 + 10

36. 1 + ⁻2

37. ⁻19 + ⁻8

38. ⁻4 + ⁻5 + 3

39. 7 + ⁻6 + ⁻2

40. ⁻8 + 3 + 5

41. ⁻3 + ⁻2 + 1

42. ⁻3 + 5 + 1

43. ⁻6 + ⁻3 + 1

44. ⁻4 + 2 + ⁻6

45. ⁻5 + ⁻5 + 1

Compare the sums. Write >, <, or =.

46. 5 + ⁻6 ● 7 + ⁻4

47. ⁻3 + 5 ● 5 + ⁻3

48. ⁻7 + 8 ● ⁻3 + 2

Mixed Applications

49. Siri was working at an archeological site. She found 230 ancient bowls. She estimated that about 75% of them were valuable finds. About how many of the bowls did she think were valuable?

50. To get to the level of a dig at the archeological site, Steve, who was at sea level, walked 8 ft down, then 3 ft up, then 4 ft down again. How many feet above or below sea level was the dig?

51. In 1963 a team of archeologists discovered a city destroyed by an earthquake in the year 1450 B.C. How long ago was the earthquake?

52. *Write a problem* that uses the following number sentence as a solution: 4 + ⁻6 = ⁻2. Solve your problem. Ask others to solve it.

EXPLORING A CONCEPT.
Subtracting Integers with Counters

The temperature dropped from 5°F to 3°F. What was the change in temperature?

WORKING TOGETHER

You can use two-color counters to model subtraction of integers. Subtracting an integer is represented by removing counters. Let a yellow counter represent a positive integer. Let a red counter represent a negative integer.

positive integer   negative integer

1. How would you use counters to show 5?

2. How would you show 3 being subtracted?

3. How many counters do you have left? What is the change in temperature?

4. Using counters, how would you model $^-5 - {}^-3$?

5. Write a number sentence to describe the situation.

6. Try to model $3 - 5$ using counters. What happens?

Here is a way to model $3 - 5$ using counters.

Show 3 with 3 yellow counters. In order to have enough yellow counters to subtract 5, add 2 yellow and 2 red counters.

Now you can take away 5 yellow counters. There are 2 red counters left. The result is $^-2$.

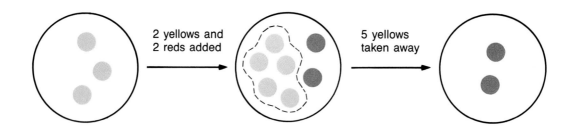

So $3 - 5 = {}^-2$.

7. Model, using two-color counters. Write a number sentence.

    a. $3 - 1$ **b.** $^-3 - {}^-1$ **c.** $^-2 - {}^-4$ **d.** $^-3 - {}^-2$

8. Why can you add pairs of yellow and red counters and not change the situation?

9. How can you tell when you need to add pairs of yellow and red counters in order to subtract?

ON YOUR OWN

Model, using two-color counters. Write a number sentence.

10. $2 - 1$ **11.** $3 - 4$ **12.** $^-3 - ^-1$ **13.** $^-4 - ^-4$

14. $2 - ^-3$ **15.** $5 - ^-2$ **16.** $^-4 - 1$ **17.** $^-2 - 2$

18. $^-1 - ^-1$ **19.** $5 - 4$ **20.** $^-2 - 4$ **21.** $^-4 - 5$

22. $3 - ^-4$ **23.** $^-6 - 3$ **24.** $^-4 - ^-5$ **25.** $5 - ^-2$

26. At 11 P.M. the temperature was 8°C. By the next morning it was $^-4$°C. What was the change in temperature?

27. The high temperature for a cold day was $^-2$°C. The low was $^-7$°C. What was the change in temperature?

28. On December 7, the temperature dropped from 9°C to 3°C. What was the change in temperature?

29. What was the change in temperature if it dropped from a high of 5°C to 0°C?

DEVELOPING A CONCEPT

Subtracting Integers

Besides using counters you can use a number line to model subtracting integers.

WORKING TOGETHER

Look at the following pairs of related number sentences.

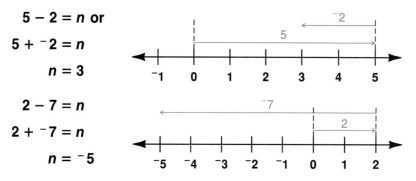

$5 - 2 = n$ **or**

$5 + {}^-2 = n$

$\quad n = 3$

$\quad 2 - 7 = n$

$\quad 2 + {}^-7 = n$

$\quad\quad n = {}^-5$

1. Write a subtraction sentence and a related addition sentence for each number-line model.

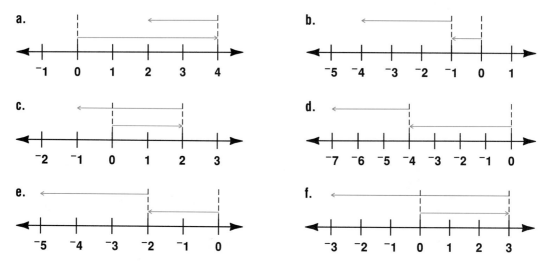

SHARING IDEAS

Look at the pairs of related sentences you found above.

2. How did the operation change?

3. What happened to the second number?

4. What rule can you write for subtracting integers?

PRACTICE

Use your rule to subtract.

5. 4 − 3   **6.** 3 − 5   **7.** 6 − 4   **8.** 5 − 6

9. ⁻2 − ⁻5   **10.** ⁻4 − ⁻2   **11.** ⁻7 − ⁻7   **12.** ⁻5 − ⁻8

13. ⁻8 − 5   **14.** ⁻7 − 2   **15.** 6 − ⁻9   **16.** 3 − ⁻3

17. ⁻4 − 16   **18.** 0 − ⁻5   **19.** 12 − ⁻9   **20.** ⁻11 − 0

21. ⁻8 − ⁻4   **22.** 13 − 7   **23.** 7 − ⁻13   **24.** ⁻11 − 5

25. 7 − 1   **26.** 0 − 6   **27.** ⁻8 − 2   **28.** 15 − ⁻15

Mixed Applications

Solve. Which method did you use?

ESTIMATION
MENTAL MATH
CALCULATOR
PAPER/PENCIL

29. On four consecutive plays the football team gained 3 yd, lost 2 yd, lost 7 yd, and gained 11 yd. How many yards did the team gain or lose all together?

30. The stock of Cal's Sports Equipment started the day at $114\frac{1}{2}$ and rose $7\frac{3}{4}$ points by closing time. What was the closing price?

31. Par for the 18-hole golf course is 72. Karen was 7 over par after the first 9 holes and 2 under par for the second 9 holes. What was her score?

32. Rick bought 25 shares of Sports World at $32.55 a share and 100 shares of Athletics Plus at $12.98 a share. How much did he spend?

UNDERSTANDING A CONCEPT

Adding and Subtracting Integers

A. The temperature in Phoenix one day was 96°F. During a storm the temperature changed by $^-28$°F. What was the resulting temperature?

You can use the following rules to add integers.

> If the integers have the same sign, add the absolute values. Then use the sign of the addends in the sum.

Add: $^-15 + {}^-9$ ***Think:*** same signs

$$^-15 + {}^-9 = |^-15| + |^-9| = 15 + 9 = 24$$

So $^-15 + {}^-9 = {}^-24$.

Add.

1. $15 + 9$ **2.** $^-4 + {}^-6$

> If the integers have different signs, subtract the absolute values. Then use the sign of the addend with the greater absolute value in the answer.

Add: $96 + {}^-28$ ***Think:*** $|96| > |^-28|$

$$96 + {}^-28 = |96| - |^-28| = 96 - 28 = 68$$

So $96 + {}^-28 = 68$. The resulting temperature was 68°F.

Add.

3. $^-46 + 28$ **4.** $23 + {}^-16$

B. You can use the following rule to subtract integers.

> To subtract an integer, add its opposite.

Subtract: $^-15 - 8$ ***Think:*** 8 is the opposite of $^-8$ $^-15 - 8 = {}^-15 + {}^-8 = {}^-23$

Subtract.

5. $^-12 - {}^-4$ **6.** $15 - {}^-6$

7. $9 + {}^-3$ **8.** $12 + {}^-17$ **9.** ${}^-2 - 9$ **10.** $14 - 22$ **11.** ${}^-8 - {}^-20$

PRACTICE

Complete the equation.

12. $4 - 6 = 4 + \blacksquare$ **13.** ${}^-3 - {}^-5 = {}^-3 + \blacksquare$ **14.** $4 - {}^-3 = 4 + \blacksquare$

15. ${}^-9 - 6 = \blacksquare + \blacksquare$ **16.** $8 - {}^-4 = \blacksquare + \blacksquare$ **17.** $14 - 9 = \blacksquare + \blacksquare$

Find the sum or difference.

18. $8 + {}^-9$ **19.** ${}^-12 + 18$ **20.** ${}^-3 - {}^-5$ **21.** ${}^-12 - 18$ **22.** $18 + {}^-14$

23. $5 + {}^-3$ **24.** $0 - {}^-6$ **25.** ${}^-8 + {}^-19$ **26.** $24 - {}^-9$ **27.** ${}^-9 - {}^-13$

28. $34 - 48$ **29.** $6 + {}^-17$ **30.** ${}^-23 -- 45$ **31.** $32 - {}^-32$ **32.** ${}^-14 - {}^-14$

33. ${}^-11 - 22$ **34.** ${}^-34 - {}^-9$ **35.** $56 - 100$ **36.** ${}^-19 + {}^-87$ **37.** $43 + 25$

38. $28 + {}^-43$ **39.** $56 - 88$ **40.** ${}^-23 + 21$ **41.** $16 - {}^-39$ **42.** ${}^-200 + {}^-300$

43. $6 - ({}^-4 + {}^-8)$ **44.** ${}^-12 + ({}^-9 - 18)$ **45.** ${}^-8 + {}^-3 - 7$

Evaluate the expression for the given value.

46. $n - {}^-22$ for $n = 43$ **47.** $24 - n$ for $n = {}^-22$

48. $n + {}^-83$ for $n = 100$ **49.** $56 - n$ for $n = 80$

Critical Thinking

50. Is the sum of two negative integers always negative? Why or why not?

51. Is the difference of two negative integers always negative? Why or why not?

Mixed Applications

52. The high temperature in Palm Desert, California, was 88°F, and that same day the low was ${}^-24$°F in Hibbing, Minnesota. What was the difference between the high and the low?

53. The greatest snowfall ever recorded in the United States in a 24-hour period was 157.5 cm. About how many centimeters of snow fell per hour, on the average?

Mixed Review

Find the answer. Which method did you use?

54. Find 68% of 100.

55. What is 75% of 1,000?

56. Find 35% of 354.

57. What is 0.9% of 7,000?

MENTAL MATH
CALCULATOR
PAPER/PENCIL

✓ UNDERSTAND
✓ PLAN
✓ TRY
CHECK
✓ EXTEND

PROBLEM SOLVING

Writing and Solving an Equation

Reggie started his vacation with $402.40. After 7 days he had $286.50 left. On the average how much did he spend per day?

Reggie plans to use an equation to solve his problem.

To set up the equation, he asks himself these questions:

- What do I know? I know the total amount and the amount left.

- What do I need to know? I need to know my expenses for the week and my average daily expenses.

He thinks: The expenses for the week are $402.40–$286.50. To find the expenses for each day, I'll divide by 7. Reggie represents the average daily expenses with x.

He sets up the equation and solves it.

$$x = \frac{\text{total amount} - \text{amount left}}{\text{number of days}}$$

$$x = \frac{\$402.40 - \$286.50}{7}$$

$$x = \frac{\$115.90}{7}$$

$$x = \$16.557$$

Reggie spent $16.56 to the nearest cent each day.

1. What other equation could Reggie have used to solve this problem?

2. **What if** Reggie had started with $113.56 and ended with $13.61? Write and solve an equation to find out his average daily expenses.

PRACTICE

Write and solve an equation to solve the problem.

3. Fred climbs 500 ft an hour for 3 hours up a mountain. For the next 2 hours, he climbs 756 ft. How high did he climb in those 5 hours?

4. The total regular airfare from Houston to Denver for 300 people is $82,500. At this rate what is the regular airfare per person?

5. Leon and his mother spent $609.12 on 2 airline tickets and cabfare. The cabfare cost $30.12. How much did each plane ticket cost?

6. Mimi's trip would cover 1,098 mi. She has 813 mi left to go. How far has she traveled already?

Strategies and Skills Review

Solve. Use mental math, estimation, a calculator, or paper and pencil.

7. In the Vacationland Mountains, 358 people were at the fair at 3:00. Between 2:00 and 3:00, 18 people left. Between 1:00 and 2:00, 58 more people came. Between 12:00 and 1:00, the number of people doubled. How many people were there at 12:00?

8. Desmond spent $985 on his vacation. This is how he spent the money. Draw a circle graph showing the percent of money spent on each item.

Carfare	$177.30
Lodging	$374.30
Food	$187.15
Recreation	$246.25

9. Kim is studying a map for her vacation. The map has a scale of 1 in. = 125 mi. Kim does not want to travel more than 1,225 mi from home. She draws a circle on the map around where she can go. What is the diameter of the circle?

10. Doug wanted to make 4 stops on his vacation: Lake Hopat, Briney Beach, Mace Mountain, and Willow Creek. How many different ordered ways can he visit these places? List the ways.

11. Catherine ended her vacation with $89.25. She had spend a total of $416 in 8 days. About how much did she spend each day?

12. **Write a problem** that can be solved by writing and solving an equation. Have someone solve the problem.

Using Number Concepts

A. Look at this multiplication problem.

$$
\begin{array}{r}
AB \\
\times\ \ BA \\
\hline
114 \\
3040 \\
\hline
3{,}154
\end{array}
$$

- Each letter stands for a digit from 0 to 9. Two letters stand for a two-digit number.
- A letter has the same value each time it appears in the problem. For example, if A = 6, it will be 6 throughout the problem.
- No two letters stand for the same digit.

What two digits do A and B stand for in the problem above?

1. Think about the first part of the multiplication.

$$
\begin{array}{r}
AB \\
\times\ \ A \\
\hline
114
\end{array}
$$

A cannot be greater than 3. Why? What are the possible values for A?

2. Next note that B × A has a ones digit of 4. List the possible values for A and B (remember what you discovered about A in Problem 1). Test each pair in the multiplication problem until you find the ones that work.

3. What did you find for A and B? Does AB × BA = 3,154? Is there another answer?

B. Here are some other problems for you to try. Make notes to keep track of the information you find at each step in a problem.

4.　ABCD　*Hint:* A must be 1 or 2. Why? Which is it? Then think
　　$\times$　4　about what D can be.
　　DCBA

5.　ABCDE　*Hint:* Start with A again. Then use the same type of
　　$\times$　4　thinking as in problem 4.
　　EDCBA

6.　　USSR　*Hint:* What must P be? Why? What must U be? Why?
　$+$　USA　Next figure out what E must be.
　　PEACE

7. This one is hard, so work with a partner. If you need an extra hint, turn the page upside down.

　　　SEND　*Hint:* What must M be? Why? Then what must O be?
　$+$　MORE　Next find S. Then decide how E and N must be related.
　　MONEY　Try different values until you discover the ones that work.

E = 5

Multiplying Integers

Mel and Bonnie were mountain climbing. During one 4-hour period, the temperature dropped 3 degrees each hour. What was the total change in temperature?

Multiply: $4 \times {}^-3$

WORKING TOGETHER

You can use a number line to model multiplication of integers. Recall that multiplication is repeated addition.

1. How can you model this multiplication using a number line?

2. Write a number sentence for the model.

3. What is the change in temperature?

Here is a way to model the situation using a number line.

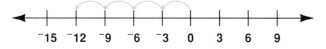

```
   ¯15  ¯12   ¯9   ¯6   ¯3    0    3    6    9
```

4. Find each product using a number line.

   a. $3 \times {}^-4$ **b.** $5 \times {}^-4$
   c. $2 \times {}^-6$ **d.** $6 \times {}^-6$

 You can use a calculator to explore patterns with integers.

5. Use a calculator to complete the number sentences in rows 1–5 of the table at the right.

6. What pattern do you see in the first column of factors?

7. What pattern do you see in the products?

8. Predict the remaining products for rows 6–9. Then use the calculator to find the products and verify your predictions.

Row	Number Sentence
1	$4 \times {}^-7 = $ ▆
2	$3 \times {}^-7 = $ ▆
3	$2 \times {}^-7 = $ ▆
4	$1 \times {}^-7 = $ ▆
5	$0 \times {}^-7 = $ ▆
6	${}^-1 \times {}^-7 = $ ▆
7	${}^-2 \times {}^-7 = $ ▆
8	${}^-3 \times {}^-7 = $ ▆
9	${}^-4 \times {}^-7 = $ ▆

SHARING IDEAS

9. Use your patterns to decide if the product is *positive* or *negative.*

    a. positive integer × negative integer
    b. negative integer × negative integer
    c. positive integer × positive integer

10. What rules can you write to multiply integers?

11. How do your rules compare with these rules?

> The product of two integers with like signs is positive.
> The product of two integers with unlike signs is negative.

12. What would the sign of the product be for 2 positive and 1 negative integer? 2 negative and 1 positive integer? 3 negative integers?

PRACTICE

Multiply.

13. 4 × 4

14. 5 × 7

15. ⁻6 × ⁻2

16. ⁻3 × ⁻8

17. ⁻9 × 2

18. ⁻7 × 6

19. 1 × ⁻6

20. 5 × ⁻4

21. 0 × ⁻7

22. 8 × 4

23. 7 × ⁻9

24. ⁻6 × ⁻6

25. ⁻12 × ⁻12

26. 8 × ⁻11

27. ⁻10 × 6

28. 4 × ⁻12

29. 3 × ⁻1 × 4

30. 1 × ⁻8 × ⁻7

31. 6 × ⁻5 × ⁻2

32. 6 × ⁻2 × 2

33. ⁻3 × ⁻5 × ⁻2

34. 1 × 4 × ⁻2

35. 2 × ⁻3 × 2

36. 3 × ⁻7 × ⁻2

Complete the table.

37.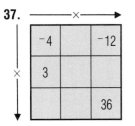

38.

Mixed Applications

39. The members of the Leary family hiked 24.8 km in 8 hours. What was their hiking speed in kilometers per hour?

40. Climbing down from the mountain, Gloria descends 12 m each minute. What is the total change in altitude for a 6-minute descent?

EXTRA Practice, page 571

DEVELOPING A CONCEPT

Dividing Integers

A. Suzanne is a member of a scuba diving club. She descends 12 m beneath the surface of the water in 3 minutes. How can you represent the average change in her position per minute as an integer?

Divide: $^-12 \div 3$

You can use what you know about the inverse relationship of multiplication and division to find this quotient.

Think: $^-4 \times 3 = {}^-12$, so $^-12 \div 3 = {}^-4$.

So Suzanne's average change in position per minute was $^-4$ m. This means she descended beneath the surface at a rate of 4 m per minute.

1. Find $^-25 \div 5$ using the related sentence $^-5 \times 5 = {}^-25$.

B. You can use a calculator to explore division patterns with integers.

2. Use a calculator to complete the number sentences in rows 1–4 of the table at the right.

3. What pattern do you see in the first column of dividends?

4. What pattern do you see in the quotients?

5. Predict the remaining quotients for rows 5–7. Then use the calculator to find the quotients and verify your predictions.

Row	Number Sentence
1	$9 \div 3 = $ ▨
2	$6 \div 3 = $ ▨
3	$3 \div 3 = $ ▨
4	$0 \div 3 = $ ▨
5	$^-3 \div 3 = $ ▨
6	$^-6 \div 3 = $ ▨
7	$^-9 \div 3 = $ ▨

6. Use a calculator to complete the number sentences in rows 1–4 of the table at the right.

7. Look for patterns to predict the quotients for rows 5–7. Then use the calculator to verify your predictions.

8. Use the patterns from both tables to predict the quotients. Then use the calculator to verify your predictions.

a. $^-15 \div 3$ **b.** $^-27 \div {}^-3$

Row	Number Sentence
1	$9 \div {}^-3 = $ ■
2	$6 \div {}^-3 = $ ■
3	$3 \div {}^-3 = $ ■
4	$0 \div {}^-3 = $ ■
5	$^-3 \div {}^-3 = $ ■
6	$^-6 \div {}^-3 = $ ■
7	$^-9 \div {}^-3 = $ ■

9. Use your patterns to decide if the quotient is *positive* or *negative*.

    a. positive integer ÷ negative integer
    b. negative integer ÷ positive integer
    c. negative integer ÷ negative integer
    d. positive integer ÷ positive integer

10. What rules can you write to divide integers?

11. How do your rules compare with these rules?

> The quotient of two integers with like signs is positive.
>
> The quotient of two integers with unlike signs is negative.

PRACTICE

Divide.

12. $28 \div 7$	**13.** $42 \div 6$	**14.** $0 \div {}^-4$	**15.** ${}^-54 \div {}^-9$
16. $40 \div {}^-8$	**17.** $8 \div {}^-4$	**18.** ${}^-30 \div 10$	**19.** ${}^-12 \div 4$
20. ${}^-56 \div 7$	**21.** ${}^-15 \div {}^-3$	**22.** $25 \div 5$	**23.** ${}^-22 \div 11$
24. $24 \div 2$	**25.** $48 \div {}^-8$	**26.** ${}^-72 \div {}^-12$	**27.** $84 \div {}^-4$
28. ${}^-12 \div {}^-3$	**29.** ${}^-108 \div 9$	**30.** $56 \div 4$	**31.** ${}^-24 \div 4$

Compare. Write $>$, $<$, or $=$.

32. ${}^-4 \div {}^-1 \, \bullet \, {}^-9 \div 3$ **33.** ${}^-12 \div 2 \, \bullet \, 15 \div {}^-3$

34. ${}^-18 \div {}^-2 \, \bullet \, 15 \div {}^-3$ **35.** ${}^-12 \times 3 \, \bullet \, 21 \div {}^-3$

36. ${}^-25 \div 5 \, \bullet \, {}^-4 \times 2$ **37.** ${}^-30 \div {}^-5 \, \bullet \, {}^-3 \times {}^-2$

Evaluate $n \div {}^-3$ for the value of n.

38. $n = 6$	**39.** $n = {}^-24$	**40.** $n = 42$	**41.** $n = {}^-120$

Evaluate $(n \div 2) - 4$ for the value of n.

42. $n = 12$	**43.** $n = 20$	**44.** $n = 16$	**45.** $n = 8$

Mixed Applications

46. A climbing party descended 33 m for the first hour and 27 m for the next two hours. Give the change in their position per hour as an integer.

47. *Write a problem* that involves multiplication or division of integers. Solve your problem. Then ask others to solve it.

Scientific Notation

A. Sirah works in a science laboratory as an entomologist. She studies insects. She is studying the parasitic wasp, a tiny insect that has a mass of only 0.000000005 kg. She records the mass using scientific notation.

Scientific notation is a way of renaming numbers as a product of two factors. The first factor is equal to or greater than 1 but less than 10. The second factor is a power of ten. You have used scientific notation to rename greater numbers, for example, $3,700,000 = 3.7 \times 10^6$.

You can also use scientific notation to rename lesser numbers. Look at the pattern.

$10^3 = 1,000$
$10^2 = 100$
$10^1 = 10$
$10^0 = 1$
$10^{-1} = 0.1$
$10^{-2} = 0.01$
$10^{-3} = 0.001$
$10^{-4} = 0.0001$

$10^3 \longleftarrow$ **exponent**
$\uparrow$
base

1. What do you notice about the value of each power of ten as the exponent decreases?

Negative integer exponents are used to rename numbers between 0 and 1. To rename the wasp's mass in scientific notation, you need to use an exponent that is a negative integer.

Step 1 Write the first factor by placing the decimal point to the right of the first nonzero digit.   **5.0**

Step 2 For the negative exponent use the number of places the decimal point was moved to the right.

$$0.000000005.0 = 5.0 \times 10^{-9}$$

B. You can rename a number expressed in scientific notation as a decimal by reversing the steps.

$6.0 \times 10^{-4} = 0.0006. = 0.0006$ $7.4 \times 10^{-7} = 0.0000007.4 = 0.00000074$

Think: Move the decimal point 4 places to the left.

Think: Move the decimal point 7 places to the left.

TRY OUT

Write the decimal.

2. 10^{-3} **3.** 10^{-4} **4.** 10^{-6} **5.** 10^{-7}

Write in scientific notation.

6. 0.06   **7.** 0.007   **8.** 0.0013   **9.** 0.000000083

Write in standard form.

10. 5.0×10^{-2} **11.** 2.4×10^{-4} **12.** 3.12×10^{-2} **13.** 1.89×10^{-5}

PRACTICE

Write as a negative power of 10.

14. 0.001   **15.** 0.0001   **16.** 0.000001   **17.** 0.0000001

Write as a decimal.

18. 10^{-2} **19.** 10^{-5} **20.** 10^{-9} **21.** 10^{-8}

Write in scientific notation.

22. 0.03   **23.** 0.005   **24.** 0.0009   **25.** 0.00008

26. 0.00012   **27.** 0.000046   **28.** 0.0000058   **29.** 0.0000124

30. 0.00038   **31.** 0.00562   **32.** 0.0000000123   **33.** 0.000412

Write in standard form.

34. 7.0×10^{-1} **35.** 4.0×10^{-4} **36.** 3.0×10^{-3} **37.** 8.0×10^{-5}

38. 5.1×10^{-5} **39.** 6.21×10^{-6} **40.** 5.63×10^{-4} **41.** 7.16×10^{-5}

Mixed Applications

42. Male banded lice may have a mass of as little as 0.005 mg each. Rename this mass in kilograms, using scientific notation.

43. The male cicada makes a sound at the rate of 7,400 pulses per minute. How many pulses per hour is that? Write your answer in scientific notation.

Mixed Review

MENTAL MATH
CALCULATOR
PAPER/PENCIL

Find the answer. Which method did you use?

44. $4\frac{1}{8} - \frac{7}{8}$ **45.** $1\frac{7}{12} + 1\frac{1}{6}$ **46.** 1.5×5

47. $2\frac{1}{4} \div 3\frac{3}{8}$ **48.** $6.3 \div (0.3 \times 1.05)$ **49.** $13\frac{5}{12} + 8\frac{1}{4}$

Integers and Coordinate Graphing   **559**

UNDERSTANDING A CONCEPT

Graphing Sentences

A. You can solve an equation and graph the solution on a number line.

Solve. $n + 14 = 21$

Think: 14 is added to n.
Subtract 14 from each side.

$$n + 14 - 14 = 21 - 14$$
$$n = 7$$

Here is the graph of the equation $n + 14 = 21$, or $n = 7$.

The graph is just one point. A solid circle at 7 means that 7 is a solution of the equation.

1. Graph the solution of each equation.

    a. $n + 2 = 4$ **b.** $x + 3 = 9$ **c.** $y - 6 = 7$

B. You can solve an inequality and graph its solution on a number line. Recall that an inequality is a number sentence that uses one of the inequality symbols, $>$ or $<$. $>$ means *is greater than* and $<$ means *is less than*.

Solve. $n + 14 > 21$

Think: Use a related equation. $n + 14 = 21$

Solve the equation. $n + 14 - 14 = 21 - 14$
$$n = 7$$

Write the solution to the inequality. $n > 7$

Here is the graph of the inequality $n + 14 > 7$, or $n > 7$.

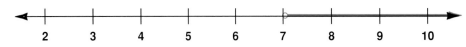

Note that an open circle at 7 means that 7 is *not* a solution. Use an arrow to show that all points to the right of 7 are solutions.

2. *What if* the solution to the inequality was $n \geq 7$? How would the graph change?

3. *What if* the solution was $n < 7$? How would the graph change?

Graph the solution.

4. $n + 6 = 9$ **5.** $n - 5 = 3$ **6.** $n + 3 < 6$ **7.** $n + 4 > 8$

PRACTICE

Write an inequality for the graph.

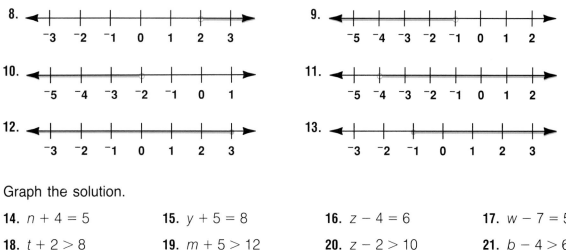

8.   ⁻3 ⁻2 ⁻1 0 1 2 3   **9.**   ⁻5 ⁻4 ⁻3 ⁻2 ⁻1 0 1 2

10.   ⁻5 ⁻4 ⁻3 ⁻2 ⁻1 0 1   **11.**   ⁻5 ⁻4 ⁻3 ⁻2 ⁻1 0 1 2

12.   ⁻3 ⁻2 ⁻1 0 1 2 3   **13.**   ⁻3 ⁻2 ⁻1 0 1 2 3

Graph the solution.

14. $n + 4 = 5$ **15.** $y + 5 = 8$ **16.** $z - 4 = 6$ **17.** $w - 7 = 5$

18. $t + 2 > 8$ **19.** $m + 5 > 12$ **20.** $z - 2 > 10$ **21.** $b - 4 > 6$

22. $p + 2 < 8$ **23.** $x + 6 < 7$ **24.** $f - 3 < 4$ **25.** $t - 6 < 10$

26. $z - 4 < {}^-3$ **27.** $t + 4 > {}^-6$ **28.** $n - 2 \leq {}^-4$ **29.** $d + 4 \geq 0$

Mixed Applications

Solve. You may need to use the Databank on page 585.

30. Reggie saw 3 plays in 4 days. At that rate how many plays will he see during the 4 weeks he will be in New York?

31. Elaine saw a play that was 3.5 hours long. She slept through two-thirds of it. How long was the part for which she was awake?

32. For the new hit play *Scarecrow,* the stage crew constructed a huge scarecrow that is taller than any ever built. Draw a graph of the inequality that expresses the height of this scarecrow.

33. *Write two problems* that can be solved by solving inequalities. Give the solution and graph for each. Ask others to match the inequality with its correct graph.

Mixed Review

Find the answer. Which method did you use?

MENTAL MATH
CALCULATOR
PAPER/PENCIL

34. 20% of 300   **35.** $n + 6 > 12$ **36.** $6.12 \div 1.8$

37. $\frac{3}{4}$ of 628   **38.** $^-4 \times {}^-3 \times {}^-5$ **39.** $3.47 \times 1{,}000$

UNDERSTANDING A CONCEPT

Graphing Ordered Pairs

A. A **coordinate plane** is represented by two perpendicular number lines that intersect at a point called the **origin.** Every point on the plane corresponds to an **ordered pair** of numbers, (x, y), the coordinates of the point. The **x-coordinate** indicates the number of units to move to the right or the left from the origin along the **x-axis.** The **y-coordinate** indicates the number of units to move up or down along the **y-axis.**

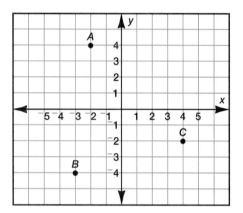

B. Find the coordinates of point A.

Point A is $^-2$ units on the x-axis, so $x = ^-2$. Point A is 4 units on the y-axis, so $y = 4$. The coordinates of point A are $(^-2, 4)$.

1. Would you expect the coordinates of point B to be positive or negative? What are the coordinates?

2. What are the coordinates of point C?

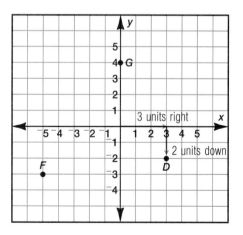

C. You can also locate a point on the plane, given its coordinates.

Graph $(3, ^-2)$.

Start at the origin. Move 3 units to the right. Then move 2 units down. Label the point D. The coordinates of D are $(3, ^-2)$.

3. **What if** you wanted to graph $(^-3, ^-2)$? What would you do differently?

TRY OUT Use graph paper to copy the coordinate grid in C.

Give the coordinates of the point.

4. F **5.** G

Graph the point.

6. $(2, ^-4)$ **7.** $(^-3, 0)$

PRACTICE

Give the coordinates of the point.

8. *A* **9.** *B* **10.** *C* **11.** *D*

12. *E* **13.** *F* **14.** *G* **15.** *H*

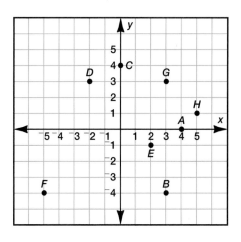

Graph the point on a coordinate grid.

16. (2, 1) **17.** (⁻4, 3) **18.** (⁻2, 0) **19.** (5, ⁻3)

20. (0, ⁻4) **21.** (⁻3, ⁻5) **22.** (4, 3) **23.** (5, 0)

24. (1, ⁻3) **25.** (⁻2, ⁻2) **26.** (⁻4, ⁻5) **27.** (0, 3)

Graph the set of points on a single coordinate axis. Connect the points in the order that they are given. Connect the last point to the first. What figure did you graph?

28. (⁻3, ⁻2), (⁻3, 3), (4, 3), (4, ⁻2)

29. (4, ⁻3), (4, 1), (0, 1), (0, ⁻3)

30. (0, 6), (4, 3), (⁻1, ⁻3)

31. (3, 3), (7, 1), (3, ⁻1), (⁻1, 1)

32. (1, 5), (5, 2), (1, ⁻1), (⁻3, 0), (⁻4, 3)

33. (⁻7.5, ⁻3.5), (⁻6, 2.25), (⁻4, 2.25), (⁻1.5, ⁻3.5)

34. Given the points (0, 3) and (6, 3), find two sets of points that can be used to complete a square.

35. Given the points (0, 4), (1, 0), and (5, 4), find the set of points that can be used to complete a parallelogram.

Critical Thinking
36. What is the *x*-coordinate of a point on the *y*-axis? What is the *y*-coordinate of a point on the *x*-axis?

Mixed Applications
Maryanne planned to make a model of her room to use when redecorating it.

37. She plotted the following points: (⁻6, ⁻4), (⁻6, 1), (⁻2, 1), (⁻2, 3), (0, 3), (0, 1), and (0, ⁻4). Plot the points and connect them to make a scale drawing of her room and the closet.

38. The main part of Maryanne's room is 10 ft by 12 ft. If she can purchase carpeting for $24.99 per yd², how much will it cost to carpet the main part of her room?

✓ UNDERSTAND
✓ PLAN
✓ TRY
✓ CHECK
✓ EXTEND

P ROBLEM SOLVING

Strategies Review

Use these problem-solving strategies to solve the problems.

- Conducting a Simulation
- Making a Model
- Conducting an Experiment
- Using Guess, Test, and Revise
- Solving a Multistep Problem
- Drawing a Diagram
- Using a Formula
- Using Spatial Thinking

- Making a Circle Graph
- Making a Table
- Using Number Sense
- Finding a Pattern
- Making an Organized List
- Solving a Simpler Problem
- Working Backward
- Writing and Solving an Equation

Solve. Tell which strategy you used.

1. A person is standing on the third rung of a ladder. The ladder has 7 rungs. Flip a coin to stimulate movement on the ladder. A flip of heads means up one rung; tails means down one rung. Keep flipping until the person reaches the top or bottom rung. How often will the person reach the bottom step? Do this simulation 10 times. Record your results.

2. A long, straight trail stretches east to west. The 0 mile marker is on the western end of the trail. A hiker is at mile marker 83 on Friday. On Thursday she hiked east 42 mi. On Wednesday she hiked west 12 mi. On Tuesday, when she started, she hiked west 6 mi and east 12 mi. What mile marker did she start from?

3. The circle graph at the right shows how Ron spent his allowance each month. If his monthly allowance was $31.00, how much did he spend on each category?

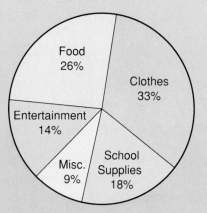

Food 26%

Clothes 33%

Entertainment 14%

Misc. 9%

School Supplies 18%

4. An architect was working on a tile design for a rectangular floor. She thought she would make a design using only one kind of triangle. Show whether or not this can be done.

5. A manufacturer is making accessories from a rectangular prism of plastic foam which measures 12 ft by 5 ft by 4 ft. If the prism is cut into three identical pieces, what is the volume of each piece?

6. An oceanographer took core samples from the ocean floor. Each sample was a cylinder 3 in. across. How much earth was in a sample 6 ft long?

7. Designers are making a scale model of a house. They use the scale of 1 cm = 1.5 ft. One room is 9 ft by 12 ft. What are the scale dimensions of the room?

8. The scout troops sell cups of juice to earn money. They make $.04 on each small cup and $.06 on each large cup. Troop 1 sells 234 small cups and 56 large cups. Troop 2 sells 132 small cups and 82 large cups. How much money will the 2 troops make from selling juice?

9. A circular room is surrounded by 5 other rooms. The designers of these rooms want to use as few doors as possible. They want to be able to get from one room to another and to pass through all the doors once and only once. Draw a diagram to show how this can be done.

10. A designer with a love of hiking devised a trail with the following patterned markers:

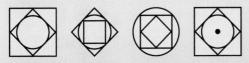

If the pattern continues what should the patterns on the next 2 markers look like?

11. Three sacks of gold coins are kept in a chest. There is a saying on the side of the chest, "Three sacks of gold in here, 171 in sum. The second sack holds twice as much as the first. The last is mean, a mean of the first two." How many coins are in each sack?

DECISION MAKING

COOPERATIVE
LEARNING

Problem Solving: Choosing a Bicycle Route

SITUATION

The bicycle club wants to have a picnic at Stoney Point. They have a
map of the area with three bicycle routes roughly indicated by
coordinates.

PROBLEM

Which bicycle route should the bicycle club choose?

DATA

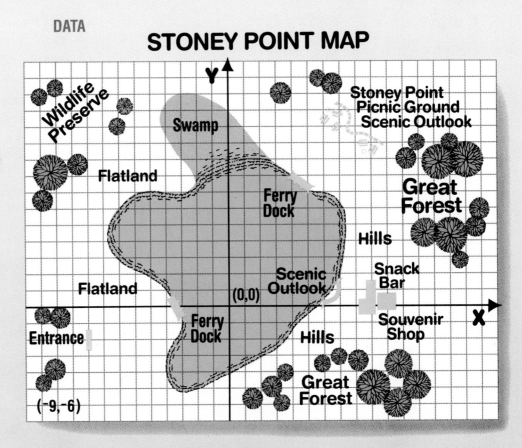

STONEY POINT MAP

● **Blue Route:** (-9,-6), (-4,-6), (0,-5), (4,-3), (6,-1), (8, 2), (8, 7), (7,10)
▲ **Red Route:** (-9,-6), (-10,-3), (-9,-1), (-8, 2), (-9, 4), (-8, 6), (-3, 8), (-5,12), (-3,14),
     (1,12), (3,10), (6, 9), (7,10)
■ **Green Route:** (-9,-6), (-8,-5), (-7,-4), (-6,-3), (-5,-2), (-4,-1), (5, 8), (6, 9), (7,10)

There is an entrance fee of $2.00 to the Wildlife Preserve.
There are a great many birds in the swamp area.
The cost of the Ferry is $3.50 one way.
There is no entrance fee to the Great Forest.

USING THE DATA

Plot the points for the route on graph paper.

1. Blue Route   **2.** Red Route   **3.** Green Route

How much does each route cost?

4. Blue Route   **5.** Red Route   **6.** Green Route

7. Which is the longest route?

8. Which route goes along flatland? over hills?

9. Which route goes by the scenic outlook and snack bar?

MAKING DECISIONS

What are the advantages of each route?

10. Blue Route   **11.** Red Route   **12.** Green Route

What are the disadvantages of each route?

13. Blue Route   **14.** Red Route   **15.** Green Route

16. *Write a list* of other factors the bicycle club should consider in choosing a bicycle route.

17. Which route would you choose? Why?

Math and Science

Rene Descartes (1596–1650) was a very young man in France when he began to revolutionize the mathematical world. While serving as a soldier, he spent a great deal of time in the study of mathematics. He developed a whole new philosophy of human thought, and in the process he developed a new branch of mathematics—analytic geometry.

One of the most useful of Descartes's gifts to mathematics was coordinate graphing.

Many cities are laid out with a main street in each direction through the center of town. Buildings are numbered in both directions from the main streets. The designations East, West, North, or South are used with the numbers to tell which side of the main streets a certain location is. A city that is laid out this way uses a coordinate system.

What if a city numbers buildings in the first block on each side of the center of town in the hundreds? Each succeeding block starts a new hundred. Give one set of directions for getting from the intersection of 400 South and 300 West to the intersection of 500 North and 600 East. How many blocks is it?

Think: There are several directions you could give. For example, you could go north 4 blocks from 400 South to the main street and 5 blocks more to 500 North. Then you would go 3 blocks east from 300 West to the center street and 6 blocks more to 600 East. The total number of blocks is 18. No matter which route is taken, the number of blocks is the same.

ACTIVITIES

1. Work with a partner to determine at least two other routes from 400 South and 300 West to 500 North and 600 East.

2. Use a map of the city, town, or county where you live. Mark where other students live. Practice giving directions to different homes using coordinates.

Calculator: Order of Operations

You can perform a series of operations on a calculator and obtain the correct answer according to the order of operations. One way is to use the calculator's memory keys.

Find: $16 + 8 \div 4 - 6$

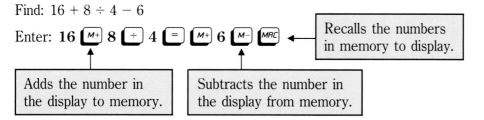

Enter: 16 **M+** 8 **÷** 4 **=** **M+** 6 **M−** **MRC** ← Recalls the numbers in memory to display.

Adds the number in the display to memory.

Subtracts the number in the display from memory.

The calculator will display 12.

When an operation involves *negative* numbers, you can use your calculator's *change-sign* key. This is the **+/−** key on the top of the first column of keys.

Find: $4 \times {}^- 6$

Enter: 4 **×** 6 **+/−** **=**. The calculator will display $\boxed{-24.}$.

$4 \times {}^- 6 = {}^- 24$

Use the memory keys *and* the **+/−** key to perform a series of operations involving negative numbers. Follow along on your calculator.

Find: $4 + 3 \times {}^- 2 - 5$

Enter: 4 **M+** 3 **×** 2 **+/−** **M+** 5 **M−** **MRC**. The calculator will display $\boxed{M \qquad 7.}$.

$4 + 3 \times {}^- 2 - 5 = {}^- 7$

USING THE CALCULATOR

Find. Use the calculator's +/− key.

1. $5 \times {}^- 4$
2. $3 \times {}^- 7$
3. ${}^- 4 \times {}^- 8$
4. ${}^- 2 \times 12$
5. $6 \times {}^- 7$
6. ${}^- 4 \times {}^- 3 \times {}^- 2$
7. $3 \times {}^- 8 \times {}^- 4$
8. ${}^- 4 \times {}^- 9 \times {}^- 2$

Find the answer. Use the calculator's memory keys and the +/− key.

9. $12 + 3 \times {}^- 3 + 5$
10. $20 - 4 \times {}^- 2 - 5$
11. $(6 \times {}^- 3) - ({}^- 4 \times 2)$
12. $25 - {}^- 5 - ({}^- 2 \times {}^- 5)$
13. $24 \times (4 + {}^- 5)$
14. $3 + {}^- 5 \times {}^- 3 - {}^- 7$

15. Explore using the memory keys and the **+/−** key. Is the order in which you have been pressing these keys the only way to get the correct answer?

EXTRA PRACTICE

Comparing and Ordering Integers, page 539

Compare. Write >, <, or =.

1. 7 ● 4

2. 12 ● 28

3. ⁻5 ● ⁻8

4. ⁻24 ● ⁻16

5. 8 ● ⁻7

6. 35 ● ⁻13

7. ⁻24 ● 12

8. ⁻35 ● 51

9. ⁻6 ● ⁻5

10. ⁻25 ● ⁻45

11. ⁻38 ● 26

12. 15 ● ⁻18

Write the integers in order from least to greatest.

13. ⁻4, 9, ⁻13

14. 3, ⁻5, ⁻11

15. ⁻342, 342, ⁻350, 347

16. ⁻5, ⁻7, 4, ⁻10, 0

17. ⁻26, ⁻28, ⁻31, 32, 27

18. 152, ⁻153, 240, ⁻257, ⁻176

Adding Integers, page 543

Add. Use a number line to check.

1. 7 + 13

2. 8 + 5

3. ⁻4 + ⁻8

4. ⁻5 + ⁻7

5. 4 + ⁻7

6. ⁻9 + 6

7. ⁻4 + 4

8. ⁻8 + 9

9. 8 + ⁻17

10. ⁻2 + 6

11. 28 + 7

12. 0 + ⁻15

13. 17 + ⁻4

14. 8 + 11

15. 1 + ⁻3

16. ⁻17 + ⁻9

17. ⁻5 + ⁻6 + 4

18. 8 + ⁻5 + ⁻3

19. ⁻9 + 4 + 5

20. ⁻4 + ⁻2 + 1

21. ⁻7 + 13 + 2

22. ⁻8 + ⁻7 + 2

23. ⁻5 + 3 + ⁻7

24. ⁻6 + ⁻6 + 2

Subtracting Integers, page 547

Use your rule to subtract.

1. 7 − 5

2. 4 − 8

3. 9 − 4

4. 7 − 8

5. ⁻3 − ⁻7

6. ⁻3 − ⁻2

7. ⁻8 − ⁻8

8. ⁻4 − ⁻9

9. ⁻7 − 3

10. ⁻9 − 2

11. 5 − ⁻9

12. 2 − ⁻2

13. ⁻5 − 17

14. 0 − ⁻7

15. 13 − ⁻9

16. ⁻12 − 0

17. ⁻7 − ⁻3

18. 14 − 8

19. 6 − ⁻12

20. ⁻10 − 4

21. 9 − 2

22. 0 − 7

23. ⁻9 − 3

24. 16 − ⁻16

Adding and Subtracting Integers, page 549

Find the sum or difference.

1. $7 + {}^-8$ **2.** ${}^-11 + 17$ **3.** ${}^-2 - {}^-4$ **4.** ${}^-11 - 17$ **5.** $17 + {}^-13$

6. $4 + {}^-2$ **7.** $0 - {}^-5$ **8.** ${}^-7 + {}^-18$ **9.** $23 - {}^-8$ **10.** ${}^-8 - {}^-12$

11. ${}^-10 - 21$ **12.** ${}^-33 - {}^-8$ **13.** $55 - 100$ **14.** ${}^-18 + {}^-86$ **15.** $42 + 24$

16. $25 + {}^-34$ **17.** $25 - 40$ **18.** ${}^-33 + 31$ **19.** $15 - {}^-29$ **20.** ${}^-150 + {}^-250$

21. $7 - ({}^-5 + {}^-9)$ **22.** ${}^-15 + ({}^-10 - 19)$ **23.** ${}^-9 - {}^-4 - 8$

24. ${}^-12 - (7 - {}^-2) + 3$ **25.** $8 + ({}^-3 + {}^-6) - 7$ **26.** ${}^-133 + ({}^-7 - {}^-90) - 9$

27. $1 - (12 + {}^-3) - {}^-5$ **28.** ${}^-13 + {}^-2 - {}^-4 + 7$ **29.** $18 - {}^-11 - {}^-2 + {}^-4$

Problem Solving: Writing and Solving an Equation, page 551

Write an equation and solve.

1. Martine opened a savings account at her company's credit union. She opened the account with a check for $348.80. After 10 days, her balance was $421.50. On the average, how much did she deposit per day?

2. Knox invited 4 of his friends to a concert and dinner. He spent a total of $267.78. The dinner for four cost $127.78. How much did Knox pay for each concert ticket?

3. Lizabeth cycled 12 mi per day for 10 days. In 6 more days she cycled an additional 78 mi. How many miles did she cycle over the 16-day period?

4. Harold bought a suit and 2 shirts for $268.50. The suit cost $198.50. How much did each shirt cost?

Multiplying Integers, page 555

Multiply.

1. ${}^-2 \times 9$ **2.** ${}^-10 \times 10$ **3.** 7×8 **4.** ${}^-7 \times 0$ **5.** $5 \times {}^-9$

6. $0 \times {}^-8$ **7.** ${}^-3 \times {}^-6$ **8.** ${}^-12 \times 5$ **9.** ${}^-4 \times {}^-4$ **10.** $4 \times {}^-9$

11. $2 \times {}^-2 \times 5$ **12.** ${}^-2 \times {}^-5 \times {}^-3$ **13.** ${}^-8 \times 1 \times {}^-2$ **14.** $0 \times {}^-4 \times {}^-6$

15. $14 \times {}^-3 \times 2$ **16.** ${}^-7 \times {}^-8 \times {}^-3$ **17.** $13 \times 3 \times {}^-7$ **18.** $20 \times {}^-4 \times {}^-3$

19. ${}^-10 \times 3 \times {}^-5$ **20.** $11 \times {}^-1 \times {}^-3$

EXTRA PRACTICE

Dividing Integers, page 557 ....

Solve.

1. 35 ÷ 7 **2.** 48 ÷ 6 **3.** 0 ÷ ⁻5 **4.** ⁻63 ÷ ⁻9

5. 32 ÷ ⁻8 **6.** 12 ÷ ⁻4 **7.** ⁻40 ÷ 10 **8.** ⁻16 ÷ 8

9. ⁻49 ÷ 7 **10.** ⁻21 ÷ ⁻3 **11.** 30 ÷ 5 **12.** ⁻33 ÷ 11

13. 36 ÷ 2 **14.** 64 ÷ ⁻8 **15.** ⁻84 ÷ ⁻12 **16.** 88 ÷ ⁻8

17. ⁻24 ÷ ⁻3 **18.** ⁻96 ÷ 8 **19.** 42 ÷ 3 **20.** ⁻28 ÷ 4

21. 27 ÷ 3 **22.** 14 ÷ ⁻2 **23.** 20 ÷ 20 **24.** ⁻132 ÷ ⁻12

Scientific Notation, page 559 ....

Write in scientific notation.

1. 0.04 **2.** 0.007 **3.** 0.0008 **4.** 0.00009

5. 0.00014 **6.** 0.000027 **7.** 0.0000078 **8.** 0.0000138

9. 0.00065 **10.** 0.00487 **11.** 0.0000000137 **12.** 0.000517

Write in standard form.

13. 8.0×10^{-2} **14.** 5.0×10^{-3} **15.** 6.1×10^{-4} **16.** 7.0×10^{-6}

17. 7.2×10^{-1} **18.** 3.81×10^{-5} **19.** 2.75×10^{-3} **20.** 9.17×10^{-6}

Graphing Inequalities, page 561 ....

Write an inequality for the graph.

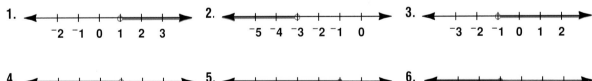

Graph the solution.

7. $n + 3 = 5$ **8.** $y + 4 = 8$ **9.** $z - 3 = 6$ **10.** $w = 8 + 5$

11. $t + 3 > 8$ **12.** $m + 4 > 12$ **13.** $n - 3 > 10$ **14.** $b - 5 > 7$

15. $p + 3 < 8$ **16.** $x + 7 < 8$ **17.** $f - 4 < 5$ **18.** $t - 6 > 11$

19. $z - 5 < ⁻4$ **20.** $t + 5 > ⁻7$ **21.** $n - 3 \leq ⁻5$ **22.** $d + 5 \geq 0$

EXTRA PRACTICE

Graphing Ordered Pairs, page 563 ....

Give the coordinates of the point.

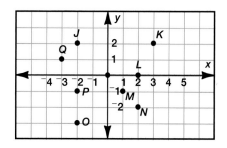

1. J   **2.** K   **3.** L   **4.** M

5. N   **6.** O   **7.** P   **8.** Q

Graph the point on a coordinate grid.

9. A (3, 1)   **10.** B (⁻5, 2)   **11.** C (⁻3, 0)   **12.** O (5, ⁻2)   **13.** E (0, ⁻3)

14. F (⁻4, ⁻5)   **15.** G (4, 2)   **16.** H (2, 0)   **17.** R (1, ⁻4)   **18.** S (⁻3, ⁻3)

Graph the set of points on a coordinate axis. Connect the points in the order that they are given. Connect the last point to the first. What figure did you graph?

19. (⁻6, 0)   **20.** (⁻3, 5)   **21.** (⁻2, 7)   **22.** (⁻1, 5)   **23.** (6, 0)   **24.** (6, ⁻1)

25. (5, ⁻2)   **26.** (3, ⁻1)   **27.** (5, ⁻3)   **28.** (4, ⁻3)   **29.** (⁻1, ⁻1)   **30.** (⁻2, ⁻6)

Problem Solving: Strategies Review, page 565 ....

Solve. Tell which strategy you used.

1. The circle graph at the right shows the most popular summer programs and activities at Green Mountain Camp. If the total number of campers is 125, how many participate in each program or activity?

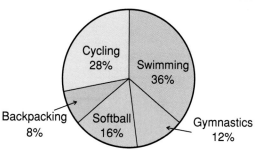

2. A certain charity sells household items to earn money. They make $.04 on each pot holder, $.06 on each dust mop, and $.09 on each broom they sell. On Monday Mona sells 282 pot holders and 57 dust mops. Gene sells 161 brooms, 48 dust mops, and 158 pot holders. How much money will the two volunteers earn for the charity?

3. Thruway 84 goes from north to south. A trucker starts at the northernmost end and drives south 173 mi on Monday morning. That afternoon he drives south another 87 mi. On Monday night he drives north 110 mi stopping at a truck depot for the night. How many miles is it from the beginning of thruway 84 in the north to the truck depot?

PRACTICE *PLUS*

KEY SKILL: Adding and Subtracting Integers (Use after page 549.)

Level A

Complete the equation.

1. $3 - 7 = 3 + \blacksquare$ **2.** $^-2 - ^-8 = ^-2 + \blacksquare$ **3.** $5 - ^-4 = \blacksquare + \blacksquare$ **4.** $^-7 - 5 = \blacksquare + \blacksquare$

5. $6 - 2 = 6 + \blacksquare$ **6.** $7 - ^-4 = 7 + \blacksquare$ **7.** $^-8 - 3 = \blacksquare + \blacksquare$ **8.** $5 - 5 = \blacksquare + \blacksquare$

Find the sum or difference.

9. $6 + ^-8$ **10.** $^-11 + 17$ **11.** $^-4 - ^-7$ **12.** $^-3 - 5$ **13.** $^-7 + ^-9$

14. $^-5 + ^-7$ **15.** $4 - 8$ **16.** $6 - ^-7$ **17.** $^-8 - ^-4$ **18.** $^-7 - ^-9$

19. The low temperature in Coldsburg was $^-12°F$ on Monday. The high was $^-8°F$. What was the difference between the low and high?

Level B

Find the sum or difference.

20. $17 + ^-22$ **21.** $^-31 + 42$ **22.** $^-51 - ^-64$ **23.** $^-75 - 78$ **24.** $^-46 + ^-54$

25. $87 - 100$ **26.** $45 - ^-45$ **27.** $26 + ^-36$ **28.** $^-17 - ^-15$ **29.** $19 - 86$

30. $20 + ^-37$ **31.** $^-17 - ^-8$ **32.** $^-43 + 62$ **33.** $71 - ^-96$ **34.** $^-83 - ^-92$

35. The temperature was $^-15°F$ at 8:00 A.M. It rose 25 degrees by noon and then dropped 8 degrees by 6:00 P.M. What was the temperature at 6:00 P.M.?

Level C

Find the sum or difference.

36. $8 - (^-7 + ^-11)$ **37.** $^-15 + (^-8 - 17)$ **38.** $^-6 - ^-2 - 5$

39. $^-17 + (32 - 58) - 12$ **40.** $(^-30 + ^-57) + (^-13 + 7)$ **41.** $(^-28 - ^-27) - 85$

Evaluate the expression for the given value.

42. $n - ^-32$ for $n = 54$ **43.** $14 - n$ for $n = ^-18$ **44.** $n + ^-52$ for $n = 100$

45. $103 - n$ for $n = ^-185$ **46.** $^-82 + n$ for $n = ^-140$ **47.** $(n - 16) - (33 + n)$ for $n = 3$

48. A company lost 4.5 million on Monday, made 6.8 million on Tuesday, lost 2.5 million on Wednesday, gained 3.2 million Thursday, lost 0.5 million Friday. What was the overall change for the week?

Practice PLUS

KEY SKILL: Dividing Integers (Use after page 557.)

Level A ···
Divide.

1. $^-28 \div ^-7$
2. $30 \div ^-6$
3. $16 \div ^-4$
4. $^-20 \div ^-10$

5. $^-12 \div 3$
6. $0 \div ^-5$
7. $^-56 \div 8$
8. $^-15 \div ^-5$

9. $35 \div 5$
10. $^-24 \div 6$
11. $48 \div ^-6$
12. $^-72 \div ^-9$

13. $^-81 \div 9$
14. $45 \div ^-5$
15. $^-96 \div ^-12$
16. $^-39 \div ^-13$

17. Annette dived 15 m beneath the surface of the water in 3 minutes. Represent the average change in her position per minute as an integer.

Level B ···
Divide.

18. $48 \div ^-8$
19. $32 \div ^-4$
20. $^-60 \div 10$
21. $^-36 \div 9$

22. $^-63 \div 7$
23. $^-25 \div ^-5$
24. $^-66 \div 11$
25. $54 \div ^-6$

26. $^-84 \div ^-12$
27. $^-30 \div ^-3$
28. $^-108 \div 12$
29. $^-169 \div ^-13$

30. $^-91 \div 13$
31. $68 \div ^-17$
32. $^-210 \div ^-14$
33. $621 \div ^-27$

34. Gregory dived 7 m below the water's surface, swam up 3 m toward the surface, and then descended for 6 m. How far from the surface was he after the last descent?

Level C ···
Compare. Write $>$, $<$, or $=$.

35. $^-5 \div ^-1$ ▆ $^-8 \div 4$
36. $^-16 \div 2$ ▆ $18 \div ^-3$
37. $^-12 \div ^-2$ ▆ $25 \div ^-5$

38. $^-9 \times 3$ ▆ $28 \div ^-7$
39. $^-35 \div 7$ ▆ $^-3 \times 3$
40. $^-40 \div ^-5$ ▆ $^-4 \times ^-2$

Evaluate $(n \div 3) - 2$ for the value of n.

41. $n = 6$
42. $n = ^-18$
43. $n = 33$
44. $n = ^-150$
45. $n = ^-30$

46. $n = ^-39$
47. $n = 78$
48. $n = ^-96$
49. $n = ^-102$
50. $n = 168$

51. Stephanie dived 18 m below the water's surface, swam up 6 m toward the surface, and then descended for 5 m. David dived 15 m below the water's surface, swam up 4 m, and then descended 7 m. Who is farther below the surface?

CHAPTER REVIEW

LANGUAGE AND MATHEMATICS

Complete the sentences. Use the words in the chart on the right.

1. Two integers that are the same distance from zero on a number line are ■. *(page 538)*

2. The distance an integer is from zero on a number line is called its ■. *(page 538)*

3. The ■ on a coordinate plane is the point where the *x*- and *y*-axes intersect. *(page 562)*

4. The coordinates of points on a coordinate plane are ■ of numbers. *(page 562)*

5. ***Write a definition*** or give an example of the words you did not use from the chart.

> **VOCABULARY**
> positive integer(s)
> negative integer(s)
> opposite(s)
> absolute value
> ordered pair(s)
> origin

CONCEPTS AND SKILLS

Compare using >, <, or =. *(pages 538, 542)*

6. 20 ● ⁻30   7. ⁻34 ● ⁻33   8. 0 ● ⁻45   9. ⁻2 + 1 ● 1 + ⁻2

Write an integer to describe the situation. *(page 538)*.

10. a loss of $37

11. an altitude of 3,250 ft

12. 12 degrees below 0

13. a depth of 6 m below sea level

14. a gain of 8 yd

15. a deposit of $125

Find the absolute value of the integer.

16. |⁻4| 17. |16| 18. |0| 19. |⁻147|

Write in order from least to greatest. *(page 538)*

20. 0, 10, ⁻20, 30, ⁻40, 50, ⁻60

21. 2, ⁻2, 41, ⁻41, 62, ⁻62, 0, 13, ⁻1

22. ⁻1, ⁻5, 4, 3, 0, ⁻2, ⁻16

23. 4, ⁻5, ⁻9, 10, ⁻8, 12, 27

Add, subtract, multiply, or divide. *(pages 548, 554, 556)*

24. ⁻12 + ⁻26   25. 23 − ⁻3   26. ⁻5 × 12   27. ⁻8 ÷ 8

28. ⁻4 − ⁻5   29. 32 + ⁻45   30. 45 ÷ 5   31. ⁻42 × ⁻1

32. ⁻6 × 5   33. ⁻3 × ⁻3   34. ⁻9 + 0   35. 0 + ⁻4

36. 9 ÷ ⁻3   37. ⁻40 ÷ ⁻8   38. 0 − 7   39. ⁻89 + ⁻100

Write in scientific notation. *(page 558)*

40. 0.03   **41.** 0.0046   **42.** 0.00000809   **43.** 0.2

Write in standard form. *(page 558)*

44. 7.0×10^{-5} **45.** 4.7×10^{-1} **46.** 9.06×10^{-2} **47.** 4.65×10^{-6}

Graph the solution on a number line. *(page 560)*

48. $n + 7 < {}^-9$ **49.** $x - 4 > 2$ **50.** $d + 5 < 0$ **51.** $f - 8 > {}^-4$

Graph each point on a coordinate grid. *(page 562)*

52. $({}^-4, 1)$ **53.** $(2, {}^-3)$ **54.** $({}^-1, 0)$ **55.** $({}^-2, {}^-4)$

56. $(3, 5)$ **57.** $(0, {}^-4)$ **58.** $(1, 9)$ **59.** $({}^-5, 6)$

Critical Thinking

60. If you connect the points (a, b) and (c, d), they form a vertical line segment. Which variables must be equal? *(page 562)*

61. The point (j, k) is to the left of the y axis. Which variable must be negative? *(page 562)*

62. The point (m, n) is the same distance from the origin as the point (p, n). What must be true about m and p? *(pages 538, 562)*

63. The point (r, t) is farther from the origin than the point (r, u). Write an inequality to show the relationship between t and u. *(pages 538, 562)*

Mixed Applications

First write an equation and then solve.

64. This morning's temperature was ${}^-3°F$. The temperature reached a high after rising $12°F$. What was the high temperature for the day? *(page 548)*

65. This evening, the temperature was ${}^-6°F$. The temperature reached a low after falling $4°F$. What was the low temperature for the day? *(page 548)*

66. Tamara and her father keep a bank account. At the start of June, she owed her father money. Her balance was ${}^-\$21$. That month she earned $\$40$. What was her balance at the end of the month? *(page 548)*

67. Frank and his mother keep a bank account. At the start of May, his balance was ${}^+\$16$. That month his mother gave him $\$20$ to spend. What was his balance at the end of the month? *(page 548)*

68. The temperature change yesterday was ${}^-6$ degrees each hour for 3 hours. What was the total change? *(page 554)*

CHAPTER TEST

Compare using >, <, or =.

1. 12 ● ⁻78
2. ⁻67 ● 67
3. ⁻1 + 2 ● 2 + ⁻1
4. ⁻7 ● ⁻2

Write in order from least to greatest.

5. 2, 0, 4, ⁻6, 8, ⁻10, 12, ⁻12
6. 8, ⁻8, ⁻11, 78, 0, 20, ⁻50

Add, subtract, multiply, or divide.

7. ⁻42 + ⁻36
8. 15 − ⁻7
9. ⁻3 × 41
10. ⁻9 ÷ ⁻9

11. ⁻34 − ⁻1
12. 89 + ⁻5
13. 62 ÷ ⁻2
14. ⁻1 × ⁻39

15. ⁻10 + 3
16. ⁻8 − 6
17. 23 × ⁻4
18. ⁻48 ÷ 3

Write in scientific notation.

19. 0.0603
20. 0.000072

Write in standard form.

21. 8.0×10^{-3}
22. 6.2×10^{-1}

Graph the solution on a number line.

23. $n + 4 < ⁻7$
24. $x − 8 > 1$
25. $d + 8 < 0$
26. $f − 18 > ⁻4$

Name the point on the coordinate grid.

27. A
28. B
29. C
30. D

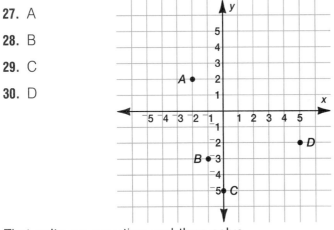

First write an equation and then solve.

31. This morning, the temperature was ⁻5°F. The high temperature was 10°F higher. What was the high temperature for the day?

32. Tracy had $210.50 in her checking account on July 1. After she paid for some clothes, she had $145.90 in her account. How much did she pay for the clothes?

33. The temperature change today was ⁻4° each hour for 8 hours. What was the total change?

GRAPHING TRANSLATIONS AND REFLECTIONS

Recall that a translation is a slide, or the movement of a figure from one position to another without turning. $\triangle A'B'C'$ is the translation of $\triangle ABC$. (Read A' as "A prime," B' as "B prime," and so on.) $\triangle ABC$ has been translated 10 units to the right.

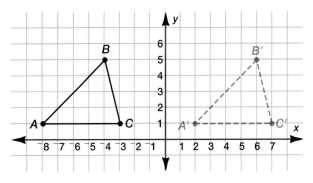

Name the coordinates.

1. A **2.** B **3.** C **4.** A' **5.** B' **6.** C'

7. Did the x-coordinates change? Why or why not?

8. Did the y-coordinates change? Why or why not?

9. Now translate $\triangle ABC$ down 7 units. Draw the new triangle, $\triangle A''B''C''$. (Read A'' as "a double prime," and so on.)

Name the coordinates.

10. A **11.** B **12.** C **13.** A'' **14.** B'' **15.** C''

16. Did the x-coordinates change? Why or why not?

17. Did the y-coordinates change? Why or why not?

A reflection is a flip of a figure about a line of symmetry. $\triangle G'H'I'$ is the reflection of $\triangle GHI$. $\triangle GHI$ has been flipped over the x-axis.

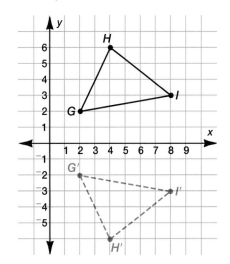

Name the coordinates.

18. G **19.** H **20.** I **21.** G' **22.** H' **23.** I'

24. Did the x-coordinate change? Why or why not?

25. Did the y-coordinate change? Why or why not?

26. Now $\triangle GHI$ is flipped over the y-axis. Draw the new triangle, $\triangle G''H''I''$. Name the coordinates of $\triangle G''H''I''$. Did the x-coordinates change? Did the y-coordinates change? Why or why not?

CUMULATIVE REVIEW

Choose the letter of the correct answer.

1. Which is true?

   a. $^-6 > 3$ **c.** $0 < {}^-2$
   b. $^-4 < {}^-1$ **d.** not given

2. $^-5 + {}^-7$

   a. $^-12$ **c.** 12
   b. $^-2$ **d.** not given

3. $6 - 9$

   a. $^-15$ **c.** 9
   b. 3   **d.** not given

4. $7 \times {}^-3$

   a. $^-21$ **c.** 21
   b. 4   **d.** not given

5. 6.3×10^{-1}

   a. 0.063   **c.** 63
   b. 0.63   **d.** not given

This graph shows Saul's budget.

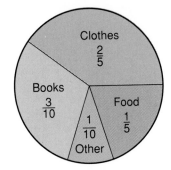

6. What percent does he spend on books?

   a. 3%   **c.** 60%
   b. 30%   **d.** not given

7. What percent does he spend on books and clothes?

   a. 7%   **c.** 30%
   b. 10%   **d.** not given

8. Find the volume of a rectangular pyramid with a base of 4 ft by 2 ft and a height of 6 ft.

   a. 12 ft³   **c.** 48 ft³
   b. 16 ft³   **d.** not given

9. In how many different orders can 4 people stand in a line?

   a. 8   **c.** 64
   b. 16   **d.** not given

10. How many faces does a triangular prism have?

   a. 3   **c.** 6
   b. 5   **d.** not given

11. What is the surface area of a cube with one edge that is 4 in. long?

   a. 16 in.²
   b. 64 in.²
   c. 96 in.²
   d. not given

A box holds 2 blue, 2 red, and 4 pink socks. Two socks are drawn at random without replacement.

12. What is $P(\text{red})$ on the first draw?

   a. 2%   **c.** 25%
   b. 20%   **d.** not given

13. What is $P(\text{blue } or \text{ pink})$ on the first draw?

   a. 0.75   **c.** 0.125
   b. 0.6   **d.** not given

14. What is $P(\text{blue, } then \text{ blue})$?

   a. $\frac{1}{2}$ **c.** $\frac{1}{28}$
   b. $\frac{1}{16}$ **d.** not given

TEN MAJOR BOX-OFFICE FAILURES

	COST TO PRODUCE (in $1,000,000)	RENTAL FROM UNITED STATES AND CANADA (in $1,000,000)	LOSS (in $1,000,000)
1. *Heaven's Gate* (1980)	36	1.5	34.5
2. *Raise the Titanic* (1980)	36	6.8	29.2
3. *Waterloo* (1969)	25	1.4	23.6
4. *Honky Tonk Freeway* (1981)	24	0.5	23.5
5. *Darling Lili* (1970)	22	3.3	18.7
6. *The Fall of the Roman Empire* (1964)	20	1.9	18.1
7. *Cleopatra* (1962)	44	26	18
8. *Hurricane* (1975)	22	4.5	17.5
9. *Sorcerer* (1977)	22	5.9	16.1
10. *Meteor* (1979)	20	4.2	15.8

OLYMPIC LONG-JUMP WINNING DISTANCES

YEAR	MEN	WOMEN
1948	25 ft 8 in.	18 ft 8.25 in.
1952	24 ft 10 in.	20 ft 5.75 in.
1956	25 ft 8.25 in.	20 ft 9.75 in.
1960	26 ft 7.75 in.	20 ft 10.75 in.
1964	26 ft 5.75 in.	22 ft 2.25 in.
1968	29 ft 2.5 in.	22 ft 4.5 in.
1972	27 ft 0.5 in.	22 ft 3 in.
1976	27 ft 4.5 in.	22 ft 0.75 in.
1980	28 ft 0.25 in.	23 ft 2 in.
1984	28 ft 0.25 in.	22 ft 10 in.
1988	28 ft 7.25 in.	24 ft 3.5 in.

DATABANK

ASTRODOME
radius = 98 meters

BASKETBALL
length = 94 feet
width = 50 feet

TENNIS
singles—length = 78 feet
width = 27 feet
doubles—length = 78 feet
width = 36 feet

HOCKEY
length = 200 feet
width = 85 feet

FOOTBALL FIELD
length = 120 yards
width = $53\frac{1}{3}$ yards

BOWLING
lane length = 62 feet $10\frac{3}{16}$ inches
lane width = $41\frac{1}{2}$ inches
gutter width = $9\frac{5}{16}$ inches

WASHINGTON D.C. SUBWAY MAP

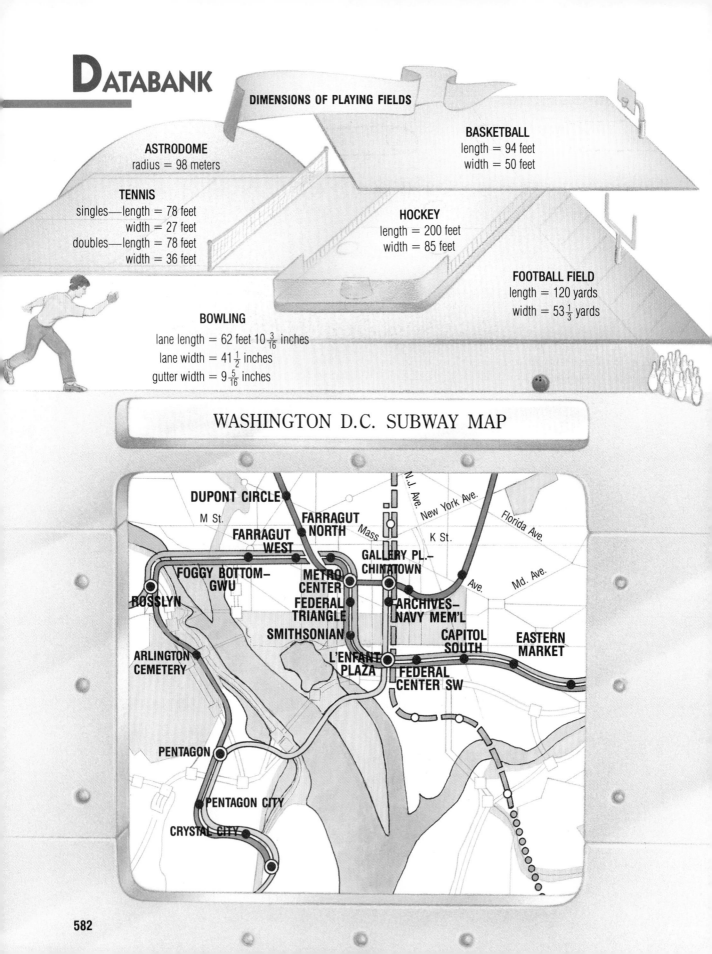

DUPONT CIRCLE
M St.
FARRAGUT NORTH
FARRAGUT WEST
FOGGY BOTTOM–GWU
GALLERY PL.–CHINATOWN
N.J. Ave.
New York Ave.
Florida Ave.
Mass
K St.
Ave.
Md. Ave.
ROSSLYN
METRO CENTER
FEDERAL TRIANGLE
ARCHIVES–NAVY MEM'L
SMITHSONIAN
CAPITOL SOUTH
EASTERN MARKET
ARLINGTON CEMETERY
L'ENFANT PLAZA
FEDERAL CENTER SW
PENTAGON
PENTAGON CITY
CRYSTAL CITY

NOTABLE TALL BUILDINGS IN THE UNITED STATES

City	Building	Height (in feet)
Atlanta	IBM Tower	825
Boston	John Hancock Tower	790
	Prudential Center	750
Chicago	Sears Tower	1,454
Detroit	Weston Hotel	720
Houston	Texas Commerce Tower	1,002
New Orleans	Energy Center	530
New York	Empire State Building	1,250
	World Trade Center	1,377
Philadelphia	City Hall Tower	548
San Francisco	Trans America Pyramid	853
Seattle	Space Needle	605

COST OF GASOLINE
(late 1980s in U.S. dollars)

Country	Typical Price per Gallon
United States	$.93
Great Britain	$2.53
France	$3.12
Spain	$2.46
Sweden	$2.71
West Germany	$2.76

CALORIES BURNED PER MINUTE ACCORDING TO WEIGHT

Activity	Calories Burned	
	Weight = 100 lb	Weight = 120 lb
Bicycling: 5.5 mi/h	3.1	3.8
Bicycling: 10 mi/h	5.4	6.5
Mountain climbing	6.6	8.0
Jogging: 8-minute mile	9.4	11.3
Jogging: 11-minute mile	6.1	7.3
Skiing: downhill	6.3	7.6
Swimming: crawl	5.8	6.9
Table tennis	2.7	3.2

DATABANK

MASSES OF THE PLANETS

Planet	Mass (in grams)
Mercury	2.390×10^{26}
Venus	4.841×10^{27}
Earth	5.976×10^{27}
Mars	6.574×10^{26}
Jupiter	1.894×10^{30}
Saturn	5.671×10^{29}
Uranus	8.785×10^{28}
Neptune	1.028×10^{27}
Pluto	4.960×10^{27}

STOCK QUOTATIONS

Stock	Dividend	Sales 100s	High	Low	Close
TrLf	1.88	2100	$38\frac{1}{4}$	$37\frac{3}{8}$	38
AcV	2.10	3112	$20\frac{1}{8}$	$19\frac{5}{8}$	$20\frac{1}{8}$
Skr	1.04	887	$59\frac{1}{2}$	$57\frac{1}{2}$	$58\frac{7}{8}$
Del	4.00	223	$69\frac{1}{4}$	$68\frac{5}{8}$	$68\frac{7}{8}$
Dmr	1.20	3329	$58\frac{3}{8}$	$57\frac{3}{8}$	58

Recipe for Tapioca Pudding

$\frac{3}{8}$ cup tapioca   2 teaspoons vanilla

2 eggs, slightly beaten $5\frac{1}{2}$ cups non-fat milk

$\frac{2}{3}$ cup sugar

1. Combine the tapioca, sugar, milk, and eggs in a saucepan. Let it stand for 5 minutes.

2. Cook and stir over medium heat until the mixture comes to a boil. (Pudding thickens as it cools.)

3. Remove the pudding from the heat. Stir in the vanilla.

4. Cool for 20 minutes; stir.

5. Serve warm or chilled; makes 12 servings.

GREATEST SNOWFALLS

Duration	Place	Date	Inches	Centimeters
1 month (U.S.)	Tamarack, CA	Jan. 1911	350	991
24 hours (U.S.)	Silver Lake, CO	Apr. 14–15, 1921	76	192.5
24 hours (Alaska)	Thompson Pass	Dec. 29, 1955	62	157.5
19 hours (France)	Bessans	Apr. 5–6, 1969	68	173
1 storm (U.S.)	Mt. Shasta Ski Bowl, CA	Feb. 13–19, 1959	189	480
1 storm (Alaska)	Thompson Pass	Dec. 26–31, 1955	175	445.5
1 season (U.S.)	Paradise Ranger Station, WA	1971–1972	1,122	2,850
1 season (Alaska)	Thompson Pass	1952–1953	974.5	2,475
1 season (Canada)	Revelstoke Mt. Copeland, British Columbia	1971–1972	964	2,446.5

GREATEST SPECIALIZED STRUCTURES IN THE WORLD

LARGEST DOME
Louisiana Superdome—outside diameter 680 ft

LARGEST DOORS
Vehicle Assembly Building near Cape Canaveral, FL—height 460 ft

TALLEST FLAGPOLE
Erected for 1915 Panama-Pacific Exposition in San Francisco—299 ft 7 in. high

TALLEST LIGHTHOUSE
Built near Brittany, France, from 1983–1985—328 ft tall

LARGEST SCARECROW
Built in Ontario, Canada, in 1936—50 ft 6 in. tall

LARGEST WINDOW
Palace of Industry and Technology, Paris, France—715.2 ft wide by 164 ft high

LONGEST WALL
Great Wall of China, built 246–210 B.C.—4,930 mi, including branches

WIDEST STREET
Monumental Axis, Brasilia, Brazil—6 lanes, 273.4 yd wide

LONGEST UNITED STATES INTERSTATE HIGHWAY
Route 90—3,087.65 mi from Boston to Seattle

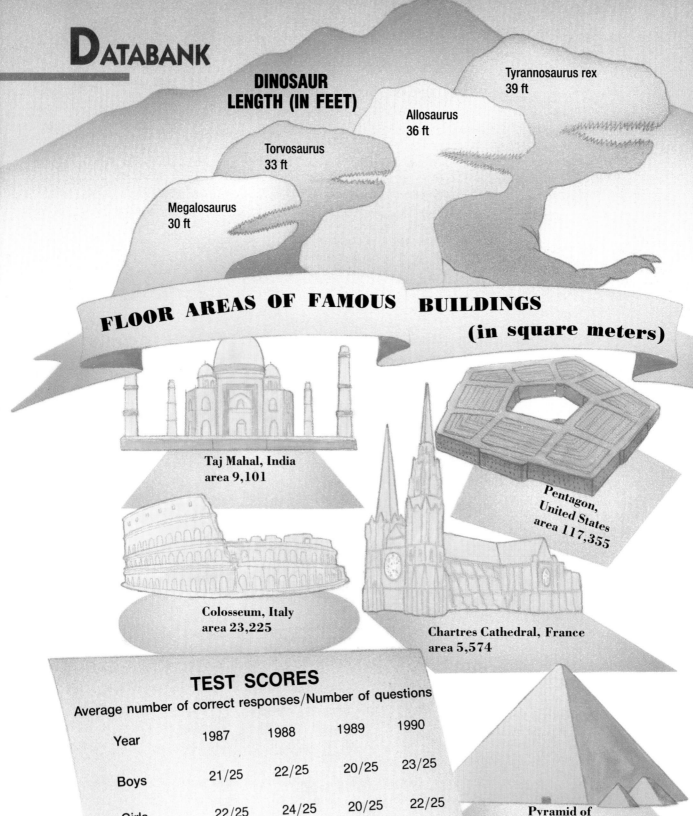

DATABANK

DINOSAUR LENGTH (IN FEET)

Tyrannosaurus rex
39 ft

Allosaurus
36 ft

Torvosaurus
33 ft

Megalosaurus
30 ft

FLOOR AREAS OF FAMOUS BUILDINGS (in square meters)

Taj Mahal, India
area 9,101

Pentagon,
United States
area 117,355

Colosseum, Italy
area 23,225

Chartres Cathedral, France
area 5,574

Pyramid of
Cheops, Egypt
area 53,100

TEST SCORES
Average number of correct responses/Number of questions

Year	1987	1988	1989	1990
Boys	21/25	22/25	20/25	23/25
Girls	22/25	24/25	20/25	22/25

GLOSSARY

A

absolute value The distance a *number* is from 0 on the number line.

adjacent angles Angles that have a common *ray* and share a common *vertex*.

algebraic expression An expression that contains *variables*, numbers, and symbols of operations.

algebraic sentence A word sentence that uses an *algebraic expression*.

angle Two rays called *sides*, with a common *endpoint* called the *vertex*. An *acute angle* measures less than 90°. A *right angle* measures 90°. An *obtuse angle* measures more than 90° but less than 180°. A *straight angle* measures 180°.

angle bisector A *ray* that divides an angle into two *congruent* angles.

area The number of square units needed to cover a region.

arithmetic sequence A sequence generated by repeatedly adding or subtracting the same number.

associative property The way *addends* or *factors* are grouped does not change the *sum* or *product*.

$$(a + b) + c = a + (b + c) \qquad (a \times b) \times c = a \times (b \times c)$$

C

capacity The amount of a substance that a container can hold.

central angle An angle whose *vertex* is at the *center* of a *circle*.

certain event The *probability* of an event that is certain is 1.

circle A simple closed figure having all points an equal distance from the *center*.

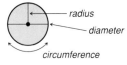

circumference The distance around a *circle*.

cluster A grouping of *data*.

combination A set of items in which order is not important.

commutative property The order of the *addends* or *factors* does not change the *sum* or *product*.

$$a + b = b + a \qquad a \times b = b \times a$$

complementary angles Two angles with a sum of 90°.

composite number A whole number greater than 1 having more than two *factors*.

congruent figures Geometric figures having the same size and shape.

coordinate plane The plane determined by a horizontal number line, called the *x-axis*, and a vertical number line, called the *y-axis*, intersecting at a point, called the *origin*. Each point of the plane corresponds to an *ordered pair* of numbers.

D

dependent events When the outcome of the first event affects the outcome of the second event.

diagonal A *line segment* other than a side that connects two *vertices* of a *polygon*.

divisibility One number is divisible by another number if the remainder is 0 after dividing.

double-bar graph Data presented visually using two bars to show comparisons.

587

double-line graph Data presented visually using two lines to show trends and changes over time.

E

equal ratios Ratios that make the same comparison.

equation An algebraic sentence that contains an *is-equal-to* (=) sign.

equivalent Decimals or fractions that have the same number.

evaluate To evaluate an *expression,* substitute a given value for the *variable.*

event The outcome of an experiment.

expanded form A number written as the sum of the value of its digits.

exponential form A number expressed using a base and an exponent.

$$2^5 \leftarrow exponent$$
$$base$$

expression A mathematical phrase made up of numbers and operation signs.

F

factor Factors are the numbers that are multiplied to give a *product.*

factorial notation A way to write the product of all counting numbers from 1 through any counting number.

$$3! = 3 \times 2 \times 1 = 6$$

factor tree A diagram used to find the *prime factors* of a number.

formula An *algebraic sentence* that states a mathematical fact or rule.

fraction A number that names part of a whole or part of a group.

$$\tfrac{1}{3} \begin{array}{l} \leftarrow numerator \\ \leftarrow denominator \end{array}$$

frequency table A listing of *data,* together with the number of times an item occurs.

G

geometric sequence A sequence generated by repeatedly multiplying or dividing the same number.

greatest common factor (GCF) The greatest whole number that is a *factor* of two or more whole numbers.

H

histogram A bar graph that presents frequency data.

hypotenuse In a *right triangle,* the longest side, which is also opposite the right angle.

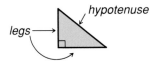

I

impossible event The *probability* of an event that is impossible is 0.

improper fraction A fraction with a *numerator* that is greater than or equal to the *denominator.*

independent events When the outcome of the first event does not affect the outcome of the second event.

integers Whole numbers and their opposites.

intersecting lines Two lines that meet at a point.

inverse operations Two operations that are opposite in effect.

L

least common denominator (LCD) The least common *multiple* of the *denominators* of two or more fractions.

least common multiple (LCM) The least nonzero number that is a *multiple* of two or more numbers.

line The endless collection of points along a straight path.

line of symmetry A line that divides a figure into two *congruent* parts.

line segment A part of a *line* having two endpoints.

M

mass The amount of matter that makes up an object.

mean The sum of a collection of *data* divided by the number of data.

median The middle number(s) when *data* is arranged in order.

midpoint A point that divides a *line segment* into two *congruent* segments.

mixed number The sum of a whole number and a fraction.

mode The number(s) that occur(s) most often in a collection of *data*.

multiples Products obtained by multiplying a number by 0, 1, 2, 3, . . .

mutually exclusive events Events that cannot occur at the same time.

N

negative integer An integer less than zero.

O

opposite integers Two different integers that are the same distance from zero on the number line, for example, $^+2$ and $^-2$.

order of operations The proper sequence of operations: raise to a power, then multiply or divide from left to right, then add or subtract from left to right.

P

parallel lines Lines in the same *plane* that never *intersect*.

parallelogram A *quadrilateral* with opposite sides *parallel*. Each pair of opposite sides and angles is *congruent*.

percent (%) The *ratio* of a given number to 100.

perfect square A number whose *square root* is a whole number.

perimeter The distance around a figure.

perpendicular bisector A line that is *perpendicular* to a *line segment* and divides the segment into two *congruent* parts.

perpendicular lines Two *lines* that *intersect* to form *right angles*.

pi (π) The *ratio* of the *circumference* of a *circle* to its *diameter* (about 3.14).

plane A flat surface that extends in all directions without end.

point An exact location in space.

polygon A closed *plane figure* formed by *line segments*. Polygons are named for the number of sides they have: *triangle* (3), *quadrilateral* (4), *pentagon* (5), *hexagon* (6), *heptagon* (7), *octagon* (8), *nonagon* (9), and *decagon* (10).

polyhedron A *space figure* whose faces are *polygons*.

positive integer An integer greater than zero.

prime factorization A *composite number* written as the product of *prime numbers*.

$$18 = 2 \times 3 \times 3$$

prime number A whole number that has only two *factors*, itself and 1.

probability The likelihood that an event will occur.

proportion An equation that states that two *ratios* are equal.

Pythagorean Theorem In a right triangle, the square of the longest side, called the *hypotenuse (c)*, is equal to the sum of the squares of the legs (*a* and *b*).

$$c^2 = a^2 + b^2$$

R

range The difference between the least and the greatest numbers in a set of *data*.

rate A *ratio* that compares different kinds of units.

ratio A comparison of two quantities.

ray A part of a *line* that has one *endpoint* and continues without end in one direction.

reciprocals Two numbers whose product is 1, for example, $\frac{1}{6}$ and $\frac{6}{1}$.

rectangle A *parallelogram* with four *right angles*.

reflection The mirror image of a figure about a line of symmetry, in a plane.

regular polygon A polygon with all sides and angles *congruent*.

relatively prime Two whole numbers whose *GCF* is 1.

repeating decimal A decimal in which a digit or group of digits repeats unendingly.

rhombus A *parallelogram* with four *congruent* sides.

rotation The image of a figure moved through an angle about a point in a *plane*.

S

sample space All possible *outcomes* of an experiment.

scale drawing A reduced or enlarged drawing of an actual object.

scientific notation A way of renaming numbers in a concise form as the product of a number between 1 and 10 and a power of 10.

$$1,800,000,000 = 1.8 \times 10^9$$

sector A region of a circle graph.

similar figures Figures with the same shape but not necessarily the same size.

simplest form A fraction form in which the *numerator* and *denominator* have no common *factors* other than 1.

space figures Three-dimensional figures.

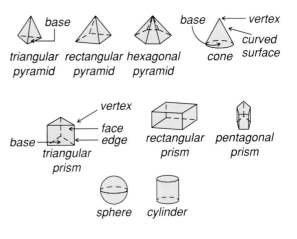

triangular pyramid · rectangular pyramid · hexagonal pyramid · cone · base · vertex · curved surface

base · vertex · face · edge · triangular prism · rectangular prism · pentagonal prism

sphere · cylinder

square A *rectangle* with four *congruent* sides.

square root One of two equal *factors* of a number. The square root of 25 is 5.

supplementary angles Two angles with a sum of 180°.

T

terms The numbers in a sequence or ratio.

terminating decimal A decimal with a limited number of nonzero digits.

translation The *slide* image of a figure in a plane.

transversal A *line* that intersects two or more lines forming *corresponding angles*.

trapezoid A *quadrilateral* with exactly one pair of *parallel* sides.

triangle A three-sided polygon.

U

unit rate An amount per single unit. The *unit price* is the price for one unit.

V

variable A symbol used to represent a number.

vertical angles *Congruent* angles formed by two *intersecting lines*.

volume The number of *cubic units* needed to fill a *space figure*.

COMPUTER TERMS

cell The way in which one unit of information such as one character, one byte, or one word is stored in a computer. Also, each individual box or square within the coordinate grid of an electronic spreadsheet.

data Information that is put into a computer.

database A group of facts and figures that are related and can be arranged in different ways. For example, the names, addresses, ages, and telephone numbers of every student in your school would be a database.

graphics Pictures created by a computer and shown on a screen, paper, or film. Graphics can range from simple line or bar graphs to colorful and complicated pictures.

program A series of instructions that tells the computer what to do with the data stored in it.

simulate To use a computer to study the possible solutions to a problem before trying them in real life.

spreadsheet A computer program that arranges data and formulas in a grid of cells.

TABLE OF MEASURES

METRIC UNITS

LENGTH
- 1 millimeter (mm) = 0.001 meter (m)
- 1 centimeter (cm) = 0.01 meter
- 1 decimeter (dm) = 0.1 meter
- 1 dekameter (dam) = 10 meters
- 1 hectometer (hm) = 100 meters
- 1 kilometer (km) = 1,000 meters

MASS/WEIGHT
- 1 milligram (mg) = 0.001 gram (g)
- 1 centigram (cg) = 0.01 gram
- 1 decigram (dg) = 0.1 gram
- 1 dekagram (dag) = 10 grams
- 1 hectogram (hg) = 100 grams
- 1 kilogram (kg) = 1,000 grams
- 1 metric ton (t) = 1,000 kilograms

CAPACITY
- 1 milliliter (mL) = 0.001 liter (L)
- 1 centiliter (cL) = 0.01 liter
- 1 deciliter (dL) = 0.1 liter
- 1 dekaliter (daL) = 10 liters
- 1 hectoliter (hL) = 100 liters
- 1 kiloliter (kL) = 1,000 liters

AREA
- 1 square centimeter (cm²) = 100 square millimeters (mm²)
- 1 square meter (m²) = 10,000 square centimeters
- 1 hectare (ha) = 10,000 square meters
- 1 square kilometer (km²) = 1,000,000 square meters

CUSTOMARY UNITS

LENGTH
- 1 foot (ft) = 12 inches (in.)
- 1 yard (yd) = 36 inches
- 1 yard = 3 feet
- 1 mile (mi) = 5,280 feet
- 1 mile = 1,760 yards

WEIGHT
- 1 pound (lb) = 16 ounces (oz)
- 1 ton (T) = 2,000 pounds

CAPACITY
- 1 cup (c) = 8 fluid ounces (fl oz)
- 1 pint (pt) = 2 cups
- 1 quart (qt) = 2 pints
- 1 quart = 4 cups
- 1 gallon (gal) = 4 quarts

AREA
- 1 square foot (ft²) = 144 square inches (in.²)
- 1 square yard (yd²) = 9 square feet
- 1 acre = 43,560 square feet
- 1 square mile (mi²) = 640 acres

TIME
- 1 minute (min) = 60 seconds (s)
- 1 hour (h) = 60 minutes
- 1 day (d) = 24 hours
- 1 week (wk) = 7 days
- 1 year (y) = 12 months (mo)
- 1 year = 52 weeks
- 1 year = 365 days
- 1 century (c) = 100 years

FORMULAS

$P = 2(\ell + w)$	Perimeter of a rectangle
$P = 4s$	Perimeter of a square
$A = \ell w$	Area of a rectangle
$A = s^2$	Area of a square
$A = bh$	Area of a parallelogram
$A = \frac{1}{2}bh$	Area of a triangle
$A = \frac{1}{2}h(b_1 + b_2)$	Area of a trapezoid
$C = \pi d$, or $2\pi r$	Circumference of a circle
$A = \pi r^2$	Area of a circle
$V = \ell wh$	Volume of a rectangular prism
$V = Bh$	Volume of any prism
$V = \pi r^2 h$	Volume of a cylinder
$V = \frac{1}{3}Bh$	Volume of a pyramid
$V = \frac{1}{3}\pi r^2 h$	Volume of a cone
$S = 2\pi r^2 + \pi dh$	Surface area of a cylinder
$a^2 + b^2 = c^2$	Pythagorean Theorem
$I = prt$	Simple interest
$d = rt$	Distance

SYMBOLS

Symbol	Meaning	Symbol	Meaning	Symbol	Meaning
$=$	is equal to	π	pi (approximately 3.14)	2:5	ratio of 2 to 5
$\neq$	is not equal to	°	degree	10^2	ten to the second power
$>$	is greater than	°C	degree Celsius	$\sqrt{\ }$	square root
$<$	is less than	°F	degree Fahrenheit	$^+4$	positive 4
$\geq$	is greater than or equal to	$\overleftrightarrow{AB}$	line AB	$^-4$	negative 4
$\leq$	is less than or equal to	$\overline{AB}$	line segment AB	$\lvert{}^-4\rvert$	absolute value of $^-4$
$\approx$	is approximately equal to	$\overrightarrow{AB}$	ray AB	$(3, {}^-4)$	ordered pair 3, $^-4$
$\cong$	is congruent to	$\angle ABC$	angle ABC	$P(E)$	probability of event E
$\sim$	is similar to	$m\angle ABC$	measure of angle ABC	sin 45°	sine of 45°
$\ldots$	continues without end	$\triangle ABC$	triangle ABC	cos 45°	cosine of 45°
$1.\overline{3}$	repeating decimal 1.333...	$\parallel$	is parallel to	tan 45°	tangent of 45°
%	percent	$\perp$	is perpendicular to		

A

Absolute value of integers, 538-539
Abundant numbers, 203
Acute angles, 328-329
Acute triangles, 340-341
Addition, *see also* Sums
  applying, 45-80
  compensation in, 46-47
  with equations, 60-61
  of fractions, 256-257
  of fractions in solving equations, 262-263
  with inequalities, 62-63
  of integers, 540-543, 548-549
  mental math in, 46-47, 53
  of mixed numbers, 258-259
  solving equations by, 182-183
  of whole numbers and decimals, 52-53
Addition properties, 46-47
Additions, equal, 46-47
Adjacent angles, 332-333
Algebra
  algebraic expressions, 174-175, 194, 195, 200, 202, 549, 557, 574, 575
  algebraic sentences, 176-177, 195, 200, 202
  equations, *see* Equations
  exponents, 94-95, 96-97, 112, 116, 118, 120, 138, 160, 164, 166, 168, 170-171, 194, 200, 202, 204, 214, 238, 279, 280, 293, 297, 509, 558-559, 572
  formulas, 98-99, 100-101, 102-103, 112, 113, 115, 117, 118, 120, 157, 168, 172-173, 186-187, 188-189, 193, 194, 197, 201, 204, 238, 460-461, 462-463, 464-465, 470-471, 472-473, 474-475, 480, 481, 482, 483, 484, 485, 486, 487, 488-489, 490, 491, 492, 536
  functions, *see* Functions
  graphing ordered pairs, 562-563, 573, 577, 578, 579
  inequalities, *see* Inequalities
  integers, *see* Integers
  order of operations, 170-171, 194, 200, 202, 204, 238, 280, 324, 569
  problem solving, 188-189, 197, 250-251, 382-383, 409, 550-551, 571
  properties, 46-47, 82-83, 287
  proportions, 378-383, 398-399, 408, 409, 411, 413, 454, 492, 536
  relations, *see* Relations
  square root, 354-357, 365, 369, 370, 372, 418, 454, 492
  variables, 60-61, 62-63, 172-173, 174-175, 194
Algebraic expressions, 174-175, 194, 195, 200, 202, 549, 557, 574, 575
Algebraic sentences, 176-177, 195, 200, 202
Angle bisectors, 338-339
Angles, 326-327
  acute, 328-329
  adjacent, 332-333
  central, 424-425
  complementary, 328-329
  congruent, 330-331
  corresponding, 332-333, 346-347
  measuring, 328-329

  obtuse, 328-329
  right, 328-329
  straight, 328-329
  supplementary, 328-329
  vertical, 332-333
Applying Addition, Subtraction: Whole Numbers, Decimals, 45-80
Applying Division: Whole Numbers, Decimals, 121-168
Applying Multiplication: Whole Numbers, Decimals, 81-120
Area
  of circles, 102-103
  estimating, 119
  lateral, of cones, 491
  of parallelograms, 100-101
  of rectangles, 98-99
  of squares, 98-99
  surface, *see* Surface area
  of trapezoids, 100-101
  of triangles, 100-101
Arithmetic sequences, 206-209
Arrangements, 518-519
Associative property
  of addition, 46-47
  of multiplication, 82-83
Axis
  horizontal, *see* Horizontal axis
  vertical, *see* Vertical axis

B

Bar graphs, 430-431
  double, 22-23
  interpreting, 22-23
  making, 24-25
Bases of exponents, 94-95
Bases of polyhedrons, 456-457
Billions, 12-13
Bisectors
  angle, 338-339
  perpendicular, 338-339
Box-and-whisker plots, 436-437

C

c (cup), 302-303
Calculators, 7, 8-9, 13, 17, 29, 32, 43, 52-53, 55, 61, 63, 65, 82-83, 84, 87, 88-89, 91, 97, 99, 103, 105, 109, 123, 127, 128-129, 131, 132-133, 134-135, 136-137, 139, 141, 147, 149, 159, 171, 181, 183, 185, 188-189, 207, 211, 212, 215, 217, 221, 243, 249, 251, 252, 257, 261, 263, 265, 285, 289, 293, 297, 299, 301, 307, 313, 333, 336-337, 339, 353, 355, 357, 377, 379, 383, 390-391, 392-393, 403, 422, 425, 427, 431, 439, 461, 462-463, 464-465, 467, 470-471, 473, 475, 477, 481, 501, 505, 509, 517, 519, 547, 549, 551, 554-555, 556-557, 559, 561, 564-565, 569
Capacity, 144-145
  in customary units, 302-303
  in metric units, 144-145
Centimeter (cm), 58-59
  cubic, 186-187
Central angles, 424-425, 443
Certain events, 496-497
Chapter opener, 11, 45, 81, 121, 169, 205, 239, 281, 325, 373, 419, 455, 493, 537

Chapter review, 40-41, 76-77, 116-117, 164-165, 200-201, 234-235, 276-277, 320-321, 368-369, 414-415, 450-451, 488-489, 532-533, 576-577
Chapter test, 42, 78, 118, 166, 202, 236, 278, 322, 370, 416, 452, 490, 534, 578
Checking for a reasonable answer, 402-403
Circle graphs, 430-431
  on a computer, 443
  making, 424-427
  reading and interpreting, 422-423
Circles, area of, 102-103
Circumference, 102-103
cm (centimeter), 58-59
Combinations, 520-521
Common denominators
  division of fractions using, 290-291
  least, 256
Common factor, greatest, 220-221
Common multiple, least, 222-223
Commutative property
  of addition, 46-47
  of multiplication, 82-83
Comparing
  decimals, 248-249
  fractions, 248-249
  integers, 538-539
  mixed numbers, 248-249
Compatible numbers, 126-127
Compensation in addition, 46-47
Complementary angles, 328-329
Composite numbers, 214-215
Compound interest on a computer, 407
Computers
  circle graphs, 443
  fractions and decimals, 269
  Logo
    star polygons, 227
    symmetry, 361
  probability, 525
  spreadsheets, 69, 157, 193, 407
  triple-line graphs, 33
Conducting an experiment, 28-29
Conducting a simulation, 504-505
Cones, 457
  lateral area of, 491
  surface area of, 491
  volume of, 474-475, 481
Congruence, 346-347
Congruent angles, 330-331
Congruent figures, 330-331, 346-347
Congruent line segments, 330-331
Constructing congruent line segments and angles, 330-331
Constructing line segment and angle bisectors, 338-339
Constructing perpendicular and parallel lines, 334-335
Constructing triangles, 371
Converting customary units, 304-305
Converting metric measures, 146-147
Cooperative learning
  chapter opener, 11, 45, 81, 121, 169, 205, 239, 281, 325, 373, 419, 455, 493, 537
  decision making, 30-31, 66-67, 106-107, 154-155, 190-191, 224-225, 266-267, 310-311, 358-359, 404-405, 440-441, 478-479, 522-523, 566-567

sharing ideas, 14, 19, 25, 27, 63, 97,
142, 153, 206, 208, 291, 347, 355,
356, 392, 395, 396, 401, 420, 422,
424, 430, 435, 437, 458, 460, 472,
474, 494, 500, 508, 513, 514, 518,
521, 541, 543, 545, 546, 555, 557
thinking mathematically, 1-10, 20-21,
56-57, 92-93, 132-133, 178-179,
218-219, 252-253, 294-295,
342-343, 384-385, 428-429,
468-469, 506-507, 552-553; *see also*
Thinking mathematically
working together, 14, 24, 26, 62, 152,
206, 354, 394, 400-401, 420, 422,
424, 430, 434-435, 436-437, 457,
460, 472, 474, 494, 500, 512, 520,
540, 542, 544, 546, 554
Coordinate plane, 562-563
Corresponding angles, 332-333, 346-347
Corresponding sides, 346-347
Counting outcomes, 518-521
Critical thinking, 13, 23, 25, 27, 40, 47, 49,
51, 61, 63, 77, 87, 89, 95, 99, 101,
103, 117, 125, 139, 141, 143, 151,
153, 165, 171, 173, 175, 177, 185,
187, 201, 207, 209, 213, 215, 221,
223, 235, 245, 247, 249, 255, 257,
261, 263, 277, 283, 285, 293, 309,
321, 329, 331, 333, 339, 341, 345,
347, 349, 351, 369, 375, 379, 399,
415, 425, 433, 451, 461, 463, 465,
471, 475, 489, 497, 499, 511, 533,
539, 549, 563, 577
Cross products, 378-379
Cubed numbers, 94-95
Cubic centimeter, 186-187
Cumulative review, 44, 80, 120, 168, 204,
238, 280, 324, 372, 418, 454, 492,
536, 580
Cup (c), 302-303
Curriculum connections
math and art, 108, 406
math and literature, 68
math and music, 226, 268
math and science, 192, 312, 360, 568
math and social studies, 32, 156, 442,
480, 524
Customary units of measurement
capacity, 302-303
converting, 304-305
length, 302-303
weight, 302-303
Cylinders, 457
surface area of, 464-465
volume of, 470-471

D

Databank, 581-586
Decagons, 344-345
Decimal powers of 10
division by, 124-125
multiplication by, 84-85
Decimals
addition of, 52-53
comparing, 248-249
division by whole numbers, 128-129
division of decimals by, 134-135
equivalent, 12-13
estimating products of, 86-87
fractions and mixed numbers and,
244-245
mental math in multiplication, 129
multiplication of, 88-89
ordering, 248-249
percents and, 388-389
place-value chart of, 12-13

products of, 89
repeating, *see* Repeating decimals
rounding quotients in, 136-137
subtraction of, 52-53
terminating, 246-247, 269
Decimeter (dm), 58-59
Decision making, 30-31, 66-67, 106-107,
154-155, 190-191, 224-225, 266-267,
310-311, 358-359, 404-405, 440-441,
478-479, 522-523, 566-567
Deficient numbers, 203
Denominators, 240-241
common, *see* Common denominators
Dependent events, 512-515, 525
Diagonals, 344-345
Diagrams, tree, 508-509
Diameter, 102-103
Differences, *see also* Subtraction
estimating by front-end estimation,
50-51
estimating by rounding, 48-49
estimating for mixed numbers, 254-255
Digits, random, 500-501
Distributive property of multiplication, 82-83
Divisibility, 212-213
Division, *see also* Divisors; Quotients
applying, 121-168
in converting customary units, 304-305
by decimal powers of 10, 124-125
of decimals by decimals, 134-135
of decimals by whole numbers, 128-129
with equations, 140-141
finding prime factors by, 214-215
of fractions using common
denominators, 290-291
of fractions using reciprocals, 292-293
of greater numbers, 138-139
with inequalities, 142-143
of integers, 556-557
of mixed numbers, 296-297
solving equations by, 184-185
solving equations with fractions,
300-301
by whole-number powers of 10,
122-123
Division patterns, 292-293
Divisors, *see also* Division
mixed numbers as, 298-299
dm (decimeter), 58-59
Double-bar graphs, 22-23
Double-line graphs, 22-23
Drawing a diagram, 104-105
Drawing a Venn diagram, 438-439

E

Edges of polyhedrons, 456-457
Enrichment for all
Buffon's needle problem, 535
constructing triangles, 371
estimating areas, 119
estimating wildlife populations, 453
exploring the lateral area of a cone, 491
generating magic squares, 79
Golden Ratio, 417
graphing translations and reflections,
579
octal numbers, 43
paradoxes, 279
Pascal's triangle, 237
perfect, deficient, and abundant
numbers, 203
perpetual calendar, 167
renaming repeating decimals as
fractions, 323
Equal additions, 46-47
Equal ratios, 374-375

Equations
applying, 186-187
with decimals, 182-183, 184-185, 196,
198-199, 201, 202, 204, 263
with fractions, 262-263, 273, 277, 278,
280, 300-301, 316, 320, 322, 324,
372, 418
with percents, 398-399, 411, 413,
414-415, 416, 418, 425, 454, 461,
471, 492, 509, 519, 536, 549
proportions, 378-379, 380-381,
382-383, 398-399, 408, 409, 411,
413, 414-415, 416, 418, 425, 454,
461, 492
solving, *see* Solving equations
using addition and subtraction, 60-61,
72, 77, 78, 80, 182-183, 196, 198,
201, 202, 204, 243, 262-263, 273,
277, 278, 280, 299, 324, 372, 418
using multiplication and division,
140-141, 160, 164, 165, 168,
184-185, 196, 199, 201, 202, 263,
299, 300-301, 316, 320, 322
Equations and Formulas, 169-204
Equilateral triangles, 340-341
Equivalent decimals, 12-13
Equivalent fractions, 240-241
Estimating/estimation
areas, 119
compatible numbers, 126-127
computation
differences, 48-51, 254-255
products, 86-87, 284-285
quotients, 126-127
sums, 48-51, 254-255
front-end, *see* Front-end estimation
measurements, *see also* Customary
units of measurement; Metric
units of measurement
capacity, 144-145, 302-303
length, 58-59, 302-303
mass, 144-145
weight, 302-303
percents, 389
percents of numbers, 396-397
rounding, *see* Rounding
Expanded form of numbers, 12-13
Experimental probability, 500-501
Experimental ratio, 500-501
Experiments, modeling, 494-495
Exploring lateral area of cones, 491
Exponential form, 94-95
Exponents, 94-95, 96-97, 112, 116, 118,
120, 138, 160, 164, 166, 168, 170-171,
194, 200, 202, 204, 214, 238, 279,
280, 293, 297, 354-355, 356-357, 509,
558-559, 572
Expressions, 170-171
with exponents, 170-171
with parentheses and brackets, 170-171
writing algebraic, 174-175
Extra practice, 34-37, 70-73, 110-113,
158-161, 194-197, 228-231, 270-273,
314-317, 362-365, 408-411, 444-447,
482-485, 526-529, 570-573

F

Faces of polyhedrons, 456-457
Factor pairs, 212-213
Factor trees, 214-215
Factorial notation, 518-519
Factorization, prime, 214-215
Factors, 212-213
greatest common, 220-221
proper, 203
Favorable outcomes, 496-497, 502-503, 525

Fibonacci Sequence, 417
Finding a pattern, 210-211
Fluid ounce (fl oz), 302-303
Foot (ft), 302-303
Formulas, 98-99, 100-101, 102-103, 112,
113, 115, 117, 118, 120, 168, 172-173,
186-187, 188-189, 194, 197, 201, 204,
238, 460-461, 462-463, 464-465,
470-471, 472-473, 474-475, 480, 481,
482, 483, 484, 485, 486, 487, 488-489,
490, 491, 492, 536
Fractions, 240-241
addition of, 256-257
comparing, 248-249
division using common denominators,
290-291
division using reciprocals, 292-293
equivalent, 240-241
improper, mixed numbers and, 242-243
mixed numbers and decimals and,
244-245, 269
multiplication by mixed numbers,
284-285
multiplication of, 282-283
on number line, 245
ordering, 248-249
percents and, 390-391
relations, *see* Relations
renaming repeating decimals as, 323
in simplest form, 240-241
solving equations by addition and
subtraction of, 262-263
solving equations by multiplication and
division of, 300-301
subtraction of, 256-257
Fractions: Addition and Subtraction, 239-280
Fractions: Multiplication and Division,
281-324
Frequency tables, 420-421
grouped, 14-15
interpreting and making, 14-15
Front-end estimation
to estimate products, 86-87
to estimate sums and differences, 50-51,
254-255
ft (foot), 302-303
Functions
function table, 193, 467

G

g (gram), 144-145
Gallon (gal), 302-303
Geometric sequences, 209
Geometry, 325-372
angles, *see* Angles
circles, 102-103
cones, *see* Cones
congruence, 346-347
constructions, 330-331, 334-335,
338-339, 371
cylinders, *see* Cylinders
line segments, *see* Line segments
lines, *see* Lines
parallelograms, *see* Parallelograms
planes, 326-327
points, *see* Points
polygons, 227, 344-345
prisms, *see* Prisms
pyramids, *see* Pyramids
Pythagorean Theorem, 354-355
quadrilaterals, 344-345
rays, 326-327
rectangles, *see* Rectangles
reflections, 348-349, 579
rhombuses, 344-345
shapes, 344-345
similarity, 346-347

spatial visualization, 456-457
spheres, 457
squares, *see* Squares
symmetry, 348-349, 361
trapezoids, *see* Trapezoids
triangles, *see* Triangles
Glossary, 587-590
Golden Ratio, 417
Golden rectangles, 417
Gram (g), 144-145
Graphing
equations, 560-561
inequalities, 560-561, 572
ordered pairs, 562-563, 573
sentences, 560-561
translations and reflections, 348-351,
365, 367, 579
Graphs
bar, *see* Bar graphs
circle, *see* Circle graphs
histograms, *see* Histograms
line, *see* Line graphs
Greatest common factor (GCF), 220-221
Grouped-frequency tables, 14-15
Guess, test, and revise, 64-65

H

Heptagons, 227, 344-345
Hexagonal pyramids, 456-457
Hexagons, 227, 344-345
Histograms, 430-431
reading and interpreting, 420-421
Horizontal axis, 22-23
in histograms, 420-421
as *x*-axis, 562-563
Hypotenuse, 354-355

I

Impossible events, 496-497
Improper fractions, mixed numbers and,
242-243
Inch (in.), 302-303
Independent events, 510-511
Inequalities
graphing, 560-561, 572, 577, 578
using addition and subtraction, 62-63,
73, 77, 78, 80, 120, 168, 204, 243
using multiplication and division,
142-143, 160, 164, 165, 168, 204,
238
Inequality symbols, 62-63, 142-143,
176-177, 560-561
Integers
absolute value of, 538-539
addition of, 540-543, 548-549, 570, 574
comparing, 538-539, 570
division of, 556-557, 572, 575
multiplication of, 554-555, 571
negative, 538-539
opposite, 538-539
ordering, 538-539
positive, 538-539
subtraction of, 544-549, 570, 574
Integers and Coordinate Graphing, 537-580
Interest, compound, 407
Intersecting lines, 332-333
Inverse operations, 182-183
Isosceles triangles, 340-341

K

Kilogram (kg), 144-145
Kiloliter (kL), 144-145
Kilometer (km), 58-59
kL (kiloliter), 144-145
km (kilometer), 58-59

L

L (liter), 144-145
Lateral area of cones, 491
lb (pound), 302-303
Leap year, 167
Least common denominator (LCD), 256
Least common multiple (LCM), 222-223
Legs of triangles, 354-355
Length
in customary units, 302-303
in metric units, 58-59
Line graphs, 69, 430-431
double, 22-23
interpreting, 22-23
making, 26-27
triple, 33
Line plots, making, 18-19
Line segments, 326-327
congruent, 330-331
perpendicular bisectors of, 338-339
Lines, 326-327
intersecting, 332-333
midpoints of, 338-339
parallel, *see* Parallel lines
perpendicular, *see* Perpendicular lines
of symmetry, 348-349, 361
Liter (L), 144-145
Logical reasoning, 10, 15, 83, 147,
178-179, 218-219, 223, 285, 428-429
Logo
star polygons, 227
symmetry, 361

M

m (meter), 58-59
Magic squares, 259
generating, 79
Making a physical model, 476-477
Making an organized list, 216-217
Making predictions, 502-503
Making a table, 466-467
Manipulative activity, 14-15, 16-17, 24-25,
26-27, 290-291, 394-395, 424-425,
434-435, 436-437, 456-457, 472-473,
474-475, 494-495, 512-513, 520-521,
540-541, 544-545
Mapmaking, 361
Mass in metric units, 144-145
Mean of numbers, 150-153, 157
Measurement
customary, *see* Customary units of
measurement
estimating, *see* Estimating/estimation,
measurements
metric, *see* Metric units of
measurement
Measurement: Surface Area and Volume,
455-492
Measuring angles, 328-329
Median of numbers, 150-153, 157
Mental math
addition, 46-47, 53
addition by zigzag method, 53
compensation, 46-47
divisibility, 212-213
division by decimal powers of 10,
124-125
division by whole-number powers of 10,
122-123
equal additions, 46-47
finding products of decimals, 89
finding squares of numbers, 95
multiplication by decimal powers of 10,
84-85
multiplication by decimals, 129
multiplication by mixed numbers, 287

multiplication by multiples of 5, 123
multiplication by whole-number powers
 of 10, 82-83
percents of numbers, 396-397
scaling up and down, 308-309
subtraction, 46-47
using rates, 376-377
Meter (m), 58-59
Metric ton or tonne (t), 144-145
Metric units of measurement
 capacity, 144-145
 converting, 146-147
 length, 58-59
 mass, 144-145
mg (milligram), 144-145
mi (mile), 302-303
Midpoints of lines, 338-339
Mile (mi), 302-303
Milligram (mg), 144-145
Milliliter (mL), 144-145
Millimeter (mm), 58-59
Millions, 12-13
Misleading statistics, 432-433
Mixed applications, 41, 47, 49, 51, 53, 59,
 61, 63, 77, 83, 85, 87, 89, 95, 97, 99,
 103, 117, 123, 125, 127, 129, 135,
 137, 139, 141, 143, 145, 147, 151,
 153, 165, 171, 173, 175, 177, 183,
 185, 187, 201, 207, 209, 213, 215,
 221, 223, 235, 241, 243, 245, 247,
 249, 255, 257, 259, 261, 263, 277,
 283, 285, 287, 293, 297, 299, 301,
 303, 305, 309, 321, 327, 329, 331,
 333, 335, 339, 341, 349, 351, 357,
 369, 375, 377, 379, 381, 387, 389,
 391, 393, 397, 399, 415, 421, 423,
 431, 451, 461, 463, 465, 473, 475,
 489, 497, 501, 503, 509, 511, 515,
 519, 533, 539, 543, 547, 549, 555,
 557, 559, 561, 563, 577
Mixed numbers
 addition of, 258-259
 comparing, 248-249
 division of, 296-297
 as divisors, 298-299
 estimating sums and differences of,
  254-255
 fractions and decimals and, 244-245
 improper fractions and, 242-243
 multiplication of, 286-287
 multiplication of fractions by, 284-285
 ordering, 248-249
 subtraction of, 258-259
Mixed review, 9, 59, 63, 85, 97, 103, 135,
 137, 185, 207, 221, 243, 261, 263,
 293, 297, 299, 331, 333, 339, 355,
 377, 379, 397, 425, 431, 461, 471,
 509, 519, 549, 559, 561
mL (milliliter), 144-145
mm (millimeter), 58-59
Mode of numbers, 150-153, 157
Modeling an experiment, 494-495
Multiples, 222-223
 least common, 222-223
Multiplication, *see also* Products
 applying, 98-99, 102-103
 in converting customary units, 304-305
 of decimal powers of 10, 84-85
 with equations, 140-141
 of fractions, 282-283
 of fractions by mixed numbers, 284-285
 of greater numbers, 96-97
 with inequalities, 142-143
 of integers, 554-555
 mental math in, 287
 of mixed numbers, 286-287
 by multiples of 5, 123

solving equations by, 184-185
solving equations with fractions, 300-301
 by whole-number powers of 10, 82-83
 of whole numbers and decimals, 88-89
Multiplication patterns, 292-293
Multiplication properties, 82-83
Mutually exclusive events, 498-499

N

Negative integers, 538-539
Nonagons, 344-345
Notation
 factorial, 518-519
 scientific, 96-97, 138-139, 558-559
Number line
 fractions on, 245
 zero on, 538-539
Number patterns, 83, 206-207
Number sense, *see* Estimating/estimation;
 Mental math
Number theory, 205-238
Numbers
 expanded form of, 12-13
 octal, 43
 powers of, 94-95
 short word name of, 12-13
 standard form of, 12-13
Numerators, 240-241

O

Obtuse angles, 328-329
Obtuse triangles, 340-341
Octagons, 227, 344-345
Octal numbers, 43
Operations
 inverse, 182-183
 order of, 170-171, 569
Opposite integers, 538-539
Order of operations, 170-171, 194, 200,
 202, 204, 238, 280, 324, 569
Ordered pairs, graphing, 562-563
Ordering
 decimals, 248-249
 fractions, 248-249
 integers, 538-539
 mixed numbers, 248-249
Origin
 as center of rotation, 350-351
 of coordinate plane, 562-563
Ounce (oz), 302-303
Outcomes
 counting, 518-521
 favorable, 496-497, 502-503, 525
 possible, 494-495, 525
 predicting, 525
 representing, 508-509
oz (ounce), 302-303

P

Pairs
 factor, 212-213
 ordered, graphing, 562-563
Paradoxes, 279
Parallel lines, 332-333
 constructing, 334-335
Parallelograms, 344-345
 area of, 100-101
Parentheses, expressions with, 170-171
Pascal's triangle, 237
Patterns, 205-238
 division, 292-293
 multiplication, 292-293
 number, 83, 206-207, 227
Patterns and Number Theory, 205-238
Patterns, relations, and functions, 60-61,
 62-63, 82-83, 100-101, 172-173,

174-175, 176-177, 182-183, 184-185,
186-187, 193, 206-207, 210-211,
262-263, 292-293, 300-301, 398-399,
400-401, 550-551, 554-555, 562-563,
564-565, 566-567, 568
Pentagonal prisms, 456-457
Pentagons, 227, 344-345
Percents, 386-387
 decimals and, 388-389
 estimating, 389
 fractions and, 390-391
 greater than 100 and less than 1,
  392-393
 of numbers, 394-399
 proportions and, 400-401
Perfect numbers, 203
Perfect squares, 356-357
Perimeter in metric units, 58-59
Periods of numbers, 12-13
Permutations, 518-519
Perpendicular bisectors, 338-339
Perpendicular lines, 332-333
 constructing, 334-335
Pi, 102-103
Pint (pt), 304-305
Place-value chart, 12-13
Plane, coordinate, 562-563
Planes, 326-327
Plots
 box-and-whisker, 436-437
 line, 18-19
 stem-and-leaf, 434-435
Points, 326-327
 intersection, 330-331
Polygons, 344-345
 regular, 227, 344-345
Polyhedrons, 456-457
Positive integers, 538-539
Possible outcomes, 494-495, 525
Pound (lb), 302-303
Powers of numbers, 94-95
Powers of 10
 decimal, *see* Decimal powers of 10
 whole number, *see* Whole-number
  powers of 10
Practice plus, 38-39, 74-75, 114-115,
 162-163, 198-199, 232-233, 274-275,
 318-319, 366-367, 412-413, 448-449,
 486-487, 530-531, 574-575
Predicting outcomes, 525
Predictions, making, 502-503
Prime factorization, 214-215
Prime numbers, 214-215
 twin, 215
Prisms, 456-457
 pentagonal, 456-457
 rectangular, *see* Rectangular prisms
 surface area of, 460-461
 triangular, *see* Triangular prisms
 volume of, 186-187
Probability, 493-536
 computer simulation, 525
 of dependent events, 512-515, 525
 experimental, 500-501
 of independent events, 510-511
 modeling an experiment, 494-495
 of mutually exclusive events, 498-499
 of simple events, 496-497
 statistics and, 502-503
 theoretical, 500-501
Problem formulation, 11, 15, 29, 30-31, 45,
 47, 55, 59, 63, 66-67, 81, 89, 97,
 104-105, 106-107, 121, 129, 131, 135,
 137, 145, 149, 153, 154-155, 169, 177,
 185, 187, 190-191, 205, 207, 209, 211,
 217, 221, 224-225, 239, 249, 251, 263,
 265, 266-267, 281, 289, 299, 303, 307,

309, 310-311, 325, 341, 353, 357, 358-359, 373, 379, 383, 387, 397, 403, 404-405, 419, 427, 439, 455, 463, 467, 475, 477, 478-479, 493, 505, 509, 517, 522-523, 537, 543, 551, 557, 561, 566-567

Problem solving
consumer mathematics, 2-3, 11, 26-27, 30-31, 45, 47, 50, 55, 61, 63, 66-67, 71, 73, 74, 77, 78, 85, 87, 88-89, 99, 103, 109, 111, 114, 117, 118, 121, 125, 127, 136-137, 141, 145, 147, 154-155, 162, 165, 166, 169, 171, 181, 185, 187, 190-191, 201, 209, 217, 247, 249, 257, 277, 281, 285, 287, 300-301, 303, 305, 308-309, 310-311, 317, 319, 329, 331, 339, 351, 376-377, 383, 403, 404-405, 407, 415, 416, 421, 426-427, 440-441, 445, 451, 452, 455, 463, 473, 478-479, 509, 524, 547, 550-551, 563, 571, 578
decision making, 30-31, 66-67, 106-107, 154-155, 190-191, 224-225, 266-267, 310-311, 358-359, 404-405, 440-441, 478-479, 522-523, 566-567
problem formulation, 11, 15, 29, 30-31, 45, 47, 55, 59, 63, 66-67, 81, 89, 97, 104-105, 106-107, 121, 129, 131, 135, 137, 145, 149, 153, 154-155, 169, 177, 185, 187, 190-191, 205, 207, 209, 211, 217, 221, 224-225, 239, 249, 251, 263, 265, 266-267, 281, 289, 299, 303, 307, 309, 310-311, 325, 341, 353, 357, 358-359, 373, 379, 383, 387, 397, 403, 404-405, 419, 427, 439, 455, 463, 467, 475, 477, 478-479, 493, 505, 509, 517, 522-523, 537, 543, 551, 557, 561, 566-567
strategies and skills review, 65, 91, 105, 131, 149, 181, 189, 217, 251, 265, 289, 307, 353, 383, 403, 427, 439, 467, 477, 505, 517, 551
thinking mathematically, 1-10, 20-21, 56-57, 92-93, 132-133, 178-179, 218-219, 252-253, 294-295, 342-343, 384-385, 428-429, 468-469, 506-507, 552-553
applying mathematics, 2-3
collecting and interpreting data, 5
estimating 8-9, 252-253
experimenting and predicting, 506-507
investigating patterns, 56-57, 92-93, 384-385
logical reasoning, 10, 15, 83, 147, 178-179, 218-219, 223, 285, 428-429
measuring, 132-133
using number concepts, 4, 20-21, 294-295, 552-553
visual reasoning, 6-7, 342-343, 468-469

Problem-solving strategies and skills
checking for a reasonable answer, 402-403
conducting an experiment, 28-29
conducting a simulation, 504-505
drawing a diagram, 104-105
drawing a Venn diagram, 438-439
finding needed information, 130-131
finding a pattern, 210-211
guess, test, and revise, 64-65
making and using a graph, 426-427
making a physical model, 476-477
making an organized list, 216-217
making a table, 466-467
solving a multistep problem, 90-91
solving a simpler problem, 250-251, 288-289
strategies review, 336-337, 564-565
using different strategies, 264-265, 516-517
using estimation, 54-55, 148-149
using the five-step process, 16-17
using a formula, 188-189
using number sense, 180-181
using proportions, 382-383
using spatial thinking, 352-353
working backward, 306-307
writing and solving an equation, 550-551

Products, *see also* Multiplication
cross, 378-379
of decimals, 89
estimating, 86-87, 284-285

Proper factors, 203
Properties, 46-47, 82-83, 287
Proportions, 378-379, 380-381, 382-383, 408, 409, 411, 413, 454, 492, 536
percents and, 400-401
percents of numbers and, 398-399
Protractors, 328-329
pt (pint), 304-305
Pyramids, 456-457
hexagonal, 456-457
rectangular, 456-457
surface area of, 462-463
triangular, 456-457
volume of, 472-473
Pythagorean Theorem, 354-355

Q

qt (quart), 302-303
Quadrilaterals, 344-345
Quart (qt), 302-303
Quotients, *see also* Division
estimating, 126-127
rounding decimal, 136-137

R

Random digits, 500-501
Random events, 496-497
Range of numbers, 150-153, 157
Rates
unit, 376-377
using, 376-377
Ratio, Proportion, and Percent, 373-418
Ratios, 374-375
equal, 374-375
experimental, 500-501
Golden, 417
scaling up or down, 374-375
Rays, 326-327
Reasonableness of answers, 9, 88, 128, 134, 258, 296, 398
Reciprocals, 282-283
division of fractions using, 292-293
Rectangles, 344-345
area of, 98-99
golden, 417
Rectangular prisms, 456-457
volume of, 186-187
Rectangular pyramids, 456-457
Reflections, 348-349
graphing, 579
Regular polygons, 227, 344-345
Related sentences, 60-61
Relations
graphing, 562-563, 579
Relatively prime numbers, 214-215

Repeating decimals, 246-247, 269
renaming as fractions, 323
Representing data, 430-431
Representing outcomes, 508-509
Rhombuses, 344-345
Right angles, 328-329
Right triangles, 340-341
Roots, square, 356-357
Rotations, 350-351
Rounding
to estimate products, 86-87
to estimate sums and differences, 48-49, 254-255
Rounding decimal quotients, 136-137

S

Sample space, 496-497
Scale drawings, 308-309, 380-381
Scalene triangles, 340-341
Scaling up and down, 308-309, 374-375
Scientific notation, 96-97, 138-139, 558-559
Sectors of circle graphs, 424-425, 443
Sentences
related, 60-61
writing algebraic, 176-177
Sequences, 206-207
arithmetic, 206-209
Fibonacci, 417
geometric, 209
sums of, 208-209
Short word name of numbers, 12-13
Sides, corresponding, 346-347
Similar figures, 346-347, 380-381
Similarity, 346-347
Simple events, 496-497
Simplest form of fractions, 240-241
Slant height of cone, 491
Solving equations
by addition and subtraction, 60-61, 72, 80, 182-183, 195, 196, 198
by addition and subtraction of fractions, 262-263, 273, 280, 324, 372, 418
by multiplication and division, 140-141, 168, 184-185, 196, 199
by multiplication and division of fractions, 300-301, 316, 398-399, 411, 413, 418
Solving a multistep problem, 90-91
Solving a simpler problem, 250-251, 288-289
Space, sample, 496-497
Space figures, 456-457
Spatial visualization, 456-457
Spheres, 457
Spreadsheets, 69, 157, 193, 407
Square roots, 356-357
Squared numbers, 94-95
Squares, 344-345
area of, 98-99
magic, *see* Magic squares
perfect, 356-357
Standard form of numbers, 12-13
Statistics, 419-454
mean, median, mode, and range, 150-153, 157
misleading, 432-433
probability and, 502-503
Stem-and-leaf plots, 434-435
Straight angles, 328-329
Strategies review, 336-337, 564-565
Subtraction, *see also* Differences
applying, 45-80
with equations, 60-61
of fractions, 256-257
of fractions in solving equations, 262-263

with inequalities, 62-63
of integers, 544-549
mental math in, 46-47
of mixed numbers, 258-259
renaming before, 260-261
solving equations with, 182-183
of whole numbers and decimals, 52-53
Sums, *see also* Addition
estimating by front-end estimation, 50-51
estimating by rounding, 48-49
estimating for mixed numbers, 254-255
magic, 79
of sequences, 208-209
Supplementary angles, 328-329
Surface area
of cones, 491
of cylinders, 464-465
of prisms, 460-461
of pyramids, 462-463
Symbols, inequality, 62-63, 142-143,
176-177, 560-561
Symmetry, 348-349, 361
lines of, 348-349, 361

T

T (ton), 302-303
t (ton or tonne, metric), 144-145
Table of measures, 592
Tables
frequency, *see* Frequency tables
of random digits, 500-501
Technology
calculators, 7, 8-9, 13, 17, 29, 32, 43,
52-53, 55, 61, 63, 65, 82-83, 84,
87, 88-89, 91, 97, 99, 103, 105,
109, 123, 127, 128-129, 131,
132-133, 134-135, 136-137, 139,
141, 147, 149, 159, 171, 181, 183,
185, 188-189, 207, 211, 212, 215,
217, 221, 243, 249, 251, 252, 257,
261, 263, 265, 285, 289, 293, 297,
299, 301, 307, 313, 333, 336-337,
339, 353, 355, 357, 377, 379, 383,
390-391, 392-393, 403, 422, 425,
427, 431, 439, 461, 462-463,
464-465, 467, 470-471, 473, 475,
477, 481, 501, 505, 509, 517, 519,
547, 549, 551, 554-555, 556-557,
559, 561, 564-565, 569
computers, 33, 69, 157, 193, 227, 269,
361, 407, 443, 525; *see also*
Computers
Ten, powers of, *see* Powers of 10

Terminating decimals, 246-247, 269
Terms
of ratios, 374-375
in sequences, 206-207
Theoretical probability, 500-501
Thinking mathematically, 1-10, 20-21, 56-57,
92-93, 132-133, 178-179, 218-219,
252-253, 294-295, 342-343, 384-385,
428-429, 468-469, 506-507, 552-553
applying mathematics, 2-3
collecting and interpreting data, 5
estimating, 8-9, 252-253
experimenting and predicting, 506-507
investigating patterns, 56-57, 92-93,
384-385
logical reasoning, 10, 15, 83, 147,
178-179, 218-219, 223, 285, 428-429
measuring, 132-133
using number concepts, 4, 20-21,
294-295, 552-553
visual reasoning, 6-7, 342-343, 468-469
Thousands, 12-13
Time intervals, 420-421
Ton (T), 302-303
Ton or tonne (t), metric, 144-145
Translations, 350-351
graphing, 579
Transversals, 332-333
Trapezoids, 344-345
area of, 100-101
Tree diagrams, 508-509
Trees, factor, 214-215
Triangles, 340-341, 344-345
acute, 340-341
area of, 100-101
constructing, 371
equilateral, 340-341
isosceles, 340-341
obtuse, 340-341
Pascal's, 237
right, 340-341
scalene, 340-341
Triangular prisms, 456-457
volume of, 186-187
Triangular pyramids, 456-457
Trillions, 12-13
Triple-line graphs, 33
Twin primes, 215

U

Unit rate, 376-377
**Understanding Numbers and Interpreting
Data,** 11-44

V

Variables, 60-61, 62-63, 172-173, 174-175,
194
Venn diagrams, drawing, 438-439
Vertex/vertices
of angles, 326-327
of circle graphs, 424-425
of polyhedrons, 456-457
Vertical angles, 332-333
Vertical axis, 22-23
in histograms, 420-421
as y-axis, 562-563
Visual reasoning, 6-7, 342-343, 468-469
Visualization, spatial, 456-457
Volume
of cones, 474-475, 481
of cylinders, 470-471
of prisms, 186-187
of pyramids, 472-473

W

Weight in customary units, 302-303
Whole-number powers of 10
division by, 122-123
multiplication by, 82-83
Whole numbers
addition of, 52-53
division of decimals by, 128-129
estimating products of, 86-87
multiplication of, 88-89
subtraction of, 52-53
Working backward, 306-307
Writing algebraic expressions, 174-175
Writing algebraic sentences, 176-177
Writing and solving an equation, 550-551

X

x-axis, 562-563

Y

y-axis, 562-563
Yard (yd), 302-303

Z

Zero on number line, 538-539
Zigzag method of addition, 53